WHAT THE CRITICS SAY:

America B*ide of its kind.*
(It is) a w *will help any*
traveler get *wit make this*
enjoyable re
You'll wan *an—its com-*
pact size mak

Getting There
...ation of Railroad Passengers

It took (Fistell) more than two years to produce this paperback, which covers everything from the history of the railroads to the fine points of planning a trip by train....Fistell is enthusiastic in telling his readers how to enjoy themselves on board.

Akron (Ohio) Beacon Journal

A handy volume about what the United States can offer. This is long overdue, for there is still plenty to savor along American tracks.
Mr. Fistell has provided a good description of Amtrak's system, and some of the special opportunities awaiting travelers.
...a good traveling companion.

The New York Times

*Ira Fistell's **America By Train** tells it as it is—and was. His guide not only helps plan a trip by train; it also includes such thoughtful details as which side to sit on for the best views on given routes.*

USA Today

...a handy guide to present-day passenger trains....You will find this book extremely helpful.

The Birmingham (Alabama) News

Ira Fistell

America ʙʏ Train

Burt Franklin & Company

HOW TO TOUR AMERICA BY TRAIN

Published by Burt Franklin & Company
235 East Forty-fourth Street
New York, New York 10017

Copyright © 1983, 1984 by Burt Franklin & Co., Inc.

SECOND EDITION

Library of Congress Cataloging in Publication Data

Fistell, Ira J.
America by train.

(The Compleat traveler's companion)
Includes index.
1. United States—Description and travel—1981–
—Guide-books.   2. Railroad travel—United States.
I. Title.   II. Series.
E158.F5   1984   917.3′04927   83-8877
ISBN 0–89102–299–6 (pbk.)

Manufactured in the United States of America

1   3   4   2

Most train photos courtesy of Amtrak.

For Chris, and for the women in my life—Marian, Kelly, Kitty,
Mary Ellen, Sara Elizabeth, and, most of all, Tonda.

Contents

Part 3: All About Everywhere: Train Trips

Part 4: Major Attractions: How to Get There by Train

Appendixes

Preface

HAVING FALLEN in love with trains during my toddling years, I have enjoyed many thousands of miles of rail travel in the past three decades. But mine has not been a common experience. Most Americans have had little or no occasion to ride the trains over the last 30 years, and indeed we now have a whole generation of young adults who have never in their lives ridden on an intercity passenger train.

Not that I blame them — for during the long decline in the quality and quantity of American passenger service that began about 1950, all too many travelers found the experience of riding U.S. passenger trains to be trying, depressing, or downright awful. With air and auto travel readily available, they simply abandoned the trains.

Today, however, that picture is changing. In the last 10 years the long decline in passenger-train service has been halted and reversed. The advent of Amtrak — the quasi-public corporation that now operates nearly all intercity passenger trains in this country — recurring energy shortages, and high gasoline prices have sparked a revival of passenger-train use. Environmental concerns and air and highway congestion have only served to stimulate interest in the passenger train as a transportation alternative. Thus the time is ripe for a practical guide to American rail passenger service.

I also have another purpose in writing this book, beyond explaining the rational advantages of rail passenger service. I hope to introduce the reader to some of the intangible factors that make the passenger train the most civilized and enjoyable form of land transportation yet devised. My hope is that this book will help the reader enjoy train travel as I do, and make even the longest trip so pleasant and interesting that it will seem to end too soon.

Acknowledgments

A project of this size could not possibly have been accomplished without the help of a number of people who contributed their valuable time, advice, and help.

John McLeod and Art Lloyd of Amtrak have been a considerable source of important information and encouragement. Irv Hirsch and Ed Von Nordeck were generous contributors of various materials and valuable advice.

Louise Brooks and Adrienne Parks read much of the manuscript and contributed valuable suggestions. And Anne Mackinnon was especially helpful in the final stages of preparing the manuscript.

Above all, I wish to thank my wife for her unfailing patience and understanding during the two years and more when she had to share me with this book.

America by Train

Amtrak's
National Rail Passenger System

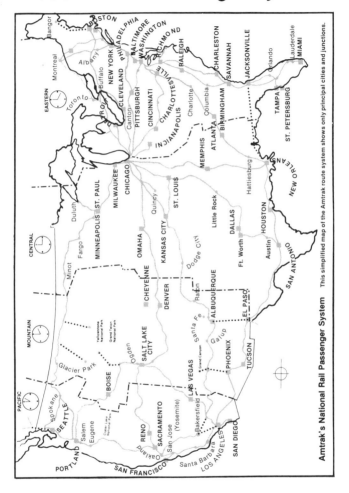

Amtrak's National Rail Passenger System   This simplified map of the Amtrak route system shows only principal cities and junctions.

PART 1

Planning a Trip by Train

Above: The *Yankee Clipper* near Sharon, Massachusetts. *Below:* Superliner cars of the *Empire Builder* departing Belton, Montana.

Planning a Trip by Train

1.1 Introduction

Like anything else, a successful trip by rail begins with good planning. You can do this yourself, and it's a lot more fun and less trouble than you might think. You must begin with an Amtrak timetable, which you can pick up free at most railroad stations or Amtrak sales offices, *or by calling Amtrak at the local phone number listed in this chapter.* Sometimes a single regional folder will be all you'll need; but if you're going to travel a long distance across country, you'll probably want the Amtrak systemwide National Timetable. This sixty-page folder includes all Amtrak train schedules, and shows connecting rail and bus schedules in the United States, Canada, and Mexico. It also contains information on fares, equipment, and services. Like the regional timetables, it's free; but you'll probably have to ask for it. (You can also request it from the Amtrak Distribution Center, P.O. Box 7717, Itasca, IL 60143.)

Important note: Amtrak has now set up a full nationwide telephone network for both reservations and information. If you wish to make a reservation to travel on an Amtrak train, or if you have any question regarding Amtrak service or facilities, or if you need a timetable, you may simply call the toll-free number below. (You may also call local numbers from selected cities and reach the same national network.) An Amtrak employee will either answer your question or put a call through for you to the appropriate Amtrak office or station anywhere in the United States. If, for example, you arrive in New York and suddenly realize that you left your wallet on the ticket counter in Kansas City, you can call either the National toll-free number or make a local call to Amtrak's New York number, and the person who answers the phone will help you to reach the Amtrak employee in Kansas City who is best able to help you. This may save you one or more costly long-distance calls.

Nationwide Reservation and Information Network

Amtrak has established a nationwide toll-free telephone number for reservations and information. The number below may be used at all times for both reservations and general information or to request a National Timetable. It is no longer necessary to call a local station. If Amtrak cannot answer your question directly, the Amtrak operator will transfer your call to the correct location or give you the telephone number you will need. The nationwide toll-free number is:

800-USA-RAIL

In addition to the toll-free number above, you may reach the Amtrak national network by calling the local telephone numbers below. Note, however, that you will be reaching one of the five regional service centers—Los Angeles, Chicago, Philadelphia, New York, or Jacksonville, Florida—for the Amtrak network, *not* your local station.

Albany, NY	(518) 465-9971
Albuquerque, NM	(505) 242-7816
Ann Arbor, MI	(313) 663-6051
Atlanta, GA	(404) 688-4417
Bakersfield, CA	(805) 327-7863
Baltimore, MD	(301) 539-2112
Boston, MA	(617) 482-3660
Bridgeport, CT	(203) 367-8002
Buffalo, NY	(716) 856-1229
Champaign, IL	(217) 352-5922
Charleston, SC	(803) 723-6679
Chicago, IL	(312) 558-1075
Cincinnati, OH	(513) 579-8506
Cleveland, OH	(216) 861-0105
Columbia, SC	(803) 779-7181
Denver, CO	(303) 893-3911
Detroit, MI	(313) 963-7396
District of Columbia	(202) 484-7540
Eugene, OR	(503) 485-1092
Harrisburg, PA	(717) 232-3916
Hartford, CT	(203) 525-4580
Indianapolis, IN	(317) 632-1905
Jackson, MI	(517) 787-9600
Jacksonville, FL	(904) 731-1600
Kalamazoo, MI	(616) 385-2993
Kansas City, MO	(816) 421-4725
Lancaster, PA	(717) 392-6717
Lansing, MI	(517) 372-7638
Long Island, NY points (Area Code 516 only)	(516) 981-9100

```
Los Angeles, CA . . . . . . . . . . . . . . . . . . . . . . . . . . . . . . . . . . . . . . . . . . . . (213) 624-0171
Milwaukee, WI . . . . . . . . . . . . . . . . . . . . . . . . . . . . . . . . . . . . . . . . . . . . . (414) 933-3081
Minneapolis, MN . . . . . . . . . . . . . . . . . . . . . . . . . . . . . . . . . . . . . . . . . . . (612) 339-2382
New Brunswick, NJ . . . . . . . . . . . . . . . . . . . . . . . . . . . . . . . . . . . . . . . . . . (201) 246-1970
New Haven, CT . . . . . . . . . . . . . . . . . . . . . . . . . . . . . . . . . . . . . . . . . . . . . (203) 777-4002
New London, CT . . . . . . . . . . . . . . . . . . . . . . . . . . . . . . . . . . . . . . . . . . . . (203) 442-5910
New Orleans, LA . . . . . . . . . . . . . . . . . . . . . . . . . . . . . . . . . . . . . . . . . . . . (504) 525-1179
New York City, NY
    (all 5 boroughs) . . . . . . . . . . . . . . . . . . . . . . . . . . . . . . . . . . . . . . . . . (212) 736-4545
Newark, NJ . . . . . . . . . . . . . . . . . . . . . . . . . . . . . . . . . . . . . . . . . . . . . . . . (201) 643-1770
Oakland, CA . . . . . . . . . . . . . . . . . . . . . . . . . . . . . . . . . . . . . . . . . . . . . . . (415) 982-8512
Philadelphia, PA . . . . . . . . . . . . . . . . . . . . . . . . . . . . . . . . . . . . . . . . . . . . (215) 824-1600
Pittsburgh, PA . . . . . . . . . . . . . . . . . . . . . . . . . . . . . . . . . . . . . . . . . . . . . (412) 621-4850
Portland, OR . . . . . . . . . . . . . . . . . . . . . . . . . . . . . . . . . . . . . . . . . . . . . . (503) 241-4290
Princeton, NJ . . . . . . . . . . . . . . . . . . . . . . . . . . . . . . . . . . . . . . . . . . . . . . (609) 921-8527
Providence, RI . . . . . . . . . . . . . . . . . . . . . . . . . . . . . . . . . . . . . . . . . . . . . (401) 751-5416
Richmond, VA . . . . . . . . . . . . . . . . . . . . . . . . . . . . . . . . . . . . . . . . . . . . . (804) 358-4936
Rochester, NY . . . . . . . . . . . . . . . . . . . . . . . . . . . . . . . . . . . . . . . . . . . . . (716) 454-5210
Sacramento, CA . . . . . . . . . . . . . . . . . . . . . . . . . . . . . . . . . . . . . . . . . . . . (916) 485-8506
San Francisco, CA . . . . . . . . . . . . . . . . . . . . . . . . . . . . . . . . . . . . . . . . . . (415) 982-8512
San Jose, CA . . . . . . . . . . . . . . . . . . . . . . . . . . . . . . . . . . . . . . . . . . . . . . (408) 280-6992
San Luis Obispo, CA . . . . . . . . . . . . . . . . . . . . . . . . . . . . . . . . . . . . . . . . (805) 541-5028
Santa Barbara, CA . . . . . . . . . . . . . . . . . . . . . . . . . . . . . . . . . . . . . . . . . . (805) 687-6848
Savannah, GA . . . . . . . . . . . . . . . . . . . . . . . . . . . . . . . . . . . . . . . . . . . . . (912) 232-0026
Schenectady, NY . . . . . . . . . . . . . . . . . . . . . . . . . . . . . . . . . . . . . . . . . . . (518) 465-9971
Seattle, WA . . . . . . . . . . . . . . . . . . . . . . . . . . . . . . . . . . . . . . . . . . . . . . . (206) 464-1930
Spokane, WA . . . . . . . . . . . . . . . . . . . . . . . . . . . . . . . . . . . . . . . . . . . . . . (509) 747-1069
Springfield, IL . . . . . . . . . . . . . . . . . . . . . . . . . . . . . . . . . . . . . . . . . . . . . (217) 753-3651
St. Louis, MO . . . . . . . . . . . . . . . . . . . . . . . . . . . . . . . . . . . . . . . . . . . . . (314) 241-8806
St. Paul, MN . . . . . . . . . . . . . . . . . . . . . . . . . . . . . . . . . . . . . . . . . . . . . . (612) 339-2382
Stamford, CT . . . . . . . . . . . . . . . . . . . . . . . . . . . . . . . . . . . . . . . . . . . . . . (203) 964-1345
Syracuse, NY . . . . . . . . . . . . . . . . . . . . . . . . . . . . . . . . . . . . . . . . . . . . . . (315) 422-8055
Toledo, OH . . . . . . . . . . . . . . . . . . . . . . . . . . . . . . . . . . . . . . . . . . . . . . . (419) 243-1084
Trenton, NJ . . . . . . . . . . . . . . . . . . . . . . . . . . . . . . . . . . . . . . . . . . . . . . . (609) 394-2604
Utica, NY . . . . . . . . . . . . . . . . . . . . . . . . . . . . . . . . . . . . . . . . . . . . . . . . . (315) 797-5510
Wilmington, DE . . . . . . . . . . . . . . . . . . . . . . . . . . . . . . . . . . . . . . . . . . . . (302) 658-1575
```

Daily Train Arrival and Departure Information

The special telephone numbers below have been established by Amtrak to provide only *arrival and departure time* information for the cities listed. For all other cities, use the regular phone numbers listed above. *Call only on the day the train in which you are interested is to arrive or depart. Do not use these numbers for making reservations or requesting fares or other train information.*

```
Albany-Rensselaer, NY . . . . . . . . . . . . . . . . . . . . . . . . . . . . . . . . . . . . . (518) 462-5763
Buffalo, NY . . . . . . . . . . . . . . . . . . . . . . . . . . . . . . . . . . . . . . . . . . . . . . . (716) 683-8440
Carbondale, IL . . . . . . . . . . . . . . . . . . . . . . . . . . . . . . . . . . . . . . . . . . . . . (618) 457-3388
```

Dallas, TX	(214) 651-8341
Denver, CO	(303) 534-2371
Detroit, MI	(313) 965-0314
Ft. Lauderdale, FL	(305) 463-8251
Ft. Worth, TX	(817) 332-2931
Fresno, CA	(209) 486-7651
Fullerton, CA	(714) 992-0530
Glenview, IL	(312) 724-2530
Houston, TX	(713) 224-1577
Hudson, NY	(518) 828-3379
Jacksonville, FL	(904) 768-1553
Joliet, IL	(815) 727-9279
Kansas City, MO	(816) 421-3622
Miami, FL	(305) 638-7321
New Orleans, LA	(504) 528-1600
Orlando, FL	(305) 843-7611
Richmond, VA	(804) 264-9194
Rochester, NY	(716) 454-2894
St. Louis, MO	(314) 231-0061
St. Petersburg, FL	(813) 522-9475
San Diego, CA	(714) 239-9021
Schenectady, NY	(518) 346-8651
Springfield, IL	(217) 753-2013
Syracuse, NY	(315) 463-1135
Tacoma, WA	(206) 627-8141
Tampa, FL	(813) 229-2473
Utica, NY	(315) 797-8962

"Metrophone"

The following telephone numbers have been established by Amtrak for both information and reservations for *Metroliner* service *only*.

New York City	(212) 736-3967
Newark, Metropark, and Trenton	800-523-8720
Philadelphia	(215) 824-4224
Wilmington, Baltimore and Beltway Sta.	800-523-8720
Washington, DC	(202) 484-5580
States of Delaware, Maryland, New Jersey, New York (except area 716)	800-523-8720
States of Connecticut, Massachusetts, New Hampshire, Rhode Island, Vermont, Virginia, West Virginia	800-523-8760
Pennsylvania	800-562-6990

Before you start planning your trip, you ought to know that Amtrak offers a unique and wonderful side benefit: unlimited stopover privileges. This means that most tickets between two points can be used as a series of tickets between intermediate stations, at no extra cost. For example, if you buy coach or sleeping-car tickets between New York and New Orleans, you can stop for days or even weeks in Washington, Atlanta, and Birmingham en route and not pay a dime extra for the privilege. If you have the time to see the country, this can be a marvelous advantage.

You should also know that Amtrak has a large fleet of comfortable sleeping cars, many of them brand new, to whisk you from city center to city center overnight. People who are in a hurry but want to enjoy the landscape and experience the feeling of journeying from place to place have always appreciated the train. And besides, sleeping-car travel is an adventure no one should miss.

Armed with your schedule, this book, and the knowledge that you can stop anyplace that suits your fancy, work out a route. Check Part 2 of this book for information on the cities, and read through Part 3, which describes sights along the train tracks. Almost anywhere you go by train, you'll see the country from a unique and fascinating perspective. Trains take you through America's most spectacular scenery and into the hearts of its cities; and, of course, the American railroads have a fascinating history of their own.

Look carefully at the schedules of the trains you want to take. (You may want to refer to the instructions on reading timetables, in section 3.1.) How often do they run? Where do you want to spend the night, and where would you like to reserve a place in the sleeping car? You may decide that you'll need several days to see a city, or you may want to stop at a station early in the day, tour the city for a few hours, and then get on a later train. (You can, for instance, leave Chicago in the morning, stop in Springfield, Illinois, for a few hours to visit the home of Abraham Lincoln, and then board a train that arrives that evening in St. Louis.) By reading the descriptions of the cities in Part 2, you'll get an idea of where you might like to stop and how long it will take you to see the sights.

Once you've worked out your route, you'll need to make reservations because space on most long-distance trains is reserved. This is an easy process. You can do it yourself or let a travel agent do it for you (see section 1.8, on reservations). Reservations for hotels and rented cars are often a good idea, too, and Part 2 of this book will give you the information you need to make them. Other information — about Amtrak's equipment and food, about packing and transporting your baggage, and about saving money with special fares — follows below.

But once you're on the train, all these things will be forgotten. Now you can sit back, turn to the description of your route, and watch the world go by, using that description as a guide to the places through which you pass.

1.2   The American Railroads and Amtrak

As recently as 40 years ago the American railroads operated a fleet of passenger trains second to none in the world. The private companies that ran those trains, however, had always regarded them as a sideline to their principal business, which was and still is the moving of freight. Only one American railroad — the commuter-hauling Long Island — earned more than half its income from carrying people. For most other lines the passenger business contributed no more than 15 percent of total revenues, and for many companies the percentage was much lower.

During the 1920s and 1930s it was still possible to make a profit in the long-distance passenger business, but the branch-line locals, suffering from the spread of paved highways, began to show consistent losses. The railroads' response was to stop running these unprofitable trains, and a good many such schedules were pared from the timetables before 1941.

World War II put a tremendous strain on the American railroads. In addition to a suddenly enormous civilian passenger business, the railroads were called upon to move 97 percent of the American military passenger traffic. The result of 4 years of this overcrowding and undermaintenance was a badly deteriorated fleet of equipment, and a backlog of passenger complaints. Combine these factors with the postwar boom in auto sales and road building, and a decline in the volume of rail passenger traffic was inevitable. At first the railroads refused to give up. Millions were spent on new streamlined equipment, but it soon became painfully obvious that the return from passenger operations just didn't justify the investment.

Meanwhile, thousands of miles of new highways were built with taxpayers' money, spent at the urging of the auto, oil, and highway lobbies. Airports, too, were constructed with public funds, and the air carriers were able to take advantage of war-developed technology to improve the speed, safety, and capacity of their planes. In short, government policies gave enormous subsidies, both direct and indirect, to the railroads' competition, while the railroads were required not only to own and maintain their rights of way, stations, and equipment but also to pay heavy taxes on their property. At the same time, fuel and labor costs rose rapidly. Even the widespread use of the efficient diesel locomotive didn't let the passenger trains bring in a profit.

By 1971, not many trains were still running, and most of those that remained were made up of rattletrap equipment pulled by aging and unreliable locomotives. There was a real chance that outside the so-called Northeast Corridor—that 450-mile stretch between Boston and Washington where heavy population density and bewildering traffic congestion kept passenger service viable—America would lose all of its remaining passenger trains.

This was the state of affairs when Congress approved, and President Nixon signed, the Amtrak Act. This legislation created an agency called the National Railroad Passenger Corporation (NRPC), a quasi-public corporation that took over operation of most of the remaining intercity trains on May 1, 1971. The railroads that joined Amtrak (the trade name for the NRPC) were relieved of their passenger deficits. In return, they paid the NRPC with title to their well-worn passenger equipment. Today every long-distance passenger railroad has either joined Amtrak or gone bankrupt.

The Secretary of Transportation designated a basic system of routes over which Amtrak was to operate, and the law permitted the corporation to run additional trains where states were willing to contribute money to finance them. Amtrak was not to operate commuter trains, and the law stated that it was to be a for-profit enterprise.

Therefore, although Amtrak was created by and receives a substantial part of its budget from Capitol Hill, it is not a state railway system like British Rail or the Japanese national railways. Amtrak has an independent board of directors, but its stock is not traded publicly. In other words, Amtrak is a hybrid: a private corporation theoretically in business to make a profit, but with important public influences and financing.

Amtrak should not be confused with Conrail, the big freight-hauling railroad formed by Congress from parts of several bankrupt Eastern railroads. In fact, Amtrak and Conrail have little in common except that both were midwifed by Congress and both run trains. The two companies are parties to a number of operating contracts, however. Amtrak runs many of its Eastern passenger trains on Conrail tracks, while Conrail operates its freight trains over Amtrak's Northeast Corridor Line.

No matter how you measure it, Amtrak is a big-time operation, America's sixth-largest commercial passenger carrier. Its trains crisscross the country from Boston to San Diego and from Miami to Seattle, covering 23,000 route miles. It employs 18,000 people, owns enough track to make it America's ninth-longest railroad, and accounts for revenues of $1.5 billion a year. Amtrak owns 1,500 passenger cars and hundreds of locomotives, and is buying more. It owns many of its 500 stations, not to mention maintenance facilities and miscellaneous real estate. Most important, it carries 19 million passengers more than 4 billion passenger miles yearly.

Amtrak calls itself "America's first national railroad passenger service," and basically that is what it is: no private railroad ever served the entire United States. But there are parts of the nation without any Amtrak service. Don't try to take a train direct from Pittsburgh to Cleveland or from Cincinnati to Atlanta—it can't be done. Five states—Maine, South Dakota, Oklahoma, Wyoming, and Hawaii—have no train service at all. Some other states have train service only three days a week or only at night. Still, the trains that are running represent a considerable accomplishment on the part of Amtrak.

At the beginning it was not clear whether Amtrak was going to promote rail passenger service or preside over its demise. Every car in its original fleet was at least 15 years old, and some dated back to before World War II. All were heated by steam (a legacy of the days before the diesel locomotives) and cooled by a bewildering and cumbersome array of battery-powered air-conditioning systems that varied from car to car. All of the original locomotives were acquired from the passenger railroads, and their average age was 29 years, well beyond the normal life expectancy of a diesel engine.

Bad as the mechanical problems may have been, they were not

Amtrak's only initial difficulties. When it began, the corporation had few employees of its own. Trains were operated, on-board services provided, cars and engines maintained, and stations and ticket agencies staffed by employees of the individual railroads, many of them old-timers nearing retirement. Morale among these people, who had worked through the long years of decline in the railroad passenger business, was often quite low. Moreover, Amtrak did not (and in most cases still does not) own or maintain the tracks or dispatch the trains. The operating railroads are frequently still responsible for those functions, and in all too many cases Amtrak trains have been slowed by bad track or sidetracked in favor of moneymaking freight trains.

Amazingly enough, Amtrak did succeed in stopping the long decline in passenger business, despite all its handicaps. In 1971 the corporation's first year of operation, it carried 11 million passengers. In 1973 that figure had risen to 15 million.

Responding to this evidence that people really will use passenger trains, Congress came up with appropriations for new cars and locomotives, and for rebuilding the best older units. Today virtually all Amtrak long-distance passengers ride in new or completely rebuilt equipment, powered by a nearly all-new locomotive fleet. Amtrak has also been able to replace or remodel decaying stations and maintenance facilities, to take over key sections of track, and to staff on-board and station jobs with its own personnel.

In 1980 these improvements were reflected in a total passenger load exceeding 20 million and revenues of $1.4 billion. Although Amtrak costs money — every important rail passenger system in the world costs money, but then so do highways and airports built at public expense — it has already accomplished many of the most difficult tasks it faced in 1971. It is now in position to become the truly modern, efficient system America has lacked.

1.3 Accommodations and Equipment

In general, Amtrak offers two types of service — coach and sleeping car — but within these areas the nature and quality of accommodations vary widely. In addition, some trains, particularly in the Northeast Corridor, offer so-called club service, roughly approximating the old parlor car, a first-class service on short daytime runs priced higher than regular coach.

Most Amtrak passengers ride in coaches, which are provided

on every train without exception. This is the lowest-priced service available, and consists of four-abreast seating, with two seats on each side of the center aisle. Doors, washrooms, and drinking water are grouped at the ends of the cars. All Amtrak coaches are air-conditioned, and all coach seats recline.

Despite these basic similarities, all Amtrak coaches are not alike. Important variables include the height above the rails at which the passenger rides; the amount of headroom; and the number of seats per coach, which varies from forty to eighty-six. Since all North American passenger cars are about the same length — 86 feet — it follows that the fewer seats in the car, the more legroom and personal space there will be.

Amtrak presently operates eight types of coaches: Metroliner, Amfleet, Amfleet II, SVP, Turboliner, Heritage, Bi-level, and Superliner. The first four of these are all variations of the same basic design, that of the original **Metroliners** of the late 1960s. These coaches were developed for America's first high-speed rail passenger service, between New York and Washington over what was then the Pennsylvania Railroad line. They were intended to operate at speeds of up to 140 miles per hour; and consequently, they were aerodynamically designed to resemble the fuselage of a DC-10 with the nose and tail cut off. Electric motors under the floors powered these cars, making separate locomotives unnecessary. The interiors were designed to move large numbers of people over short distances, so seats were placed close together and lounging space was kept to a minimun. Coupled with the low ceilings inherent in the airliner-influenced design, these features made the Metroliners a little cozy inside; but since they were used only on short runs, this was not considered a problem.

Several years later, when Amtrak was shopping around for new coaches to replace the antiques it had inherited from the private railroads, it found that American car builders could not or would not come up with an economical design. The Metroliner plans were at hand, however; Amtrak dusted them off, discarded the electric self-propelling equipment (which could be used only on the New York–Washington line anyway), and came up with what it calls its **Amfleet** cars. There are 492 of them, and they are found in short-run service all over the country. Some of these cars have been refitted inside and out for Metroliner service.

Because they are a variation of the original Metroliner design, which had been planned for use on the electrified New York–Washington route, the Amfleet cars have all-electric heating, air-conditioning, and other equipment. By contrast, Amtrak's older cars had been heated by steam—a legacy from the old days of steam locomotives—and each car had carried its own cooling equipment. Since mechanical failures had been all too frequent, Amtrak, therefore, made a momentous decision: It converted all of its cars to the all-electric system. The results have been a marked improvement in equipment performance, a great reduction in the number of complaints, and a healthy cut in maintenance costs.

Two other types of Amtrak coaches are also variations of the Metroliner design. **Amfleet II** cars are used on long-distance trains running from New York to the South and the Midwest. These cars have more interior room and larger windows than their Amfleet precursors and are more appropriate for long trips. Amtrak added 150 of these Amfleet II cars in 1983. In addition, there are self-propelled, diesel-powered **SVP** cars, used principally in New England.

Turboliners are used on runs in New York State. These trains, powered by a gas-turbine engine at each end, are American-built variations of a French design. They are clean, roomy, and comfortable, and they have large picture windows—an especially welcome feature on the scenic New York–Albany line.

Other trains in the east use what is called the **Heritage Fleet** equipment. These coaches are the best of those acquired by Amtrak from the private railroads, rebuilt from the rails up at Amtrak's Beech Grove, Indiana, shops. The Heritage rebuilding program included sleeping cars, dining cars, and lounges, in addition to coaches, and Beech Grove did such a splendid job that when the first Heritage Fleet cars went into service, many passengers thought they were riding on all-new equipment. These cars are good for another ten to fifteen years on the rails, and Amtrak is already working on designs for the new cars that will eventually replace them.

Heritage coaches have as few as forty seats per car, less than half the number in an Amfleet car. Because the car bodies are squared at the top, rather than curved, there is a good deal more interior room. Their weight makes the Heritage cars ride smoothly, and conversion to all-electric temperature control has done away with the greatest single source of passenger complaints—air-conditioning and heating failure. In short, the

Heritage coaches are very comfortable vehicles for long-distance travel.

Restricted clearances in the East demand low-level cars in that part of the country, but west of the Chicago—New Orleans axis Amtrak can use the taller, roomier **Bi-level** coaches. These first appeared on the Santa Fe Railroad as early as 1956 and were so successful that Amtrak is still using them, in conjunction with the newest and most beautiful cars on the rails—the Superliners.

Superliners are the highest, heaviest, most elegant, and most expensive railroad passenger vehicles ever built, and they are worth every cent of the million or so dollars each one cost. Most Superliner coach seats are on the upper level, which means a quieter, smoother ride and a panoramic view of the Western scenery. Even the lower level seats give you a smooth passage, because the heavy weight of these larger cars smooths out ordinary bumps in the track.

When the Superliners were first delivered, they rode rather roughly. Amtrak has since made adjustments in the trucks, however, and today Superliner coach passengers need not fear two nights on the train. You float through the West well above the tracks, and if you can't sleep on a Superliner, you can't sleep on any train.

From Amtrak's point of view, the Superliners are good business. Long-distance coaches must have low-density seating to be comfortable, but that drives up costs on a per-passenger basis. The Superliners, with up to seventy-eight seats on two levels, nearly double the number of passengers per coach without sacrificing comfort while reducing overall operating costs. Superliner or bilevel equipment is now assigned to all long-distance trains in the West, and it has proved to be extremely popular with passengers.

Coach passengers account for most of Amtrak's customers. But there has always been a segment of the traveling public that is not content with these facilities, and for this market Amtrak offers a custom "club class" service on certain day trains, plus sleeping cars on all overnight runs.

Club service, found on the Metroliners and some Amfleet trains, offers special seating (individual chairs) and meal service at your seat. For this, a premium fare is charged, roughly 33 percent above the regular coach tariff. The service approximates the old-time "parlor car" featured on many day trains thirty or forty years ago and is designed primarily for business travelers.

Sleeping-car service on overnight trips is another kettle of fish. As comfortable as a coach may be, it doesn't offer a private room with a clean, comfortable bed whose turned-down sheets are practically irresistible. To enjoy long-distance rail travel at its delightful best, the more expensive but uniquely satisfying sleeping car is the way to go.

I say "sleeping car" because that's the correct term — but it's hard for anybody raised in America before, say, 1965 not to call it a Pullman by force of habit. George M. Pullman did not invent the sleeping car, but the company he founded made his name practically synonymous with the cars it ran.

The Pullman Company not only built sleeping cars. It also operated them by contract with the railroads. Pullman cars were staffed by Pullman employees, and the service standards were always high. Old-timers will remember how a Pullman porter would shine your shoes each night and bring your beer along with a carefully iced glass. In the days before the Civil Rights Act of 1964, when rigid job discrimination prevailed nationwide, blacks could hold few more prestigious jobs than that of Pullman porter. You may recall that the nation's most important black labor leader was A. Philip Randolph of the Brotherhood of Sleeping Car Porters. Thirty years or so ago, however, the Pullman Company was forced by the federal government to either give up building cars or stop operating them, and it chose the latter alternative.

Today, under Amtrak auspices, the sleeping car is making something of a comeback. The NRPC operates three types of sleeping cars, including the first new sleepers built in this country in a quarter of a century, the Superliners.

Nowhere short of a space capsule will you find such ingenuity as in a sleeping car. Everything you could possibly want is there — you just have to look around a little. Heritage Fleet sleeping cars (but not Superliners) have a tiny toilet and a folding washbasin in every room (Amtrak provides the soap and hand towels). The toilet has a cover that turns the commode into a small table. Seats magically fold down to become beds, and beds descend from the ceiling or from behind apparently solid walls. If you want to see pure delight, take a child for a trip on a sleeping car — and I'll bet the kid claims the upper berth!

Speaking of berths, sleeping-car mattresses tend to be a little on the soft side, but linens are always cool, crisp, and impeccably clean, and blankets are warm. Temperature controls are within your reach. There's a bright reading light over each berth, and a blue night light for those who abhor total darkness. If you wear glasses, you'll frequently find a neat little pocket in which to keep them right at the head of the bed. And, of course, there's a button at hand that will bring the porter if there's anything you need. Passengers need not worry about security, either. Sleeping-car rooms may be locked from the inside, and nothing is more difficult to break into than a sealed room on a Heritage car.

All overnight trains east of the Mississippi, and some long-distance runs elsewhere, carry rebuilt **Heritage sleeping cars** offering two types of sleeping accommodations. The **roomette** is designed for a single person. It contains one bed, which folds down for nighttime use and can be raised for daytime use. The **bedroom** is larger and has two fold-down beds. It can be used as a comfortable sitting room during the day. Adjacent bedrooms may be converted into a four-bed suite by opening the connecting panel. Whichever type of room suits you best, you may wish to ask for space near the center of the car — the rooms over the wheels tend to be noisier and perhaps a bit rougher riding.

Riding in a Heritage sleeping car does have its inconveniences: You'll find that when the bed is lowered, there's no room to stand up while changing your clothes. Also, you must raise the bed in order to use the commode — another case where you'll need to plan ahead. In the long run, though, these minor difficulties are well worth the fun of traveling in a sleeping car.

Several of Amtrak's Eastern trains also offer, in addition to regular sleeping-car service, an economy service known as **Slumbercoach.** Slumbercoach rooms, like those in Heritage sleeping cars, come as singles or doubles, but they are very small. The beds are shorter, narrower, and considerably less comfortable than in regular sleeping cars. Amtrak also doesn't provide the usual complimentary morning coffee. This is a no-frills service designed for people who want economy but don't want to sit up all night in a coach. If you're neither claustrophobic nor very tall, Slumbercoach can be a big money-saver for you. This service is currently available on the *Crescent, Broadway Limited, Lake Shore Limited, Silver Meteor, Montrealer,* and *Silver Star.*

West of Chicago and New Orleans, most Amtrak trains are

Above: Superliner coaches. *Below:* Superliner family bedrooms, which extend the full width of the railroad car. *Next page:* Various features of the Superliner deluxe bedroom, including sofa, swivel chair, basin, and mirror. Bottom photo illustrates how some adjoining bedrooms can be opened to form a suite.

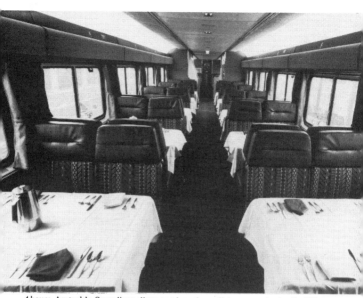

Above: Amtrak's Superliner diner used on long-distance routes in the West.
Below: The Heritage Fleet cafeteria-lounge used on several Eastern routes. Photos on the next page show Superliner economy bedrooms.

equipped with the brand-new **Superliner sleeping cars.** These double-deck cars offer a wider range of accommodations than the older Heritage cars, and anyone planning a long trip through the West should consider them. Each Superliner sleeping car contains fourteen **economy bedrooms** accommodating one or two persons, and one **family bedroom** suitable for two adults and two children. These rooms do not have their own toilet facilities. In addition, each car contains five **deluxe bedrooms** with lavatories and an extra-wide lower berth, and a **special bedroom** designed for a disabled person traveling with a companion. This spacious room extends all the way across one end of the car and has its own toilet area, large enough to accommodate a wheelchair. When not reserved for a handicapped traveler, this room will be sold to other passengers. All of the deluxe rooms and ten of the economy bedrooms are on the upper level; the rest of the sleeping spaces are on the lower. There are rest rooms on both levels and a dressing room downstairs. Deluxe bedrooms can be converted into a suite by opening the connecting door. All Superliner berths are designed to be raised and lowered without the aid of a porter, and all rooms are planned to permit the upper berth to remain down while the lower is converted into a seat for daytime use. Most deluxe bedrooms now have showers, and all will have them soon. Many interior walls are made of glass, which means that you can open the curtains and avoid the claustrophobic feeling that sometimes comes over you in an older car.

Superliner sleeping cars are smooth-riding, owing partly to their heavy weight, and are cheerful and comfortable inside. Incidentally, the washrooms have a folding infant-changing table for travelers with babies.

Whatever sleeping-car space you choose, you're bound to enjoy the experience. Also, think of it another way. When you ride an overnight train to your destination, you avoid a night's hotel bill. With accommodations in major cities running upward of $50 a night, you may enjoy substantial savings by getting transportation and a bed for the price of a hotel room alone.

Auto Train service between Washington, D.C., and Florida was revived in 1983 on a three-times-a-week basis. Beginning on March 1, 1984 Auto Trains will run daily in both directions between Lorton, Virginia (20 miles from Washington), and Sanford, Florida. For a reasonable fare, the train will carry you and your car over the entire distance in one night. You save the time and trouble of driving, and you won't have to rent a car when you reach your destination. Bedrooms and roomettes are available at higher rates. Dinner and breakfast are included at no extra cost.

1.4 Food Service

All Amtrak passengers, whether coach or sleeping car, use common dining facilities, which vary from train to train as well as from one section of the country to another.

All Superliner-equipped trains, most Heritage Fleet trains, and Metroliner trains between New York and Boston have full **dining cars** with table service. Many Amfleet trains offer dinette cars, and in some cases food may be served at your seat. On some short-distance trains, notably the Chicago—Milwaukee runs, there is no meal or beverage service at all.

Before recent budget cuts, Amtrak food service was one of the true delights of rail travel. There was relaxed waiter-service, using elegant silver on immaculately clothed tables, with real glassware and fresh flowers daily. Menus were tailored to reflect the cuisine of the region through which each train passed. But all that cost a great deal of money, and the reasonable prices charged did not begin to cover the costs of the service. Amtrak's food-service deficit in 1980 was close to $60 million. The budget cuts spared the Amtrak system, but they have done away with the delights of traditional dining.

It's difficult to write about Amtrak dining service today, however, because it's in such a state of flux that everything may be different tomorrow. Although we can't expect a quick return to the high-quality service Amtrak offered before their budget was cut, the NRPC is experimenting, and some improvements—such as fresh-cooked breakfasts or Haagen-Dazs ice cream for dessert—have been made. The service has improved too. Some of the furloughed employees have been rehired, so waiting time has been reduced. While Amtrak dining may not be the luxury it once was, it's better today then in the past two years.

Meal service on most shorter-run trains was less elaborate in the first place, so it was less affected by the cuts. Amtrak owns 492 Amfleet cars—but not one of them is a full diner. **Amcafe** and **Amdinette** service is limited to sandwiches and precooked food heated in a convection oven, plus a variety of snack foods—pastry, potato chips, soda, and candy. Passengers usually buy food at a counter and then take it back to their seats or the lounge. Some trains offer limited table service, with paper placemats and plastic forks.

1.5 Lounging Around

Many Amtrak trains have a lounge car open to all passengers, where drinks are served and passengers may play cards or board games and converse informally, and where the relaxed ambience of train travel is most fully felt. These cars are one of the big reasons for taking a train instead of an automobile, bus, or plane; those forms of travel offer neither the spaciousness, the feeling of camaraderie, nor the picture windows.

One caution: Alcohol sales are subject to the laws of the states through which Amtrak's trains pass, and some of these states are dry on Sunday. Dining-car stewards and lounge-car attendants will inform you if you're approaching an area where alcoholic beverages may not be served.

Each **Superliner lounge** has a glass roof and nearly all-glass walls for better viewing of the spectacular Western scenery. Upper levels have a service bar with twenty-two seats; other seats swing toward the windows or toward closed-circuit TV monitors, which Amtrak plans to use someday to show feature films. On the lower level are tables for snacking or card playing, plus couches with cocktail tables.

Nice as the Superliner lounges are, however, they lack the forward view that was such an attractive feature in the **dome cars** they have replaced. Fortunately, Amtrak has restored a few of those beautiful bubble-topped cars where you can sit above the roof level of the rest of the train and see in all directions. They are already in use on the *Capitol Limited* and the Auto Trains. Look for more on the *City of New Orleans*. They are available to all passengers on a first come, first served basis.

1.6 Baggage

One of the nicest things about Amtrak is its baggage service. With a paid ticket a passenger may check up to 150 pounds of baggage through to his destination absolutely without additional charge—and Amtrak assumes liability for loss up to $500. Checked-baggage service is available at most stations (exceptions are always noted in the timetable), and most trains carry a baggage car. The only requirements are that each passenger check no more than three pieces, that each piece be clearly marked with name and address, and that no piece weigh more than 75 pounds. You can bring more baggage at extra cost, and you can buy additional insurance for your baggage from the clerk at the check-in counter.

This is one of the best travel bargains available. When we travel with our children from California to Wisconsin, their trunks full of summer camp clothes ride along on our Amtrak tickets. That saves us hundreds of dollars in express charges — we know, because we had to ship them one year when we didn't take the train.

Cost savings aren't the only attraction of Amtrak's checked-baggage service. If your trip involves a change of train, it's a nuisance to have to switch your own luggage from one train to another. Your best bet is to check as much of your baggage in advance as possible. Keep with you just one small suitcase containing the things you'll actually need while on the train: toiletries, sleepwear, a casual change of clothes, and something to wear for dinner in the diner and to meet friends or business associates when you arrive.

Bring any baggage you want to check to the baggage office 30 minutes before your train departs, and it should be ready at the end of your trip about 30 minutes after your train pulls in. If you want your baggage to be waiting for you when you arrive, however, it's wise to check it at the station a day or two before your own scheduled departure. That way, all you do is take your claim checks to the baggage room when your train pulls in, and presto! there's your gear.

Many people prefer to carry their baggage onto the train, especially if the trip is not a long one. Amtrak allows this, as long as you keep your things out of the aisles and, if the train is crowded, off the seats. There is room next to and under your seat for small items, and there is a long shelf above the seats where larger items may be stowed. People who have trouble lifting need not worry. There's always someone on the train who will help you put your bags up or take them down. Bulky items — like skis — should usually be checked, but you may be allowed to carry them on with you if the train is not too crowded. A bicycle may be taken on the train, but only if the handlebars are removed and the bicycle is boxed; Amtrak sells an inexpensive carton for this purpose.

Although there are still a few "redcap" porters to help you with your baggage in major stations, they are very rare today. Therefore you will probably have to transport your luggage from your car to the checking area yourself. Amtrak supplies some very useful carts to help you with this task, and you should try to find one when you get to the station. If you really do need a redcap, however, tell a conductor at the platform, and he or she will page a porter for you. Better yet, identify your special needs when you make your reservation, and Amtrak will arrange for assistance.

1.7 Fares

Like everything else in our inflation-plagued economy, Amtrak fares keep going up. The days when a hundred dollars would buy you 5,000 miles of rail travel are gone, probably forever. Today basic fares range from about 15 cents a mile for short-run trips in the East to a bargain 8 cents a mile on long runs in the West. Either way, Amtrak is competitive with driving.

Round-trip excursion fares are the first and most important discount. Available on most Amtrak runs, they save approximately 30 percent of the cost of two one-way tickets. There are some restrictions on departure times. (Consult the agent.) This discount may not be combined with the discounts listed below, although there is a savings of about 50 percent for children aged two through eleven traveling with an adult.

If you are traveling as a family, Amtrak offers big savings. The **family plan,** good on all Amtrak trains except the Metroliners and Auto Trains, works like this: The head of household pays full fare, spouse and children from twelve through twenty-one pay half fare, children from two through eleven pay only 25 percent of the regular tariff—and babies under two go free. Another nice feature of family-plan travel is that you no longer have to start your trip on a particular day. Family-plan fares are in effect whenever you are ready to go.

Even if you can't travel together and don't qualify for the family-plan rate, you can still save money on **children's tickets.** Children from two through eleven pay half fare when traveling with a passenger twelve years old or older; one infant under two travels free. Unaccompanied children (aged eight through eleven only, and with prior approval by Amtrak) pay full fare, however, and children traveling by Auto Train pay 75 percent of full fare.

Senior citizens and **handicapped people** can also get a break on Amtrak fares. Those who qualify (check with an Amtrak agent, but generally you are eligible if you're over sixty-five) save a flat 25 percent of the regular rate on any round-trip ticket, except the Metroliners and Auto Trains.

Even if you're over twelve and under sixty-five, have no family, and are going one way, you can still get a discount from Amtrak if you can travel as part of a group. Any party of fifteen or more persons going together is entitled to **group plan** rates: 25 percent off round-trip tickets and 15 percent off one-way tickets. This group plan applies to all trains except the Auto Trains.

Military personnel also get a discount of 25 percent on all trains except the Metroliners and the Auto Trains.

In addition to the regular system-wide fare discounts already discussed, Amtrak offers, from time to time, money-saving **weekend excursion rates** on various routes. Often these rates are well below the regular round-trip excursion fare. Check with an Amtrak agent before buying tickets, to find if there's a special bargain fare offered for the trip you wish to make.

Amtrak also offers a series of **USA Rail Passes** to foreign visitors. These passes must be purchased abroad and are good for unlimited travel within a specified area and time period. Nationwide passes are available for 7-, 14-, 21-, or 30-day periods, and regional passes are sold for 14-day periods. The family discount (see above) applies to these passes. The regional passes are new, and they are quite a bargain. The regions are Western, Central, Southern, and Eastern; and their boundaries have been generously drawn. See the Appendix for more information.

Sleeping-car fares, while substantially higher than coach charges, are relatively less expensive than they were before Amtrak took over passenger service in 1971. That is because you no longer need to buy a special first-class rail ticket in order to get sleeping-car space. Today you pay only the regular fare plus the room charge, which varies with the type of accommodation selected. If it's within your budget, I recommend taking a sleeper for overnight travel—you'll enjoy the trip far more.

The **Metroliners** along the Northeast Corridor are more expensive than the regular, slower trains. You'll need a special ticket to ride one, or if you change your mind at the last minute, you can upgrade a regular ticket by trading it in and paying the difference.

Auto Train passenger fares are about the same as regular fares. There is an additional fee for your car.

1.8 Reservations and Tickets

Most Amtrak trains require advance reservations. All sleeping-car space, all club-class space, all Metroliner seats, all space on the Auto Trains, all coach seats on long-distance trains, and some seats on short-distance day trains must be reserved in advance of departure. This means that except on nonreserved, short-distance trains, you can't just walk into the station, buy a ticket, climb on board, and grab the first seat you see.

This system has both positive and negative aspects. It does guarantee space to those who reserve first, and it does away with long lines to get a seat on popular trains. Theoretically, at least, it gives Amtrak better control of equipment demands and on-board food and beverage requirements. But people who make advance reservations sometimes don't show up, and a train may leave with empty seats after potential passengers have been turned away.

To make your reservations, call the appropriate reservations and information number for your city (see the back of the Amtrak National Timetable or section 1.1 of this book). There are special numbers to call for reservations on the Metroliners and a special teletypewriter line for deaf persons. Make separate reservations for each portion of your journey, if you are planning to make stopovers.

When you make your reservations, you will be given a date by which your tickets must be picked up or your reservations will be canceled. This date depends on how far in advance you are making the reservation. If you call a month before your trip, you'll probably have to pick up your tickets in about two weeks. If you wait until the day before you leave, you run the risk of finding the train full, but you don't have to pick up your tickets until the day of your departure. Amtrak also offers a ticket-by-mail service for people who reserve at least two weeks in advance and who don't want to make an extra trip to the station.

If you should need to cancel a reservation, be sure to call Amtrak at least 30 minutes before your train is scheduled to leave, or you will be assessed a service charge. Besides, if you cancel, someone else may be able to take your seat.

Amtrak reservations are now handled by a new computer system known as "Arrow," which went into service late in 1981, replacing a less successful computer. In addition, the corporation shares Trans World Airlines's automated reservations system. Recently, Amtrak and VIA, the Canadian passenger rail line, began to make reservations for all trains in both countries; so even if you're not buying Amtrak tickets, you can still arrange a Canadian trip at any Amtrak office.

In ticketing, too, Amtrak has made great progress. It will accept practically any major credit card: Visa, MasterCard, American Express, Diners Club, Carte Blanche, C & S, Choice, and even Eurocard. These cards may be used to charge on-board meal service aboard club cars and long-haul dining cars. You can also use personal checks for these purposes, as long as you present adequate identification.

If your trip includes stopovers, be sure to get the ticket agent to write separate coupons for each portion of your journey. If you decide later to skip a stop or to add one, you can ask to have the tickets adjusted at any station.

At major stations like New York and Chicago, and especially at peak travel times, the lines at Amtrak ticket windows can sometimes get pretty long. Whenever possible, it's a good idea to buy your ticket at least a day or two in advance of your departure. This will spare you the nerve-racking experience of waiting in line while the clock ticks relentlessly away toward departure time. It's especially nice to avoid the ticket lines if you're taking one of the short-distance coach trains where seats are not reserved.

1.9   Visiting Cities

Although visiting American cities is always exciting, getting around them without a car can be anything but easy. You can make things much more convenient for yourself if you arrange to stay in a hotel near the railway station (if the station is downtown) or centrally located for sight-seeing. (All hotels listed in Part 2 of this book have been chosen according to these criteria.)

Make hotel reservations in advance, if possible, and mention that you'll be arriving by train—occasionally you'll be offered a ride from the station, but you may at least get some advice about the best way to get to your hotel. Unless you carry very little luggage, you will probably want to take a taxi to your hotel when you arrive, although you may be able to rely on city buses or subways once you get settled in. Ask about local bus routes at the hotel desk, or call the local public-transit authority (numbers are listed for each city in Part 2). Most likely there will be a major bus route within a block or two of your hotel.

Centrally located hotels are more expensive than out-of-town motels, but a downtown hotel is close to interesting things and often reflects the character of its city in a unique way. You'll be able to walk around and get to know the city — and you may even save money by avoiding taxi and bus fares.

Day trips out of the cities are a great way to see some of the best historical and scenic attractions. You can always rent a car for these trips, and you'll probably want to do so if you are traveling with a group or your family. For a single person or a couple, however, a bus tour may be less expensive than driving, and of course it's always easier. Some companies run full-day excursions to places more than 100 miles from the base city, and many offer a wide variety of tours. Call and see what they have to offer before you rent a car. By the way, a 3-hour city-bus tour is a good way to get a broader picture of a city than you can get on foot, and a boat tour will let you see many cities from an entirely different perspective.

Another good way to take a day trip is by traveling on commuter trains, or even on Amtrak. From Boston, for instance, you can go to Concord and Lexington; from Washington, D.C., you can go to Harpers Ferry by B&O or Amtrak; and from Chicago, you can go to the beautiful Indiana Dunes on the shore of Lake Michigan. Check suggested day trips in Part 2 of this book, and commuter schedules.

If you're stopping in a city for only a few hours, you may want to leave your luggage in a locker at the station. These lockers are quite safe, and you needn't be afraid that your bags will be stolen. If the station is out of town, a taxi is probably the quickest way to get to the center of the city, though most stations do have city bus service during the daytime.

All cities listed in Part 2 have visitors' bureaus or chambers of commerce. Most have visitors' centers, where you can stop in or call for information. All will be pleased to send you information on their cities in advance, if you request it. You will probably receive helpful advice if you explain that you will be arriving without a car. Don't forget to ask for local bus schedules, tour brochures, and a map of the city.

1.10 Packaged Tours

For people who don't want to work out their own itineraries, packaged tours offer an agreeably easy way to travel. There are many different kinds of tours by rail. Some offer luxurious travel in private cars; others employ regular Amtrak accommodations.

Amtrak offers 144 packaged tours in its Rail America program, ranging from an $18.50 1-day group excursion from Chicago to Springfield, Illinois, to a $3,500 deluxe escorted 22-day extravaganza from New York. These tours are generally operated by private companies in association with Amtrak, and the stated tour price may not include the rail fare. Be sure of the actual cost before you sign up. Amtrak publishes free brochures describing tours in various areas of the country, which are available at most stations or from the Amtrak Distribution Center, P.O. Box 7717, Itasca, IL 60143. Ask for the folders on the parts of the country that interest you most.

There are also special tours put together by various travel agencies and aimed primarily at that remarkable creature, the railfan. (Incidentally, the term is always "railfan," never "railbuff." That's used only by people who aren't part of the hobby.) The railfan literally doesn't care where he's going, so long as he gets there by train, and to travel with him is an experience you won't soon forget. Examples of railfan-oriented tours are the annual Colorado excursions run by Slotsy Tours of Fullerton, California, and the Iron Horse Vacations operated by Free Enterprise Tour–USA of Metairie, Louisiana. If you're interested in trips of this sort, you should check the "Running Extra" pages at the back of *Trains Magazine*. This monthly publication is available at some newsstands and many hobby shops, or from the Kalmbach Publishing Company, 1027 North Seventh Street, Milwaukee, WI 53233. The price is a steep $1.75 a copy, but you'll find listings of some unusual and interesting trips, including overseas excursions, that aren't advertised elsewhere. Also watch the travel section of the Sunday *New York Times*, which frequently carries advertisements from private-tour operators seeking a general clientele.

My favorite tours are those which go by private cars. An excursion on one of these rolling palaces, some of which were formerly owned by millionaires, is beyond all doubt the most elegant travel experience available. If money is no object, this is *the* way to see the United States. Four Winds Travel and Continental Rail are major packagers of luxury rail tours.

Besides tours, Amtrak offers a series of rail-hotel packages known as Escapades. Brochures are available from the Amtrak Distribution Center (address above), listing the packages available for different regions of the country.

1.11 Notes for Foreign Visitors

Visitors to the United States from Europe or Japan will find American trains quite different from those they are used to. There, the passenger train is the most important mode of intercity travel; here, it is much less universally used. As a result, in the United States there is often just one train a day between cities that in Europe would have frequent service. In fact, more than a few routes have no passenger service at all.

Nevertheless, there are many good passenger trains in America — and there's no better way to get to know and understand the United States than to travel through it by rail. The country's awesome size and stunning natural beauty simply cannot be appreciated from the air, and meeting Americans is much easier and more pleasant on the train than on a bus. For foreign visitors who really want to get to know America and its people, the train is definitely the way to go.

American trains are universally air-conditioned, which means that you can't open the windows, and doors are always opened by employees. Coaches in the United States are simply long, open cars with rows of seats all facing forward. There is no trace of the intimate six- or eight-seat compartment found in Europe.

Meal service on American trains is reasonably good, when there is a dining car, and American dining-car meals are much less expensive than those on European trains. In Europe it is common for passengers to bring their own food aboard, and share with other passengers. This practice is much less common in the United States.

Visitors to the United States should be forewarned that aboard the trains, as everywhere else in the country, they should not count on finding employees who speak even a word of any language other than English. Even with the enormous influx of Spanish-speaking people from Mexico, Cuba, and Puerto Rico, which has visibly changed American life in the last twenty years, most Americans still speak no language but their own. Likewise, signs arc generally printed in English only, although some—especially in New York, Los Angeles, and other cities with large Spanish-speaking populations—are now in Spanish as well. Amtrak does print time-tables and information in French for those trains serving Montreal, but other than these exceptions the rule is that a visitor must know at least some English to function in the United States.

Europeans are used to seeing schedules printed in the 24-hour system (also used in Canada), but American train schedules—not to mention bus, airline, and theater times—are always given in the 12-hour system. Thus, a train scheduled to leave at 1630 according to the 24-hour clock is shown departing at 4:30 P.M. in the United States.

American railroad stations are also very different from those abroad, and a word of warning is not out of place. Stations in Europe and Japan are centers of activity. They are always clean, busy, and full of special services like restaurants and money-exchange counters. In the United States, despite Amtrak's progress in rebuilding and modernizing many facilities, too many buildings tend to be old, dirty, and occupied only by vagrants except at train times. Except in New York City, Washington, D.C., Philadelphia, and Chicago, *foreign visitors should not expect to find many facilities in railroad stations* and should not plan on spending much time in them. For instance, do not plan on eating meals in American stations—the food service is likely to be minimal or even non-existent. Likewise, toilet facilities at many American passenger stations are primitive at best; public rest rooms in hotels and department stores are generally more congenial.

Also, no American railroad station that I know of offers that marvelous and nearly universal European institution, the lodging bureau. In the United States you cannot be sure of obtaining help in finding a place to stay on arriving in town. You must make your own hotel reservations (or have a travel agent make them for you), and this should be done in advance if you're traveling during a busy season.

Money Exchange: Foreign visitors should also remember that they will have few opportunities to exchange foreign currency for U.S. dollars. International airports usually have exchange counters, but train stations do not. In fact, there are some smaller American cities where a foreign visitor will have a difficult time finding a bank to exchange money. Therefore it is a good idea to

exchange your money when you first arrive, and to buy traveler's checks. Nearly any American business will accept a traveler's check in dollars, though few are likely to accept a traveler's check in another currency. Commercial banks in most large cities will exchange currency during business hours, or they will be able to give you the name of a local bank that can. American Express offices often exchange money, and they usually have longer hours, but they are rarely found outside the major cities. For assistance in an emergency, call the Travelers Aid office in the city or state where you're staying.

San Xavier del Bac mission, known as the "White Dove of the Desert," was built by missionaries visiting what is now the Tuscon, Arizona, area in the 1770's. (See section 2.48.)

PART 2

The Cities: Facilities and Services

The Saguaro (pronounced sah-war-oh) grows only in Arizona and Mexico, with a few scattered along the Colorado River in California. This cactus grows to a height of from 40 to 50 feet and lives to an age of from 150 to 200 years. These unusual plants can be seen at the Arizona-Sonora Desert Museum at the Saguaro National Monument. The Museum and National Monument can be reached from Tucson, Arizona. (See section 2.48) (Photo, courtesy of the Arizona Office of Tourism).

2.1 Albuquerque, New Mexico

Albuquerque, with a population of about a third of a million, is the largest city in New Mexico. It was named for the Spanish viceroy, the Duke of Albuquerque, who governed here from 1702 to 1712.

If you like clean air and bright sunshine, this is the place for you. The city is 5,354 feet above sea level; and although it's hot during the daytime, it cools off at night. The climate is dry, there's no ragweed pollen, and perhaps most important, the mountains surrounding the city are beautiful.

Albuquerque is a commercial center and the home of the University of New Mexico. Old Town Albuquerque, the oldest part of the city, has been restored in the style of the city's Spanish period. Visitors may explore this area of historic adobe houses on foot; it's a good place to purchase the handmade silver and turquoise jewelery characteristic of this region.

From Albuquerque, you can visit the Sandia Mountains and the pueblos and national monuments of northwestern New Mexico. Santa Fe, the historic capital of New Mexico, is about an hour's drive north.

Amtrak Station: 314 1st St., SW (downtown).

Tourist Information: Albuquerque Convention and Visitors' Bureau, Convention Center, 401 Second St., N.W., Albuquerque, NM 87102, 505-243-3696.

Lodging: The Regent of Albuquerque, 3rd and Marquette, 505-247-3344 (deluxe). Quality Inn Central, 717 Central Ave., N.W. (near Old Town), 505-247-1501 (moderate). Town House Motor Hotel, 400 Central Ave., S.E., 505-247-0703 (budget).

Car Rental: Avis, Albuquerque International Airport, 505-842-4080. Hertz, Albuquerque International Airport, 505-842-4235 (railroad-station pickup available). Gelco, 2601 Yale St., S.E., 505-345-6668 (inexpensive).

Taxis: Yellow Cab, 505-247-8888. Checker Cab, 505-243-7777.

Public Transportation: Sun Tran (buses), 505-766-7830.

Bus Stations: Greyhound, 505-243-4435. Trailways, 505-842-5511. Both at 302 2nd St., N.W.

Tours: Gray Line, 505-243-5501. Piper Tours, 505-842-1184.

Attractions: Sandia Peak Aerial Tramway, Cibola National Forest, 505-298-8518. Take I-25 north to Tramway Road, then 4.5 miles east. Spectacular view over the city from the top, which is above 10,000 feet. Open daily, daytimes and evenings; call for hours. Also, be sure to stop at Bien Mur Indian Market, on Tramway Road.

Indian Pueblo Cultural Center; 2401 Twelfth St., N.W., 505-843-7270. Museum of Pueblo Indians. Dances performed weekend afternoons in summer. Open Mon–Fri. 9–5, Sat–Sun. 11–5 in summer; Mon.–Sat. 9:30–5:30 rest of year.

Old Town; fifteen blocks west of downtown Albuquerque, off Rio Grande Blvd.

Rio Grande Zoo; 903 10th St., S.W., 505-843-7413. Rain forest, reptile house, prairie-dog colony. Open daily 9–5.

Day Trips: Santa Fe, 60 miles north on I-25. Information available from Santa Fe Chamber of Commerce; 200 W. Mary St., 505-983-7317.

Isleta Pueblo and Mission, about 10 miles south off I-25, 505-869-3111. An interesting pueblo, more accessible from Albuquerque than most. Extensive tours of this and other pueblos are available from the tour companies listed above; brochures for driving tours are available at the Albuquerque visitors' center (see above).

2.2 Atlanta, Georgia

Standing on a high plateau above the Chattahoochee River, Atlanta is one of America's top twenty metropolitan areas in population and is the financial and commercial capital of the Southeast, as well as the political capital of Georgia.

Atlanta had an unusual origin. In 1837 Georgia began construction of a railroad to connect the northwestern portion of the state with the Tennessee River at Chattanooga. At that time, however, there was no town in northwest Georgia to serve as a starting point; so the surveyors simply planted their stakes at a convenient place and established a community called Terminus. As the starting point of the new line to Tennessee, the town attracted connecting railroads from the east and began to grow. In 1847 it was incorporated under its present name. With the railroads came industry, and Atlanta had developed into the South's leading manufacturing center by the 1850s.

Atlanta's importance to the South during the Civil War made it a prime Union objective, and fighting around the city was heavy. It was under siege for two months and finally fell to the Union forces in September 1864. Two months later, before setting out on his famous march to the sea, General William T. Sherman made sure that the city would be of little use to the Confederates: His men expelled the population, then burned the city to the ground. After the war, however, Atlanta revived, bigger and more important than ever.

Atlanta today can practically be called a boom town—so many people and businesses have moved in during the past few years. Famous for its showplace hotels and glistening new architecture, Atlanta embodies the vibrant spirit of the "new South." Although much of its tradition has been left behind in the race for progress, many people have called this city the best place to live in the United States.

Peachtree Station: 1688 Peachtree St., NW (about 2 miles out of town; in daytime take bus 23 to Art Center metro station).

Tourist Information: Atlanta Convention and Visitors' Bureau, 233 Peachtree St., NE, Suite 200, Atlanta, GA 30043, 404-521-6633. Sights, Delights, and Savings Program, 800-241-3803.

Lodging: Hyatt Regency Atlanta; 265 Peachtree St., NE, 404-577-1234 (deluxe). Ramada Inn Central, 1630 Peachtree St., 404-875-9711 (expensive; across from railway station). Days Inn Atlanta Downtown; 300 Spring St., 404-623-1144 (moderate). For bed-and-breakfast accommodations, contact Bed and Breakfast Atlanta, 1221 Fairview Rd., NE, Atlanta, GA 30306, 404-378-6026.

Car Rental: Budget, 140 Courtland St., NE, 404-530-3030. Avis, 143 Courtland St., NE, 404-659-4814 (railroad-station pickup available). Hertz, 202 Courtland St., NE, 404-659-3000 (railroad-station pickup available).

Taxis: Checker Cab, 404-872-2318. Yellow Cab, 404-521-0200.

Public Transportation: MARTA (buses and rapid rail), 404-522-4711.

Bus Stations: Greyhound, 81 International Blvd., NW, 404-522-6300. Trailways, 200 Spring St., NW, 404-524-2441.

Tours: Gray Line, 404-767-0594. AAtlanta Tours, 404-762-7991.

Currency Exchange: American Express Co., Colony Sq., 1175 Peachtree St., NE; 404-892-8175.

Attractions: Georgia State Capitol, Washington St., 404-656-2844. Open Mon.-Fri. 9-5, Sat. 10-2, Sun. 1-3.

Cyclorama, Grant Park, 404-624-1071. A panoramic painting of the Battle of Atlanta. Open daily 9-5.

Atlanta Historical Society, 3101 Andrews Dr., 404-261-1837. (9 miles north of city center). Archives, museum, restored homes and other buildings, craft demonstrations, children's program. Museum open Tues.-Sat. 10:30-4, Sun. 2-4.

Grave of Reverend Martin Luther King, Jr., Ebeneezer Baptist Church, 413 Auburn Ave., NE Martin Luther King, Jr., and his father were both pastors of this church. For more information call the Martin Luther King, Jr., historic district at 404-524-1956.

Robert W. Woodruff Art Center, 1280 Peachtree St., 404-892-3600. Brand new, $20 million art center. Open Tues.-Sat. 10-5, Sun. 12-5.

Day Trips: Stone Mountain, off I-285 east, via I-78, 404-469-9831. Giant mountainside carvings of Confederate heroes. Also historical museums, restored plantation, water sports, picnicking, and scenic mountain railroad. Attractions open 10–9 June–Aug., 10–5:30 Sept.–May. Take bus 120 from Avondale metro station.

Six Flags over Georgia, I-20 west, 404-948-9290. Portrays history of Georgia under flags of Spain, France, England, the Republic of Georgia, the Confederacy, and the United States. Amusement park. Fireworks nightly. Open daily in summer, weekends in spring and fall. Closed in winter. Call for hours. Take special bus from High Tower metro station.

2.3 Baltimore, Maryland

Baltimore was named for George Calvert, Lord Baltimore, the founder of Maryland. It stands at the northern tip of the Patapsco River, an arm of Chesapeake Bay, and is one of America's most important ports. The city has plenty going for it, although it tends to be obscured by its more illustrious neighbors, New York, Philadelphia, and Washington, D.C. It is the home of Johns Hopkins University, the first American institution of higher learning to reorganize itself on the European model, stressing postgraduate study and independent research. The city has a first-class art museum, famous libraries, and the oldest ship in the U.S. Navy—the frigate *Constellation,* built in 1797. Edgar Allan Poe came from Baltimore; so did Babe Ruth. Francis Scott Key wrote "The Star-spangled Banner" here while watching the bombardment of Fort McHenry from the deck of a British warship in 1814. The Maryland Historical Society has the manuscript. The old Inner Harbor area is being restored.

Baltimore has a special place in American railroad history, for it was here that the first line in the United States, the Baltimore and Ohio (B & O), opened in 1830. It was also the site of the famous race between the steam engine Tom Thumb and a horse. The horse won when the engine broke down, but the locomotive, of course, was the ultimate victor. The B & O's original Mount Clare station is still standing and is now part of the Transportation Museum, which houses a number of well-preserved old locomotives and other exhibits.

Pennsylvania Station: 1515 N. Charles St. (about a mile north of city center; about 6 blocks northeast of the State Center metro station, at Eutaw and Preston streets); all Amtrak trains and Conrail commuter trains to Washington, D.C.

Tourist Information: Baltimore Office of Tourism and Promotion, 110 W. Baltimore St., Baltimore, MD 21201, 301-752-8632.

Lodging: Belvedere Hotel, 1 E. Chase St., 301-547-1080 (deluxe). Howard House, 8 North Howard, 301-539-1680 (moderate). Best Western Harbor City Inn, 1701 Russell St., 301-727-3400 (moderate). For bed-and-breakfast accommodations, contact Sharpe-Adams, Inc., 8 Gentry Ct., Annapolis, MD 21401, 301-269-6232.

Car Rental: Hertz, Holiday Inn Downtown, 301 W. Lombard St., 301-332-0015 (direct line from station). Budget, 202 S. Paca St., 301-837-6955. Avis, Lombard and Charles sts., 301-685-6000.

Taxis: Yellow Cab, 301-685-1212. Arrow Cab, 301-358-9696.

Public Transportation: MTA (buses and new metro system, opened November 1983), 301-539-5000.

Bus Stations: Greyhound, Howard and Center sts., 301-744-9311. Trailways, 210 W. Fayette St., 301-752-2115.

Tours: American Excursions, 301-889-8889. Alexander Tours, 301-664-5577. Baltimore Patriot Boat Tours, 301-685-4288.

Attractions: B & O Railroad Museum, Pratt and Poppleton sts., 301-237-2387. Open Wed.–Sun. 10–4.

National Aquarium, Pier 3, 501 Pratt St., 301-576-3800. Open Mon.–Thurs. 10–5, Fri.–Sun. 10–8, May 16–Sept. 15; Sat.–Thurs. 10–5, Fri. 10–8, Sept. 16–May 15.

U.S Frigate *Constellation,* dock at foot of Pratt and Light sts., 301-539-1797. Open 10–dusk June 16–Labor Day; 10–6 Labor Day–Oct. 15; 10–4 Oct. 16–May 15; 10–6 May 16–June 15.

Fort McHenry National Monument, 301-962-4290. Take MTA bus from Pratt St. (for information, call number above) or the ferry that leaves every half hour (Memorial Day—Labor Day) from the dock at the end of Light St. Open daily 9–8 in summer, 9–5 the rest of the year.

2.4   Birmingham, Alabama

Birmingham is the largest city in Alabama and the home of the Southern steel industry. It lies in the Jones Valley, in the southernmost reaches of the Appalachian Mountains.

Look for the city on a Civil War map, and you'll find nothing but cotton fields and a hamlet called Elyton. By 1871, however, railroads from four directions had met in these cotton fields, and the railroads made this an obvious location for new steel works. The town that grew up here was named Birmingham, after the British steel capital; and it soon began to resemble the northern steel city Pittsburgh, complete with noise and pollution.

Birmingham today, happily, is a good deal cleaner and more pleasant than it once was. The steel mills are still very much in evidence, however, and Birmingham's continuing preeminence among Southern industrial cities is symbolized by the 55-foot statue of Vulcan, the Roman god of fire and metalworking, which overlooks the city from the top of Red Mountain. Visitors to Birmingham have plenty of opportunities to learn about the steel-making process and its role in the history of the area.

Amtrak Station: 1819 Morris Ave. (about 3 blocks south of city center, but most hotels are about 10 blocks away).

Tourist Information: Greater Birmingham Convention and Visitors' Bureau, Tourist Division, 2027 1st Ave. N., Birmingham, AL 35203, 205-252-9825.

Lodging: Hyatt Birmingham, 901 21st St. N., 205-322-1234 (deluxe). Holiday Inn–Convention Center, 2230 10th St. N., 205-328-6320 (moderate). EconoLodge, 2224 5th Ave. N., 205-324-6688 (moderate). For bed-and-breakfast accommodations, contact Bed and Breakfast Birmingham, P.O. Box 31328, Birmingham, AL 35222, 205-591-6406.

Car Rental: Avis, 2023 5th Ave. N., 205-251-3223. National, 2315 5th Ave. N. 205-252-6087. Dollar, 7700 5th Ave. N., 205-833-2900.

Taxis: Anderson Taxi, 205-252-5373.

Public Transportation: Birmingham Transit Authority (buses) 205-322-7701.

Bus Stations: Greyhound, 618 N. 19th St. N., 205-252-7171. Trailways, 2324 5th Ave. N. 205-323-1678.

Attractions: Arlington Historic House and Museum, 331 Cotton Ave., SW, 205-780-5656. Birmingham's oldest home, elegantly restored. Open Tues.–Sat. 9–4:30, Sun. 1–4:30.

Red Mountain Museum, 1425 22nd St. S., 205-254-2757. Natural history. Walkway carved into the side of the mountain displays geologic formations. Fossils. Open Tues.–Sat. 10–5, Sun. 12–5.

Vulcan Park, Route 31 and Valley Ave., 205-254-2628. Elevator to observation deck. Vulcan's torch usually burns green but is changed to red after a traffic fatality in the area. Open daily 8:30–10.

The Sloss Furnace, 1st Ave. N. at 32nd St., 205-254-2367. Site of early steel production, declared a National Historic Landmark in 1983. Open Sat. 10–5, Sun. 12–5, Mon.–Fri. by appointment.

Day Trip: Tannehill Historical State Park, off I-59 near Bessemer (Bucksville exit), 205-477-6101. Birthplace of Birmingham iron industry. Ruins of Tannehill furnaces, reconstructed grist mill, cotton gin, pioneer homes, church. Open 24 hours daily.

2.5   Boise, Idaho

Boise, the capital of Idaho and its largest city, is at the edge of a huge national-forest system that covers half the state. In fact, the city's name derives from the French word *boisé,* meaning "wooded." French Canadians heading west used the site as a resting place after crossing the Snake River plain. The first American settlers arrived in 1863, many in quest of gold. Agriculture, state government, and the tourist trade support Boise's economy.

Boise's Amtrak station is a lovely Spanish-style structure. The state capitol building stands at the other end of the thoroughfare, with parks, museums, the University of Idaho, and the Boise River in between. The capitol is built of a distinctive local sandstone, which has been used in many buildings throughout the city.

Amtrak Station: 1701 Eastover Terrace (at the end of Capitol Blvd.).

Tourist Information: Boise Convention and Visitors' Bureau, Hoff Building, 802 W. Bannock, Suite 308 (P.O. Box 2106, Boise, Idaho 83701), 208-344-7777, from out of state 800-635-5240.

Lodging: Red Lion Motor Inn—Riverside, 2900 Chinden Blvd., 208-343-1871 (beautiful location with all services, but not downtown; expensive). Red Lion Inn—Downtowner, 1901 Main St., 208-344-7691 (expensive). Statehouse Inn, 981 Grove St., 208-342-4622 (from out of state 800-635-5628) (moderate). Sands Motel, 1111 W. State St., 208-343-2533 (budget).

Car Rental: Hertz, Municipal Airport, 3201 Airport Way, 208-383-3100 (railroad-station pickup with advance reservation). Avis, Municipal Airport, 3201 Airport Way, 208-383-3350.

Taxis: Orange Taxi, 208-345-3535. AOK Cab, 208-384-9198.

Public Transportation: Boise Urban Stages (buses), 208-336-1010.

Bus Stations: Greyhound, 1212 W. Bannock, 208-343-3681. Trailways, 1009 S. 8th St., 208-343-7531.

Attractions: State Capitol, Capitol Boulevard, 208-334-2120. Open Mon.–Sat. 8:30–5.

Old Idaho Penitentiary, Penitentiary Rd. (off Warm Springs Rd.), 208-334-2844. Built in 1872 by convicts. Gardens, interesting architecture, visitors' center with slide show. Open daily 12–4.

Boise Green Belt Riverside Park. 8 miles of parkland along the Boise River through the center of the city.

Day Trips: Boise National Forest. Just outside the city, the forest has many scenic drives and walks. Write or call for maps and information: Public Information Officer, Office of Information, Boise National Forest, 1750 Front St., Boise, ID 83702, 208-334-1516. This office also serves as a visitors' center.

Sun Valley. About 160 miles from Boise, Sun Valley is actually more than a day's trip away. Stay overnight, and enjoy the sports facilities and magnificent surroundings. Call 800-635-8261 for information.

2.6   Boston, Massachusetts

Boston is the most important city in New England and one of America's most beautiful cities. A major urban center on a small scale, it is certainly one of the finest walking cities in America. Historical sites, museums, lovely parks and gardens, picturesque streets, and colorful ethnic neighborhoods are all within walking distance of one another or are easily reached by public transportation.

Boston was first settled in 1630 and was immediately named the capital of the Massachusetts Bay Colony. (The first capital was Salem.) The Puritan founders of Boston hoped to make their city an example for the rest of the world, a "city on a hill." They may not have succeeded as they would have liked, but they did establish Boston as a center of theology and education, as well as of commerce and government.

Ironically, Boston, the center of British colonial government, was also the seat of the American Revolution. The Boston Massacre in 1770 and the Boston Tea Party in 1773 were important signals of the popular discontent that led to the war. Fighting actually began in 1775, just outside Boston in the towns of Lexington and Concord. Boston has managed to preserve many colonial and Revolutionary buildings, which continue to give the old city a strong and exhilarating sense of the past.

The Amtrak train brings you to South Station, a grand old edifice built in the 1890s and now being restored.

Amtrak Stations: South Station, Atlantic Ave. and Summer St. Several blocks south of the city center. Subway station outside. Amenities in South Station include newspapers and snacks. Amtrak trains and commuter trains to the southern and western suburbs use this terminal.

Back Bay Station (temporarily closed).

Tourist Information: Boston Convention and Tourist Bureau, Prudential Plaza, P.O. Box 490, Boston, MA 02199, 617-536-4100. Events line: 617-267-6446. Information centers are at the Prudential Center and on Boston Common at Tremont St., near the Park Street subway station.

Lodging: Ritz Carlton Hotel, Arlington and Newbury sts., 800-225-7620 (deluxe). Marriott Longwharf, 296 State St., 800-228-9290 (deluxe). Copley Square Hotel, 47 Huntington Ave., 800-225-7062 (expensive). Harvard Motor House, 110 Mt. Auburn St. (in Harvard Square, Cambridge), 617-864-5200 (moderate to expensive). For bed-and-breakfast accommodations, contact New England Bed and Breakfast, 1045 Centre St., Newton, MA 02159, 617-498-1819, or Bed and Breakfast Brookline/Boston, Box 732, Brookline, MA 02145, 617-277-2292.

Car Rental: Avis, 60 Park Sq., 617-267-8500. Budget, 62 Eliot St., 617-426-3043 (railroad-station pickup available). Mr. Rent-A-Car, 200 Milk St., 617-482-9010. Brodie's Auto Rental, 106 Mt. Auburn St. (in Harvard Square), 617-491-7600.

Taxis: Yellow Cab, 617-422-0055. Checker Cab, 617-536-7000.

Public Transportation: MBTA (buses and subways), 617-722-3200.

Bus Stations: Greyhound, 10 St. James Ave., 617-423-5810 (frequent service to Maine). Trailways, 555 Atlantic Ave., 617-482-6620.

Tours: Freedom Trail Walking Tour. Get information at the booth on the Common (see ''Tourist Information,'' above) or at visitors' center at 15 State St. Bus tour available from Brush Hill Shuttle, 617-472-0925.

Gray Line, 617-426-8805. Massachusetts Bay Line Harbor Tours, 617-542-8000. Bay State Spray Cruises, 617-723-7800.

Currency Exchange: American Express, 10 Tremont St., 617-723-8422. Deak-Perera, 160 Franklin St., 617-426-0016. Major downtown banks will exchange most foreign currencies.

Attractions: Boston Common, between Arlington, Beacon, Park, Tremont, and Boylston Sts. The oldest public park in America. The public gardens and famous swan boats are at the western end, adjoining Arlington St. The gold-leaf dome of the State House overlooks the park.

Faneuil Hall, Faneuil Hall Square at Merchant's Row, 617-523-1999. An eighteenth-century market and meeting hall, now restored to include museums, restaurants, and shops.

Museum of Fine Arts, Huntington Ave. and the Fenway, 617-267-9300. Open Tues. 10–5, Wed. 10–10, Thurs.–Sun. 10–5. West wing open until 10 Wed.–Fri.

New England Aquarium, Central Wharf on Atlantic Ave., 617-742-8870. World's largest tank, full of sharks, tortoises, etc. Open Mon.–Thurs. 9—5, Fri. 9–9, Sat.–Sun. 9–6.

Old State House, Washington and State sts., 617-242-5655. Built in 1657. The Boston Massacre occurred outside. Open daily 9:30–5 April–Oct.; Mon.–Fri. 10–4, Sat. 9:30–5, Sun. 11–5 rest of year.

Old North Church (Christ Church), 193 Salem St., 617-523-6676. Oldest church building in Boston, it held Paul Revere's lanterns on the eve of the Battle of Lexington. The church is in the heart of Boston's Italian North End, a wonderful area for strolling and sampling the wares of the many small shops that line the streets. Open daily 9–5.

Harvard University, Harvard Square, Cambridge. America's oldest university has museums and fine architecture. Tours leave the information center at 1350 Massachusetts Avenue. Call 617-495-1573 for schedule.

Day Trips: Minuteman National Historical Park, Concord. Visitors' center open daily 9–5 (617-369-6993). The North Bridge, where the first fighting of the Revolution took place, is just inside the Concord entrance to the park. To get here from Boston, take a commuter train from North Station, 1200 Causeway Street (there are several each day), to Concord. Walk away from the station to Main Street or Sudbury Road, and continue on either of these to the Concord Green. From there, walk on Monument Street to the park. The total walking distance is about a mile.

Salem. Walking-tour brochure available from Salem Chamber of Commerce, 221 Derby St., Salem, MA 01970, 617-744-0004. Interesting sites include the House of the Seven Gables, which inspired Hawthorne's novel (617-744-0991).

Cape Cod. Tours available from Gray Line, Brush Hill, and Bay State Spray Cruises.

2.7   Burlington, Vermont

Ethan Allen, leader of the Green Mountain Boys in Revolutionary War times, was one of the first residents of Burlington, founded in 1773 on the shore of Lake Champlain. During the War of 1812, British ships sailing on the lake fired on the town. Today, however, Burlington is a quiet city, the home of the University of Vermont and the shopping and cultural center of northern Vermont. Its many shops and restaurants make it an ideal place from which to explore the small towns that surround it. Driving and hiking in the nearby Green Mountains are favorite pastimes, especially during the autumn, when the foliage is most spectacular. During the summer, visitors will enjoy the Lake Champlain Shakespeare Festival, staged annually. Amtrak passengers detrain at Essex Junction, about 5 miles from Burlington.

Amtrak Station: 29 Railroad Ave., Essex Junction. Connecting bus to Burlington meets the train daily except Sunday, scheduled to arrive within 30 minutes of the arrival of the train.

Tourist Information: Lake Champlain Regional Chamber of Commerce, Box 453, Burlington, VT 05402, 802-863-3489.

Lodging: Radisson Burlington Hotel, Battery St., 802-658-6500 (expensive). Midtown Motel, 230 Main St., 802-862-9686 (budget).

Car Rental: Hertz, Burlington Airport, 802-864-7409 (will reimburse for cab fare, with receipt). Budget, Burlington Airport, 802-658-1211.

Taxis: B and B Taxi, 802-862-3300. Benway's Cab, 802-862-1010.

Public Transportation: Burlington Transit Authority (buses), 802-864-0211.

Bus Station: Vermont Transit, 135 St. Paul St., 802-864-6811.

Attractions: Lake Champlain Ferry to Port Kent, N.Y., King St. Dock, 802-864-9804. Runs daily when the lake is not frozen. Call for schedule.

Champlain Shakespeare Festival (July and August), 802-656-2094.

Shelburne Museum, Shelburne (on U.S.-7, south of Burlington), 802-985-3344. Museum of New England life: restored homes and public buildings, workshops, gardens. Open daily 9–5 May–Oct.; only Sun. 1–4 Nov.–April. City bus to the museum gate is available (call Burlington Transit Authority, above).

Day Trip: Mount Mansfield, Stowe, about 45 miles from Burlington. Take I-89 south to Waterbury, Route 100 to Stowe, then Route 108 north to Mount Mansfield. Toll road to the top of the mountain open mid-June through mid-October 9–5. Gondola ski lift open mid-June through mid-October 9–4. After leaving Mount Mansfield, drive north on Route 108 through Smugglers Notch and return to Burlington on Routes 15 and I-89.

2.8   Charleston, South Carolina

Charleston, founded in 1680, is one of America's most interesting cities. It lies on a peninsula between the Ashley and Cooper rivers, at the head of a great natural harbor, and is known for its graceful homes and wide streets. The city is named for King Charles II, who in 1663 gave eight of his friends a charter for a new colony to be planted south of Virginia. The most important of these men was Anthony Cooper, Lord Ashley. (The rivers of Charleston were named after him.) The South Carolina colony was a success from the beginning. Rice and tobacco plantations, worked by slave laborers, flourished, and the great harbor made the port of Charleston the most important trading center of the Atlantic South.

To protect Charleston harbor, the U.S. Government established Fort Sumter on an island off the coast. When South Carolina became the first state to secede, in December 1860, its governor asked that the fort be turned over to the state. Major Robert Anderson, commanding the garrison, refused the request, with the backing of President Abraham Lincoln. Anderson's men were short of supplies, however, and so Lincoln decided to send a provisioning vessel carrying no arms or reinforcements. Lincoln notified the South Carolina authorities of his intention. This put the secessionist leaders to a stern test: If they permitted the ship to land, they would be bowing to federal authority; if they prevented it from doing so by force, there would be war. The Confederate leaders chose to bombard the fort, and so at dawn on April 12, 1861, the cannon on shore opened fire on Fort Sumter. Two days later, Major Anderson surrendered. The Civil War was on.

Because it lay out of the way of Sherman's march through South Carolina, Charleston was largely undamaged by the war, and therefore, it retains much of its antebellum character. The annual Festival of Houses attracts visitors from all over the nation, as does the Spoleto festival of music and drama. The city is world famous for its gardens. Visitors can tour the old city market and the slave auction block, which remain much as they were before that fateful April morning.

Amtrak Station: 4565 Gaynor Ave., North Charleston. About 8 miles west of the city on Route 52; bus service to Charleston available.

Tourist Information: Visitor Information Center, 85 Calhoun St. (P.O. Box 975, Charleston, SC 29402), 803-722-8338.

Lodging: Mills House Hotel, 115 Meeting St., 803-577-2400 (deluxe). Two Meeting Street Inn, 2 Meeting Street, 803-723-7322 (expensive; breakfast and use of bicycles included). Best Western King Charles, 237 Meeting St., 803-723-7451 (moderate; includes breakfast). For bed-and-breakfast accommodations, contact Historic Charleston Bed and Breakfast, 23 Wentworth St., Charleston, SC 29405 (803-722-6606).

Car Rental: Hertz, Heart of Charleston Motel, 200 Meeting St., 803-723-2016. Avis, 170 Lockwood Blvd., 803-722-2977. National, 252 Meeting St., 803-723-8266.

Taxis: Veteran Taxi, 803-577-5577. Safety Cab, 803-722-4066.

Public Transportation: Downtown Area Shuttle (DASH), 803-577-6970 ext. 500. City Bus Service, 803-722-2226.

Bus Stations: Greyhound, 89 Society St., 803-722-7721. Trailways, 85 Calhoun St., 803-723-8649.

Tours: Gray Line Water Tours, 803-722-1112. Gray Line Bus Tours, 803-722-4444. Palmetto Carriage Tours, 803-723-8145.

Attractions: Edmondston-Alston House, 21 E. Battery St., and Nathaniel Russell House, 51 Meeting St., 803-722-3405. Two of Charleston's most opulent mansions. Combined or separate admissions. Mon.–Sat. 10–5, Sun. 2–5.

Fort Sumter, 803-722-1691. Tour boat leaves from Municipal Marina off Lockwood Blvd.

For information on Festival of Houses and Spoleto Festival, contact visitors' center, above.

Day Trips: Middleton Place, Route 61 (14 miles north), 803-556-6020. Home of Henry Middleton, president of First Continental Congress. The landscaped gardens, originally planted by slaves, are the oldest in America. Open 9–5; house open Tues.–Sun. 10–4:30, Mon. 1:30–4:30.

Cypress Gardens, I-52 (24 miles north of Charleston), 803-553-0515. Not the Florida tourist attraction. Native cypress forest on old rice plantation, accented with flowers. Boat rides through the gardens available. Open weekdays 8–4, weekends 9–5.

2.9   Charlottesville, Virginia

The city is named for Charlotte, queen of England and wife of George III, during whose reign it was founded in 1762. Although the city bears her name, Queen Charlotte takes second place to another person, even though he has been dead for more than a century and a half: Charlottesville is Thomas Jefferson's town.

Jefferson was born at Shadewell, 6 miles east of the present city of Charlottesville, in 1743, and lived his entire life in the area except when serving his country in Washington or abroad. His adult home, the mountaintop estate called Monticello, which he designed himself, is a short distance south of town. The University of Virginia, which he founded and whose first building, the Rotunda, he also designed, is in Charlottesville.

By any standard, Jefferson was a formidable personality. Of course, he was the primary author of the Declaration of Independence and the third president of the United States. He was for a time minister to France and secretary of state. He wrote the Virginia Statute of Religious Liberty and engineered the Louisiana Purchase. But Jefferson was much more than a statesman and politician. He was an architect, an accomplished musician, a great correspondent, and a brilliant philosopher.

The town of Charlottesville itself is known for its graciousness and hospitality, and these traditions are maintained in the many old-fashioned inns and guest houses that are found here. An especially good time to visit is in the fall, when the leaves have turned.

Union Station: 810 W. Main St. (downtown).

Tourist Information: Charlottesville–Albemarle County Chamber of Commerce, 415 E. Market St., 804-295-3141. The Chamber of Commerce also operates a visitors' center, but it is outside of town on Route 20 (P.O. Box 161, Dept. A, Charlottesville, VA 22902; 804-293-6789).

Lodging: Boar's Head Inn, I-250 (3 miles from the station), 804-296-2181 (not downtown, but a resort hotel that offers all services; hotel desk will arrange taxi service and car rental, if requested; deluxe). Howard Johnson's, 13th and W. Main sts., 804-296-8121 (moderate). University Lodge, 140 Emmett St., 804-293-5141 (near University of Virginia; budget). For bed-and-breakfast accommodations, contact Guesthouses Bed and Breakfast, P.O. Box 5737, Charlottesville, VA 22903, 804-979-7264. Many elegant accommodations available.

Car Rental: Avis, Route 29N, 804-973-3336 (railroad station pickup usually available). Hertz, 1283 Seminole Trail, 804-973-6040 (4–5 miles from station).

Taxis: Yellow Cab, 804-295-4131. Pace's Taxi, 804-293-8121.

Public Transportation: Charlottesville Transit Service (buses), 804-296-7433.

Bus Station: Trailways, 310 W. Main St., 804-295-5131.

Tours: VIP Tours (individual van or limo tours), 804-296-5219.

Attractions: Monticello, off Route 53 southeast of Charlottesville, 804-295-8181. Thomas Jefferson's home. Open 8–5 March–Oct., 9–4:30 rest of year.

    Michie Tavern, Route 53, near Monticello, 804-977-1234. Tavern built in 1735, where you can get a colonial-style lunch. Museum open 9–5 daily.

    Ash Lawn, off Route 53, past Monticello, 804-293-9539. James Monroe's home. Open 9–6 daily March–Oct., 10–5 rest of year.

    University of Virginia Rotunda, I-29 and I-250 business routes, 804-924-7969.

Day Trip: Skyline Drive and Shenandoah National Forest. Take I-64 west about 30 miles to Skyline Drive, then travel north along the Blue Ridge to Front Royal. This is the most beautiful section of the mountain drive.

2.10 Cheyenne, Wyoming

In 1983, Amtrak trains ceased to run along the Wyoming route and were rerouted along the former Denver and Rio Grande Railroad line from Denver to Salt Lake City. There are no plans at present for resuming service to Cheyenne, although service may be restored at some time in the future.

2.11 Chicago, Illinois

Chicago stands at the heart of the continent and has long been the transportation crossroads of North America. Its original stimulus came from waterways. The city grew up around the portage, and then the canal, between the Great Lakes and the Mississippi Valley.

The first railroads from Chicago were built westward to the fertile grain lands. Later, developers constructed lines from the east, hoping to obtain a share of the heavy traffic pouring into the city from the rich land around it. Chicago was hardly more than a trading post in 1820 and a town of a few hundred people in 1835; but it was a lusty metropolis by 1860. Few cities in the world have grown so big so fast. Not only is Chicago now the railroad capital of the nation and a major inland port, but its O'Hare Field is also the world's busiest air terminal.

Union Station, on the west bank of the South Branch at Jackson Boulevard, is conveniently close to the Chicago financial district (a short walk away), to hotels, and to shopping. It serves all Amtrak trains and a couple of busy commuter lines as well. It stands in the shadow of the world's tallest building—the Sears Tower. The tower, the station, the river, and the railroads symbolize perfectly what Chicago is all about.

Union Station: 210 S. Canal St. Downtown, with full station services. Serves all Amtrak trains. Commuter trains run from this station to Fox Lake, Elgin, Aurora, Joliet, Orland Park, Valparaiso (Ind.), and intermediate stations (312-346-5200).

Illinois Central Station: 151 N. Michigan Ave. The South Shore Line runs from this station (312-782-0676), as do commuter trains to southern suburbs (312-332-0295).

Northwestern Station: Canal and Madison sts., 2 blocks north of Union Station. Commuter trains to northern, northwestern, and western suburbs. Call 312-836-7860 or 312-836-7000 for information.

Tourist Information: Chicago Convention and Tourism Bureau, McCormick Place on the Lake, Chicago, IL 60616, 312-225-5000. Visitor Information Center, Chicago and Michigan aves. (in the historic Water Tower).

Lodging: The Drake, 140 E. Walton Place, 312-787-2200 (deluxe). Essex Inn, 800 S. Michigan Ave., 312-939-2800 (courtesy car service available; expensive). Avenue Motel, 1154 S. Michigan Ave., 312-427-8200 (moderate).

Car Rental: Hertz, 9 W. Kinzie St., 312-372-7600 (will refund cab fare from station, with receipt). Budget, 200 N. Dearborn St., 312-236-2145.

Taxis: Yellow Cab, 312-829-4222. Checker Cab, 312-829-4222.

Public Transportation: Chicago Transit Authority (buses, subways, and "els"), 312-836-7000.

Bus Stations: Greyhound, W. Randolph and N. Clark sts., 312-781-2900. Trailways, 20 E. Randolph St., 312-726-9500.

Tours: American Sightseeing Tours, 312-427-3100. Gray Line, 312-346-9506. Mercury Sightseeing Boats, 312-332-1353.

Currency Exchange: Foreign currency can be exchanged at major downtown banks or at American Express, 20 S. Michigan Ave., 312-435-2595, or Deak-Perera, 17 N. Dearborn St., 312-236-0583.

Attractions: Art Institute of Chicago, Michigan Ave. at Adams St., 312-443-3500. Open Mon., Tues., Wed., Fri. 10:30–4:30, Thurs. 10:30–8, Sat. 10–5, Sun. 10–6:30. Thurs. free.

Field Museum of Natural History, Lake Shore Dr. (in Grant Park), 312-922-9410. Open daily 9–5. Thurs. free.

Museum of Science and Industry, 57th St. and Lake Shore Dr., 312-684-1414. In Jackson Park, site of the 1893 World's Columbian Exposition, in one of the original buildings. Includes a coal mine and a German submarine. Open 9:30–5:30 in summer, 9:30–4 rest of year.

University of Chicago. Tours leave at 10 A.M. during the school year from 5801 S. Ellis Ave. (Mon.-Fri.) or 121 E. 59th St. (Sat.). Call 312-753-4429 for information.

Day Trips: Springfield. The Lincoln Home National Historical Site is at 8th and Jackson sts., 9 blocks from the Springfield railroad station. The visitors' center, 426 S. 7th St., 217-789-2357, is open 8–5. The current Amtrak schedule allows for sightseeing and return in one day.

Indiana Dunes. The South Shore Line stops at the National Lakeshore. It leaves Chicago from the Illinois Central Station (above).

2.12   Cincinnati, Ohio

Cincinnati got its name from the followers of the Roman general Cincinnatus, who at the end of a war put down his sword and picked up his plow. Early Americans saw themselves in the same mold, and a number of ex-Revolutionary soldiers organized themselves into an association they called the Society of the Cincinnati.

The city owes its existence to the Ohio River, which before the railroads and paved roads was the main commercial artery of the trans-Appalachian west. It first became known as a packing center—indeed, one of Cincinnati's early nicknames was ''Porkopolis,'' because so many hogs were slaughtered here. A sidelight of the meat-packing industry was the city's preeminence in the manufacture of tallow candles and soap, made from by-products of the packing plants—and even today Cincinnati's biggest industrial firm is that super soap seller Procter and Gamble.

Amtrak trains from the east enter the city over a long bridge across the Ohio. The downtown area is to the east (right side of the train), with Riverfront Stadium prominent in the foreground. But the *Cardinal* no longer uses the big Union Terminal. Instead, Amtrak has a small, somewhat out-of-the-way stop at River Road.

Amtrak Station: 1901 River Road, about 1 mile from town. No local bus from station.

Tourist Information: Cincinnati Convention and Visitors' Bureau, 200 W. 5th St., Cincinnati, OH 45202, 513-621-2142. 24-hour information line: 421-INFO.

Lodging: Westin Hotel Cincinnati, 4th and Vine sts., 513-621-7700 (deluxe). Clarion Hotel, 141 W. 6th St., 513-352-2110 (expensive). Milner Hotel, 108 Garfield Pl., 513-241-3570 (budget–moderate).

Car Rental: Budget, 300 Walnut St., 513-241-6134 (railroad-station service usually available). Hertz, Westin Hotel, Fountain Sq. S., 513-241-8079. Avis, 308 Walnut St., 513-621-1479.

Taxis: Yellow Cab, 513-241-2100.

Public Transportation: Queen City Metro (buses), 513-621-4455.

Bus Stations: Greyhound, 1065 Gilbert Ave., 513-352-6000. Trailways, 721 Reading Rd., 513-241-2620.

Tours: BB Riverboats (Covington, Ky.), 513-261-8500. Blue Chip Tours, 513-871-BLUE.

Attractions: Cincinnati Zoological Gardens, Dury Ave., 513-281-4700. One of the country's great zoos. Open daily 9–5.

Carew Tower Observatory, 5th and Vine sts., 513-381-3443. Observation deck in Cincinnati's tallest building. Overlooks the riverfront and Fountain Square, the city's central plaza. Open Tues.–Sat. 9–5.

Day Trips: U.S. Air Force Museum, Springfield Pike, Dayton, Ohio, about 60 miles north of Cincinnati. 513-255-3284. Open Mon.–Fri. 9–5, Sat.–Sun. 10–6.

Seven Caves, off U.S.-50, west of Bainbridge, Ohio, about 60 miles east of Cincinnati, 513-365-1283. Trails wind through spectacular caverns. Open 8A.M.–dark. Nearby (3 miles east of Bainbridge) is the Siep Mound State Memorial, site of an ancient Indian mound.

2.13 Cleveland, Ohio

In 1796 General Moses Cleaveland surveyed the area at the mouth of the Cuyahoga River, which was part of the Western Reserve, land once claimed by Connecticut but ceded to Congress upon the adoption of the Constitution. Cleaveland laid out a town site around a central public square, as was the New England practice. In the years since then, however, industry transformed Cleveland into a major city. With its deteriorated inner city surrounded by a ring of beautiful suburbs, its symphony orchestra and art museums, its chronic financial problems, its miserable pollution, and its outstanding universities and medical-research facilities, Cleveland typifies the triumphs and troubles of the American city.

Amtrak's new downtown station is next to Municipal Stadium, where the Browns and the Indians play. Unfortunately, downtown Cleveland is not safe at night, when the eastbound *Lake Shore* gets in. You will probably want to take a taxi to your hotel.

Lakefront Station: 200 E. Memorial Shoreway. Downtown, by the lake.

Tourist Information: Convention and Visitors' Bureau of Greater Cleveland, 1301 E. 6th St. (at St. Clair), Cleveland, OH 44114, 216-621-4110.

Lodging: Stouffer's Inn on the Square, 24 Public Square, 216-696-5600 (deluxe). Bond Court Motel, E. 6th St. and St. Clair Ave., 216-771-7600 (expensive). Holiday Inn Lakeside, 111 Lakeside Ave., 216-241-5100 (moderate). For bed-and-breakfast accommodations, contact Private Lodgings, P.O. Box 18590, Cleveland, OH 44118, 216-321-3213.

Car Rental: Hertz, 708 St. Clair Ave., 216-696-6066 (direct line from station; pickup available). Avis, 1180 Lakeside Ave., 216-623-0800 (railroad-station pickup available). National, 55 W. 6th St., 216-861-1691.

Taxis: Yellow Cab, 216-623-1500.

Public Transportation: Greater Cleveland Regional Transit Authority (buses and rapid-transit trains), 216-621-9500.

Bus Stations: Greyhound, 1465 Chester Ave., 216-781-1400. Trailways, 70 Chester Ave., 216-861-3161.

Tours: *Goodtime II* Lake and River Cruises, 216-531-1505.

Attractions: Cleveland Museum of Art, 1150 East Blvd. (University Circle), 216-421-7340. Open Tues., Thurs., Fri. 10-6; Wed. 10-10; Sat. 9-5; Sun. 1-6.

Western Reserve Historical Society, 10825 East Blvd. (University Circle), 216-721-5722. Open Tues.-Sat. 10-5, Sun. 12-5.

Cleveland and Akron Steam Train, P.O. Box 49, Peninsula, Ohio 44264, 216-657-2474. Old-fashioned steam train runs on the Cuyahoga Valley Line from Independence (a suburb about 8 miles from Cleveland) to Hail Farm (a restored village), and to Akron's Quaker Square. Runs Saturdays June–Oct.

The Cleveland Indians and the Cleveland Browns play at Municipal Stadium, W. 3rd and E. 9th sts. Call 216-861-1200 for information on the Indians' games. For information on the Browns, call 216-781-5600.

2.14   Dallas, Texas

Dallas is the second-largest city in Texas, with a population of nearly a million—only Houston, its sworn rival, is bigger. Dallas was founded on the Trinity River by John Neely Bryan, who settled here in 1841 and probably named it for George M. Dallas, then vice-president under James K. Polk.

Dallas was originally a cotton city—its Cotton Exchange still prospers—but the discovery of the eastern Texas oil fields in 1930 made oil the city's most important commodity. Dallas is also the banking capital of the Southwest and one of the country's leading convention centers.

President John F. Kennedy was assassinated in Dallas on November 22, 1963. The cenotaph and memorial park at Dealy Plaza mark the site, and the JFK Museum commemorates the president.

Dallas has restored and rebuilt its old railroad station into a modern transportation center, conveniently located in the heart of town.

Union Station: 400 S. Houston St. (downtown, at Young St.). One of the few American stations that offer a full line of services: restaurants, car-rental desks, snack bars, newsstand, and the city's visitors' information center, in addition to full Amtrak baggage service.

Tourist Information: Convention and Visitors' Bureau Information Center, Union Station, 400 S. Houston St., Dallas, TX 75202, 214-747-2355.

Lodging: Hyatt Regency Dallas, 300 Reunion Blvd., 214-651-1234 (deluxe). Grenelefe Hotel, 1011 S. Alcard St., 214-421-1083 (expensive). Plaza Hotel, 1933 Main St. (at Harwood St.), 214-742-7251 (moderate). For bed-and-breakfast accommodations in the Dallas/Fort Worth area, contact Bed and Breakfast Texas Style, 214-298-5433.

Car Rental: Avis, Union Station, 400 S. Houston St., 214-748-8411. Budget, 200 S. Industrial St., 214-741-6843.

Taxis: Yellow Cab, 214-426-6262. Taxidallas, 214-631-8588.

Public Transportation: Dallas Transit System (buses), 214-826-2222.

Bus Stations: Trailways, 1500 Jackson St., 214-655-7000. Greyhound, Commerce and Lamar sts., 214-741-1481.

Tours: Silver Cloud; 214-521-1664. Texas Express; 214-357-4274. Gray Line, 214-824-2424.

Currency Exchange: Deak-Perera, 717 N. Harwood St., 214-748-7403.

Attractions: Dallas Hall of State, State Fair Park, 214-421-5136. Museum of Texas history, with special emphasis on the independence struggle. Open Mon.–Sat. 9–5, Sun. 1–5.

The Age of Steam Railroad Museum, State Fair Park, 214-565-9935. Open Sun. 1–5.

Dallas Science Place State Fair Park, 214-428-8351. Exciting exhibits; wonderful for children. Planetarium (call for show schedule). Open Tues.–Sat. 9–5, Sun. 1–5.

John Fitzgerald Kennedy Memorial, Main and Market sts. (Dealy Plaza). Marker and enclosed space for meditation.

Day Trips: Fort Worth has many outstanding museums, and you can get a taste of several in a day trip from Dallas. The Amos Carter Museum of Western Art (817-738-1933) specializes in the art of the Western United

51

States. The Kimbell Art Museum (817-332-8451) has a fine collection of European Renaissance art. The Fort Worth Art Museum (817-738-9215) displays twentieth-century art. All are within a few blocks of one another and are accessible by city bus from Dallas. (Amtrak also serves Fort Worth.) The tour companies listed above also offer tours of Fort Worth and environs, featuring such attractions as the Chisholm Trail and Billy Bob's, the honky-tonk night spot.

Six Flags over Texas, Route 360 (off I-30, west of Dallas), 817-461-1200. Historical theme park depicting Texas under flags of Spain, France, Mexico, the Republic of Texas, the Confederacy, and the United States. More than 100 rides. Open daily mid-May–Aug.; closed Dec.–mid-March; open weekends only during rest of year. Opens 10 A.M.; closing times vary.

2.15   Denver, Colorado

Denver is called the "Mile High City" with good reason: The U.S. Geological Survey has established that the second step of the state capitol building here is exactly 5,280 feet above sea level.

In 1858 gold nuggets were discovered at the mouth of Cherry Creek, just where it empties into the South Platte River. News of the discovery brought 100,000 would-be prospectors to Colorado, and although the Cherry Creek diggings were quickly played out, big strikes were soon made in the high mountains to the west. Denver, the town that grew up at Cherry Creek, later settled into the role it still plays as the administrative and distribution center of the whole Rocky Mountain region.

After the Civil War, the Indians remaining in Colorado were forcibly subdued. The state entered the Union in 1876, with Denver as its capital. Gold and silver mining was the main industry.

Since World War II Denver has experienced a new boom. The metropolitan-area population has tripled to more than 1.6 million. As a result, you'll find modern steel-and-glass buildings generously mixed with the Victorian gingerbread that graces the older architecture of the city.

Denver's Union Station is conveniently located near the central business district and state-capitol building. It's a fairly long walk to these places, though, so you may prefer to take a bus or taxi.

Union Station: 17th and Wynkoop sts., 303-534-2812. In town, several blocks west-northwest of the business district.

Tourist Information: Convention and Visitors' Bureau of Denver and Colorado, 225 W. Colfax Ave., Denver, CO 80202, 303-892-1505.

Lodging: Brown Palace Hotel, 321 17th St., 303-297-3111 (deluxe). Oxford Hotel, 1600 17th St., 303-628-5400 (expensive; newly renovated; half block from Union Station). Holiday Chalet Hotel Apartments, 1829 E. Colfax, 303-321-9975 (restored brownstone; some suites; moderate). Broadway Plaza, Broadway and 10th Ave. (on Capitol Hill), 303-893-3501 (budget–moderate). For bed-and-breakfast accommodations, contact Bed and Breakfast Colorado, P.O. Box 20596, Denver, CO 80220, 303-333-3340.

Car Rental: Hertz, 2001 Welton St., 303-861-2128. Avis, 1900 Broadway, 303-839-1280.

Taxis: Yellow Cab, 303-292-1212. Ritz Cab, 303-294-9199.

Public Transportation: Denver Regional Transportation District (buses), 303-778-6000.

Bus Stations: Both Greyhound, 303-623-6111, and Trailways, 303-534-2291, are at 19th and Arapahoe sts.

Tours: Gray Line, 303-289-2841 (city and mountain tours available, some offered in summer only). Mountain Men, 303-750-0090 (individual van tours). Historic Denver Tours, 303-534-1858 (walking or van tours).

Currency Exchange: Deak-Perera, 918 16th St., 303-571-0808.

Attractions: Forney Transportation Museum, 1416 Platte St., 303-433-3643. Open Mon.–Sat. 9–5, Sun. 11–6 in summer; Mon.–Sat. 9:30–5, Sun. 11–5:30 in winter. In the old Denver Tramways Power House. Railroad and auto exhibits. Railfans will also want to visit the Colorado Railroad Museum, on West 44th Ave. near Garden, 15 miles west of Denver—a must if you are interested in Colorado's colorful railroad history.

Molly Brown House. 1340 Pennsylvania St., 303-832-4092. Tours Tues.–Sat. 10–4, Sun. 12–4 in summer; reduced off-season hours (call for information).

U.S. Mint, W. Colfax Ave. at Cherokee St., 303-837-3582. All coins with little D's on them were made here. Open daily 8–3 May–Aug.; 8:30–3 rest of year. No tours during the last week of each fiscal year (late June—early July).

Day Trips: Rocky Mountain National Park, off U.S.-36, about 65 miles northwest of Denver. Stop at the visitors' center near the park entrance for literature and maps. For information in advance, write or call the superintendent, Rocky Mountain National Park, Estes Park, CO 80517, 303-586-2371. You can rent a car for this trip or, in summer, join a tour from Denver. Alternatively, you can take a train to Granby, which is nearer to the park. To rent a car from there, call National Car Rental at 303-887-2411. In winter call the park superintendent's office to find out if the road from Granby is open.

Pike's Peak, off U.S.-24, about 75 miles south of Denver. A highway goes from Colorado Springs to the top of the mountain, but many people prefer not to drive this difficult road themselves. Gray Line offers a tour to the top from Denver. There is also a cog railway to the top, which begins in Manitou Springs. Call 303-685-5401 for reservations.

2.16 Detroit, Michigan

One look at a map will tell you how Detroit was founded. The city sits on the Detroit River, the narrow channel that connects Lake Huron with Lake Erie and so commands all water traffic from the western Great Lakes to the east. Likewise, the city is squarely on the land route from Canada to the West, making its location doubly strategic. The French recognized the importance of the site and established a fort here in the seventeenth century. Today the French influence remains in a number of names found in and around the area. "Detroit" itself comes from the French word for "strait".

When the British drove the French from North America in 1763, the old French outpost became an important British fort. Despite the American Revolution, the British held onto Detroit until 1796, and they recaptured it during the War of 1812. Not until the Treaty of Ghent was implemented in 1815 did Detroit become firmly and finally an American city. It grew slowly during the nineteenth century; but after 1900, as the auto industry settled in the city, it didn't just grow—it exploded. In 10 years the population of Detroit doubled to more than a million; by 1920 it was the fourth-largest city in the United States, and its character as the nation's automotive center was fixed.

The city has had more than its share of ups and downs, but today it is enjoying a renaissance as hundreds of millions of dollars are being invested in new downtown construction. After seeing the new Detroit, however, visitors should be sure to walk through Detroit's ethnic neighborhoods, where some things never change. Visit colorful Greektown or Chinatown, or come in the summer, when a different ethnic festival is held each weekend on Philip A. Hart Plaza.

Amtrak Station: Vernor Hwy. and Michigan Ave. About 1 mile from the city center.

Tourist Information: Visitor Information Center, 2 E. Jefferson Ave. at Hart Plaza, 313-567-1170. Or write the Metropolitan Detroit Convention and Visitors' Bureau, Suite 1950, 100 Renaissance Center, Detroit, MI 48243. For travel or entertainment information, call 313-298-6262.

Lodging: Westin Hotel, Renaissance Center, 300 E. Jefferson Ave., 313-568-8000 (deluxe). Downtown Detroit TraveLodge, 1999 E. Jefferson Ave., 313-567-8888 (moderate). Shorecrest Motel, 1316 E. Jefferson Ave., 313-568-3000 (moderate).

Car Rental: Avis, 1101 Washington Blvd., 313-964-0494. Hertz, 1041 Washington Blvd., 313-964-2678. National, 510 Cass Ave. 313-963-2701.

Taxis: Checker Cab, 313-963-7000. City Cab, 313-833-7060.

Public Transportation: Detroit Department of Transportation (buses) 313-933-1300. Southeast Michigan Transportation Authority (buses; Dearborn and outlying areas), 313-962-5515.

Bus Stations: Greyhound, 130 E. Congress St., 313-963-9840. Trailways, 1205 Washington Blvd., 313-963-1322.

Tours: Gray Line, 313-224-1555.

Attractions: The Renaissance Center, on the Detroit waterfront, is the centerpiece of the city's redevelopment. It is a complex of glass towers containing shops, hotels, and restaurants.

Greenfield Village and Henry Ford Museum, Village Rd. and Oakwood Blvd., Dearborn, 313-271-1620. Lively and fascinating museums and restored buildings relating to the industrialization of the United States. Open daily 9–5. Call Southeast Michigan Transportation Authority (above) for bus information.

Detroit Zoological Park, 8450 Ten Mile Rd., 313-398-0900. Open daily 10–5.

Detroit Institute of Arts, Woodward and Kirby Aves., 313-833-7900. One of the finest collections in the country; noted for its seventeenth-century Flemish and Dutch paintings and its African art. Open Tues.–Sun. 9:30–5:30.

2.17   El Paso, Texas

El Paso, a booming Sun Belt city, now has almost half a million people; it has absorbed the suburb Ysleta, the oldest town in Texas and site of the Mission Del Carmen.

Modern El Paso grew from Fort Bliss, a frontier outpost; and the military is still an important part of the city's economy. The current Fort Bliss surrounds the old frontier fort. Biggs Air Force Base and the Beaumont Army Medical Center are also in El Paso, and the White Sands Missile Range is 50 miles away in southern New Mexico.

El Paso is a good place from which to visit Mexico and the nearby desert country of Texas and New Mexico. You can walk across the bridge into Ciudad Juárez for the day. (Bus tours are also available.) English is widely spoken in Juárez, especially in the markets. United States citizens do not need passports as long as they are not traveling beyond the border city and are returning to the States within 72 hours.

Amtrak Station: 700 San Francisco St. Downtown; newly refurbished. For connections to Mexico City, take a taxi across the bridge to the National Railways of Mexico station in Ciudad Juárez.

Tourist Information: El Paso Convention and Visitors' Bureau, Visitors' Information Center, 5 Civic Center Plaza, El Paso, TX 79999, 915-544-3650.

Lodging: Sheraton—El Paso, 325 N. Kansas St., 915-533-8241 (expensive). Holiday Inn—Downtown, El Paso and Missouri sts, 915-544-3300 (moderate). Bel Air Motor Lodge, 1811 N. Mesa St., 915-533-5961 (budget). Plaza Motor Inn, Oregon and Mills sts., 915-532-5661 (budget).

Car Rental: Budget, 3003 N. Mesa St., 915-544-4321 ext. 279. Avis, El Paso International Airport, 6520 Convair Rd., 915-779-2700.

Taxis: Red Cab, 915-545-2121. Checker Cab, 915-532-2626.

Public Transportation: Sun City Area Transit (buses), 915-533-3333.

Bus Stations: Greyhound, 111 San Francisco St., 915-544-7200. Trailways, 200 W. San Antonio St., 915-533-6378.

Tours: Gray Line, 915-598-8878. Golden Tours, 915-779-0555.

Attractions: Magoffin Home State Historic Site, 1120 Magoffin Ave., 915-533-5147. An eclectic adobe house, built in 1875, that combines Mexican, Eastern, and Greek motifs. Open Wed.–Sun. 9–4.

Tigua Indian Reservation and Pueblo, 122 S. Old Pueblo Rd., Ysleta (14 mi. east of El Paso), 915-859-3916. Mission, pueblo, dancing area, museums, and craft center. Dancing June–Aug. Call for hours.

Ciudad Juárez, Mexico. Simply walking around the markets, sampling food, and buying a piece or two of jewelry will make an interesting day. You can ask the U.S. Customs Service (915-541-7444) questions about customs. During the summer there are bullfights on Sunday afternoons at the Plaza de Toros Monumentals on Av. 16 de Septiembre, about 2 miles south of the Stanton St. Bridge.

Day Trip: Carlsbad Caverns National Park is not accessible by public transportation for day visitors. To visit, rent a car and spend the night near the park. Write or call Carlsbad Caverns National Park, 3225 National Parks Hwy., Carlsbad, NM 88220, 505-885-8884.

2.18   Houston, Texas

Fast-growing Houston has emerged as the fifth-largest city in the United States. Home of the Lyndon B. Johnson Space Center, third-largest port in the country, and the capital of the American oil industry, Houston has been America's number-one boomtown since World War II.

Houston was founded in 1836 by a couple of land speculators who convinced the Texas legislature to locate the capital of the new Republic of Texas on their site. The first railroad came in 1858, and during the Civil War the city was an important port for Southern blockade runners. Houston did not really begin to boom, however, until 1901, when oil was discovered; the petrochemical and aerospace industries followed. The city limits now enclose 450 square miles, the population is rocketing toward 2 million, and the city has America's worst traffic congestion. Sheer bigness is not the city's only claim to fame, however: Houston is the cultural and educational center of Texas, and its influence is felt throughout the world.

Amtrak Station: 902 Washington Ave., northwest of city center, across Route I-45. Take a taxi downtown.

Tourist Information: Greater Houston Convention and Visitors' Center, 3300 Main St., Houston, TX 77002, 713-523-5050.

Lodging: Hyatt Regency Houston, 1200 Louisiana St., 713-654-1234 (deluxe). Best Western Savoy, 1616 Main St., 713-659-1141 (expensive). University of Houston Downtown Center, 101 Main St. (at Franklin), 713-225-1781 (budget–moderate). For bed-and-breakfast accommodations, contact Bed and Breakfast Society of Houston, 713-666-6372.

Car Rental: Avis, 2120 Louisiana St., 713-659-6537. Hertz, 2020 Milam St., 713-659-8190. Budget, 1010 Webster St., 713-659-8352.

Taxis: Yellow Taxi, 713-236-1111.

Public Transportation: Metro Transit Authority (buses), 713-635-4000.

Bus Stations: Greyhound, 1410 Texas Ave., 713-222-1161. Trailways, 2121 Main St., 713-759-6500.

Tours: Gray Line, 713-757-1252.

Attractions: Houston Astrodome, Kirby Dr. at I-610. Call 713-799-9544 for information. Call 713-799-9555 for tickets to sporting events. Metro bus available from downtown.

Bayou Bend, 1 Westcott St., 713-529-8773. Former home of Ima Hogg, the philanthropist daughter of a late Texas governor. Tours Tues.–Fri. 10–2:30, Sat. 10–1. Call to make reservations.

Sam Houston Park, Allen Pkwy. and Bagley St., 713-223-8367 (on weekends 759-1292). Restored early Houston homes. Open Tues.–Sat. 10–4, Sun. 2–5.

Day Trip: Lyndon B. Johnson Space Center, Nasa Rd. (2 miles from I-45, southeast of city), 713-483-4321. Tours are run daily 9–4. No public transportation available from Houston, but Gray Line (above) features day-long trips.

2.19 Indianapolis, Indiana

Indiana's capital and largest city, and about as typically Midwestern and middle-American as a city could be, Indianapolis has stockyards and railroad yards, drug companies and insurance companies, and a pervasive conservatism that extends even to its architecture. Once a year, though, Indianapolis really hops—every May, during the Indy 500 auto race and the preceding weeks.

The Amtrak passenger terminal here is a fine example of an old-fashioned city station. Pay no attention to the gloomy train shed, which was built in 1924; but take a good look at the Victorian station building, with its glorious circular stained-glass window. Unfortunately, the old structure was neglected for many years, and it needs a lot of refurbishing; but if your have any affection for gingerbread architecture, you can look past the grime and see this grand old lady for the beauty she once was.

Amtrak Station: 39 Jackson Place. Downtown, between Capitol and Illinois sts. Currently under renovation.

Tourist Information: Indianapolis Convention and Visitors' Bureau, 100 S. Capitol St., Indianapolis, IN 46225, 317-635-9567.

Lodging: Hyatt Regency Indianapolis, Washington and Capitol sts., 317-632-1234 (deluxe). Atkinson Hotel, Georgia and Illinois sts. 317-639-5611 (moderate). Howard Johnson's, 501 W Washington St., 317-635-4443 (moderate).

Car Rental: Hertz, Hyatt Regency Indianapolis, Washington and Capitol sts., 317-634-6464 (2 blocks from station; will refund cab fare, with receipt).

Taxis: Yellow Cab, 317-637-5421.

Public Transportation: Metro Transit (buses), 317-635-3344.

Bus Stations: Greyhound, 127 N. Capitol St., 317-635-4501. Trailways, 248 S. Illinois St., 317-635-8671.

Tours: Gray Line, 317-635-4433. ABR Tour De Jour, 317-634-TOUR.

Attractions: Benjamin Harrison Memorial Home, 1230 N. Delaware St., 317-631-1898. Built by Harrison in 1872, before he became president; he owned this home until his death in 1901. Open Mon.-Sat. 10–3:30, Sun. 12:30–3:30.

Home of James Whitcomb Riley, 528 Lockerbie St., 317-631-5885. Built by the Hoosier Poet in 1872. Open Tues.-Sat. 10–4, Sun. 12–4.

Indianapolis Motor Speedway, Speedway, 317-241-2501. Museum open daily 9–5; bus ride around track available. For tickets to the annual Indianapolis 500 race, write to Indianapolis Motor Speedway, P.O. Box 24152, Speedway, IN 46224, for a ticket-order form.

Conner Prairie Pioneer Settlement, 13400 Allisonville Rd. (6 miles north of I-465), 317-773-3633. Reconstructed 1836 Indiana village. Open Tues.–Sat. 10–5, Sun. 12–5 May–Oct.; Wed.–Sat. 10–5, Sun. 12–5 April and Nov.

2.20   Jacksonville, Florida

"Gateway to Florida" and the state's leading commercial and industrial center, Jacksonville now has more than half a million people. The first European settlement near the site was a Huguenot colony established in 1564, but the present city was laid out only after the War of 1812. It is named for a leading American hero of that war, Andrew Jackson, in recognition not only of his great victory over the British at New Orleans but also of his part in adding Florida to the United States.

Florida was still a Spanish colony in 1817 when Jackson received a military commission to fight the Seminole Indians. Believing that the Spanish and British were inciting the Indians, Jackson led his force over the boundary, captured several Spanish outposts, and hanged a couple of British subjects whom he accused of being spies. The effect of this illegal raid was to convince the Spanish authorities that they could never hold on to Florida; so in 1819 they ceded the territory to the United States in exchange for $5 million in claims that were assumed by the U.S. Government. The new town on the St. Johns River was accordingly named for the rambunctious general whose exploits had led to the cession.

Jacksonville today has relatively few tourists, and some areas in and around the city remain uncommercialized. Historic sites in nearby towns include forts, early settlements, and plantations. Mayport, a 300-year-old fishing village, is a short drive away; and beautiful St. Augustine can be reached in less than an hour by car. The history of Florida before the tourist boom—of the Spanish settlers, the fishermen, the plantation owners, and the slaves—still echoes in this region.

Clifford Lane Station: 3570 Clifford Lane. A couple of miles out of town, but only 2 blocks from Edgewood Ave., a major artery on which run local buses into the city center.

Tourist Information: Jacksonville Convention and Visitors' Bureau, 206 N. Hogan St., Jacksonville, FL 32202, 904-353-9736.

Lodging: Sheraton at St. Johns Place, 1515 Prudential Dr., 904-396-5100 (deluxe). Sea Turtle Inn, 1 Ocean Blvd., Atlantic Beach, 904-249-7402 (on the beach; moderate).

Car Rental: National, Jacksonville Hilton, 565 Main St. S., 904-396-9491. Holiday, 110 N. Julia St., 904-353-5333 (railroad-station pickup available for rentals of 2 days or more).

Taxis: Checker Cab, 904-764-2472. Yellow Cab, 904-354-5511.

Public Transportation: Jacksonville Transit Authority (buses), 904-633-7330.

Bus Stations: Greyhound, 10 N. Pearl St., 904-356-5521. Trailways, Pearl and Duvall sts., 904-354-8543.

Tours: Gray Line, 904-396-8687.

Attractions: Cummer Gallery of Art, 829 Riverside Ave., 904-356-6857. Fine collections and gardens. Open Tues.–Fri. 10–4, Sat. 12–5, Sun. 2–5.

Day Trips: St. Augustine. About 45 miles south of Jacksonville, on the coast. The oldest city in the United States, with a beautiful historic district. The city's visitors' center is at 75 King St. (904-829-5681).

North Florida Historical Tour. Route is described in detail in a brochure available from Jacksonville's visitors' bureau; Gray Line offers a similar trip. The route includes Fort Caroline, Mayport, Kingsley Plantation, Fort Clinch, Fernandina Beach, a drive along beaches and causeways, and a short ferry trip. Kingsley Plantation, on an island, is especially interesting. The oldest plantation in Florida, it was once the headquarters of a slaver, who landed his ships here.

2.21   Kansas City, Missouri

Kansas City, the starting point of the old Santa Fe Trail, was named for the Kansas (sometimes called the Kaw) Indians. Today Kansas City is a well-kept secret, a town that is loved by its residents but never overrun by tourists. It is also up-to-date to a degree Rodgers and Hammerstein could never have foreseen when they wrote their song about the city for the musical *Oklahoma.*

Kansas City is a city of parks, commerce, and culture. It is built on the south bank of the Missouri River, where the Kansas River flows into it. The Missouri does not form the state boundary at this point, contrary to common belief. On the Kansas side of the state line are stockyards.

Amtrak trains use the large, old Union Station, which while it needs sprucing up, remains an excellent example of big-city railroad-station architecture. This station is unusual in that it faces away from the city.

Union Station: Main St. and Pershing Rd., downtown, but a long walk from most hotels.

Tourist Information: Convention and Visitors' Bureau of Kansas City, 1100 Main St., Kansas City, MO 64105, 816-221-5242.

Lodging: Crown Center Hotel, 1 Pershing Rd. (very near the station), 816-474-4400 (deluxe). Radisson Muehlebach Hotel, 12th and Baltimore sts., 816-471-1400 (deluxe). Holiday Inn City Center, 1301 Wyandotte St., 816-221-8800 (moderate). TraveLodge Downtown, 921 Cherry St., 816-471-1266 (moderate). For bed-and-breakfast accommodations, contact Kansas City Bed and Breakfast, 913-268-4214.

Car Rental: Avis, 1415 Baltimore St., 816-471-2421 (railroad-station pickup available). Budget, 1227 Wyandotte St., 816-471-5955 (railroad-station pickup available).

Taxis: Yellow Cab, 816-471-5000.

Public Transportation: Kansas City Area Transportation Authority (buses), 816-221-0660.

Bus Stations: Greyhound, 12th and Holmes sts., 816-221-1775. Trailways, 1023 McGee St., 816-421-7427.

Tours: Kansas City Excursion Boats, 816-842-0027. Gray Line, 816-471-5996. Surreys LTD Horse and Buggy Tours, 816-268-6580.

Attractions: Nelson–Atkins Museum of Fine Art, 4525 Oak St., 816-561-4000. Excellent collection of Eastern art. Open Tues.–Sat. 10–5, Sun. 2–6.

　　Liberty Memorial, 26th and Main sts., 816-221-1918. World War I museum and observation tower. Open Tues.–Sun. 9:30–4:30.

　　Harry S. Truman Library and Museum, Delaware St. (at U.S.-24), Independence, Mo., 816-833-1400. Open daily 9–5. City bus from Kansas City (transfer to "red" route in Independence).

2.22   Las Vegas, Nevada

Las Vegas must be seen to be believed—and even then it's a fantasy world. Until after World War II this was just a dusty railroad town. After the war, however, a Chicago hoodlum named Benjamin "Bugsy" Segal got to thinking. Nearby Hoover Dam, finished in 1937, offered cheap electricity; Nevada had legalized casino gambling during the Depression; and booming southern California, with its moneyed population, was just a few hours away. The potential of these three factors inspired Segal to borrow syndicate money and build the first resort-gambling hotel in Las Vegas in 1947. Segal was murdered when he neglected to pay the money back on time, but the Las Vegas he had created continued to grow, using big-name entertainment, luxurious accommodations, and opulent meals to attract potential gamblers.

　　Over the years these tactics have lured millions of visitors, and the profits have built the startling display of flashing neon known as the Strip.

The Amtrak station and the Union Plaza Hotel, in whose lobby the train stops, are downtown; but most of the big hotels now extend along Las Vegas Boulevard, south of town.

Amtrak Station: Union Plaza, 1 Main St. (downtown).

Tourist Information: Las Vegas Convention and Visitors' Bureau, 3150 S. Paradise Rd., Las Vegas, NV 89109, 702-733-2323.

Lodging: Downtown—Union Plaza Hotel, 1 Main St., 702-386-2110 (the railroad station shares the lobby; expensive). Mint Hotel, 100 E. Fremont St., 702-385-7440 (moderate–expensive). California Hotel, 1st and Ogden sts., 702-385-1222 (moderate).

The Strip—Caesar's Palace, 3570 Las Vegas Blvd., 702-731-7110 (deluxe). Aladdin Hotel, 3667 Las Vegas Blvd., 702-736-0111 (expensive). Circus Circus Hotel, 2880 Las Vegas Blvd., 702-734-0410 (circus entertainment; moderate).

Car Rental: Avis, Caesar's Palace, 3570 Las Vegas Blvd., 702-731-7790. Budget, 3396 Las Vegas Blvd., 702-735-9311. Brooks, 3041 Las Vegas Blvd., 702-735-3344.

Taxis: Checker Cab, 702-382-1234. Yellow Cab, 702-382-4444.

Public Transportation: Las Vegas Transit System, 702-384-3540 (buses run every 15 to 30 minutes, 24 hours a day, along Las Vegas Blvd.).

Bus Stations: Greyhound, 220 S. Main St., 702-382-2640. Trailways, 217 N. 4th St., 702-385-1141.

Tours: Grand Canyon Air and Bus Excursions, 702-739-1900. Gray Line, 702-384-1234.

Attractions: Liberace Museum, 1775 E. Tropicana Ave., 702-798-5595. Open Mon.–Sat. 10–5, Sun. 1–5.

Day Trips: Hoover Dam, about 25 miles southeast of Las Vegas on Route 93. Information and film on the construction of the dam are available at the Lake Mead visitors' center, 601 Nevada Highway, Boulder City, 702-293-4041. At the dam itself is an exhibit building (702-293-8367), and an elevator that takes visitors down to the power plant. You may walk across the crest of the dam, which spans Black Canyon. Boat rides on Lake Mead are available from the Boulder City Marina; ask for directions at the visitors' center.

Valley of Fire State Park, Route 169, about 40 miles northeast of Las Vegas, 702-394-4088. Spectacular red sandstone formations and ancient petroglyphs. The place is named for its fiery appearance at sunset.

2.23 Los Angeles, California

Third-largest city in the United States, center of the aircraft and motion-picture industries, spiritual home of the fast-food franchise and the drive-in movie theater—what can be said about Los Angeles that hasn't been said already? It's the Shangri-la of America, the Disneyland of the world.

You won't see the Pacific Ocean from Los Angeles; it's several miles away at Santa Monica to the west or Long Beach to the south. But you can give your visit to Los Angeles a wonderful beginning by walking across from the station to the plaza on Olvera Street. This is the original site of the city, established in 1781, and is surrounded by historic buildings. Street vendors sell tasty Mexican food, with or without hot sauce, which you can eat while watching the interesting people who pass by. Once you leave this spot, unfortunately, Los Angeles becomes a difficult city in which to get around. A taxi is often out of the question because distances are so long, and public transportation is unreliable. Bus tours are a good solution, if they suit your taste; otherwise rent a car. And don't worry—it's not easy to drive in Los Angeles, but it's not nearly as hard as the city's reputation suggests. Obey all traffic laws carefully. You'll find that driving is easier that way, and you won't get a ticket from California's notoriously efficient traffic and highway police.

Amtrak Station: Union Passenger Terminal, 800 N. Alameda St. (downtown; all services).

Tourist Information: Greater Los Angeles Visitors' and Convention Bureau, 505 S. Flower St., Level B, Arco Plaza, Los Angeles, CA 90071, 213-488-9100.

Lodging: Biltmore Hotel, 515 S. Olive St. (at 5th St.), 213-624-1011 (deluxe). Mayflower Hotel, 535 S. Grand Ave., 213-624-1331 (expensive). Best Western Dragon Gate Inn, 818 N. Hill St., 213-617-3077 (Chinatown area; moderate). Executive Motor Inn-Mariposa, 457 S. Mariposa St., 213-380-6910 (moderate). For bed-and-breakfast accommodations, contact Bed and Breakfast of Los Angeles, 32074 Waterside Lane, Westlake Village, CA 91361, 213-889-8870 or 213-889-7325.

Car Rental: Hertz, 1055 W. 6th St., 213-482-5365 (railroad-station pickup available). Avis, 1207 W. 3rd St., 213-481-2000 (railroad-station pickup available). Budget, Union Station, 800 N. Alameda St., 213-617-1087.

Taxis: Red Top, 213-934-6700. Independent, 213-385-8294. Checker, 213-258-3231.

Public Transportation: Southern California Rapid Transit District, 213-626-4455.

Bus Stations: Trailways, Union Passenger Terminal, 800 N. Alameda St., 213-742-1200. Greyhound, 6th and Los Angeles sts., 213-603-0141.

Tours: Gray Line, 213-481-2121. Starline Tours, 213-463-3131 (stars' homes).

Currency Exchange: Deak-Perera, Hilton Hotel Center, 677 S. Figueroa St., 213-624-4221.

Attractions: Universal Studios Tour, U.S.-101 at Lankershim Blvd., Universal City, 213-877-1311. Open daily 8–6 in summer; Mon.–Fri. 10–3:30, Sat.–Sun. 9:30–4 rest of year.

Los Angeles County Museum of Art, 5905 Wilshire Blvd., 213-937-2590. Open Tues.–Fri. 10–5, Sat.–Sun. 10–6.

Olvera Street, between N. Main and Alameda sts. Mexican marketplace. Open daily 10–8.

Venice Beach. Lined with shops and cafés and widely known as the funkiest and most interesting place to watch people in the Los Angeles area. The beach itself is beautiful. There are bikes to rent and a bicycle path along the beach, and you can watch acrobatic roller skating and body building that you'll never see back home.

1984 summer Olympics, July 28–Aug. 14. For information, contact the Los Angeles Olympic Organizing Committee, Los Angeles, CA 90084, 213-741-6789. Ticket order forms are available at Sears stores throughout the country. All tickets must be ordered by mail.

Day Trips: Santa Catalina Island. Boat trips are available from Long Beach and San Pedro. Write or call Catalina Cruises, P.O. Box 1948, San Pedro, CA 90733, 213-775-6111.

Disneyland, 1313 Harbor Blvd., Anaheim, 714-999-4565. Open Sun.–Fri. 9 A.M.–midnight, Sat. 9 A.M.–1 A.M. in summer; call for hours during rest of year. (1984 summer hours will be extended because of the Olympic Games. Call for exact hours.)

San Juan Capistrano Mission, about 1 ¼ hours from Los Angeles. Amtrak offers frequent service. The mission is near the station and is open daily. Call 714-493-1424 for information.

2.24   Memphis, Tennessee

Memphis, a river town built on a bluff facing one of the Mississippi's many loops, has a long and colorful history. This land belonged to the Chickasaw Indian nation until white settlers from the Carolinas and Virginia began moving in during the nineteenth century. Those pioneers, who brought their slaves with them, were seeking new cotton lands to replace the worn-out soil farther east. The area around Memphis became a major cotton-producing region, and Memphis became—and remains—the nation's most important cotton market.

Memphis was a prime Union objective during the Civil War, not only because of its strategic location by the Mississippi but also because it stood astride the Confederacy's best rail route between the Eastern states and the rich states west of the river. This route was attacked by Union forces in April 1862, and the Confederates fought and lost the great battle of Shiloh to protect it.

More recently Elvis Presley lived in Memphis; and his home, now open to the public, has become something of a shrine. Elvis isn't the only celebrated musician to come from Memphis, however—W. C. Handy, said to be the originator of the blues, played in clubs along Beale Street, now a restored area. The river heritage of Memphis still colors the city, and no visit is complete without a ride on a Mississippi riverboat.

Amtrak Station: 545 S. Main St. (downtown, on Mid-America Mall, a pedestrian plaza).

Tourist Information: Memphis Convention and Visitors' Bureau, Beale and 3rd sts., Memphis, TN 38103, 901-526-1919.

Lodging: The Peabody, 149 Union Ave., 901-529-4100 (deluxe). Holiday Inn Rivermont, 200 W. Georgia Ave., 901-525-0121 (expensive). Admiral Benbow Inn—Midtown, 1200 Union Ave., 901-725-0630 (moderate). For bed-and-breakfast accommodations, contact Bed and Breakfast in Memphis, P.O. Box 41621, Memphis, TN 38174, 901-726-5920.

Car Rental: Hertz, Holiday Inn Rivermont, 200 W. Georgia Ave., 901-527-2508. Budget, Union Ave. and Belvedere Blvd., 901-725-1771 (railroad-station pickup available). Dollar, 2031 E. Brooks Rd., 901-345-3890 (railroad-station pickup available).

Taxis: Yellow Cab, 901-526-8358.

Public Transportation: Memphis Area Transit Authority (buses) 901-274-6282.

Bus Stations: Greyhound, 203 Union Ave., 901-523-7676. Trailways, 235 Union Ave. 901-523-0200.

Tours: Gray Line, 901-345-8687. Memphis Queen Riverboat Lines 901-527-5694. Bluff City Buggy Co., 901-521-1118.

Attractions: Graceland Manor, 3764 Elvis Presley Blvd., 901-332-3322 (from out of state 800-238-2000). Home and grave site open to the public. Call ahead for reservations. Open daily May–Oct., Wed.–Sun. Nov.–April.

Mud Island, 125 N. Main St., 901-528-3595. Historical theme park on an island across from the city center. A commercialized but fun treatment of life on the Mississippi, on a grand scale. Open daily 10–10 April–Oct., Wed.–Sun. Nov.–March. Museums close at 5:30 P.M.

Day Trips: Shiloh National Military Park, about 90 miles east of Memphis, near Savannah, Tenn. Commemorates Civil War Battle of Shiloh, April 6–7, 1862. Visitors' center open daily 9–5.

Casey Jones Home and Railroad Museum, about 75 miles northeast of Memphis, off I-40 near Jackson, 901-668-1222. Home of the legendary engineer. Open daily 8–8 in summer; Mon.–Sat. 9–5, Sun. 1–5 rest of year.

2.25   Miami, Florida

Miami did not exist in 1890; it boomed from 1910 through the 1920s; it slumped from then until World War II; and then, after 1945, it boomed again. The rapid influx of Cubans into the area since 1960 has made Miami more a Latin American city than an Anglo one. It's not only the jumping-off place for American visitors to the Carribean, but also the jumping-on spot for Latin Americans coming to North America.

Miami and Miami Beach owe their existence to developers who sought to exploit the sunny climate of this part of Florida. Henry M. Flagler, an oil and railroad magnate, was the first of many. Owner of the Florida East Coast Railroad, he built a line to the Miami area around the turn of the century and established a town. He realized that the long growing season and warm weather made the area desirable both for agriculture and as a resort, and the town of Miami began to grow. Miami Beach, however, remained a mangrove swamp until about 1930, when developers cleared and dredged the little off-shore island and started to erect homes.

Today Miami and Miami Beach have almost everything anyone could want in the way of recreation, entertainment, glitter, and glamour. They may have been wilderness less than a century ago, but they are a hive of human activity today.

Amtrak Station: 8303 NW 37th Ave. (several miles from both the beach and downtown).

Tourist Information: Metro Dade County Dept. of Tourism, 234 W. Flagler St., Miami, FL 33130, 305-579-4694. Miami Beach Visitor and Convention Authority, 555 17th St., Miami Beach, FL 33139, 305-673-7070.

Lodging: (all are in Miami Beach): Sheraton Bal Harbour, 9701 Collins Ave., Bal Harbour, 305-865-7511 (deluxe). The Palms on the Ocean, 9449 Collins Ave., Surfside, 305-865-3551 (expensive). Sandy Shores Motel, 16251 Collins Ave., 305-947-3681 (inexpensive–moderate, depending on season). For bed-and-breakfast accommodations, contact Bed & Breakfast Company, 305-661-3270.

Car Rental: Hertz, Fontainbleu Hotel, 4441 Collins Ave., 305-534-4661. Avis, Miami International Airport, 305-526-3005 (cab fare refunded with receipt). Budget, 6742 Collins Ave., 305-865-4446.

Taxis: Yellow Cab, 305-633-3333. Central Taxi, 305-532-5555.

Public Transportation: Metro Transit Agency (buses), 305-638-6700 or 638-6600.

Bus Stations: Greyhound, 950 NE 2nd Ave., Miami (or 1622 Collins Ave., Miami Beach), 305-374-2222. Trailways, 99 NE 4th St., 305-373-6561.

Bicycle Rental: Miami Beach Bicycle Center, 305-531-4161.

Tours: American Sightseeing Tours, 305-871-4992. Island Queen, 305-379-5119. Nikko Gold Coast Cruises, 305-945-5461. Trolley Tyme Tours, 305-948-8823. Nationwide Tour Lines, 305-893-1300.

Currency Exchange: Deak-Perera, 1 SE 3rd Ave., 305-372-8888. American Express, 1351 Biscayne Blvd., 305-358-7350. Most major Miami and Miami Beach banks are prepared to exchange many currencies.

Attractions: Miami Seaquarium, Rickenbacker Causeway, 305-361-5703. Tanks and outdoor shows, featuring whales, porpoises, and sea lions. Open 9–6:30. Last tour of shows begins at 3:50.

Villa Vizcaya, 3251 S. Miami Ave., 305-579-2708. Ornate villa on Biscayne Bay. Built as a private home in 1912, it now houses the Dade County Art Museum. Open 9:30–4:30.

Day Trips: Fishing boats of all descriptions leave Miami every day with paying visitors on board. You and your party can charter a boat, or you can join a drift-fishing boat. Most boat owners rent out equipment, and many will show you how to fish if you need help. Different boats go off in search of different kinds of fish; so you can choose what suits you best. Write or call Metro Dade County Dept. of Tourism (see above) for details.

Everglades National Park, Route 27, just south of U.S.-1 and Florida City, about 45 miles south of Miami. There is a visitors' center at the park entrance. You can drive through the park as far as Flamingo, where there are restaurants and shops; bicycles are available for rent. Write to Superintendent, Everglades National Park, P.O. Box 279, Homestead, FL 33030.

2.26 Milwaukee, Wisconsin

Milwaukee means beer to most Americans, and it's true that the city has been a leading brewing center since the 1840s. It may surprise you to know, however, that Milwaukee's leading industry is manufacturing: Electrical products, machine tools, and heavy equipment are made here; and they are far more important to the city's economy than beer. In fact, Milwaukee has only two big breweries left—Pabst and Miller—since Schlitz closed its facility in the city in 1981.

Despite the popular conception, Milwaukee is not a thoroughly German city either. It's true that the Teutonic influence, which is reflected in the city's brewing tradition, has been strong for a century and a half, but the largest single ethnic bloc in Milwaukee is Polish. The South Side of the city is nearly as Polish as Warsaw.

Milwaukee is a conservative, traditional city—not an exciting place, anything but trendy, but a clean and sometimes elegant place with a river-trading past. It was developed by its inhabitants' hardworking immigrant ancestors. If you're looking for old-time American values, this is the place.

Amtrak's station is three blocks south of the city's main business street, Wisconsin Avenue. The visitors' center, the museums, and the breweries are all a good hike from the station.

Amtrak Station: 433 W. St. Paul Ave. (downtown, south of the city center). All services, including restaurant, during daytime hours.

Tourist Information: Greater Milwaukee Convention and Visitors' Bureau, 756 N. Milwaukee St., Milwaukee, WI 53202, 414-273-7222.

Lodging: Pfister Hotel, 424 E. Wisconsin Ave., 414-273-8222 (deluxe). Ramada Inn, 633 W. Michigan Ave., 414-272-8410 (moderate-expensive). Astor Hotel, 924 E. Juneau Ave., 414-271-4220 (moderate). For bed-and-breakfast accommodations, contact Bed and Breakfast Milwaukee, 414-342-5030.

Car Rental: Hertz, Amtrak Station, 414-271-1147 (after hours: 414-747-5200). Budget, 804 N. 4th St., 414-276-1633 (from out of state: 800-558-5238). Avis, 603 N. 4th St., 414-272-0892.

Taxis: Yellow Cab, 414-271-1800.

Public Transportation: Milwaukee County Transit System (buses), 414-344-6711 (ask for brochure "Discover Milwaukee by Bus," which outlines attractions in the area and how to reach them by city bus).

Bus Stations: Greyhound, 606 N. 7th St., 414-272-8900. Badger, 635 N. 7th St., 414-276-7490 (bus service throughout Wisconsin).

Tours: Iroquois Boat Line, 414-332-4194. Emerald Isle Boat Tours, 414-241-5631. Transit System Bus Tours, 414-344-6711 (summer only).

Attractions: Brewery tours. Miller Brewery, 4251 W. State St., 414-931-2153. Open Mon.–Fri. 9–3:30. Pabst Brewery, 917 W. Juneau Ave., 414-347-7327. Open Mon.–Fri. 10–11, 1–3:30; also Sat. 9–11 June–Aug. Call for exact tour schedules and reservations.

Pabst Mansion, 2000 W. Wisconsin Ave., 414-931-0808. Open Mon.–Sat. 10–3:30, Sun 12–4 March 15—Nov. 30; Mon.–Fri. 11–2, Sat. 10–3:30, Sun. 12–3:30 Dec.–March 14.

Milwaukee Public Museum, 800 W. Wells St., 414-278-2700. Natural history, with emphasis on development of different cultures. Open daily 9–5.

Horticultural Domes, Mitchell Park, 524 S. Layton Blvd., 414-278-4383. Three giant glass domes housing horticultural exhibits. Open Sat.–Thurs. 9–8, Fri. 9–5 in summer; Mon.–Fri. 9–5, Sat.–Sun. 9–8 rest of year.

2.27   Minneapolis-St. Paul, Minnesota

They're called the Twin Cities, but Minneapolis and St. Paul are by no means alike. St. Paul is essentially Irish, Catholic, and blue collar; Minneapolis is largely Scandinavian, Protestant, and managerial. St. Paul is the state capital; Minneapolis has the state university. St. Paul has the railroad shops and manufacturing plants; Minneapolis has the flour mills. Yet, despite all this, it is virtually impossible for an outsider to tell where one of the twins ends and the other begins.

St. Paul grew out of a trading post and was once known by the much less dignified name of Pig's Eye. Minneapolis owes its location to the Falls of St. Anthony, which mark the northern limit of navigation on the Mississippi river and which provided natural water power for the great flour mills. The two cities have always been rivals, and they remain so today, although Minneapolis gets more national attention.

These cities are the cultural capitals of the entire northern Midwest. They have excellent parks and other recreational facilities, distinguished museums, fine music, and some of the best theater outside New York. The Guthrie Theatre, in Minneapolis, is known for its excellent productions of new plays and the classics. Go on an opening night and you'll see the aristocracy of a Midwestern city in its element.

Midway Station: 730 Transfer Rd., St. Paul. About 5 miles from the center of each city. To catch a bus to either city center, walk south to University Ave. (2 blocks) and take bus 16 west to Minneapolis or east to St. Paul.

Tourist Information: Minneapolis Convention and Tourism Commission, 15 S. 5th St., Minneapolis, MN 55402, 612-348-4313. Information center at IDS Crystal Court, S. 8th St.

St. Paul Convention and Tourism Commission, Landmark Center B-100, St. Paul, MN 55102, 612-292-4360.

Lodging: Hyatt Regency Minneapolis, 1300 Nicollet Mall, 612-370-1234 (deluxe; the mall is an appealing feature during the winter). Radisson St. Paul, 11 E. Kellogg Blvd., 612-292-1900 (expensive). Holiday Inn

Nicollet Mall, 1313 Nicollet Mall, Minneapolis, 612-332-0371 (moderate). The Inn—St. Paul, 175 W. 7th St., 612-292-8929 (moderate). For bed-and-breakfast accommodations, contact Bed and Breakfast Upper Midwest, P.O. Box 28036, Minneapolis, MN 55428, 612-535-7135.

Car Rental: Avis, 829 3rd Ave. S., Minneapolis, 612-332-6321. National, 64 E 6th St., St. Paul, 612-227-8588.

Taxis: Yellow Cab—St. Paul, 612-222-4433; Minneapolis, 612-379-7171. City-Wide Cab, 612-292-1616.

Public Transportation: Metropolitan Transit System (buses), 612-221-0939.

Bus Station: Greyhound, 29 9th St. N., 612-371-3311.

Tours: Gray Line, 612-827-4071. Jonathan Padelford and Josiah Snelling Boat Trips, 612-227-1100.

Attractions: Walker Art Center, Hennepin Ave. and Vineland Pl., Minneapolis, 612-375-7600. Open Tues.–Sat. 10–8, Sun. 11–5.

American Swedish Institute, 2600 Park Ave., Minneapolis, 612-871-4907. Open Tues.–Sat. 12–4, Sun. 1–5.

IDS Center, 8th St. S., Minneapolis. See the city from the top of the 57-story tower. Observation deck open Sun.–Thurs. 10–10, Fri.–Sat. 10 A.M.—11 P.M. May–Aug.; Sun.–Thurs. 10–6:30, Sat.–Sun. 10A.M.—11P.M. rest of year.

State Capitol, University Ave., St. Paul, 612-297-3521. Tours on the hour Mon.–Fri. 9–4, Sat. 10–3, Sun. 1–3.

Day Trip: Duluth. The current Amtrak schedule makes it possible to visit Duluth in a single day, but in winter the train runs on weekends only. In Duluth, the St. Louis County Heritage and Arts Center, 506 W. Michigan St., houses a transportation museum in a restored railroad station. Visitors who stay more than a day will enjoy driving along the north shore of Lake Superior on U.S.-61, one of the most beautiful lakeshore routes in North America. The fabulous Mesabi Range, source of much of America's iron ore, is 65 miles northwest of Duluth; here you can see huge open-pit mines.

2.28   New Orleans, Louisiana

New Orleans is, by any measure, America's most unusual big city. It has a unique culture and history, woven together from French, Spanish, black, and English influences; and it has long been famous as a city whose inhabitants know how to live well.

The heart of New Orleans, its oldest and most colorful section, is an area along the Mississippi River known as the French Quarter, the Vieux Carré. Famous for its ironwork balconies, mysterious old buildings, and excellent restaurants, it keeps its exotic flavor and life-style despite the encroachments of tourism. The Bourbon Street jazz clubs represent one side of life in the quarter; the busy Mississippi, whose traffic you can watch from a park behind the old French market, represents another.

Southwest of the French Quarter and just south of the route of the St. Charles Avenue trolley is the Garden District, with its beautiful nineteenth-century homes. Downtown New Orleans, between the French Quarter and the Garden District, is a modern commercial and convention center, as fast-paced as many a northern city, in spite of the hot and humid climate. The Amtrak station is on the edge of the downtown area, adjacent to the Superdome.

Union Passenger Terminal: 1001 Loyola Ave. (downtown, about 10 blocks southwest of the French quarter).

Tourist Information: Greater New Orleans Tourist and Convention Bureau, 334 Royal St., New Orleans, LA 70140, 504-566-5011.

Lodging: Pontchartrain Hotel, 2301 St. Charles Ave., 504-524-0581 (in Garden District; deluxe). Le Richelieu Motor Hotel, 1234 Chartres St., 504-529-2492 (expensive). Cornstalk Fence Guest House, 915 Royal St., 504-523-1515 (expensive). French Quarter Maisonnettes, 1130 Chartres St. 504-524-9918 (moderate). Park View Guest House, 7004 St. Charles Ave., 504-861-7564 (near Audubon Park; moderate). For bed-and-breakfast accommodations, contact New Orleans Bed and Breakfast, 3658 Gentilly Blvd. (P.O. Box 8163, New Orleans, LA 70812), 504-949-6705.

Car Rental: Hertz, 1540 Canal St., 504-568-1645 (cab fare refunded up to $5 with receipt). National, 324 S. Rampart St., 504-525-0416.

Taxis: United Cab, 504-522-9771. Checker Cab, 504-943-2411.

Public Transportation: New Orleans Public Transit (buses and streetcars), 504-486-6338.

Bus Stations: Greyhound, Union Passenger Terminal, Loyola Ave. and Earhart Blvd., 504-525-9371. Trailways, 1314 Tulane Ave., 504-525-4201.

Tours: American Sightseeing Tours, 504-246-1991. Gray Line, 504-525-0138. Steamboat Natchez Cruises, 504-524-9787. Voyageur River, Plantation, and Bayou Cruises, 504-523-5555.

Attractions: Preservation Hall, 726 St. Peter St. Famous hall where pure Dixieland jazz can be heard nightly. Open daily 8:30 P.M.—12:30 A.M.

St. Louis Cathedral, Jackson Square. Built in 1794, this is still an active house of worship. Open daily between services, 9–5.

St. Charles Avenue Streetcar, 504-524-2626. Runs from Canal St. along St. Charles Ave., past the Garden District to Audubon Park and the zoo. For zoo information, call 504-861-2537. Zoo open 9:30–5 Mon.–Fri., 9:30–6 Sat.–Sun.

French Quarter, bounded roughly by Canal, Rampart, Esplanade, and Decatur sts. Garden District, centered south of St. Charles Ave.

between Washington and Jackson sts.

Metairie Cemetery, Metairie Rd. and City Park Ave. Largest cemetery in New Orleans, full of ornate tombs. Tombs in this city are built above ground because of the dampness of the delta soil.

2.29 New York, New York

The great city of New York is unlike any other in the United States and, for that matter, the world. Its skyscrapers and busy streets make it the epitome of the modern city, and the fast-paced life-style of its residents sets the standard for urban chic. A visit to New York can be bewildering, educational, and even shocking—but it's always exhilarating.

Some of the city's most famous attractions are listed below, but these examples hardly begin to suggest the richness and variety of New York's cultural life. Simply walking around the city—through its posh shopping districts, Greenwich Village, Central Park, or the Lower East Side, for instance—can be exciting. Check the newspapers for events that interest you—you're sure to find plenty—and don't hesitate to go to the famous, "touristy" places. Many of New York's attractions are anything but tourist traps; the Statue of Liberty is a good example. Be sure to get a map of the city at the railroad station before you try to find your way around. If you plan to use the subway, get a transit map at one of the subway stations. You may find it difficult at first to get around; but once you get the hang of the patterns, you'll see that most of the streets and subways are arranged logically.

Grand Central Terminal: E. 42nd St. and Park Ave. All services. Amtrak trains to the Hudson Valley use this terminal, as do commuter trains to Connecticut and Westchester County (call Metro-North: 212-532-4900 for information).

Pennsylvania Station: 8th Ave., from W. 31st to W. 33rd sts. All services. All Amtrak trains, except those going up the Hudson Valley, use this station, as do commuter trains to New Jersey and Long Island (call Long Island Railroad, 212-739-4200, for information).

Tourist Information: New York Convention and Visitors' Bureau, 2 Columbus Circle (59th St. and Broadway), New York, NY 10019, 212-397-8222 (maps, information, assistance to foreign visitors). Times Square Information Center, 42nd St. and Broadway.

Lodging: Algonquin Hotel, 59 W. 44th St., 212-840-6800 (famous old hotel; deluxe). Hotel Empire, 44 W. 63rd St., 212-265-7400 (across from Lincoln Center; expensive). Gorham Hotel, 136 W. 55th St., 212-245-1800 (expensive). For bed-and-breakfast accommodations, contact the B and B Group, 301 E. 60th St., New York, NY 10022, 212-838-7015, or Urban Ventures, 322 Central Park W., New York, NY 10025, 212-662-1234.

Car Rental: Avis, 217 E. 43rd St., 212-593-8378. Hertz, Pennsylvania Station, 250 W. 34th St., 800-654-3131. Budget, 225 E. 43rd St., 212-883-1133.

Taxis: XYZ Two Way Radio Taxi Service, 212-685-3333. Minute Men Taxi, 212-899-5600.

Public Transportation: New York City Transit Authority, (buses and subways; subways not safe late at night) 212-330-1234. Subway maps available at subway stations.

Bus Station: Port Authority Bus Terminal, 8th Avenue and W. 42nd St., 212-564-8484.

Tours: Circle Line Boat Tours (March–Nov.), 212-563-3200. Crossroads Sightseeing Tours, 212-581-2828. Gray Line, 212-397-2600. Horse-drawn carriages can be hired to tour Central Park. They line up all day and in the evening at the south end of the park, at 59th St. and 5th Ave.

Currency Exchange: Thomas Cook Travel, 18 E. 48th St., 212-310-9400 (limited hours). Deak-Perera, 41 East 42nd St., 212-883-0400. Downtown commercial banks exchange foreign currency during banking hours.

Attractions: Empire State Building, 5th Ave. and 34th St., 212-736-3100. Observation tower open 9:30 A.M.—11:25 P.M.

Statue of Liberty, Liberty Island, 212-269-5755. Ferry leaves from Battery Park, at southern tip of Manhattan. Call for schedule.

Museum of Natural History, Central Park West at 79th St., 212-873-1300. Open Mon., Tues., Thurs., Sun., 10–5:45; Wed., Fri., Sat. 10–9.

Metropolitan Museum of Art, 5th Ave. at 82nd St., 212-535-7710. Open Tues. 10–8:45, Wed.-Sat. 10–4:45, Sun. 11–4:45.

United Nations, 1st Ave. between 42nd and 48th sts., 212-754-7710. Open daily 9–4:45.

Solomon R. Guggenheim Museum, 5th Ave. at 89th St., 212-860-1300. Art museum designed by architect Frank Lloyd Wright. Open Tues. 11–8, Wed.-Sun. 11–5.

New York Zoological Park (Bronx Zoo), Fordham Rd. and Southern Blvd., 212-220-5100. Open Mon.-Sat. 10–5, Sun. 10–5:30 Feb.-Oct.; daily 10–4:30 Nov.-Jan.

Day Trips: Atlantic City, about 130 miles south. The major bus companies offer frequent service to the city. The bus-tour companies offer low-cost one-day tours, many of which include admission to a casino.

Hudson River Day Line Cruises, 212-279-5151 These scenic Hudson River cruises include stops at Bear Mountain and West Point. Trips leave daily mid-May through mid-September.

2.30   Omaha, Nebraska

Today the largest city in Nebraska, Omaha was once the starting point of the old Oregon Trail. It was Abraham Lincoln who ordered that the first transcontinental railroad be built westward from Omaha, and the Union Pacific still has its headquarters and eastern terminus here.

When you think of Omaha these days, however, you don't think of railroads—you think of meat. Omaha has replaced Chicago as the meat-packing capital of the United States. The reason is simple: It's cheaper and easier to ship dressed meat than live animals; so the stockyards have moved closer to the beef-cattle herds.

Just outside Omaha is Father Flanagan's Boys Town, a 1,500-acre community of a thousand boys, run by the youngsters themselves. It is the subject of a somewhat sentimental old film, and it will always be associated with the slogan "He ain't heavy—he's my brother."

Amtrak trains serving Omaha use the back of the Burlington station, on the eastern edge of the downtown area. Nearby is the old Union Station, which houses the Western Heritage Museum. Also nearby is the Union Pacific Museum, which has plenty to interest any train aficionado.

Amtrak Station: 1003 S. 9th St. (behind the old Burlington station). Trains arrive at night or early in the morning, so take a taxi to the city center (about a mile).

Tourist Information: Omaha Convention and Visitors' Council, Suite 1200, 1819 Farnum St., Omaha, NE 68183, 402-444-4660. The Nebraska-Omaha Information Center is at 10th St. and Deer Park Blvd.

Lodging: Red Lion Inn Omaha, 1616 Dodge St., 402-346-7600 (expensive). Conant Motel, 1913 Farnum St., 402-341-1313 (moderate). Hilltown Inn, 16th and Howard sts., 402-341-9332 (budget). For bed-and-breakfast accommodations, contact Bed & Breakfast of Nebraska, 402-564-7591.

Car Rental: Avis, 1409 Dodge St., 402-422-6482. Hertz, 202 N. 19th St., 402-341-2200. Budget, 1755 E. Locust St., 402-348-0455.

Taxis: Happy Cab, 402-339-0110. Checker Cab, 402-342-8000.

Public Transportation: Omaha Metro Area Transit (buses), 402-341-0800.

Bus Stations: Greyhound, 1802 Farnum St., 402-341-1900. Trailways, 16th and Jackson sts., 402-342-7303.

Tours: Western Sightseeing Tours (individual limo or van tours), 402-399-9300.

Attractions: Union Pacific Museum, 1416 Dodge St., 402-271-3530. Open Mon.–Fri. 9–5, Sat. 9–1.

Western Heritage Museum, 801 S. 10th St., in the old Union Station, 402-444-5071. Open Tues.–Fri. 10–5, Sat.–Sun. 1–5.

Joslyn Art Museum, 2200 Dodge St., 402-342-3300. Open Tues.–Sat. 10–5, Sun. 1–5.

Ak-sar-ben Coliseum, 63rd and Shirley sts., 402-556-2300. Events include horseracing, rodeos, and "baby beef" shows. City bus available from downtown.

Boys Town, U.S.-6, about 10 miles from downtown, 402-498-1111. Visitors welcome Mon.–Sat. 8–4:30, Sun. 9–4:30. City bus available from downtown.

Day Trip: Lincoln, about 55 miles southwest. The unusual State Capitol (402-471-2311) is open Mon.–Fri. 8–5, Sat. 10–5, Sun. 1–5. Tours of the building are available. Amtrak runs from Omaha to Lincoln, but the train stops in these cities in the middle of the night. Greyhound and Trailways, however, provide frequent bus service, and they deliver passengers to downtown stations.

2.31   Philadelphia, Pennsylvania

Philadelphia was founded by William Penn in 1682, partly as a refuge for Quakers, a sect persecuted in England. Charles II owed a substantial debt to William's father, who had been an admiral in the Royal Navy; and he paid it in the form of a land grant in America. The grant was known as Pennsylvania—Penn's Woods—after the admiral. Indians and some Swedish colonists occupied the tract at the time, but William Penn saw to it that they were compensated for their rights. Thus, the City of Brotherly Love was founded in a manner entirely consistent with its name. At the beginning of the American Revolution, Philadelphia not only was the largest city in the colonies but was second only to London in the entire British Empire. It was chosen as the meeting place for the Continental Congress and was also the new nation's first capital.

The Amtrak station is in West Philadelphia, near the University of Pennsylvania. From the second floor of the station, you can take a train to Penn Center near City Hall, which is close to many points of interest, including the Pennsylvania Academy of Fine Arts, the Academy of Natural Sciences, and the Franklin Institute Science Museum and Planetarium. The area around Independence Hall is where you'll find most of the historic shrines of the Revolutionary period: the Liberty Bell, the Betsy Ross house, the old City Hall, and Christ Church, to name a few. Independence Hall is about ten blocks east of Penn Center and about 2 miles east of the Amtrak station.

Thirtieth Street Station: 30th and Market sts. All Amtrak trains arrive here. A big-city station with all services, about 10 blocks from the city center. Suburban station is upstairs.

Suburban Station: 30th and Market sts., upstairs from Amtrak station. Serves Philadelphia's western suburbs including Paoli, Chestnut Hill, and Swarthmore. Your Amtrak ticket stub will let you travel free from this station to Penn Center (downtown Philadelphia).

Reading Terminal: 12th and Market sts. Commuter station serving Philadelphia's northern and eastern suburbs (215-574-7800; if no answer, call 800-462-0928).

Tourist Information: Philadelphia Convention and Visitors' Bureau, 1525 John F. Kennedy Blvd., Philadelphia, PA 19107, 215-568-6599.

Lodging: Franklin Plaza Hotel, 16th and Race sts., 215-448-2000 (expensive-deluxe). Holiday Inn-Independence Mall, 4th and Arch sts., 215-923-8660 (expensive). Penn Centre Inn, 20th and Market sts., 215-569-3000 (moderate–expensive). For bed-and-breakfast accommodations, contact Bed & Breakfast of Philadelphia, P.O. Box 101, Oreland, PA, 215-884-1084.

Car Rental: Avis, 30th St. Station, 215-386-2332. Hertz, 30th St. Station, 215-492-2958. Budget, 1819 John F. Kennedy Blvd., 215-492-3900.

Taxis: United Taxi, 215-854-0750. Yellow Cab, 215-922-7186.

Public Transportation: Southeastern Pennsylvania Transportation Authority (buses and subways), 215-574-7840. Subways not safe at night.

Bus Stations: Greyhound, 17th and Market sts., 215-568-4800. Trailways, 13th and Arch sts., 215-569-3100.

Tours: Gray Line, 215-569-3666. Fairmont Park Trolley Buses, 215-879-4044.

Currency Exchange: American Express, 1710 John F. Kennedy Blvd., 215-587-2350.

Attractions: Pennsylvania Academy of Fine Arts, Broad and Cherry sts., 215-972-7600. Open Tues.–Sat. 10–5, Sun. 1–5.

Academy of Natural Sciences, 19th St. and Benjamin Franklin Pkwy., 215-299-1000. Open Mon.–Fri. 10–4, Sat.–Sun. 10–5.

Franklin Institute Science Museum and Planetarium, 20th St. and Benjamin Franklin Pkwy., 215-564-3375. Open Mon.–Sat. 10–5, Sun. 12–5.

Independence Hall National Historical Park, mainly from 2nd to 6th St. between Walnut and Chestnut sts. Buildings in this area and others in the city that played a role in the Revolution are included in the park. There is a visitors' center at Chestnut and 3rd sts., 215-597-8974. Open daily 9–5.

Independence Hall, Chestnut St. between 5th and 6th sts., 215-597-8974. Open daily 9–8 in summer; 9–5 rest of year. The Liberty Bell Pavilion is in front, near Market St.

Betsy Ross House, 239 Arch St., 215-627-5343. Open daily 9–6 in summer; 9–5 rest of year.

Christ Church, 2nd St. between Market and Arch sts., 215-922-1695. Open daily 9-5 March-Dec.; Wed.-Sun. 9-5 Jan.-Feb. (Church may open on Mon. and Tues. in 1984. Call for information). Fifteen signers of the Declaration of Independence belonged to this church, and visitors can sit in pews belonging to Benjamin Franklin, George Washington, and Betsy Ross. The Burial Ground, where Benjamin Franklin was buried, is on 5th St. at Arch. His grave can be seen from the street when the grounds are closed. Open daily 9:30-4:30 June-mid-Oct..

Day Trips: Lancaster, about 70 miles west. Frequent Amtrak service between Philadelphia and Lancaster, the capital of Pennsylvania Dutch country, makes this a likely day trip by train. Many of the more interesting Pennsylvania Dutch homes and farms, however, are in the countryside and are accessible only by car or, in some cases, tour bus. For information, write or call the Lancaster Chamber of Commerce, 30 W. Orange St., Lancaster, PA 17601, 717-397-3531.

Atlantic City, about 60 miles east. Connecting buses run from 30th St. Station and Trailways terminal. Call Transport of New Jersey, 215-569-3100.

2.32   Phoenix, Arizona

In ancient times Indians built an extensive irrigation system in what is now the Salt River valley, then inexplicably abandoned it about A.D. 1300. When the first white settlers arrived, they found the ruins of this ancient irrigation system and believed that what had been done before could be done again. Therefore, they named the town Phoenix after the legendary bird that rose again from its ashes.

Phoenix was incorporated in 1881 but didn't really mushroom until after World War II. In the 1950s alone the population quadrupled. Phoenix today has close to 800,000 people, although in 1950 there were only 105,000. More than half of all Arizonans live in the Phoenix metropolitan area. The city is the capital of the state and its largest commercial and industrial center.

Probably the most attractive thing about Phoenix is its climate. The sun shines nearly every day with a dry heat, and the city cools off each night.

Amtrak Station: 401 W. Harrison St. (downtown).

Tourist Information: Phoenix Valley of the Sun Convention and Visitors' Bureau, Suite 1460, 4455 E. Camelback Rd., Phoenix, AZ 85018. 602-952-8687.

Lodging: Phoenix Hilton (formerly Adams Hotel), Central and Adams sts., 602-257-1525 (deluxe). Los Olivos Hotel, 202 E. McDowell Rd.,

602-258-6911 (moderate). Western Village Motor Hotel, 1601 Grand Ave., 602-258-1631 (moderate). For bed-and-breakfast accommodations, contact Bed and Breakfast in Arizona, Suite 160, 8433 N. Black Canyon, Phoenix, AZ 85201, 602-939-2180.

Car Rental: Avis, Hyatt Regency Hotel, 122 N. 2nd St., 602-257-0807. Dollar, Hyatt Regency Hotel, 122 N. 2nd St., 602-257-1557.

Taxis: Checker Cab, 602-257-1818. Village Cab, 602-994-1616.

Public Transportation: Phoenix Transit Corp. (buses), 602-257-8426.

Bus Stations: Greyhound, 5th and Washington sts., 602-248-4040. Trailways, 433 E. Washington St., 602-246-4341.

Tours: Gray Line, 602-254-4550. Arizona Bus Tours, 602-254-5451. Dons Club, 602-258-6016. Phoenix by Night, 602-957-9801.

Attractions: Heard Museum, 22 E. Monte Vista Rd., 602-252-8848. Exhibits on Southwestern anthropology and primitive art. Good museum shops. Open Mon.–Sat. 10–5, Sun. 1–5.

State Capitol, Washington St. and 17th Ave., 602-255-4581. Open Mon.–Fri. 8–5; tours at 10 and 2:30.

Day Trip: Tonto National Monument, about 60 miles east. Take U.S.-60 to Apache Junction, then go northeast on Route 88. Prehistoric cliff dwellings. Visitors' center open daily 8–5; trail to ruins 8–4. The drive on Route 88 is spectacular.

2.33   Pittsburgh, Pennsylvania

Pittsburgh has long been the Steel City, but it is no longer the Smoky City. In fact, Pittsburgh is America's outstanding example of what urban renewal and pollution control can accomplish. Laid out on a series of hills, Pittsburgh has more bridges than any other American city, and its street pattern is so confusing that the late Ernie Pyle once remarked that the place must have been laid out by a mountain goat. Despite this, Pittsburgh is a very livable city. It has money and culture as well as industry and commerce.

Lying as it does between coal fields and iron-ore regions, with good transportation by both rail and water, Pittsburgh is ideally situated for making steel. And as the head of navigation on the Ohio, the city has long been a major distribution center for goods of all descriptions. The city's cultural institutions—including the University of Pittsburgh and the Carnegie Institute of Art—are widely respected. If you're not familiar with Pittsburgh, you should take the time to get to know this vibrant city.

Amtrak Station: Liberty and Grant sts. (downtown).

Tourist Information: Pittsburgh Convention and Visitors' Bureau, Visitors'

Center, Gateway Center, Pittsburgh, PA 15222, 412-281-9222. 24-hour information line: 412-391-6840.

Lodging: Hyatt Regency Pittsburgh, 112 Washington Pl., 412-471-1234 (deluxe). William Penn Hotel, 530 William Penn Way, 412-281-7100 (expensive). Best Western Viking, 1150 Banksville Rd., 412-531-8900 (not downtown but on a main thoroughfare; moderate).

Car Rental: Hertz, Chatham Center, 412-391-0364 (railroad-station pickup available). Budget, 700 5th Ave., 412-261-3320. Avis, 625 Stanwix St., 412-261-0540.

Taxis: Yellow Cab, 412-665-8100.

Public Transportation: Port Authority of Allegheny County (buses), 412-231-5707.

Bus Stations: Greyhound, 11th St. and Liberty Ave., 412-391-2300. Trailways, 210 10th St., 412-261-5400.

Attractions: Carnegie Institute of Art, 4400 Forbes Ave., 412-622-3172. Open Tues.–Sat. 10–5, Sun. 1–5.

Fort Pitt Museum, in Point State Park, 412-281-9284. Exhibits on early history of the region, with emphasis on the French and Indian War. Open Wed.–Sat. 9–5, Sun. 12–5.

Phipps Conservatory, in Schenley Park, 412-255-2375. Thirteen greenhouses with exotic plants. Open daily 9–5.

2.34   Portland, Oregon

Called the City of Roses for its beautiful flower gardens, Portland was founded in 1845 and quickly became a leading shipping center, even though it is 100 miles from the ocean. The Columbia River, however, is navigable by seagoing vessels to its junction with the Willamette River, making Portland a world outlet for the grain and timber of the interior and an important entry port for Asian products.

Portland got its name in an unusual way. Amos Lovejoy of Boston and F. W. Pettygrove of Portland, Maine, co-owners of the original town site, flipped a coin to decide what to call the place, and when Pettygrove won, he named it after his hometown.

Portland is the largest city in Oregon and one of the most attractive big cities in the United States. The business district is on the west side of the Willamette, and most of the residential section is to the east. The Columbia flows placidly to the north of the city, forming the boundary between Oregon and Washington.

Amtrak Station: 800 N.W. 6th Ave. About a mile north of city center.

A pleasant old station with many services, including a restaurant. Buses downtown run on 6th Ave.

Tourist Information: Greater Portland Convention and Visitors' Bureau, 26 S.W. Salmon St., Portland, OR 97204, 503-222-2223.

Lodging: Westin Benson Hotel, 309 S.W. Broadway, 503-228-9611 (deluxe). Portland Motor Hotel, 1414 S.W. 6th Ave., 503-221-1611 (from out of state: 800-547-4262) (moderate–expensive). Imperial Hotel, 400 S.W. Broadway, 503-228-7221 (moderate). For bed-and-breakfast accommodations, contact Northwest Bed and Breakfast, 707 S.W. Locust St., Portland, OR 97223, 503-246-8366.

Car Rental: Avis, Old Towne Chevron Service, 400 W. Burnside, 503-226-1456. Hertz, 1009 S.W. 6th Ave., 503-224-7700 (railroad-station pickup available). Budget, 1139 S.W. Broadway, 503-222-9123.

Taxis: Broadway Cab, 503-227-1234. Radio Cab, 503-227-1212.

Public Transportation: Tri-Met (buses), 503-233-3511. Downtown bus service is free, except from 3 to 7 P.M.

Bus Stations: Greyhound, 509 S.W. Taylor St., 503-243-2323. Trailways, 500 N.W. Broadway, 503-228-8571.

Tours: Gray Line, 503-226-6755. Aviation Enterprises, 503-667-1877 (flights over Mount St. Helens). AES, Inc., 503-239-8393 (ski and hiking trips, or shuttle to mountain areas).

Attractions: Washington City Park, W. Burnside Rd., 503-226-1561. In the park are the International Rose Test Gardens and Japanese Gardens. The annual Rose Festival is held in early June.

Pittock Mansion, 3229 N.W. Pittock Dr., off W. Burnside Rd., 503-248-4469. 1914 mansion of the founder of the *Daily Oregonian* newspaper. Magnificent views from the grounds. House open Wed.–Sun. 1–5; grounds open daily all day.

Day Trips: Columbia River Gorge, U.S.-30, east of the city. The road follows the river, passing through the gorge and near many waterfalls and rock formations. A number of state parks along this route offer good spots for picnics. There is Amtrak service through the gorge twice daily in each direction.

Mount St. Helens, about 65 miles northeast. Take I-5 north to exit 49, then take Route 504 past Silver Lake and along the Toutle River to the area devastated by the volcano. Gray Line offers bus tours from Portland; fly-over tours are also available (see above).

2.35 Providence, Rhode Island

Providence was founded in 1636 by Roger Williams and his followers, whose religious views had caused them to be banished from the Massachusetts Bay Colony. The city was named in gratitude to God for having brought them safely to this site.

Providence has been a shipping and commercial center since colonial times. Merchants' mansions built in the nineteenth century (many now restored and open to the public) reveal the seafaring heritage of the city. Providence is also an educational center: The Rhode Island School of Design and prestigious Brown University stand on the hill east of the Providence River.

Providence has an unusually large Roman Catholic community because of its long tradition of religious toleration, and the church is an important force in the city. Much of the city's Italian community lives in ethnic neighborhoods where annual festivals draw thousands of persons.

Amtrak Station: Railroad Terrace. Downtown: Dorrance St. and City Hall are a few blocks south. A new station, at the foot of the Capitol building, is scheduled to open in late 1984.

Tourist Information: Greater Providence Convention and Visitors' Bureau, 10 Dorrance St., Providence, RI 02903, 401-274-1636. Visitor Information Center, 401-274-1776. Call or write for information on annual festival of historic houses in early May and on annual Christmas festival.

Lodging: Providence Marriott, 1 Orms St., 401-272-2400 (from out of state: 800-228-9290) (deluxe). Biltmore Plaza, 11 Dorrance St., 401-421-0700 (from out of state 800-228-2121) (courtesy limo from station available; expensive–deluxe). Holiday Inn–Providence, 21 Atwells Ave., 401-831-3900 (from out of state 800-238-8000) (courtesy limo from station available; moderate).

Car Rental: National, 29 Eddy St., 401-801-6500. Hertz, Washington and Eddy sts., 401-274-9600. Avis, 1 Dorrance St., 401-521-7900.

Taxis: Laurel-Sweeney Cab, 401-521-4200. Economy Cab, 401-944-6700.

Public Transportation: RIPTA (buses), 401-781-9400 (frequent service to Newport).

Bus Station: Greyhound and Bonanza, W. Exchange St., 401-751-8800.

Tours: Janet Rochon Tours, 401-831-5273. Preservation Society Tours, 401-831-7440 (walking tours). Festive Tours, 401-438-8500.

Currency Exchange: Old Stone Bank, 86 S. Main St., 401-278-2000.

Attractions: Rhode Island School of Design Museum of Art, 224 Benefit St., 401-331-3511. Call for hours.

John Brown House, 52 Power St., 401-331-8575. Brick mansion, built in 1786 for a local China trader, slave trader, privateer, and patriot. Open Tues.–Sat. 11–4, Sun. 1–4.

State House, Smith St. between Francis and Gaspee sts., 401-277-2311. Designed by McKim, Meade, and White, the state-capitol building has the second-largest marble dome in the world, after Saint Peters in Rome. Open Mon.–Fri. 9:30–3:30.

Day Trip: Newport, about 35 miles south. Walk along the Cliff Walk or tour the mansions of the famous rich. Frequent bus service from Providence (call 401-781-9400). Information on sightseeing and lodging is available from the Newport Chamber of Commerce, 10 Americas Cup Ave., Newport, RI 02840, 401-847-1600. Bus and boat tours are available from Viking Tours of Newport, 401-847-6921.

2.36   Raleigh, North Carolina

The capital of North Carolina, Raleigh was established in 1792 near the center of the state, specifically to serve as the seat of North Carolina's state government. It is named, of course, for Sir Walter Raleigh, the English statesman, diplomat, poet, historian, and military leader who was a favorite of Elizabeth I's. In 1587, Raleigh planted a colony at Roanoke Island, home of Virginia Dare, the first English child born in the New World. Sometime before 1590, however, the colony disappeared, leaving no clue behind but the enigmatic word "Croatan" carved in a tree. The fate of Virginia Dare and the other Roanoke Island settlers remains a mystery to this day.

Visitors to Raleigh may tour the state-government buildings and the executive mansion. Many of these gracious antebellum structures were built by slaves; their initials can be seen, here and there, carved into the bricks.

Raleigh is the home of a number of colleges and universities. It contains Amtrak's station for the University of North Carolina, at Chapel Hill, and for Duke University, at Durham, both about 30 miles away by car or bus.

Amtrak Station: 707 Semart Dr. About 1 mile north of the capitol area; bus downtown stops in front of station.

Tourist Information: North Carolina Travel Division, Dept. of Commerce, Raleigh, NC 27611. Capitol Area Visitors' Center, 301 N. Blount St., 919-733-3456.

Lodging: Radisson Plaza, 420 Fayetteville St. Mall, 919-834-9900 (from out of state: 800-228-9822) (deluxe). Holiday Inn State Capitol, 320

Hillsborough St., 919-832-0501 (moderate–expensive). Journey's End Motel, 300 N. Dawson St., 919-828-9081 (moderate).

Car Rental: Budget, 1820 North Blvd., 919-834-6751. Hertz, 3415 Old Wake Forest Rd., 919-872-9047.

Taxis: Checker Cab, 919-832-5814. Safety Cab, 919-832-8801.

Public Transportation: Capital Area Transit Service (buses), 919-833-5701.

Bus Stations: Greyhound, 314 W. Jones St., 919-828-2567. Trailways, 313 New Bern Ave., 919-832-5536.

Tours: Topics, Inc., 919-362-8013 (individual van and auto tours).

Attractions: State Capitol Building, Capitol Square. Mon.–Sat. 8–5, Sun. 1–5.

North Carolina Museum of History, 109 E. Jones St., 919-733-3894. Contains exhibit on the Lost Colony. Tues.–Sat. 9–5, Sun. 1–6.

Executive Mansion, 200 N. Blount St. Tours can be arranged through the visitors' center (see above).

Day Trips: American Tobacco Co., Pettigrew and Blackwell sts., Durham, 919-682-2101. Open 9–2 but closed on and around many major holidays. Frequent bus service to Durham available daily from Greyhound and Trailways. Tour reservations are required.

Morehead Planetarium, University of North Carolina, East Franklin St. (I-501), Chapel Hill, 919-962-1248. One of the best planetariums in the United States. Shows nightly at 8; special constellation show Fri. at 7 P.M. Frequent Greyhound and Trailways bus service available to the university.

2.37 Reno, Nevada

"The Biggest Little City in the World," says the banner across the main street. Reno got its start more than a hundred years ago as the gateway to Virginia city and the fabulous Comstock Lode. It was laid out by Joseph Graham, a Central Pacific construction engineer, who established the town on the north bank of the Truckee River on April Fools' Day, 1868. It was named for J. L. Reno, a popular Union general in the Civil War who was killed in action in 1862. The town immediately became the commercial center of western Nevada.

Today the mining era is over and Reno is better known for gambling and quick divorces. Gaming here dates back to 1931, when the state legalized gambling to pep up its Depression economy. The move was so successful that Nevada now supports itself largely on tax revenues generated in the casinos. Residents pay no state income tax.

Near Reno is beautiful Lake Tahoe, Mecca for skiers and other sportsmen. Like Reno, Lake Tahoe offers casino gambling and nightclub entertainment. Virginia City also has much to offer the visitor who wants to get a firsthand look at what's left of the Gold Rush.

Amtrak Station: Commercial Row and Lake St. (downtown).

Tourist Information: Visitors' Information Center, Reno Chamber of Commerce, 133 N. Sierra St., Reno, NV 89504, 702-786-3030.

Lodging: Harrah's Hotel, Center and 2nd sts., 702-786-3232 (casino; expensive). Circus Circus Hotel, 500 N. Sierra St., 702-329-0711 (casino; moderate). Pick Hobson's Riverside Hotel, 17 S. Virginia St., 702-786-4400 (moderate).

Car Rental: Hertz, MGM Grand Hotel, 2500 E. 2nd St., 702-785-2605. National, Reno Hilton, N. Sierra St., 702-786-3757.

Taxis: Yellow Cab, 702-331-7171.

Public Transportation: Citifare (buses), 702-826-3273.

Bus Stations: Greyhound, 155 Stevenson St., 702-322-4511. Trailways, 500 W. 2nd St., 702-323-6163. Lake Tahoe–Reno Line (LTR) buses leave from here.

Tours: Gray Line, 702-329-1147. Reno Tahoe Tours, 702-322-6343.

Attractions: Mining Museum, Mackay School of Mines, end of N. Center St., 702-784-6987. Exhibits focus on mining in this area, past and present. Open Mon.-Fri. 8-5.

Harrah's Automobile Collection, Glendale Road, Sparks, 702-788-3242. Free shuttle bus leaves from Harrah's Hotel (Center and 2nd sts.) every hour. Open daily 9-6.

Day Trips: Virginia City, about 25 miles southeast on Route 341. This once great gold- and silver-mining city is now practically a ghost town, except for the tourist trade. The Chollar Mine, saloons, the opera house, and a mansion are open to the public. To some this may be a tourist trap, but read Mark Twain's *Roughing It* and you may enjoy the place as a living illustration of a way of life. There is a visitors' center on C Street, between Taylor and Union sts., 702-847-0311. Other than renting a car, there's only one way to get here—by LTR bus (see above), which stops in Virginia City only once a day and stays only half an hour.

Lake Tahoe, about 30 miles southwest. The lake is beautiful, and the sports facilities are superb. You can get here by Greyhound or LTR (see above), either directly or with a short stop in Virginia City. Bus tours from Reno are also available.

2.38 Richmond, Virginia

Richmond became the capital of Virginia in 1779. In 1861 it was named capital of the Confederacy as well, and it held this title until the city was captured by Grant's army in April 1865. This site was known to some of Virginia's earliest settlers, who came here in the 1630s; but the present town was not established until 1737. It was named for Richmond-upon-Thames, England; and like the first Richmond, it stands astride a river—the James—which is navigable to this point. Richmond has long been an important industrial and commercial center. Tobacco and cotton markets are here, as well as the Federal Reserve Bank.

The state-capitol building was designed by Thomas Jefferson; other important buildings include the Confederate capitol and the home of John Marshall, chief justice of the United States for 34 years. The Richmond Battlefield Park occupies scattered sites to the east of the city center. Here Lee beat off Union general George McClellan's attempt to take the city in June 1862.

The railroad station is a few miles out of town; visitors must take a taxi to reach the state-capitol area and hotels.

Amtrak Station: 7519 Staples Mill Rd. Several miles north of the city. Newspapers available at the station.

Tourist Information: Visitor Information Center, 1700 Robin Hood Rd., Richmond, VA 23219, 804-358-5511.

Lodging: John Marshall Hotel, 5th and Franklin sts., 804-644-4661 (expensive). Downtowner Motor Inn, 7th and Marshall sts., 804-649-0316 (moderate). Massad House Hotel, 11 N. 4th St., 804-648-2893 (budget). For bed-and-breakfast accommodations, contact Benson House of Richmond, P.O. Box 15131, Richmond, VA 23227, 804-321-6277.

Car Rental: Hertz, Turpin's American Cars, 5210 W. Broad St., 804-282-5333. Avis, 6th and Franklin sts., 804-643-6691.

Taxis: Yellow Cab, 804-355-4321.

Public Transportation: Greater Richmond Transit Co. (buses), 804-358-4782.

Bus Stations: Greyhound, 412 E. Broad St., 804-353-8903. Trailways, Broad and 9th sts., 804-643-1886.

Tours: Gray Line, 804-644-2901. Richmond-on-the-James, 804-780-0107 (self-guided and guided tours of historic neighborhoods, also river cruises).

Attractions: State Capitol, Capitol Square. Open daily 9–5.

Confederate Museum, 1201 E. Clay St., 804-649-1861. Open Mon.–

Sat. 10–5, Sun. 2–5.

Philip Morris, U.S.A., 3601 Commerce Rd., 804-274-3342. Tour of cigarette production process. Open Mon.–Fri. 9–4. Closed around major holidays.

Richmond National Battlefield Park. Main visitors' center is in Chimborazo Park, in a converted Civil War hospital. Call 804-226-1981 for information. Open daily 9–5.

Day Trip: Berkeley Plantation, about 27 miles south on Route 5, 804-795-2453. The first Thanksgiving was celebrated on this spot in 1619, even before it was celebrated by the Massachusetts Pilgrims. The house was built in 1726 and was the birthplace of President William Henry Harrison. It was Union general George McClellan's headquarters during the Civil War, and "Taps" was written here. Open daily 8–5.

2.39   Sacramento, California

The capital of California, Sacramento has been a strategic transportation center since long before the railroads came. It was founded in 1839 by John Sutter—on whose land gold was found 9 years later. A native of Switzerland, he had come to America and obtained a land grant from the Mexican authorities. Here, at the head of navigation on the Sacramento River, where the American River flows in, he established his town.

Sutter's vision of a miniature Switzerland was never fulfilled, but his settlement boomed when the discovery of gold nearby brought thousands of fortune seekers to California. Owing to its location, at almost the exact center of the state and conveniently close to both the gold diggings and San Francisco, Sacramento was made the capital of California in 1854. Today it has more than a quarter of a million people and is an important agricultural center as well as the seat of state government.

Sacramento has a special place in railroading history. It was here that Collis Huntington and Mark Hopkins, a couple of hardware dealers, joined forces with Leland Stanford and Charles Crocker to build a railroad over the Sierras. They were called the "Big Four," and their project, the Central Pacific Railroad, turned them from small-time merchants into four of the richest and most powerful men on the continent.

To commemorate its role as the original terminus of the Central Pacific, Sacramento was selected as the site of the California State Railroad Museum, opened on May 10, 1981—112 years to the day after the Golden Spike ceremony marking the completion of the nation's first transcontinental railroad. The museum, well worth a visit, is just west of the Amtrak passenger

The Phoenix, Arizona, skyline. Phoenix has been one of America's fastest growing cities since World War II,

Seattle, Washington, is a city of contrasts, with the Space Needle, downtown, and Mt. Rainier in the distance.

station in downtown Sacramento. Here, too, is the reconstructed area known as Old Sacramento, lying along the river front.

Amtrak Station: 401 I St. (downtown).

Tourist Information: Sacramento Convention Center and Visitors' Bureau, 1311 I St., Sacramento, CA 95814, 916-442-5542.

Lodging: Best Western Ponderosa, 1100 H St., 916-441-1314 (from out of state: 800-528-1234) (expensive). Mansion Inn, 700 16th St., 916-444-8000 (expensive). Capitol Plaza Holiday Inn, 300 J St., 916-446-0100 (moderate).

Car Rental: Hertz, 1025 16th St., 916-444-2414. Budget, 830 L St., 916-444-3455.

Taxi: Yellow Cab, 916-444-2222. River City Jitney, 916-441-0279.

Public Transportation: Sacramento Regional Transit (buses), 916-444-2877.

Bus Stations: Greyhound, 715 L St. 916-444-6800. Trailways, 1129 I St., 916-443-2044.

Tours: River City Transportation, 916-447-2208. Sacramento Sightseeing, 916-442-7564 (individual van tours).

Attractions: State Capitol, 10th and L sts., 916-324-0333. Distinctive building with 40 acres of grounds. Open daily 7 A.M.–9 P.M. Tours available.

Sutter's Fort, 27th and L sts., 916-445-4209. Exhibits on early white settlers and local Indians. Open daily 10–5.

California State Railroad Museum, 2nd and I sts., 916-445-4209. Large, fascinating exhibit on railroading and its history. Open daily 10–5.

Day Trips: Lake Tahoe. This resort center is about 100 miles east of Sacramento. Rent a car and drive, or take one of many Greyhound buses scheduled daily.

California Wine Country. Napa and Sonoma counties are about 60 miles west of Sacramento. Rent a car and visit several wineries in a single day. Good inexpensive guide pamphlets are available at the visitors' bureau in Sacramento (see above).

2.40 St. Louis, Missouri

St. Louis was named for King Louis IX of France, who was canonized in recognition of his charitable works and religious faith. It was founded by French fur traders about 1764, a few miles below the point where the Missouri River flows into the Mississippi. By 1803, when it became an American city, it had a thousand citizens. With the coming of the steamboats, St. Louis assumed its position as a gateway to both the West and the South. Today it is second only to Chicago as a transportation center and remains one of America's great inland cities.

The population of St. Louis is widely diverse. The French, of course, have been here from the beginning. Missouri was a slave state, and descendants of Southern whites and freed slaves account for a large percentage of the city's inhabitants. Around 1850 St. Louis, like many other Midwestern cities, acquired a large German community made up largely of refugees from the revolution in that country that was suppressed in 1848. St. Louis is, therefore, a mixture of old and new, traditional and progressive. It's also hot and humid in summer.

That fact has something to do with another St. Louis distinction. During the 1904 World's Fair (the occasion celebrated in the song "Meet Me in St. Louis") it got so hot that the ice cream seller ran out of bowls. He had plenty of ice cream left but nothing on which to serve it. Ah, but nearby another vendor was selling German cookies. The two businessmen put their heads together, and soon people were lapping up ice cream served on a wafer. That American staple the ice cream cone was born.

The 1904 World's Fair was also the occasion for the construction of the magnificent St. Louis Union Station, once the biggest structure of its kind in the United States. Today, however, with only five or six trains a day rolling into the city, Amtrak has moved out of the huge old station to a nearby smaller facility in an effort to cut maintenance and operating costs. The new station may be more efficient, but it lacks the glamour and grandeur of the old terminal.

Amtrak Station: 550 S. 16th St. (downtown).

Tourist Information: St. Louis Convention and Visitors' Bureau, 10 S. Broadway, Suite 300, St. Louis, MO 63101, 314-421-1023 (or 800-325-7962).

Lodging: Marriott Pavilion Hotel, 1 Broadway, 314-421-1776 (deluxe). Mayfair Hotel, St. Charles and 8th sts., 314-231-1500 (expensive). Ramada Inn, 303 S. Grand Blvd., 314-534-8300 (moderate). For bed-and-breakfast accommodations, contact Bed and Breakfast St. Louis, 16 Green Acres, St. Louis, Mo., 314-868-2335.

Car Rental: Hertz, 400 N. Tucker Blvd., 314-421-3131. Avis, 925 Washington Ave., 314-241-5780. Budget, 202 Mansion House Center, 314-231-6822.

Taxis: Yellow Cab, 314-361-2345.

Public Transportation: Bistate Transit (buses), 314-773-1120.

Bus Stations: Greyhound, 801 N. Broadway, 314-231-7800. Trailways, 706 N. Broadway, 314-231-7181.

Tours: Gray Line, 314-241-1224. Huck Finn and Tom Sawyer Cruises, 314-621-4040.

Attractions: Gateway Arch—Jefferson National Expansion Memorial at the end of Market St., 314-425-4465. Visitors' center open daily 8 A.M.—10 P.M. in summer, 9–6 rest of year. Museum open daily 9–6 (open later in summer; call for hours). Tram to observation deck open daily 8:30 A.M.—9:30 P.M. in summer, 9:30–5:15 rest of year.

Shaw's Garden (Missouri Botanical Garden), 4344 Shaw Ave., 314-577-5100. Beautiful exotic gardens modeled on London's Kew Gardens. Open daily 9–7:30 mid-April–Sept., 9–5 Oct.–mid-April.

Anheuser-Busch Brewery, Broadway and Pestalozzi St., 314-577-2626. Tour of plant, beer tasting, and a glimpse of the Clydesdale horses. Open Mon.–Fri. 9:30–3:30. Closed weekends and company holidays.

Steamship Dock. Mississippi riverboats dock here, east of the downtown area, on the river front.

Day Trip: Hannibal, about 120 miles north. Boyhood home of Samuel Clemens, known as Mark Twain, and the setting for many of his books. His home is open to the public, as is the cave that Twain wrote about in *The Adventures of Tom Sawyer.* Visitors may also want to take a riverboat trip. Call 314-221-9010 for information, or write to Mark Twain's Boyhood Home, 208 Hill St., Hannibal, MO 63401.

2.41 St. Petersburg, Florida

Believe it or not, this sunny city was named for icebound St. Petersburg (now known as Leningrad), once the capital of imperial Russia. St. Petersburg, Florida, has little industry besides tourism. It is in business to provide vacations. Attractions include the Sunken Gardens, the Salvador Dali Museum, and a replica of the H. M. S. *Bounty,* of mutiny fame. St. Petersburg and nearby islands offer excellent beaches. And, of course, there is fishing in Tampa Bay and the Gulf of Mexico, where you have a chance to pull in a really big one. Lively Tampa, with its Latin quarter, is across the bridge.

Amtrak Station: 3601 31st St. N.

Tourist Information: St. Petersburg Chamber of Commerce, Visitors' Information Center, 800 2nd Ave. NE, St. Petersburg, FL 33731, 813-821-4715. There is another center at 401 3rd Ave. S. (813-821-4069).

Lodging: Bay Front Concourse Hotel, 333 1st St. S., 813-896-1111 (expensive). Edgewater Beach Motel, 631 N. Shore Dr. N.E., 813-898-0811 (budget–moderate, depending on season).

Car Rentals: Hertz, 2950 Central Ave., 813-327-4357 (railroad-station pickup available). Budget, 500 34th St., 813-327-0010.

Taxis: Independent Cab, 813-327-3444. St. Pete Taxi, 813-367-3705.

Public Transportation: St. Petersburg Transit Authority (buses), 813-893-7433.

Bus Stations: Greyhound, 110 Central Ave., 813-895-4455. Trailways, 105 2nd St. S., 813-823-3140.

Tours: Transit Authority Downtown Tour, 813-893-7433. Gray Line, 813-832-3577. Captain Anderson Cruises, 813-360-2619.

Attractions: H. M. S. *Bounty,* 345 2nd Ave. N.E., 813-896-3117. Ship built by MGM for the film *Mutiny on the Bounty.* Open 9 A.M.—10 P.M.

    Salvador Dali Museum, 1000 3rd St. S., 813-823-3767. Largest collection of Dali's works in the world. Open Tues., Wed., Fri., Sat. 10-5; Thurs. 10-8; Sun. 12-5.

    Sunken Gardens, 1825 4th St. N., 813-896-3186. Native Florida plants and birds in a natural setting. Open daily 9-5:30.

Day Trip: Ringling Museums, Sarasota, about 35 miles south of St. Petersburg on U.S.-41, the Tamiami Trail, 813-355-5101. The estate of the circus family, the complex includes a museum of art, the Museum of the Circus, the Ringling Residence, and the Asolo Theatre. Overlooks the water. Open Mon.–Fri. 9-7, Sat. 9-5, Sun. 11-6. Tours from St. Petersburg are available, and there is frequent bus service to Sarasota.

2.42   Salt Lake City, Utah

"This is the place!" said Brigham Young, when after an exhausting trek across the Great Plains from Nauvoo, Illinois, the Mormons saw the Salt Lake Valley. They were looking for a homesite outside what was then the United States, where they would be free to practice polygamy without interference from their neighbors or the courts; and they had found it here. Within an amazingly short time the wilderness had become a thriving commercial city, crossroads of western trade routes.

    Today Salt Lake City has about 165,000 inhabitants, two-thirds of whom belong to the Mormon Church—the Church of Jesus Christ of Latter-Day Saints. The city was planned around Temple Square, which includes the Temple itself, the Mormon Tabernacle, and a number of other church buildings. North of Temple Square is the state capitol, atop a commanding hill. Farther east, at the edge of the Wasatch Mountains, is the campus of the University of Utah. To the northwest is Great Salt Lake. Salt Lake City is famous for its broad streets, its sparkling clean atmosphere—it is more than 4,000 feet above sea level—and the industry and efficiency of its people. The Amtrak station, which formerly served the Union Pacific, is at the west end of the downtown area, at the foot of South Temple Street.

Amtrak Station: 4th West and S. Temple sts. (downtown).

Tourist Information: Salt Lake City Convention and Visitors' Bureau, 180

SW Temple St., Salt Lake City, UT 84101, 801-521-2822. Information center at Trolley Sq., 7th St. between 5th S. and 6th S. sts.

Lodging: Hotel Utah, S. Temple and Main sts., 801-531-1000 (deluxe). Temple Square Hotel, 75 W. S. Temple St., 801-355-2961 (moderate-expensive). Palace Motel, 210 W. S. Temple St., 801-532-4400 (moderate). For bed-and-breakfast accommodations, contact Bed and Breakfast Association of Utah, P.O. Box 16465, Salt Lake City, UT 84116, 801-532-7076.

Car Rental: Avis, Municipal Airport, 801-539-2177 (railroad-station pickup available). Hertz, 445 S. Main St., 801-521-4100 (railroad-station pickup available). Budget, 750 S. Main St., 801-322-5581.

Taxis: Yellow Cab, 801-521-2100. Ute Cab, 801-359-7788.

Public Transportation: Utah Transit Authority (buses), 801-531-8600.

Bus Stations: Greyhound, 160 W. S. Temple St., 801-355-4684. Trailways, 77 W. S. Temple St., 801-328-8121.

Tours: Gray Line, 801-521-7060. Greater Salt Lake Tours, 801-364-0185.

Attractions: Temple Square. Visitors' center open 8 A.M.—10 P.M. The Mormon Temple, which holds the sacred ordinances of the church, is the building with the gold-leaf roof (not open to the public). The Mormon Tabernacle is open 8 A.M.—10 P.M. April–Aug., 9–9 Sept.–March. Choir rehearses Thurs. 8 P.M.; broadcasts Sun. 9:30 A.M. (get there by 9). Call 801-531-2534 for information.

Pioneer Trail State Park, 2601 Sunnyside Ave., 801-533-5881. At the mouth of Emigration Canyon, the park includes Brigham Young's farm and the "this is the place" monument. Open 7–10 May–Oct., 10–6 rest of year.

Great Salt Lake. South Shore Beach is off I-80, about 20 miles west of Salt Lake City. Public bathhouses and cold showers available if you want to float around a bit—just don't duck your head under water! Gray Line operates buses to this beach.

2.43   San Antonio, Texas

Founded in 1718, San Antonio is much older than Houston or Dallas, its larger rivals. It is also the most Hispanic large city north of the border.

Say, "San Antonio," and somebody is sure to mention the Alamo, the mission where a group of Texans headed by William Travis, Davy Crockett, and Jim Bowie was besieged and eventually wiped out in 1836, during the Texas Revolution. The cry "Remember the Alamo" spurred Sam Houston's force to victory over General Santa Anna at San Jacinto a month and a half later. The Alamo is, of course, San Antonio's top tourist attraction.

Today San Antonio is noted as the commercial center of southern Texas. It is also an air-force city, with the Randolph and Lackland bases nearby.

San Antonio is also known for its beautiful river walk, the Paseo del Rio. City planners from around the world have praised this promenade, where the river has been used to lend focus and unusual charm to the city.

Amtrak Station: 1174 E. Commerce St. A few blocks west of the city center. Walk west on Commerce St. to reach the Paseo del Rio.

Tourist Information: San Antonio Visitors' Information Center, 321 Alamo Plaza (P.O. Box 2277, San Antonio, TX 78298), 512-299-8123 (from out of state: 800-531-5700; in Texas: 800-292-1010).

Lodging: Hotel St. Anthony Inter-Continental, 300 E. Travis St., 512-227-4392 (deluxe). Menger Hotel, Alamo Plaza, 512-223-4361 (expensive). TraveLodge on the River, 100 Villita St., 512-226-2271 (moderate). Texian Motel, 211 N. Pecos St., 512-225-1111 (800-531-1000) (moderate; includes breakfast and downtown limo; near El Mercado). For bed-and-breakfast accommodations, contact Bed and Breakfast Hosts of San Antonio, 166 Rockhill, San Antonio, TX 78209, 512-824-8036.

Car Rental: Hertz, Marriott Hotel, 711 E. Riverwalk, 512-222-1695. Budget, 410 E. Commerce St., 514-349-4441.

Taxis: Yellow Cab, 512-226-4242. Checker Cab, 512-222-2151.

Public Transportation: VIA Metropolitan Transit (buses), 512-227-2020.

Bus Stations: Greyhound, 500 N. St. Mary's St., 512-227-8351. Trailways, 301 Broadway, 512-226-6136.

Tours: Gray Line, 512-227-5251. Band T Fuller Double-Decker Bus Tours, 512-734-8706. Yellow Rose Horse and Carriage Tours, 512-225-6490. Paseo del Rio Boats, 512-222-1701.

Attractions: The Alamo, Alamo Plaza, near the river, 512-225-1391. Open Mon.–Sat. 9–5:30, Sun. 10–5:30.

La Villita, Villita St. between S. Presa and S. Alamo sts., 512-299-8610. A restored area of craft shops and galleries, La Villita is the oldest part of the city.

San José Mission State and National Historical Site, 6539 San José Dr., 512-922-2731. The largest of San Antonio's missions, famous for stone carvings. Open daily 9–6 Sept.–May; 9–8 June–Aug.

El Mercado, 514 W. Commerce St., 512-299-8600. Colorful market. Open daily 10–6.

2.44   San Diego, California

There's more to San Diego than tuna boats and retired naval officers these days. The city has grown rapidly and is now much more dynamic and cosmopolitan than it used to be. With its beautiful bay and hills and its ever blooming flowers, this is an ideal vacation spot. Sea World, the Maritime Museum on the waterfront, and the world-famous zoo in Balboa Park are additional attractions. Tijuana, Mexico, is a short bus ride away, or you can take the "Tijuana Trolley," whose route begins across the street from the Amtrak station. The waterfront is also within walking distance of the station.

Amtrak Station: 1050 Kettner Blvd. (at Broadway). Near the city center. Traditional California architecture distinguishes the station.

Tourist Information: San Diego Convention and Visitors' Bureau, Suite 824, 1200 3rd Ave., San Diego, CA 92101, 619-232-3101.

Lodging: The Westgate Hotel, 1055 2nd Ave., 619-238-1818 (deluxe). Royal Lodge—Downtown, 833 Ash St., 619-239-2285 (expensive). Friendship Inn Town House, 810 Ash St., 619-233-8826 (moderate). For bed-and-breakfast accommodations, contact Caroline's Bed and Breakfast, P.O. Box 84776, San Diego, CA 92138, 619-481-7662.

Car Rental: Avis, Stardust Hotel, 950 Hotel Circle, 714-231-7130. Hertz, 1420 Kettner Blvd., 714-232-6801 (railroad-station pickup available). Thrifty, 2100 Kettner Blvd., 714-239-2281.

Taxis: Silver Cab, 619-280-2667. Coast Cab, 619-226-8294.

Public Transportation: San Diego Trolley, 619-231-1466 (runs between Amtrak station and Mexican border). San Diego Transit (buses) 619-233-3004. Mexicoach, 619-232-5049 (to Tijuana).

Bus Stations: Greyhound, 1st Ave. and Broadway, 619-239-9171. Trailways, Union and C sts., 619-232-2001.

Tours: Gray Line, 619-231-9922. El Paso Tours, 619-427-8630 (tours to Mexico). Bahia Belle, 619-488-0551. *The Invader* Tours, 619-298-8066 (largest schooner in U.S.).

Currency Exchange: Deak-Perera, 531 C St., 619-235-0900.

Attractions: Balboa Park. Large public park, site of 1915–16 California International Exposition. Many exhibits still open, and most of the city's museums are here.

   San Diego Zoo, in Balboa Park, 619-234-3153. One of the finest zoos in the world; many exotic animals in natural habitats. Open daily 8:30–6:30.

Old Town San Diego, northwest of Balboa Park and downtown area, 619-237-6770. Most of San Diego's oldest buildings are in this state historic park, which preserves the site of the original town.

Cabrillo National Monument, Cabrillo Memorial Dr., 619-293-5450. At the tip of Point Loma a lighthouse and statue commemorate the Spanish explorer Juan Cabrillo. Overlooks the city and harbor; whales are sometimes seen from here. Open daily 9–5:15.

Maritime Museum of San Diego, 1306 N. Harbor Dr. (a block west of the Amtrak station), 619-234-9153. Three historic ships to tour. Nautical exhibits. Open daily 9–8.

Sea World, Sea World Dr., Mission Bay, 619-224-3562. Aquarium and marine-life center, including whale show, shark exhibits, dolphin and porpoise tanks. Open daily 9–sunset.

Day Trip: Tijuana, Mexico. Frequent public transportation is available if you want to spend a few hours exploring the city on your own. Bus tours, half or full day, also available. American citizens do not need passports for day trips. Tijuana, though commercialized and full of tourists, is worth a visit, especially if you like Mexican food.

2.45   San Francisco, California

Train travelers who enter San Francisco over the Bay Bridge get a suitable introduction to this cosmopolitan city set in the midst of imposing natural beauty. San Francisco Bay is spectacular, and so are the hillsides of this gateway city.

San Francisco is built on a hilly peninsula between the Pacific Ocean and the bay. The Spanish were the first to settle here, and they established a military post and a mission on the site. The mission was dedicated to Saint Francis of Assisi, and his name was passed on to the city as well.

In the nineteenth century the city grew with the flood of westward migration. Although San Francisco itself remained off the main railroad lines until the twentieth century, newly wealthy railroad and mining barons chose to build their houses here. Those homes, especially the ones on Nob Hill, reveal the eclectic tastes of this new American aristocracy.

The hills, whose steepness inspired the building of cable cars, make for hard walking but marvelous sightseeing around the city. The Coit Tower, atop Telegraph Hill, gives a view in all directions; to the west you can see Lombard Street zigzagging alarmingly. Nob Hill overlooks the ocean and much of the city. From the Golden Gate National Recreation Area, along the northern waterfront, you can get an unforgettable view of the Golden

Gate Bridge, floating dramatically in a blanket of fog. Unfortunately, the cable cars are not running now, while the century-old system is undergoing a thorough restoration.

Transbay Terminal: 425 Mission St. at 1st St., 2 blocks southeast of Market St. Passengers from Oakland arrive here by bus.

Southern Pacific Terminal: 4th St. between Townsend and Key sts. Serves commuter trains to Palo Alto and San Jose 415-495-4546.

Tourist Information: San Francisco Visitor Information Center, Hallidie Plaza, Powell and Market sts., San Francisco, CA 94102, 415-391-2000.

Lodging: Mark Hopkins Hotel, 1 Nob Hill (California and Mason sts.), 415-392-3434 (deluxe). Wharf Inn, 2601 Mason St., 415-673-7411 (expensive). Beck's Motor Lodge, 2222 Market St., 415-621-8212 (moderate). For bed-and-breakfast accommodations, contact Bed and Breakfast International, 151 Ardmore Rd., Kensington, CA 94707, 415-525-4569, or American Family Inn, 2185-A Union St., San Francisco, CA 94123, 415-931-3083.

Car Rental: Avis, 675 Post St., 415-885-5011. Hertz, 433 Mason St., 415-771-2200 (railroad-station pickup available). Budget, 321 Mason St., 415-928-7863.

Taxis: Yellow Cab, 415-626-2345. Veterans' Taxi, 415-552-1300.

Public Transportation: San Francisco Municipal Railways (MUNI) (buses, streetcars, and cable cars), 415-673-6864. Bay Area Rapid Transit (BART) (subways), 415-788-BART.

Bus Stations: Greyhound, 7th and Market sts., 415-433-1500. Trailways, 1st and Mission sts., 415-982-6400.

Ferries: Red and White Fleet, 415-546-2815 (Pier 41 to Tiburon). Golden Gate Transit District Ferries, 415-332-6600 (Ferry Building to Sausalito and Larkspur).

Tours: Red and White Fleet, 415-546-2810. Gray Line, 415-771-4000. City Guides (free historic walking tours), 415-558-3770.

Currency Exchange: Thomas Cook Travel, 175 Post St., 415-392-2378. Deak-Perera, 100 Grant Ave., 415-362-3452.

Attractions: Chinatown, roughly from Broadway to Bush St., between Stockton St. and Grant Ave. Largest Chinese community in the Americas. Call the Chinese Culture Center, 415-986-1822, for information on walking tours.

Fisherman's Wharf, end of Taylor St., at the north end of the city. Shops and seafood restaurants line the wharf.

Lombard St., between Hyde and Leavenworth sts. One of the crookedest streets in the world.

Alcatraz Island, 415-546-2805. 2-hour tours daily 8:45–2:45. Boats leave from Pier 41, at foot of Powell St. Tickets go on sale at 8:30 each day for that day's tours. Advance tickets available through Ticketron.

Nob Hill, centered around Grace Cathedral, on California St. between Jones and Taylor sts. Nob Hill was the fashionable place to build a house in nineteenth-century San Francisco, and the houses still show the pride of their owners.

Old U.S. Mint, 5th and Mission sts., 415-974-0788. This former mint building now houses a museum of Western paintings and exhibits on California gold mining. Open Tues.–Sat. 10–4.

Day Trips: Wine Country. Most California vineyards offer visitors tours with wine tasting, and these can be an interesting and civilized way to spend a day in the beautiful California countryside. Pick up a winery guide at any bookstore or newsstand in San Francisco, or take a bus tour. The famed Napa Valley is just north of the city.

The Monterey Peninsula, with its 17-mile coastline drive, is about a 3-hour drive south of San Francisco, off U.S.-101. If you spend the night, Big Sur is about an hour farther south.

2.46 Savannah, Georgia

Savannah is the oldest settlement in Georgia, having been founded in 1733 by General James Oglethorpe. The colony was intended to be a military post to protect the English colonies to the north from the Spanish in Florida. Oglethorpe, therefore, set down strict regulations for the new settlement: Large-scale landholding and slavery were prohibited, and Roman Catholics were excluded from the community for fear that their true loyalties might be with their Spanish coreligionists. Moreover, Oglethorpe and his fellow trustees had a second purpose in mind: to give inmates of British debtors' prisons a new start in life. Thus a number of the early settlers of Savannah were delivered from incarceration. It wasn't long, however, before Georgia evolved into a more typical antebellum Southern state with plantation agriculture.

Today Savannah is a lovely Southern city with a strong flavor of its seafaring past. Oglethorpe's arrangement of streets and public squares has been retained, and the result is a well-ordered city. Begin your tour at the restored railroad station on West Broad Street (unfortunately, this is not the Amtrak station), where the visitors' center is located.

Amtrak Station: 2611 Seaboard Coast Line Dr. About 10 miles from the city.

Tourist Information: Savannah Visitor's Center, 301 W. Broad St., Savannah, GA 31401, 912-233-6651.

Lodging: Eliza Thompson House, 5 W. Jones St., 912-236-3620 (expensive). Quality Inn, 300 W. Bay St., 912-236-6321 (moderate). Bed and Breakfast Inn, 117 Gordon St., 912-238-0518 (moderate).

Car Rental: Avis, Downtowner Motor Inn, 201 W. Oglethorpe Ave., 912-236-3096 (railroad-station pickup available, with reservation). National, 401 W. Bay St., 912-234-8913.

Taxis: ABBA Cab, 912-354-6911. Adam Cab, 912-927-7466.

Public Transportation: Savannah Transit Authority (buses), 912-233-5767.

Bus Stations: Greyhound, 610 Oglethorpe Ave., 912-233-7723. Trailways, 266 W. Broad St., 912-233-4104.

Bicycle Rental: Historic Savannah Foundation, 912-233-7703.

Tours: Historic Savannah Foundation Tours, 912-233-3597. Black Heritage Trail, 912-233-2027. Gray Line, 912-236-9604.

Attractions: Owens-Thomas House, 124 Abecorn St., 912-233-9743. Fine Regency-style villa. Open Tues.–Sat. 10–5, Sun.–Mon. 2–5. Closed Sept.
Savannah Waterfront (Bay Street, Factors Walk, and River Street). Cobblestones and ironwork highlight this restored historic area.

Day Trip: Tybee Island, Route 80, east of Savannah. A quiet beach-resort town with excellent swimming. A lighthouse and a museum are open to the public (912-786-4077).

2.47 Seattle, Washington

With nearly half a million residents, Seattle is the metropolis of the Pacific Northwest. The city is built on a series of hills and islands, with Elliott Bay—part of Puget Sound—on the west side and Lake Washington on the east. Seattle, named for a local Indian chief, was first settled in 1852; but it remained a small and relatively unimportant lumbering town until 1897, when the discovery of gold in the Klondike caused a rush to Alaska. Then as now Seattle was the jumping-off place for Alaska; and traffic to and from the largest state, as well as Asian shipping, has ensured Seattle's position as one of the nation's leading ports. Unfortunately, the city is surrounded by rain forest, and there is precipitation here much of the time. In other respects, Seattle is as pleasant a city as America has to offer, with economic and cultural opportunities in a scenic setting.

King Street Station: 3rd and Jackson sts. Downtown, a few blocks southeast of the city center.

Tourist Information: Seattle–King County Convention and Visitors' Bureau, 1815 7th Ave., Seattle, WA 98101, 206-447-7273.

Lodging: Warwick Hotel, 401 Lenora Ave., 206-625-6700 (deluxe). Vance Downtown Hotel, 620 Stewart St., 206-623-2700 (moderate). Mayflower Park Hotel, 4th St. and Olive Way, 206-623-8700 (moderate). For bed-and-breakfast accommodations, contact Pacific Bed and Breakfast, 701

NW 60th St., Seattle, WA 98107, 206-784-0539, or Travellers' Bed and Breakfast, P.O. Box 492, Mercer Island, WA 98040, 206-232-2345.

Car Rental: Avis, 1919 5th Ave., 206-622-1000. Dollar, 2001 6th Ave., 206-682-1316.

Taxis: Farwest Cab, 206-622-1717. Yellow Cab, 206-622-6500.

Public Transportation: Seattle Metropolitan Transit System (buses, streetcar, and monorails), 206-447-4800. Free bus service in downtown area.

Bus Stations: Greyhound, 8th and Stewart sts., 206-624-3456. Trailways, 1936 Westlake Ave., 206-624-5955.

Ferries: Washington State Ferry, Pier 52 at foot of Marion St., 206-464-6400 (to Olympic Peninsula, Bremerton, and Bainbridge Island). British Columbia Steamship Co., Pier 69 at foot of Wall St., 206-623-5560 (to Victoria, B.C.; April–Oct. only).

Tours: Gray Line, 206-343-2000. American Sightseeing, 206-624-5077. Bill Speidel Underground Tours, 206-682-4646 (tours of Underground Seattle). City and Country Tours, 206-282-2301. Seattle Harbor Tours, 206-623-1445. Emerald City Excursions, 206-631-8232. Day Tours, 206-624-2377 (unusual tours, worth investigating).

Attractions: Tillicum Village, 206-329-5700. Northwest Indian village in Baker Island State Park. 45-minute ferry to island and salmon dinner included. Several trips each day May—mid-Oct., weekends only during off season. Call for information and reservations.

Klondike Gold Rush National Historical Park, 117 S. Main St., Pioneer Sq., 206-442-7220. Open daily 9–7 in summer; Mon.-Fri. 9–5, Sat.-Sun. 9–6 rest of year.

Seattle Center, 1 mile north of downtown. Former grounds of the Seattle World's Fair, now includes Seattle Art Museum Pavilion, the Space Needle, and the Pacific Science Center. Accessible by monorail (see above).

Lake Washington Ship Canal and Locks, Gilman Ave., 206-783-7000. Windows allow visitors to watch trout and salmon climb the fish ladders.

Day Trips: Olympic National Park and Mount Rainier National Park are both within a short driving distance of Seattle. Olympic National Park visitors' centers are at Port Angeles, Hoh Rain Forest, and Lake Crescent. Write to Superintendent, Olympic National Park, 600 E. Park Ave., Port Angeles, WA 98362, for information. Mount Rainier has four visitors' centers: Sunrise, Ohanapecosh, Longmire, and Paradise. Write to Superintendent, Mount Rainier National Park, Tahoma Woods–Star Route, Ashford, WA 98304. Information is also available from the Seattle–King County Convention and Visitors' Bureau, above. Remember that road conditions vary with the season, and many roads are impassable in winter. In summer, tour companies run bus trips from Seattle to both parks.

2.48   Tucson, Arizona

Tucson, Arizona's second-largest city and the home of the University of Arizona, is as old as the United States, having been established in 1776 by Spaniards from Mexico. At about the same time, missionaries who had been visiting the area for years built the nearby San Xavier del Bac mission. This spectacular mission, known as the "White Dove of the Desert," is still dedicated to its original work and includes an active house of worship. The city, however, has changed over the years, despite persistent Spanish influence. Today it is best known as a Mecca for people looking for a dry climate and sunny weather, and it is a popular and profitable health resort.

Both east and west of the city are sections of the Saguaro National Monument, where the rare giant cacti grow in awesome stands. The Arizona–Sonora Desert Museum, one of the of the finest and most unusual museums in the country, is near the national monument; visitors to this part of the country should make a stop here and learn about the desert environment. Old Tucson, a movie set built in the 1940s and now open to the public, is an amusement theme park unlike any other, where you can learn about the history of the city and the area and have fun at the same time.

Amtrak Station: 400 E. Toole St. (downtown).

Tourist Information: Tucson Convention and Visitors' Bureau, 450 W. Paseo Redondo (P.O. Box 3028), Tucson, AZ 85702), 602-624-1817.

Lodging: Marriott Hotel, 180 W. Broadway, 602-624-8711 (deluxe). Santa Rita Hotel, 88 E. Broadway, 602-791-7581 (moderate). There are several deluxe guest ranches in the Tucson area that offer complete resort features, including horseback riding—e.g., Hacienda del Sol, 602-299-1501; Sundancer Resort, 602-743-0411; Tanque Verde Guest Ranch, 602-296-6275.

Car Rental: Avis, Doubletree Hotel, 445 S. Alvernon Way, 602-746-3278 (cab fare refunded up to $5). Budget, 723 E. 22nd St., 602-623-5743 (railroad-station pickup available). Road Runner, 338 W. Drachman St., 602-624-5132.

Taxis: All-State Taxi, 602-881-2227.

Public Transportation: Sun Tran (buses), 602-792-9222.

Bus Stations: Greyhound, 2 S. 4th Ave., 602-792-0972. Trailways, 201 E. Broadway, 602-882-0005.

Tours: Gray Line, 602-622-8811. Hoot Gibson's Desert Tours, 602-297-1000. Ghost Town Excursions, 602-884-0777.

Attractions: Arizona State Museum, Park Ave. and University Blvd.,

602-621-6302. Southwestern archaeology. Open Mon.–Sat. 9–5, Sun 2–5.

Mission San Xavier del Bac, 1 Mission Rd., 602-294-2624. Called the "White Dove of the Desert," this is one of the most beautiful missions in America. Open daily 8–5. Taped lectures Mon.–Sat. 9:30–4:30.

Day Trips: The Arizona-Sonora Desert Museum, Saguaro National Monument, and Old Tucson can all be visited by car in one day. The museum (602-883-1380) is 14 miles west of the city in Tucson Mountain Park (opens at 7 A.M. in summer, 8:30 rest of year; closes at sunset), a few miles beyond Old Tucson. The national monument is just beyond the museum; its visitors' center (602-883-6366) is open daily 8–5. Old Tucson (602-883-0100) is open daily 9:30–5. To reach all three sites, take Speedway Blvd. west to Saguaro Rd.

2.49 Washington, D.C.

There is no more beautiful or interesting city in the United States than Washington, D.C., and its highlights alone would fill an entire book. Everyone should try to visit here at least once.

The site of Washington was chosen by George Washington himself, after Congress decided to move from Philadelphia and build a capital city farther south. In 1793 Pierre L'Enfant, a French officer and architect, laid out a plan for the new capital. Although the land was nothing but a mosquito-infested swamp, L'Enfant envisioned a great city of broad avenues and grand vistas. Unfortunately, it took years to transform the marsh into a habitable town, and most people agreed well into the nineteenth century that the new capital was a terrible place to live. All that has changed, however, and today's Washington lives up to L'Enfant's expectations.

Just south of Union Station, where Amtrak trains arrive, is the Mall, Washington's green centerpiece, which runs from the Capitol to the Washington Monument. Branches of the Smithsonian Institution line both sides of the Mall, and the White House is several blocks north of its western end, adjoining the Ellipse. Broad avenues named for the states cross the city diagonally; these are punctuated by parks, squares, and circles, many of which contain lovely gardens and statues.

The old Union Station was refurbished at the time of the U.S. Bicentennial and was turned into a National Visitors Center. Unfortunately, problems with the roof have closed the center indefinitely, and it has not been relocated. The railroad station is now behind the old station building.

Visitors will have no trouble getting around in Washington, for the city has one of the newest and best subway systems in the country.

Union Station: 50 Massachusetts Ave., NE 3 blocks north of the Capitol. Serves all Amtrak trains and commuter trains to Baltimore, Md.; Martinsburg, W. Va.; and intermediate stations. For information on commuter routes and schedules, call 202-789-0344. Station services include newsstands, snack bars, car-rental counters, and travelers' aid facilities. Subway (Metro) station in front.

Tourist Information: Washington Visitors' Information Center, 1400 Pennsylvania Ave., Washington, D.C. 20005, 202-789-7000. International Visitors' Center, 801 19th St., NW, 202-872-8747 (language assistance and travel information).

Lodging: Hotel Washington, 15th St. and Pennsylvania Ave., NW, 202-638-5900 (from out of state: 800-424-9540) (a block from the White House; deluxe). Hyatt Regency Hotel, 400 New Jersey Ave., NW, 202-737-1234 (3 blocks from Union Station; deluxe; ask about special weekend rates). Intrigue Hotel, 824 New Hampshire Ave., NW, 202-337-6620 (rooms have small kitchens; near subway; expensive). Connecticut Inn, 4400 Connecticut Ave., NW, 202-244-5600 (near zoo and subway; moderate). Windsor Park South Hotel, 2116 Kalorama Blvd., NW, 202-483-7700 (near subway; moderate). For bed-and-breakfast accommodations, contact Bed and Breakfast League, 2855 29th St., NW, Washington, D.C. 20008, 202-232-8718, or Sweet Dreams and Toast, P.O. Box 4835, Washington, D.C. 20035, 202-483-9191.

Car Rental: Hertz, Union Station, 50 Massachusetts Ave., NE, 202-789-0460 (from out of state: 800-331-1212). Avis, Union Station, 50 Massachusetts Ave., NE, 202-789-0742. Thrifty, 628 Mass. Ave., NW, 202-737-6767 (from out of state: 800-331-4200) (railroad-station pickup available).

Taxis: Capitol Cab, 202-546-2400. Diamond Cab, 202-387-6200.

Public Transportation: Metro (buses and subways), 202-637-2437.

Bus Stations: Greyhound, 12th St. and New York Ave., NW, 202-565-2662. Trailways, 1200 Eye St., NW, 202-737-5800.

Tours: Gray Line, 202-479-5900. Spirit of 76 Tours, 202-529-2575 (double-decker London buses). American Sightseeing, 202-393-1616. Tourmobile, 202-554-7950 (stops at major sites, including several locations on the Mall, Arlington National Cemetery, and Union Station; passengers buy a day ticket and can get on and off as often as they like). Washington Boat Lines, 202-554-8000.

Currency Exchange: American Express, 1150 Connecticut Ave., NW, 202-457-1300. Deak-Perera, 1800 K St., NW, 202-872-1233. Most major banks will exchange foreign currency. In the Union Station area is the First American Bank of North America, 444 N. Capitol St.

Attractions: Smithsonian Institution (including the Museum of American History, the National Gallery, and other sites). Call 202-357-2020 for information and hours.

U.S. Capitol, atop Capitol Hill, between Independence and Constitution avenues. Free tours leave the rotunda every 15 minutes. If you want to stay for more than a few minutes in one of the galleries, call or write your congressman for a special pass. The Senate and House office buildings adjoin the Capitol.

Lincoln Memorial, W. Potomac Park at the intersection of Independence Ave. and 23rd St., SW. The Washington Monument and the new Vietnam Veterans' Memorial are in the same area.

White House, 1600 Pennsylvania Ave., NW, 202-456-7041. Tickets necessary in late spring and in summer. Get them at the tent on the Ellipse. Open Tues.–Sat. 10–12 noon.

National Zoological Park, 3000 block of Connecticut Ave., NW, 202-673-4800. Gates open 6 A.M., buildings open 9–4:30 (open later in summer). Gates close 1 hour after buildings. The Chinese giant pandas are fed at 11 A.M. and 3 P.M.

National Air and Space Museum (a branch of the Smithsonian), 7th St. and Independence Ave., SW. Excellent exhibits and films; children will love it. Call 202-357-1300 for hours and information.

Day Trips: Harpers Ferry, W. Va. Commuter-train lines offer frequent service to this historic town. The arsenal where the abolitionist John Brown was captured is open to the public. For information, call the National Historical Park, 304-535-6371.

Mount Vernon, Va., about 15 miles south. The home of George Washington overlooks the Potomac. Take the George Washington Parkway south. Call 703-780-2000 for hours and other information.

PART 3

All About Everywhere: Train Trips

·

3.1 Experiencing Travel by Rail

Traveling by train is a unique experience, unlike going by plane, bus, or car. You can relax and take in the sights and sounds of the train. Immerse yourself in the feeling of actually journeying from place to place. If you appreciate the world of railroading around you, you're bound to enjoy your trip that much more.

Stations

It's a good idea to start your trip by getting to the station early and taking a good, long look around and up. Railroad stations are usually interesting structures, and as the gateways to their communities, they are often designed to make an architectural statement. Absorb the style and the use of materials in the building: you'll often find it a refreshing and rewarding experience.

Long before Louis Sullivan and Frank Lloyd Wright proclaimed that in American architecture form should follow function and buildings should harmonize, rather than clash with, their natural surroundings, many railroad stations in smaller communities were expressing these very principles.

The classic station in American small towns contained three major areas: a waiting room for passengers, a baggage room, and an office from which the agent-operator sold tickets and reported and helped dispatch the trains. Characteristically, the office had a bay window on the track side of the building. The operator sat there, Morse key at hand, with a view up the rails in either direction. Between the office space and the waiting room was the familiar grilled ticket window, permitting the operator to sell tickets when he wasn't working his telegraph key.

The building was generally built of wood or, where more style was desired and the cost was not excessive, of brick. Most stations were one-story structures, often with peaked roofs to allow rain and snow to run off. Sometimes, however, there was a second story containing living quarters for the agent-operator and his family. Though many Victorian-era homes and commercial buildings were heavily ornamented, small town stations were designed for low-cost and easy maintenance. As a result, they tend to display strikingly clean lines.

In the larger cities, however, contrary forces were at work. Each community and each railroad company sought to make its terminal outshine its competition. The result was a series of grandiose structures, often of highly ornate design, which were among the best (or worst, depending on your viewpoint) examples of American Victorian architecture. Many of these monuments have been destroyed, victims of the decline in rail passenger traffic and the rising costs of upkeep and taxes. A few, however, remain in service. Perhaps the most notable is the grand old dowager station in Indianapolis, which may be the best standing example of the ornate style of the Gaslight Era.

When you talk about the American railroad station as a civic monument, one building stands out above all the others: New York's Grand Central Terminal. The present Grand Central was completed in 1914, and stands right in the middle of Manhattan at 42nd Street and Park Avenue. It is a classic example of French Renaissance style adapted to American commercial use. It is especially notable for its enormous windows, through which slanting light bathes the interior; for its famous ceiling, decorated with drawings of the constellations as the ancient Greeks imagined them and studded with tiny electric lights to simulate the stars; and for its central information desk and clock, probably the best-known meeting place in New York for the last three generations.

About as far from Grand Central as you can get — and not just in distance — is the Los Angeles Union Passenger Terminal, completed in 1939. This station is a striking example of harmonizing a railroad station with its surroundings. Located right across the street from the old plaza where pioneers from Mexico founded Los Angeles in 1781, the modern building clashes not at all with the historic structures and Spanish atmosphere of Olvera Street. The exterior resembles the old missions; graceful courtyards within the station grounds add to the restful atmosphere, which disguises the fact that hundreds of thousands of people use this building each year. The interior, too, harmonizes with the Spanish atmosphere, with its high ceilings and polished wood beams and furnishings. Look carefully, however, and you'll notice that the Spanish Mission style is tempered by a strong Art Deco influence expressed in,

Above: Rebuilding cars at Beech Grove, Indiana. *Below:* Rebuilding from the ground up by laying track at 1,200 feet per hour. *Next page:* Traditional architecture (top) in the San Diego station and Philadelphia's 30th Street Station, serving passengers since 1933, is contrasted with Amtrak's modern station.

among other things, the waiting-room furniture and the station signs. The combination is pure Los Angeles.

The Amtrak facility seen by more long-distance passengers than any other is, of course, Chicago's Union Station. It is actually made up of two buildings. The first, completed in 1926, contains the waiting room, baggage room, and office space upstairs. Inside, it has the high ceilings and airy feeling characteristic of many great American stations.

The concourse building, unhappily, is a different story. Once it too was lofty and airy, laced with steel girders on the model of the old Pennsylvania Station in New York. But, like the old Penn Station, the Chicago copy was replaced by an office building. Now the concourse is a cramped, low-ceilinged area that looks more like a subway station than a busy railroad terminal.

Of course, there are many other stations to be appreciated. I might mention in passing a brace of Victorians in the Northwest, King Street Station in Seattle and Union in Portland; there's businesslike South Station in Boston, which harmonizes with the State Street financial center that is its neighbor; the elegantly restored stations in Little Rock and Dallas; and the brand-new, airport-like facility at Minneapolis-St. Paul. Washington's large and beautiful old Union Station is now being restored for passenger service, and Amtrak may move back into the historic St. Louis Union Station, now being rehabilitated. For the time being, the Art Deco masterpiece in Cincinnati is not in use by Amtrak, but it survives as a shopping center and may someday once again see trains. Countless other American cities and towns are discovering and restoring their old depots. Take the time to look, and you're sure to appreciate these elegant structures.

Boarding the Train

Once you've had a good look at the station, and checked whatever baggage you don't need during the trip, you're ready to board the train.

At terminal cities the gates usually open 15 or 20 minutes before departure time, although Amtrak discourages visitors from going onto the platform. If you do go out to help with luggage or to say good-bye, don't get caught on the train as it gets under way — they probably won't stop to let you off.

Sometimes, when space is reserved, you'll be asked to check in at the gate, as you would on an airplane. This allows Amtrak to confirm that reservations will actually be used. Space held by no-shows can then be sold to other passengers. If you're traveling on an unreserved train, it's obvious that the earlier you line up at the gate, the better choice of seat you'll have.

But even if you have reserved space, there are other reasons to avoid last-minute arrivals at the station. One of them is luggage carts—these wonderful little devices always seem to be in short supply. They can carry as much or more luggage than a porter, and they never ask for a tip. Besides, there are no more squadrons of redcaps available at a moment's notice. At Los Angeles's Union Passenger Terminal, for example, there are usually only two porters on duty.

A note on the luggage carts. Many of them are equipped with a brake that you release by squeezing the bar below the handle. When you let go of the bar, the brake goes on.

Finding Your Space

Each car on Amtrak's reserved-space trains, whether coach or sleeping car, is identified by a number beginning with the number of the train of which it is a part. For example, cars on Train 48, the eastbound *Lakeshore Limited,* are designated 4801, 4802, 4803, etc., while on train number 5, the westbound *San Francisco Zephyr,* you'll find cars 501, 502, 503, and so forth. Your ticket will tell you which car your space is in.

As you walk along the train, you'll find an attendant at each door who will tell you where your proper car is and will help you board at the right door. He or she will stay with the car for the duration of the trip. Although operating crews change period-ically, service personnel (they don't call them porters anymore) do not.

On-Train Employees

In general, on-train personnel fall into two categories: service employees who see to passenger comfort, and railroad employees who actually run the train. Service people, who are all Amtrak employees, wear dark red, white, and blue uniforms, while the railroaders generally wear blue suits with the traditional peaked cap. They are generally not Amtrak employees. They work for the operating railroads and are assigned on a seniority basis.

The operating crew on an American passenger train usually consists of five people: the engineer and fireman, who are stationed in the locomotive and are not seen by passengers; a conductor; and two trainmen. The engineer actually runs the train, while the fireman—who is often, in fact, a qualified engineer—tends the diesel engines and acts as a safety lookout.

The conductor is the head crewman. He is in charge of the train and has ultimate responsibility for the safe arrival of the passengers. The engineer moves the train only on his signal. He is usually in radio communication with the dispatcher as well as with his engine crew and with other trains on the line. Along with his other responsibilities, he takes tickets and sells unused space en route.

The trainmen (sometimes called brakemen because years ago they had to set the brakes by hand) assist the conductor and operate the doors at stations. They also serve as safety lookouts, and the rear-end trainman has the additional responsibility of protecting his train from a rear-end accident whenever it stops outside a terminal. Another part of the job is inspecting other trains as they pass by, looking for anything dragging, smoking, or out of the ordinary. Rear brakemen signal one another as they pass, as do other railroad employees who work along the line. So, if you see a towerman motioning toward your train, don't think he's just waving to his friends on board.

The conductor and trainmen are the people to ask if you want to know if the train is on time or if connections will be made. They also know the scenery intimately. After all, they've been traveling over their divisions for years, day after day.

In contrast to the operating crews, the service people—attendants, dining-car staff, and bartenders—don't necessarily know any more about the actual operation of the train than you do. Just as you would not properly ask a trainman to bring you a glass of water, you wouldn't ask a dining-car waiter if you'll arrive on time in Chicago.

On some trains you'll find an additional Amtrak employee, the passenger service representative, whose job is simply to be helpful. He or she wears a red jacket and may be found anywhere on the train. This person can usually solve any minor problem you may have, and sometimes the major ones, too.

Living on Board

Once you're settled in your assigned seat or sleeping-car room, don't stay in it. On a plane, on a bus, or in an auto, you sit where you are until the next stop, but the beauty of train travel is that you can get up and move around, and you should. In fact, the key to enjoyable train travel is this: Don't just sit there — do something.

In my case, the first thing I usually do is take off my tie, loosen my collar, and exchange my suit jacket for a loose sweater or a lightweight shirt. Then I grab my timetable and itinerary, head for the lounge car, and settle down in a comfortable seat with a beer or a soft drink. There's nothing like getting into the spirit of a trip by starting out relaxed.

In fact, there's no rush to do anything on a train. Don't go bounding to answer the first call for dinner, unless you're famished or have young children who must be fed early. Instead, enjoy the scenery as long as it's light outside. There will be plenty of time to eat later. Don't be afraid to strike up a conversation with a fellow passenger, either. On a train, most people loosen up and like to meet strangers. And if you're squeamish about opening up too much, you needn't give your right name. In fact, it's kind of fun to travel under an alias — a *nom du voyage,* if you will. After all, what does it matter? You're all just strangers on a train, thrown together for a few hours in a situation where everybody wants companionship.

If you are traveling with children, buy them a Coke and let them romp up and down the aisles. Kids seem to have a natural love affair with trains, and their excitement and delight will infect you and your fellow travelers. Nobody breaks the ice better than a friendly, happy child.

Before you know it, you'll have been camped out in the lounge car for a couple of hours, and you'll be ready for a walk before dinner. Go all the way to the front of the train, then walk all the way back. It's good exercise, of course, but seeing the train is also useful in other ways. First, it gives you an idea of what facilities are available and where they are, and second, it gives you an idea of conditions in other parts of the train. Suppose, for example, that the air conditioning in your coach goes on the fritz. You have two choices — stay and swelter, or move to that empty seat you saw up ahead.

Now it's time to think about dinner. As a rule, I prefer to eat late. It breaks up the trip, and by lingering over the coffee you can shorten the evening considerably. You can add something to the feeling of a special occasion by changing clothes before heading for the dining car. That's another way to use time and shorten your trip. Although Amtrak food isn't what it was before the 1981 budget cuts, you can still enjoy the unique experience of dining at 75 miles per hour on most Amtrak trains. At least once during your trip, you owe it to yourself to enjoy a sit-down dinner on wheels.

With dinner over, it's time for books or board games, cards or conversation. If you're traveling with children, coloring books are a good idea, and old-favorite games like Monopoly are a surefire bet. If you're a bridge player and can find four to play, you'll pass the evening in total bliss. Whatever you do, however, the longer you can stretch out the evening, the better — the worst thing you can do on an overnight trip is go to bed too early. If you aren't dead on your feet, it's likely that the excitement of the trip and the unaccustomed rumble of the wheels will leave you tossing in your berth half the night. Because 5 or 6 hours of deep sleep is better than 8 hours of fitful wakefulness, stay up later and sleep better!

Timetables and How to Read Them

One of the prime tools for enjoying a trip by rail is a timetable. Of course, its most apparent and most important purpose is to indicate arrival and departure times at various stations. But if you know how to read it, a detailed timetable can also tell you much more: average speed between designated points; places where trains pass each other, and where delays are likely to occur; locations of tunnels and rivers and other natural features; and through the names of the places you pass, a feeling for the country and its people. If you're on the *Broadway Limited,* for example, and you pass through towns called Mount Joy and Bird in Hand, you know just from the names that you're in the Pennsylvania Dutch country.

Reading timetables is really quite simple, but a lot of people are intimidated by having to read up and down columns of figures or to decipher the footnotes that decorate many schedules. Don't be put off, however — you, too, can learn to read and understand timetables, and when you do, you'll be surprised at the amount of information that can be condensed into one of these folders.

Chicago-Kalamazoo-Jackson-Detroit-Toledo-Port Huron-(Toronto)

READ DOWN ⟶ / ⟵ READ UP

354	364	352	350	374	Mi	Km	Train Number / Name / Station	365	351	353	355	373
The Twilight Limited	The Blue Water Limited	The Lake Cities	The Wolverine	The Michigan Executive			**Train Name**	The Blue Water Limited	The Wolverine	The Lake Cities	The Twilight Limited	The Michigan Executive
Daily	Daily	Daily	Daily	⊙ Ex Sa Su			**Frequency of Operation**	Daily	Daily	Daily	Daily	⊙ Ex Sa Su
LD	LD	LD	LD				**Type of Service**	LD	LD	LD	LD	
5 15 P	4 10 P	11 50 A	7 45 A		0	0	**Chicago, IL** -Union Sta (CT) Dp	11 40 A	1 00 P	5 45 P	9 20 P	
	5 21 P		8 56 A		52	84	Michigan City, IN ● (CT)	10 20 A	12 05 P			
7 57 P	6 58 P	2 32 P	10 32 A		88	141	Niles, MI (ET)	10 42 A	11 50 A	4 49 P	8 19 P	
8 10 P					101	163	Dowagiac, MI ●				8 00 P	
8 47 P	7 44 P	3 19 P	11 14 A		138	221	**Kalamazoo, MI** ●■ (Grand Rapids)	9 55 A	11 15 A	4 05 P	7 35 P	
9 17 P	8 25 P	3 49 P	11 44 A		160	258	Battle Creek, MI	9 25 A	10 45 A	3 35 P	7 05 P	
							(Grand Trunk Western)					
	9 22 P				208	335	**East Lansing, MI** ● *(Lansing)*	8 10 A				
	9 48 P				238	382	Durand, MI ●	7 42 A				
	10 13 P				254	409	Flint, MI ●	7 22 A				
	10 34 P				274	441	Lapeer, MI ●	7 00 A				
	11 35 P				318	513	Port Huron, MI ● Ar / Dp	6 15 A				
							(Conrail)					
		4 22 P			185	298	Albion, MI ●			3 00 P		
10 07 P		4 47 P	12 39 P	6 15 A	205	331	**Jackson, MI** ●		9 55 A	2 35 P	6 15 P	7 00 P
				6 37 A	227	365	Chelsea, MI ●					6 35 P
10 47 P		5 27 P	1 19 P	7 00 A	243	390	Ann Arbor, MI ●		9 15 A	1 55 P	5 35 P	6 15 P
				7 10 A	252	405	Ypsilanti, MI ●					6 00 P
D 11 22 P		⊙ 6 02 P	⊙ 1 54 P	7 30 A	273	439	Dearborn, MI ⊕		R 8 45 A	⊙ 1 25 P	⊙ 5 05 P	5 40 P
11 48 P		6 28 P	2 20 P	⊙ 7 55 A	280	450	**Detroit, MI** -Amtrak Sta. Ar			12 50 P		
		6 48 P			280	450	**Detroit, MI** -Amtrak Sta. Dp		8 30 A	1 10 P	4 50 P	⊙ 5 25 P
		8 38 P			337	542	**Toledo, OH** -Central Union Trml (ET) Dp			11 00 A		
		48					**Connecting Train Number**			**49**		
		9 05 P			337	542	**Toledo, OH** -Central Union Trml (ET) Ar / Dp			10 17 A		
		11 25 P			444	714	**Cleveland, OH** -Lakefront Sta. Dp			7 46 A		
		3 20 A			631	1016	**Buffalo, NY** -Depew Sta.			3 57 A		
		8 47 A			920	1480	Albany-Rensselaer, NY			10 32 P		
		12 12 P			1062	1709	**New York, NY** -Grand Central Terminal					
		2 12 P			1120	1801	**Boston, MA** -South Sta. (ET) Ar			5 15 P		

Amtrak issues many timetables, each covering a particular region of the country, but the one I prefer is the system-wide National Timetable. This folder is issued twice a year (generally coincident with the spring and fall time changes) and runs to about sixty pages. It contains the schedules of all Amtrak passenger trains.

Below you'll find Amtrak's schedule for the Chicago — Port Huron line as it appeared during the summer of 1981. You'll notice that the names of the towns and cities along the route are in the center, with columns of figures to each side. Each column represents a train. Those on the left side represent eastbound runs from Chicago to Detroit, and read from top to bottom. Those to the right of center represent westbound trains, and read up from bottom to top.

Immediately to the left of the station list is a column showing the distance from Chicago, in miles and kilometers, of each station. For example, Ann Arbor, Michigan, is 243 miles, or 390 kilometers, from Chicago.

At the top of each column representing a train, you will find its designating number. The train names, such as *Lake Cities* or *Twilight Limited,* are used to give the train some public identity, but railroaders always and without exception refer to a train by its number alone. You can tell in which direction a train is going by its number. All eastbound runs have even numbers, all westbound trains have odd numbers.

Just below the train number and name are its days of operation. Note that while trains 350, 352, 354, and 364 run daily, number 374, the *Michigan Executive,* does not operate on Saturdays and Sundays. There is also a little circled number 9 in this column; referring to the key at the bottom of the page, we find that this train will not run on May 25, July 3, or September 7, which are business holidays.

Below the Frequency of Operation line, you'll find another little box containing some mysterious symbols and labeled Type of Service. These symbols are supposed to tell you what kinds of baggage and meal service are offered, but I find them more confusing than helpful. You need only look on the next page of the timetable to find out in plain English that each of these trains offers snack and beverage service and that baggage may be checked on the *Twilight, Blue Water,* and *Lake Cities.*

Now let's read the time schedule. Suppose you are in Chicago, and you want to spend a weekend in Ann Arbor. A look at the timetable tells you that Train 350, the *Wolverine,* leaves Chicago's Union Station every day at 7:45 A.M. Central Time (note the little CT beside the Chicago listing). Looking down the column representing this train, we find that it stops in Michigan City, Indiana, at 8:56 A.M. Central Time; and in Niles, Michigan, at 10:32 Eastern Time. Because there is no time shown beside the listing for Dowagiac, Michigan, we understand that the *Wolverine* does not serve this station. It stops next at Kalamazoo at 11:14 A.M. and arrives in Battle Creek at 11:44. This train does not serve any of the stations along the Grand Trunk line to Port Huron, nor does it stop at Albion. It arrives in Jackson at 12:39, and is due in Ann Arbor at 1:19 P.M.

Returning to Chicago, you have a choice of three trains daily: the *Wolverine* leaves each morning at 9:15; the *Lake Cities* departs at 1:55 P.M.; and the aptly named *Twilight Limited* pulls out at 5:35. You decide to take the *Twilight.* Reading up the column, we find that it stops at Jackson at 6:15; Battle Creek at 7:05; Kalamazoo at 7:35; Niles at 8:19 Eastern Time; Michigan City at 8:00 Central Time; and arrives in Chicago at 9:20 P.M.

But there's much more information buried in these columns than simple arrival and departure times. For example, compare the schedule of Train 350, the eastbound *Wolverine,* with that of Train 355, the westbound *Twilight Limited.* The eastbound train takes from 7:45 A.M. Central Time to 10:32 Eastern Time to cover the 88 miles between Chicago and Niles. Subtracting an hour to allow for the time difference, it takes one hour and 47 minutes, or 107 minutes of actual running time, to cover this stretch—not bad, when you consider that there is a good deal of slow-speed running through the congested Chicago metropolitan area included. Coming west, however, the *Twilight* takes from 8:19 Eastern Time to 9:20 Central, or 121 minutes of actual running time, to do the same distance. Does it actually take 14 minutes longer to go that 88 miles westbound?

Of course not. What we see here is an example of the common practice of "padding" the last part of a train's schedule, so that time lost earlier in the trip can be recovered to give an on-time arrival at the terminal.

Timetables contain much other interesting data, and they

reflect a lot of careful planning. Most of the Chicago‖Detroit line (and indeed most American railroads outside the Northeast Corridor) is single track. Provision must be made, therefore, for trains going in opposite directions to meet at locations where there are side tracks for passing. Notice, then, that Train 365, the *Blue Water,* leaves Niles for Chicago at 10:42, 10 minutes after Train 350, the eastbound *Wolverine,* is due at Niles. Likewise, we find that Train 350 meets its opposite number, 351, at Kalamazoo. Suppose, however, that 350 is delayed and leaves Chicago 15 minutes late. It will accordingly delay each train it is supposed to meet along the way, for if the eastbound doesn't arrive on time, the westbound must wait for it—it cannot proceed beyond the siding into the face of an oncoming train. This is one of the possible delays that makes it necessary to add additional time to schedules at the end.

This timetable also gives information on connecting services. The *Lake Cities* arrives at Toledo at 8:38 P.M. There it connects with Train 48, the *Lake Shore,* scheduled to leave at 9:05 for Cleveland, Buffalo, Albany, Boston, and New York. Connecting trains are shown in italic figures.

It is not apparent in this timetable, which covers a flatland operation, but sometimes a schedule can tell you a lot about the nature of the country through which the train passes. For example, it takes the *California Zephyr* 145 minutes to cover the 75 miles from Denver to its first stop at Granby. The slow speed gives you an idea of what those 75 miles of track are like. This stretch includes 50 miles of stiff uphill grades, tortuous curves, and mountain hazards.

Amtrak's timetables hold a lot of information, but they have been simplified to show only the stations where the trains stop; the passing tracks, tank towns, and natural features of the land are no longer noted. To make good this deficiency, I have prepared detailed station lists or itineraries for each of Amtrak's routes. These have been compiled from pre-Amtrak timetables and official guides, and from employee time cards not generally available to the public. The itineraries also show division points, places where the train stops to change engine crews; each such point is indicated in the lists in this book by a horizontal line and repetition of the station's name. By using these detailed itineraries, you can follow the progress of your train much more accurately than you can with Amtrak's condensed schedules. The names of the stations where the train is scheduled to stop are capitalized in the lists and the related text.

Maps

Maps, too, can tell you a lot about your trip. One of the most helpful aids to take along is an ordinary Rand-McNally *Road Atlas* of the United States, Canada, and Mexico. Using this, and referring to the detailed station lists to be found in this book, plot the route of your train for yourself. You'll often be surprised at how the rails deviate from a straight-line route, often for reasons of geography and sometimes because of local politics. Notice that Amtrak trains stop to change engine crews every 100 to 175 miles, sometimes at towns so small you can hardly find them on the map. This is because the range of a steam locomotive back in the nineteenth century rarely reached 200 miles.

Today, with diesel power, engines don't need to be changed so frequently—but the towns and cities that owe their origin to the steam locomotive still dot the American landscape.

Railroad Operations

Speed: Speed limits aren't just for automobiles. Railroads have them too, and sometimes they are set by the federal government. The Federal Railroad Administration limits most U.S. passenger trains to 79 miles per hour except where the track is equipped with cab signals or automatic train stop for additional safety protection. (Cab signals present the engineer with signal indications right in his cab. He needn't depend on seeing lineside indicators. Automatic train stop is a device that automatically slows or stops the train if the engineer doesn't respond to signals.) High-speed districts in operation today include the Northeast Corridor line, where trains may reach 120 miles per hour; the Illinois Central Gulf line in southern Illinois; and the Santa Fe main line west of Kansas City, used by the *Southwest Limited.*

Administrative restrictions aside, the speed of a train is limited by two factors: the capabilities of the locomotive and the condition of the track. The top speed of most Amtrak trains today, outside the Northeast Corridor electrified zone, is 97 miles per hour. Most must travel more slowly than that, however, because of the condition of the track. Over the years, rising wages and equipment costs have demanded more efficient operation from the railroads, with the result that engines and freight cars are built bigger and freight trains run faster. The track takes a terrific pounding, and track maintenance is expensive. Thus, as many railroads got into financial trouble, they cut or deferred maintenance on the track. In some places the track got so bad that speeds were held to 10 miles per hour.

Track reconstruction work has been carried out in many parts of the nation, including the Northeast Corridor, and the situation is considerably better today than it was 5 years ago. But "slow orders" can still be a problem from time to time.

Figuring Your Speed

There are no speedometers in the passenger sections of Amtrak trains, so if you want to know how fast you are traveling, you'll have to figure it out for yourself. Fortunately, that is an easy process.

The mileage of each American railroad is measured from some point, and little white posts with numbers on them mark off each mile. These mileposts, which aren't hard to spot if you're looking for them, can tell you your speed. Just count on your watch the number of seconds it takes your train to go from one to the next, and consult the table below.

Seconds per Mile	Speed in Miles per Hour
120	30
90	40
72	50
60	60
52	70
45	80
40	90
36	100
33	110
30	120

Finding Your Place

You'll also note that, in addition to the mileposts, there are numbers and perhaps a letter painted on each lineside shack, signal, or bridge. For example, on the Burlington Northern stretch between Chicago and Galesburg, there are two tracks. If you sit in the lounge car and watch the signals (supported on overhead bridges), you'll see that each signal is marked "N-1245," for example, or "S-987." This indicates the north or south track and the distance from Chicago in miles, with the decimal point omitted. Thus, signal N-1245 would be protecting the north track and would be located 124.5 miles west of Chicago's Union Station. A glance at the detailed station list for the Chicago–Galesburg line puts this spot just west of Neponset, Illinois. In this way, the mileposts and other lineside markings can tell you not only your speed but exactly where you are on the railroad at any time. All you need to know is from what point the mileposts are numbered, and you can usually figure this out from the station list.

What Makes the Train Go?

In the Northeast Corridor (except between New Haven and Boston) and between Philadelphia and Harrisburg, Pennsylvania, the answer is electricity drawn from overhead wires. During the Depression, the Pennsylvania Railroad (which then owned these lines) obtained a federal loan and electrified its heavily trafficked main lines in New Jersey, Pennsylvania, Delaware, and Maryland. This improvement raised train speeds, increased the capacity of the track, improved on-time performance, cut pollution, saved money on fuel bills, and generally made operations much more efficient. No other project in American railroad history has returned such brilliant results.

Power is transmitted to the locomotives at 11,000 volts AC. It enters the train through a device called a pantagraph, a boxlike or armlike device mounted on the roof, and turns the traction motors that are mounted on the axles.

Not all trains in the electrified corridor are pulled by locomotives. The original Metroliners, the *Jersey Arrow* commuter trains, and some other equipment have their own motors under the floor. Self-propelled cars of this type are called "Multiple Unit" or "MU" cars, for the cars may be operated by a single engineer from his control stand at the front car. MU equipment has both advantages and drawbacks. On the positive side, MU's are flexible and inexpensive to operate, but they are expensive to maintain and cannot be used where there is no overhead electric wire. Lately,

Amtrak has favored locomotives in the Northeast Corridor, and the Metroliner service is now operated with conventional, rather than MU, equipment.

Outside the electrified zones in the East, all North American passenger trains except some local runs are powered by diesel locomotives. Beginning in the 1930s, diesel demonstrated its enormous advantages over steam power, but it was not until the mid-1950s that diesels took over nearly all American operations. Diesels are rugged, powerful, and relatively simple machines, which thrive on hard work and can go anywhere with relatively little maintenance and without long halts for coal or water. They operate on low-grade oil and are somewhat like auto engines, except that they have no spark plugs. The diesel is an internal combustion engine. That is, the fuel is burned inside the cylinder where the power is produced. The explosion of the oil drives the piston down; the piston is connected to a crankshaft, and this in turn distributes the power. In European locomotives, as in your car, that crankshaft is geared directly to the wheels. This is known as a direct-drive diesel.

North American locomotives, however, use the power from the crankshaft to turn not the wheels but an electric generator. The power thus developed then drives traction motors on the wheels. Thus, American diesels are more properly called diesel-electric types. They are electric locomotives that carry their own power plants with them.

Obviously this is less efficient than transmitting power directly from a central source, as is done in the Northeast Corridor. Why, then, when the American railroads did away with steam after 125 years of relying on the Iron Horse, did they turn to the diesel-electric rather than straight electrification? The answer is the relatively low traffic density of American railroads and the enormous capital investment required for electrification. The diesel-electric was a low-cost compromise, offering many of the operating characteristics and economies of the electric locomotive without the necessity of stringing miles of overhead wires.

What Makes the Train Stop?

During the last quarter of the nineteenth century, as trains grew longer and heavier, the railroads could no longer rely on the muscle power of burly brakemen and the steam brakes on the engine as the only means of stopping a train. George Westinghouse first demonstrated that compressed air, when released suddenly from a reservoir, could be used to apply brakes evenly on each car of a train, thus bringing it to a stop smoothly and quickly.

Early air brakes, called "straight air," used a compressor to pump up the brake cylinders. When the engineer opened the valve, the air pushed the brake shoes against the wheels. However, if an air hose broke, or if all the air in the compressor was used up and the pumps lacked time to build up a new supply, it was just too bad—there would be no braking power at all.

Today, therefore, air brakes work on the reverse of Westinghouse's original idea. Instead of using air pressure to *apply* the brakes, modern trains use the compressed air to hold the brakes off the wheels. Thus, if the pressure fails, the train stops automatically. This system also gives the engineer more control of his train. The more air he releases from the compressor, the faster the train will stop. This is not to say, however, that a heavy, fast-moving train can stop on a dime. A passenger train running at 79 miles per hour takes more than a mile to stop, even with the brakes in full emergency.

Safety on the Rails

Automatic train control, cab signaling, and air brakes are not the only safety devices that make riding the train by far the safest form of intercity travel.

Another protective device is the so-called "deadman control," a pedal or lever that the engineer must activate at intervals. Should he fail to respond, the brakes will be set automatically and the train will come to a stop. This feature is designed to protect the passengers in case the engineer should suffer a disabling injury or fail to pay attention to his responsibilities.

Since the end of World War II, train radio has come into widespread use. Engine crews, trainmen, and off-train officials can now talk to each other, making operations safer and more efficient than ever before.

But the primary device for avoiding accidents between trains is still signals—the so-called silent sentinels. Signals prevent collisions between trains running in opposite directions and maintain space between trains going in the same direction to ward off rear-end accidents.

On most American railroads, automatic block signals, operated electronically, are used. Generally they display the three traditional color indications — green for proceed, yellow for caution, red for stop. But not all signals are the same. On the lines of the former Pennsylvania Railroad (including the Northeast Corridor south of New York), position lights are used. Yellow bulbs are arranged to give indications, as below:

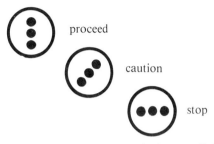

proceed

caution

stop

Lines of the Baltimore and Ohio, between Baltimore, Washington, Cumberland, and Pittsburgh, use an interesting combination of the colored light and position systems:

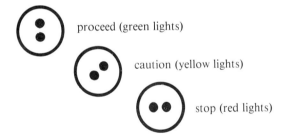

proceed (green lights)

caution (yellow lights)

stop (red lights)

In addition, trains are operated under strict control from a dispatcher. No conductor simply takes his train out of the terminal when he feels like it, but only when he has authority to start. For a hundred years this authority was conveyed on American railroads by train order and timetable, but today many main lines are operated by an electronic marvel called Centralized Traffic Control (CTC, for short), first used in 1927.

The CTC dispatcher sits before an electronic panel represent-

ing the entire district under his jurisdiction; each train is represented by a light. As two trains converge, the dispatcher determines where they should meet, then sets the appropriate signals and even throws the switches—all by remote control. Delays are minimized, manpower is saved, and trains get over the road more efficiently. It gives a single-track line three-fourths of the capacity of a double-track one, and thus allows railroads to reduce maintenance costs by eliminating one line of a double track. CTC can also be used to increase the capacity of multiple-track lines in busy areas by permitting all tracks to be used for operation in either direction, as the flow of traffic demands.

This discussion of a few of the technical aspects of modern railroading should give you, the passenger, at least an inkling of the fascinating things going on around you—the things that make it possible for you to ride in safety and comfort for hundreds or even thousands of miles. The more you understand about how your trip is proceeding, the more you'll agree that getting there is half the fun!

3.2 Boston — Albany

This is one of America's older railroad lines, completed in 1841. It was built by Boston capitalists who were dismayed that their city was losing Western trade to its rival, New York, after the opening of the Erie Canal. Originally known as the Boston and Albany, it later became part of the New York Central system. That in turn was merged into Penn Central, and today the line is part of Conrail, the big freight line created by Congress out of a number of Eastern railroads.

The scenic highlight of the line is its crossing of the Berkshire Mountains in western Massachusetts. The Berkshires are actually part of the Appalachian chain, the mountains that separate the eastern coastal plain from the interior of North America. They were a formidable barrier to commerce, and by the time the Boston and Albany was finished, New York had forged permanently ahead of Boston in the race for commercial supremacy among the East Coast cities.

0.0 **BOSTON (South Station)** *199.8.*   For information on the city, see section 2.6.

Just out of the station, trains bound for New York and Albany swing to the right and dive under the Fitzgerald Expressway, named for Boston's legendary mayor, John "Honey Fitz" Fitzgerald, an ancestor of President Kennedy's. The tracks parallel the Massachusetts Turnpike through an open cut that skirts the south edge of the city's central business district.

1.0 **Back Bay** *198.8.*   At one time Back Bay, a low-lying area west of Boston neck, was covered by the slow water of the Charles River. When the railroads came, two lines built causeways across this shallow bay, the two causeways meeting at the present site of Back Bay station. Later, the Charles was channeled into its present course and the bay was filled in. Today Back Bay, with its beautiful tree-lined streets and late-Victorian mansions, is one of the most elegant urban areas in the United States. At Copley Square, a block or two north of the station, stands the Boston Public Library, the first in the United States.

As the train leaves the city, it skirts the Fens, a meandering watercourse and park, past Fenway Park, home of the Red Sox, and along the edge of the Boston University campus.

7.1 **Newton** *192.7.*   Just to give you an idea of how they name towns in New England, there are around Newton the following places: Newtonville, Newton Center, Newton Highlands, Newton Upper Falls, Newton Lower Falls, and West Newton.

Westbound/miles   *miles/Eastbound*

Westbound/miles		miles/Eastbound
0.0	BOSTON (South Station)	199.8
1.0	Back Bay	198.8
4.3	Allston	195.5
7.1	Newton	192.7
10.9	Riverside	188.9
14.7	Wellesley	185.1
17.6	Natick	182.2
21.4	FRAMINGHAM	178.4
24.2	Ashland	175.6
27.5	Cordaville	172.3
28.1	Southville	171.7
31.9	Westboro	167.9
37.9	North Grafton	161.9
44.3	WORCESTER	155.5
47.9	Jamesville	151.9
53.1	Rochdale	146.7
57.5	Charlton	142.3
61.9	South Spencer	137.9
67.0	Brookfield	132.8
72.6	Warren	127.2
74.9	West Warren	124.9
83.6	Palmer	116.2
88.7	North Wilbraham	111.1
98.3	SPRINGFIELD	101.5
100.9	West Springfield	98.9
107.9	Westfield	91.9
112.9	Woronoco	86.9
115.4	Russell	84.4
119.3	Huntington	80.5
125.8	Chester	74.0
130.6	Middlefield	69.2
134.1	Becket	65.7
137.7	Washington	62.1
141.9	Hinsdale	57.9
145.3	Dalton	54.5
150.6	PITTSFIELD	49.2
156.7	Richmond Summit	43.1
158.8	Richmond	41.0
161.8	State Line, Mass.	38.0
163.6	Edwards Park, N.Y.	36.2
167.0	Canaan	32.8
171.4	East Chatham	28.4
177.2	Chatham	22.6
182.1	Chatham Center	17.7
184.7	Niverville	15.1
187.4	Post Road Crossing	12.4
190.1	Van Hoesen	9.7
192.4	Brookview	7.4
195.4	East Greenbush	4.4
199.8	ALBANY-RENSSELAER, N.Y.	0.0

10.9 **Riverside** *188.9.*   Here the rails cross the Charles River, which swings through the area in a series of serpentine loops on its way to Boston and the sea.

14.7 **Wellesley** *185.1.*   This is the site of Wellesley College, the prestigious women's school. Town and college are named for the aristocratic Wellesley family of Great Britain, whose most famous member was Arthur, Duke of Wellington, the general who defeated Napoleon at Waterloo in 1815.

21.4 **FRAMINGHAM** *178.4.*   There is a General Motors assembly plant here.

44.3 **WORCESTER** *155.5.*   It looks like *Wor-sester,* but please don't say it that way: the correct pronounciation is *Wooster.* Holy Cross College is here.

98.3 **SPRINGFIELD** *101.5.*   Springfield is on the Connecticut River, whose valley bisects New England all the way from Vermont to the sea. The area was settled in the 1630s by pioneers from Boston, who found life in the Massachusetts Bay colony too restrictive for their taste. The town really began to develop about 1794, when the Springfield Arsenal was established here by the federal government. Springfield still manufactures arms, together with machinery, electrical products, and other goods. The city is also the site of Springfield College, where, in 1891, James A. Naismith hung a couple of peach baskets above the gymnasium floor and invented basketball.

Leaving the Connecticut Valley, the rails start the long climb toward the highest crossing point over the Berkshire Mountains, 60 miles west.

150.6 **PITTSFIELD** *49.2.*   This is the station for Lenox, Tanglewood, and the entire Berkshire area. At Lenox, Nathaniel Hawthorne had his summer home, Tanglewood, where he wrote the *Tanglewood Tales.* The estate is now the home of the Tanglewood summer music festival, which features the Boston Symphony Orchestra and the world's finest musicians.

156.7 **Richmond Summit** *43.1.*   This is the highest point between Boston and Albany, in the Berkshire Mountains.

161.8 **State Line, Mass.** *38.0.*   The State Line Tunnel is just east of the New York State border. A few miles southeast is Chesterwood, the home of Daniel Chester French, the American sculptor whose works include the statue at the Lincoln Memorial in Washington, D.C.

177.2 **Chatham, N.Y.** *22.6.*   The town was named for William Pitt, Lord Chatham, Britain's prime minister during the French and Indian War, Between Chatham and Rensselaer trains operate over some of the newest track on the Amtrak system, though the alignment is more than a century old. After passenger service on the old Boston and Albany ended in 1971, the Penn Central company tore up some 20 miles of track west of Chatham, which was not needed for freight trains. When Amtrak reinstituted passenger service, trains were forced to detour around this missing 20 miles until, in 1979, Amtrak relaid the old grade with new rails.

199.8 **ALBANY-RENSSELAER** *0.0.* Albany grew from a Dutch military post called Fort Nassau, which was established on the site in 1614. It received its present name fifty years later when it was conquered by the English, who named it for James, Duke of Albany, brother of King Charles II. The city still operates under its 1686 charter, making it one of the oldest corporations in North America.

Albany owes its importance to its strategic location. It can be reached by seagoing vessels coming up the Hudson and sits at the entrance to the Mohawk Valley, a natural water route westward through the Appalachian mountain chain. The city has been capital of New York state since 1797.

Amtrak's Albany station is actually located across the Hudson in the town of Rensselaer; this community stands on what was once the site of the greatest of the Dutch Colonial manors, Rensselaerswick. These large manors, or patroonships, were an attempt to introduce European land-holding patterns into the New World, but they failed because working people soon realized that they could easily own land themselves if they only moved further west. With no peasant class to work the large manors, they were eventually broken up into smaller tracts.

3.3   Boston — New York

This 232-mile route, comprising the northern half of the so-called North-east Corridor, is owned and operated by Amtrak itself. It was once the main line of the old New York, New Haven, and Hartford; later, that company was merged into the ill-fated Penn Central. When that giant went bankrupt (still the largest business failure in U.S. history), Amtrak bought the track.

The Boston — New York segment is known as the Shore Line because much of it lies within sight of Long Island Sound. This makes for a picturesque route, and now the new Metroliner service has cut the running time to 4 hours. The line, so far, is electrified only between New York and New Haven, where all trains must change engines. In time, the overhead electric wires should extend all the way to Boston.

The great attraction of the Shore Line route is the shoreline. There are many charming scenes as the train crosses rivers and inlets that run down to the sea. You can almost taste the clam chowder as you look out the windows. This is an easy way to get a quick glimpse of old New England.

0.0 **BOSTON** *231.5.* The train follows the same route as the Boston–Albany train as far as Back Bay. For notes on the city, see section 2.6.

1.0 **Back Bay** *230.5.* At this point the Shore Line swings away from the Albany line and heads southward toward Rhode Island. A mile or so south of Back Bay, the tracks pass through the Roxbury section, where much of the city's black population lives.

12.0 **ROUTE 128** *219.5.* Circling Boston at a radius of from 10 to 15 miles, Route 128 is a key traffic artery. The station here gives easy access to passengers from anywhere in the suburbs.

But Route 128 is more than a convenient highway around central Boston. It is also the home of many of the electronics firms that have settled in New England, and it has come to symbolize brainpower and high technology.

BOSTON – NEW YORK

Westbound/miles		*miles/Eastbound*
0.0	BOSTON (South Station)	231.5
1.0	Back Bay	230.5
12.0	ROUTE 128	219.5
15.0	Canton Junction	216.5
18.5	Sharon	213.0
23.0	East Foxboro	208.5
25.0	Mansfield	206.5
32.0	Attleboro, Mass.	199.5
39.5	Pawtucket, R.I.	192.0
44.0	PROVIDENCE	187.5
49.0	Auburn	182.5
54.5	Apponaug	177.0
57.3	EAST GREENWICH	174.2
60.8	Davisville	170.7
63.3	Wickford Junction	168.2
71.0	KINGSTON	160.5
75.5	Kenyons	156.0
76.0	Shannock	155.5
78.0	WESTERLY, R.I.	153.5
93.5	Stonington, Conn.	138.0
96.5	MYSTIC	135.0
97.5	West Mystic	134.0
99.0	Noank	132.5
106.0	NEW LONDON	125.5
113.0	East Lyme	118.5
124.0	OLD SAYBROOK	107.5
132.5	Clinton	99.0
136.0	Madison	95.5
140.0	Guilford	91.5
143.0	Leete's Island	88.5
144.5	Stony Creek	87.0
145.5	Pine Orchard	86.0
148.0	Branford	83.5
157.0	NEW HAVEN	74.5

157.0	NEW HAVEN	74.5
166.0	Milford	63.5
170.2	Stratford	61.3
173.7	BRIDGEPORT	57.8
178.7	Fairfield	52.8
180.4	Southport	51.1
182.1	Green's Farms	49.4
185.1	Westport/Saugatuck	46.4
187.2	East Norwalk	44.3
188.3	Norwalk/South Norwalk	43.2
190.1	Rowayton	41.4
191.6	Darien	39.9
192.8	Noroton Heights	38.7
194.1	Glenbrook	37.4
196.0	STAMFORD	35.5
198.0	Old Greenwich	33.5
199.0	Riverside	32.5
199.7	Cos Cob	31.8
201.2	Greenwich, Conn.	30.3
203.6	Port Chester, N.Y.	27.9
205.2	RYE	26.3
207.1	Harrison	24.4
208.8	Mamaroneck	22.7
210.6	Larchmont	20.9
212.7	New Rochelle	18.8
	Hell Gate Bridge	
	East River Tunnels	
231.5	NEW YORK (Penn Station)	0.0

A few miles east of the Route 128 station is Braintree, home of America's second president, John Adams, his wife, the outspoken Abigail Adams, and his son John Quincy Adams.

23.0 **East Foxboro, Mass.** *208.5.* Foxboro is the site of Schaefer Stadium, home of the New England Patriots football team. To the east is Brocton, hometown of former world's heavyweight champion Rocky Marciano.

39.5 **Pawtucket, R.I.** *192.5.* Pawtucket has a special place in American history; it is the site of Slater's Mill, the first textile mill ever built in this country.

Samuel Slater emigrated from England to Rhode Island, and though England had tried to prevent the export of its technology, he carried the plans for an integrated textile mill in his head. He found a sponsor, and, in 1790, Slater's Mill was opened, marking the beginning of the American textile industry and the factory system in the New World. The expensive, water-powered machinery had to be housed in one building, and so workers were brought from the surrounding farms to the new factory. Slater's Mill is still standing and can be visited by the public.

44.0 **PROVIDENCE** *187.5.* See section 2.35 for notes on the city. This is also the Amtrak station for Newport, 25 miles south, and for Fall

The *Senator* crossing the Mystic River at Mystic, Connecticut, on its way to New York and Washington, D.C. This train swaps its diesel locomotive for an electric locomotive at New Haven. From New Haven the line is fully electrified all the way to Washington. Eventually, the entire Northeast Corridor run from Boston to Washington will be electric. Mystic, Connecticut, is the site of Mystic Seaport, with its restored sailing ships. An especially popular attraction for families and nautical fans, the Seaport is easily accessible from the train.

The Hunter House, built in 1748, is perhaps the finest example of pre-Revolutionary Newport, Rhode Island. *Below:* The Elms, representative of the vast wealth of those who built Newport's mansions, was once a private residence. Newport can be reached from Providence. (See sections 2.35 and 3.3.)

River, Massachusetts 15 miles east, where Lizzie Borden wielded her ax.

71.0 **KINGSTON** *160.5.* This is the home of the University of Rhode Island. Here the route turns west to parallel the shores of Block Island Sound and Long Island Sound all the way to New York, although the track here is still several miles inland.

78.0 **WESTERLY, R.I.** *153.5.* This is the last town in Rhode Island. Three miles west of here the railroad comes within sight of the sea on the south side (left side of the train, going from Boston to New York). For the next 120 miles, passengers are treated to some picturesque scenery as the Shore Line lives up to its name. The train passes through a small fishing town every few miles, and a series of bridges takes the track over inlets and wetlands.

96.5 **MYSTIC, CONN.** *135.0.* This old whaling port, with its restored historic district, is the most picturesque of all the Connecticut coastal towns. If you want to feel the ambience of the great days of the whaling ships and the clippers, Mystic is the place for you.

106.0 **NEW LONDON** *125.5.* The restored station here is an outstanding example of the work of the American architect H. H. Richardson. Just east of the city, the tracks pass through Groton, where Electric Boat makes nuclear submarines, then cross the Thames River. A few miles upstream, the U.S. Navy maintains its principal submarine base. New London is also the home of the U.S. Coast Guard Academy.

124.0 **OLD SAYBROOK** *107.5.* The train crosses the Connecticut River just above its mouth before reaching the station. The Connecticut is the great river of New England. Rising in the White Mountains near the Canadian border, it drains four states. To its fertile valley the Reverend Thomas Hooker and his followers came from Boston in 1636 to found Connecticut, the "land of steady habits." It was also the scene of some of the bloodiest battles between Indians and settlers in colonial times.

148.0 **Branford** *83.5.* One of America's largest and oldest museums devoted to the preservation and operation of streetcars is located here.

157.0 **NEW HAVEN** *74.5.* New Haven has a long history, having been founded in the mid-seventeenth century. By 1662 it was joined with Thomas Hooker's settlements in the Connecticut Valley to make the Royal Colony of Connecticut, and since 1701 it has been the home of Yale University, third-oldest institution of higher learning in the United States. For many years New Haven has been the northern end of electric operation. All trains change engines here, and if the lights go off, don't be alarmed. They'll come on again as soon as an electric locomotive replaces the diesel that has brought your train from Boston.

The Metro-North commuter line to New York begins here; connections to intermediate stations that are bypassed by Amtrak can be made in New Haven, Bridgeport, or Stamford, or at Grand Central Terminal, New York. Connections to Hartford, Conn., and Springfield, Mass., should also be made at New Haven.

170.2 **Stratford** *61.3.*   Just east of the town, the tracks cross the Housatonic, another of the important rivers that flow southward through New England.

Stratford takes its name from the English town and birthplace of William Shakespeare. Stratford, Connecticut, is the site of the American Shakespeare Festival.

173.7 **BRIDGEPORT** *57.8.*   Although much of Connecticut was settled early in the colonial period, Bridgeport, incorporated as late as 1836, is a different case. Its growth has been tied directly to the products of its factories. Bridgeport makes electric machinery, munitions, textiles, and aircraft parts, among other things.

Bridgeport is most famous, however, as the home and headquarters of the Fabulous Showman himself, P. T. Barnum. He had several homes in and around Bridgeport, owned a good deal of land in the area, and had his winter quarters here during much of his career. Those quarters were, unfortunately, fire traps, and Barnum was burned out more than once. Each time, however, he rebuilt his museum and menagerie bigger and better than before. Today the Barnum Institute of Science and History is one of Bridgeport's attractions.

Incidentally, P. T. Barnum was not primarily a circus man. His name and fortune were made in the museum and menagerie field, and it was only late in his life that he entered his partnership with James A. Bailey.

Amtrak trains pass through Bridgeport on an elevated structure, giving passengers a good look at this busy industrial community. Connections for Waterbury, Connecticut, are made here.

178.7 **Fairfield** *52.8.*   The town is notable as the home of Fairfield University, whose athletic teams are called the Stags. Do you suppose that after Fairfield victories they have Stag parties?

185.1 **Westport/Saugatuck** *46.4.*   This is the heart of the New York commuting belt; every morning the local trains bring the men in the gray flannel suits into Manhattan, and every afternoon they bring them back to the country. Look for posters advertising Broadway shows along the platform.

191.6 **Darien** *39.9.*   This is also a very prosperous commuter town. This residential area, located on Long Island Sound, was incorporated in 1820.

196.0 **STAMFORD** *35.5.*   This is the new home of countless corporate headquarters. The companies moved here to get out of New York City, but their skyscrapers have turned Stamford itself into a metropolis. Change here for Danbury and New Canaan.

199.7 **Cos Cob** *31.8.*   The big building next to the tracks is the old powerhouse that generates the electricity along the old New Haven Railroad tracks. Note that the overhead wires form a triangle over each track.

This unique form of suspension is used nowhere else in the United States but on this former New Haven line.

201.2 **Greenwich, Conn.** *30.3.* Pronounced *Grenitch* and named after the city in England through which the prime meridian runs, this is the last town in Connecticut.

205.2 **RYE, N.Y.** *26.3.* There's a first-class amusement park here — Playland.

210.6 **Larchmont** *20.9.* This was the home of the late American mystery writer Frederic Dannay, who with his partner and cousin, the late Manfred B. Lee, created the works signed "Ellery Queen."

212.7 **New Rochelle** *18.8.* This city was named for the French city of La Rochelle, citadel of the Protestant Huguenots in the religious wars of the sixteenth century. Near here the Hell Gate Bridge line to Pennsylvania Station, used by Amtrak, diverges from the commuter line to Grand Central. Through trains peel off to the southeast, running through part of the Bronx to reach the bridge approach.

Hell Gate Bridge is a key link in the only rail route through New York City. This line, which also includes the East River and Hudson River tunnels and Pennsylvania Station, is the creation of Alexander Cassatt, turn-of-the-century president of the Pennsylvania Railroad and brother of the artist Mary Cassatt.

Cassatt realized that as long as his Pennsylvania line terminated across the Hudson at Jersey City, it could not hope to compete on even terms with the New York Central, at that time the only line to enter Manhattan. His answer was to build a long tunnel under the Hudson — but he did not stop there. Canny enough to see that the cost of real estate on Manhattan prohibited the building of terminal yards on the island, he continued his tunnel through the new Pennsylvania Station and under the East River to Long Island. There, where land prices were more reasonable, he built a huge yard to service and store the passenger trains that came from all over the United States to his new New York station. The Penn Station project, including the tunnels and the big Sunnyside Yard, was finished in 1910.

Cassatt envisioned a connection from Long Island to the New Haven Railroad's Boston line up in the Bronx, but he died before it could be built. Not until 1917 was the missing link, the Hell Gate Bridge, finished.

The great bridge takes its colorful name from the narrow strait connecting the East River with Pelham Bay, over which it passes. This waterway is used by oceangoing ships, so the bridge had to be high enough to clear large vessels and wide enough to span the channel without obstructing pillars.

Including its approaches, the Hell Gate Bridge is 3½ miles long, and the center span soars 977 feet across open water. The structure cost $19 million in 1917 money. The northern approach to the bridge is relatively unspectacular until you see the spires of Manhattan rising off to the southwest, on the right side of the train when coming into New York. The long downgrade off the bridge slopes over the rooftops of Queens and finally ends at Sunnyside Yard, so called because it is built on the west or sunny side of Richmond Hill. At this point, Amtrak trains from New England join the commuter lines of the Long Island Rail Road, and together they dive into Alexander Cassatt's East River Tunnels to cross into Manhattan.

231.5 **NEW YORK (Pennsylvania Station)** *0.0.* Occupying the west side of Seventh Avenue between 31st and 33rd Streets is the Penn Center–Penn Station–Madison Square Garden comlex. It stands on the site of the original Pennsylvania Station, which was completed in 1910. Built by Cassatt and designed by Stanford White on the model of the Baths of Caracalla in Rome, it was torn down to make way for the present nondescript but efficient complex, which makes use of air rights over the tracks. Underground, Penn Station is as efficient as ever. Trains move from the coach yards at Sunnyside, load rapidly at the floor-level platforms, and are quickly dispatched. Thousands of trains carrying millions of passengers pass through the station each year, all completely out of sight beneath the busy streets of the busiest city in the world.

For information on the city, see section 2.29.

3.4   New York—Albany

The Hudson River Valley line is one of America's most beautiful railroad routes. For 130 miles the tracks follow the east bank of the majestic river that Henry Hudson took to be the mysterious Northwest Passage when he discovered it in 1609.

This was formerly the main line of the New York Central system, and today it is part of Conrail; passenger operations are conducted by Amtrak and the State of New York. In the last few years, the state has financed major track repairs on this route, and today some trains make the New York—Albany run in as little as two hours and twelve minutes—the best time ever for this trip. Most schedules operate with Turboliner equipment, although Amfleet II and Heritage cars are also in regular service. The *Lake Shore Limited* is scheduled for Amfleet II coaches as soon as enough new cars are delivered.

0.0 **NEW YORK (Grand Central Terminal)** *141.6.* In 1869, Cornelius Vanderbilt, the former ferryboat captain who ran the New York Central lines, moved his New York passenger station up into the country at 42nd Street and Park Avenue. That was a long carriage ride from Wall Street, and pooh-poohers said nobody would ever ride the

Northbound/miles   *miles/Southbound*

0.0	NEW YORK (Grand Central)	141.6
4.2	125th Street	137.4
4.9	Bronx (138th Street)	136.7
7.1	High Bridge	134.5
9.6	Marble Hill	132.0
10.4	Spuyten Duyvil	131.2
12.2	Riverdale	129.4
12.9	Mount St. Vincent	128.7
14.5	Yonkers	127.1
18.7	Hastings-on-Hudson	122.9
20.0	Dobbs Ferry	121.6
21.0	Ardsley	120.6
22.0	Irvington	119.6
24.5	Tarrytown	117.1
28.7	Scarborough	112.9
30.2	Ossining	111.4
32.7	CROTON-HARMON	108.9
33.9	Croton-on-Hudson	107.7
35.7	Oscawana	105.9
36.7	Crugers	104.9
38.1	Montrose	103.5
40.6	Peeksill	101.0
45.4	Manitou	96.2
49.1	Garrison	92.5
51.8	Cold Spring	89.8
56.5	Dutchess	85.1
58.3	Beacon	83.3
61.8	Chelsea	79.8
64.4	New Hamburg	77.2
67.5	Camelot	74.1
72.8	POUGHKEEPSIE	68.8
78.5	Hyde Park	63.1
82.9	Staatsburg	58.7
88.4	RHINECLIFF (Kingston)	53.2
94.0	Barrytown	47.6
98.3	Tivoli	43.3
103.7	Germantown	37.9
105.4	North Germantown	36.2
113.7	HUDSON	27.9
118.0	Stockport	23.6
121.2	Newton Hook	20.4
123.6	Stuyvesant	18.0
129.6	Schodack Landing	12.0
133.6	Castleton-on-Hudson	8.0
141.6	ALBANY-RENSSELAER	0.0

Commodore's trains anymore. But Vanderbilt knew better. Anticipating the growth of the city, he put his station right in the path of future development and then prudently bought up all the surrounding land. Within a few years New York surrounded Grand Central, and Vanderbilt made countless millions from his real-estate holdings in the area.

By the turn of the century the old Grand Central, big as it was, was no longer adequate; and plans were drawn up for the present building—the most famous railroad station in America.

Opened in 1914, Grand Central is in the heart of midtown New York. The site is so valuable that several efforts have been made to tear down the French Renaissance structure and put up a profitable high rise, as was done at Penn Station, but so far, Grand Central continues to survive.

Amtrak trains use the top level of this bilevel terminal. Only passengers for points in upstate New York, the *Adirondack* to Montreal, the *Maple Leaf* to Toronto, and the *Lake Shore Limited* to Cleveland and Chicago now join the regular flood of commuters to Grand Central. All other Amtrak trains operate from Penn Station. Half the former ticket windows now dispense $2 tickets on the horses. *Sic transit gloria!*

Leaving the terminal, trains run for 3 miles through a tunnel under Park Avenue, emerging at last at 96th Street. This four-track tunnel, and the New York City smoke-control ordinance, long ago demanded electrification of all trains running into Grand Central. Thus, third-rail direct current extends for 33 miles north, to Croton-Harmon.

On emerging from the tunnel, trains pass through the Spanish Harlem section of Upper Manhattan on an elevated structure that threads its way between the tenements and housing projects above Park Avenue.

4.2 **125th Street** *137.4.* This is the main street of Harlem. Famous landmarks like the Hotel Theresa are farther west, however.

Beyond the station is a four-track lift bridge over the Harlem River. Here the rails leave Manhattan for the Bronx, the only one of New York's five boroughs located on the U.S. mainland.

At Mott Haven, the line divides. A commuters-only branch goes north to points in suburban Connecticut and Westchester County; Amtrak trains turn west, passing Yankee Stadium (on the right side, leaving New York) and eventually coming out along the east bank of the Harlem River.

9.6 **Marble Hill** *132.0.* At Marble Hill the Harlem River turns suddenly westward. The rails follow, cutting through imposing rock formations.

10.4 **Spuyten Duyvil** *131.2.* Pronounced *Spy-ten Die-vil,* the name means "spitting devil" and was given to the place by the Dutch, who feared the tricky currents where the Harlem River issues into the Hudson.

Spuyten Duyvil station is on the north bank of the Harlem (here known as Spuyten Duyvil Creek), just opposite the northernmost tip of Manhattan Island and under the shadows of the Henry Hudson Bridge. Here Amtrak trains turn north to begin the long run up the east bank of the Hudson to Albany. A freight-only branch crosses the Harlem at its mouth and runs southward along Manhattan's West Side. This is the most important freight route into New York proper. This track may someday be used to allow Amtrak trains from Albany to reach Pennsylvania Station, which would permit the NRPC to move out of Grand Central entirely.

14.5 **Yonkers** *127.1.* This industrial city is just across the border from New York. Otis elevators, among other things, were made here until recently.

Yonkers got its unusual name from the original Dutch landholder at the site, a youthful patroon named Van der Donck who was known locally as *Der Jonkheer,* "the young nobleman."

22.0 **Irvington** *119.6.* The "Irving" of Irvington is Washington Irving, America's first great literary figure. The writer's home, "Sunnyside," is nearby; it has been restored and is open to the public. Irving's two best-known stories, "Rip Van Winkle" and "The Legend of Sleepy Hollow," are set in this picturesque valley where the Dutch influence still lingers.

Just north of Irvington the Hudson widens into what is called the Tappan Zee. The train passes beneath the highway bridge that spans the river at this point.

24.5 **Tarrytown** *117.1.* Across the wide, smooth Tappan Zee are the Catskills, the mysterious mountains where Rip Van Winkle went to sleep one summer afternoon and didn't wake up for twenty years.

30.2 **Ossining** *111.4.* Here trains pass between the buildings of Ossining Correctional Facility, more popularly, and at one time officially, known as Sing Sing Prison. Guard towers and the overhead bridges connecting the prison buildings give Amtrak passengers a brief vision of prison life.

32.7 **CROTON-HARMON** *108.9.* Formerly called Harmon, this is the northern end of the third-rail electrification that extends from Grand Central. There are facilities here for maintaining both diesel and electric engines.

51.8 **Cold Spring** *89.8.* Directly across the Hudson is West Point, a fortress during the Revolutionary War and since 1802 the site of the U.S. Military Academy. Benedict Arnold turned over the plans of this post to Major John André of the British army in 1779 and earned his reputation as a traitor.

58.3 **Beacon** *83.3.* Across the river is the city of Newburgh, where George Washington maintained his headquarters from April 1782 to August 1783, at the end of the Revolutionary War.

A couple of miles south of Beacon, on a small island in the Hudson, stands a weird structure called Bannerman's Castle. North of Beacon, a highway bridge across the Hudson carries Route I-84.

72.8 **POUGHKEEPSIE** *68.8.* This is the site of Vassar College, formerly one of the "Seven Sisters" women's schools, which now admits men. The school colors have been changed to red and white; the former pink and gray was simply too much for the men's basketball team to bear.

Just beyond the station, the train passes under the Poughkeepsie Bridge, once a principal rail-freight route to New England but no longer in use. This spectacular structure was one of the highest bridges in the east.

78.5 **Hyde Park** *63.1.* On the bluffs above the tracks is the estate and burial place of Franklin D. Roosevelt, President of the United States from 1933 to his death in 1945. Adjacent to the home is a library and museum.

A few miles north is the Vanderbilt mansion, all fifty rooms of it. Built in 1898, it contains elegant furnishings, tapestries, and rugs. This was the home of the tycoons who for years dominated the affairs of the New York Central system, whose tracks these used to be.

88.4 **RHINECLIFF** *53.2.* Across on the west bank of the river is the city of Kingston, the first capital of New York State.

113.7 **HUDSON** *27.9.* A picturesque town chartered in 1785, Hudson was the home of Frederick Church, the nineteenth-century painter and most noted member of the Hudson River School. His exotic house, overlooking the river, is open to the public.

123.6 **Stuyvesant** *18.0.* The town was named for Peter Stuyvesant, the cantankerous Dutch governor of New Netherlands who in 1664 was forced to turn over control of the colony to the English. They renamed it in honor of the brother of King Charles II, James, Duke of York.

Five miles from Stuyvesant is the village of Kinderhook, birthplace of Martin Van Buren. The eighth president of the United States, he served from 1837 to 1841. Known for his political maneuvering and the distinctive color of his beard, he was sometimes called the "Red Fox of Kinderhook."

141.6 **ALBANY-RENSSELAER** *0.0.* For notes on Albany, see section 3.2.

3.5 (New York)—Albany—Montreal

Between the biggest city in the United States and the biggest city in Canada lies some of the most beautiful scenery in the East. This is the route of Amtrak's *Adirondack,* which makes a daily daylight trip in each direction up the Hudson and along the west shore of Lake Champlain and the Richelieu River to Montreal.

This is not only one of the prettiest but also one of the most historic routes in America. It follows the ancient Indian trail that later served the French *voyageurs* and, still later, the British army during the Revolutionary War. Along the route are Fort Ticonderoga, where independence was nearly lost, and Saratoga, where it was practically won. At the end of the trip is bilingual Montreal, everybody's favorite city.

Seats on the *Adirondack* are unreserved, so here's a tip: The best views are on the west (left side of the train) between New York and Albany and on the east (right side) beyond. Switch sides at Albany–Rensselaer, and you'll be in the best position to see everything.

For notes on the route from New York to Albany, see section 3.4. For information on Albany, see section 3.2.

141.6 **ALBANY–RENSSELAER** *234.5.* Just beyond the station, Amtrak trains turn sharply to the left and cross the Hudson into Albany proper. From this point to Schenectady, 17 miles, the modern railroad follows the path of one of America's first passenger-carrying lines, the Mohawk and Hudson, built in 1831. This was the route of the DeWitt Clinton, the third steam engine in America, which pulled a train of stagecoach bodies on iron wheels at the startling speed of 15 miles per hour. The rails were wood stringers covered with strips of iron that sometimes broke loose and came stabbing up through the car floors. These "snakeheads" were only one hazard of early railroad travel. Today the rails are steel, but the route is the same.

159.0 **SCHENECTADY** *217.1.* Home of the giant research laboratories of the General Electric Company, Schenectady is at the mouth of the Mohawk Valley—the natural gate in the Appalachian barrier through which the commerce of the West has flowed since settlement began.

Montreal-bound trains leave the Conrail main line to Buffalo (the old New York Central) just west of the new Schenectady station, turning northward onto the tracks of the Delaware and Hudson. This is another of America's oldest railways, having begun as a canal company in the early nineteenth century. The D & H soon realized the value of rails, and as early as 1830—a year before the DeWitt Clinton made its first run—it experimented with a steam engine brought from England. Unfortunately, this machine proved to be too heavy for the company's flimsy track, and it never ran again.

It is appropriate to be thinking about locomotives while passing through Schenectady on the D & H, for just to the west of the tracks (left side, going north) is the old American Locomotive Company factory, which used to build them by the hundreds.

(NEW YORK)—ALBANY—MONTREAL

Northbound/miles		miles/Southbound
0.0	NEW YORK (Grand Central)	376.1
141.6	ALBANY-RENSSELAER	234.5
141.6	ALBANY-RENSSELAER	234.5
159.0	SCHENECTADY	217.1
159.0	SCHENECTADY	217.1
162.6	Alplaus	213.5
166.7	Ballston Lake	209.4
173.1	Ballston Spa	203.0
179.8	SARATOGA SPRINGS	196.3
190.6	Gansevoort	185.5
197.1	FORT EDWARD	179.0
204.6	Smith's Basin	171.5
208.5	Fort Ann	167.6
212.4	Comstock	163.7
219.1	WHITEHALL	157.0
226.0	Clemons	150.1
228.9	Dresden	147.2
233.9	Putnam	142.2
238.9	Wrights	137.2
241.1	Montcalm Landing	135.0
243.0	FORT TICONDEROGA	133.1
250.6	Crown Point	125.5
258.2	PORT HENRY	117.9
269.3	WESTPORT	106.8
272.1	Wadhams	104.0
275.7	Whallonsburg	100.4
278.7	Essex	97.4
283.5	WILLSBORO	92.6
292.5	Douglass	83.6
296.0	PORT KENT	80.1
302.3	Valcour	73.8
305.7	Bluff Point	70.4
307.2	Cliff Haven	68.9
310.0	PLATTSBURGH	66.1
314.1	Beekmantown	62.0

315.9	Spellman's	60.2
319.3	West Chazy	56.8
325.6	Chazy	50.5
329.4	Cooperville	46.7
333.3	ROUSES POINT, N.Y. (U.S.)	42.8

333.3	ROUSES POINT, N.Y. (U.S.)	42.8
339.3	LACOLLE, P.Q. (CANADA)	36.8
347.3	Napierville	28.8
353.3	St. Edouard	22.8
358.3	St. Mathieu	17.8
362.3	Delson Junction (C.P. Ry.)	13.8
369.0	LaSalle	7.1
371.4	MONTREAL OUEST	4.7
374.2	WESTMOUNT	1.9
376.1	MONTREAL, P.Q. (Windsor Sta.)	0.0

179.8 **SARATOGA SPRINGS** *196.3.* It's too bad that you can't see any of the town from the station, for Saratoga Springs was once the resort for the rich and socially prominent—and it's still quite a spa, especially during the summer racing season.

Saratoga has further historical significance: This was the site of the defeat and surrender of British General "Gentleman Johnny" Burgoyne, probably the most important colonial victory of the Revolutionary War.

Burgoyne had planned to march from Canada down the Richelieu–Champlain–Hudson corridor, capturing the American outposts and cutting New England off from the rest of the colonies. Had he succeeded, the revolution would probably have been crushed. His failure, however, cost the British even more than the five thousand irreplaceable soldiers who surrendered with Burgoyne on October 17, 1777. The colonial victory at Saratoga was the catalyst that led to the Franco-American alliance, the alliance that brought essential French money, arms, troops, and finally naval help to the struggling Americans.

197.1 **FORT EDWARD** *179.0.* Before entering the town, the train crosses the Hudson for the final time.

Three miles upstream, at Glens Falls, the Hudson comes within 9 miles of the southern tip of Lake George. Early explorers carried their boats over this portage when traveling the water route from Canada to the sea. The Champlain Canal was built to avoid this portage, and at the south end of the canal, Fort Edward was established to protect this important commercial route.

208.5 **Fort Ann** *167.6.* Twin to Fort Edward, Fort Ann guarded the northern end of the Champlain Canal, where it enters the Halfway River. The Halfway, in turn, connects directly with Lake Champlain, thus bypassing Lake George and the portages at its northern and southern ends and making an all-water route from Montreal to New York.

219.1 **WHITEHALL** *157.0.* Whitehall features a picturesque setting, complete with an old silk mill across the river from the railroad station. Leaving town, the train passes through a short tunnel and emerges along the southern tip of Lake Champlain, crossing to the west shore of the lake. Here the train enters the Adirondack State Park, a vast expanse of state and privately owned land that constitutes the largest wilderness area in the East.

243.0 **FORT TICONDEROGA** *133.1.* Built on a high bluff commanding the short overland portage from Lake Champlain to Lake George, Ticonderoga was the key to control of the route from Canada to New York. Accordingly, the colonials spared no expense in making the site as formidable as possible—only to have British General Burgoyne capture the fort, together with a huge cache of arms and supplies, early in the summer of 1777. The surrender of Ticonderoga was a terrific blow to the patriot cause, but Burgoyne's later defeat at Saratoga reversed its ill effects.

258.2 **PORT HENRY** *117.9.* Well-manicured lawns, fine old houses, and a classic fire station mark this lovely old lakeside town. Across the water to the east is Vermont; to the west rise the Adirondack Mountains, capped by Mount Marcy (5,344 feet), the highest point in New York State.

269.3 **WESTPORT** *106.8.* This little station, on a high bluff overlooking Lake Champlain, is the closest Amtrak stop to Lake Placid and the Whiteface Mountain ski area, both about 35 miles west and accessible by a bus that meets the train. John Brown, the abolitionist famous for his exploits in "Bleeding Kansas" and at Harpers Ferry, is buried at his farm near here.

The next 27 miles, from Westport to Port Kent, is the most scenic stretch on this generally scenic route. Near Willsboro the train runs along a narrow shelf cut into the bluffs, with a sheer cliff rising to one side and a sheer drop down to Lake Champlain on the other.

296.0 **PORT KENT** *80.1.* Nearby is Ausable Chasm, which features boat trips through a spectacular gorge. A ferryboat crosses Lake Champlain from here to Burlington, Vermont. Beyond Port Kent the track leaves the Adirondack Park. The train runs away from the lake shore, and the scenery, while still attractive, is much less spectacular.

310.0 **PLATTSBURGH** *66.1.* Here are located an old roundhouse and shop facility and a tidy old two-story station. Paper mills are seen at the crossing of the Saranac River, which flows into the lake here.

Between Plattsburgh and Rouses Point the land is increasingly flat, and farming replaces lumbering. This stretch is a good time to purchase beer and cigarettes if you want them, because they are not available once the train crosses into Canada.

333.3 **ROUSES POINT, N.Y.** *42.8*. Rouses Point is a railroad town, pure and simple—the junction where American and Canadian lines meet. The international border is a mile or so north of the town.

339.3 **LACOLLE, QUEBEC** *36.8*. Canadian customs and immigration personnel check the train here. The procedure is fast—it probably won't take more than 10 minutes—and American citizens do not need a passport to enter Canada. Remember, when reentering the United States, more than a quart of alcohol is subject to duty.

362.3 **Delson Junction** *13.8*. This is not a town but simply a railroad junction where the D & H meets the main line of the Canadian Pacific, over which Amtrak trains operate into Montreal. The name is derived from contracting *Del*aware and Hud*son*.

Seven miles beyond the junction, the rails cross the St. Lawrence River and the St. Lawrence Seaway on a lift bridge. Downtown Montreal is visible from the bridge. Look to the east (right side, going north).

371.4 **MONTREAL OUEST** *4.7*. An important junction where Canadian Pacific lines radiate in four directions. The station is convenient to Montreal's international airport and to the suburbs of Verdun, Lachine, and Dorval.

374.2 **WESTMOUNT** *1.9*. Montreal may be two-thirds French-speaking, but English is the primary language in Westmount. Close by is the Montreal Forum, home of the Canadiens hockey team.

376.1 **MONTREAL (Windsor Station)** *0.0*. The largest French-speaking city in North America, Montreal is Canada's second-largest city and perhaps the world's greatest example of bicultural living. Old Windsor Station, however, despite recent remodeling, is as Victorian as England herself. The waiting room looks as if Prince Albert might have passed through yesterday. This very British station in the midst of French Canada is a fitting terminal for the trip up the Lake Champlain valley, where British redcoats once marched.

3.6   *Montreal—New Haven—(New York)*

Seventy miles longer than the Lake Champlain route but serving the Connecticut River valley and the Vermont ski slopes, this is the route of the *Montrealer*. Famous during Prohibition as the "Bootlegger" because of the Canadian whiskey smuggled aboard for its southbound trips, the *Montrealer* had been discontinued by its operators and was revived by Amtrak. It's not particularly fast, and its overnight schedule allows only a minimum of scenic viewing; but this is a chummy, friendly train nonetheless. A large number of its winter passengers are skiers going to Stowe, and skiers are notorious party-lovers. Sometimes Le Pub, the *Montrealer's* bar car, seems like an après-ski lounge itself.

The route follows the Richelieu River from Montreal to the U.S. border, skirts the east shore of Lake Champlain for 50 miles, then follows the Winooski and White rivers to the Connecticut. From White River Junction, Vermont, to Hartford, Connecticut, the route follows the Connecticut River valley, the principal north-south artery of New England.

North of Springfield, Massachusetts, the *Montrealer* provides once-a-day service, offering through Washington–Montreal sleeping cars, coaches, and slumbercoaches.

South of Springfield, Massachusetts, Amtrak runs eight trains a day through the Connecticut Valley, with connections at New Haven for New York and points south.

0.0 **MONTREAL, P.Q. (Central Station)** *368.1*. Central Station is a world removed from old Windsor Station, just a few blocks away. Central occupies the basement of a big hotel and commercial complex, and from the outside you'd never guess it was a railroad terminal. This is the new Montreal, as Windsor is the old, but neither station has a truly Gallic atmosphere. English capital built Canada's railroads, and English culture dominates Montreal's stations.

1.9 **Bridge Street** *366.2*. The *Montrealer* leaves by the Victoria Bridge over the St. Lawrence. The seaway locks are on the south bank, immediately beneath the bridge.

Upriver (left side of the train, leaving Montreal) two islands are visible. Nearest the bridge is the Ile Notre Dame; farther on, and right in the center of the river, is the Ile St. Helene, which was the site of Expo '67, the Montreal World's Fair.

MONTREAL—NEW HAVEN—(NEW YORK)

Southbound/miles   *miles/Northbound*

0.0	MONTREAL, P.Q. (Central Sta.)	368.1
1.9	Bridge Street	366.2
4.0	St. Lambert	364.1
9.1	Brosseau	359.0
17.0	Lacadie	351.1
23.2	St. Jean	344.9
29.7	Grande Ligne	338.4
32.1	Girard	336.0
35.8	St. Valentin	332.3
40.3	CANTIC, P.Q.	327.8
50.1	East Alburgh, Vt.	318.0
56.7	Swanton	311.4

23.3 **St. Jean** *344.9.* Here the train enters the valley of the Richelieu River, running due north and south and connecting the St. Lawrence with Lake Champlain. The river was named for Armand Jean du Plessis, Cardinal Richelieu, the prime minister of France under Louis XIII from 1624 to 1642. It was under his administration that an expedition under de Maisonneuve founded Montreal in 1642.

The Richelieu valley is typical of Quebec. Small farms and villages have changed little over the last two centuries, and the area is so thoroughly French that English is no more familiar to most residents than, say, Italian.

40.3 **CANTIC, P.Q.** *327.8.* The U.S. Customs and Immigration personnel board the train here and conduct their inspection en route.

50.1 **East Alburgh, Vt.** *318.0.* East Alburgh is built on a peninsula protruding into Lake Champlain between the Richelieu to the west and Missisquoi Bay to the east. East of the station, the train crosses the bay on a mile-long causeway.

65.7 **ST. ALBANS** *302.4.* The town stands at the base of the Green Mountains a few miles inland from Lake Champlain. East of here is the birthplace of President Chester A. Arthur, who served from 1881 to 1885.

St. Albans earned a footnote in the history books in 1864, when a band of Confederates based in Canada attacked the town. They burned a number of buildings and did significant damage before retreating back across the border. This raid was the northernmost land combat of the American Civil War.

89.5 **ESSEX JUNCTION** *278.6.* This is the Station for Burlington, which is 5 miles west on the shore of Lake Champlain. At this point the railroad turns southeast to begin its passage through the Green Mountains by way of the Winooski River valley. Mount Mansfield, at 4,393 feet above sea level the highest point in Vermont, is about 20 miles due east of here.

111.8 **WATERBURY** *256.3.* This is skiers' paradise. Stowe's slopes are 5 miles north, and within 25 miles of the Waterbury station are six other major ski areas. The *Montrealer* does a lively business at this station, especially on winter weekends.

121.4 **MONTPELIER JUNCTION** *246.7.* This is the station for Montpelier, Vermont's capital since 1808, and for Barre with its stone quarries 7 miles away. Vermont is the nation's leading producer of granite.

At Montpelier Junction the route turns south along the Third Branch of the White River.

165.2 **South Royalton** *202.9.* Here the three branches of the White River join. A mile or two out of town is a monument marking the birthplace of Joseph Smith, founder of the Mormon Church.

182.9 **WHITE RIVER JUNCTION** *185.2.* A typical picturesque New England town at the confluence of the White River and the Connecticut, this is the transportation crossroads of upper New England, where highways and rail lines from New York, Boston, Montreal, and Quebec converge.

It's also the station for Dartmouth College, 5 miles up the Connecticut River valley at Hanover, New Hampshire. And 30 miles west of White River Junction, at Plymouth, is the home of President Calvin Coolidge. He was vice-president when in 1923 he came to Plymouth to visit his father, a local judge. Then the news of President Warren G. Harding's death arrived, and by the light of an oil lamp in the parlor of his family home, Calvin Coolidge was sworn in as President of the United States by his own father.

197.0 **Windsor, Vt.** *171.1.* Across the Connecticut River in New Hampshire is the Saint-Gaudens National Historic Site, honoring the New England sculptor who lived from 1848 to 1907. Below Windsor the train crosses the Connecticut River to the New Hampshire side.

204.9 **Claremont Junction, N.H.** *163.2.* This is the station for Claremont, 4 miles east. Nearby are Lake Sunapee, the Mount Sunapee and King Ridge ski areas, and the town of Newport with its unusual clock-museum.

222.1 **BELLOWS FALLS, VT.** *146.0.* Here the rails recross the Connecticut back into Vermont. Near Bellows Falls is the Steamtown, USA, museum, where the late Nelson Blount assembled a large collection of old steam locomotives. Excursions are run during the summer months.

245.8 **BRATTLEBORO, VT.** *122.3.* The first permanent white settlement in Vermont was Fort Dummer, built at this site in 1724 by settlers from Massachusetts. The station here serves Keene, New Hampshire, and Bennington, Vermont, both within driving distance. This, too, is ski country, with a number of slopes nearby.

270.0 **Greenfield, Mass.** *98.1.* Old Deerfield Village, a restored pioneer settlement, is nearby. Twenty-five miles west of Greenfield, on the Boston–Troy line of the B & M, is the Hoosac Tunnel. Hoosac is 5 miles in length and took more than 25 years to build. It's the longest tunnel east of the Mississippi, and the third longest in North America. Unfortunately, only freight trains use it today.

289.0 **NORTHAMPTON** *79.1.* Colleges abound in and all around Northampton. Smith, another of the "Seven Sisters," is in the town; its rival, Mount Holyoke, is at nearby South Hadley. Amherst College and the University of Massachusetts are about 8 miles away, at Amherst.

Northampton was the home of Jonathan Edwards, perhaps the greatest revivalist preacher of them all. Edwards (1703–58), minister at the local church for more than 20 years, was the leading figure in the Great Awakening, a widespread religious revival of the mid-eighteenth century. He is legendary for his hellfire and brimstone sermons.

306.1 **SPRINGFIELD, MASS.** *62.0.* For information on Springfield, see section 3.2.

314.1 **ENFIELD, CONN.** *54.0.* Here, in 1741, Jonathan Edwards delivered his sermon "Sinners in the Hand of an Angry God." It's powerful to read even today; 200 years ago, it must have had the congregation cringing in terror.

331.5 **HARTFORD** *36.6.* Capital of Connecticut and the state's largest city, Hartford has long been known as the "insurance city"—more than thirty major insurers have headquarters here. This is also an important manufacturing city; the Gun That Won the West, Samuel Colt's .45, was made here.

Hartford has also been an intellectual center, going back to Federalist times and the group of satirists who called themselves the "Hartford Wits." Three of the most important literary figures of the nineteenth century made their homes here: Noah Webster, author of the first American dictionary; Mark Twain, the creator of Huck Finn and Tom Sawyer; and Harriet Beecher Stowe, whose *Uncle Tom's Cabin* stirred antislavery sentiment throughout the country. Their homes are all open to the public.

Passengers to intermediate stations between here and New Haven should change to a local train.

368.1 **NEW HAVEN, CONN.** *0.0.* For information on New Haven and the route from there to New York City, see section 3.3.

3.7   The Mid-Atlantic Seaboard

Connecting the nation's political and economic capitals, and running through the most densely populated area of the United States, the New York–Washington run is by far Amtrak's most important route.

The track is actually owned and operated by Amtrak, which purchased this former Pennsylvania Railroad line from Conrail on April 1, 1976. Since then, a major improvement program has seen Amtrak put down a quarter of a million new concrete cross ties and 40 miles of welded rail, permitting safe operation at speeds in excess of 110 miles per hour today with a goal of 120 miles per hour by 1985. All passenger equipment used on the line is either new or recently rebuilt.

A brand new fleet of electric locomotives hauls the trains.

South of Washington, Amtrak operates four trains daily in each direction to Richmond. In the long run, it hopes to electrify this track and, in effect, extend the present corridor southward for another 100 miles.

3.8 New York—Philadelphia— Baltimore—Washington

Between Penn Station, New York, and Union Station, Washington, Amtrak most closely aproximates European or Japanese high-speed, mass-movement passenger railroading. The entire line is electrified, and much of it is grade separated—no highway crossings to worry about. From two to six tracks are provided for the ceaseless flow of trains carrying America's heaviest rail passenger traffic.

This route once belonged to the Pennsylvania Railroad, which assembled it from shorter lines built in the first half of the nineteenth century. The last link—the Hudson River tunnels into New York—was finished in 1910.

Service on this line is fast, frequent, and reasonably comfortable. It is not particularly scenic or glamorous, which is not to say that this "strictly business" line may not offer the best passenger service in North America today. Center city to center city, Amtrak consistently beats buses and autos and is competitive with air shuttle. Just don't expect the ambience of luxury travel, which some of the Western trains offer.

0.0 **NEW YORK, N.Y. (Penn Station)** *225.3.* For information on Penn Station, see section 3.3. For information on the city, see section 2.29.

Leaving Penn Station, Philadelphia-bound trains pass under the main post office and emerge briefly into daylight at Ninth Avenue; then they dive into the double-tracked tunnel under the Hudson River. The exit from the tube is on the west side of the Palisades, the steep cliffs that rise along the river on the Jersey side. The tracks cross a swampy area, running parallel to the New Jersey Turnpike. A drawbridge spans the Hackensack River.

Near Harrison the Penn Station tunnel line, built in 1910, joins the original route from the Jersey City ferry slip. At this point there used to be a curious station called Manhattan Transfer, where the electric locomotives originally used in the Hudson River tunnels were replaced by steam engines. During the Depression, however, the Pennsylvania

147

Southbound/miles   *miles/Northbound*

0.0	NEW YORK, N.Y. (Penn Sta.)	225.3
	Hudson River Tunnel	
10.0	NEWARK, N.J. (Penn Sta.)	215.3
10.6	South Street	214.7
14.4	North Elizabeth	210.9
15.5	Elizabeth	209.8
16.1	South Elizabeth	209.2
18.7	Linden	206.6
20.8	Rahway	204.5
22.9	Colonia	202.4
24.1	Iselin	201.2
24.6	METROPARK	200.7
25.4	Menlo Park	199.9
27.2	Metuchen	198.1
30.3	Stelton	195.0
32.7	NEW BRUNSWICK	192.6
36.9	Adams	188.4
39.9	Deans	185.4
42.4	Monmouth Junction	182.9
46.9	Plainsboro	178.4
48.4	PRINCETON JCT.	176.9
58.1	TRENTON, N.J.	167.2
59.5	Morrisville, Pa.	165.8
64.5	Tullytown	160.8
65.3	Edgely	160.0
67.8	Bristol	157.5
70.6	Croydon	154.7
72.3	Eddington	153.0
73.5	Cornwells Heights	151.8
74.6	Andalusia	150.7
75.6	Torresdale	149.7
78.1	Holmesburg Junction	147.2
79.2	Tacony	146.1
80.3	Wissinoming	145.0
81.1	Bridesburg	144.2
82.7	Frankford Junction	142.6
84.8	North Penn	140.5
85.9	NORTH PHILADELPHIA	139.4
90.1	PHILADELPHIA (30th St.)	135.2
90.1	PHILADELPHIA (30th St.)	135.2
96.2	Darby	129.1
96.9	Curtis Park	128.4
97.3	Sharon Hill	128.0
97.8	Folcroft	127.5
99.1	Norwood	126.2
99.6	Moore	125.7
100.5	Ridley Park	124.8
101.2	Crum Lynne	124.1

101.8	Baldwin	123.5
102.4	Eddystone	122.9
103.4	CHESTER	121.9
104.4	Lamokin St.(Chester)	120.9
107.2	Marcus Hook, Pa.	118.1
109.6	Claymont, Del.	115.7
112.2	Bellvue	113.1
114.0	Edge Moor	111.3
116.8	WILMINGTON	108.5
128.8	NEWARK, DEL.	96.5
134.7	ELKTON, MD.	90.6
141.0	North East	84.3
143.6	Charlestown	81.7
149.0	PERRYVILLE	76.3
150.2	Havre de Grace	75.1
155.0	ABERDEEN	70.3
158.6	Perryman	66.7
164.7	EDGEWOOD	60.6
166.7	Magnolia	58.6
169.5	Harewood Park	55.8
170.6	Chase	54.7
173.0	Bengies	52.3
174.9	Middle River	50.4
176.5	Stemmer's Run	48.8
183.9	Biddle Street	41.4
185.2	BALTIMORE (Penn Sta.)	40.1
187.9	EDMONDSON AVE.	37.4
189.3	Frederick Road	36.0
192.4	Halethorpe	32.9
196.1	BALT.-WASH. INT. AIRPORT	29.2
203.0	ODENTON	22.3
208.9	Jericho Park	16.4
210.0	BOWIE	15.3
212.5	Glendale	12.8
214.1	Seabrook	11.2
217.0	NEW CARROLLTON	8.3
218.2	Landover	7.1
219.7	Cheverly, Md.	5.6
225.3	WASHINGTON, D.C.	0.0

Railroad electrified the line all the way to Washington and Harrisburg, Pennsylvania, using 11,000-volt AC from overhead wires. The DC tunnel motors disappeared, and so did Manhattan Transfer. Today its name survives in the title of a John Dos Passos novel.

10.0 NEWARK, N.J. *215.3.* Newark may be one of America's most troubled cities, but its station remains an important transfer point. Amtrak trains from New York enter the city over a large drawbridge across the Passaic River, which they share with New Jersey commuter trains and the Port Authority Trans-Hudson line (formerly called the Hudson Tubes). PATH operates two tunnels of its own to Manhattan: one to the World Trade Center in the financial district, the other to midtown. Amtrak passengers can make convenient across-the-platform connections to PATH trains and also to central New Jersey commuter trains.

15.5 **Elizabeth** *209.8.* The tracks skirt the downtown area on a broad reverse curve, which was eased in recent years after extensive and costly construction.

20.8 **Rahway** *204.5.* At this junction, trains bound for the Jersey coast branch off from the main line to Philadelphia.

24.6 **METROPARK** *200.7.* This station just south of Iselin is convenient to the New Jersey Turnpike, the Garden State Parkway, and Route I-287. There's hardly anyplace in New Jersey that can't be reached easily from this point.

25.4 **Menlo Park** *199.9.* Here, before the turn of the century, Thomas Edison established his laboratory. The lab and accompanying machine shop were themselves two of Edison's greatest inventions—well-equipped facilities designed to research and develop new products.

32.7 **NEW BRUNSWICK** *192.6.* New Brunswick is at the head of navigation on the Raritan River and was once the terminus of the Delaware and Raritan Canal, which connected the two rivers in its title, thus creating an inland water route between Philadelphia and New York.

Rutgers—which is, despite its name, the State University of New Jersey—has its main campus here.

48.4 **PRINCETON JUNCTION** *176.9.* This is the station for Princeton, with its university (the fourth oldest in the nation), the Institute for Advanced Studies (where Einstein worked), and the Educational Testing Service. A shuttle train connects the town and university with the main line station at Princeton Junction.

58.1 **TRENTON, N.J.** *167.2.* The capital of New Jersey, Trenton lies on the east bank of the Delaware River (the opposite shore is Pennsylvania). The site was originally known as Trent's Town, after a royal magistrate named William Trent, and it has an interesting history.

After the British victories around New York in the summer of 1776, George Washington and his army were forced to retreat across New Jersey, taking up a defensive position on the Pennsylvania side of the Delaware. The British then occupied New Jersey. A detachment of Hessian mercenaries was posted to hold Trenton.

It was not customary for eighteenth-century European armies to fight during the winter, but George Washington was not the man to let the seasons dictate his strategy. On Christmas night he led a force across the Delaware (and no, he didn't stand up in the boat) and routed the Hessian troops.

Trenton today is primarily an industrial city, but it nearly became the capital of the United States. In 1784, Congress voted to establish a new federal city here, but under the Articles of Confederation, in force at that time, it had no power to levy taxes and thus had no money to make good the scheme. Three years later, as part of the negotiations that produced the present Constitution, Washington, D.C., was chosen as the permanent capital at the insistence of the Southern states.

Immediately after leaving the Trenton station, Amtrak trains cross the Delaware River and enter Pennsylvania. The river and the state were named for Lord Delaware, a colonial governor.

59.5 **Morrisville, Pa.** *165.8.* In the hills on the south side of the Delaware, Washington posted his army in the winter of 1776. Here he was secure from attack if the British had attempted a winter campaign.

At Morrisville, freight trains to and from the west leave the main line to bypass Philadelphia.

64.5 **Tullytown** *160.8.* From here to Wilmington, Delaware, the route runs parallel to the Delaware River, which is sometimes within sight.

82.7 **Frankford Junction** *142.6.* At this point the crack *Congressional Limited* derailed at high speed back in 1943—the worst American railroad disaster in the last half century. The cause of the wreck was an overheated bearing. With today's roller-bearing equipment, this accident could not have occurred.

85.9 **NORTH PHILADELPHIA** *139.4.* This neighborhood station owes its importance to the fact that the direct route from New York to Harrisburg and the west bypasses the main station in Philadelphia.

Between North Philadelphia and downtown lies Zoo Tower, one of the most important railroad junctions in America. Here the heavy stream of traffic from New York divides. Part goes south to Washington, part west to Harrisburg. The junction takes its unusual name from the adjacent Fairmont Park Zoological Gardens. Zoo is so planned that north and southbound traffic never have to cross at grade. A subway takes the Harrisburg line under the southbound Washington tracks.

90.1 **PHILADELPHIA (30th Street Station)** *135.2.* For information on the city, see section 2.31.

102.4 **Eddystone** *122.9.* To the east of the tracks (left side, leaving Philadelphia) stand the buildings that once made up the Baldwin Locomotive Works, America's biggest manufacturer of steam locomotives. Thousands of iron horses were built here in a plant opened by Matthias Baldwin, a watchmaker by trade. They made engines here until the early 1950s, when diesels made steam engines obsolete.

103.4 **CHESTER** *121.9.* Chester is the oldest city in Pennsylvania, having been settled by Swedish colonists in 1644—nearly 30 years before William Penn founded Philadelphia. It was originally called Upland but received its present name when Penn took over the colony in 1682. Today it's an industrial city and a Delaware River port. The river is on the east side of the tracks (left side, going south).

107.2 **Marcus Hook, Pa.** *118.1.* This is another industrial center, with oil-refining facilities.

109.6 **Claymont, Del.** *115.7.* In 1664, when the British took New York from the Dutch, they also acquired New Jersey and Delaware. All these lands were owned by James, Duke of York. The duke, however, had no desire to leave England to live in the American wilderness, and so he gave some of his possessions to his friends. Delaware he deeded to William Penn, proprietor of neighboring Pennsylvania, in 1682. Delaware was then treated as part of Pennsylvania until 1703, when it began to elect its own legislature. Delaware's motto is "The First State," but this is based on its being the first to ratify the Constitution, not the first to be settled.

116.8 **WILMINGTON** *108.5.* The largest city in Delaware, Wilmington is the home base of the far-flung Du Pont interests. The Du Ponts first made their fortune selling munitions to the Union army during the Civil War. Today the company is active in many fields, especially chemicals.

Du Pont has long been a Delaware firm, but the state is also "home" to many other corporations that actually do most of their business elsewhere. This is because little Delaware, seeking revenue from franchise taxes, deliberately made its corporation laws among the most lenient and flexible in the nation. Business firms from across the nation have found it useful to incorporate under Delaware law, and the state receives substantial revenue as a result.

128.8 **NEWARK, DEL.** *96.5.* The Univerity of Delaware is situated here. Its athletic teams have one of the nation's most unusual and colorful nicknames; they're called the "Blue Hens," after Delaware's state bird.

134.7 **ELKTON, MD.** *90.6.* Maryland was founded by Lord Baltimore as a combination land speculation and refuge for persecuted Catholics. Its charter was granted in 1632 by Charles I, who named the territory after his consort, Henrietta Maria. Settlement began in 1634, making Maryland the third permanent English colony in America after Virginia and Massachusetts. Elkton takes its name from the Elk River, an arm of Chesapeake Bay.

149.0 **PERRYVILLE** *76.3.* The town stands on the north bank of the Susquehanna River just above the point where it empties into Chesapeake Bay. A long bridge spans the river between here and Havre de Grace. Although the rest of the railroad from Philadelphia to

Baltimore was finished in 1838, it wasn't until after the Civil War that the Susquehanna was bridged at this point. For 28 years ferryboats shuttled across the river, filling the gap between railheads. However, one winter the Susquehanna froze so solidly that it became possible to lay tracks across the ice and move freight and passenger cars from one bank to the other by horsepower. This unusual arrangement continued for a month until the ice began to melt and the ferryboats went back to work.

155.0 **ABERDEEN** *70.3.* Named after the Scottish city, Aberdeen, Maryland, is the site of the U.S. government's Aberdeen Proving Grounds where rockets and military equipment are tested. The government reservation occupies a long peninsula jutting into Chesapeake Bay south of the railroad.

164.7 **EDGEWOOD** *60.6.* The Edgewood Arsenal fills another of those inaccessible peninsulas, this one separated from the proving grounds by the mouth of the Bush River.

166.7 **Magnolia** *58.6.* The long bridge south of this station crosses the Gunpowder River.

174.9 **Middle River** *50.4.* At this point, at another of the many streams that flow into Chesapeake Bay, the railroad turns west toward the city of Baltimore.

176.5 **Stemmer's Run** *48.8.* Important railroad yards are here, at the eastern edge of Baltimore. The route through the city is mostly underground, however, so the Baltimore row houses you glimpse near here are about all of the city you'll see.

185.2 **BALTIMORE** *40.1.* The Baltimore station is approached through a series of tunnels built in 1874 that today constitute one of the most serious bottlenecks on the Northeast Corridor line.

For information on the city, see section 2.3.

196.1 **BALTIMORE–WASHINGTON INTERNATIONAL AIRPORT** *29.2.* This new station—it opened in October 1980—is a unique attempt to develop intermodal traffic. The station isn't actually in the airport—a free shuttle bus takes you around to the terminal—but it is close enough to allow convenient connections between plane and train.

210.0 **BOWIE** *15.3.* If you look at a map, you'll see that Bowie is well off the direct route between Baltimore and Washington. The railroad runs due south from Baltimore to Bowie, then makes a right-angle turn and runs due west to Washington. This round-Robin-Hood's-barn route has an interesting historical explanation.

Years ago the Baltimore and Ohio had a monopoly on the Baltimore–Washington traffic, and by buying up competitors and using its influence with the Maryland legislature, it was working hard to keep it. But the rival Pennsylvania Railroad was determined to crack the monopoly, and its managers hit upon a stratagem. They leased a sleepy little railroad that meandered through Maryland from Baltimore to an insignificant Potomac River port called Pope's Creek. As the Pennsylvania had anticipated, the B & O made no objection, for the Pope's Creek line did not go near Washington.

What the B & O people had overlooked was that the Pope's Creek charter permitted the construction of branch lines anywhere in Maryland, so long as they were not more than 20 miles long. The Pennsylvania company realized that Bowie, on the Pope's Creek route, was just under 20 miles from Washington, and so, by building a "branch line" from the insignificant little railroad, the Pennsylvania reached the nation's capital and broke the B & O monopoly.

217.0 **NEW CARROLLTON** *8.3.* Amtrak's new station at New Carrollton is shared with the Washington Metro (the capital's subway system) and many local bus routes, making it a convenient transfer point for passengers destined for suburban Maryland.

218.2 **Landover, Md.** *7.1.* About 2 miles west on Route 202 is the town of Bladensburg, where the British army camped during its raid on Washington in August 1814. The story is not well known by Americans, probably because it isn't very glorious from the local point of view, but the British did, in fact, capture Washington and burn several buildings, including the president's house. When that structure was rebuilt, it was painted white to cover up the smoke damage, and it's been called the White House ever since.

225.3 **WASHINGTON, D.C.** *0.0.* Washington's Union Station is at the foot of Capitol Hill, on the northeastern edge of the central city. For information on the city, see section 2.49.

3.9   *Washington—Richmond*

There is no more beautiful or historic area in the United States than the hundred miles between Washington and Richmond. Northern Virginia had already been settled for a century and a half at the time of the American Revolution; George Washington lived here all his life, and during the Civil War practically every foot of the region was disputed by the armies of the North and the South. To ride an Amtrak train through this region is to take a rolling history lesson.

The Richmond, Fredericksburg and Potomac Railway, the operating company, is one of the shortest major railroads in the United States, but also one of the busiest. Amtrak runs four trains a day each way over the R F & P's track, making the run in about 2 hours.

0.0 **WASHINGTON, D.C.** *108.3.* For notes on the city, see section 2.49.

Trains to and from the south use the lower concourse of Washington's bilevel Union Station. Immediately after leaving the platform, they plunge into the Capitol Hill Tunnel—and while Congress may not be meeting directly over your head, the tunnel does run almost under the Capitol.

The tunnel ends at New Jersey Avenue and D Street, and the tracks climb to an elevated right-of-way that snakes its way between a number of important government buildings. On the north (right side of the train, leaving Washington) are the Department of Health and Social Services, NASA, the Federal Aviation Agency, and the Bureau of Printing and Engraving, where dollar bills are made. The Mall, where the Smithsonian Institution stands, is one block farther north. To the other side are the Department of Transportation and the L'Enfant Plaza office complex, named for the French officer who developed the original plan for the city.

Passing 14th Street, the tracks swing to the south, cross the Tidal Basin (where the Japanese cherry trees bloom every spring), and pass

WASHINGTON—RICHMOND

Southbound/miles		miles/Northbound
0.0	WASHINGTON, D.C.	108.3
	Capitol Hill Tunnel	
	Potomac River	
7.5	Potomac Yard, Va.	100.8
8.2	ALEXANDRIA	100.1
17.8	Newington (Accotink)	90.5
21.1	Lorton	87.2
24.1	Woodbridge (Occoquan)	84.2
31.1	Cherry Hill	78.2
33.5	Possum Point	74.8
34.7	QUANTICO	73.6
39.1	Wide Water	69.2
45.4	Brooke	62.9
52.8	Dahlgren Jct.	55.5
54.1	FREDERICKSBURG	54.2
62.0	Summit	46.3
66.6	Guinea	41.7
69.0	Woodford	39.3
75.7	Milford	32.6
80.5	Penola	27.8
86.4	Ruther Glen	21.9
91.7	Doswell (C & O Crossing)	16.6
98.7	Ashland	11.6
105.3	Glen Allen	3.0
108.3	RICHMOND, VA. (Staples Mill Rd.)	0.0

the Jefferson Memorial (right side of the train, leaving Washington). The tall spire of the Washington Monument is also on the same side. Beyond the Jefferson Memorial and Potomac Park is the river, spanned by a long steel bridge with a swing span at the center.

Immediately after crossing the Potomac, and again to the right side of the train leaving Washington, is the Pentagon Building, headquarters for the U.S. Army and other military offices. Although this is Virginia territory today, it was once part of the District of Columbia, which was originally planned to form a perfect square. Congress, in its wisdom, later decided that it did not need the Virginia land, however, and gave it back.

On the other side of the train is Washington's National Airport, convenient to both the Pentagon and the other government offices across the river.

7.5 **Potomac Yard, Va.** *100.8.* The freight yard to the east of the train (left side, leaving Washington) is Potomac Yard, one of the nation's most complex facilities. From all over the South and from parts of the Midwest, freight cars arrive here to be shuffled into new trains, given fresh engines and crews, and sent north. Freight trains bypass the cramped Capitol Hill Tunnel and Washington's Union Station by using a route through Anacostia in southern Maryland. The electric wires that extend all the way south from New Haven end at Potomac Yard; south of here all trains are pulled by diesel engines.

8.2 **ALEXANDRIA** *100.1.* Alexandria is a good deal older than Washington, having been founded in 1749. It is named, not for the Egyptian city, but rather after John Alexander, an early landowner in this vicinity.

The odd-looking structure to the right side of the train (as you go south) is the George Washington National Masonic Memorial. Washington's adult home, the Mount Vernon plantation, is located along the Potomac a few miles south of Alexandria. At the Alexandria station, the railroad turns inland, away from the river.

17.8 **Newington** *90.5.* Nearby is the army post called Fort Belvoir. This station used to be called Accotink, after the creek which flows past the town.

21.1 **Lorton** *87.2.* This is the northern terminal for the Auto Train, the take-your-car-along-to-Florida service which was resumed in late 1983.

24.1 **Woodbridge (Occoquan)** *84.2.* This is another place where the name of a nearby suburban town has replaced the former Indian name. Occoquan Creek has a tributary, the little stream called Bull Run, made famous by the two Civil War battles that took place along its banks. From this point all the way to Richmond, nearly every mile raises echoes of the Revolutionary and Civil wars.

34.7 **QUANTICO** *73.6.* This station serves the Marine Corps Base in nearby Quantico.

39.1 **Wide Water** *69.2.* Here the Potomac turns sharply east, flowing into Chesapeake Bay, while the railroad continues straight south. At this point, passengers get their last look at the broad river (left side of the train).

Beyond Wide Water is a little stream called Aquia Creek. In Civil War times this was the northern terminal of the railroad from Richmond. The rest of the trip to Washington had to be made by riverboat.

52.8 **Dahlgren Junction** *55.5.* A branch runs from here to Dahlgren, on the Potomac 25 miles east. George Washington and James Monroe, the first and fifth presidents of the United States, were both born within a few miles of Dahlgren.

Just west of here is Falmouth, where the Union army camped from late 1862 until the following spring while the Confederates occupied Fredericksburg on the other side of the Rappahannock River.

54.1 **FREDERICKSBURG** *54.2.* This historic town—the home of George Washington's mother—was the focal point of four great Civil War battles fought in and near the city. Fredericksburg occupies a strategic position behind the Rappahannock, where Robert E. Lee and his Army of Northern Virginia disputed the passage of any major Northern force. The Federal Army of the Potomac tried to storm across in December 1862. The Confederates, fortified on the hills behind the town, turned them back in the bloodiest Union defeat of the entire war.

The men in blue tried again 5 months later. This time they attempted a flanking movement and had Lee half caught in a trap. Yet, despite having been surrounded on three sides and outnumbered two to one as the fighting began, he whipped the Federals for a second time at the battle of Chancellorsville, probably his greatest victory.

In 1864 the Federals, now under Grant, tried again. In two frightfully bloody battles, Wilderness and Spotsylvania, Grant lost 30,000 men in 10 days but kept pushing southward. Lee had fewer casualties, but he had fewer troops to begin with and could not replace those who fell. This so-called Hammering Campaign permanently weakened Lee's army.

At Fredericksburg the railroad crosses the Rappahannock at the same spot where General Ambrose Burnside sent the Union soldiers across on pontoon boats under heavy Rebel fire during the first attack on the town.

66.6 **Guinea** *41.7.* At this station, far behind the Confederate lines, General Stonewall Jackson died of complications that set in after he was wounded at Chancellorsville on May 2, 1863. He had been Lee's most brilliant and most trusted subordinate.

75.7 **Milford** *32.6.* Here the rails cross the Mattaponi, another of the rivers that flow down to Chesapeake Bay from the Virginia highlands. The Mattaponi is unusual in that its name, as well as the river itself, is a combination of its four principal tributaries: the Mat, the Ta, the Po, and the Ni.

86.4 **Ruther Glen** *21.9.* Just south of the station is another river crossing, this one over the North Anna. The existence of navigable streams reaching far into the interior was an important factor in the development of Virginia, for it meant that ships from England could sail right up to the plantation docks, unload manufactured goods, and take on cotton for export directly from the growers. Thus, Virginia grew up as a rural society without commercial cities, other than Richmond; this fact profoundly colored the economic and social character of the Old Dominion.

91.7 **Doswell** *16.6.* Once called Hanover Junction, this station marks the crossing of the R F & P line from Washington with the C & O route from Richmond to western Virginia. This was an important Union objective during the Civil War. South of Doswell the line crosses the South Anna River.

105.3 **Glen Allen** *3.0.* Nearby is the site of Yellow Tavern, where in 1864 a Union cavalry force defeated and killed Confederate General James Ewell Brown ("Jeb") Stuart, the most romantic and adventurous of all cavalry officers. Stuart used to ride into battle with his personal banjo player at his side; his death deprived Lee of a subordinate almost as important as Jackson had been, for it was Stuart who supplied much of Lee's intelligence about the Union armies.

108.3 **RICHMOND** *0.0.* For information on the city, see section 2.38.

3.10   Richmond—Newport News

This line extends down the length of the Peninsula of Virginia, between the York and the James rivers. Jamestown, the first permanent English colony in America, is on this peninsula; nearby is Yorktown, where Cornwallis surrendered to assure the independence of the United States. Here, too, General George MacClellan and an army of 100,000 Union soldiers attempted to capture Richmond and reunite a divided nation in 1862. Colonial Williamsburg, the painstaking and magnificent restoration of the early capital of the commonwealth, is the leading tourist attraction.

Amtrak's original mandate from the secretary of transportation included a line from Newport News to Chicago via Richmond and Cin-

158

cinnati; but this service never attracted many passengers. Wisely, Amtrak severed the Newport News to Richmond segment and instead combined it with the New York, Washington, and Richmond line, giving a daily through service between the Northeast and the peninsula.

0 **RICHMOND** *83*. Trains pass through much of the old part of Richmond, running along the north bank of the James River to reach the east side of the city. Here General George McClellan with 100,000 Union soldiers threatened Richmond in May 1862. He was so close that his men could hear the church bells ringing in the Confederate capital, but Robert E. Lee led a Southern counterattack that drove McClellan off. It would be nearly 3 years before the Union army finally captured Richmond.

26 **Roxbury** *57*. To the south, on the James River, is perhaps the most beautiful and famous of all Virginia plantation homes, Berkeley. Built in 1726, it was the home of the aristocratic Harrison family and the birthplace of two presidents—William Henry Harrison and his grandson Benjamin. McClellan used it as his headquarters during the campaign of 1862, and "Taps," the famous evening bugle call, was written here at that time.

Great plantations like this one predated the Cotton Kingdom in the South. Virginia's first great crop was tobacco, and it was to cultivate the tobacco fields that the early English settlers first turned to slave labor. Tobacco, however, is hard on the soil, and by the time of the Civil War, production in Virginia had slipped to the point where there were more slaves in the state than work. Thus one of Virginia's chief economic functions was to supply slaves to the states farther south.

RICHMOND—NEWPORT NEWS

Eastbound/miles		miles/Westbound
0	RICHMOND (Staples Mill Rd.)	83
8	Main Street (C & O)	75
15	Fort Lee	68
21	Elko	62
26	Roxbury	57
31	Providence Forge	52
37	Walker	46
41	Diascund	42
46	Toano	37
49	Norge	34
56	WILLIAMSBURG	27
60	Grove	23
65	LEE HALL (Fort Eustis)	18
70	Oriana	13
76	Morrison	7
83	NEWPORT NEWS	0

56 **WILLIAMSBURG** *27.* In the eighteenth century Williamsburg served as the capital of Virginia. Here Patrick Henry delivered his fiery call to arms, "Give me liberty, or give me death!" The Virginia legislature, adjourned by order of the royal governor, met in unofficial session at Williamsburg's Raleigh Tavern and drew up resolutions for independence. The College of William and Mary, founded in 1693, is the second oldest university in America. It has occupied the same campus since colonial times.

Williamsburg is unique in its faithful restoration of the old town to its colonial appearance. Original buildings were rehabilitated and repaired; those that had been destroyed were replaced with carefully reconstructed replicas. Millions of Rockefeller dollars paid for the work. Today, arts and crafts of the colonial period are practiced in the shops, and employees wear period costumes. No autos are permitted in the restored area, shuttle buses take tourists from the visitors' center to the colonial village. The Amtrak station is a short taxi ride from the center.

83 **NEWPORT NEWS** *0.* Founded in 1621, Newport News is almost as old as Jamestown. It is named for Captain Christopher Newport, who originally landed the Jamestown colonists in 1607 and who later made a timely return with more people and supplies to bolster the colony.

Today Newport News is not only a large port but also a major shipbuilding and naval center. Langley Air Force Base is served by this station.

Hampton Roads, the natural harbor on which Newport News is built, was the scene of history's first battle between ironclad, steam-powered warships. On March 9, 1862, the Union *Monitor* met the Confederate *Virginia* (sometimes incorrectly called the *Merrimack* because it was built on the hull and engines of that burnt-out Union ship). The battle was technically a draw, but the *Monitor* clearly showed itself to be the faster and better vessel.

3.11   The Trunk Lines

In American railroad parlance, those companies connecting the East Coast with Chicago and St. Louis are known as "trunk lines," those operating between Chicago and the Missouri River are called "granger roads," and those running from the Missouri to the West Coast are called "transcontinentals." In fact, no American railroad is truly transcontinental, because none owns tracks extending from the Atlantic to the Pacific, though both the Canadian Pacific and the Canadian National do so north of the border.

The trunk lines—the east-west routes across the northeastern quarter of the country—used to be the Big Berthas of American railroading. Indeed, the Pennsylvania Railroad, biggest of the big, went so far as to call itself the "Standard Railroad of the World"—and few argued with the claim. Other principal trunk lines included the New York Central, the Erie, the Baltimore and Ohio, and the two Pocohontas region roads, the Chesapeake and Ohio, and the Norfolk and Western.

Today Amtrak operates four routes between the East Coast and the Midwest, two between New York and Chicago and two others between Washington and Chicago. Each of these lines has scenic highpoints, and in general the trains are comfortable if not excessively fast. But the standards of service that prevailed on the *Twentieth Century Limited* are gone, probably forever.

3.12   Albany—Buffalo

The Mohawk Valley, stretching across the length of New York State from the Hudson River to Lake Erie, has been an artery of commerce since Indian times. In 1825 the State of New York constructed the Erie Canal, diverting much of the western trade to Albany and New York City. Just six years later, the third railroad in the United States, the Mohawk and Hudson, went into operation between Albany and Schenectady. Within a few years it was connected with other lines, and shortly after the Civil War, Cornelius Vanderbilt, called "Commodore" because he had run a steamboat line before entering the railroad business, combined it with a number of smaller lines into the New York Central route (now part of Conrail).

The railroad parallels the Mohawk River from Schenectady to Utica, then cuts across the state to Buffalo. On a map, however, the route appears to wiggle its way through central New York. It's anything but a beeline. This is a legacy of the way the through route was put together by combining many short, local railroads.

Amtrak presently offers four trains daily in each direction between Albany and Buffalo. One of these, the *Lake Shore,* goes on to Chicago, and another, the *Maple Leaf,* continues to Toronto. The other two run to Niagara Falls.

0.0 **ALBANY-RENSSELAER** *297.1.* For information on Albany, see section 3.2.

17.4 **SCHENECTADY** *279.7.* For information on Schenectady, see section 3.5.

From Schenectady west as far as Rochester, the railroad parallels the Erie Canal, finished in 1825. This canal, which took 8 years to build, was a major factor in the growth of New York City. For several years after the first railroads were built, those lines paralleling the canal were prohibited from carrying freight, to protect the canal boats from competition. Eventually, however, the superiority of the faster, more flexible railroad became manifest, and the ban was withdrawn.

33.3 **AMSTERDAM** *263.8.* The Hudson River valley is full of Dutch names, but Amsterdam is the last outpost of Dutch influence.

81.3 **Herkimer** *215.8.* The town is named for Nicholas Herkimer, who was killed in 1777 while leading an army of German immigrant farmers to victory in a battle against a force of British, Indians, and Tories at Oriskany.

Thirty miles south of here, on the shore of Lake Otsego, is the picturesque village of Cooperstown. This was the home of the writer James Fenimore Cooper, whose father founded the community—but it's better known to millions of Americans as the site of the National Baseball Hall of Fame. Cooperstown was chosen for this honor because it was the hometown of Major General Abner Doubleday, the Civil War hero who is supposed to have invented baseball. Actually, it's now pretty clear that whatever General Doubleday's accomplishments, he did not invent the national passtime. The game almost certainly was derived from an English predecessor called "rounders," and the first code of rules was the work of a man called Alexander Cartwright.

95.0 **UTICA** *202.1.* An industrial center that grew up next to the Erie Canal.

101.9 **Oriskany** *195.2.* Near here, on August 6, 1777, General Nicholas Herkimer and his farmer patriots had an important encounter with a force of British, Indians, and Tories. By closing the Mohawk Valley to the advance of British Colonel Barry St. Leger and his troops, Herkimer and his men made it impossible for St. Leger to aid or reinforce General Burgoyne when he reached Saratoga, so the little-known Battle of Oriskany had an important bearing on the course of the American Revolution.

108.8 **ROME** *188.3.* Here the railroad line leaves the course of the Erie Canal for some distance, running south to Syracuse. Fort Stanwix, a mile or so south of town, was an important American outpost during the Revolution. Herkimer was actually defending the fort when he fought his battle at Oriskany, 5 miles away.

121.9 **Oneida** *175.2.* This was the site of one of the many experi-

Westbound/miles		miles/Eastbound
0.0	ALBANY-RENSSELAER	297.1
17.4	SCHENECTADY	279.7
33.3	AMSTERDAM	263.8
43.9	Fonda	253.2
49.2	Yosts	247.9
55.3	Palatine	241.8
58.4	Fort Plain	238.7
64.3	St. Johnsville	232.8
74.0	Little Falls	223.1
81.3	Herkimer	215.8
83.4	North Ilion	213.7
95.0	UTICA	202.1
101.9	Oriskany	195.2
108.8	ROME	188.3
117.4	Verona	179.7
121.9	Oneida	175.2
124.7	Wampsville	172.4
127.0	Canastota	170.1
137.2	Kirkville	159.9
139.8	Minoa	157.3
143.1	East Syracuse	154.0
147.9	SYRACUSE	149.2
159.9	Memphis	137.2
165.0	Jordan	132.1
169.4	North Weedsport	127.7
172.8	North Port Byron	124.3
176.2	Fox Ridge	120.9
179.8	Savannah	117.3
185.4	Clyde	111.7
192.4	Lyons	104.7
197.9	Newark	99.2
202.1	East Palmyra	95.0
205.4	Palmyra	91.7
209.2	Walworth	87.9
211.0	North Macedon	86.1
214.0	Wayneport	83.1
218.5	Fairport	78.6
220.4	East Rochester	76.7
227.8	ROCHESTER	69.3
235.3	Cold Water	61.8
239.0	Chili	58.1
243.3	Churchville	53.8
246.4	Bergen	50.7
253.2	South Byron	43.9
260.3	Batavia	36.8
272.3	Corfu	24.8
276.5	Crittenden	20.6
279.5	Wende	17.6
289.8	BUFFALO (Depew Sta.)	7.3
297.1	BUFFALO (Exchange St.)	0.0

mental societies that sprang up in the United States during the first half of the nineteenth century. The Oneida Community practiced simple socialism and plural marriage; it was more successful than most so-called perfectionist experiments because it rested on a solid economic basis—Oneida made a superior brand of animal trap!

Today the experimental community of the 1840s has been replaced by a conventional town, and the animal traps have been replaced as the leading product by Oneida silverware.

127.0 **Canastota** *170.1.* This is the home of former boxing champion Carmen Basilio, who had an onion farm near here. Lake Oneida is a few miles north.

147.9 **SYRACUSE** *149.2.* Named after the Greek colony on the island of Sicily, Syracuse, New York, occupies the site of an Indian village that was the capital of the Iroquois Confederacy. Until after the Civil War the town was the nation's leading source of salt; today it's primarily a manufacturing center and the home of the New York State Fair.

169.4 **North Weedsport** *127.7.* There are several communities with "port" in their names between Syracuse and Rochester. All of them were stops on the Erie Canal.

Ten miles south of this point is the town of Auburn, center of the Finger Lakes region and home of William Seward, secretary of state under Lincoln and the man responsible for purchasing Alaska, known as "Seward's Folly," in 1867. This area takes its name from the five narrow lakes—Cayuga, Otisco, Owasco, Seneca, and Canandaigua—that look on a map like the fingers of a hand.

179.8 **Savannah** *117.3.* Fifteen miles south is Seneca Falls, the town where in 1848 the Women's Rights movement may be said to have begun. Elizabeth Cady Stanton and Lucretia Mott issued a call to a convention to be held at Seneca Falls, where the delegates adopted resolutions based on the Declaration of Independence proclaiming the rights of women to equal status with men. On the southern tip is the city of Ithaca, where "far above Cayuga's waters" stands Cornell University.

197.9 **Newark** *99.2.* Not to be confused with the New Jersey city of the same name, Newark is a pleasant small town. To the south is Seneca Lake.

205.4 **Palmyra** *91.7.* This was the home of Joseph Smith, the most important of all American prophets. In 1830 Smith, who was then twenty-two, claimed to have discovered a set of gold plates on a hillside at nearby Manchester, New York. Several years later he published what he claimed was a translation of the words found on those plates. It was called the Book of Mormon.

The Mormons were not popular with their New York neighbors,

The border between Canada and the United States passes through the 176-foot high Horseshoe Falls at Niagara. (Section 3.13.)

An array of cannons at Fort Ticonderoga, which was captured twice from the British during the Revolutionary War. (See section 3.5.)

so Smith took his followers first to Ohio, then to Missouri, and finally to Nauvoo, Illinois, where a temple was built. But the neighbors in Illinois proved to be even less hospitable than in New York. In 1844 Joseph Smith and his brother Hyrum were murdered by an angry mob while being held at the jail in nearby Carthage, Illinois. A new leader, Brigham Young, then took most of the Mormons across the continent to a new home in Utah.

227.8 **ROCHESTER** *69.3*. This city is named for Colonel Nathaniel Rochester, who planned it at the falls of the Genesee River in 1811. Rochester is the home of the Eastman Kodak company, the great film and camera firm, and as the site of the University of Rochester with its Eastman School of Music. It was also the home of Frederick Douglass, the escaped slave and eloquent speaker who led the abolitionist fight in this country and in England. He is buried in Rochester's Mount Hope Cemetery.

260.3 **Batavia** *36.8*. Eleven miles south is Attica, site of the state prison where serious rioting focused national attention on prison conditions in 1972. The "Attica Accords" brought humanized standards to New York State's prison system.

Batavia was the site of the famous Holland Land Office (now a museum) where millions of dollars' worth of public lands were sold in the early nineteenth century.

Between Batavia and Buffalo the track is straight and level, and it was here one day in May 1893 that engine number 999 set her famous speed record. Engineer Charles Hogan opened the throttle all the way, and the 999 responded by pulling the crack *Empire State Express* at the then unheard-of speed of 112.5 miles per hour. The 999 quickly became the most famous locomotive in America, and you can see it today at the Museum of Science and Industry in Chicago.

289.8 **BUFFALO (Depew Station)** *7.3*. Depew is an eastern suburb of Buffalo, named after Chauncey M. Depew, a former railroad executive. The station here has replaced Buffalo's Art Deco–style Central Terminal, which was too expensive to keep up. Depew Station is convenient to the New York Thruway (Route I-90), to Route I-290, which runs around the city of Buffalo to Niagara Falls, and to the Buffalo airport.

297.1 **BUFFALO (Exchange Street))** *0.0*. Buffalo is the metropolis of western New York State, and it owes its growth primarily to its position at the eastern end of Lake Erie. Until the Welland Canal was built to bypass Niagara Falls, Buffalo was the head of navigation on the western lakes, and the construction of the Erie Canal made it an important transshipment point between lake steamers and canalboats. Buffalo is still a great flour-milling center and an important manufacturing and distribution point.

Exchange Street, convenient to the central business district, is served by through trains from New York to Toronto and Niagara Falls. The *Lake Shore,* en route to Chicago, does not run through this station.

3.13   Buffalo—Toronto

In April 1981 Amtrak and its counterpart north of the border, VIA of Canada, initiated one-seat through service from New York to Toronto. The *Maple Leaf* uses Amfleet equipment and makes the 546-mile run in a little under 12 hours—the best service offered between these cities in many years.

Only the *Maple Leaf* travels as far as Toronto; but two other trains, the *Empire State Express* and the *Mohawk,* go to Niagara Falls each day from New York and Buffalo.

For information on Buffalo, see section 3.12.

17.7 **Tonawanda** *96.4.* The route follows the east bank of the Niagara River, which connects Lake Erie with Lake Ontario. The Niagara (which flows northeast) is also the international boundary. The west side of the river is in Canada. The Canadian shore is not visible, however, because Grand Island (which is American territory) occupies the center of the river between Buffalo and Niagara Falls.

Just beyond Tonawanda the train crosses the New York State Barge Canal, the updated version of the famous old Erie Canal, just above its western terminus at the river.

29.3 **NIAGARA FALLS, N.Y.** *84.8.* No place in America is better known than Niagara, one of the three greatest waterfalls in the world. The falls, about 200 feet high, are divided into the American and Canadian (or Horseshoe) falls by Goat Island. Niagara isn't the highest or the broadest waterfall in the world, but it is easily the most visible and the most spectacular, because the flow of water is always heavy.

Amtrak's Niagara Falls station is located inland, away from the falls, so you can't see much from the train.

31.1 **Suspension Bridge, N.Y.** *83.0.* The great suspension bridge over the Niagara River is some distance north (downstream) from the falls. It was designed by the great bridge builder John A. Roebling, who later created the Brooklyn Bridge. In 1851 Roebling began to string cables across the Niagara, using wire rope that he manufactured himself. Years later the bridge attained notoriety when Big Ed Delahanty, one of baseball's top stars during the Gaslight Era, disappeared while cross-

Northbound/miles   *miles/Southbound*

0.0	BUFFALO (Depew Sta.)	114.1
7.3	BUFFALO (Exchange Street Sta.)	106.8
11.7	Black Rock	102.4
17.7	Tonawanda	96.4
18.3	North Tonawanda	95.8
20.0	Gratwick	94.1
24.3	LaSalle	89.8
27.1	Echota	87.0
29.3	NIAGARA FALLS	84.8
31.1	Suspension Bridge, N.Y. (U.S.)	83.0
31.7	NIAGARA FALLS, ONT. (CANADA)	82.4
40.6	Meritton	73.5
42.9	ST. CATHARINES	71.2
48.6	Jordan	65.5
50.0	Vineland	64.1
54.4	Beamsville	59.7
58.6	GRIMSBY	55.5
63.3	Winona	50.8
68.7	Stoney Creek	45.4
74.8	HAMILTON	39.3
79.2	Aldershot	34.9
82.1	BURLINGTON WEST	32.0
88.5	Bronte	25.6
92.7	OAKVILLE	21.4
98.0	Clarkson	16.1
99.1	Lorne Park	15.0
101.3	Port Credit	12.8
103.0	Lakeview	11.1
107.3	Mimico	6.8
110.6	Sunnyside	3.5
114.1	TORONTO (Union Sta.)	0.0

ing it on a train. No one knows what happened to him.

31.7 **NIAGARA FALLS, ONT.** *82.4.* The stop here includes time for Canadian customs and immigration officials to complete their work.

Downriver (north) from Niagara Falls is the whirlpool in the Niagara River and the town of Queenston, Ontario. This is the site of the Sir Adam Beck power station. Here on a November afternoon in 1965 a simple relay failed to work properly. A surge of power went out over the wires, causing equipment at other plants to shut off. Power went out in Massachusetts at 5:21; Buffalo went dark at 5:22; Syracuse succumbed at 5:25; and 2 minutes later Consolidated Edison's big generators shut down and New York City blacked out. Eight hundred thousand rush-hour commuters were trapped in the subways alone; countless others found themselves stuck in elevators. It took the better

167

part of the night before most power was restored—and all because of a little relay failure at Queenston.

42.9 **ST. CATHARINES** *71.2.* Here the train crosses the Welland Canal, one of the most important artificial waterways on the continent. Extending from Lake Ontario at St. Catharines to Lake Erie at Port Colborne, it bypasses Niagara Falls and opens the way for oceangoing ships to reach the Great Lakes.

Between St. Catharines and Hamilton the tracks follow the southern shore of Lake Ontario, smallest and most northerly of the Great Lakes chain.

74.8 **HAMILTON** *39.3.* With a metropolitan population of half a million, Hamilton is Canada's leading industrial center. The city produces steel, autos, heavy machinery, and other goods. Located at a natural harbor at the western end of Lake Ontario, Hamilton was founded in 1813. The city occupies a narrow strip of flat land along the lake shore.

From beyond the passenger station, trains follow the shoreline around the tip of the lake. The best views are from the right-side windows (going toward Toronto.)

Just west of Hamilton is Bayview Junction, the busiest railroad junction in Canada, where lines converge from three directions. At this point the route curves around to the north shore of Lake Ontario, so that trains that headed west from Buffalo now head east for the last 30 miles into Toronto.

114.1 **TORONTO** *0.0.* Trains approach the city along the lake shore. Unfortunately, an expressway lies between the roadbed and the waterfront, somewhat impeding the view of Exhibition Park, the site of Canada's annual National Exhibition (right side of the train, going into the city).

3.14 Buffalo—Chicago

This is the remainder of the former New York Central's "Water Level Route" to Chicago. Until the early 1950s this was one of the most heavily used passenger routes in America, served by a fleet of trains headed by the famed *Twentieth Century Limited.* But the *Century* made its last run in 1967, and the desultory service still running at the advent of Amtrak was terminated when this route was not included in the original mandate from the secretary of transportation. That left Cleveland, Toledo, and other major cities with no rail passenger service at all, a clearly intolerable situation eventually corrected by the inauguration of the *Lake Shore Limited,* which has proved to be one of Amtrak's most popular Eastern trains. It offers coach, slumbercoach, and sleeping-car accommodations, has connections at Toledo for Detroit and other points in Michigan, and connects at Chicago with the Western streamliners. Recent schedule changes have cut two hours from this train's time, so it is now the fastest thing on rails between the East Coast and Chicago.

The Buffalo–Chicago segment follows the south shore of Lake Erie all the way from Buffalo to Toledo, then takes off across northwestern Ohio and northern Indiana to Chicago. The scenery en route is pleasant if not spectacular, and although there's only one train a day, it serves every station west of Buffalo at a reasonably convenient hour.

0.0 **BUFFALO (Depew Station)** *528.7.* Depew, well east of the city and beyond the airport, is the only Buffalo stop for the *Lake Shore Limited*. On the way through Buffalo it crosses the Buffalo River on a drawbridge. A passing boat will occasionally hold up traffic at this point.

25.6 **Angola** *503.1.* Angola is just north of the Cattaraugus Indian Reservation: it may surprise you that New York State has a substantial Indian population.

While the railroad runs parallel to the Lake Erie shoreline for the entire 295 miles to Toledo, the tracks are often a few miles inland and the lake out of sight, as it is along here.

53.5 **Brocton** *475.2.* Birthplace of George M. Pullman, the carpenter turned carbuilder who put Americans in beds on wheels.

61.7 **Westfield, N.Y.** *467.0.* Six miles south, at the northern tip of a rustic lake, is Chautauqua—site of the Chautauqua Institute. Before the advent of radio, television, and movies, the lecture circuit was almost the only communication between people in the small towns of the west and the great world outside. Chautauqua lecturers brought entertainment and intellectual stimulation to many a small town.

77.2 **North East, Pa.** *451.5.* Fifty miles wide, the neck of Pennsylvania reaches up to the Lake Erie shore. Due south of this point is Titusville, the spot where in 1859 Edwin Drake drilled the first successful oil well. People laughed and called it "Drake's Folly," but when the well began to gush, the whaling industry was doomed.

91.2 **ERIE, PA.** *437.5.* Pennsylvania's only Great Lakes port, Erie is on Presque Isle Bay, formed by a narrow neck of land that curves out into the lake and forms a near island, hence the name.

Presque Isle Bay was the home base of Commodore Oliver Hazard Perry, the American naval officer who was given the task of driving the British from the Great Lakes during the War of 1812. Here he built a small fleet, and late in the summer of 1813 he sailed, looking

BUFFALO—CHICAGO

Westbound/miles   *miles/Eastbound*

Westbound	Station	Eastbound
0.0	BUFFALO (Depew Sta.)	528.7
12.3	Bay View	516.4
21.5	Derby	507.2
25.6	Angola	503.1
35.7	Silver Creek	493.0
44.5	Dunkirk	484.2
53.5	Brocton	475.2
61.7	Westfield	467.0
69.5	Ripley, N.Y.	459.2
77.2	North East, Pa.	451.5
91.2	ERIE	437.5
102.0	Fairview	426.7
106.7	North Girard	422.0
111.1	Springfield, Pa.	417.6
118.7	Conneaut, Ohio	410.0
132.0	Ashtabula	396.7
141.3	Geneva	387.4
146.8	Madison	381.9
151.7	Perry	377.0
157.5	Painesville	371.2
163.6	Mentor	365.1
168.0	Willoughby	360.7
179.4	Collinwood	349.3
181.6	East Cleveland	347.1
189.3	CLEVELAND (Lake Front Sta.)	339.4
189.3	CLEVELAND	339.4
194.8	Linndale	333.9
200.7	Berea	328.0
203.4	Olmstead Falls	325.3
209.4	Shawville	319.3
213.8	ELYRIA (Lorain)	314.9
220.3	Amherst	308.4
227.8	Vermilion	300.9
237.2	Huron	291.5
248.4	SANDUSKY	280.3
251.2	Venice	277.5
253.8	Baybridge	274.9
256.0	Danbury	272.7
258.1	Gypsum	270.6
261.3	Port Clinton	267.4
267.1	Lacarne	261.6
272.5	Oak Harbor	256.2
275.8	Rocky Ridge	252.9
278.5	Graytown	250.2
283.0	Martin	245.7
287.7	Millbury Junction	241.0
295.3	TOLEDO	233.4
295.3	TOLEDO	233.4

for the British squadron. He ran them down at Put-In Bay near Sandusky, Ohio, at the other end of the lake. On September 10, 1813, in a bloody day-long engagement, the British fleet was destroyed. After this battle Perry made his famous report: "We have met the enemy and they are ours."

Erie is today a heavy manufacturing center as well as a lake port. General Electric has a big plant here that turns out locomotives, among other things. Like the lake on which it is built, the city is named for the Erie Indians, whose lands these once were. The town was laid out in 1795 and incorporated as a city in 1851.

118.7 **Conneaut, Ohio** *410.0.* Conneaut is an Indian word meaning "fish," and this was a fishing village from its founding in 1793 until the ore boats began to dock here in the late nineteenth century. Today the town is one of several ports through which ore and coal reach Pittsburgh's steel mills.

Conneaut is also a railroad town. The old Nickel Plate Road (now Norfolk and Western) has yards here. The Nickel Plate, built primarily to annoy the Vanderbilt monopoly into buying it, and officially known as the New York, Chicago, and St. Louis Railroad, acquired its unusual nickname because the price Vanderbilt paid for it was so inflated that some wag observed that it must have been plated with nickel.

132.0 **Ashtabula** *396.7.* Another Lake Erie port city, Ashtabula is, like its neighbor Conneaut, an important unloading point for ore shipments going to the Pittsburgh steel mills. Ashtabula was the site of one of America's most disastrous train wrecks when a passenger train fell through a collapsing bridge here in 1876.

163.6 **Mentor** *365.1.* Nearby is the home of James A. Garfield, third of the six Ohio presidents. Garfield's career is the epitome of the American success story. He really was born in a log cabin and he spent his youth as a canal boy, driving mules. He worked his way through college, became a teacher, studied law, and was admitted to the Ohio bar. When the Civil War came, he was commissioned as a Union officer and served with distinction.

After Lee surrendered, Garfield entered politics as a member of the Ohio legislature before receiving the 1880 Republican presidential nomination as a dark-horse candidate. In a close election he defeated Democrat Winfield Hancock—another former Union general—but served only 4 months in the White House before he was fatally shot by Charles Guiteau, a disappointed office-seeker. His home has been preserved as a museum.

179.4 **Collinwood** *349.3.* No passenger stop here, but an important service stop at the big engine terminal east of Cleveland. From 1930 until 1953 passenger trains running through Cleveland's Union Terminal changed to electric engines at this point, but after the diesels came, the electrics were no longer necessary.

181.6 **East Cleveland** *347.1.* Just across the city boundary is the Lake View Cemetery, where James A. Garfield and John D. Rockefeller are buried. It was in Cleveland that Rockefeller got his start, as a commission merchant. The profits that he made in that venture he invested in the oil business—but old John D. was shrewd enough to see that the big money in oil was not in drilling wells but in monopolizing the refining process. At one time Rockefeller's Standard Oil combine controlled 90 percent of all American refining capacity.

189.3 **CLEVELAND** *339.4.* For information on the city, see section 2.13.

213.8 **ELYRIA (Lorain and Oberlin)** *314.9.* Lorain is a lake-shore town about 15 miles northwest. Oberlin, site of Oberlin College, is about the same distance southwest. Oberlin College has a number of important distinctions. It was the first American institution of higher learning to enroll black students, and the first to admit women on an equal basis with men.

220.3 **Amherst** *308.4.* The town was named for Amherst, Massachusetts. Most of the early settlers in northern Ohio came from New England.

227.8 **Vermilion** *300.9.* At this point the rails return to the Lake Erie shore. Vermilion is the home of the Great Lakes Historical Society Museum. The lakes have both a fascinating and tempestuous history, and many a good ship has gone to the bottom while navigating these, the largest chain of freshwater lakes in the world.

237.2 **Huron** *291.5.* Eight miles inland is the hamlet of Milan (pronounced *My-lan* in Ohio), where Thomas Alva Edison was born in 1847. He had only 3 months of formal schooling, yet he owned more patents than any other inventor. When he died in 1931, the *New York Times* calculated that the total value of his inventions, at that time, was more than $25 billion.

248.4 **SANDUSKY** *280.3.* Sandusky enjoys a fine natural harbor, protected from the storms of the open lake by a peninsula and a number of islands. Off one of these, South Bass Island, is Put-In Bay, where Oliver Hazard Perry destroyed the British fleet in 1813. The Perry Victory and International Peace Memorial on the island can be reached by ferryboat.

Broad, shallow Sandusky Bay extends westward and inland for several miles. Its north shore is formed by the Marblehead Peninsula. The railroad and Route 2 cross the bay to reach Toledo by the shortest practical route.

253.8 **Baybridge** *274.9.* The town is at the south end of the bridge-and-fill across Sandusky Bay. It's about 2 miles from here to Danbury, on the opposite shore.

295.3 **TOLEDO, OHIO** *233.4.* Built on the Maumee River where it enters Lake Erie, Toledo stands near the site of Fort Miami. Just south, in 1794, General "Mad Anthony" Wayne (who was in reality anything but mad), defeated the Indians at Fallen Timbers, opening the way for white settlement of northwestern Ohio and all of northern Indiana.

Modern Toledo dates from 1833, and for a short time, in 1835,

Ohio and Michigan actually came to the brink of civil war over who would own Toledo before Congress awarded possession to Ohio. To compensate, however, Congress gave Michigan the Northern Peninsula—geographically part of Wisconsin.

With its strategic location at the western end of Lake Erie, Toledo has grown into a major inland port with particularly heavy traffic in coal, iron ore, and grain.

Toledo is also a manufacturing town, known for its glass factories and auto-parts plants. Oil refineries, chemical plants, machine tool works, and railroad yards complete the industrial picture.

At Toledo connections are made for Detroit and points in southern Michigan. Between Toledo and Elkhart, Indiana, Amtrak trains operate over the so-called Air Line route. This has nothing to do with DC-10s; it's called the Air Line because from the outskirts of Toledo to Butler, Indiana, a distance of 68½ miles, there isn't a single curve.

386.7 **Kendallville, Ind.** *142.0.* This is the so-called Limberlost Country recollected in the novels of Gene Stratton Porter. Mrs. Porter is commemorated by a nearby state memorial.

Although Indiana isn't commonly thought of as Indian country, the state got its name because early white settlers were amazed at the number of Indians they encountered here.

428.2 **ELKHART** *100.5.* Elkhart is a railroad division point where engine crews change, but it's much better known for the musical instruments made here. From 1880, when Charles G. Conn made the first American-produced cornet in Elkhart, until 1970, when a new owner moved production out of town, this was the undisputed brass instrument capital of America. What's more, it may soon be again, for an Elkhart businessman and musician has purchased the Conn Company from the conglomerate, moved the offices back to town, and plans to bring production back as well. So, the trumpet you refused to practice on probably came from Elkhart, and the one your kids will refuse to play 10 years from now may come from here too.

445.3 **SOUTH BEND** *83.4.* Named for a bend in the St. Joseph River, this was the site of the portage used by La Salle, the French explorer, to cross from the Lake Michigan watershed to the Kankakee River, which eventually reaches the Mississippi.

To most Americans, South Bend means Notre Dame, the university that football made famous. Today, however, Rockne, Leahy, and Parseghian are not all Notre Dame is about; the university has achieved recognition for its academic programs, admitted women, and made great strides toward becoming the preeminent Catholic institution in the nation. Oh, yes—they still have a pretty good football team.

South Bend was never a true "college town" like, say, Ann Arbor. It has always been a manufacturing city, but its best-known industry belongs to the past—the Studebaker Company. This firm began by building wagons and ended by producing the small cars of the future at a time when Americans were buying gas-guzzlers. Throughout, Studebaker maintained a reputation for fine craftsmanship, and many of its products are still on the road.

470.0 **La Porte** *58.7.* *La Porte* means "the door" in French. The door in this case opens on the Indiana Dunes, the fascinating "moving mountains" whose beauty and fragile ecology has attracted sportsmen and scientists for a century and more. The dunes are found along the southern and eastern shores of Lake Michigan. They extend from west of La Porte to a point just east of Gary.

488.5 **Porter** *40.2.* This is an important junction point where two railroads from Michigan join the line from Toledo and share the tracks for the rest of the way into Chicago.

502.6 **Gary** *26.1.* Gary makes steel, and steel literally made Gary; the town was built from the ground up when the United States Steel Company located its new plant here in 1906. The Gary Works are visible on the north side of the train (right side, going west) and are one of the biggest steel mills in the United States.

507.0 **Pine Junction** *21.7.* At this point trains from Pittsburgh join the *Lake Shore Limited's* route from Buffalo sharing the track for the remainder of the distance to Chicago.

509.4 **Indiana Harbor** *19.3.* Like neighboring Gary, this is a steel town; the major producers are Inland and Youngstown. The area takes its name from the Indiana Harbor canal used by the big ore boats that dock here to feed the steel mills.

512.8 **HAMMOND-WHITING** *15.9.* This new station serves more than half a million residents of the Calumet area of northern Indiana; it is also convenient for passengers to and from the South Side of Chicago. The big Lever Brothers soap factory stands beside the tracks to the south (left side, going west), and you may get a glimpse of Lake Michigan to the north.

If Gary and Indiana Harbor mean steel, Whiting is synonymous with oil. Several big refineries are here, and the tracks are lined with huge storage tanks protected by earthen fire walls. The flames you may see leaping from the tops of tall steel towers result from the burning of impure, combustible gases to prevent explosions.

513.3 **Roby, Ind.** *15.4.* This point is just short of the Illinois state line. It is marked by a power plant and a couple of large grain elevators. The Indiana Toll Road (I-90) comes up from the south and parallels the railroad into Chicago.

516.1 **South Chicago, Ill.** *12.6.* Actually part of the city of Chicago, this is the site of still another major steel mill—U.S. Steel's South Works. Trains cross the Calumet River on a large lift bridge.

The adjacent Chicago Skyway rises high into the air and crosses the river on a fixed bridge with clearance enough to let the tall-masted ore boats pass underneath.

521.7 **Englewood** *7.0.* At one time Englewood was a stop for trains entering Chicago from the south and east; but with the decline of the surrounding neighborhood, the station was closed. Amtrak trains cross the old Rock Island Line, now bankrupt, at Englewood. The part of its track is today used mostly by commuter trains.

527.1 **21st Street** *1.6.* This is one of the most important and busiest junctions in Chicago—a city full of junctions. Here trains from St. Louis and Los Angeles join the eastern lines; together they cross the South Branch of the Chicago River on a double-tracked lift bridge.

Just north of the bridge is Amtrak's 16th Street coach yard and engine terminal, where maintenance is performed on the cars that carry passengers to every corner of the United States (right side of the train, coming into the city). To the left is the Burlington Northern's suburban coach yard.

528.7 **CHICAGO (Union Station)** *0.0.* All Amtrak trains serving Chicago now use Union Station, on the west bank of the South Branch of the Chicago River at Canal and Adams streets. You no longer have to change stations in Chicago unless you're taking a commuter train or the electric South Shore Line. One thing has not changed, however—no passenger train runs *through* Chicago; all trains entering the city terminate here, just as they have for 130 years.

For information on the city, see section 2.11.

3.15   *Philadelphia—Pittsburgh*

This is one of the oldest, most historic, and most interesting railroad routes in America. It was formerly the main line of the Pennsylvania Railroad, once the giant of the American transportation industry. Today the eastern section, from Philadelphia to Harrisburg, is owned by Amtrak, while the trans-Allegheny line from Harrisburg to Pittsburgh is a Conrail property.

The country traversed ranges from Philadelphia and its "Main Line" suburbs, through the Pennsylvania Dutch country, to the rugged crossing of the Allegheny Mountains including the Horseshoe Curve. Parts of the route incorporate sections of the Pennsylvania Main Line of Public Works, that fantastic combination of canals, railways, and inclined planes by means of which Pennsylvania attempted to meet the competition of the Erie Canal.

0.0 **PHILADELPHIA** *347.9.* For information on the city, see section 2.31. For notes on the route from New York to North Philadelphia, see section 3.8.

4.1 **52nd Street** *343.8.* A hundred years ago this was called Hestonville and was outside the city limits. A branch line to the anthracite coal fields of east central Pennsylvania diverges here. At one time, anthracite or "hard" coal was highly sought as a heating and cooking fuel because it burns relatively cleanly. Today there is little need for anthracite, but a century ago it was an important factor in Pennsylvania's economy.

5.6 **OVERBROOK** *342.3.* From Overbrook, which marks the Philadelphia city limits, to Paoli, 14 miles west, lies a string of beautiful suburbs collectively known as the Main Line. This elegant residential area was laid out by the Pennsylvania Railroad after the Civil War. The company encouraged its executives to buy homes here, and soon this chain of towns became *the* place to live for wealthy Philadelphia families. They commuted to work on the Pennsylvania's "main line," hence the name.

PHILADELPHIA—PITTSBURGH

Westbound/miles		miles/Eastbound
0.0	PHILADELPHIA (Penn Center)	347.9
0.9	30th STREET	347.0
4.1	52nd Street	343.8
5.6	OVERBROOK	342.3
6.1	Merion	341.8
7.0	NARBETH	340.9
7.6	Wynnewood	340.3
8.6	ARDMORE	339.3
9.3	Haverford	338.6
10.3	BRYN MAWR	337.6
11.0	Rosemont	336.9
12.1	Villanova	335.8
13.1	RADNOR	334.8
13.9	St. Davids	334.0
14.6	WAYNE	333.3
15.5	Strafford	332.4
16.6	Devon	331.3
17.7	Berwyn	330.2
18.7	Doylesford	329.2
20.0	PAOLI	327.9
21.7	MALVERN	326.2
24.0	EXTON (Frazer)	323.9
25.5	Glen Loch	322.4

26.8	Ship Road	321.1
27.5	Whiteland	320.4
28.5	WHITFORD	319.4
31.6	DOWNINGTOWN	315.3
38.6	COATESVILLE	309.3
42.2	Pomeroy	305.7
44.3	PARKESBURG	303.6
47.1	Atglen	300.8
48.5	Christiana	299.4
51.1	Gap	296.8
54.4	Vintage	293.5
56.5	Leaman Place	291.4
58.0	Gordonville	289.9
61.1	Bird in Hand	286.8
62.8	Witmer	285.1
67.9	LANCASTER	280.0
75.4	Landisville	272.5
76.1	Salunga	271.8
79.4	MOUNT JOY	268.5
80.6	Florin	267.3
84.0	Rheems	263.9
86.2	ELIZABETHTOWN	261.7
93.3	Royalton	254.6
93.7	MIDDLETOWN	254.2
98.0	Highspire	249.9
101.2	Steelton	246.7
103.2	HARRISBURG	244.7
103.2	HARRISBURG	244.7
110.4	Marysville	237.5
118.0	Duncannon	229.9
130.6	Newport	217.3
135.9	Millerstown	212.0
140.9	Thompsontown	207.0
143.7	Van Dyke	204.2
149.4	Port Royal	198.5
152.2	Mifflin	195.7
159.1	Hawstone	188.8
163.8	LEWISTOWN	184.1
175.7	McVeytown	172.2
179.9	Ryde	168.0
182.0	Pa. Sand Glass Corp.	165.9
185.7	Newton Hamilton	162.2
188.3	Mount Union	159.6
191.5	Mapleton	156.4
200.2	HUNTINGDON	147.7
204.4	Warrior Ridge	143.5
208.3	Petersburg	141.6
209.8	Barree	138.1
213.5	Union Furnace	134.4
218.5	Tyrone Forge	129.4
219.8	TYRONE	128.1
226.9	Bellwood	121.0

234.0	ALTOONA	113.9

234.0	ALTOONA	113.9
245.8	Gallitzin	102.1
248.5	Cresson	99.4
251.5	Lilly	96.4
255.4	Portage	92.5
260.2	Summerhill	87.7
261.2	Ehrenfeld	86.7
262.1	South Fork	85.8
269.0	Conemaugh	78.9
271.5	JOHNSTOWN	76.4
275.8	Seward	72.1
284.9	New Florence	63.0
290.5	Bolivar	57.4
295.6	Torrance	52.3
302.9	Derry	45.0
307.8	LATROBE	40.1
313.0	Donohoe	34.9
317.1	GREENSBURG	30.8
319.0	Radebaugh	28.9
320.7	Grapeville	27.2
321.2	Jeanette	26.7
322.7	Penn	25.2
324.2	Manor	23.7
325.6	Shafton	22.3
326.5	Irwin	21.4
327.2	Larimer	20.7
328.8	Ardara	19.1
330.9	Trafford	17.0
332.5	PITCAIRN	15.4
334.1	Wilmerding	13.8
335.2	Turtle Creek	12.7
335.7	East Pittsburgh	12.2
337.0	Bessemer	10.9
337.8	Braddock	10.1
338.3	Copeland	9.6
338.9	Hawkins (Rankin)	9.0
339.8	Swissvale	8.1
340.6	Edgewood	7.3
341.3	Wilkensburg	6.6
342.3	Homewood	5.6
343.3	East Liberty	4.6
344.2	Roup	3.7
344.7	Shadyside	3.2
347.9	PITTSBURGH	0.0

Several of the Main Line suburbs have Welsh names—Bryn Mawr, Radnor, St. David's, Narbeth—but not because of any real Welsh influence in the area. The promoters of Main Line real estate gave the towns these names simply because they sounded high class.

9.3 **Haverford** 338.6. Quaker-sponsored Haverford College is located here.

10.3 **BRYN MAWR** *337.6.* This is the home of Bryn Mawr College for women, one of the "Seven Sisters."

12.1 **Villanova** *335.8.* One of the few Main Line suburbs that date back to the pre–Civil War period, this is the site of Villanova University, a well-known Catholic school.

20.0 **PAOLI** *327.9.* This station marks the end of the Main Line commuting district. It is named for a tavern and stagecoach stop built at this site about 1775 and named in honor of a Corsican general, Pasquale de Paoli. The tavern was an important stop on the Philadelphia-Lancaster Turnpike, and when the Philadelphia and Columbia Railroad was laid out in 1834, the former coaching inn became a railroad station.

Paoli is the closest Amtrak station to the Valley Forge National Historic Site, marking the place where George Washington's ragged and hungry Continental Army camped through the miserable winter of 1777–78.

25.5 **Glen Loch** *322.4.* From approximately this point the route passes through the so-called Pennsylvania Dutch country, home of hex signs on barns and shoo-fly pie. Of course, the Pennsylvania Dutch are not Dutch at all, but *Deutsch*—German. William Penn himself was responsible for the original German settlement in Pennsylvania. In his search for sober, hardworking colonists for his new land grant, he traveled to the Rhineland, where he made a deal with a Protestant minister called Daniel Francis Pastorius. The minister and his associates bought 15,000 acres of Penn's Pennsylvania farmland. They proved to be industrious people and ideal colonists, and they prospered to such a degree that thousands of their countrymen followed them to this area.

26.8 **Ship Road** *321.1.* Like Paoli, this community owes its name to a coaching inn, The Ship, which once stood at this site.

44.3 **PARKESBURG** *303.6.* Parkesburg sprang into existence in 1834 when the Philadelphia and Columbia Railroad chose this spot— midway between its terminal cities—as the site of its repair shops.

51.1 **Gap** *296.8.* The name is derived from a gap in the hills through which the railroad passes from the Delaware watershed into that of the Susquehanna.

58.0 **Gordonville** *289.9.* Some of the Pennsylvania Dutch people belong to a sect called the Amish. They refer to themselves as "the plain people." They refuse to ride in automobiles, they wear somber clothes of black or gray, fastened with hooks instead of buttons, and they shun public schools in their efforts to raise their children in the old tradition. Some important Amish settlements are located around Gordonville.

This part of Pennsylvania has colorful and unusual town names. In the vicinity are Intercourse, Blue Ball, Fivepointville, Goodville, and Paradise. Robert Fulton, inventor of the steamboat, was born about 20 miles south of here at Chestnut Level.

61.1 **Bird in Hand** *286.8.* This is another name derived from a stagecoach inn, and as quaint as any you'll find.

About 12 miles due north of here is one of the most interesting places in the United States—the Ephrata Cloisters. This religious community was founded by a German immigrant minister named Conrad Beissel, who must have been an exceptionally brilliant and forceful personality: he was pastor, colonizer, social reformer, farmer, builder, inventor, and musician.

67.9 **LANCASTER** *280.0.* This is the largest city in the region, unofficial capital of the Pennsylvania Dutch country, and one of the oldest communities in Pennsylvania outside of Philadelphia itself.

Thus far the current Amtrak route follows the right-of-way of the old Philadelphia and Columbia Railroad, constructed in 1834 as the easternmost link in the Commonwealth of Pennsylvania's ambitious Main Line of Public Works.

The completion of the Erie Canal in 1825 had diverted much trans-Allegheny trade to New York. Dismayed, Philadelphia businessmen countered with a complicated system of railroads, canals, and inclined planes designed to surmount the mountains and draw the trade of the Ohio valley to Philadelphia.

Construction began in 1826, but the system was not completed for another 9 years. The Main Line of Public Works began at the Philadelphia Exchange, where canalboats were loaded on flatcars and carried 82 miles by rail to Columbia, west of Lancaster on the Susquehanna River. There the boats were lowered into the water, using the Susquehanna and Juniata Rivers and a series of canals to reach Hollidaysburg, at the base of Allegheny Mountain (near Altoona). From there a series of fourteen inclined planes took the boats, in sections, over the summit of the mountains. Another short section of railroad then brought them to Johnstown, where they were reassembled and put back into the water for the remainder of the canal trip to Pittsburgh. The size of the undertaking may be grasped if you consider that the western section alone included 68 locks, 16 aqueducts, 10 major dams, and 2 canal tunnels, including one under downtown Pittsburgh.

The Main Line system operated for two decades but was never as efficient as the Erie Canal. The completion of the Pennsylvania Railroad (opened in 1854) made the inclined planes instantly obsolete, and in June 1857 the entire state system was sold to the only interested buyer—the Pennsylvania Railroad—for less than a quarter of its original cost. The railroad incorporated parts of the system into its own lines, including the strategic segment of the Philadelphia and Columbia east of Lancaster, but the cumbersome, colorful inclined planes were immediately abandoned. The last of the canals was used until 1903, but today little remains of the Pennsylvania Main Line of Public Works except the national historic site near Portage, where the inclined planes surmounted the crest of the Alleghenies.

93.3 **Royalton** *254.6.* Beyond this point the rails follow the east bank of the Susquehanna River into Harrisburg.

98.0 **Highspire** *249.9.* Just beyond the town the Pennsylvania Turnpike passes overhead. The original turnpike extended from a point just west of Harrisburg to Irwin, near Pittsburg, crossing the Alleghenies through a series of tunnels. It was built on the unfinished grade of the South Penn Railroad, a nineteenth-century attempt to compete with the Pennsylvania that was never completed.

103.2 **HARRISBURG** *244.7.* This is the capital of Pennsylvania. Nearby Three Mile Island is where a nuclear power plant malfunctioned in 1979. Had the radiation release been larger, the authorities would have had to put a fence around Harrisburg and seal off the whole area for the next 150,000 years. Also nearby is Gettysburg, where the Civil War battle was fought and where Lincoln delivered his famous address.

Harrisburg is the end of the electrification that extends all the way from New York. Diesel locomotives pull all trains west of this point. Also, beyond Harrisburg trains are operated by Conrail, which owns the track. Amtrak owns the rail facilities east of here.

Five miles beyond Harrisburg the rails swing west to cross the Susquehanna River on a graceful stone arched bridge three-fifths of a mile long—the longest structure of its type in the world. From here to Duncannon the rails follow the west bank of the river.

118.0 **Duncannon** *229.9.* Just beyond this point is the junction of the Juniata River with the Susquehanna. The Juniata valley forms a natural gate through the Buffalo, Shade, and Tuscarora mountains— the three easternmost ridges of the Alleghenies. Following the path of the old Main Line canal route, the present railroad turns up the Juniata, following its course for the next hundred miles.

163.8 **LEWISTOWN** *184.1.* This is the station for State College, home of Penn State university.

188.3 **Mount Union** *159.6.* Near here the Juniata squeezes through a gap in Jacks Mountain called "Jacks Narrows." The old canal and the present railroad follow the river. At one time, canal locks were located in the narrows to help lift boats up and over this hump.

191.5 **Mapleton** *156.4.* This is the western end of the Jacks Narrows passage.

200.2 **HUNTINGDON** *147.7.* The town was founded in 1777 by Reverend William Smith of Philadelphia, who was an official of the

University of Pennsylvania as well as a land speculator. He named the place for the countess of Huntingdon, who had given money to the University.

A short distance east of here the Little Juniata River comes down from the north to join the Juniata. The rails now follow the course of the Little Juniata almost to its source, near Altoona.

218.5 **Tyrone Forge** *129.4.* In the nineteenth century much iron smelting was done in the vicinity. One of these works was here.

219.8 **TYRONE** *128.1.* Still following the Little Juniata, the rails turn sharply southwest here as they enter Logan Valley, which parallels Allegheny Mountain, the highest peak in the range to which it gives its name.

234.0 **ALTOONA** *113.9.* Altoona has always been a railroad town. It was first settled as a construction camp for the Pennsylvania Railroad in 1849, and the Pennsylvania later established its principal shops in the city. More than 6,000 steam locomotives were built in Altoona, not to mention countless cars and other equipment.

The city stands at the base of the big grade over Allegheny Mountain. From here on there's no watercourse to follow—it's just a hard pull up and over the hump. In 11 miles from Altoona to the summit at Gallitzin, the rails must climb over 1,000 feet; that's a good, stiff 1.8 percent grade, enough to tax any locomotive.

The climb begins immediately after leaving the Altoona station, with the tracks climbing the west side of Logan Valley. At Burgoon Run, the route turns west and follows the northern side of this little stream to its head. Here, about 6 miles from Altoona, is the Horseshoe Curve, probably the best-known piece of railroad engineering in the United States. The curve begins when the train rounds Kittanning Point into a little valley. Across the way, but more than 100 feet higher up, the route doubles back on itself. The horseshoe is about 1,400 feet across, but nearly a mile around, and by using this extra distance the engineers were able to gain enough elevation to reach the summit without employing even steeper grades.

The Horseshoe Curve was opened to traffic in February 1854. It was the last segment of the Pennsylvania Railroad to be built, and almost from the first day it became a landmark and tourist attraction. During World War II it was considered so important to the defense effort that it was placed under 24-hour guard—and indeed, Nazi saboteurs captured on Long Island were found to have marked the Horseshoe as a prime target. The curve was designated a national historic landmark in 1966, and a souvenir shop here attracts a quarter of a million visitors every year.

Speaking of souvenirs, at the center of the Horseshoe you will see a steam locomotive on exhibit. This is a class K-4 "Pacific" type, number 1361, used on the Pennsylvania Railroad for a quarter of a century. This engine ran more than 2 million miles in its working career, mostly in fast passenger service. Now it watches the younger, stronger diesels negotiate the big curve where it once ran.

For the best views of the Horseshoe, take a left-side window seat when traveling west from Philadelphia.

245.8 **Gallitzin** *102.1*. This is at a crest of the Alleghenies, 2,200 feet above sea level. This point marks the divide between the Atlantic and Mississippi watersheds. Three tunnels, side by side, are necessary to carry the heavy rail traffic under the crest; two were built in 1852 and the third was added in 1904.

Gallitzin is named for a pioneer Roman Catholic priest who gave up the life of a Russian nobleman to become a missionary. He came to Pennsylvania in 1789 and settled at nearby Loretto (now home of the College of St. Francis). When he died in 1840, his name was given to this mountaintop town.

248.5 **Cresson** *99.4*. Here, in a pretty mountain setting with pure, clean air, Andrew Carnegie once had a summer home. Other Pittsburgh millionaires joined him, and in the 1870s Cresson was a popular resort, complete with grand hotel and grand mansions.

But it had one serious drawback. There was no lake at Cresson, no boating or fishing, and because of this a number of Pittsburgh nabobs remained unsatisfied with the place. In 1879 some of them bought the old earth dam at South Fork, 15 miles above Johnstown, and filled the reservoir behind it to create Lake Conemaugh, 2 miles long, a mile wide, and 70 feet deep. Along its western shore they erected a large clubhouse and a number of elegant summer homes. After that, Cresson's popularity declined, and Lake Conemaugh replaced it as Pittsburgh's favorite mountain retreat.

About 4 miles east of Cresson on U.S.-Route 22 is the Allegheny Portage National Historic Site. Here the Main Line of Public Works topped the summit of Allegheny Mountain; boats were hauled up the series of inclined planes by stationary steam engines. The Lemon House, at the summit of the planes, served as a station for the Main Line and is still standing, as a museum.

251.5 **Lilly** *96.4*. The descent from Gallitzin is much less steep than the climb up the east side of the mountain. The grade is only about 1 percent (52 feet to the mile) down to the Conemaugh River at Lilly. From this point the rails follow the Conemaugh for 45 miles.

262.1 **South Fork** *85.8*. The station takes its name from the South Fork of the Little Conemaugh River, which flows into the Conemaugh here. About 3 miles up the South Fork stood the earth dam that those Pittsburgh millionaires bought in 1879, when they abandoned lakeless Cresson as a summer resort.

This dam had originally been built to supply water for the Main Line of Public Works canal system. When the Main Line was sold to the Pennsylvania Railroad in 1857, the dam was no longer of any use and was simply abandoned. At that time it had little water behind it.

After 1879, however, when Lake Conemaugh was filled, the structure was holding back 20 million tons of water. No attention was paid to the ominous facts: The dam had had virtually no maintenance since its construction 40 years before; there was an inadequate spillway and no sluice gates; and the thriving industrial town of Johnstown was just 15 miles down the Conemaugh. Any break in the earth dam would clearly threaten disaster, but there had been a number of previous false alarms and nobody took the possibility of a break in the dam very seriously.

On Thursday, May 30, 1889, a titanic rainstorm struck western Pennsylvania, drenching the land so that it could hold no more water. The runoff from the surrounding hills began to pour into Lake Conemaugh, which rose 2 feet during the night. By the next morning it was clear that the lake would soon reach the top of the 72-foot earthen dam and begin to pour over the rim. When that happened, the water would soon cut a groove into the center of the dam and, as the groove got deeper and wider, the dam would collapse. Warnings of the coming disaster were sent to Johnstown, but ignored.

At 11:00 A.M. on Friday morning, Lake Conemaugh began to wash over the lip of the dam. By 2:00 there was a gash 10 feet deep in the center of the structure. At 3:00 the old dam collapsed, and millions of tons of water came charging down the valley at 20 miles per hour, destroying everything it hit. The force of the 40-foot wall of water was so great that it scoured the valley clean of trees, buildings, animals, and everything else. From South Fork to Johnstown, today's railroad follows the path of that rampaging flood of 1889.

269.0 **Conemaugh** *78.9.* At this suburb of Johnstown a strange drama was played out on the afternoon of the flood. An engine was coming down from South Fork to Johnstown, when the crew heard a roaring sound behind them. Looking back, they saw the menacing 40-foot wall of flood water. The engineer opened the throttle and, with the whistle screaming a warning, that locomotive raced the flood to Conemaugh, where the valley widens out. The engine won by seconds. Just as it burst from the valley and into the clear, the flood hit the town and leveled everything in sight. Because of the warning whistle, however, many lives were saved in Conemaugh.

271.5 **JOHNSTOWN** *76.4.* Since the Civil War, Johnstown has been an iron and steel center. It lies at the confluence of the Conemaugh and the Stony Creek rivers, walled in on all sides by the Alleghenies.

Lying as it does, the city is in constant peril from floods. The disaster of 1889 was by no means the only inundation Johnstown has experienced, but none of Johnstown's other drenchings compares to the disaster of May 31, 1889. At 4:07 P.M., that devastating wall of water came pounding through the same gap used by Amtrak trains today and struck Johnstown with all its force. In 10 minutes practically every building in town was destroyed, and one of every ten residents of the city died. The Johnstown Flood is the second worst natural disaster in American history. Only the Galveston Hurricane of 1900, in which at least 6,000 people perished, took more lives.

In the wake of the Johnstown disaster, Clara Barton and her American Red Cross proved their value for the first time. Miss Barton got to Johnstown 5 days after the disaster and stayed 5 months, supervising the distribution of half a million dollars' worth of aid to the stricken town.

Within 10 days of the disaster the Johnstown mills announced their intention to rebuild, and they are there today. Also still in place is a stone viaduct across the Conemaugh, north of the station. It was against this substantial stone bridge that the Johnstown flood finally broke. Because the bridge held, communities downstream were spared Johnstown's fate.

290.5 **Bolivar** *57.4.* Near here the tracks pass through the Packsaddle Gap, cut by the Conemaugh River through Laurel and Chestnut hills. These are the westernmost ridges of the Alleghenies.

307.8 **LATROBE** *40.1.* The town is named for Benjamin Latrobe (1764–1820), the first major professional architect to work in the United States. His influence was enormous, for it was Latrobe who introduced Greek and Renaissance forms to this country. His best-known work is the south wing of the U.S. Capitol in Washington.

Latrobe, Pennsylvania, is the hometown of golfer Arnold Palmer.

317.1 **GREENSBURG** *30.8.* This town is surrounded by a great coal mining area. Appropriately enough, Westmoreland County was the birthplace of the steel-and-coke millionaire Henry Clay Frick.

334.1 **Wilmerding** *13.8.* Here, along the banks of Turtle Creek, is the Westinghouse plant. George Westinghouse was only twenty-three when, in 1869, he perfected the first air brake, the device that made high-speed travel possible. Later he went into electricity, developing alternating current for industrial use in competition with direct current, which was promoted by Thomas Edison.

From a shack on these factory grounds, in November 1920, KDKA broadcast returns from the Harding-Cox presidential election, thus becoming the first commercial radio station to go on the American airwaves.

337.0 **Bessemer** *10.9.* In 1856 a British inventor, Sir Henry Bessemer, developed a new process for turning iron into steel. Eight years later Andrew Carnegie introduced the Bessemer Converter to the United States at a plant near here.

337.8 **Braddock** *10.1.* On approximately this site British General Edward Braddock and his force were attacked and defeated by the French and their Indian allies on July 9, 1755. Braddock was mortally wounded, and he died during the subsequent British retreat. He was succeeded by a young colonel from Virginia named Washington, who led the British and colonial troops to safety.

Three years later the British returned in force and captured the French outpost at Fort Duquesne, which had been Braddock's objective. They renamed this fort, which stood at the head of the Ohio River, after the prime minister of England, William Pitt. The town that grew up around Fort Pitt was called Pittsburg; later the spelling was altered to Pittsburgh, the form we know today.

339.8 **Swissvale** *8.1.* A residential borough of Greater Pittsburgh that acquired its name from the original developer, a man named Swisshelm. The U.S. Steel plant at Homestead, just across the Monongahela River to the south, was the site of a bitter strike in 1892, which ended in a pitched battle between striking workers and Pinkerton detectives brought in by the company under the management of Henry Frick. It took 8,000 National Guardsmen to restore order at Homestead.

344.7 **Shadyside** *3.2.* This is part of the city of Pittsburgh. To the south are the University of Pittsburgh campus, with its unique skyscraper, the Tower of Learning; Carnegie-Mellon University; the Carnegie Museum of Art; the Frick Fine Arts Building; and Schenley Park.

347.9 **PITTSBURGH** *0.0.* Trains approach the Steel City along the south bank of the Allegheny River. The passenger station, at 11th and Grant streets, stands at the site of what was once the western terminal of the Main Line canal system and has been used as a railroad station since 1865. The current building, completed in 1902, is the third structure to occupy this site.

For information on the city, see section 2.33.

3.16 Washington—Pittsburgh

In 1981 Amtrak built a connecting track at Pittsburgh that allows it to route its Chicago–Washington train, the *Capitol Limited,* over the Baltimore and Ohio line up the Potomac Valley. This line is almost

200 miles shorter than the previous routing through Philadelphia, and passengers are now treated to some of the prettiest scenery in the east.

The Baltimore and Ohio, begun in 1830, was America's first common-carrier railroad. It was planned to connect the Ohio River valley with Baltimore, whose merchants hoped for a share of the Western trade that had begun to stream into New York with the completion of the Erie Canal 5 years before.

Amtrak offers two round trips daily between Washington and Martinsburg, West Virginia, and the *Capitol Limited* continues on to Pittsburgh and Chicago.

0.0 **WASHINGTON, D.C.** *296.1.* Leaving Union Station, the route parallels the new Washington subway (called the Metro) out into the Maryland suburbs. A short distance out of the station the Ivy City engine terminal and passenger coach yards are on the east (right side, leaving the city).

2.6 **University, D.C.** *293.5.* The Catholic University of America is here, within the boundaries of the District of Columbia.

WASHINGTON—PITTSBURGH

Westbound/miles		miles/Eastbound
0.0	WASHINGTON, D.C.	296.1
2.6	University, D.C.	293.5
5.7	Takoma Park, Md.	290.4
6.9	SILVER SPRING	289.2
9.2	Forest Glen	286.9
10.4	Kensington	285.7
11.9	Garrett Park	284.2
16.0	ROCKVILLE	280.1
20.1	Washington Grove	276.0
21.1	GAITHERSBURG	275.0
25.9	Germantown	270.2
28.4	Boyd	267.7
29.8	Buck Lodge	266.3
32.6	Barnesville	263.5
34.8	Dickerson	261.3
38.5	Tuscarora	257.6
42.1	Point of Rocks	254.0
45.2	Catoctin	250.9
49.0	BRUNSWICK	247.1
52.2	Weverton, Md.	243.9
55.1	HARPERS FERRY, W.VA.	241.0
62.4	Shenandoah Junction	233.7
73.3	MARTINSBURG	222.8
80.9	North Mountain	215.2
87.0	Cherry Run	209.1
96.4	Hancock	199.7

99.2	Sir John's Run	196.9
103.3	Great Capacon	192.8
116.1	Green Ridge	180.0
119.7	Magnolia	176.4
121.8	Paw Paw	174.3
126.6	Okonoko	169.5
131.8	Green Spring, W. Va.	164.3
145.9	CUMBERLAND, MD.	150.2
145.9	CUMBERLAND	150.2
146.5	Viaduct Jct.	149.6
152.0	Ellerslie, Md.	144.1
154.8	Cook's Mills, Pa.	141.3
159.8	Hyndman	136.3
161.9	Hoblitzell	134.2
165.3	Fairhope	130.8
169.4	Glencoe	126.7
172.0	Philson	124.1
175.8	Mance	120.3
177.6	Manila	118.5
179.2	Sand Patch	116.9
180.2	Keystone	115.9
183.0	Meyersdale	113.1
184.2	Salisbury Jct.	111.9
187.9	Garrett	108.2
190.6	Atlantic	105.5
194.8	Rockwood	101.3
199.0	Casselman	97.1
201.7	Markleton	94.4
203.0	Pinkerton	93.1
209.2	Ursina	86.9
211.2	Confluence	84.9
216.1	Bidwell	80.0
221.3	Ohiopyle	74.8
223.9	Kaufmann	72.2
230.7	Indian Creek	65.4
238.1	CONNELLSVILLE	58.0
240.7	Broad Ford	55.4
243.5	Dawson	52.6
250.9	Layton	45.2
254.2	Banning	41.9
255.1	Jacobs Creek	41.0
256.9	Smithton	39.2
258.4	Fitz Henry	37.7
262.8	West Newton	33.3
266.8	Suter	29.3
268.2	Scott Haven	27.9
270.8	Shaner	25.3
273.6	Coulter	22.5
278.2	Versailles	17.9
281.1	McKEESPORT	15.0
285.1	Bessemer	11.0
286.4	Braddock	9.7
296.1	PITTSBURGH	0.0

6.9 **SILVER SPRING, MD.** *289.2.* This suburban station just across the district line is convenient for Maryland residents, who don't have to go into the city to catch the train. The area used to be casual and suburban, but today Silver Spring is practically a big city itself.

Just across the line, in Washington proper, is the Walter Reed Army Medical Center. Also nearby is the site of Fort Stevens, where President Lincoln came to watch the fighting when Confederate General Jubal Early led a flying column of Rebels to the edge of Washington in August 1864. Early knew he lacked the strength to capture and hold the city, but he threw a good scare into everybody except Lincoln. The president stood up on the battlements in his tall stovepipe hat, making what must have been a tempting target for Confederate sharpshooters. The Union commander persuaded him to step down only after an argument, and later wrote that he would have pulled Lincoln down by force if he'd had to.

10.4 **Kensington** *285.7.* Between Silver Spring and Rockville the route passes through a beautiful suburban residential area. Near Kensington are Bethesda, where the naval hospital is located, and Chevy Chase—not named for the comedian. Between Kensington and Garrett Park the train crosses Rock Creek, the same stream that meanders through the city of Washington on its way to the Potomac.

20.1 **Washington Grove** *276.0.* The National Bureau of Standards has headquarters here. I don't know of a more beautiful part of the United States than the next 35 miles to Harpers Ferry. This part of Maryland is an area of gently rolling hills and rich farms.

34.8 **Dickerson** *261.3.* To the east (right side, leaving Washington) Sugar Loaf Mountain rises in the distance. To the west, the Potomac comes into view, paralleled by the Chesapeake and Ohio Canal bed. This old canal was surveyed by George Washington himself. It fell into disuse after the railroads came and is now a national historical park. Robert Kennedy used to jog here.

42.1 **Point of Rocks** *254.0.* At this quaint old depot—a masterpiece of Victorian gingerbread—the line from Washington joins the original Baltimore and Ohio main line from Baltimore to Cumberland, Maryland.

In 1829 Baltimore merchants, seeing the success of New York's Erie Canal, planned their own system of canals to reach the Ohio Valley. But they also agreed to try out a newfangled scheme called a railway, which had been used successfully in England. Charles Carroll of Carrollton, the last surviving signer of the Declaration of Independence, turned the first spadeful of dirt, fully conscious that it might be as important an act as the Revolution itself. The first 13 miles of track were soon finished, but the question of motive power remained. The Baltimore and Ohio tried everything: horses, a treadmill car, even a sail car that looked like a small boat on wheels. None of these schemes worked very well, and when a New York inventor named Peter Cooper asked the Baltimore officials to try out his tiny steam engine, the Tom Thumb, they readily agreed. The Tom Thumb broke down on its first run while racing a horse, but steam power soon proved its superiority.

Beyond Point of Rocks the rails follow the north bank of the Potomac River (left side of the train, leaving Washington).

49.0 **BRUNSWICK, MD.** *247.1.* About 20 miles north of here is the town of Frederick, the home of Francis Scott Key, the lawyer who wrote some new words to the tune of an old British drinking song and so produced "The Star-Spangled Banner." The town is also known to Americans as Barbara Frietchie's home in John Greenleaf Whittier's poem. Unfortunately, the story of how the 96-year-old Barbara waved the American flag in Stonewall Jackson's face may be rousing poetry, but it's pure fabrication from first line to last.

55.1 **HARPERS FERRY, W. VA.** *241.0.* Where the Shenandoah River empties in to the Potomac, and where Virginia, West Virginia, and Maryland meet, stands the picturesque and historic town of Harpers Ferry. Trains from the east approach it in dramatic fashion—through a tunnel under Maryland Heights and then over a long bridge across the Potomac.

Harpers Ferry was the sight of an important arsenal, and this was the objective when in October 1859 John Brown, his sons, and some followers attacked the town. Brown was a fanatic who was convinced that he was God's chosen instrument to destroy slavery. His hands had been bloodied in Kansas long before the Harpers Ferry plot. His plan was to seize the arsenal, use the town as a base, and raid the countryside, freeing and arming the slaves. The local militia and a battalion of Federal troops trapped Brown's men at the arsenal. Ten men were killed and Brown was wounded and captured before the incident ended. His attempt to incite a slave insurrection ended on the gallows, where he and six of his men were hanged for treason against the Commonwealth of Virginia.

If John Brown's raid was futile, however, it did in a sense help to bring about the destruction of slavery. For more than any other single factor, this fanatical act convinced Southern leaders that their section could not hope to remain in the Union with safety and, therefore, contributed to the secession movement, which began a little over a year later in South Carolina.

The Harpers Ferry arsenal was destroyed early in the Civil War, but the ruins and some foundations can be seen to the south (left side, going west) of the train. Harpers Ferry remained a military objective throughout the war by virtue of its location, and it changed hands several times. The most significant action occurred in September 1862, when Lee's army captured the town on its way north to Antietam. Lee had been to Harpers Ferry before. Three years earlier he had commanded the Federal troops who captured John Brown.

The Battle of Antietam, which took place 17 miles north of Harpers Ferry, was probably the most vicious combat of the Civil War. The two armies suffered more than 23,000 casualties in a single day. The Union here stopped the Rebel invasion, which helped to persuade the English and French not to join the war on the side of the South, and Abraham Lincoln took the opportunity to issue the Emancipation Proclamation.

62.4 **Shenandoah Junction** *233.7.* Here the B & O's east-west line crosses beneath the Norfolk and Western's freight line, which comes up the length of the fertile Shenandoah Valley from Lynchburg. This route continues north to Hagerstown, Maryland, where it connects with other railroads. It's a major bypass route for freight trains going to and from the South.

West of Shenandoah Junction the rails cut overland across one of the Potomac's big loops.

73.3 **MARTINSBURG** *222.8.* This has always been a railroad town, with the usual yards and shops. The interesting old roundhouse dates back to Civil War times.

Martinsburg has a place in American labor history, for it was here that the first great nationwide strike began. It happened in 1877 when a number of railroads including the B & O announced unilateral wage cuts of 10 percent. Workers at Martinsburg struck rather than take the pay cut, and within a few days the work stoppage spread to many other cities. There was violence on an unprecedented scale; at Pittsburgh, the station was burned and a number of men were shot before order was restored.

96.4 **Hancock, W.Va., Md., Pa.** *199.7.* Hancock straddles the Potomac, with part of the town on the south bank, in West Virginia, and most of the rest on the north side, in Maryland. But because this is the narrowest point of Maryland's slender neck, the northern edge of Hancock spills over into Pennsylvania as well. Thus Hancock spreads into three states—a unique distinction for a community with fewer than 2,000 inhabitants.

West Virginia, of course, was once part of Virginia proper, but the mountain counties were far from Richmond economically and politically as well as geographically. There were few slaves in the area and little sentiment for secession; so when Virginia left the Union in 1861, the mountain counties announced their refusal to go along. The Constitution provides, however, that no state may be carved from the territory of an existing state without its permission, which Virginia would hardly give.

The Lincoln Administration, however, found a way to get around that difficulty. Since early in the Civil War, Union troops had occupied a small piece of Virginia territory just across the Potomac from Washington. A civilian "government" of Virginia was set up there, and this authority granted the necessary permission for West Virginia to enter the Union as the thirty-fifth state.

145.9 **CUMBERLAND, MD.** *150.2.* Located where Evitts Creek spills into the Potomac, Cumberland is a railroad division point, with a major freight yard. It is also a junction where the Baltimore and Ohio splits, one route going straight west to Parkersburg, Cincinnati, and St. Louis, the other leg turning north toward Pittsburgh and Chicago.

Cumberland, like Hancock, sits on a narrow strip of Maryland soil squeezed between West Virginia to the south and Pennsylvania to the north. Just 25 miles away, in fact, is Bedford, the historic Pennsylvania town where George Washington led an army of 15,000 men— not against the French or the British, but against rebellious American farmers who refused in 1794 to pay the new federal excise tax on whiskey. The massive show of force dispersed the would-be revolutionaries and established the authority of the U.S. Government.

From Cumberland to the summit of the Alleghenies at Sand Patch, the rails must rise more than a quarter of a mile into the air. This next 33 miles is a stiff test of railroad workers and equipment, especially in bad weather.

146.5 **Viaduct Junction** *149.6.* Here the Grafton and Pittsburgh lines diverge.

152.0 **Ellerslie, Md.** *144.1.* The Pennsylvania state line is just beyond the town. Willis Mountain rises to the east.

159.8 **Hyndman, Pa.** *136.3.* Here the rails, following the course of Willis Creek, turn westward to assault the Alleghenies. Hyndman, population 1,100, is the base station for helper engines, which boost heavy freight trains up the hill to Sand Patch. You may see some waiting helpers standing near Q Tower as you pass.

175.8 **Mance** *120.3.* At this point Willis Creek is left behind, and the railroad rounds a horseshoe curve (less well known than Horseshoe Curve near Altoona, but impressive enough in its own right). Look to the south (left side of the train, going west), and you'll see the engines up front as they round the bend.

177.6 **Manila** *118.5.* The steepest part of the climb up the Alleghenies is right here, with a grade of 2 percent—110 feet up for every mile of forward progress. Beyond Manila is Sand Patch Tunnel, three-quarters of a mile long, leading from the Potomac watershed to that of the Ohio.

179.2 **Sand Patch** *116.9.* Opposite SA Tower is a trackside marker indicating an altitude of 2,258 feet above sea level. From here on it's all downgrade, with an easier slope on the western side of the hill. From Sand Patch summit the tracks follow little Flaugherty Creek down to its junction with the Casselman River.

183.0 **Meyersdale** *113.1.* Due west of this little town rises Mount Davis, at 3,213 feet the highest point in Pennsylvania. From just beyond Meyersdale the rails follow the Casselman River to Confluence, 28 miles of twisting, curving track.

187.9 **Garrett** *108.2.* John B. Garrett was for many years the president of the Baltimore and Ohio. Garrett is the west-side helper station, but because the grade is less steep fewer trains require assistance to get up to Sand Patch on this side of the mountain.

203.0 **Pinkerton** *93.1.* West of here a couple of short tunnels take the rails through rock spurs, cutting off a couple of the many sharp loops made by the Casselman River. Every curve eliminated makes railroad operations that much easier and more efficient.

211.2 **Confluence** *84.9.* The town takes its name as the meeting point of the Casselman and Youghiogheny rivers. Youghiogheny (pronounced something like *Yock-i-heny*) is an Indian name said to mean "the river that twists against itself." It's certainly appropriate, because this river hardly has a straight stretch anywhere.

221.3 **Ohiopyle** *74.8.* About the last thing you'd expect to find in the middle of Pennsylvania mountain wilderness is one of the greatest landmarks in American architecture, but just a few miles north on Route 381 is Fallingwater, the magnificent house designed by Frank Lloyd Wright for the wealthy Kaufmann family of Pittsburgh. Fallingwater is cantilevered over a small waterfall, which is completely hidden from view but can be heard throughout the house. The structure follows Wright's dictim that a building should mesh with its natural surroundings, and everything in the house down to the furniture was designed by Wright himself. The home is open to the public by appointment.

Five miles south of Ohiopyle is the site of Fort Necessity, the outpost built by George Washington during the French and Indian War. Washington buried the British General Braddock here, while retreating from a battle near Pittsburgh. Afraid that Indians might find the corpse, Washington ordered that the grave be dug in the middle of the road.

223.9 **Kaufmann** *72.2.* The Kaufmann family, owners of the biggest department store in Pittsburgh, had a large tract of land here. For a time it was used as a recreation area for employees of the store, who came down for weekend picnics. Later, Fallingwater was constructed on the property.

238.1 **CONNELLSVILLE** *58.0.* Everywhere you look between Connellsville and Pittsburgh, there are signs of the coal mines that fired the mills of the Steel City. In fact, the proximity of the coal fields led to the steel industry's locating in Pittsburgh in the first place. Now many of these older mines are closed, and the coke ovens are cold.

262.8 **West Newton** *33.3.* About 7 miles west is the town of Donora, where a smog killed twenty persons in 1948. The Donora tragedy had one positive result; it focused attention on air pollution problems in nearby Pittsburgh, where a massive cleanup was begun. Donora also has another, pleasanter distinction—it was the hometown of Stan "The Man" Musial, the St. Louis Cardinals baseball star.

278.2 **Versailles** *17.9.* Although it's named after the French city where the World War I peace treaty was signed, the name is pronounced *Ver-sails* in Pennsylvania, not *Ver-sigh,* as in France.

281.1 **McKEESPORT** *15.0.* Here at last the Youghiogheny empties into the Monongahela, which in turn joins the Allegheny at Pittsburgh to form the mighty Ohio. Between this point and Pittsburgh, the rails run past several of the big steel mills that have made this area world famous. The mills can be a spectacular sight at night.

286.4 **Braddock** *9.7.* This is the site of Braddock's wounding and defeat in 1755. Washington retreated from here to Fort Necessity.

296.1 **PITTSBURGH** *0.0.* For information on the city, see section 2.33.

3.17   Pittsburgh—Chicago

Once the busy main line of the Pennsylvania Railroad, this direct Pittsburgh–Chicago route is now merely a secondary freight line west of Bucyrus, Ohio, and most of it sees just one passenger train daily in each direction—the combined *Broadway Limited* and *Capitol Limited,* which operate as one train west of Pittsburgh. There is additional local service over the extreme western segment of the route, between Valparaiso, Indiana, and Chicago.

Leaving Pittsburgh, the rails follow the Ohio River for 26 miles to Rochester, Pennsylvania, then continue north along the valley of its tributary, the Beaver River, for a few miles more. The best scenery of the route is along these valleys. Unfortunately, the *Broadway* passes in darkness in both directions most of the year.

The train twists and turns through eastern Ohio until it reaches Mansfield. From this point all the way to Chicago the track is almost arrow straight. In fact, the American speed record for steam-powered trains was set on this route near Lima, Ohio—127 ½ miles per hour.

No such heroics take place these days; what used to be called the "Racetrack" is now just another piece of flatland railroad.

0.0 **PITTSBURGH** *468.4*. For information on the city, see section 2.33.

Leaving the station, Chicago-bound trains curve sharply to the right and cross the Allegheny River. Some brief views of downtown Pittsburgh and the Golden Triangle can be had from the left side (leaving Pittsburgh); but unfortunately, the bridge has high sides, and the sight lines are mostly blocked.

1.0 **Federal Street** *467.4*. A junction at which the Chicago main line joins the Allegheny Division of Conrail, which comes in along that river. From this point the track runs inside a cut through the North End of Pittsburgh; little of the city can be seen.

18.0 **Economy** *450.4*. In the nineteenth century a great number of experimental communities were started in response to the rapid social changes that seemed to call into question virtually every institution from private property to monogamy. One of these communities, Economy, was established here. Its buildings have been preserved as a historic attraction. Incongruously, the industrial town of Aliquippa is directly across the river, standing for the very social institutions that were anathema to the reformers.

PITTSBURGH—CHICAGO

Westbound/miles		miles/Eastbound
0.0	PITTSBURGH	468.4
1.0	Federal St.	467.4
3.4	Woods Run	465.0
5.1	Bellevue	463.3
6.0	Avalon	462.4
6.5	Ben Avon	461.9
7.0	Emsworth	461.4
8.4	Dixmont	460.0
9.4	Glenfield	459.0
11.0	Haysville	457.4
12.5	Sewickley	455.9
13.4	Edgeworth	455.0
14.1	Shields	454.3
14.9	Leetsdale	453.5
16.5	Ambridge	451.9
18.0	Economy	450.4
20.6	Baden	447.8
22.4	Conway	446.0
23.9	Freedom	444.5
25.8	Rochester	442.6
29.0	New Brighton	439.4

30.3	Beaver Falls	438.1
32.8	Morado	435.6
40.1	New Galilee	428.3
45.2	Enon, Pa.	423.2
49.9	E. Palestine, Ohio	418.5
54.3	New Waterford	414.1
59.7	Columbiana	408.7
63.1	Leetonia	405.3
69.6	Salem	398.8
75.6	Garfield	392.8
77.8	Beloit	390.6
79.0	Sebring	389.4
83.0	Alliance	385.4
87.0	W. Alliance	381.4
89.2	Maximo	379.2
94.8	Louisville	373.6
101.7	CANTON	366.7
104.5	Buck Hill	363.9
105.7	Reedurban	362.7
109.5	Massillon	358.9
112.2	Newman	356.2
116.6	North Lawrence	351.8
124.0	Orrville	344.4
128.5	Smithville	339.9
135.1	Wooster	333.3
144.5	Shreve	323.9
150.1	Lakeville	318.3
156.5	Loudonville	311.9
160.9	Perrysville	307.5
168.5	Lucas	299.9
175.3	Mansfield	293.1
188.8	CRESTLINE	279.6
188.8	CRESTLINE	279.6
195.2	Robinson	273.2
201.2	Bucyrus	267.2
209.7	Nevada	258.7
218.0	Upper Sandusky	250.4
224.8	Kirby	243.6
229.7	Forest	238.7
236.8	Dunkirk	231.6
239.2	Dola	227.2
246.1	Ada	222.3
252.6	Lafayette	215.8
260.7	LIMA	207.7
267.0	Elida	201.4
271.6	Auglaize	196.8
275.1	Delphos	193.3
280.8	Middlepoint	187.6
288.0	Van Wert	180.4
295.3	Convoy, Ohio	173.1
300.8	Dixon, Indiana	167.6
304.8	Monroeville	163.6

309.8	Maples	158.6
315.1	Adams	153.3
320.4	FORT WAYNE	148.0

320.4	FORT WAYNE	148.0
328.8	Arcola	139.6
331.3	Columbia City	129.1
346.9	Larwill	128.5
351.3	Pierceton	117.1
357.8	Winona Lake	110.6
359.7	Warsaw	108.7
366.2	Atwood	102.2
370.0	Etna Green	98.4
373.8	Bourbon	94.6
378.5	Inwood	89.9
384.6	Plymouth	83.8
391.4	Donaldson	77.0
395.0	Grovertown	73.4
398.9	Hamlet	69.5
409.3	Hanna	59.1
415.6	Wanatah (ET)	52.8
424.8	VALPARAISO (CT)	43.6
431.4	WHEELER	37.0
435.3	HOBART	33.1
437.4	New Chicago	31.0
438.2	Liverpool	30.2
441.0	BROADWAY	27.4
443.4	GARY (5th and Chase)	25.0
444.5	Clarke	23.9
446.2	Clarke Junction	22.2
448.5	INDIANA HARBOR	19.9
451.6	HAMMOND-WHITING	16.8
452.5	Lake Jct., Ind.	15.9
461.4	Englewood, Ill.	7.0
468.4	CHICAGO (Union Sta.)	0.0

22.4 **Conway** *446.0.* Site of the biggest and most modern freight yard between Harrisburg and Chicago, this is Conrail's principal facility for handling tonnage in the Pittsburgh area.

25.8 **Rochester** *442.6.* Here the Ohio, after flowing north from Pittsburgh, reverses itself and turns west. The railroad continues north along the banks of the Beaver River.

30.3 **Beaver Falls** *438.1.* This is the hometown of the former football star "Broadway Joe" Namath.

45.2 **Enon, Pa.** *423.2.* Spell it backward and it comes out "None." The same trick of spelling a word backward to make a place name was used by a solitary telegraph operator at a lonely spot near Harrisburg. He named the place "Enola," which spelled the right way around is "Alone."

49.9 **East Palestine, Ohio** *418.5.* All of a sudden the hills and valleys of Pennsylvania disappear, and the land turns flat. Twenty miles north is the steel city of Youngstown, which is now having some hard times because a couple of big mills there shut down.

59.7 **Columbiana** *408.7.* About 15 miles south of here is the town of West Point, where the Confederate cavalry raider John Morgan was finally trapped and forced to surrender after a ride that took him across three Northern states with half the Union army in pursuit. This 1863 exploit was the longest and boldest Rebel invasion of the North.

69.6 **Salem** *398.8.* Many towns in the northern part of Ohio were settled by New Englanders, and in more than one case the early residents named the spot for their hometown farther east. Salem, Ohio, recalls Salem, Massachusetts, the port city north of Boston where the witchcraft trials took place in 1692.

75.6 **Garfield** *392.8.* The town was named for President James A. Garfield, elected in 1880 but assassinated the next year. Garfield was a native Ohioan; his home at Mentor, near Cleveland, has been preserved.

83.0 **Alliance** *385.4.* A branch line to Cleveland, now used only by freight trains, diverges here.

Like many Ohio towns, Alliance is built around the campus of a small college. In this case, the school is Mount Union, a Methodist-affiliated liberal arts institution with an enrollment of a little over a thousand.

101.7 **CANTON** *366.7.* This was the home of another martyred Ohio president, William McKinley, who served in the White House from 1897 until his assassination in 1901.

Running as a Republican, McKinley won over William Jennings Bryan in the bitterly fought election of 1896. He did it with a strategy designed by his savvy campaign manager, Mark Hanna. Because Bryan was known as a spellbinding orator, McKinley simply refused to debate him at all, or even to make campaign speeches in his own behalf. Instead, he stayed home in Canton, letting Bryan hang himself with his "radical" talk about free coinage of silver. This was called the "Front Porch" campaign, because McKinley supposedly spent his time rocking on the swing on his front porch.

As president, the affable McKinley presided over America's emergence as a world power, with its victory in the Spanish-American War and its first acquisition of overseas territories. He was reelected in 1900, but with a different running mate—the former governor of New York, who was being kicked upstairs because he made too much trouble for the political bosses in that state. When McKinley was shot by Leon Czolgos in 1901, Theodore Roosevelt became the youngest president in American history.

Canton also has another distinction in the sports world. It was here, in the showroom of a local Hupmobile dealer who also owned a professional football team, that the National Football League was founded. In honor of Canton's position as the cradle of the game, the Pro Football Hall of Fame was established here, and an annual exhibition game is played between two NFL teams.

Canton contains Amtrak's station for Akron, the Rubber City, which is 20 miles north.

109.5 **Massillon** *358.9*. This is the twin of Canton. A hot football rivalry exists between the local high schools.

124.0 **Orrville** *344.4*. This is the home of the J. M. Smucker Company, the preserves and jelly manufacturer. Bobby Knight, the successful but controversial basketball coach, is an Orrville native.

135.1 **Wooster** *333.3*. Here's one Wooster that's spelled the way it sounds, unlike the city in Massachusetts. Wooster is another town built around a college, a Presbyterian school called the College of Wooster.

150.1 **Lakeville** *318.3*. Don't be confused; there's no lake at Lakeville. The town gets its name from the Lake Fork of the Mohican River, which the train crosses here.

188.8 **CRESTLINE** *279.6*. Crestline may have only 6,000 people, but it's a big railroad town with the usual yards and shops. Crews change here on the Pittsburgh–Chicago line; moreover, the Cleveland–Columbus–Cincinnati line crosses here. If you like trains, you'll find plenty of them at Crestline.

Six miles south, at Blooming Grove, is the birthplace of Warren G. Harding, another Ohio president, who died in office under somewhat mysterious circumstances while on a tour of the West in 1923. Harding, it should be noted, was voted the worst president in U.S. history in a recent poll of American historians.

201.2 **Bucyrus** *267.2*. This is a small industrial city. Marion, Ohio, where Harding had his adult home, is 18 miles southwest. He owned a department store and a newspaper there before going into politics. Harding also owned the Marion team in the Ohio State League, making him the only president who ever owned a professional baseball franchise. His predecessor in the White House, Woodrow Wilson, had also been involved in sports—he was once Princeton's football coach.

218.0 **Upper Sandusky** *250.4*. This town gets its name from its position on the Sandusky River, some 50 miles upstream from its mouth. Forty miles south is Delaware, hometown of still another Ohio president, Rutherford B. Hayes.

246.1 **Ada** *222.3*. Another little town built around a campus—Ohio Northern University this time.

Thirty miles south of Ada is Bellefontaine, where the first concrete pavement in the United States was laid, back in 1891. Talk about little-known sites of massive importance—what would America be like without concrete pavement?

260.7 **LIMA** *207.7.* It may be pronounced *Lee-ma* in Peru, but it's *Lye-ma,* as in "lima beans," in Ohio. This industrial city used to turn out steam locomotives; now its factories produce heavy machinery. Neil Armstrong, the first man on the moon, hails from nearby Wapakoneta. At the Lima station the Pittsburgh–Chicago main line crosses the Chessie system's Detroit–Cincinnati route.

267.0 **Elida, Ohio** *201.4.* The track here is straight and level, and over a 3-mile stretch east of Elida, Pennsylvania Railroad engine number 7002 set the world's record for speed with steam power. The date was June 12, 1905, and the occasion was the first westbound run of the crack *Pennsylvania Special* on an accelerated 18-hour schedule, New York to Chicago.

Engineer Jerry McCarthy and the 7002 took over the train at Crestline, leaving 25 minutes late owing to delays farther east. McCarthy had instructions to make up as much time as he could, and he sent the *Special* over the 3 miles between AY Tower and Elida in just 85 seconds. It's a record that will never be broken, now that there aren't any steam engines left to challenge it. The feat is all the more remarkable when you remember that it was done in 1905, before the advent of modern safety devices and in the course of regular operations with no special preparation at all. And by the way, the *Special* arrived in Chicago 3 minutes early.

320.4 **FORT WAYNE, IND.** *148.0.* Located on the Maumee River, Fort Wayne is the metropolis of northeastern Indiana. It is named for "Mad Anthony" Wayne, who won this part of the country from the Indians. Wayne, a Virginian and a friend of George Washington's, earned his nickname not because he frothed at the mouth, but because he was such a daring commander. He died in 1796 at the age of fifty-one.

Twenty-five miles north of Fort Wayne is the town of Auburn, where the Duesenberg, Cord, and Auburn cars were once built. Indiana was the first home of the American auto industry, before it became concentrated in Detroit, and the state is still a leader in production of auto parts and accessories. The Indianapolis 500 didn't originate in Indiana by chance.

Fort Wayne is the burial place of Johnny Appleseed, the itinerant preacher and seed sower who wandered over much of the Midwest around the turn of the nineteenth century.

In addition to its other distinctions, Fort Wayne is also a railroad division point, where engine crews change.

357.8 **Winona Lake** *110.6.* Grace Theological Seminary is nearby, and this resort area has long been a favorite spot for religious retreats and summer camps.

384.6 **Plymouth** *83.8.* A freight-only branch line connecting South Bend and Logansport crosses the Pittsburgh–Chicago main line here. The train passes into the Central Time Zone about 10 miles west of town, but don't change your watch until you read the explanation, under Valparaiso, below.

398.9 **Hamlet** *69.5.* It is a hamlet, too: population 700. You can add this little town to your list of Shakespearean place names in the United States, together with Othello, Washington; Romeo, Illinois; and Caesar, Texas.

424.8 **VALPARAISO** *43.6.* The correct Indiana pronunciation is *Val-pa-ray'-so,* rather than *Val-pa-rye-so,* but don't worry about it. Most local folks just call it "Valpo" and have done with it.

Valparaiso is the end of the line for commuter trains from Chicago, and in effect it marks the edge of the Chicago metropolitan area. Accordingly, Valpo is always on Chicago time, together with the rest of northwestern Indiana, and this situation demands clarification.

In the rest of the nation, either an entire state goes on Daylight Savings Time in the summer or none of it does. (Arizona is the only state that has never adopted Daylight Time.) But in Indiana, while most of the state is on Eastern Time, the six northwestern counties, which are actually part of the Chicago area, are on Central.

That would be confusing enough, but the story gets even more complex. Indiana has generally elected to remain on Eastern Standard Time in the summer, but the northwestern counties follow Chicago and go on Central Daylight. This means that from October to April most of Indiana is an hour ahead of the northwestern corner, while from April through October the whole state runs on the same time—except that most of Indiana calls it Eastern Standard, while the northwestern counties are on Central Daylight. Got that?

443.4 **GARY (5th and Chase Streets)** *25.0.* Amtrak has three stations in Gary: the *Broadway Limited* and the *Capitol Limited* use the former Pennsylvania Railroad facility at 5th and Chase streets, west of the central business district.

For notes on Gary and on the remaining 25 miles to Chicago, see section 3.14.

3.18 Washington—Cincinnati

This is one of the most scenic routes in the United States, but unfortunately it is also Amtrak's least well exploited. The one train on the run, the New York to Chicago *Cardinal,* has led a Perils of Pauline existence and was actually discontinued in 1981, only to be revived by congressional mandate on a three-day-a-week basis. It's scheduled to pass through some of the best scenery in darkness, it's slow, and it manages to miss every possible connection in Chicago.

Yet despite all this, the Heritage Fleet cars on the *Cardinal* are roomy and comfortable, the leisurely pace is relaxing, and this is the only rail passenger service to Cincinnati. The *Cardinal* has shown increases in ridership lately, and one wonders what a truly first-class train could do on this run.

For notes on the line from Washington to Orange, see section 3.28.

85 **Orange** *514.* Between Washington and Orange the *Cardinal* uses the tracks of the Southern Railway. At Orange it reaches the rails of the Chesapeake and Ohio, which likes to call itself "George Washington's Railroad" because its original, predecessor company—which operated a canal, not a railroad—was founded by Washington in 1785.

The C & O is one of America's more profitable rail lines, mostly because of its heavy coal traffic moving from the mines in Kentucky and West Virginia to Chesapeake Bay and the Great Lakes. Today the C & O is part of the CSX holding company, which also owns the Family Lines in the South and the Baltimore and Ohio in the East and Midwest.

94 **Gordonsville** *505.* Here at the big, white, empty frame station the line coming down from Washington meets another C & O line coming from Richmond. In Civil War times this line was called the Virginia Central, and it was the main railroad from the Confederate capital to the Shenandoah, an essential source of men and supplies. Thus, the junction at Gordonsville was crucial to the Confederacy, which defended it strongly throughout the war.

WASHINGTON—CINCINNATI

Westbound/miles		miles/Eastbound
0	WASHINGTON, D.C.	599
8	ALEXANDRIA, VA.	591
15	Springfield	584
20	Burke	579
22	Sideburn	577
23	Fairfax	576
34	MANASSAS	565
37	Bristow	562
44	Catlett	555
46	Claverton	553
53	Bealeton	546

204

```
363 .......................  MONTGOMERY .....................  236
367 ...........................Pratt Jct......................  232
373 ..................... Cabin Creek Jct. .................  226
388 ..................... CHARLESTON ......................  211
400 .......................  St. Albans .....................  199
414 ...........................Hurricane.......................  185
420 ........................... Milton .......................  179
429 ..................... Barboursville .....................  170
438 .......................HUNTINGTON.......................  161
```

```
438 .......................HUNTINGTON.......................  161
446 ..................... Kenova, W.Va. .....................  153
448 .......... TRI-STATE STATION (Catlettsburg, Ky.) ..........  151
454 ......................... Ashland .........................  145
458 ......................... Russell ........................  141
467 ......................... Greenup ........................  132
485 ..................... S. PORTSMOUTH ....................  114
497 ......................... Garrison ........................  102
506 ..................... Vanceburg .....................  93
536 .....................MAYSVILLE.....................  63
559 ...........................Wellsburg .......................  40
568 ...........................Carntown .......................  31
596 ......................... Newport .........................  3
598 ..................... Covington, Ky. .....................  1
599 ........... CINCINNATI, OHIO (River Road Sta.) ...........  0
```

111 **Shadwell** *488.* This is the birthplace of Thomas Jefferson.

116 **CHARLOTTESVILLE** *483.* For information on this historic city, see section 2.9.

Just after leaving the station, look for the campus of the University of Virginia, designed by Jefferson, to the south side (left side, westbound) of the tracks.

123 **Ivy** *476.* This is the birthplace of Meriwether Lewis, leader of the Lewis and Clark expedition. He had been Jefferson's private secretary and friend, and when the United States purchased the unmapped Louisiana Territory from France, Jefferson chose him to explore the vast new land. Lewis, in turn, named William Clark his second in command; so, although we always speak of the Lewis-and-Clark expedition, Lewis was actually its leader.

138 **Afton** *461.* Immediately west of Charlottesville the rails begin the long climb over the Blue Ridge Mountains, the first range of the Appalachians and the hills that separate Tidewater Virginia from the Shenandoah Valley. At Afton the train surmounts the Blue Ridge through Rockfish Gap, an indescribably beautiful and picturesque location.

142 **Waynesboro** *457.* Standing at the southern end of the Shenandoah Valley, Waynesboro is a transportation crossroads. The Appalachian Trail and the famous Skyline Drive are accessible from this point, and the east-west Chesapeake and Ohio line used by Amtrak crosses over the Norfolk and Western's Shenandoah Valley freight line here. That line is a principal route for northbound freight, since it bypasses the coastal cities and their congested freight yards.

155 **STAUNTON** *444.* Staunton, pronounced *Stanton,* just as if it had no *u* in it, was the birthplace of Thomas Woodrow Wilson, President of the United States from 1912 to 1920. The city stands at the point where the railroad from Richmond crossed the old Valley Turnpike, the main road up and down the Shenandoah Valley. Today Route I-81 follows roughly the line of the old pike. This region was once the home turf of Stonewall Jackson, and many of his victories were won here.

To the west of Staunton lie the main ridges of the Appalachians, which the rails must surmount to reach the Ohio valley.

212 **CLIFTON FORGE** *387.* This is an important railroad division point and junction. Here the line from Washington meets a low-grade freight route that comes from Richmond along the banks of the James River. Over this route, the endless trains of American coal head for the docks at Newport News, where the "black diamonds" are loaded onto ships for export to virtually every corner of the world.

224 **Covington, Va.** *375.* Nearby is Virginia Hot Springs, site of the Homestead resort hotel. Also in the vicinity are the towns of Warm Springs, Healing Springs, and Falling Springs.

246 **WHITE SULPHUR SPRINGS, W.VA.** *353.* At 1,923 feet above sea level, this is the highest point of any Appalachian pass. Since Charlottesville the rails have climbed 1,500 feet in 130 miles.

White Sulphur Springs is a pretty resort town, site of the Greenbriar Hotel. The Greenbriar is a worthy rival to the Homestead at Hot Springs and is also the home course of the golfer Sam Snead.

257 **Ronceverte** *342.* From this point westward for 150 miles, the tracks follow the valleys of the Greenbriar and Kanawha rivers, which make a natural pathway through the rugged mountains of West Virginia.

270 **ALDERSON** *329.* This is the site of a federal prison for women.

291 **HINTON** *308.* This railroad division point marks, approximately, the halfway point between the Potomac and Cincinnati. Crews change here.

314 **PRINCE** *285.* There is not much to be seen here but the station, which serves the city of Beckley.

325 **THURMOND** *274.* If anything, Thurmond is even smaller than Prince—there's just room in the narrow canyon for the river and the railroad. The station here serves the town of Mount Hope, a few miles away by road.

363 **MONTGOMERY** *236.* Once capital of the state, Montgomery is today a coal town distinguished by the presence of the West Virginia Institute of Technology campus.

373 **Cabin Creek Junction** *226.* Nearby Cabin Creek is the hometown of one of the greatest players in the history of basketball, Jerry West, who went on to fame at the University of West Virginia and with the professional Los Angeles Lakers.

388 **CHARLESTON** *211.* Capital of West Virginia and the state's largest city, Charleston lies on the Kanawha River, 70 miles above its mouth.

Southwest of Charleston is isolated Logan County, home of the Hatfield clan. America's most celebrated blood feud erupted here in 1882, when young Johnse Hatfield ran off with Rosanna McCoy. The Hatfields and the McCoys went at it for ten years before the feud was patched up, and it ended as it began—with a wedding.

438 **HUNTINGTON** *161.* Here at last the railroad reaches the Ohio River valley, the leading artery of commerce west of the Appalachians before the railroads came. Huntington was named for Collis P. Huntington, the nineteenth-century railroad baron best known as one of the four builders of the Central Pacific, part of the first transcontinental railroad. He also controlled the Chesapeake and Ohio for a time. This town is a railroad division point where engine crews change.

Huntington is also the home of Marshall University, whose athletic teams bear the colorful nickname ''The Thundering Herd.''

446 **Kenova, W.Va.** *153.* The name is derived from Kenova's location at a point where three states meet: *Ken*tucky, *O*hio, and West *Va*. The Big Sandy River, which flows into the Ohio here, forms the Kentucky–West Virginia boundary.

448 **TRI-STATE STATION (Catlettsburg, Ky.)** *151.* Amtrak constructed this new facility to serve the entire area, which includes Ironton, Ohio, and Ashland, Kentucky.

458 **Russell** *141.* Russell is an important spot to the Chesapeake and Ohio Railroad. At this point the long coal trains are made up and head east to Tidewater or west to Toledo or Chicago.

485 **SOUTH PORTSMOUTH** *114.* This is the station for Portsmouth, Ohio, across the river.

568 **Carntown** *31.* Across the river is Point Pleasant, Ohio, birthplace of Ulysses S. Grant. A failure all his life until his Civil War victories, he was then elected to the Presidency, where he proved to be a failure again.

598 **Covington, Ky.** *1.* Here the C & O line from the east joins the Louisville and Nashville tracks from the south; together they cross the Ohio on a long steel bridge to enter Cincinnati. The downtown area of the city is to the east of the bridge (right side, coming into the city), with Riverfront Stadium, home of the Reds and the Bengals, in the foreground.

599 **CINCINNATI, OHIO** *0.* The *Cardinal* no longer uses the big Union Terminal. Instead, Amtrak has a small, somewhat out-of-the-way stop at River Road. This spot was chosen several years ago because it allowed trains to pass through Cincinnati without having to back into the terminal. Ironically, the Conrail line to Chicago over which Amtrack used to run was declared unfit for use, and the *Cardinal* was shifted to the Chessie system's track. That move left River Road off the main line, so Amtrak must again back up to reach its Cincinnati station.

For information on the city, see section 2.12.

3.19   Cincinnati—Chicago

Amtrak's current route between these two cities is patched together from parts of four separate main lines and one branch line. Service is minimal—one train a day in each direction, 3 days a week. Heritage cars are used, and they are more than adequate.

It's difficult to recommend this service to anybody but a confirmed railfan. It's painfully slow, to begin with. The 297-mile run takes about 8 hours, at an average speed of less than 40 miles per hour. You can drive the distance in 6 hours and frequent air service takes just an hour. Nor is the run particularly scenic, although the Indiana countryside is pleasant. The best aspect of the present service is that it keeps Amtrak alive in Cincinnati, offering at least a hope of better service in the future.

0.0 **CINCINNATI** *296.7*   For information on Cincinnati, see section 2.12.

1.6 **Union Terminal** *295.1*. The beautiful Cincinnati Union Terminal, in Mill Creek Valley west of the central-city district, was once unique. Its concourse has a peculiar appearance. It looks like a band shell, or as one of my friends put it, like a raised eyebrow looking over the city. The building is again in use as a shopping center after a few years of standing idle, but it has been shorn of one of its greatest glories: The colorful murals that used to grace the interior walls of the concourse have been moved to the Greater Cincinnati Airport. Despite some talk, there are no firm plans right now to reopen the station for trains.

Until a couple of years ago, the Chessie system's Chicago line, over which Amtrak operates, began to climb out of the valley immediately after leaving the terminal, traveling from Cincinnati by way of Cheviot. This route, which included some spectacular high bridges, has been closed because of new yard construction in the valley, and so Amtrak passenger trains now use the Chessie line to Toledo as far as Hamilton,

Ohio. The new route is slightly longer and, unhappily, much less interesting than the steep track up Cheviot Hill, but it's easier to operate and serves more potential traffic.

26.3 **HAMILTON** *270.4*. The city is built on the site of Fort Hamilton, which was established to guard the area from Indian attacks. It was named after Alexander Hamilton, secretary of the treasury under Washington and the architect of much federal policy between 1791 and 1800. Hamilton is Amtrak's closest station to Dayton, 50 miles farther up the Great Miami River. The Miami takes its name from the Indian tribe once dominant in this area.

40.4 **Oxford, Ohio** *256.3*. To its very name, Oxford is a university town. While most people would probably connect ''Miami'' with Florida, this is the original Miami University, antedating the Florida institution (and its city) by many years. Miami of Ohio is a state-supported coeducational institution that numbers a president of the United States, Benjamin Harrison, among its alumni. It also has been called the ''mother of coaches'' because so many fine football coaches have worked here.

49.0 **Cottage Grove, Ind.** *247.7*. At this tiny village Amtrak trains switch onto the Chessie system's Cincinnati–Chicago route after completing the detour through Hamilton.

CINCINNATI—CHICAGO

Westbound/miles		miles/Eastbound
0.0	CINCINNATI (River Road Sta.)	296.7
1.6	Union Terminal	295.1
6.2	Winton Place	290.5
9.0	Ivorydale	287.7
9.9	Elmwood Place	286.8
12.0	Hartwell	284.7
13.2	Wyoming	283.5
16.4	Glendale	280.3
20.0	Stockton	276.7
26.3	HAMILTON	270.4
40.4	Oxford	256.3
45.8	College Corner, Ohio	250.9
49.0	Cottage Grove, Ind.	247.7
54.9	Kitchell	241.8
56.9	Witts	239.8
58.9	Boston	237.8
65.9	S. Richmond	230.8
67.0	RICHMOND	229.7
73.0	Webster	223.7
77.9	Williamsburg	218.8
83.6	Economy	213.1

86.3	Thornburg	210.4
90.5	Losantville	206.2
94.4	Blountsville	202.3
100.7	Medford	196.0
107.1	MUNCIE	189.6
114.3	Benadum	182.4
117.6	Gaston	179.1
121.8	Janney	174.9
125.0	Fowlerton	171.7
131.3	Jonesboro (Gas City)	165.4
136.4	MARION	160.3
142.0	Sweetser	154.7
147.7	Converse	149.0
150.8	Amboy	145.9
156.7	Santa Fe	140.0
164.4	PERU (Logansport)	132.3
164.4	PERU	132.3
174.0	Hoover	122.7
178.5	Twelve Mile	118.2
184.4	Fulton	112.3
193.8	Kewanna	102.9
198.1	Lake Bruce	98.6
202.0	Lawton	94.7
206.7	Beardstown	90.0
214.0	Lena Park	82.7
217.3	North Judson	79.4
221.5	English Lake	75.2
224.5	La Crosse	72.2
230.6	Thomaston	66.1
233.4	Hanna	63.3
239.6	Wellsboro	57.1
246.8	Alida	49.9
249.3	Coburg	47.4
252.6	Suman	44.1
258.6	Babcock	38.1
260.8	McCool	35.9
262.7	Willow Creek	34.0
267.2	GARY (Miller)	29.5
269.5	East Gary	27.2
270.8	Gary	25.9
272.9	Curtis Yard	23.8
275.0	Pine Jct.	21.7
275.0	Pine Jct.	21.7
277.4	Indiana Harbor	19.3
278.1	Mahoning	18.6
279.9	HAMMOND-WHITING	16.8
281.3	Roby, Ind.	15.4
284.1	S. Chicago, Ill.	12.6
289.7	Englewood	7.0
295.1	21st Street	1.6
296.7	CHICAGO (Union Station)	0.0

67.0 **RICHMOND** *229.7.* James Whitcomb Riley, the Hoosier poet and humorist, lived 30 miles west of here at Greenfield. Although the Wright brothers are most closely associated with the city of Dayton, Ohio, Wilbur was actually an Indiana native, born in nearby Millville in 1867.

107.1 **MUNCIE** *189.6.* Many communities can lay claim to being typical of something or other, but no town has a better reason to call itself the typical American Midwestern small city than does Muncie. This was the place the sociologists Robert and Helen Lynd used as their subject when they wrote *Middletown* and *Middletown in Transition,* the landmark studies of their type.

In real life, Muncie makes auto parts and other machine products and is the home of the Ball Company, makers of glass jars and metal lids for home canning and preserving. The influence of the Ball family pervades the town—even the local university is called Ball State.

117.6 **Gaston** *179.1.* This town's name is pronounced *Gas-tun,* not the French *Gas-toe.* It is derived from the large natural-gas reserves that were discovered in this part of Indiana a century ago. The gas wells fueled a short boom (pardon the pun!), but the prosperity didn't last. Today only the town names recall Indiana's natural-gas industry.

131.3 **Jonesboro** *165.4.* Jonesboro is the twin of nearby Gas City, another town that owes its name to the long-ago gas boom.

136.4 **MARION** *160.3.* Named after Francis Marion, the Revolutionary War hero who was called the "Swamp Fox," Marion is a city of 50,000 that seems to be on the road to anyplace you're going in eastern Indiana. Highways and railroads enter it from ten directions. The *Cardinal,* however, is its only passenger train.

164.4 **PERU** *132.3.* For a small town (population 13,000) Peru has quite an interesting history. Until 1930, when the Depression closed them down, several of America's most famous circuses had their winter quarters here. Why here? Because Peru offered a central location with good railroad connections in all directions, and the rich farm lands in the area provided plenty of inexpensive fodder for the circus animals and workhorses. Now, however, all that remains is Peru's glorious tradition as a circus town.

Just north of Peru the rails cross the Wabash, Indiana's favorite river. Remember "When I dream about the moonlight on the Wabash, then I think about my Indiana home"? That song, "Back Home Again in Indiana," is the state's anthem. It was written by novelist Theodore Dreiser's brother Paul. And speaking of Indiana songwriters, Peru was the hometown of one of the best—Cole Porter—who was born here in 1893.

198.1 **Lake Bruce** *98.6.* Here's one for Ripley: 3 miles from the town of Lake Bruce is the town of Bruce Lake.

217.3 **North Judson** *79.4*. There's not much of a town to be seen here, but North Judson is an important railroad junction with tracks of four companies converging. This is one of many such multiple junctions around Chicago.

224.5 **La Crosse** *72.2*. Here the *Cardinal* leaves the direct Cincinnati–Chicago route and turns northeast over a branch line in order to reach the Baltimore and Ohio's Pittsburgh–Chicago main line at Wellsboro, 15 miles away. This awkward detour was made necessary when the abandonment of the Erie-Lackawanna Railroad, whose tracks the Chessie system used to use to get into Chicago, left a gap in the direct route.

230.6 **Thomaston** *66.1*. The train crosses the Norfolk and Western Railroad's Buffalo–Chicago main line, the former Nickel Plate road that was merged into the N & W some years ago.

233.4 **Hanna** *63.3*. This is another junction—this time the branch crosses the Conrail main line from Pittsburgh to Chicago, the former Pennsylvania Railroad. This track is used by Amtrak's *Broadway Limited*.

239.6 **Wellsboro** *57.1*. Here Chicago-bound passenger trains leave the C & O branch and turn west on the B & O's Pittsburgh–Chicago main line. From here on, good track and high-speed signals make for decidedly faster running.

246.8 **Alida** *49.9*. Here the train crosses the Louisville and Nashville Railroad's Michigan City branch, formerly the Monon Railroad. At this point, you are 13 miles due north of La Crosse, but Amtrak's roundabout route via Wellsboro has added another 10 miles or so.

Between Alida and Miller, 20 miles, the train passes through part of the Indiana Dunes country, a region of shifting sand hills thick with foliage and various kinds of trees. This is an ecologist's paradise, so naturally it has been the subject of a long fight between preservationists and developers. Both sides have scored victories: the Dunes State Park and the National Lakeshore have preserved large tracts in their wild state, pleasing the nature lovers, while the Burns Harbor facility and its adjacent steel mill represent a victory for industry.

260.8 **McCool** *35.9*. This is another of those ubiquitous railroad junctions: the crossing of the B & O main line (on which you are traveling) and the Elgin, Joliet and Eastern, which circles the city from Gary to Waukegan.

262.7 **Willow Creek** *34.0*. This is still another multiple junction: the B & O, Norfolk and Western (the former Wabash Railroad), and a Conrail branch that was once the old Michigan Central all come together here.

267.2 **GARY (Miller)** *29.5*. The *Cardinal*'s stop in Gary is at Lake

Street, several miles east of the frightfully deteriorated downtown area. This station is convenient to the Indiana Tollway (I-90) and Routes I-65 and I-94, making it easily accessible from anywhere in northern Indiana.

269.5 **East Gary** *27.2.* The great steel mills of Gary are to the north (right side of the train, approaching Chicago).

275.0 **Pine Junction** *21.7.* From this point into Chicago, the route is shared with other Amtrak lines from the east. See section 3.14.

3.20   The South

Amtrak passenger service in the South is spotty. Along the Eastern Seaboard, between Richmond and Florida, it's very good. Both day and overnight trains run as far south as Savannah; good coverage is available throughout Florida, and while there's only one train a day between Washington and New Orleans, via Atlanta and Birmingham, that train is the *Crescent*—one of the corporation's biggest success stories.

On the other hand, Amtrak does not serve such important Southern cities as Louisville, Nashville, Chattanooga, or Mobile; there's no passenger service at all between the Midwest and Florida or between Memphis and the mid-South and points east. In other words, Amtrak can take you from the Northeast to the Deep South in ease and comfort—but you can't cross the region in any other direction.

Because they operate through the Capitol Hill Tunnel and on to New York in the Northeast Corridor, Southern passenger trains cannot use bilevel or Superliner cars: therefore, the *Crescent* operates with Heritage equipment, and the *Silver Star* and the *Silver Meteor* have the new Amfleet II cars. The *Star* and *Meteor* offer sleeping-car passengers extra amenities—complimentary meals, wine and cheese, and even shoe shines. This is Amtrak's "Florida First Class" service.

3.21   Richmond—Savannah via Florence

This former Atlantic Coast Line route is served by the *Silver Meteor* on an overnight schedule and by the daytime *Palmetto*. Both trains operate through from New York to Washington and Richmond. The Auto Train, which has no passenger stops between Virginia and Florida, runs on the same track. The roadbed is in good shape, and speeds average more than 60 miles per hour over the whole 500 mile route.

0.0 **RICHMOND** *495.6.* For information on this former Confederate capital, see section 2.38.

Leaving from the new Staples Mill Road station on the northwestern outskirts of Richmond, Amtrak passenger trains avoid running through the old downtown area of the city. Instead, they cross the James River farther west and rejoin the old line at the southern city limits of Richmond.

From June 1864 until April 1865, 100,000 Union troops under General Grant were lined up along a front 30 miles long, from the

RICHMOND—SAVANNAH VIA FLORENCE

Southbound/miles		miles/Northbound
0.0	RICHMOND (Staples Mill Road)	495.6
13.1	Falling Creek	482.5
15.1	Bellbluff	480.5
17.9	Centralia	477.7
20.4	Chester	475.2
29.2	PETERSBURG (Ettrick)	466.4
43.7	Carson	451.9
49.7	Stony Creek	445.9
59.8	Jarratt	435.8
69.2	Emporia, Va.	426.4
80.8	Pleasant Hill, N.C.	414.8
86.8	Garysburg	408.8
89.0	Weldon	406.6
96.6	Halifax	399.0
108.5	Enfield	387.1
113.7	Whitakers	381.9
117.9	Battleboro	377.7
126.3	ROCKY MOUNT	369.3
126.3	ROCKY MOUNT	369.3
127.3	So. Rocky Mount	368.3
131.7	Sharpsburg	363.9
136.1	Elm City	359.5
142.4	WILSON	353.2
150.8	Lucama	344.8
158.2	Kenly	337.4
168.2	SELMA (Smithfield)	327.4
178.7	Four Oaks	316.9
186.9	Benson	308.7
193.0	Dunn	302.6
200.4	Godwin	295.2

north side of Richmond to south of Petersburg. Robert E. Lee, with 60,000 haggard and battle-weary Confederate veterans, held off the Union army for nearly a year, though he had so few men that he was forced to arm the sutlers and storekeepers. The object of the Union siege was not primarily Richmond: it was to capture Petersburg, the railroad center through which nearly all the supplies for Lee's army had to come.

13.1 **Falling Creek** *482.5.* The line of Falling Creek marks, roughly, the southern city limits of Richmond. Just to the east is the Richmond National Battlefield Park, which contains the remnants of the Confederate defenses that protected Richmond, the Confederate capital, from the Union army from June 1864 to April 1865. At this point the James River flows south; a bit farther on it turns east again.

The river was named by the first permanent English colonists in

America in honor of their king, James I, who was on the throne when Jamestown colony was established in 1607.

29.2 PETERSBURG (Ettrick) *466.4.* Amtrak's Petersburg station is actually in the suburb of Ettrick, across the Appomattox River to the north of central Petersburg. Trains on the Columbia route stop here.

The Petersburg National Battlefield Park, east of the town, marks the site of one of the most unusual events of the Civil War—the Battle of the Crater. During the bitter siege of Petersburg, a Union officer named Colonel Henry Pleasants showed up at General Burnside's headquarters with an idea. He had been a mining engineer in civilian life, and the regiment he commanded—the 48th Pennsylvania Infantry—contained many miners. They could, said Pleasants, dig a long shaft under the Confederate trench line and blow it up, leaving a gap through which the Union army could rush forward and take Petersburg. Burnside approved the idea, so Colonel Pleasants and his men went to work. They dug a tunnel 500 feet long, planted 8,000 pounds of explosives beneath the Confederate defenses, and ran a long fuse back to the Union Lines. A couple of Union divisions were told to attack when the mine exploded.

After some trouble with the fuse, the powder charge went off early on the morning of July 30, 1864. Sure enough, Colonel Pleasants's idea worked like a charm. A gap 500 yards wide was blown open in the Rebel fortifications, and the way was prepared for a decisive Union assault.

Unhappily, General Burnside had not done a thorough job of planning the attack; the two subordinates who were supposed to lead it got drunk instead and never left the safety of their headquarters. Advancing without orders and without leadership, the Union infantry went marching straight ahead—into the crater left by the explosion! Once there, they found it impossible to climb the steep walls; and the Confederates, soon recovering, killed five thousand of the storming party before General Grant called the whole fiasco to a halt. So, instead of taking Petersburg in the summer of 1864, the Union army had to besiege the place for 8 more miserable months before Lee was finally forced to evacuate the town in April 1865.

59.8 Jarratt *435.8.* At this little South Side Virginia hamlet, you cross the former Virginian Railway, now part of the Norfolk and Western system. The Virginian was designed and built for one purpose: to haul Pocahontas coal from the West Virginian mines to the port of Norfolk as cheaply and efficiently as possible. It was the creation of Henry H. Rogers, a close associate of John D. Rockefeller, Sr.'s, and a friend, business adviser, and sometime financial angel of Mark Twain's.

69.2 Emporia, Va. *426.4.* Twenty-seven miles east is Courtland, formerly known as Jerusalem—the scene of the Nat Turner Rebellion, the most important slave uprising in American history.

Nat Turner was no overworked field hand; on the contrary, he was a house slave who had never been ill-treated. He appeared to be quiet, respectful, and religious—anything but the type to lead a bloody revolt.

Yet, in the summer of 1831, he did just that. Turner and his followers killed some fifty whites before they were finally captured. Turner and several others were hanged.

White Southerners tended to blame the event on Northern abolitionist propaganda, especially the *Liberator* of William Lloyd Garrison. Their response was to tighten controls everywhere, to fortify themselves mentally and their section politically. Before 1830 there were serious antislavery movements within the South. Indeed, the Virginia legislature even considered compensated emancipation, rejecting the idea only because of the cost. But after Nat Turner's Rebellion, the South closed ranks in support of slavery and against any agitation to end it. From the intellectual point of view, Nat Turner's Rebellion was thus a major step in the increasing isolation of the South, which helped to bring on the Civil War 30 years later.

89.0 **Weldon, N.C.** *406.6.* In earlier times this was an important river port. Oceangoing ships from England would sail up the Albemarle Sound and the Roanoke River and dock here, just below the rapids that made the stream impassable farther inland. When the first railroad was built south from Petersburg, it pointed on Weldon, where the goods carried from the interior could be transferred to ships.

126.3 **ROCKY MOUNT** *369.3.* This is the Amtrak station for eastern North Carolina. Some 150 miles east, at Roanoke Island, Sir Walter Raleigh established the Lost Colony, from which all residents disappeared without a trace between 1587 and 1590. On the sand spit between Roanoke Sound and the Atlantic, the Wright brothers made the first successful powered flight in December 1903.

142.4 **WILSON** *353.2.* Twenty miles south is the birthplace of Charles Aycock, North Carolina's turn-of-the-century governor and the man most responsible for wresting the state from its post–Civil War backwardness.

178.7 **Four Oaks** *316.9.* About 15 miles due south is the site of Bentonville, where one of the last big battles of the Civil War was fought.

216.6 **FAYETTEVILLE** *279.0.* This is the station for the Fort Bragg Military Reservation nearby, which is named after Confederate General Braxton Bragg. Unfortunately, in spite of his colorful name, his Civil War record left him little to Bragg about. His armies marched from one defeat to another almost without interruption. True, he did command at Chickamauga, which was at least technically a Rebel victory, but the engagement cost so many Southern casualties that it actually amounted to a defeat.

237.1 **Rennert, N.C.** *258.5.* Between here and the next siding, Buie, 6 miles farther south, in December 1943, one passenger train jumped the track and a second ran into the wreckage. It was one of the worst train disasters in American history.

269.2 **DILLON, S.C.** *226.4.* This whole northeastern section of South Carolina is pervaded by memories of Francis Marion, the "Swamp Fox," the Revolutionary War hero whose headquarters were at Snow Island in the nearby Pee Dee River. Marion's guerrillas gave the British headaches, striking suddenly and without warning, then vanishing back into their stronghold in the South Carolina swamps.

299.4 **FLORENCE** *196.2.* An important railroad division point, Florence is the largest community in this part of South Carolina. It is also the closest Amtrak station to the Myrtle Beach resort area on the seacoast, 70 miles east by car.

From Florence to Charleston the rails run due south across the coastal plain, hurdling four major rivers in this 94-mile stretch.

337.3 **KINGSTREE** *158.3.* The train crosses the Black River just south of town.

355.9 **St. Stephen** *139.7.* Just north of town, the train crosses the Santee River.

362.8 **Bonneau** *132.8.* The French name is a reminder that Huguenot Protestants were in South Carolina from early colonial times.

393.9 **CHARLESTON** *101.7.* Amtrak trains do not enter the old part of the city, but use a station at River Road, west of town. For information on the city, see section 2.8.

423.1 **Jacksonboro** *72.5.* The town is named for General Andrew Jackson, who was born in South Carolina, although much of his adult life was spent in Tennessee. At this town the tracks cross the Edisto, one of the major rivers of the state.

446.8 **YEMASSEE** *48.8.* This is the station for Beaufort, Port Royal, and the U.S. Marine Corps base at Parris Island, all about 30 miles southeast.

477.5 **Hardeeville, S.C.** *18.1.* Twenty-five miles away, on the coast, is Hilton Head Island with its beautiful beaches and Sea Pines plantation. This fine natural harbor was captured by the Federals in November 1861 and afterward served as a base for Union vessels blockading the Southern ports. Today it's a resort area.

495.6 **SAVANNAH, GA.** *0.0.* For information on the city, see section 2.46. For passengers continuing on to Florida, see section 3.23.

3.22   Richmond—Savannah via Columbia

Amtrak's second Richmond–Savannah route lies somewhat west of the line through Florence, missing Charleston but serving the capitals of both North and South Carolina, Raleigh and Columbia. This was once the Seaboard Air Line Railroad, so called because it proudly promoted its long stretches of straight track. Straight or not, however, this route is 14 miles longer than the route through Florence.

One passenger train daily in each direction runs over this route—the *Silver Star,* en route from New York to Florida. It covers the 509 miles in about 10 hours.

For notes on the line from Richmond to Petersburg, see section 3.21. Leaving the Petersburg area, the route turns southwest, crossing the Appomattox River, the route of Lee's retreat from Petersburg in April 1865.

45.5 **Dinwiddie** *463.3.* The town, as well as the surrounding county, are named after Robert Dinwiddie, the lieutenant governor of colonial Virginia from 1751 to 1758. Nearby is the battlefield of Five Forks, where the Army of Northern Virginia fought its last major engagement, on April 1, 1865. It was attempting to protect Lee's remaining supply lines into Petersburg, but it failed. The day after the battle, Lee had to evacuate Richmond and Petersburg; and a week later his army surrendered.

69.2 **Alberta, Va.** *439.6.* Here you cross the former Virginian Railway, now part of the Norfolk and Western system.

106.4 **Norlina, N.C.** *402.4.* ''Norlina'' is an obvious contraction of North Carolina; the town lies just south of the Virginia state line. This used to be an important railroad operating point but is less significant nowadays.

138.0 **Franklinton** *370.8.* The town is in Franklin County, which got its name in a most unusual way. Originally, the seaboard colonies, by virtue of their English charters, had extensive claims on western lands. These claims had to be resolved before a new constitution could be adopted, and so North Carolina agreed to cede her claim to what is now eastern Tennessee on condition that Virginia do likewise. When a legal dispute arose over the Virginia cession, North Carolina tried to reclaim her western land and incorporate it as a county. Meanwhile, pioneer settlers attempted to detach the area and create a new state,

RICHMOND—SAVANNAH VIA COLUMBIA

Southbound/miles   *miles/Northbound*

0.0	RICHMOND (Staples Mill Rd.)	508.8
13.1	Falling Creek	495.7
15.1	Bellbluff	493.7
17.9	Centralia	490.9
20.5	Chester	488.3
29.2	PETERSBURG (Ettrick)	479.6
45.5	Dinwiddie	463.3
49.8	DeWitt	459.0
55.6	McKenney	453.2
65.1	Warfield	443.7
69.2	Alberta	439.6
71.9	Cochran	436.9
75.8	Grandy	433.0
82.0	Skelton	426.8
86.9	LaCrosse	421.9
94.4	Bracey, Va.	414.4
99.0	Paschall, N.C.	409.8
106.4	Norlina	402.4
108.6	Ridgeway	400.2
111.4	Manson	397.4
114.3	Middleburg	394.5
117.7	Greystone	391.1
121.6	HENDERSON	387.2
129.7	Kittrell	379.1
138.0	Franklinton	370.8
144.2	Youngville	364.6
148.2	Wake Forest	360.6
155.1	Neuse	353.7
158.8	Millbrook	350.0
165.4	RALEIGH	343.4
165.4	RALEIGH	343.4
173.9	Cary	334.9
179.7	Apex	329.1
185.9	New Hill	322.9
188.5	Bonsal	320.3
190.8	Merry Oaks	318.0
195.5	Moncure	313.3
203.8	Colon	305.0
207.5	Sanford	301.3
214.1	Lemon Springs	294.7
219.7	Cameron	289.1
225.2	Vass	283.6
226.4	Lake View	282.4
230.4	Niagra	278.4
232.2	Manley	276.6
233.4	SOUTHERN PINES	275.4
237.2	Aberdeen	271.6
239.5	Pine Bluff	269.3

220

which they wanted to call ''Franklin.'' Not until 1796 was the confusion finally resolved and Tennessee admitted to the union under its present name. North Carolina then gave the name Franklin to this Piedmont county.

165.4 **RALEIGH** *343.4*. For information on the city, see section 2.36.

233.4 **SOUTHERN PINES** *275.4*. The name is a reminder of the extent of the forests of North Carolina: three fifths of the state's area is covered by trees. The Loblolly pine is the most common in the eastern part of the state, hence the name of the town.

Southern Pines serves as Amtrak's station for Pinehurst, about 6 miles west, a golfing resort and home of the World Golf Hall of Fame.

262.0 **HAMLET, N.C.** *246.8.* Hamlet is an important railroad operating point, where rail lines converge from five directions. In addition to the north-south main line, a branch comes in from the port city of Wilmington. This line includes the longest stretch of ruler-straight track in the United States, 79 miles without a curve. Another freight-only route goes west from Hamlet to Atlanta and Birmingham, Alabama. And there is also a freight-only branch to Charlestown. Vast yards and engine-servicing facilities are at Hamlet.

277.8 **Wallace, S.C.** *231.0.* Just west of the town, the rails cross the Pee Dee River, one of South Carolina's major rivers. The Pee Dee rises in the Piedmont region of North Carolina and flows southward to the Atlantic. Together with its tributaries, it drains the entire northeastern quadrant of South Carolina.

321.5 **Cassatt** *187.3.* Alexander Cassatt, president of the Pennsylvania Railroad in the early part of the century, also had an interest in southern railroad development—an interest recalled by this town name.

335.0 **CAMDEN** *173.8.* This town is notable as the birthplace (in 1870) of Bernard Baruch, financier, statesman, and adviser to every president from Wilson to Eisenhower. Baruch made his fortune in Wall Street and was appointed chairman of the War Industries Board by Wilson. He also served as an adviser to Wilson at the Versailles Peace Conference. Later in his career he was named U.S. delegate to the United Nations Atomic Energy Commission, where he proposed a plan for international control of nuclear weapons, which was rejected by the Soviet Union. He died in 1965 at the enviable age of ninety-five.

Camden was the scene of a British victory during the Revolutionary War. General Cornwallis, marching north from Charleston, met and soundly defeated a Colonial force under the incompetent Horatio Gates on August 16, 1780.

At Camden the train crosses the Wateree River—marvelous name!

367.9 **COLUMBIA** *140.9.* Capital of the state and home of the University of South Carolina, Columbia lies along the Congaree River. Its planners chose a site in the dead center of the state. Columbia was nearly destroyed at the end of the Civil War, when 100,000 Union troops under William T. Sherman came marching northward through the town. The Northern soldiers were in an ugly mood, burning to take out their resentment on the state that had been first to secede. Sherman himself wrote that he almost trembled at what was in store for South Carolina.

When Columbia was occupied, some local residents made a misguided effort at conciliation: They bought barrels of whiskey for their conquerors. While everybody was getting well lubricated, fire broke out in the city and burned the place to the ground. To this day the cause of the conflagration is in dispute. Rebels accused the drunken Federals, but the Yankees claimed that the fire started when Southerners tried to destroy the piled-up cotton crop. Whoever was responsible, the result was that modern Columbia dates almost entirely from the postwar period.

Today Columbia is an important marketing, educational, and governmental center.

397.9 **North** *110.9.* This has to be one of the greatest place names in America. How would you like to explain to people that you live in North, South Carolina? Actually, the name derives from the north fork of the Edisto River, which the rails cross just south of the town.

From here to Savannah the railroad is built across the natural drainage pattern. Five major rivers had to be bridged in the next 110 miles. Sherman's army had to cross them on its advance from Savannah, and in 1865 there were no bridges. Yet the Federals advanced so fast that the opposing Confederate general is supposed to have said that the Northern army was the most awesome military force since Julius Caesar's.

409.9 **Norway** *98.9.* Between Norway and Denmark (*sic!*) the railroad crosses the south fork of the Edisto River.

418.5 **DENMARK** *90.3.* From Hamlet to Denmark, via Norway, is 157 miles. Take that, William Shakespeare!

428.9 **Olar** *79.9.* South of town the railroad breasts the swamps to cross the Salkehatchie River. Sherman reached this river and found no less than fifteen separate channels barring his way. Fifteen bridges were built across them in a single day. No wonder the Rebels became discouraged!

468.9 **Garnett, S.C.** *39.9.* The town was named for Richard Garnett, a Confederate general who was killed in action at Gettysburg while leading a brigade during Pickett's Charge.

A few miles south of Garnett the route crosses the Savannah River, the boundary line between South Carolina and Georgia. The last 30 miles into Savannah are in the latter state.

508.8 **SAVANNAH, GA.** *0.0.* For information on this historic old port city, see section 2.46. For passengers continuing on to Florida, see section 2.23.

3.23   Savannah—Jacksonville

As late as the 1960s there were three separate passenger routes between Savannah and Jacksonville, but today Amtrak traffic is concentrated on the former Atlantic Coast Line route through Jesup and Folkston. The *Silver Meteor* and *Silver Star,* en route from New York to Florida, provide service twice a day in each direction. The Auto Train also uses this route.

0.0 **SAVANNAH** *147.6.* For information on Savannah, see section 2.46.

15.4 **Richmond Hill** *132.2.* Here you'll cross the Ogeechee, one of the three major rivers between Savannah and Jacksonville. The U.S. Army Flight Training Center at Fort Stewart is just west of town. At Richmond Hill the former ACL line, used today by Amtrak, diverges from the former SAL route through Thalmann; the two meet again at Jacksonville.

53.2 **Doctortown** *94.4.* I don't know the number of physicians in Doctortown, but there can't be many. This is just a tiny hamlet at the south end of the Altamaha River bridge.

56.7 **JESUP** *90.9.* Jesup is Amtrak's station for Brunswick and

SAVANNAH—JACKSONVILLE

Southbound/miles		*miles/Northbound*
0.0	SAVANNAH	147.6
11.2	Burroughs	136.4
15.4	Richmond Hill	132.2
19.8	Daniel	127.8
23.2	Fleming	124.4
30.8	McIntosh	116.8
38.1	Walthourville	109.5
45.8	Ludowici	101.8
53.2	Doctortown	94.4
56.7	JESUP (Brunswick)	90.9
85.1	Nahunta	62.5
111.1	Folkston, Ga.	36.5
122.7	Hilliard, Fla.	24.9
132.9	Callahan	14.7
143.0	Dinsmore	4.6
147.6	JACKSONVILLE (Clifford Lane Sta.)	0.0

Jekyll Island, the former millionaires' playground that is now an attractive state park. It's a crossroads town, with rail and highway routes diverging in five directions.

111.1 **Folkston, Ga.** *36.5*. Just south of town, you'll go across the St. Mary's River into Florida. West of Folkston lies the wild Okefenokee Swamp, a national wildlife refuge filled with sawgrass, Spanish moss, and hungry alligators. Incidentally, the alligator differs from its cousin the crocodile in that it inhabits freshwater areas and has a broader jaw and snout.

122.7 **Hilliard, Fla.** *24.9*. Florida's name, Spanish for ''full of flowers,'' is singularly appropriate. Florida was discovered on Easter Sunday 1513 by a romantic Spanish explorer named Juan Ponce de Leon; he was searching for the legendary Fountain of Youth. So many older folks have retired to Florida that you'd think the place really was the Fountain of Youth that Ponce was looking for. Florida's population is the fastest growing in the Union—up more than 1,000 percent since the end of World War II. More than 100,000 people a year move to Florida from other states—not to mention the enormous influx of refugee Cubans that has occurred since 1960.

147.6 **JACKSONVILLE** *0.0*. Amtrak no longer uses the old Union Station in Jacksonville; today trains stop at a station at the edge of the city. For information on the city, see section 2.20. Passengers continuing on to Miami should see section 3.25 or 3.26; to Tampa and St. Petersburg, see section 3.24.

3.24   Jacksonville—St. Petersburg via Orlando

Amtrak covers Florida like a blanket, with two routes between Jacksonville and Miami and another from Jacksonville to the Tampa—St. Petersburg area.

The west-coast section of the *Silver Meteor,* the *Silver Star,* and the *Auto Train* operate via De Land; the Miami section of the *Silver Meteor* runs via Ocala. There is also cross-Florida day service between Miami and Tampa. The only part of Florida that Amtrack does not serve is the panhandle.

Note that two mileage figures are given for communities between Auburndale and Jacksonville on the De Land route, northbound. The larger figure is the distance from Miami; the smaller, the distance from St. Petersburg.

0.0 **JACKSONVILLE (Clifford Lane Station)** *291.7/419.8.* (Jacksonville's new suburban station is 291.7 miles from St. Petersburg and 419.8 miles from Miami, via Orlando.) For information on the city, see section 2.20.

Between Jacksonville and Sanford this former Atlantic Coast Line route follows the St. Johns River, which flows northward parallel to the coast but always a few miles inland. At Sanford the train swings westward through the central-Florida resort area, where some of the greatest tourist attractions in North America, headed by Walt Disney World, are found.

33.0 **Green Cove Springs** *258.7/386.8.* Twenty-five miles east, on the seacoast, is St. Augustine, the oldest European settlement in North America. The town was founded by the Spaniards in 1565 and has been inhabited continuously ever since.

58.1 **PALATKA** *233.6/361.7.* This is the station for points on

JACKSONVILLE—ST. PETERSBURG

Southbound/miles		miles/Northbound
0.0	JACKSONVILLE (Clifford Lane Sta.)	291.7
12.6	Yukon	279.1
17.2	Orange Park	274.5
23.6	Doctor's Inlet	268.1
33.0	Green Cove Springs	258.7
43.4	West Toccoi	248.3
48.9	Bostwick	242.8
58.1	PALATKA	233.6
67.1	Satsuma	224.6
72.6	Pomona Park	219.1
77.4	Huntington	214.3
79.6	Crescent City	212.1
86.6	Seville	205.1
92.3	Pierson	199.4
97.0	Barberville	194.7
102.2	DeLeon Springs	189.5
105.4	Glenwood	186.3
110.4	DE LAND	181.3
115.2	Orange City	176.5
121.5	Benson Junct.	170.2
127.5	SANFORD	164.2
127.5	SANFORD	164.2
137.0	Longwood	154.7
139.9	Altamonte Springs	151.8
142.5	Maitland	149.2
145.0	WINTER PARK	146.7
149.8	ORLANDO	141.9

149.8	ORLANDO	141.9
165.2	Pine Castle	126.5
167.6	KISSIMMEE	124.1
171.6	Campbell	120.1
183.9	Davenport	107.8
188.6	Haines City	103.1
195.3	Lake Alfred	96.4
199.6	Auburndale	92.1
204.8	Carters	86.9
210.2	LAKELAND	81.5

210.2	LAKELAND	81.5
214.3	Winston	77.4
220.7	Plant City	71.0
226.9	Dover	64.8
230.9	Seffner	60.8
232.4	Mango	59.3
238.1	Uceta	53.6
241.3	TAMPA	50.4

241.3	TAMPA	50.4
247.7	Sulphur Springs	44.0
250.3	Lake Carroll	41.4
255.5	Tarpon	36.2
261.4	Oldsmar	30.3
266.3	Safety Harbor	25.4
269.4	Coachman	22.3
273.9	CLEARWATER	17.8

273.9	CLEARWATER	17.8
278.5	Largo	13.2
283.3	Cross Bayou	8.4
285.3	Pinellas Park	6.4
287.7	Lellman (St. Petersburg)	4.0
291.7	ST. PETERSBURG	0.0

the coast between St. Augustine and Ormond Beach, including Marineland with its aquatic animal shows and Flagler Beach, named after Henry M. Flagler, the oil man turned real-estate magnate who was most responsible for the development of Florida around the turn of the century.

East of Palatka the railroad crosses the St. Johns River and runs along its east bank to Satsuma. From there to Sanford the route is parallel to the river but some distance to the east.

110.4 **DE LAND** *181.3/309.4.* Here is the station for the city of Daytona Beach, site of the Daytona Speedway. At Daytona, Mary McLeod Bethune (1875–1955) founded an industrial-training school for black girls in 1904. Today it has grown into Bethune-Cookman College. Mrs. Bethune was a remarkable lady—a leading educator and civil-rights activist for more than half a century. She was active in the

Urban League and the NAACP and was a special adviser to President Franklin D. Roosevelt.

De Land also has a college of its own, Stetson University—and, yes, it was named after the hat-making people. The school's athletic teams, in fact, are called the Stetson Hatters.

115.2 **Orange City** *176.5/304.6.* As evident from the name, this is real citrus country now. Florida is the nation's largest producer of citrus fruits. The annual crop is worth billions of dollars. Florida oranges, grapefruits, and tangerines are marketed everywhere in the United States, even—would you believe?—in California.

121.5 **Benson Junction** *170.2/298.3.* A branch line extends from this point to Titusville, on the coast, the nearest large town to Cape Canaveral and the Kennedy Space Center. Between Benson Junction and Sanford, the tracks skirt the western shore of Lake Monroe, actually a wide place in the St. John's River. The train soon leaves the river after following its course on and off all the way from Jacksonville.

127.5 **SANFORD** *164.2/292.3.* The Sanford Amtrak station is the one most convenient to the Kennedy Space Center, which is about 40 miles away by auto.

Sanford marks the approximate edge of the central Florida recreation area, which includes innumerable attractions. It is the southern terminus of the Auto Train. Sanford is also a railroad division point where engine crews change. All trains stop here for a few minutes.

145.0 **WINTER PARK** *146.7/274.8.* Actually a suburb of Orlando, Winter Park still maintains its own identity. Rollins College is located here.

149.8 **ORLANDO** *141.9/270.0.* This is the principal city of central Florida, with a population of 150,000. Orlando is convenient to Cape Canaveral by the Bee Line Expressway, a toll highway through the orange groves, which also serves such communities as Winter Garden, Leesburg, and Eustis. Orlando is convenient to almost anyplace on the Florida peninsula; it lies near the center of the state, and express highways extend outward from the city in five directions, like the spokes of a wheel.

Major tourist attractions within an hour's drive of Orlando include Walt Disney World, Sea World, and the Ringling Brothers and Barnum and Bailey Circus World, in addition to the Kennedy Space Center, fresh- and saltwater fishing and swimming, and sunning. Orlando thus has become a convenient headquarters city for many Florida visitors.

167.6 **KISSIMMEE** *124.1/252.2.* This is Amtrak's closest station to Walt Disney World, which is about 20 miles west. Kissimmee is also a convenient station for such East Coast communities as Melbourne, Vero Beach, and Fort Pierce—all accessible via the Florida Turnpike, which runs southeast from here.

228

199.6 **Auburndale** *92.1/220.2.* There isn't much to see here—a few factories in the fields— but Auburndale is Amtrak's most important Florida junction, the point where the two Florida lines cross and where the *Silver Star* is split into sections bound for St. Petersburg and Miami. So, while you won't find the place in Amtrak's timetables—there isn't even a station here—Auburndale is extremely important.

210.2 **LAKELAND** *81.5.* Despite Lakeland's name, there isn't a lake in sight. Lake Hancock, the nearest body of water, is 10 miles southeast.

Lakeland has been the spring-training base of the Detroit Tigers for many years. The team has a big complex of diamonds and buildings called Tigertown, which is occupied every year from February to early April by Tiger players of today and tomorrow.

241.3 **TAMPA** *50.4.* Florida's biggest Gulf Coast port and home of the American cigar industry, Tampa grew out of Fort Brooke, established in 1823. It is therefore three quarters of a century older than Miami. The Latin quarter, known as Ybor City, is a tourist attraction.

The city is built on the north edge of Hillsborough Bay, itself an arm of Tampa Bay. Part of the town is on a peninsula extending out into the water; from this peninsula two highway bridges extend across to St. Petersburg. Amtrak trains, however, must circle all around the bay to reach St. Pete, a slow hour and a half trip; by car on Route I-275, you can do it in less than a third of that time. So if you're late for your train north at St. Petersburg, you needn't worry—catch it at Tampa. Amtrak would prefer, in fact, that all trains someday terminate at the newly rebuilt Tampa station. Eliminating the last 50 miles into St. Petersburg would save the NRPC $1.6 million a year while causing little inconvenience.

273.9 **CLEARWATER** *17.8.* Here the train reaches the Gulf Coast at last. From Clearwater south, the rails run along the peninsula between the coast and Tampa Bay, on which St. Petersburg is built.

291.7 **ST. PETERSBURG** *0.0.* For information on the city, see section 2.41.

3.25   Jacksonville—Miami via Wildwood

This, the former Seaboard Air Line main line through Florida, goes west from Jacksonville for 20 miles before turning south. It runs through the center of the state to Sebring, then cuts across the swamplands to reach the Atlantic coast at West Palm Beach.

From Jacksonville to Auburndale, service is limited to one train daily in each direction, the *Silver Meteor* to and from New York. South of Auburndale the *Meteor* is joined by the East Coast section of the *Silver Star,* which comes from Jacksonville by way of Orlando.

0.0 **JACKSONVILLE (Clifford Lane Station)** *408.5*. For information on the city, see section 2.20.

20.8 **Baldwin** *387.7*. Baldwin is the junction of the Jacksonville line and a cutoff route, used by fast freight trains, that bypasses Jacksonville altogether. At Baldwin the train turns due south to begin its run through the middle of the Florida peninsula.

58.3 **WALDO** *350.2*. This is the station for Gainesville, home of the University of Florida, which is 17 miles southwest by car. Just north of Waldo the rails cross the Santa Fe River, a tributary of the famous Suwannee River.

79.1 **Lochloosa** *329.4*. The name is a peculiar combination of Scottish and Indian words. The lake itself may be seen on the west side of the train (left side, going south).

103.6 **OCALA** *304.9*. You may not think of Florida as horse country, but there are Thoroughbred farms around here. The big Ocala National Forest lies a few miles east—a reminder that not all of Florida grow citrus fruit. The northern part of the state produces lumber, paper, resins, and other by-products from its thick stands of timber.

JACKSONVILLE—MIAMI VIA WILDWOOD

Southbound/miles		miles/Northbound
0.0	JACKSONVILLE (Clifford Lane Sta.)	408.5
9.3	Marietta	399.2
12.9	White House	395.6
20.8	Baldwin	387.7
28.4	Maxville	380.1
34.8	Highland	373.7
39.8	Lawtry	368.7

46.7	Starke	361.8
52.9	Hampton	355.6
58.3	WALDO	350.2
63.6	Orange Heights	344.9
67.6	Campville	340.9
72.6	Hawthorne	335.9
79.1	Lochloosa	329.4
82.7	Island Grove	325.8
85.2	Citra	323.3
90.7	Sparr	317.8
94.0	Anthony	314.5
103.6	OCALA	304.9
111.4	Santos	297.1
115.3	Belleview	293.2
119.3	Summerfield	289.2
125.1	Oxford	283.4
129.7	WILDWOOD	278.8

129.7	WILDWOOD	278.8
134.3	Coleman	274.2
138.7	Sumterville	269.8
145.8	Center Hill	262.7
149.8	Mabel	258.7
168.3	Withla	240.2
179.1	Polk City	229.4
184.6	Noxon	223.9
188.3	Auburndale	220.2
194.3	WINTER HAVEN	214.2

194.3	WINTER HAVEN	214.2
204.0	West Lake Wales	204.5
215.9	West Frostproof	192.6
226.7	Avon Park	181.8
235.7	SEBRING	172.8
251.5	Fort Bassenger	157.0
267.2	Okeechobee	141.3
281.9	Sherman	126.6
305.8	Indiantown	102.7
338.4	WEST PALM BEACH	90.1
345.0	Lake Worth	63.5
349.2	Hypoluxo	59.3
351.8	Boynton Beach	56.7
356.0	DELRAY BEACH	52.5
359.6	Yamato	48.9
366.8	DEERFIELD BEACH	41.7
373.6	Pompano Beach	34.9
380.8	FORT LAUDERDALE	27.7
385.3	Dania	23.2
388.2	HOLLYWOOD	20.3
390.0	Hallandale	18.5
398.5	Opa-Locka	10.0
402.4	MIAMI (Amtrak Sta.)	6.1
404.9	Hialeah	3.6
408.5	Miami (SAL Sta.)	0.0

129.7 **WILDWOOD** *278.8.* Wildwood is a railroad division point with freight yards and other facilities.

134.3 **Coleman** *274.2.* This is the junction between the St. Petersburg and Miami legs of the old Seaboard Air Line. The track to Miami, used by Amtrak's *Silver Meteor,* is one of America's newer main lines. It was completed in 1927. Until then, service to Miami had been a monopoly of Henry M. Flagler's Florida East Coast system. The FEC is still in the freight business, but all Miami-bound passenger trains now use the former Seaboard route.

Between Coleman and Auburndale the tracks run through the middle of a vast swamp—there's not even a village for 30 miles.

188.3 **Auburndale** *220.2.* This is the junction point where Amtrak's two Florida routes cross.

194.3 **WINTER HAVEN** *214.2.* Here is the station for Cypress Gardens. Waterskiing here was the first to be promoted nationally. Nearby are Lake Wales, with its Bok Singing Tower, and Bartow.

235.7 **SEBRING** *172.8.* To millions of auto-racing fans around the world, Sebring means the Grand Prix racecourse. Lake Jackson laps at the edge of the town.

251.5 **Fort Bassenger** *157.0.* The railroad and the Florida highway department spell the name differently; all highway maps say "Basinger." At this point the tracks cross the Kissimmee River.

267.2 **Okeechobee** *141.3.* To the south lies Lake Okeechobee, the largest lake in Florida. Beyond it stretch the endless miles of the Everglades and Big Cypress swamps, where there is virtually no human habitation except along the two coasts. Indeed, the Everglades Parkway across the area is known as Alligator Alley.

338.4 **WEST PALM BEACH** *90.1.* This is the station for ritzy Palm Beach. From here south the scene changes. Instead of the forlorn miles of scrub pines, sand, and reeking swamps, there is one nearly continuous urban area all the way to Miami. The railroad parallels the seashore, but the Atlantic is out of sight to the east.

402.4 **MIAMI** *6.1.* Amtrak's new Miami station is well north of the downtown area, out by the Hialeah freight yards. The location is less inconvenient than it sounds, however, because expressways connect the site with just about anyplace you'd want to go in southern Florida.

For information on the city, see section 2.25.

3.26   Jacksonville—Miami via Orlando

This is the route used by the East Coast section of the *Silver Star*. The *Star* comes down from New York as a single train, splitting at Auburndale into Miami and St. Petersburg sections. North of Auburndale, this line is also used by the Gulf Coast section of the *Silver Meteor;* south of Auburndale, the *Silver Meteor*'s East Coast section uses these tracks too. There are, therefore, two trains daily in each direction over the entire 420-mile distance from Jacksonville to Miami. Note that from Jacksonville to Auburndale, the line via Orlando is 11 miles longer than the route through Wildwood.

JACKSONVILLE—MIAMI VIA ORLANDO

Southbound/miles		miles/Northbound
0.0	JACKSONVILLE	419.8
12.6	Yukon	407.2
17.2	Orange Park	402.6
23.6	Doctor's Inlet	396.2
33.0	Green Cove Springs	386.8
43.4	West Tocco	376.4
48.9	Bostwick	370.9
58.1	PALATKA	361.7
67.1	Satsuma	352.7
72.6	Pomona Park	347.2
77.4	Huntington	342.4
79.6	Crescent City	340.2
86.6	Seville	333.2
92.3	Pierson	327.5
97.0	Barberville	322.8
102.2	DeLeon Springs	317.6
105.4	Glenwood	314.4
110.4	DELAND	309.4
115.2	Orange City	304.6
121.5	Benson Junction	298.3
127.5	SANFORD	292.3
127.5	SANFORD	292.3
137.0	Longwood	282.8
139.9	Altamonte Springs	279.9
142.5	Maitland	277.3
145.0	WINTER PARK	274.8
149.8	ORLANDO	270.0

165.2	Pine Castle	254.6
167.6	KISSIMMEE	252.2
171.6	Campbell	248.2
183.9	Davenport	235.9
188.6	Haines City	231.2
195.3	Lake Alfred	224.5
199.6	Auburndale	220.2
205.6	WINTER HAVEN	214.2

205.6	WINTER HAVEN	214.2
215.3	West Lake Wales	204.5
227.2	West Frostproof	192.6
238.0	Avon Park	181.8
247.0	SEBRING	172.8
262.8	Fort Bassenger	157.0
278.5	Okeechobee	141.3
293.2	Sherman	126.6
317.1	Indiantown	102.7
349.7	WEST PALM BEACH	90.1
356.3	Lake Worth	63.5
360.5	Hypoluxo	59.3
363.1	Boynton Beach	56.7
367.3	DELRAY BEACH	52.5
370.9	Yamato	48.9
378.1	DEERFIELD BEACH	41.7
384.9	Pompano Beach	34.9
392.1	FORT LAUDERDALE	27.7
396.6	Dania	23.2
399.5	HOLLYWOOD	20.3
401.3	Hallandale	18.5
409.8	Opa-Locka	10.0
413.7	MIAMI (Amtrak Sta.)	6.1
416.2	Hialeah	3.6
419.8	Miami (SAL Sta.)	0.0

For notes on the route from Jacksonville to Auburndale, see section 3.24. For notes on the route from Auburndale to Miami, see section 3.25.

3.27 Miami—Tampa

There had not been rail service connecting the east and west coasts of Florida for many years until Amtrak introduced the new *Silver Palm* in late 1982. Financed in part by the state, this unreserved, all-coach train makes a daily round trip between Miami and Tampa by way of the junction at Auburndale.

Northbound/miles   *miles/Southbound*

0.0	MIAMI	255.8
3.9	Opa-Locka	251.9
12.4	Hallandale	243.4
14.2	HOLLYWOOD	241.6
17.1	Dania	238.7
21.6	FORT LAUDERDALE	234.2
28.8	Pompano Beach	227.0
35.6	DEERFIELD BEACH	220.2
42.8	Yamato	213.0
46.4	DELRAY BEACH	209.4
50.6	Boynton Beach	205.2
53.2	Hypoluxo	202.6
57.4	Lake Worth	198.4
64.0	WEST PALM BEACH	191.8
96.6	Indiantown	159.2
120.5	Sherman	135.3
135.2	Okeechobee	120.6
150.9	Fort Bassenger	104.9
166.7	SEBRING	89.1
175.7	Avon Park	80.1
186.5	West Frostproof	69.3
198.4	West Lake Wales	57.4
208.1	WINTER HAVEN	47.7
214.1	Auburndale	41.7
219.3	Carters	36.5
224.7	LAKELAND	31.1
228.8	Winston	27.0
235.2	Plant City	20.6
241.4	Dover	14.4
245.4	Seffner	10.4
246.9	Mango	8.9
252.6	Uceta	3.2
255.8	TAMPA	0.0

For notes on the Miami–Auburndale segment, see section 3.24. For notes on the route from Auburndale to Tampa, see section 3.25.

3.28 Washington—Atlanta—Birmingham—New Orleans

This is the route of the *Crescent,* one of Amtrak's most popular trains. It takes its name from its southern terminus, New Orleans, which is called the Crescent City because it sits in a crescent-shaped loop of the Mississippi. Before Amtrak took it over, it was the premier train of the Southern Railway system. The *Crescent* is equipped with Heritage Fleet cars and provides daily coach and sleeping-car service from the Northeast to Atlanta, Birmingham, and New Orleans.

The Southern did not join Amtrak when the latter was formed in 1971, and for eight years it continued to operate the *Crescent* on its own account. But the cars were aging, the old diesels needed replacement, and the service did not justify large capital investments in new equipment. Thus, after protracted negotiations, the Southern turned its pride and joy over to Amtrak in 1979.

Happily, the results have been good. The *Crescent* has scored big gains in ridership and is consistently among the most popular trains in the East. And in conjunction with the *Sunset Limited,* it offers an alternative New York—Los Angeles route, with an overnight stay in New Orleans.

For notes on the route between Washington and Alexandria, see section 3.9.

8.2 **ALEXANDRIA** *1146.0.* Between Alexandria and Orange the *Crescent* runs over what was once the Orange and Alexandria Railroad, which was a key line important to both sides during the Civil War. It was destroyed and rebuilt several times during the Virginia fighting and served as a vital supply line for both Union and Confederate armies.

23.3 **Fairfax** *1130.9.* As a young man George Washington surveyed the lands of Lord Fairfax. Today this area is well within the suburbs of Washington, D.C.

32.6 **MANASSAS** *1121.6.* When Virginia seceded from the United States in April 1861, Confederate troops took up positions near Washington. They soon retreated 20 miles or so to a position near here, on the hills above a little stream called Bull Run, commanding the junction of the Orange and Alexandria and Manassas Gap railroads at Manassas station. This junction was vital because it controlled the route from the Shenandoah Valley by which Confederate reinforcements would come.

Under pressure from Washington, Union commander Irvin McDowell attacked the Confederates here on July 21, 1861; but the attack came too late. Confederate General Joe Johnston and his troops arrived during the fighting, in time to turn the battle into a rout. At the height of the Union attack a Confederate officer, trying to rally his men, pointed to the Virginia brigade commanded by Thomas J. Jackson and shouted, "Look! There stands Jackson like a stone wall!" It was "Stonewall Jackson" from then on.

The most important things about the First Battle of Manassas were that a railroad junction was the objective and that troops transported by rail won the day—a clear indication of the importance of railroads in the Civil War, the first of the so-called modern conflicts.

Nor was this first big fight of the war the only action to take place on this ground. Thirteen months later, in August 1862, the Confederate Army of Northern Virginia under Robert E. Lee and Stonewall Jackson inflicted a severe defeat on a Union force commanded by the hapless John Pope. This was the high point of the Confederacy, the only time when all the major Confederate forces were victorious and advancing.

61.5 **Brandy** *1092.7.* Every foot of this beautiful part of northern Virginia is rich in Civil War history, and this spot, formerly called Brandy Station, is no exception. Here, Union General Alfred Pleasanton sent his horsemen against Jeb Stuart's Confederates in the biggest cavalry clash of the entire war. The battle ended as a draw.

84.7 **Orange** *1069.5.* This was once called Orange Court House. It was the custom in early Virginia to establish a courthouse by itself

WASHINGTON—ATLANTA—BIRMINGHAM—NEW ORLEANS

Southbound/miles		*miles/Northbound*
0.0	WASHINGTON, D.C.	1154.2
	Capitol Hill Tunnel	
	Potomac River Bridge	
8.2	ALEXANDRIA, VA.	1146.0
9.6	Seminary	1144.6
13.5	Edsall	1140.7
15.1	Springfield	1139.1
18.0	Ravensworth	1136.2
19.9	Burke	1134.3
22.1	Sideburn	1132.1
23.3	Fairfax	1130.9
26.8	Clifton	1127.4
32.6	MANASSAS	1121.6
36.6	Bristow	1117.6
39.4	Nokesville	1114.8
44.0	Catlett	1110.2
46.3	Calverton	1107.9
50.0	Midland	1104.2
52.8	Bealeton	1101.4
56.3	Remington	1097.9
61.5	Brandy	1092.7
64.4	Inlet	1089.8
67.4	CULPEPER	1086.8
71.9	Winston	1082.3
74.4	Mitchell	1079.8
79.1	Rapidan	1075.1
84.7	Orange	1069.5
88.8	Montpelier	1065.4
91.5	Somerset	1062.7
95.8	Barboursville	1058.4

101.7	Gilbert	1052.5
105.7	Proffit	1048.5
109.4	Rio	1044.8
112.2	CHARLOTTESVILLE	1042.0
115.7	Hickory Hill	1038.5
119.2	Arrowhead	1035.0
120.5	Red Hill	1033.7
123.1	North Garden	1031.1
128.0	Covesville	1026.2
132.4	Faber	1021.8
134.8	Rockfish	1019.4
138.8	Elma	1015.4
142.1	Shipman	1012.1
146.7	Arrington	1007.5
149.9	Tye River	1004.3
153.0	New Glasgow	1001.2
158.0	Amherst	996.2
160.0	Sweetbriar	994.2
162.1	Coolwell	992.1
164.2	McIver	990.0
165.1	MONROE	989.1

165.1	MONROE	989.1
166.6	Winesap	987.6
172.5	LYNCHBURG	981.7

172.5	LYNCHBURG	981.7
173.5	Durmid	980.7
176.6	Montview	977.6
180.7	Lawyer	973.5
186.8	Evington	967.4
193.1	Clarion	961.1
195.8	Alta Vista	958.4
203.2	Sycamore	951.0
208.3	Gretna	945.9
213.3	Whittle	940.9
218.2	Chatham	936.0
235.8	DANVILLE	918.4
241.1	Stokesland, Va.	913.1
244.3	Pelham, N.C.	909.9
250.7	Ruffin	903.5
259.9	Reidsville	894.3
268.8	Benaja	885.4
272.4	Brown Summit	881.8
284.1	GREENSBORO	870.1

284.1	GREENSBORO	870.1
294.2	Jamestown	860.0
299.2	HIGH POINT	855.0
306.0	Thomasville	848.2
316.8	Lexington	837.4
323.0	Linwood	831.2
331.1	Spencer	823.1
333.7	SALISBURY	820.5

239

564.0	Alto	590.2
571.4	Belton	582.8
572.2	Lula	582.0
578.8	White Sulphur	575.4
584.6	GAINESVILLE	569.6
590.3	Oakwood	563.9
594.1	Flowery Branch	560.1
600.9	Buford	553.3
607.0	Suwanee	547.2
612.5	Duluth	541.7
618.4	Norcross	535.8
623.1	Doraville	531.1
624.5	Chamblee	529.7
626.7	Oglethorpe Univ.	527.5
633.5	ATLANTA (Peachtree Sta.)	520.7

633.5	ATLANTA	520.7
647.7	Mableton	506.5
650.9	Austell	503.3
659.4	Douglasville	494.8
668.3	Villa Rica	483.9
677.6	Temple	476.6
685.4	Bremen	468.8
688.3	Waco	465.9
695.6	Tallapoosa, Ga. (ET)	458.6
702.4	Muscadine, Ala. (CT)	451.8
705.5	Fruithrust	448.7
710.8	Edwardsville	443.4
716.9	Heflin	437.3
722.4	Iron City	431.8
725.2	Choccolocco	429.0
728.6	DeArmanville	425.6
735.4	ANNISTON	418.8
748.2	Eastaboga	406.0
754.2	Lincoln	400.0
759.3	Riverside	394.9
764.7	Pell City	389.5
772.1	Cook Springs	382.1
777.0	Brompton	377.2
781.7	Leeds (C of G)	372.5
787.1	McCombs	367.1
790.4	Weems	363.8
793.4	Irondale	360.8
799.3	BIRMINGHAM	354.9

799.3	BIRMINGHAM	354.9
810.7	Bessemer	343.5
812.4	Burstall	341.8
816.5	McCalla	337.7
828.6	Woodstock	325.6
834.1	Vance	320.1
840.6	Coaling	313.6
843.2	Grimes	311.0
847.4	Cottondale	306.8

854.8	TUSCALOOSA	299.4
865.0	Hull	289.2
869.6	Moundville	284.6
877.0	Stewart	277.2
880.4	Akron	273.8
886.7	McClure	267.5
889.3	EUTAW	264.9
899.1	Boligee	255.1
906.5	Epes	247.7
915.3	Livingston	238.9
918.8	Hixon	235.4
924.6	York	229.6
930.9	Cuba, Ala.	223.3
934.9	Kewanee, Miss.	219.3
939.0	Toomsuba	215.2
944.5	Russell	209.7
951.7	MERIDIAN	202.5
951.7	MERIDAN	202.5
968.6	Enterprise	185.6
978.4	Pachuta	175.6
987.9	Vossburg	166.3
991.6	Heidelburg	162.6
995.7	Markwald	158.5
999.5	Sandersville	154.7
1002.8	Hawkes	151.4
1008.4	LAUREL	145.8
1015.7	Ellisville	138.5
1024.7	Moeselle	129.5
1037.3	HATTIESBURG	116.9
1037.3	HATTIESBURG	116.9
1042.9	Richburg	111.3
1048.3	Okahola	105.9
1053.6	Purvis	100.6
1058.8	Talowah	95.4
1064.4	Lumberton	89.8
1070.1	Hillsdale	84.1
1077.0	Poplarville	77.2
1083.6	Derby	70.6
1086.3	Millard	67.9
1087.5	Tyler	66.7
1091.0	McNeil	63.2
1094.5	Carriere	59.7
1098.7	Richardson	55.5
1101.1	PICAYUNE	53.1
1104.6	Nicholson, Miss.	49.6
1112.1	Pearl River, La.	42.1
1119.3	SLIDELL	34.9
1124.1	North Shore, Lake Pontchartrain	30.1
1130.5	South Point	23.7
1136.1	Little Woods	18.1
1143.7	Seabrook	10.5
1151.8	Carrollton Ave.	2.4
1154.2	NEW ORLEANS	0.0

out in the fields, for there were few established towns. Gradually the courthouse would become the center of a settlement, which is what happened here.

Orange was the home of James Madison, fourth president of the United States. A protégé and disciple of Jefferson, Madison served under him as secretary of state before winning the presidency in 1808. He is regarded today as a strong chief executive who led the nation into war in 1812 rather than capitulate to British pressure.

At Orange, the double-tracked main line of the Southern Railway veers away to the southwest; the Chessie system's single track (used by Amtrak's *Cardinal*) goes straight ahead. The two lines meet again at Charlottesville.

112.2 **CHARLOTTESVILLE** *1042.0.* For information on the city, see section 2.9.

165.1 **MONROE** *989.1.* This Virginia town is the home of Sweet Briar College, a women's school widely known in the South. Otherwise, Monroe is pure railroad: The Southern Railway maintains a division point and engine terminal here.

172.5 **LYNCHBURG** *981.7.* On the James River 100 miles west of Richmond, Lynchburg is Amtrak's station for Roanoke to the west and, to the east, for Appomattox Court House, where Lee surrendered in April 1865. There's an interesting story about that event. The first big battle of the Civil War was fought at Manassas, practically on the front lawn of a house owned by a man named MacLean. Mr. MacLean decided that the neighborhood was too dangerous for his family, so he moved to a new home farther south. Four years later Lee surrendered—in the living room of Mr. MacLean's new house!

From Lynchburg south, the road climbs a long grade through the hills of South Side Virginia (South Side is that part of the commonwealth south of the James River) to Danville.

235.8 **DANVILLE, VA.** *918.4.* The town is on the Dan River, just above the North Carolina border. After the Confederate Government evacuated Richmond in April 1865, it moved here. Danville was technically the last capital of the Confederacy.

244.3 **Pelham, N.C.** *909.9.* John Pelham commanded the artillery under the Confederate calvary general Jeb Stuart and was an extremely able soldier, later killed in action.

250.7 **Ruffin** *903.5.* Edmund Ruffin was a leading expert on agriculture and also a strong exponent of the Southern plantation system. His works on deep plowing, crop rotation, and fertilization were written to encourage Southern agriculture, and he was such a strong advocate of secession that when General Beauregard opened fire on Fort Sumter to begin the Civil War, he invited Ruffin to touch off the first cannon. When the last Confederate armies surrendered,

Thomas Jefferson, third President of the United States, designed and built Monticello on a plateau on the top of a small mountain near Charlottesville, Virginia. Although construction began in 1768, it was not completed until 1809. (See sections 2.9 and 3.28.)

Mount Vernon, plantation home of America's first President, George Washington. Here Washington lived the life he loved best, that of a prosperous country squire. Mount Vernon was originally constructed in 1743 by Washington's half-brother, Lawrence, and acquired by George from his sister-in-law. To support the mansion, Washington built an extensive village-like group of flanking service buildings, or "dependencies," most of which still survive. (See section 2.9.)

Ruffin committed suicide. So, just as it could be said that the war began and ended on Mr. MacLean's property, so it could be said that Edmund Ruffin fired both the first and the last shots of the conflict—the first at the Federals, the last at himself.

Incidentally, no state sent a higher percentage of its citizens to the Confederate armies than North Carolina, and none suffered a higher percentage of casualties—yet the Tar Heel State had few slaves, was not anxious to secede, and left the Union only when all her neighbors pulled out, leaving her surrounded and isolated. North Carolina has been called a valley of humility between two mountains of conceit: Virginia and South Carolina. Today it is one of the more progressive and prosperous Southern states.

284.1 **GREENSBORO** *870.1.* Central North Carolina—the part of the state that lies between the fall line to the east and the Blue Ridge Mountains to the west—is called the Piedmont region, and Greensboro is right in the middle of it. Together with nearby Winston-Salem and High Point, it forms the most important urban complex in North Carolina. Tobacco processing, cotton mills, and furniture manufacturing help make this the most prosperous part of the state.

299.2 **HIGH POINT** *855.0.* It's not generally realized, but three-fifths of North Carolina's total area is forested. Native hardwoods supply the state's big furniture industry, which is centered here in High Point. Twice a year, furniture buyers from across the nation come to the big market held in the city.

323.0 **Linwood** *831.2.* Between Linwood and Spencer (the next town), the railroad crosses the Yadkin River, one of North Carolina's most important, rising in the Blue Ridge Mountains and draining the north central part of the state.

North Carolina—unlike, say, Virginia—has few rivers reaching the interior and, because of stormy Cape Hatteras and a number of reefs, few good natural harbors. These facts account for the state's slow growth during the colonial period and for its relatively low slave population. It was easier for ships from Europe and Africa to land in Virginia or South Carolina. North Carolina, unlike its neighbors, was settled largely by pioneers moving into the region from other colonies.

333.7 **SALISBURY** *820.5.* An important railroad division and crew-change point, Salisbury is also Amtrak's station for Kannapolis and Statesville and for the Lake Norman recreational area 25 miles west.

377.1 **CHARLOTTE** *777.1.* This is the largest city in North Carolina and the nation's leading production center of cotton cloth. Like the town in Virginia, Charlotte is named for the wife of George III, Queen Charlotte, who was on the throne at the time the city received its charter in 1768. Ironically, however, Charlotte and surrounding Mecklenburg County were hotbeds of opposition to the British crown.

A declaration of independence was actually issued here in May 1775—more than a year before Jefferson's document was approved by the Continental Congress in Philadelphia.

389.1 **Belmont** *765.1.* Just west of here, you'll cross the Catawba River. Like the Yadkin, it is one of North Carolina's two principal rivers. About 15 miles north, the Catawba has been dammed at Cowans Ford, creating Lake Norman, the largest body of water in the state.

399.3 **GASTONIA** *754.9.* Like Charlotte, Gastonia is a textile center. It has a population of about 50,000 and is the seat of Gaston County.

411.1 **Kings Mountain, N.C.** *743.1.* This was the site of an important Revolutionary War engagement. When Lord Cornwallis invaded the South, he expected and relied upon the aid of a large number of American Tories. But on October 7, 1780, a force of over a thousand loyalists was destroyed at Kings Mountain by a patriot army of Carolina backwoodsmen. Without this army, Cornwallis was considerably weakened.

443.4 **Cowpens, S.C.** *710.8.* If Kings Mountain meant trouble for the British, Cowpens meant disaster. Three months after his Tory auxiliaries were wiped out, Cornwallis was attacked at Cowpens by an American force led by the brilliant General Nathanael Greene, probably the best commander in the colonies after Washington himself. Even Cornwallis admitted that this was a damaging defeat, and two months later, after meeting Greene again at Guilford Court House (near Charlotte), Cornwallis was forced to retreat to Virginia where he was eventually trapped and forced to surrender. The *Crescent's* route passes close to all three of these battlefields. It might be called "the route of Cornwallis' defeat."

452.6 **SPARTANBURG** *701.6.* Humming textile factories and roaring diesel engines play the tune to which Spartanburg's economy dances. This is upland South Carolina—not a rice field or a tobacco plant in sight. Instead, Spartanburg manufactures and ships. The city is a junction of the Southern and the Clinchfield, a little-known railroad that connects the southeast with the Kentucky coal fields by the only north-south railroad route across the Alleghenies east of Chattanooga.

Spartanburg also has the nearest Amtrak station to Asheville and the "Land of the Sky" across the North Carolina border. Asheville has long been known for its beautiful setting and clear mountain air, which have made it a major summer resort. The Vanderbilt family chose it as the site for their Biltmore mansion, the largest home in the United States. Asheville was also the home of Thomas Wolfe, the novelist who immortalized the town under the name "Altamont" in *Look Homeward, Angel.*

484.1 **GREENVILLE** *670.1.* Greenville is a classic textile-mill town, with several big plants located here.

It was also the hometown of the man Babe Ruth called "the greatest hitter in baseball"—Shoeless Joe Jackson. He got his nickname from a writer who saw him play the outfield in his socks one day when he had blisters on his feet, and it suited him perfectly, for Jackson was a real backcountry boy who could neither read nor write. But how he could hit—he had a lifetime major-league average of .356, third highest in the history of the game.

But you will not find Shoeless Joe Jackson's name in the Baseball Hall of Fame at Cooperstown; in fact, it's a good bet that most fans know nothing of him except that marvelous nickname and perhaps the poignant phrase, "Say it ain't so, Joe." Joe Jackson was one of eight Chicago White Sox players who were banned from baseball by the new commissioner, Judge Landis, after the fixing of the 1919 World Series. Shoeless Joe hit .375 in that series and never got a cent of gamblers' money, but that made no difference to Landis. Nor did the fact that the eight players involved were acquitted of conspiracy to throw the series when the case came up in court. Landis was out to save baseball's reputation for honesty, and Jackson and his teammates paid the price.

514.2 **CLEMSON** *640.0.* Clemson University, one of the state's two major institutions of higher learning, is here. (The other is the University of South Carolina at Columbia.)

On the Clemson campus is Fort Hill, the home of John C. Calhoun. First elected to the House of Representatives in 1811, Calhoun spent the rest of his life defending the interests of his state. When those interests coincided with those of the federal government (as they did in the War of 1812), Calhoun was a nationalist. Later he became the strongest advocate of nullification and eventually of secession. In addition to his three terms in the House, he also served as secretary of state, secretary of war, vice-president (twice), and senator from South Carolina for three terms.

Clemson is also Amtrak's station for the textile center of Anderson, 18 miles southeast, and for the Lake Keowee recreation area to the north. The railroad crosses a narrow neck of the lake just west of town.

531.6 **Westminster, S.C.** *622.6.* About 10 miles west of this station, the railroad crosses the Tugaloo River and enters Georgia.

547.3 **TOCCOA, GA.** *606.9.* This station serves the entire northeastern part of the state—a mountain wilderness area cut with gorges, not at all like the popular conception of the South. But in fact Georgia, like most of the region, is far more complex than is generally thought. It is the largest state east of the Mississippi and one of the most diversified. In addition to the traditional cotton crop, it also produces peaches and peanuts. But agriculture is only one facet of Georgia's economy. Industry is the state's leading source of income, and surprisingly Georgia is a leader in production of electric power. In addition, more than 70 percent of the state is covered by forests, and pine resin, turpentine, timber, and paper are leading products. Georgia also has a thriving cattle industry and mines granite and nonferrous metals. No simple stereotype can describe such a big, rich state.

584.6 **GAINESVILLE** *569.6.* Among its other industries, Georgia counts poultry—and Gainesville means chickens. Georgia markets half a billion broiler chickens a year, many of them raised right here.

In Gainesville is Amtrak's station for Athens, site of the University of Georgia. Technically, this is the oldest state university in America, having received its charter in 1785, but it did not actually enroll students until 1801.

North of Gainesville is the largest body of water in Georgia, Lake Sidney Lanier. It was named for an obscure nineteenth-century poet and was created by damming the Chattahoochee River. It is 20 miles long, covers more than 40,000 acres, and has over 500 miles of shoreline.

600.9 **Buford** *553.3.* At Buford the railroad enters Gwinnett County. Button Gwinnett, a Georgia delegate to the First Continental Congress, has a peculiar distinction: his signature is the most valuable one on the Declaration of Independence. It seems he died young, and very few copies of his authenticated signature exist. Discover a Button Gwinnett on some old document, and you can retire.

626.7 **Oglethorpe University** *527.5.* Founded in 1835 and named for James Oglethorpe, the father of Georgia, this is a small liberal-arts college best known for its programs in English for foreign students. The English Language Service Center here enrolls a large number of visitors from other nations who spend a month improving their command of the language before going on to study elsewhere.

633.5 **ATLANTA** *520.7.* For information on the city, see section 2.2.

650.9 **Austell** *503.3.* Due north about 15 miles is Kennesaw Mountain National Battlefield Park. In his effort to capture Atlanta, Sherman ordered a general assault on the Rebel fortifications at Kennesaw in June 1864. It was beaten off with ghastly losses by General Joseph Johnston's Confederate army. The father of baseball's first commissioner was wounded in action here; he named his son Kennesaw Mountain Landis in honor of the battle.

At Austell the Southern Railway splits: One branch turns north to Chattanooga and Cincinnati, the other (used by Amtrak) continues west to Alabama and New Orleans.

695.6 **Tallapoosa, Ga.** *458.6.* The town is named for the Tallapoosa River, which rises in Georgia but flows mostly through

Alabama. It was at Horseshoe Bend on the Tallapoosa that Andrew Jackson and a force of Tennessee riflemen avenged a Creek Indian attack on an American fort by slaughtering Indian men, women, and children indiscriminately back in 1814.

Just west of the town of Tallapoosa the train crosses the river and enters Alabama. The time zone changes at the border.

702.4 **Muscadine, Ala.** *451.8.* Alabama calls itself ''Heart of Dixie,'' and geographically it is. The rich soil of the ''Black Belt'' is some of the best growing land in the South. In antebellum days cotton was the dominant crop, but today the state's agriculture is diversified. For example, Alabama grows fruit, including the muscadine grapes that give their name to this town.

716.9 **Heflin** *437.3.* Lying halfway between Atlanta and Birmingham, Heflin is at the east edge of the Talladega National Forest, through which the rails run for the next 5 miles.

735.4 **ANNISTON** *418.8.* This is the station for the Army's Fort McClellan and for the city of Gadsden 30 miles north. Gadsden is named for James Gadsden, an Alabama railroad man who negotiated the purchase of land in southern New Mexico and Arizona on behalf of the federal government in 1853.

781.7 **Leeds** *372.5.* The town was named for an English city noted for its textile industry. From here to Birmingham the Southern Railway operates its own and Amtrak's trains over the rails of the Central of Georgia.

793.4 **Irondale** *360.8* The iron industry has been a part of Alabama's economy since 1818, but it was only after the Civil War that a huge infusion of Northern capital turned the state into the steel center of the South.

799.3 **BIRMINGHAM** *354.9.* For information on the city, see section 2.4.

810.7 **Bessemer** *343.5.* This was the site of the first forge built in the Birminham region; it was named for Sir Henry Bessemer, the British inventor who developed the Bessemer process for turning iron into steel. (See the notes for Bessemer, Pennsylvania in section 3.15.)

854.8 **TUSCALOOSA** *299.4.* Home of the University of Alabama, Tuscaloosa is named for a Choctaw Indian chief defeated by Hernando De Soto, the Spanish explorer who was the first European to visit Alabama.

In 1963, Alabama's Governor George Wallace made his famous stand at the doorway of the university, in an attempt to prevent its integration. Despite his defiance, a black woman was enrolled—and life at 'Bama has gone on quite peacefully ever since.

At Tuscaloosa the rails turn south to follow the Black Warrior River for about 40 miles.

889.3 **EUTAW** *264.9.* This is the Alabama Black Belt, prime cotton land where plantations flourished before the Civil War. Twenty miles southeast is one of Alabama's most elegant mansions, Magnolia Grove, near Greensboro.

915.3 **Livingston** *238.9.* Robert Livingston was the special envoy to France who helped to negotiate the biggest real-estate deal in history—the sale of the Louisiana Territory to the United States in 1803.

Not far from Livingston is the town of Demopolis, site of another of those elegant antebellum plantations, Gaineswood.

924.6 **York, Ala.** *229.6.* First Leeds, then Birmingham, now York—an English visitor should feel right at home in Alabama.

939.0 **Toomsuba, Miss.** *215.2.* Many of the odd-sounding names in this part of the South derive from Choctaw or Chickasaw Indian language. These tribes inhabited most of Mississippi until the early nineteenth century.

951.7 **MERIDIAN** *202.5.* This is a railroad division point, with lines radiating in six directions.

1008.4 **LAUREL** *145.8.* Laurel's living claim to fame is Leontyne Price, the great soprano of the Metropolitan Opera, who is a native of the town.

1037.3 **HATTIESBURG** *116.9.* Hattiesburg calls itself the "Hub City," because of the many railroad lines that intersect here.

Virtually all of Mississippi was once covered by forests, and 60 percent of its land area still is. It should not come as a surprise, then—although to most people it does—that lumbering has long been one of the state's leading industries. Near Hattiesburg is the De Soto National Forest, covering parts of five counties.

1042.9 **Richburg** *111.3.* Charles Rich was a nineteenth-century lumber baron and this site was once one of his camps.

Richburg has a place in boxing history. At one time, prizefighting, though popular, was technically illegal in most states, including Mississippi. That, however, deterred neither the fans nor the ambitious promoters. Late on the night of July 3, 1889, the world's heavyweight champion John L. Sullivan, challenger Jake Kilrain, and a mob of reporters and fans climbed aboard a train at New Orleans and headed for a fight. The only problem was that nobody knew where it was going to be held. The governor of Mississippi had called out the militia to keep the fighters from entering the state, so the train's destination—the site of the match—was kept strictly secret. It turned out to be Richburg, where a temporary ring had been set up. There Sullivan whipped Kilrain in 75 rounds to retain his title; it was the last bare-knuckles championship bout in history. The fight ended only when a doctor advised the referee that Kilrain would probably be killed if he were allowed to continue in the stifling Mississippi heat.

It also seems that the railroad would not permit the reporters covering the bout to use its telegraph line to send out their stories. One enterprising scribe, looking for a way to score a scoop, is supposed to have scribbled his blow-by-blow account on little strips of paper, which he then pushed into rubber balls. Between rounds he threw the balls to a confederate, who mounted a fast horse and rode to a neighboring town where the telegraph lines were open.

1064.4 **Lumberton** *89.8.* The town's name is another indication of the importance of timbering to this part of the state.

1077.0 **Poplarville** *77.2.* This is Pearl River County, part of the Mississippi Panhandle, the corner of the state that extends down to the Gulf Coast, forming a panhandle between Mobile and New Orleans.

1101.1 **PICAYUNE** *53.1. Picayune* is a French word meaning "small" or "of little importance." New Orlean's leading newspaper is called the *Times-Picayune.*

1104.6 **Nicholson, Miss.** *49.6.* Southwest of the town, the tracks cross the Pearl River and enter Louisiana.

Having first been settled by the French, and long controlled by Spain, Louisiana has a unique cultural heritage. Its people are a mixture of Anglo Protestants, French and Spanish Catholics, blacks, and Creoles of mixed blood.

The state has quietly become the nation's second-largest producer of petroleum, as well as its leading grower of rice and sweet potatoes; and only Hawaii grows more sugarcane. But the real surprise is this—Louisiana is America's second-largest mining state, producing mostly salt and sulfur.

1119.3 **SLIDELL, LA.** *34.9.* John Slidell was one of the Confederacy's ablest diplomats. He spent most of the Civil War years as its representative in France. On his way to that post aboard a British mail boat, he was captured by the U.S. Navy, and the British were so insulted that they seemed ready to go to war. Only the most careful diplomacy saved the Union from a potentially disastrous confrontation.

1124.1 **North Shore** *30.1.* Here begins the 7-mile-long causeway that takes the railroad across a narrow neck of Lake Pontchartrain. The main part of the lake lies to the west (right side of the train, coming into New Orleans). This is the largest body of fresh water in Louisiana, with an area of 630 square miles. The highway paralleling the tracks across the lake is Route I-10.

1130.5 **South Point** *23.7.* This is Orleans Parish (parishes, not counties, in Louisiana).

Amtrak passengers arriving in New Orleans from the east are treated to a tour of a large part of the city. The rails follow the south shore of Lake Pontchartrain past the Lakefront Airport, cross the Inner Harbor Navigation Canal (which connects the lake with the Mississippi and the Intracoastal Waterway), then skirt the campus of Louisiana State University at New Orleans (the school's main campus is at Baton Rouge). Then the tracks turn south away from the lake shore and pass through City Park, site of the beautiful Delgado Art Museum, one of New Orleans's many treasures. Then the route curves southeast, passing between Metairie and Greenwood Cemeteries.

In New Orleans, cemeteries are different. Since the city actually lies below sea level, digging in the ground produces unsanitary ooze and groundwater. Consequently, burials are made in vaults above ground. No traveler to the Crescent City should miss these most unusual and interesting sites.

1151.8 **Carrollton Avenue** *2.4*. No longer a passenger stop, this is the junction where lines from the east, north, and west join for the approach to New Orleans's Union Passenger Terminal.

1154.2 **NEW ORLEANS** *0.0*. For information on the city, see section 2.28. For passengers continuing on to Houston, San Antonio, El Paso, Tuscon, Phoenix, or Los Angeles, see section 3.42. For Memphis-bound and Chicago-bound passengers, see section 3.33.

3.29 Main Lines of Mid-America

One look at a map tells you what Chicago means to the American transportation industry. For example, Amtrak passenger trains enter the city from ten directions. On an ordinary weekday, more than fifty long-distance passenger trains use Union Station, not to mention the hundreds of commuter trains and freights.

In the sections that follow, we'll consider Amtrak service from Chicago to Toronto, New Orleans, and such Midwestern cities as Detroit, Indianapolis, St. Louis, Quincy, Milwaukee, and the Twin Cities. Other lines entering Chicago are discussed in the sections on the Eastern trunk lines and the Western routes (sections 3.11–19 and 3.40–45, respectively).

3.30   Chicago—Detroit

The 280-mile Chicago-Detroit route has been one of Amtrak's success stories. This former New York Central line connects two of the nation's six largest cities, yet service had deteriorated badly: ranshackle engines towed tired, worn-out cars on unreliable schedules, and most of the public just ignored them.

Amtrak today runs three daily trains between Chicago and Detroit. One of these, the *Lake Cities,* continues on to Toledo, Ohio, making convenient connections with the *Lake Shore Limited* for New York and Boston. There is also service between Chicago and Battle Creek and between Ann Arbor and Detroit. Trains are modern and clean, and they usually run on time. As a result, this line is now carrying half a million people a year, with every reason to expect further increases in the future.

The Chicago-Detroit route uses Conrail tracks most of the way, but one segment near Kalamazoo is actually owned by Amtrak, which purchased it in order to keep the route intact when Conrail no longer needed it for freight service.

For notes on the route between Chicago and Porter, Indiana, see section 3.14.

40.2 **Porter** *241.3.* At this junction, the Detroit line leaves the Toledo–Buffalo route used by the *Lake Shore.* Porter is a quaint, arty-looking village with a string of small shops along the one main street visible from the north side of the train (left side, going east).

54.0 **MICHIGAN CITY, IND.** *227.5.* Michigan City—which despite its name is not in Michigan, but on the Indiana side of the state line—started out with ambitions to become a great lake port, but today it is just a small, pleasant community on the east edge of the Indiana Dunes region popular with summering Chicagoans. Many permanent residents commute all the way into the big city every day. As you pass through the town you may get a quick look at the lake to the north side (left side, going east) of the train.

63.9 **New Buffalo, Mich.** *217.6.* Its name gives this town away; New Buffalo, at the extreme southwestern corner of Michigan, hoped to become for that state what Buffalo is to New York State, a great lake port. (Does this sound familiar?) Like its neighbor, Michigan City, however, it failed to develop in competition with Chicago and is now a resort town.

Eastbound/miles		miles/Westbound
0.0	CHICAGO	281.5
1.6	21st Street	279.9
7.0	Englewood	274.5
12.6	South Chicago, Ill.	268.9
15.4	Roby, Ind.	266.1
16.8	HAMMOND/WHITING	264.7
18.6	Mahoning	262.9
19.3	Indiana Harbor	262.2
21.7	Pine Junction	259.8
26.1	Gary	255.4
40.2	Porter	241.3
54.0	MICHIGAN CITY, IND. (CT)	227.5
63.9	New Buffalo, Mich. (ET)	217.6
71.1	Three Oaks	210.4
76.8	Galien	204.7
84.3	Buchanan	197.2
90.9	NILES	190.6
103.3	DOWAGIAC	178.2
114.5	Decatur	167.0
122.2	Lawton	159.3
126.4	Mattawan	155.1
139.5	KALAMAZOO	142.0
143.3	Comstock	138.2
148.3	Galesburg	133.2
152.7	Augusta	128.8
162.3	BATTLE CREEK	119.2
162.3	BATTLE CREEK	119.2
175.4	Marshall	106.1
187.1	ALBION	94.4
196.6	Parma	84.9
207.4	JACKSON	74.1
217.7	Grass Lake	63.8
228.8	Chelsea	52.7
236.1	Dexter	45.4
245.6	ANN ARBOR	35.9
253.5	YPSILANTI	28.0
265.4	Wayne	16.1
272.4	DEARBORN	8.1
281.5	DETROIT (Amtrak Sta.)	0.0

84.3 **Buchanan** *197.2.* This town was named for James Buchanan, the fifteenth president of the United States, who was elected in 1856 and was the only American chief executive who never married. His sister served as hostess during his single term in the White House.

90.9 **NILES** *190.6.* Niles lies in the valley of the St. Joseph River, which meanders northward from Indiana to empty into Lake Michigan at the twin towns of St. Joseph and Benton Harbor, 20 miles northwest of here.

Southwestern Michigan is fruit country, and between Niles and Kalamazoo the route passes through berry fields and cherry and peach orchards, in addition to the familiar Midwestern corn fields.

103.3 **DOWAGIAC** *178.2.* The name honors an Indian chief once prominent in this area. Dowagiac is in Cass County, named for the former territorial governor of Michigan and later U.S. senator from the state, Lewis Cass. He was an unsuccessful presidential candidate in 1848 and also served as secretary of war under Andrew Jackson and as minister to France in the Van Buren administration. Cassopolis, 9 miles southeast, is also named after him.

114.5 **Decatur** *167.0.* Stephen Decatur, the naval hero of the early nineteenth century, was a popular figure in the trans-Appalachian west. There are towns bearing his name in at least seven states.

122.2 **Lawton** *159.3.* Three miles north is a town with an irresistible name—Paw Paw, Michigan.

139.5 **KALAMAZOO** *142.0.* Speaking of unusual names—Kalamazoo is derived from an Indian word said to mean "bubbling pot," referring to natural springs in the area.

Producing a variety of manufactured goods and serving as the shipping and marketing center for the fruit and vegetables produced in the vicinity, Kalamazoo is the metropolis of southwestern Michigan and the home of Western Michigan University.

The region northwest of Kalamazoo has a large population of Dutch ancestry; it's said that some of the first colonists from the Netherlands were blown ashore here by a lake storm and decided to stay. The area has become a leading center of Dutch-American culture, expressed through the annual Tulip Festival at Holland and through such institutions as Hope College and Calvin College, both controlled by the Dutch Reformed Church.

162.3 **BATTLE CREEK** *119.2.* Chances are your breakfast was processed and packaged at Battle Creek, for this is the dry-cereal capital of America. Both Kellogg and Post (now part of General Foods) have their main plants here, and if you ever have a couple of hours in Battle Creek, you should take a factory tour and watch corn become cornflakes.

A short distance east of Amtrak's new Battle Creek passenger station, Detroit trains branch off to the right. The line continuing straight ahead goes to Port Huron.

187.1 **ALBION** *94.4.* The town is built around Albion College, and there's no need to question what nationality dominated here. "Albion" is another name for England and the college's athletic teams are called the Britons. The Dutch may hold sway in western Michigan, but it's the British who dominate here.

207.4 **JACKSON** *74.1.* Jackson is perhaps best known as the site of the notorious Southern Michigan Prison, where riots have made national headlines more than once. Jackson is also the site of the Michigan Space Center and vies with Ripon, Wisconsin, as the birthplace of the Republican Party. Lansing, the state capital, is 30 miles north.

At Jackson the track surmounts the low ridge between the Lake Michigan and Lake Huron watersheds.

245.6 **ANN ARBOR** *35.9.* Ann Arbor is synonymous with the University of Michigan, one of the oldest, largest, and finest public institutions of higher learning in the nation. Founded in 1817—20 years before Michigan entered the Union—the university now enrolls 35,000 students, from every state and a hundred foreign countries, on the Ann Arbor campus. The university libraries contain over 5 million books; its research programs cover every aspect of human experience, at a cost of more than $100 million every year; and its faculty is so distinguished that of its 36 graduate programs, Michigan rates in the nation's top 10 in 35. Any way you look at it, this university is both big and good.

The same adjectives describe its football teams, for which it is best known to the general public. Since it began playing the game in 1879, Michigan has graduated more than a hundred All-Americans. (Former President Gerald Ford was *not* one of them, although he was captain of the 1935 squad.)

253.5 **YPSILANTI** *28.0.* Ypsilanti (pronounced *Yip-si-lant-ee*) is the center of Michigan's Hellenic culture. It's also the home of Eastern Michigan University, another of the many former teachers' colleges that have grown into full universities since World War II.

265.4 **Wayne** *16.1.* This town was named (as is Wayne County, which contains Detroit) for "Mad Anthony" Wayne, whose victory over the Indians in 1794 opened the Midwest to white settlement.

272.4 **DEARBORN** *8.1.* This is the site of the Henry Ford Museum and Greenfield Village, probably the top tourist attraction in the Detroit area. Three hundred years of American history are represented in the collections, and the village contains more than a hundred historic buildings, some restored, some replicas. See section 2.16 (attractions).

Greenfield Village, like nearly everything else in Dearborn, was created by Henry Ford. The Ford Motor Company is still dominant here; the Proving Grounds are at Dearborn, and so is the famous River Rouge plant where Fords are built. (Right side of the train, going into Detroit.)

Henry Ford did not invent the automobile, nor did he originate the idea of mass production from standardized parts. His contribution was the assembly line: no longer did one workman build an entire car. Under Ford's system each employee performed one step of the assembly process, over and over again. The result was more efficient production, which allowed Ford to cut the price of his product so much that automobiles became affordable to ordinary working people. The cost was the progressive dehumanization of the labor force, so much so that today employers are experimenting with alternatives to the assembly line. Whatever you think of Ford's idea, there is no doubt that he revolutionized industry when he set up the first assembly line in Dearborn on January 14, 1914.

281.5 **DETROIT (Amtrak Station)** *0.0.* Amtrak decided to use the former Michigan Central Station, which is not in the central business district, to allow for approaches to the Detroit River tunnel, which leads across the international border to Windsor, Ontario. Unfortunately, this tunnel is now used only by freight trains. Passengers wishing to connect at Windsor with Canadian trains must make their own transfer arrangements. Don't try to walk the mile or so to downtown—this is a high crime area, and it's best to take a cab.

Windsor, Ontario, by the way, lies due *south* of Detroit—an accident of geography that may win you a free drink someday.

For information on Detroit, see section 2.16.

3.31   *Chicago—Port Huron—Toronto*

In cooperation with its sister agency, VIA Rail of Canada, Amtrak has restored through service between Chicago and Toronto for the first time since 1971. The new *International Limited* makes a daily round trip, using both American and Canadian equipment. Coach seats are unreserved, and there is sandwich and beverage service.

Between Chicago and Battle Creek, the route is shared with the Detroit trains. Beyond Battle Creek, the *International Limited* branches off to the north, serving East Lansing and the twin border cities of Port Huron, Michigan, and Sarnia, Ontario, en route to Bayview, Ontario. At that point it joins the route of the *Maple Leaf* (another shared Amtrak-VIA train) for the remainder of the trip into Toronto.

For notes on the route from Chicago to Battle Creek, see sections 3.14 and 3.30.

162.3 **BATTLE CREEK** *156.8.* The Detroit and Port Huron lines split at a crossing east of the new Battle Creek station, next to the cereal plants.

180.0 **Olivet** *139.1*. The railroad detours from a direct north-eastward route to reach this town. Such little meanders, found all too frequently on American railroads, are often the result of crafty nineteenth-century bargaining between the railroad promoters and the town fathers. In general, the towns wanted the tracks, while the railroads wanted money from the towns. Often, the townspeople were reluctant to pay; then the railroad would announce that its route would miss the village altogether. This was a ploy to get the towns to ante up. Sometimes they did, and the route was changed at the last moment. Sometimes they didn't, and then it was the railroad that had to knuckle under, if the town was big enough and important enough to make the company need its business.

206.6 **Lansing** *112.5*. Lansing is the capital of Michigan, largely because of its geographical position in the middle of the state (not counting the Upper Peninsula). Before paved highways and railroads, such a central location was important because access to the state capital and its public business was both difficult and important. Farmers in their horse-and-buggy rigs were not about to go all the way to Detroit (the first capital), and they had the voting power to enforce their demands for a more centrally located capital.

Incidentally, Amtrak trains do not stop in Lansing proper: the sta-

CHICAGO—PORT HURON

Eastbound/miles		miles/Westbound
0.0	CHICAGO (Union Sta.)	319.1
1.6	21st Street	317.5
7.0	Englewood	312.1
12.6	South Chicago, Ill.	306.5
15.4	Roby, Indiana	303.7
15.9	HAMMOND-WHITING	303.2
19.3	Indiana Harbor	299.8
21.7	Pine Junction	297.4
26.1	Gary	293.0
40.2	Porter	278.9
54.0	Michigan City, Ind. (CT)	265.1
63.9	New Buffalo, Mich. (ET)	255.2
71.1	Three Oaks	248.0
76.8	Galien	242.3
84.3	Buchanan	234.8
90.9	NILES	228.2
103.3	Dowagiac	215.8
114.5	Decatur	204.6
122.2	Lawton	196.9
126.4	Mattawan	192.7

139.5	KALAMAZOO	179.6
143.3	Comstock	175.8
148.3	Galesburg	170.8
152.7	Augusta	164.4
162.3	BATTLE CREEK	156.8
162.3	BATTLE CREEK	156.8
174.9	Bellevue	144.2
180.0	Olivet	139.1
188.1	Charlotte	131.0
194.4	Potterville	124.7
206.6	Lansing	112.5
210.3	EAST LANSING	108.8
227.9	Morrice	91.2
234.2	Bancroft	84.9
239.0	DURAND	80.1
247.2	Swartz Creek	71.9
255.8	FLINT	63.3
264.4	Davison	54.7
275.2	LAPEER	43.9
287.1	Imlay City	32.0
294.5	Capac	24.6
303.1	Emmett	16.0
308.1	Goodells	11.0
319.1	PORT HURON	0.0

tion serving the state capital is actually in adjacent East Lansing, where Michigan State University is located. This in itself says a lot about the nature of the passenger business today. The state capital is not a stop, but the university town next door is.

210.3 **EAST LANSING** *108.8*. In 1862 Congress passed, and President Lincoln signed, a bill granting federal land to the states. They were empowered to sell this property and use the revenues for the support of education in agriculture, engineering, and military science (this was during the Civil War, of course). Michigan was the first state to make use of its grant, and thus the institution we now know as Michigan State University came into being; it was the first of the so-called land grant colleges. Today MSU has an enrollment of more than 35,000 students on the 2,000-acre East Lansing campus and is a worthy rival of its older sister, the University of Michigan at Ann Arbor, with which it should never be confused. The Amtrak station is practically right on the campus, and MSU students are an important source of business at this station.

227.9 **Morrice** *91.2*. A little way east of the town the tracks cross Looking Glass River.

239.0 **DURAND** *80.1*. Durand is of vital importance to the Grand Trunk Railroad and of practically none to anybody else. The town is so small you can hardly find it on the map without a magnifying glass, but it's the hub of the Grand Trunk system, with lines radiating to Detroit, Grand Rapids, Saginaw, and Bay City, in addition to Chicago and Port Huron.

255.8 **FLINT** *63.3.* Flint is a General Motors town. GM has a number of plants in and around the city turning out Chevrolets, Buicks, and AC sparkplugs, among other things.

Flint is also the closest Amtrak station to the Saginaw–Midland–Bay City complex 25 miles north, an area noted for its major chemical works.

294.5 **Capac** *24.6.* This town is notable because its name is a palindrome—that is, it's spelled the same backward and forward.

303.1 **Emmett** *16.0.* You know there must have been some Irishmen among the early settlers in this town, for it's named after Robert Emmett, the Irish patriot who was hanged by the British after leading an unsuccessful rebellion in Dublin in 1803.

319.1 **PORT HURON, MICH. (U.S.)** *0.0.* Port Huron stands at the southern tip of Lake Huron, just where it flows into the St. Clair River. The St. Clair forms the international boundary between the United States and Canada and flows, in turn, into Lake St. Clair, the Detroit River, and eventually Lake Erie.

Though it isn't very big, Port Huron has historic significance as the boyhood home of Thomas Alva Edison, whose father moved the family from Milan, Ohio, in 1854 when young Tom was seven. Father Sam took a job tending the lighthouse at the mouth of the river, and it is possible that his young son first developed an interest in mechanics while watching his father at work.

At Port Huron, young Edison ran away from one school and so discouraged his teacher at another that she thought he had brain damage and was beyond teaching. After that, Sam got his son a job selling newspapers on the local train between Port Huron and Detroit. That lasted a year, until the chemical laboratory Tom had set up in the baggage car caught fire one day. Edison learned telegraphy at the age of sixteen, and shortly thereafter he left Port Huron for good.

0.0 **PORT HURON, MICH. (U.S.)** *177.1.* Westbound, the *International Limited* stops here for 40 minutes to allow U.S. Customs and Immigration personnel to inspect the train and passengers.

Between Port Huron and Sarnia, on the Canadian side of the St. Clair River, the train passes through the St. Clair Tunnel, built in 1891 to eliminate the bottleneck caused by ferryboat operations. This tunnel was a notable engineering feat for its time, for it was one of the first projects to employ the new shield method of digging. Construction took almost 3 years; when it was finished, the St. Clair Tunnel saved $50,000 a year in ferry-operating costs and reduced travel time by 2 hours.

Smoke and gas, however, caused two serious accidents in the bore, in which several men were killed. In 1908 the St. Clair became the first major tunnel in North America (other than the pioneering Howard Street Tunnel in Baltimore) to convert to electric operation. The elec-

PORT HURON—TORONTO

Eastbound/miles		miles/Westbound
0.0	PORT HURON, MICH. (U.S.)	177.1
3.1	SARNIA, ONT. (Canada)	174.0
16.7	Wyoming	160.4
28.8	Watford	148.3
42.1	STRATHROY	135.0
52.1	Komoka	125.0
57.9	Hyde Park	119.2
62.0	LONDON	115.1
71.7	Dorchester	105.4
81.2	INGERSOLL	95.9
85.8	Beachville	91.3
90.7	WOODSTOCK	86.4
102.4	Princeton	74.7
110.0	Paris	67.1
117.2	BRANTFORD	59.9
126.2	Lynden	50.9
130.6	Copetown	46.5
135.5	DUNDAS	41.6
140.2	Bayview	36.9
142.2	Aldershot	34.9
145.1	BURLINGTON WEST	32.0
151.5	Bronte	25.6
155.7	OAKVILLE	21.4
161.0	Clarkson	16.1
162.1	Lorne Park	15.0
164.3	Port Credit	12.8
166.0	Lakeview	11.1
170.3	Mimico	6.8
173.6	Sunnyside	3.5
177.1	TORONTO (UNION STA.)	0.0

tric engines ran until 1955, when introduction of diesel power made them no longer necessary.

3.1 **SARNIA, ONT. (Canada)** *174.0.* The petrochemical center of Canada, Sarnia is an industrial city. Eastbound trains pause here for 30 minutes for Canadian Customs and Immigration work.

16.7 **Wyoming** *160.4.* The region just south of here was Canada's most important early oil center. Nearby are the towns of Petrolia, Oil

City, and Oil Springs. Today, of course, the Ontario oil field is of miniscule importance compared with the huge petroleum reserves in Alberta.

62.0 **LONDON** *115.1.* Like its namesake in England, London, Ontario, an industrial city of 175,000, is on the Thames River. The University of Western Ontario has its campus here. London is the closest passenger station to Stratford, site of the Canadian Shakespeare Festival, 40 miles away.

117.2 **BRANTFORD** *59.9.* The station here also serves the towns of Galt, Preston, Waterloo-Kitchener, and Guelph, all of which are within easy driving distance.

140.2 **Bayview** *36.9.* At the extreme western end of Lake Ontario, just outside the steelmaking city of Hamilton, this is Canada's most important and busiest railroad junction. Here trains from the west meet trains from the east; together they procede north along the shoreline to Toronto.

For notes on the route from Bayview to Toronto, see the final portion of section 3.13.

3.32   Chicago—Indianapolis

This run was begun partly to cut the cost of shuttling cars to and from Amtrak's Beach Grove shop near Indianapolis, which was left isolated when the *National Limited* quit running in 1979. But it has attracted reasonable passenger loads, too, and operates on a convenient, if not extremely rapid, schedule.

The route passes through the attractive lake country of northern Indiana, down the main street of Lafayette, through Hoosierland towns and villages, and past the Indianapolis Motor Speedway. Much of the run is over the former Monon Railroad (now L & N), which was a local institution in Indiana with a particular tradition of service to the state's many colleges and universities. Amtrak's *Hoosier State* continues this tradition.

The train makes a daily round trip, into Chicago in the morning and back to Indianapolis in the afternoon. Amfleet cars are used and offer the usual snack-meal service.

In its own folksy way, this short but picturesque trip is one of Amtrak's most enjoyable runs—a journey through the American heartland.

0.0 **CHICAGO, ILL. (Union Station)** *191.1.* For information on Chicago, see section 2.11.

20.7 **Hammond, Ind.** *170.4.* At the Illinois-Indiana state line is a busy junction; beyond, the train crossses the Calumet River and angles its way right through the central business district of Hammond, crossing the principal streets and the Indiana Harbor Belt Line railroad at grade.

25.5 **Maynard** *165.6.* This is another of the many multiple railroad crossings so common in and around Chicago. At Maynard the Grand Trunk Western's Toronto line, the Conrail freight route from Cincin-

CHICAGO—INDIANAPOLIS

Southbound/miles   *miles/Northbound*

0.0	CHICAGO (Union Sta.)	191.1
1.6	21st Street	189.5
6.6	Englewood, Ill.	184.5
20.7	Hammond, Ind.	170.4
25.5	Maynard	165.6
29.0	DYER	162.1
33.5	St. John	157.6
39.5	Cedar Lake	151.6
44.8	Lowell	146.3
52.6	Shelby	138.5
54.1	Thayer	137.0
56.5	Rose Lawn	134.6
62.2	Fair Oaks	128.9
73.0	RENSSELAER	118.1
76.9	Pleasant Ridge	114.2
80.0	McCoysburg	111.1
88.4	Monon	102.7
95.8	Reynolds	95.3
102.1	Chalmers	89.0
106.2	Brookston	84.9
110.2	Ash Grove	80.9
112.9	Battle Ground (CT)	78.2
120.0	LAFAYETTE (ET)	71.1
126.5	Taylor	64.6
129.5	South Raub	61.6
132.9	Romney	58.2
137.0	Linden	54.1
147.3	CRAWFORDSVILLE	43.8
147.3	CRAWFORDSVILLE	43.8
153.3	Linnsburg	37.8
158.3	New Ross	32.8
163.4	Jamestown	27.7
169.1	Lizton	22.0
173.5	Pittsboro	17.6
177.4	Brownsburg	13.7
186.5	Speedway	4.6
191.1	INDIANAPOLIS	0.0

nati, and the Louisville and Nashville (former Monon) all meet. You won't find the spot on an Indiana highway map, but it's just south of the Hammond city limits in the town of Munster, Indiana.

29.0 **DYER** *162.1.* Another railroad junction, although there's actually a town at this one. Here the L & N line used by Amtrak crosses the Elgin, Joliet and Eastern—the Chicago Outer Belt. This line, owned by U.S. Steel, starts at Gary, on Lake Michigan, and describes a giant half circle around the city at a radius of about 30 miles, ending at Waukegan on the lake north of Chicago. The E J & E connects with every railroad entering the city, and expedites the exchange of freight cars from one line to another.

The station at Dyer serves not only northern Indiana but also Chicago Heights and other communities across the state line in Illinois.

39.5 **Cedar Lake** *151.6.* This is a summer resort area, with swimming, fishing, and boating on the lake. Until 1948 the tracks used to run right along the shore, but wandering pedestrians and the danger that a locomotive might derail and fall into the lake caused the construction of a new line on higher ground west of the lakeshore. While riding over the present bypass, you can see traces of the old line to the east.

73.0 **RENSSELAER** *118.1.* Named for the New York town across the Hudson River from Albany, this is the home of St. Joseph's College. Like its neighbor Ohio, Indiana is full of small, mostly church-affiliated liberal arts colleges.

88.4 **Monon** *102.7.* Originally called Bradford, the town changed its name in 1879 and now is named after the creek that runs through it. "Monon" is a Potawatomi Indian word meaning "fast running"; evidently the creek must have had a snappy current.

Monon is another of those tiny towns that are important to particular railroads. On a highway map it looks quite insignificant—there isn't even a crossroad through town. But Monon is the junction between the Chicago–Indianapolis and Michigan City–Louisville lines of the former Monon Railroad, which took its name from the town.

110.2 **Ash Grove** *80.9.* Here the rails begin their descent into the Wabash River valley. In the old days, steam-powered freight trains used to require the aid of pusher engines to get up this grade from Lafayette, 10 miles away.

112.9 **Battle Ground** *78.2.* The battle referred to was Tippecanoe, fought on November 7, 1811, and it was a key event in the opening of the West to white settlement.

Rarely were the various Indian tribes able to cooperate against the whites, but a Shawnee chief, Tecumseh, was one of the few Indian leaders who was able to inspire unity. He was aided by his brother, a one-eyed, epileptic medicine man called "The Prophet," who led a religious revival coinciding with Tecumseh's military alliance; toward the autumn of 1811 the Indians appeared to be developing a potent force. The headquarters were at The Prophet's camp, at the confluence of the Wabash and Tippecanoe rivers just upstream from Battle Ground.

Late in 1811, Tecumseh left the camp on a voyage down the Mississippi. His purpose was to bring the southern tribes into his alliance. William Henry Harrison, the Virginian military commander, saw an opportunity to attack the Indians while their military leader was absent. On November 7, Harrison and his force of 1,000 whites moved in. The fighting was bloody, and both sides suffered serious casualties, but at the end of the day, despite The Prophet's promises, the white men's guns had proved to be as deadly as ever and the Indians' faith in the medicine man was gone. Tecumseh returned to find his confederation in ruins; it was the beginning of the end for Indian power in the region. Two years later Tecumseh himself was killed while fighting for the British at the Battle of the Thames during the War of 1812. At the end of that conflict, the Indians were forced to move west of the Mississippi.

Today a state memorial at Tippecanoe Battlefield commemorates the fighting here that led to the downfall of the greatest Native American leader and made William Henry Harrison president of the United States for a month. He caught pneumonia at his inauguration and died shortly after at the age of sixty-nine.

120.0 **LAFAYETTE** *71.1.* Named for George Washington's friend and aide, the Marquis de Lafayette, who came to America to offer his services in the revolutionary cause, Lafayette stands on the east bank of the Wabash River, surrounded on all sides by hills. Purdue University is built on the bluffs across the river.

North of Lafayette the train passes the yards and shops of the old Monon Railroad. These shops have a quaint connection with the university. Back in 1888, Purdue's football team walloped the daylights out of tiny Wabash College. Chagrined, Wabash claimed that Purdue had cheated by bolstering its squad with some brawny boilermakers from the railroad shops, and the Purdue football team has been "the Boilermakers" ever since.

At Lafayette, Amtrak trains run right down the middle of 5th Street for more than a mile—one of the few places in the United States where you can lean out the Dutch doors of a passenger train and feed the parking meters as you go by.

From Lafayette to Linden, 17 miles, there's a continuous upgrade as the rails climb out of the Wabash valley to reach high ground again.

147.3 **CRAWFORDSVILLE** *43.8.* This pretty little Indiana town is the home of Wabash College, the school Purdue and its boilermakers beat up on in 1888, and of Lew Wallace, author of *Ben Hur*. Wallace was not very successful as a Union general in the Civil War; at the Battle of Shiloh he and his troops got lost and spent an entire day wandering around the back roads, looking for somebody to fight. But as a novelist, he did very well indeed—his story about the early Christians in Rome has been popular for a hundred years now.

At Crawfordsville, Amtrak trains curve to the east and use the old Peoria and Eastern line (now part of Conrail) to reach Indianapolis. Before the *Hoosier State* began operating in 1980, this track hadn't seen a passenger train in 30 years. Unfortunately, it's still in no condition to permit high-speed running. It parallels U.S. 136 and then U.S. 40 all the way to Indianapolis, passing through a number of hamlets, each with its grain elevator, feed store, gas station, and café.

186.5 **Speedway** *4.6.* On the west edge of Indianapolis, the Motor Speedway (not visible from the train) is the home of the annual 500-mile race. The track has been an Indiana institution since 1911, when driver Ray Haroun won the first 500 in a Marmon Wasp. Each Memorial Day weekend a crowd of more than 300,000 people comes to the Speedway to watch the race, making this the biggest single sporting event in North America. During the 1960s somebody sagely referred to the Indy 500 as "Mid-America's Woodstock"—as good a description as I can think of.

191.1 **INDIANAPOLIS** *0.0.* For information on the city, see section 2.19.

3.33 Chicago—New Orleans via Carbondale

This is the most important north-south route in the country, other than those on the East and West coasts, and it connects the Great Lakes with the Gulf of Mexico. The northern end of the route sees three daily passenger trains in each direction; south of Carbondale, once-a-day service is provided by the *City of New Orleans*.

The *City* was an all-coach day train before Amtrak took over the route from the Illinois Central Railroad in 1971; overnight service was provided by the luxury streamliner *Panama Limited*. Amtrak discontinued the *Panama,* but shortly found that this 924-mile run was too long for a day train. The *City of New Orleans* frequently ran late because of bad track, and whenever it ran late, it would arrive at its terminal cities about 3 A.M. No wonder the passenger loads were low.

Amtrak then reinstated overnight service, but the train bears the name *City of New Orleans*. It was recently upgraded with Heritage Fleet cars, including a dome coach; but it still lacks a full dining car.

Its route is interesting. The first 250 miles run through rich Illinois farm land and then continue through surprisingly rugged hill country rich with seams of coal. In western Kentucky the track passes through low-lying swamp and then, beyond Fulton, through cotton fields in Tennessee and Mississippi. Finally, in Louisiana, the terrain changes again, and the final miles pass through low, flat land where rice and strawberries are the leading crops. At the end of the run is graceful, happy-go-lucky New Orleans.

0.0 **CHICAGO (Union Station)** *923.8*. Before Amtrak, trains on the New Orleans line used to leave from the quaint Central Station on the lakefront, which was built for the 1893 World's Fair. Now all Amtrak trains use the more modern Union Station, but the gain in convenience is partially offset by trains on this route having to back in or out of the station. This move adds from 15 to 25 minutes to the running time, as compared with schedules in the old days when Central Station was in use.

1.6 **21st Street** *922.2*. At this important junction, trains back across the big lift bridge over the South Branch of the Chicago River, then back around a curve far enough to clear the switches. They then proceed forward, crossing the main line to points east, and follow one of the most interesting pieces of railroad in the United States.

This is the St. Charles Air Line, which connects the eastern and western railroads at 21st Street with the Illinois Central Gulf on the

CHICAGO—NEW ORLEANS VIA CARBONDALE

Southbound/miles   *miles/Northbound*

0.0	CHICAGO (Union Sta.)	923.8
1.6	21st Street	922.2
9.4	Woodlawn (63rd St.)	914.4
17.0	Kensington	906.8
23.3	Markham	900.5
24.9	HOMEWOOD	898.9
30.7	Richton	893.1
33.0	Stuenkel	890.8
35.6	Monee	888.2
41.9	Peotone	881.9
48.1	Manteno	875.7
52.2	Indian Oaks	871.6
55.6	Bradley	868.2
56.7	Kankakee Junction	867.1
57.3	KANKAKEE	866.5
61.7	Otto	862.1
65.7	Chebanse	858.1
70.5	Clifton	853.3
74.5	Ashkum	849.3
78.8	Danforth	845.0

82.5	Gilman	841.3
86.1	Onarga	837.7
89.0	Del Rey	834.8
94.5	Buckley	829.3
100.1	Loda	823.7
104.2	Paxton	819.6
109.7	Ludlow	814.1
115.2	RANTOUL	808.6
120.1	Thomasboro	803.7
124.0	Leverett	799.8
125.5	Leverett Junction	798.3
129.2	CHAMPAIGN-URBANA	794.6

129.2	CHAMPAIGN-URBANA	794.6
133.6	Savoy	790.2
138.5	Tolono	785.3
143.3	Pesotum	780.5
147.0	Hayes	776.8
151.2	Tuscola	772.6
155.5	Galton	768.3
159.3	Arcola	764.5
165.0	Humboldt	758.8
168.9	Dorans	754.9
173.8	MATTOON	750.0
180.7	Aetna	743.1
185.7	Neoga	738.1
192.6	Sigel	731.2
200.6	EFFINGHAM	723.2

200.6	EFFINGHAM	723.2
207.1	Watson	716.7
212.9	Mason	710.9
216.0	Edgewood	707.8
219.9	Laclede	703.9
224.5	Farina	699.3
230.3	Kinmundy	693.5
235.0	Alma	688.8
240.4	Tonti	683.4
245.6	Odin	678.2
251.4	Branch Junction	672.4
253.8	CENTRALIA	670.0

253.8	CENTRALIA	670.0
261.4	Irvington	662.4
264.1	Richview	659.7
267.7	Ashley	656.1
275.2	Bois	648.6
281.1	Tamaroa	642.7
289.9	Du Quoin	633.9
294.7	Dowell	629.1
296.9	Elkville	626.9
303.4	DeSoto	620.4
309.6	CARBONDALE	614.2

640.8	Duck Hill	283.0
651.9	WINONA	271.9
662.5	Vaiden	261.3
672.4	West	251.4
682.0	DURANT	241.8
689.9	Goodman	233.9
696.9	Pickens	226.9
703.6	Vaughn	220.2
717.2	CANTON	206.6
717.2	CANTON	206.6
728.4	Madison	195.4
740.4	JACKSON	183.4
740.4	JACKSON	183.4
756.2	Terry	167.6
764.8	Crystal Springs	159.0
774.0	HAZLEHURST	149.8
785.7	Wesson	138.1
794.5	BROOKHAVEN	129.3
804.6	Bogue Chitto	119.2
815.5	Summit	108.3
818.4	McCOMB	105.4
822.3	Fernwood	101.5
825.4	Magnolia	98.4
831.4	Chatawa	92.4
835.3	Osyka, Miss.	88.5
840.4	Kentwood, La.	83.4
844.8	Tangipahoa	79.0
848.4	Fluker	75.4
852.3	Roseland	71.5
855.0	Amite	68.8
861.4	Independence	62.4
865.5	Tickfaw	58.3
867.7	Natalbany	56.1
870.5	HAMMOND	53.3
875.3	Ponchatula	48.5
886.0	Manchac	37.8
904.3	LaBranch	19.5
913.2	Kenner	10.6
921.4	Carrollton Ave.	2.4
923.8	NEW ORLEANS	0.0

lakefront. Although it's less than a mile long, it's a vital connecting artery that sees many trains. It was once owned by the penurious lady financier Hetty Green, to whose fortune it made substantial contributions.

The Air Line follows the river for a short distance, then strikes straight east, crossing the Rock Island tracks and threading its way between gloomy warehouses until it reaches the lakefront, where it curves south to join the Illinois Central Gulf main line at 16th Street.

The Chicago skyline is visible briefly as the train makes this curve (left side, leaving the city).

From 16th Street to 49th Street, about 4 miles, Lake Michigan is on the east (left) side of the majestic multitrack right-of-way. The ICG's predecessor company, the Illinois Central, was one of the first railroads to enter Chicago and was therefore able to preempt the best possible route—right along the lakeshore. In fact, part of this route was once actually in the lake, built on a low-pile trestle through the shallow water. In later years the shoreline was brought out to the tracks by landfills, and eventually a titanic legal battle over ownership of the Chicago lakefront developed between the railroad and the city. The case dragged on for many years before the city finally won title to its front door.

At 49th Street the tracks curve away from the lakeshore and pass a number of high-rise apartment houses; and at 57th Street it passes the Museum of Science and Industry (left side, leaving Chicago). This world-famous museum, with its coal mine and captured German submarine, is one of Chicago's unique attractions.

Two blocks farther on, at 59th Street, trains cross the Midway. This wide boulevard, connecting Jackson and Washington parks, got its name because during the 1893 World's Fair that's exactly what it was—the carnival midway where the world's biggest Ferris wheel stood and where "Little Egypt" did her shocking hoochy-koochy dance. Today the Midway is somewhat more sedate; it's flooded for ice-skating during the winter, and sometimes used for softball games in summer. The huge equestrian statue (right side of the train, leaving the city) is a monument to Jan Masaryk, the father of modern Czechoslovakia.

Farther to the west are a number of great, gray buildings lining both sides of the Midway. These are part of the campus of the University of Chicago, one of the world's greatest centers of higher learning and research. The university was created with the intention of making it a worthy rival of Harvard and Yale, and it has been both outstanding and controversial from the day it opened in 1893.

9.4 **Woodlawn (63rd Street)** *914.4*. Since Amtrak took over passenger operations on what was once the Illinois Central Railroad, through trains have not stopped here (though suburban trains still do). Yet, the ramshackle Woodlawn station deserves some comment because of its social significance. It was the entry port for thousands of Southern blacks who came to Chicago looking for a better life. The influx is slower now, and the people don't get off here anymore. But somebody should remember Woodlawn, which to many, many people was the first thing they saw in the North.

A mile or so south of Woodlawn is Grand Crossing, where the Illinois Central Gulf line passes under the Conrail lines used by Amtrak trains going to and from New York and Detroit. This crossing was grade separated in 1914. Before that, it had the reputation of being about the most congested junction in the world.

About 3 miles farther on, at 111th Street, look to the east side (left side, leaving Chicago) for a glimpse of some of the buildings of the old town of Pullman. This village was built in 1880 by George M. Pullman, the sleeping-car magnate, to house his car-building shops and the people who worked in them. It was an extreme example of the company town. Every house was owned by Pullman, every store, all city services—all were provided by the company, at prices higher than those prevailing elsewhere. Workers found that virtually every cent they made from Pullman at the plant went back to Pullman in rents and fees. It was an impossible situation, which culminated in the great Pullman strike of 1894.

23.3 **Markham** *900.5.* Here is Illinois Central Gulf's biggest and most important Chicago-area freight yard (left side).

24.9 **HOMEWOOD** *898.9.* The station stop here serves not only the southern suburbs of Chicago but also Hammond and other communities in the Calumet area of northern Indiana, which are just across the state line to the east.

Most of Chicago's wealthiest residential suburbs are clustered along the Lake Michigan shoreline north of the city or in the Fox River valley west of it. Some executives, however, prefer to live close to the big industrial plants south of the city, which accounts for the presence of elegant Homewood and its neighbor, Flossmoor.

57.3 **KANKAKEE** *866.5.* An industrial town bisected by the Kankakee River, a tributary of the Illinois.

65.7 **Chebanse** *858.1.* This is classic, rich Illinois farmland; the principal crops are corn and soybeans. A major Chicago dairy maintains its headquarters here, close to the cows.

115.2 **RANTOUL** *808.6.* This is the station for the U.S. Air Force base at Chanute Field. Octave Chanute, for whom the base is named, was an aviation pioneer and sometime associate of the Wright brothers.

129.2 **CHAMPAIGN-URBANA** *794.6.* Champaign and its adjacent twin, Urbana, are the home of the University of Illinois, renowned for its schools of engineering and agriculture.

Like all the Big Ten schools except Northwestern, Illinois is very big. The Champaign campus has well over 30,000 students; another campus in Chicago serves 20,000 more. And, like all the Big Ten schools (Northwestern again is the exception), Illinois is athletically minded. The school's football field, Memorial Stadium, has 70,000 seats. It can be seen to the east side (left side of the train, going south) just after leaving the Champaign station. Adjacent to the stadium is the 16,000-seat Assembly Hall, home of the Fighting Illini basketball team. The Illinois State High School Association basketball tournaments are

Amtrak's National Rail Passenger System

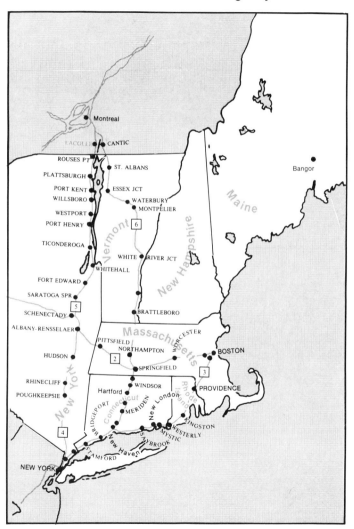

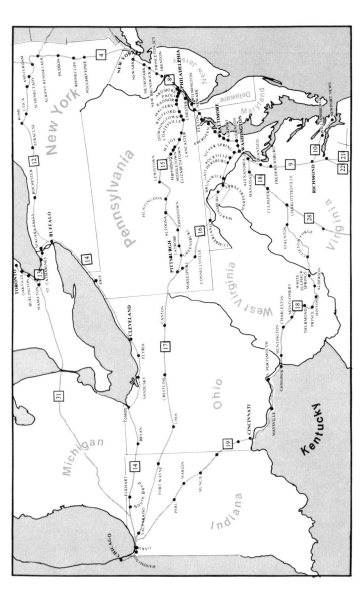

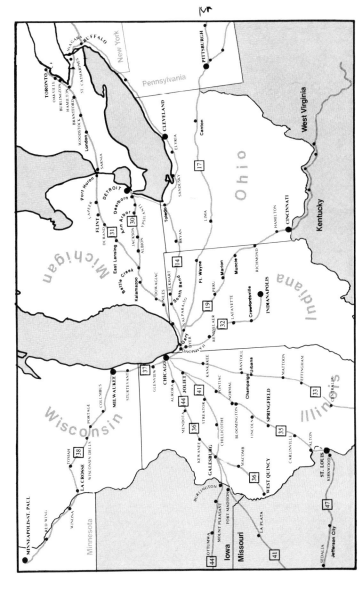

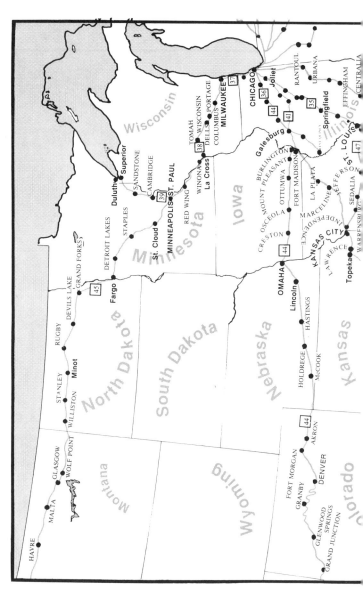

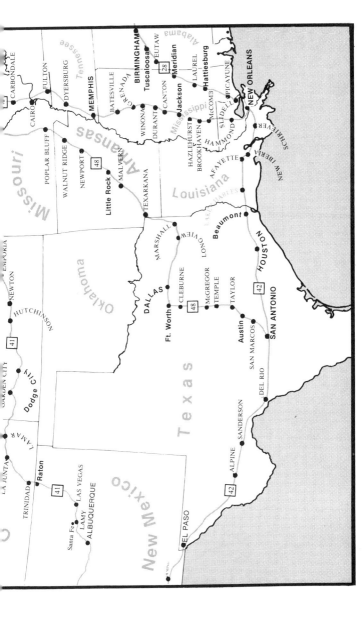

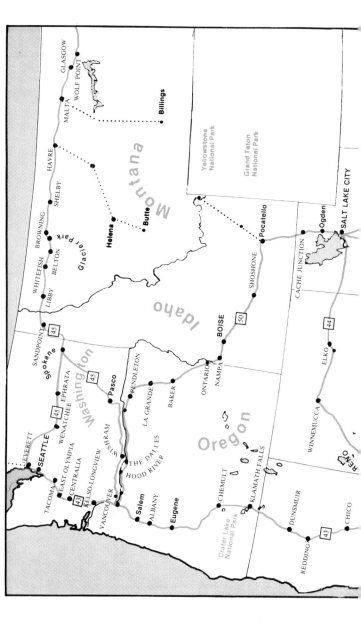

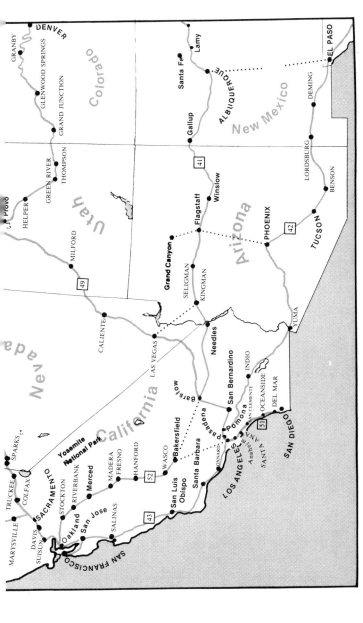

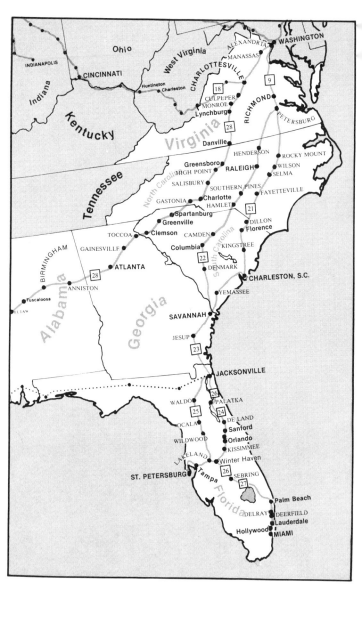

also played here each March.

Champaign is more than a university town, however. It is a railroad division point where engine crews change, and it also has considerable industry. It remains the trading center for the surrounding farmlands—a reminder that although Illinois is one of the nation's leading industrial states, it is also the fourth largest agricultural producer in the United States. Only California, Texas, and neighboring Iowa produce more farm products.

173.8 **MATTOON** *750.0.* This is the station for Charleston, site of Eastern Illinois University, which is 11 miles east.

A few miles from Mattoon is the site of a log cabin once occupied by the Lincoln family. Though he was born in Kentucky and lived for a while in Indiana, Abraham Lincoln is considered Illinois' greatest native son. He spent his young adulthood at New Salem and practiced law in Springfield, his home until he went to Washington as the sixteenth president of the United States. The cabin near Mattoon was his first Illinois residence; he lived there while still a boy.

200.6 **EFFINGHAM** *723.2.* Effingham is a major crossroads town, where the east-west route from Pittsburgh and Indianapolis to St. Louis crosses the north-south line from Chicago to the Gulf.

Route I-70, which passes through Effingham on the way to the West, marks a rough, but important, unofficial boundary line. Above it, Illinois is a Northern state, originally settled largely by natives of New England and New York. This part of the state was staunchly anti-slavery before and during the Civil War, to which Illinois contributed more than a quarter of a million Union soldiers, among them General Grant. South of Route I-70, however, Illinois is nearly as Southern as its neighbor Kentucky. Most of the original settlers in this part of the state came down the Ohio or up the Mississippi, bringing their attitudes with them. Schools in this part of the state were racially segregated, by law, as late as the 1960s. If the northern part of Illinois has been rock-ribbed Republican since Lincoln's time, the southern section has been just as strongly conservative Democratic. In speech, too, the natives of southern Illinois seem much more than 200 miles removed from the clipped tones of bustling, dynamic Chicago. South of Effingham, the Midwest ends and the South begins.

216.0 **Edgewood** *707.8.* Although you won't notice it until you get farther south, southern Illinois differs from the northern part of the state in topography as well as in history and culture. There are hills and valleys down here, quite unlike the flat prairies between Effingham and Chicago. As a result, the Illinois Central Railroad, predecessor of the Illinois Central Gulf, originally had some steep grades and heavy curves south of Du Quoin. This section was a bottleneck to the road's growing freight traffic, and in the 1920s the company bypassed it with a brand-new line for freight trains that runs from Edgewood to Fulton, Kentucky. This 169-mile line has nominal grades and few curves. To construct it required one of the biggest railroad-building jobs of the century. It saves 22 miles and countless hills and curves, making for faster, more efficient, and safer freight operations. It's known as the Edgewood Cutoff.

240.4 **Tonti** *683.4.* Henri de Tonti was La Salle's assistant and companion on his voyage of discovery down the Mississippi in 1682. Tonti was a colorful character; he is said to have had an artificial hand made of iron.

245.6 **Odin** *678.2.* South of Odin, huge deposits of bituminous coal lie beneath the fields and hills of southern Illinois. For more than a century Illinois has been among the leading coal-producing states, and part of Chicago's amazing growth as an industrial center was due to these conveniently located coal fields. Today, however, Illinois coal is less important than it used to be, because it has a high sulfur content. Thus, some big coal-users have switched to low-sulfur coal from Montana and Wyoming to meet environmental-protection standards.

251.4 **Branch Junction** *672.4.* When the Illinois Central Railroad was first built, in 1854, it was conceived of as a connection between the producing centers and farms of the north and the Ohio and Mississippi River steamboats at Cairo. At Branch Junction the line split—with one route going north to Freeport and Galena; the other, northeast to Champaign and Chicago. The Freeport section was considered the main line, and the Chicago route was thought of as a branch. Of course, it soon became clear that the latter route would carry far heavier traffic. Today the Freeport line is a very lightly traveled, freight-only secondary branch.

253.8 **CENTRALIA** *670.0.* This is a coal and railroad town named for the Illinois Central, which created it. Centralia has seen better times, but even in its best years it was never free from work and sorrow: Two terrible mine disasters took place near here.

289.9 **Du Quoin** *633.9.* North of Du Quoin the land is quite flat. South of here are the real hills.

For 23 years Du Quoin had its moment of glory each August when the Hambletonian—the Kentucky Derby of trotting races—was run at the county fairgrounds here. But in 1981 the Hambletonian Society moved the race to the new Meadowlands complex in New Jersey. The race may get more media coverage there, as its sponsors hope, but the folksy, down-home atmosphere that made the Hambletonian unique is gone forever.

The southern part of Illinois has an unusual nickname: It's often called "Egypt." This is because early in the state's history there were serious crop failures in the north while the south remained fertile; the

272

biblical parallel was too clear to miss. The theme is carried out in a number of southern-Illinois place names. You'll find, in addition to Cairo, towns called Thebes and Karnak, to name just a couple.

But never, never call Egypt "Little Egypt." She was the exotic dancer who scandalized the 1893 World's Fair.

309.6 **CARBONDALE** *614.2.* Its very name means "valley of coal," and Carbondale has been Old King Coal's town for many years. Nearby are many mining towns such as Marion, West Frankfort, and Orient, all owing their existence to rich coal veins below the surface. Carbondale is also a railroad town. Tracks of the Illinois Central Gulf converge on it from six directions, and it is the terminus of Amtrak's *Shawnee* from Chicago. This train, by the way, might be better called the *Education Express,* because so many of its passengers are students at Illinois, Eastern Illinois, or Carbondale's own school, Southern Illinois.

Southern Illinois is another teachers' college that has expanded into a university. It now has 22,000 students, a library of nearly 2 million volumes, and several doctoral programs. Its athletic teams are called the Salukis, a nickname adopted from the exotic Egyptian hunting dog.

324.8 **Cobden** *599.0.* You wouldn't expect it in coal-conscious southern Illinois, but Cobden is known for apples. Its high school team is the "Appleknockers." Apparently an appleknocker is the person who climbs the tree and shakes the apples loose—although I've never heard the word except in Cobden.

330.2 **Anna** *593.6.* From Anna to the Ohio River crossing at Cairo is a steady 30-mile downgrade for southbound trains, but a stiff uphill pull coming north. Avoidance of this hill was one reason for building the Edgewood Cutoff in 1926.

362.9 **CAIRO, ILL.** *560.9.* Cairo (pronounced *Care-o* hereabouts; don't say *Kye-ro* or they'll know you for a tourist) sits at the southern tip of Illinois, where the Ohio and the Mississippi come together. To give you an idea of just how far south it is—well, believe it or not, Cairo, Illinois, is farther south than Richmond, Virginia!

Cairo was of great importance in the steamboating days, but it's been bypassed by the new highroads of progress. The spot has never been a healthy place to live. It lies in the swamps and has been flooded out many times. When Charles Dickens came here in 1842, he found the inhabitants suffering from ague and general disease. But Cairo also meant freedom for slaves running from the South to freedom up the Ohio. Remember your *Huckleberry Finn?*

Amtrak trains do not actually enter Cairo but stop at the North Cairo station, on high ground north of town. Leaving this point, trains curve to the east to cross the Ohio River on a long, impressive bridge.

On the Kentucky side of the Cairo Bridge the tracks pass through a low-lying, swampy area for several miles before reaching high ground. This swamp was a key element in the defense system planned by the Confederate military in 1861. Since no army could march across it, the Rebels concentrated their efforts on a huge fortress on the high bluffs at Columbus, Kentucky, less than 20 miles south.

371.7 **Wickliffe, Ky.** *552.1.* To the west of the train (right side, going south) passengers get their last look at the Mississippi River for 150 miles. From this point south as far as Memphis, the railroad runs inland. Near Wickliffe there are traces of an ancient buried city.

385.4 **Arlington** *538.4.* Six miles west, on the Mississippi, is Columbus, site of the fortress that was supposed to protect the Confederacy from Union invasion.

At the beginning of the Civil War, Kentucky was badly split, and the state therefore issued a proclamation of neutrality.

The Confederates, however, needed to block the Mississippi to Union shipping, and to do it they marched into Kentucky and seized the steamboat landing at Columbus, which was then also the northern terminus of the railroad from New Orleans. Here they built an imposing fortress, armed mainly with guns taken from the Norfolk Navy Yard when it surrendered.

As a result of this "invasion," the Confederacy lost support in Kentucky, which though a slave state remained in the Union throughout the war.

407.5 **FULTON, KY.** *516.3.* Fulton is a railroad town: a division point, a junction (the Edgewood Cutoff rejoins the main line here), and the site of a big freight yard. At Fulton, passenger trains snake their way around a sharp curve. This elbow is a legacy of the time when the Illinois Central Railroad was pieced together from segments of shorter lines. The original route from the Ohio River to the Gulf ran through Jackson, Tennessee. Later, the IC acquired a railroad from Louisville to Memphis that crossed its own route at Fulton, and they incorporated the southern end of this route into a new, more advantageous main line to New Orleans. This is the track used by Amtrak today, and the sharp curve at Fulton is the connection between the original line and the newer Memphis–Louisville route.

About 10 miles west of Fulton is a little town called Cayce, Kentucky—locally pronounced *Casey*. This was the hometown of John Luther Jones, a locomotive engineer on the Illinois Central in the Gay Nineties.

It was John Luther Jones's good fortune to work, early in his career, on a division in which a number of employees were named Jones. When the foreman asked him his hometown, he replied, "Cayce, Kentucky," and he was known thereafter as "Casey Jones." There can hardly be an American who has not heard of Casey Jones, the brave engineer, but few people know that he was a real man, for his legend has obscured the facts of his life and death. From Fulton to Canton, Mississippi, however, the current Illinois Central Gulf main line has many recollections of Casey's career.

Twenty-five miles west of here—near where Missouri, Tennessee, and Kentucky come together—is a huge oxbow in the Mississippi River. This loop and Reelfoot Lake, in Tennessee, are the scars left by America's strongest earthquake, the New Madrid tremor of 1811. It took few lives and destroyed little property, but it changed the course of the Mississippi.

Between Cairo and Fulton the railroad runs southeast, tending away from the Mississippi. Between Fulton and Memphis the road runs southwest, approaching the great river again at Memphis.

463.4 **Halls, Tenn.** *460.4.* This is the halfway point between the Great Lakes and the Gulf.

482.0 **Henning** *441.8.* Remember *Roots,* the immensely popular book and TV series of a few years back? At the end, the family leaves the Deep South for a new home in Tennessee, at Henning. This is the hometown of the book's author, Alex Haley.

528.5 **Poplar Avenue (Memphis)** *395.3.* There's no station here anymore, but in Casey Jones's day this was an important spot. It was from this point that Casey and his fireman, Sim Webb, pulled out with Train Number 1 on a rainy Sunday night in April 1900. This was the beginning of Casey's last trip: he never reached his terminal at Canton, Mississippi.

529.9 **MEMPHIS, TENN. (Central Station)** *393.9.* The river is visible from the west side of the train (right side, going south).

For information on the city, see section 2.24.

588.8 **BATESVILLE, MISS.** *335.0.* Twenty-five miles east is Oxford, site of the University of Mississippi (commonly called Ole Miss) and the home of one of America's literary giants, William Faulkner. Winner of the Nobel prize for literature in 1949, Faulkner is famous for his novels of Mississippi—its land and its people.

629.0 **GRENADA** *294.8.* Although it's *Gre-nah-da* in Spain, they say *Gre-nay-da* in Mississippi. The town stands on the Yalobusha, one of many rivers flowing into the Mississippi Delta.

On the night of his last run, Casey Jones left Memphis 3 hours late, determined to make up all that time before reaching the end of his run at Canton. He sent Number 1 racing through the midnight darkness at speeds up to 70 miles per hour, and when he reached Grenada, 100 miles from Memphis, he had already gained an hour and a half on his schedule.

651.9 **WINONA** *271.9.* Say it *Wye'-nona,* with the accent on the first syllable.

682.0 **DURANT** *241.8.* By the time he made his stop at Durant—the last scheduled halt before Canton—Casey Jones had made up all but 30 minutes of the lost time. He planned to pick up the rest in the next 25 miles to Way and then coast into Canton on time. He did not know that at Vaughn, 4 miles north of Way, a freight-train accident had left the main line blocked—and there were no signals on this line in 1900.

703.6 **Vaughn** *220.2.* Approaching Vaughn from the north there is a reverse curve. Casey Jones and Number 1 came flying around the upper end at 60 miles per hour. Fireman Sim Webb, leaning out from the left side of the locomotive, suddenly saw a dark shape on the track dead ahead. He shouted a warning; Casey threw his brakes into full emergency, reversed his engine, and yelled, "Jump, Sim!" Those were his last words; he stayed in the cab and died when his engine crashed into the stalled freight train. Sim Webb was dazed and shaken up but otherwise unhurt. He lived for many years after the accident and told the story often.

But it's unlikely that the saga of Casey Jones would have entered American folklore had it not been for an illiterate engine-wiper named Wallace Saunders, who made up the original ballad of the brave engineer.

740.4 **JACKSON** *183.4.* Capital of Mississippi and the largest city in the state, Jackson is named for General Andrew Jackson, the seventh president of the United States. Jackson was immensely popular among the farmers of the West and South, and when he was elected president in 1828 his supporters regarded the event as a triumph of the common man over the forces of place and privilege. The celebration at the White House reached almost riotous proportions as Jackson's followers mobbed the place in honor of their hero's victory.

Forty miles due west of Jackson is Vicksburg. Here the Confederates blocked the Mississippi to Union shipping and protected Rebel communications to Arkansas and Texas. The Southerners repelled eight Northern attacks, but lost this vital post on July 4, 1863, after Grant starved them out.

794.5 **BROOKHAVEN** *129.3.* This is the station for Natchez, the historic old river town that lies 60 miles to the west. Natchez dates to French and Spanish times, long before there was a United States; moreover, it escaped serious damage during the Civil War and so contains many gracious antebellum homes.

818.4 **McCOMB, MISS.** *105.4.* McComb looks (from the train, anyway) like the set for a Hollywood movie about the Deep South.

870.5 **HAMMOND, LA.** *53.3.* Home of Southeast Louisiana University, Hammond is in the midst of the northern Louisiana strawberry country. Uncounted loads of berries are shipped each year from Tangipahoa Parish.(Remember, this is Louisiana, where parishes, rather than counties, are the units of local government.)

Hammond is the nearest Amtrak station to Baton Rouge, which is 35 miles west by Route I-12. Baton Rouge is not only the state capital but also the home of Louisiana State University. Huey Long was assassinated here, in the rotunda of the state capitol building he had caused to be built.

886.0 **Manchac** *37.8.* Here the railroad passes over a series of causeways and bridges between Lake Maurepas to the west and Lake Pontchartrain to the east. Route I-55 parallels the railroad across the passage.

913.2 **Kenner** *10.6.* This suburb of New Orleans is built on the narrow neck of land that lies between Lake Pontchartrain and the Mississippi River. New Orleans International Airport is nearby, on the north side of the train (left side, coming into New Orleans).

921.4 **Carrollton Avenue** *2.4.* This is a junction point where eastern, northern, and western railroads come together.

923.8 **NEW ORLEANS** *0.0.* For information on the city, see section 2.28. Passengers continuing on to Houston, San Antonio, El Paso, Tucson, Phoenix, or Los Angeles should refer to section 3.42. Those bound for Birmingham, Atlanta, or Washington, D.C., should refer to section 3.28.

3.35   Chicago—Springfield—St. Louis

Connecting Lake Michigan with the Mississippi, linking the nation's two top railroad centers, and bisecting the heart of Illinois, Land of Lincoln—this is one of Amtrak's busier and more interesting short runs.

A glance at a map will show that this route is practically straight between Chicago and the Mississippi River port city of Alton, Illinois, but awkwardly roundabout between there and St. Louis. This is because the predecessor Chicago and Alton Railway was designed as a link between lake boats at Chicago and river steamers at Alton, rather than as a connection between the great rail centers. Thus the thinking of the mid-nineteenth century is reflected in Amtrak's out-of-the-way approach to St. Louis even today.

Originally called the Chicago and Alton—and later the Gulf, Mobile and Ohio—this line is now part of the Illinois Central Gulf system. No matter what name it has operated under, however, this has always been the main passenger route between Chicago and St. Louis. Amtrak now operates three daily trains in each direction over this track. The *Eagle,* which goes on to Texas, rates Superliner cars, while Amfleet coaches are used on other trains. Coach seats are unreserved, so get to the station early if you're traveling during a peak period.

0.0 CHICAGO (Union Station) *283.9.* Like all Amtrak trains going south, east, and west from Chicago, St. Louis trains leave from the south side of Chicago's Union Station, passing under the main post office. This, incidentally, is a unique spot, for although the railroad tracks go under the building, the Eisenhower Expressway goes right through it, crossing over the railroad tracks at right angles. Is there another place where a multilane superhighway crosses over a railroad inside a building?

5.2 **Brighton Park** *278.7.* An important railroad junction, where the ICG St. Louis line crosses the Baltimore and Ohio Chicago terminal's busy freight line. A safety stop is made here.

Beyond Brighton Park, trains parallel both Route I-55, the main Chicago–St. Louis highway, and beyond it the Chicago Sanitary and Ship Canal. This waterway (locally called the Drainage Canal, for short) is one of the most remarkable engineering accomplishments in the world. Not only does it connect the Great Lakes with the Mississippi River, it also assures Chicago of pure drinking water by reversing the direction of the Chicago River.

The Chicago is a little river, neither long nor deep. Nature made it drain into Lake Michigan. As the great city grew during the nine-

CHICAGO—SPRINGFIELD—ST. LOUIS

Southbound/miles   *miles/Northbound*

0.0	CHICAGO (Union Sta.)	283.9
1.6	21st St.	282.3
2.6	Halsted Street	281.3
5.2	Brighton Park	278.7
10.3	Glenn	272.6
11.9	Summit	272.0
17.5	Williow Springs	266.4
25.3	Lemont	258.6
32.9	Lockport	251.0
35.8	State Prison	248.1
37.2	JOLIET	246.7
45.8	Elwood	238.1
52.5	Wilmington	231.4
57.3	Braidwood	226.6
61.2	Braceville	222.7
64.5	Gardner	219.4
73.6	Dwight	210.3
81.7	Odell	202.2
86.9	Cayuga	197.0

91.9	PONTIAC	192.0
97.7	Ocoya	186.2
102.3	Chenoa	181.6
110.3	Lexington	173.6
118.2	Towanda	165.7
124.1	NORMAL	159.8
126.6	BLOOMINGTON	157.3
132.2	Shirley	151.7
136.3	Funk's Grove	147.6
140.9	McLean	143.0
145.8	Atlanta	138.1
149.7	Lawndale	134.2
156.4	LINCOLN	127.5
163.4	Broadwell	120.5
167.3	Elkhart	116.6
173.0	Williamsville	110.9
177.6	Sherman	106.3
185.1	SPRINGFIELD	98.8
185.1	SPRINGFIELD	98.8
194.5	Chatham	89.4
200.6	Auburn	83.3
204.3	Thayer	79.6
207.0	Virden	76.9
210.8	Girard	73.1
214.5	Nilwood	69.4
223.8	CARLINVILLE	60.1
229.7	Macoupin	54.2
234.2	Plainview	49.7
238.3	Shipman	45.6
243.2	Miles	40.7
246.0	Brighton	37.9
252.1	Godfrey	31.8
257.0	ALTON	26.9
274.9	Granite City, Ill.	9.0
	Mississippi River	
283.9	ST. LOUIS, MO.	0.0

teenth century, its industries poured their pollutants into the stream. They wound up in the lake, source of the city's drinking water. Something had to be done. The twentieth-century answer would have been to reduce the level of pollution, but the nineteenth-century response was this canal, which made the river flow backward, out of the lake! This had the effect of shipping Chicago's pollution down the Illinois to the Mississippi. Nobody but Chicagoans liked that result much, but the realities of power at the time left the protesters helpless to do more than complain.

The canal is controlled by locks at the mouth of the Chicago River at the east end of the system and at Lockport on the west end, where it flows into the Des Plaines River, a tributary of the Illinois.

11.9 **Summit** *272.0.* The Drainage Canal was not the first attempt to connect Lake Michigan with the Mississippi waterway. In 1673 Father Jacques Marquette and his *voyageur* companion, Louis Joliet, discovered that they could carry their canoe between the little Chicago River and the Des Plaines. This short portage offered the most convenient route between the Great Lakes and the Mississippi. The site of this portage was just west of present-day Harlem Avenue, just outside the Chicago city limits, in the county forest preserve near the village of Summit. Summit, of course, got its name because it stands on the low glacial ridge that divides the Lake Michigan watershed from the Illinois valley.

Although a portage was adequate for a couple of Frenchmen in a canoe, it was hardly efficient for boats carrying heavy loads of grain, and in 1833 the State of Illinois built a canal across the glacial ridge. It was called the Illinois and Michigan Canal, and parts of it still exist. Much of the labor on the project was done by Irish immigrants, many of whom settled at the Chicago end in an area called Bridgeport (near the present Brighton Park crossing). The neighborhood is still predominantly Irish and was the lifelong home of Chicago's late mayor and political boss Richard J. Daley.

25.3 **Lemont** *258.6.* To the north, across the two canals and the Des Plaines River, is Argonne National Laboratory, a world center of nuclear research.

32.9 **Lockport** *251.0.* Lockport was founded by the builders of the original Illinois and Michigan Canal, which ended here. A canal museum is maintained at the site. Here also are the locks that form the western end of the present Drainage Canal.

35.8 **State Prison** *248.1.* The Illinois State Prison at Joliet is still in use but it has been supplemented by Stateville, a bigger and more modern correctional institution on the other side of the Des Plaines River and a few miles farther north.

37.2 **JOLIET** *246.7.* This industrial town is named for the French explorer Louis Joliet, who accompanied Father Jacques Marquette on his trip through the Illinois country in 1673. The expedition had a dual purpose: to explore the territory and claim it for France and to convert the Indians to Christianity. Marquette and Joliet explored a large part of what is now Wisconsin, as well as the Illinois valley.

Incidentally, the name of the Illinois city is pronounced *Jolly-ette,* despite its French origins.

45.8 **Elwood** *238.1.* A large U.S. Army arsenal is located here. The railroad bisects the military reservation.

52.5 **Wilmington** *231.4.* Just south of the town the tracks cross the Kankakee River, another tributary of the Illinois. La Salle, a Frenchman who followed the Mississippi all the way to the Gulf and claimed its watershed for his king, used this river rather than the Des Plaines in his 1682 voyage of discovery. He portaged from the St. Joseph River to the Kankakee near the present site of South Bend, Indiana, missing the Chicago portage altogether.

91.9 **PONTIAC** *192.0.* Pontiac was the name of an Indian chief once powerful in this region.

I'll never forget this town, because I was once snowed in here while driving from St. Louis to Chicago. There were drifts 17 feet high on I-55, and most of the local snowplows were out of commission. So, four hundred truckers and yours truly spent the night on the floor of the National Guard armory, with food and bedding supplied by the Red Cross. Next time I'll take the train!

124.1 **NORMAL** *159.8.* The town gets its name from the old Illinois Normal School, a teacher-training college here. Today, Illinois Normal has become Illinois State University, a major institution with 20,000 students and range of graduate programs.

126.6 **BLOOMINGTON** *157.3.* This is the twin sister city of Normal, and the Amtrak station for both towns is here. Bloomington has its own university—Illinois Weslyan, a private Methodist-affiliated institution.

A railroad history footnote involves Bloomington, as well as the entire line from Chicago to Springfield. Contrary to popular belief, George M. Pullman did not invent the sleeping car, but he did build one far more luxurious and comfortable than any earlier product. Appropriately, he called it a "Palace." Trouble was, Pullman's Palace car was too wide to operate on most railroads of the time, and until Abraham Lincoln was assasinated, it appeared that luxury would never reach the rails. Pullman saw potential benefit in that terrible act: He offered his elegant Palace car to Mrs. Lincoln, gratis, for use on the presidential funeral train. She accepted, and rather than cause a fuss the railroad made the necessary clearance adjustments to let the Lincoln train through, Palace car and all.

This done, Pullman got the Alton to begin operating his car on the regular night train between Chicago and Bloomington. So superior were Pullman's accommodations that it wasn't long before passengers began to demand Pullman cars on other runs, and the former cabinet-maker from Brocton, New York, was in the sleeping-car business in a big way.

156.4 **LINCOLN** *127.5.* Abraham Lincoln never actually lived here, but the town's name is not a misnomer. All of this part of central Illinois is Lincoln country. As a young attorney, he rode the circuit from courthouse to courthouse. As a youth, he lived at New Salem (30 miles west of Lincoln), where he kept store, split rails, and unsuccessfully wooed Ann Rutledge.

Incidentally, Miss Rutledge holds an interesting distinction: she remains the only woman to be honored by having an Amtrak train named after her. The *Ann Rutledge* operates on the Chicago—St. Louis line, and it stops in Lincoln every day.

185.1 **SPRINGFIELD** *98.8.* Springfield has two important industries—state government and Abraham Lincoln, not necessarily in that order. The town was founded in 1818, and Lincoln settled here in 1837, when he was twenty-eight. He opened a law office and soon led a successful campaign to move the state capital to his adopted hometown. He lived the rest of his adult life in Springfield, except for his 4 years as president. His home—the only house he ever owned—still stands at the corner of 8th and Jackson streets; it is now a museum. It was from this house that he left, one rainy morning early in 1861, for Washington. He was returned to Springfield 4 years later to be interred in the cemetery on the north edge of town where Mrs. Lincoln and three of their children are also buried.

The Amtrak station in Springfield is conveniently located within sight of the state capitol (left side, going south) and within walking distance of the Lincoln home.

257.0 **ALTON** *26.9.* Alton was once a great river port, but it lost much of its economic importance when the railroads muscled steamboats out of the transportation picture. Historically, the city is memorable as the home of Elijah Lovejoy, a crusading antislavery newspaper editor who suffered martyrdom when some of his proslavery neighbors lynched him during a riot in 1837. A state memorial on the Alton riverfront commemorates the event.

Amtrak trains do not enter the waterfront area, however; they stop at the College Avenue station in the northern part of the city, then continue on down the Illinois side of the Mississippi to Granite City. Unfortunately, the right of way lies somewhat inland, so passengers do not get to see the point where the Missouri River empties into the Mississippi a few miles south of Alton. This was the starting point of the Lewis and Clark expedition of 1803–6.

274.9 **Granite City, Ill.** *9.0.* Though situated in Illinois, Granite City is actually part of the St. Louis metropolitan area. Years ago, when Missouri was dry on Sundays, the local trolley line to Granite City was mobbed once a week with thousands of thirsty St. Louisans seeking their beloved beer.

In common with other "east side" communities, Granite City is an industrial town—in this case, steel and heavy manufacturing. The National Stock Yards are farther south.

Amtrak trains enter St. Louis by way of the Merchants Bridge, northernmost of the four railroad bridges over the river. The bridge is several miles upstream from the city center, so passengers are treated to a ride down the west bank of the Mississippi.

283.9 **ST. LOUIS, MO.** *0.0.* On the way into town, trains pass under the historic Eads Bridge and past the Jefferson National Expansion Memorial with its Gateway Arch.

The Eads Bridge, finished in 1874, crosses the river just north of the arch. Until its construction it was generally believed that the Mississippi was too wide and the current too swift to be bridged at St. Louis. But James B. Eads, an entirely self-taught engineer, dared to use steel, which had not been tested, to build an arch longer than any that had been built before. This bridge, the first Eads had ever designed, is as secure today as it ever was.

The Gateway Arch, just beyond the bridge (right side of the train, entering the city) was designed by Eero Saarinen and commemorates St. Louis's historic role as a jumping-off place for westward expansion. It honors Thomas Jefferson, who acquired the Louisiana Territory for the United States in the greatest real-estate deal in history—half a continent for $15 million.

For information on the city, see section 2.40.

3.36   Chicago—West Quincy

In Greek mythology, Zephyrus was the spirit of the West Wind, so the Burlington Route displayed quite a literary turn of mind when they gave the name "Zephyr" to their new streamliner back in 1934. The *Illinois Zephyr,* partly funded by the state, makes a daily round trip from Quincy, on the Mississippi River in west-central Illinois, to Chicago. As with other such short-run trains, seats are unreserved, there is no checked-baggage service, and meals are limited to snacks and sandwiches. The train is quite fast, even though it stops frequently. It covers the 263-mile route in about 4½ hours, which is substantially faster than you could drive. Equipment is usually double-decker coaches, offering plenty of seats and a smooth ride.

0.0 **CHICAGO (Union Station)** *263.5.* Leaving the station, trains pass beneath the main post office and between the Burlington Northern suburban coach yard on the left and the Amtrak coach yard on the right. At 16th Street the Burlington Northern turns sharply to the west.

6.9 **Cicero** *256.6.* This station is just west of the Chicago city limits. Al Capone once had his headquarters here.

10.0 **Harlem Avenue** *253.5.* Due south and not over a mile away

Southbound/miles   *miles/Northbound*

Southbound	Station	Northbound
0.0	CHICAGO (Union Sta.)	263.5
1.7	Halsted St.	261.8
3.7	Western Avenue	259.8
6.9	Cicero	256.6
8.5	Clyde	255.0
9.0	La Vergne	254.5
9.6	Berwyn	253.9
10.0	Harlem Avenue	253.5
11.0	Riverside	252.5
11.7	Hollywood	251.8
12.2	Brookfield	251.3
13.0	Congress Park	250.5
13.8	LA GRANGE ROAD	249.7
14.1	Stone Avenue	249.4
15.4	Western Springs	248.1
16.3	Highlands	247.2
16.8	Hinsdale	246.7
17.8	West Hinsdale	245.7
18.2	Clarendon Hills	245.3
19.4	Westmont	244.1
20.3	Fairview Avenue	243.2
21.1	Downers Grove	242.4
22.6	Belmont	240.9
24.4	Lisle	239.1
28.4	Naperville	235.1
33.4	Eola	230.1
37.8	AURORA	225.7
40.0	Montgomery	223.5
45.5	Bristol	218.0
51.5	PLANO	212.0
55.9	Sandwich	207.6
59.2	Somonauk	204.3
65.3	Leland	198.2
72.1	Earlville	191.4
78.1	Meriden	185.4
82.7	MENDOTA	180.8
91.4	Arlington	172.1
95.3	Zearing	168.2
98.4	Malden	165.1
104.2	PRINCETON	159.3
110.7	Wyanet	152.8
116.6	Buda	146.9
123.0	Neponset	140.5
131.0	KEWANEE	132.5
139.3	Galva	124.2
146.7	Oneida	116.8
155.1	Wataga	108.4
157.7	Bishop	105.8
162.4	GALESBURG (Seminary Street Sta.)	101.1

162.4	GALESBURG	101.1
166.2	Waterman	97.3
172.3	Abingdon	91.2
182.8	Avon	80.7
191.4	Bushnell	72.1
202.3	MACOMB	61.2
209.3	Colchester	54.2
211.7	Tennessee	51.8
217.4	Colmar	46.1
221.9	Plymouth	41.6
225.9	Augusta	37.6
235.2	Golden	28.3
240.9	Camp Point	22.6
245.9	Coatsburg	17.6
248.2	Paloma	15.3
254.3	Ewbanks	9.2
258.8	QUINCY, ILL. (24th Street)	4.7
263.5	WEST QUINCY, MO.	0.0

is the site of the original Chicago portage, used first by the Indians and later by the French explorers to pass from Lake Michigan to the Mississippi Valley. This portage, the shortest and easiest route from the Great Lakes and Canada to the Gulf, was the first stimulus to the growth of what was to become America's second largest city.

11.0 **Riverside** *252.5.* An old and elegant suburb along the Des Plaines River, which the train crosses here.

12.2 **Brookfield** *251.3.* The Brookfield Zoo here is one of Chicago's two major zoological parks and universally acknowledged as one of the finest zoos anywhere.

13.8 **LA GRANGE ROAD** *249.7.* This suburban station in the town of La Grange is convenient to Route I-294, the Illinois Tollway, which brings it within easy driving distance of virtually any Chicago suburb. O'Hare International Airport is about 10 miles north via the highway.

16.8 **Hinsdale** *246.7.* This residential suburb is the hometown of former Davis Cup tennis star Marty Riesen.

24.4 **Lisle** *239.1.* Half a mile north of the right-of-way is the Morton Arboretum, endowed by the salt family and containing an amazing variety of flowers and trees.

28.4 **Naperville** *235.1.* A few miles north, in the adjoining town of Wheaton, is Cantigny, the estate of the late Robert R. McCormick, the blustering former publisher of the *Chicago Tribune.*

McCormick became editor and publisher of the paper in 1920, and under his regime the *Tribune*'s editorial policy was somewhere to the right of Attila the Hun. The paper also insisted on its own private reform of English orthography. In the *Tribune,* "freight" came out "frate" and "straight" was "strate," among other idiosyncrasies. But there is one thing you can say about McCormick and his newspaper—neither one was ever dull.

37.8 **AURORA** *225.7.* The town gets its name from the Greek word for dawn. Aurora is on the Fox River, a tributary of the Illinois. This was the birthplace of the Burlington Railroad, which started out as a small line known as the Aurora Branch; there are still extensive shops here, visible to the north (right side, going west). Aurora is at the outer end of suburban service from Chicago.

Just west of the passenger station, the line divides: One fork goes to Savannah and eventually to the Twin Cities, St. Paul and Minneapolis; the other goes to Omaha and Denver. Amtrak trains use the left, or southern, fork.

82.7 **MENDOTA** *180.8.* Here the rails curve sharply to the left, pass by the station building, then turn right and cross the Illinois Central's freight-only branch from Rockford. About 7 miles south is Troy Grove, birthplace of Wild Bill Hickok.

91.4 **Arlington** *172.1.* As the train approaches this tiny hamlet, look out the south side windows (left side, going west), and you will see in the distance two pyramids rising up above the cornfields. These are all that is left of the Cherry Mine, scene of one of America's worst disasters and most inspiring stories of survival against odds.

Back in 1909, the Cherry Coal Mine was regarded as one of the newest and safest in America, until a freak fire broke out in the main gallery and 259 miners died. Some 20 men, however, barricaded themselves deep in the mine, away from the fatal smoke and gas. There they stayed, self-entombed, for a week. Search parties hunting for bodies found them, weak but alive, 7 days after the fire. They had survived underground for a full week without food, water, or light.

104.2 **PRINCETON** *159.3.* Ten miles south along the Illinois River is the town of Hennepin with its steel plant. Peoria, Illinois' second largest city, is 50 miles away.

116.6 **Buda** *146.9.* Sweeping reverse curves take the train through this tiny town. Twenty miles south is another little Illinois hamlet, called Tampico—worth mention as the birthplace of President Ronald Reagan.

131.0 **KEWANEE** *132.5.* Kewanee is a market town for the surrounding farms, but it has an industrial past as well. The old buildings of the Kewanee Boiler Works line the tracks.

162.4 **GALESBURG** *101.1.* Birthplace of the poet and historian Carl Sandburg and site of Knox College, Galesburg is an archetypical midwestern small town. It was founded in 1836 by the Reverend George Washington Gale, who selected the site as a likely place for a college dedicated to the training of Presbyterian ministers. The town was named for the Reverend Gale; the college, for John Knox, the founder of

Scottish Presbyterianism. Today, Knox is a nonsectarian liberal-arts college with an outstanding academic reputation. If you look quickly, you can catch a glimpse of the campus just after leaving the passenger station (right side of the train, going west).

Galesburg is a Burlington Northern division point and hub of all its lines east of the Missouri River. Quincy trains leave the main line here, operating over the Kansas City branch for the last hundred miles of their runs. The Galesburg freight yards are located along the track south of town.

A century ago a Swedish immigrant named Sandburg earned his living in these railroad shops. In 1878 his wife gave birth to an infant son who grew to be one of the best-loved poets and writers America has produced. Carl Sandburg's boyhood was spent in Galesburg; then, as a young man, he moved to Chicago, where he became a reporter. In 1916 he published his "Chicago Poems"—who has not heard that verse about the fog that comes on little cat feet? Later he won two Pulitzer prizes, one for his poetry and one for his biography of Abraham Lincoln. His home in Galesburg is open to the public.

202.3 **MACOMB, ILL.** *61.2.* Western Illinois University, with its twelve thousand students, dominates the town. Many of the passengers on the *Illinois Zephyr* are WIU students going back and forth between the campus and their homes in the Chicago area.

258.8 **QUINCY, ILL. (24th Street)** *4.7.* Quincy is an old Mississippi River town, perhaps a trifle tarnished but still maintaining plenty of nineteenth-century charm. Until recently, Amtrak passengers visiting the town had to use the station at West Quincy, Missouri, across the river, but a new passenger stop has been established at the northeastern part of the town.

After leaving the new Quincy station, trains skirt the northern edge of town, swing to the south, and then turn westward again to cross the great Mississippi on an impressive bridge.

263.5 **WEST QUINCY, MO.** *0.0.* West Quincy is not a town—just a railroad junction and station that serves as the terminal for the *Illinois Zephyr*. It is within 20 miles or so of one of America's most wonderful and best-known sites: Hannibal, Missouri, hometown of Mark Twain.

Twain (whose real name was Samuel L. Clemens) lived in Hannibal as a child and until his young manhood, when he left for good. He has immortalized the town in *Tom Sawyer* and *Huckleberry Finn,* calling it St. Petersburg; all the features of the books are there. The Clemens house is now a museum, with the famous fence that Tom got his friends to whitewash still standing out front. Cardiff Hill, a tall bluff along the river just north of town, is today decorated by a statue of Tom and Huck. The cave where Tom and Becky Thatcher were lost is an attraction south of town; you can see Injun Joe's cup and the rocky den where the treasure box was hidden.

3.37 Chicago—Milwaukee—(Minneapolis —Seattle)

No Amtrak service suffered more from the budget cuts of 1981 than this 85-mile mini-corridor. Two daily trains each way were eliminated altogether, and two of the three remaining runs lost all meal and beverage service. What remains is essentially glorified commuter service, with morning and afternoon trains in each direction making connections at Chicago to Amtrak's long-distance runs. The only first-class service is provided by the *Empire Builder,* which uses this route on its way from Chicago to the Twin Cities and the Northern Pacific Coast.

The route parallels the shoreline of Lake Michigan but lies several miles inland, so that passengers never see the lake at all. The line bypasses the cities of Waukegan, Kenosha, and Racine. There has long been agitation to move Amtrak's trains from the Milwaukee Road to the lakefront Chicago and North Western line so as to provide service to these population centers. To date, however, there are no concrete plans for this move.

0.0 **CHICAGO** *85.0.* Unlike all other Amtrak trains using Chicago's Union Station, Milwaukee-bound runs use the north side of the terminal.

Just after leaving, look to the right side of the train for an unusual view of the city. The north and south branches of the Chicago River join the immediate foreground. The huge Art Deco building across the river is the Merchandise Mart, one of the world's largest commercial buildings. It is owned by the politically minded Kennedy family. The twin round towers beyond the Mart, which look a little like corncobs on end, are the Marina City apartment complex, and the John Hancock Center with its twin TV antennas forms a towering backdrop to the scene.

At Lake Street, where this vista opens up, there are five levels of transportation stacked one atop another. Underground is the subway; above are the river, the railroad, and the street; and overhead is the Chicago elevated line.

Just beyond Lake Street there is a sharp curve to the left. Milwaukee-bound trains run straight west for the next 2½ miles.

Look to the south side of the train (left side, leaving Chicago) and you will see, a few blocks away, a massive, squat gray building. This is the Chicago Stadium, home of the Bulls and Blackhawks and site of political conventions, ice shows, and once upon a time (believe it or not) a National Football League championship game.

2.9 **Western Avenue** *82.1.* At this interlocking tower, Milwaukee-bound trains curve to the north (right), cross the Chicago and North Western line to Omaha, and pass the coach yards where suburban equipment and some Amtrak cars are serviced.

9.0 **Mayfair** *76.0.* Here the train crosses a North Western suburban line and the Kennedy Expressway. The John Hancock building,

CHICAGO—MILWAUKEE

Northbound/miles		miles/Southbound
0.0	CHICAGO (Union Sta.)	85.0
2.9	Western Ave.	82.1
6.4	Healy	78.6
8.2	Grayland	76.8
9.0	Mayfair	76.0
10.2	Forest Glen	74.8
11.6	Edgebrook	73.4
14.3	Morton Grove	70.7
16.2	Golf	68.8
17.4	GLENVIEW	67.6
20.9	Northbrook	64.1
23.9	Deerfield	61.1
28.0	Lake Forest	57.0
32.3	Rondout	52.7
34.0	Abbott Park	51.0
38.3	Gurnee	46.7
42.9	Wadsworth, Ill.	42.1
52.6	Truesdell, Wis.	32.4
57.5	Somers	27.5
61.8	STURTEVANT	23.2
66.0	Franksville	19.0
69.4	Caledonia	15.6
72.8	Oakwood	12.2
77.9	Lake	7.1
82.9	Kinnickinnic River Br.	2.1
83.9	Washington St.	1.1
85.0	MILWAUKEE	0.0

9 miles away, can be seen plainly in clear weather (right side of the train, leaving Chicago).

10.2 **Forest Glen** *74.8.* This attractive residential area is still within the Chicago city limits. Beyond the station the train passes through a part of the Cook County Forest Preserve. The little stream crossed here is the North Branch of the Chicago River.

14.3 **Morton Grove** *70.7.* First of the many suburbs north of the city, Morton Grove is home for young account executives and junior corporate officers. (The senior executives generally live in the more exclusive suburbs closer to Lake Michigan.) The town was in the news not long ago when it passed an ordinance, subsequently upheld by the U.S. Supreme Court, forbidding ownership of hand guns.

17.4 **GLENVIEW** *67.6.* This busy station serves all the northern suburbs of Chicago. Just north of the station is the Glenview Naval Air Station (left side of the train, leaving Chicago).

Three miles beyond Glenview is Tower A-20. At this point mainline freight tracks join the passenger tracks. They do not run into Chicago proper, but come around the edge of the city from Bensenville Yard near O'Hare Field. This junction is at a place called Techny, after the Catholic seminary that can be seen on the hill in the distance (right side, leaving Chicago).

23.9 **Deerfield** *61.1.* This is the site of the Sara Lee bakery, which makes the popular cakes seen in supermarkets. The firm got its name from its founder, Charles Lubin, who named his product after his infant daughter.

28.0 **Lake Forest** *57.0.* Lake Forest is Chicago's most exclusive suburb, but you'd never know it by looking out the window of an Amtrak train. The elegant gaslit, tree-shaded, curving streets with their beautiful mansions are a couple of miles east, near the lake.

32.3 **Rondout** *52.7.* Here the Milwaukee Road crosses the Elgin, Joliet and Eastern tracks (the Chicago Outer Belt) at grade. Here, too, the suburban trains to Fox Lake leave the main line, branching off to the west (left side, going north). The North Shore interurban line used to cross overhead at this point; the bridge abutments are still in place.

34.0 **Abbott Park** *51.0.* Abbott Park is named for Abbott Laboratories, which has a large office and manufacturing complex here.

A mile or two north of here, where Buckley Road crosses the tracks, is the site of America's greatest train robbery. It happened, appropriately, on Friday the 13th, in June 1924. A gang of six armed men held up a mail train and got away with $3 million worth of cash and securities. Circumstances of the robbery indicated that it was an inside job. Quick police work rounded up all six of the active thieves, and 2 months later the cops caught up with the masterminds—an ace postal inspector and a Chicago politician. All the robbers went to prison for terms of up to 25 years, but at least $1 million of the stolen money was never recovered. Compared to the Rondout gang, Butch Cassidy and the Sundance Kid were small potatoes.

42.9 **Wadsworth, Ill.** *42.1.* The town is named for Union General James Wadsworth, who was killed in action at the battle of the Wilderness in May 1864.

About 6 miles northeast of Wadsworth, on the shore of Lake Michigan, is the town of Zion. This unusual community was planned and built by the followers of John Alexander Dowie, a once famous evangelist and religious leader. He preached communal living and plural marriage, and there was a fair amount of whispering about goings-on in Zion. Today, though, it's just another little suburban town, with only some of the old white frame buildings and the broad streets remaining from its earlier, more scandalous times.

52.6 **Truesdell, Wis.** *32.4.* To the east (right side, going north) is a huge parking lot, the shipping point for new American Motors cars, which are built at nearby Kenosha.

61.8 **STURTEVANT** *23.2.* Sturtevant is a very small town, but it's an Amtrak station because it serves Racine, an industrial city 10 miles east. Racine is the home of the Johnson Wax Company and of two important Frank Lloyd Wright structures, masterpieces of American architecture. The first is the office building at Johnson's, shaped like a big bottle of wax. The second is the Wingspread Conference Center, the former home of the Johnson family, on the lake shore north of town.

66.0 **Franksville** *19.0.* Just to the left of the tracks going north is the structure that gives the town its name—the Franks Sauer Kraut company.

77.9 **Lake** *7.1.* Lake Tower sits at the top of a 7-mile grade that drops the railroad down to the valley of the Menomonee river at Milwaukee. Just beyond the tower to the east (right side, going toward Milwaukee) is Billy Mitchell Field, the city's commercial air terminal.

82.9 **Kinnickinnic River Bridge** *2.1.* The Kinnickinnic (accent on the last "ic") is one of the three little rivers that empty into Lake Michigan at Milwaukee.

Just beyond the bridge are the big coke ovens of the Milwaukee Solvay Coke Company, which make a brilliant fiery picture at night if you happen to pass while one of the ovens is open. Beyond the coke ovens is more of the port of Milwaukee, which sees ocean-going ships from all over the world, thanks to the St. Lawrence Seaway. Grain and manufactured goods make up much of the outgoing traffic. You may see some ships in port to the east side (right side of the train, going north).

83.9 **Washington Street** *1.1.* To the west (left side of the train, going north) is the Allen-Bradley factory, topped by what the company claims is the biggest four-sided clock in the world. Beyond the plant is a sharp left curve where a freight line diverges, avoiding the downtown passenger station. Amtrak trains then curve immediately to the right again, pass the Pittsburgh Paint factory to the east, cross the Menomonee River on an interesting old side-swing bridge, swing to the west under the new post office, and come to a stop at Milwaukee's functional new passenger station, just three blocks from the main business street of the city.

85.0 **MILWAUKEE** *0.0.* For information on the city, see section 2.26. For passengers continuing on to Minneapolis-St. Paul, Seattle, or Portland, see sections 3.38 and 3.45.

3.38 (Chicago)—Milwaukee— Minneapolis-St. Paul— (Seattle)

This route includes a ride through the dairylands of central Wisconsin, an unexpected tunnel, and 125 scenic miles along the banks of the Mississippi River. It's part of the 2,200-mile run of the *Empire Builder,* one of Amtrak's finest trains, which operates daily between Chicago and the Pacific Northwest. There used to be a second daily train between Chicago, Milwaukee, and the Twin Cities; but it vanished as a result of budget cuts in 1981.

Before Amtrak, the *Empire Builder* used to go by way of the Burlington Northern route through Aurora and Savannah, Illinois. Since 1971, however, the train has operated by way of Milwaukee in order to serve larger population centers. For a time the new route was plagued by poor track on the Milwaukee Road, but today extensive repairs have been carried out and the *Empire Builder* now covers the 417 miles between Chicago and the Twin Cities in a respectable 8 hours. Accommodations include Superliner coaches, sleeping cars, lounge car, and dining car.

For notes on the route from Chicago to Milwaukee, see section 3.37.

85.0 **MILWAUKEE, WIS.** *331.7.* Leaving the Milwaukee station, the tracks run along the floor of the Menomonee River valley to the north of the river.

87.0 **Cut Off** *329.7.* Here the freight line that bypasses the Milwaukee passenger station rejoins the main line. The engine terminal and West Milwaukee shops are adjacent (left side, leaving Milwaukee).

88.2 **Grand Avenue** *328.5.* Three miles west of downtown Milwaukee, the Menomonee Valley turns sharply north. The rails follow, past County Stadium on the west (left side, leaving Milwaukee) to Grand Avenue Tower. At this point the line divides: One branch goes straight north to Green Bay and upper Michigan; the other fork turns left, crosses the river, and heads for La Crosse, on the western edge of the state. Amtrak trains use this left fork.

Incidentally, Grand Avenue is the name of the tower, but there is no such street. Some years ago the city of Milwaukee changed the name of its principal thoroughfare to Wisconsin Avenue, but the railroad didn't bother; therefore, the tower still bears the old name. The Miller Brewery, on the hill above the valley to the east, towers over the tracks (right side, going west).

90.4 **Wauwatosa** *326.3*. This is a residential suburb of Milwaukee.

(CHICAGO)—MILWAUKEE—MINNEAPOLIS-ST. PAUL

Westbound/miles		*miles/Eastbound*
0.0	CHICAGO, ILL. (Union Sta.)	416.7
85.0	MILWAUKEE, WIS.	331.7
87.0	Cut Off	329.7
88.2	Grand Ave.	328.5
90.4	Wauwatosa	326.3
94.9	Elm Grove	321.8
99.2	Brookfield	317.5
101.9	Duplainville	314.8
105.3	Pewaukee	311.4
109.9	Hartland	306.8
112.6	Nashotah	304.1
114.8	Okauchee	301.9
117.8	Oconomowoc	298.9
123.5	Ixonia	293.2
131.0	Watertown	285.7
132.8	Voltz	283.9
135.3	Richwood	281.4
140.6	Reeseville	276.1
145.9	Astico	270.8
149.7	COLUMBUS	267.0
153.3	Fall River	263.4
159.1	Doylestown	257.6
163.9	Rio	252.8
168.9	Wyocena	247.8
176.7	Portage Junction	240.0
177.9	PORTAGE	238.8
181.0	Silver	235.7
186.7	Lewiston	230.0
194.8	WISCONSIN DELLS	221.9
203.4	Lyndon	213.3
214.0	Mauston	202.7
221.0	New Lisbon	195.7
227.0	Camp Douglas	189.7

233.3	Oakdale	183.4
239.8	TOMAH	176.9
243.2	Tunnel City	173.5
245.9	Raymore	170.8
249.3	Camp McCoy	167.4
256.2	Sparta	160.5
262.8	Rockland	153.9
266.4	Bangor	150.3
271.0	West Salem	145.7
278.0	Medary	138.7
279.6	Grand Crossing	137.1
280.8	LA CROSSE, WIS.	135.9
280.8	LA CROSSE, WIS.	135.9
282.8	Bridge Switch, Minn.	133.9
289.9	Dakota	126.8
293.7	Donehower	123.0
298.5	Lamoille	118.2
307.5	WINONA	109.2
313.6	Minnesota City	103.1
318.3	Whitman	98.4
326.9	Weaver	89.8
334.4	Kellogg	82.3
340.5	Wabasha	76.2
353.0	Lake City	63.7
359.3	Frontenac	57.4
369.9	RED WING	46.8
373.5	Duke	43.2
377.8	Stroms	38.9
390.3	Hastings	26.4
391.1	St. Croix Jct.	25.6
391.5	St. Croix Tower	25.2
395.5	Chemolite	21.2
401.8	Newport	14.9
406.3	Oakland	10.4
407.3	St. Paul Yard	9.4
409.9	St. Paul (Union Depot)	6.8
410.8	Chestnut St.	5.9
411.7	Fordson Jct.	5.0
414.9	Snelling Ave.	1.8
415.7	Merriam Park	1.0
416.7	MINNEAPOLIS-ST. PAUL (Midway Sta.)	0.0

The syllable "wau" is an Indian world meaning water. The names of many Wisconsin towns and villages contain this word element.

101.9 **Duplainville** *314.8.* An interlocking tower here controls the crossing of the Milwaukee Road and the Soo Line. The Soo is a freight-only railroad extending from Canada and North Dakota to Minneapolis and Chicago. "Soo" is short for "Sault Sainte Marie," the Michigan town that is the site of the Soo Locks.

105.3 **Pewaukee** *311.4.* The rails skirt the shore of Pewaukee Lake, a favorite vacation spot (left side, going west). During the warm months you will surely see plenty of swimmers and boaters on the lake.

149.7 **COLUMBUS** *267.0.* Columbus wouldn't rate an Amtrak stop if it didn't also serve as the station for Madison, Wisconsin's capital and second-largest city, 30 miles southwest. A connecting bus takes passengers back and forth.

Madison is interesting geographically because it is laid out on an isthmus between two lakes. The streets radiate from the capitol building, and all the original thoroughfares were named for the signers of the Constitution. The main campus of the University of Wisconsin, with its forty thousand students, is within the city, and Madison has one of the highest educational levels in America, as well as one of the highest levels of per capita income.

177.9 **PORTAGE** *238.8.* Portage owes its name and historical importance to its site at the short overland portage between the Fox and Wisconsin rivers. Father Marquette came this way in 1673 on his way from Green Bay to the Mississippi valley.

Portage is also notable as the hometown of Frederick Jackson Turner, one of the most influential American historians. Turner taught at Madison for a time but was on the Harvard faculty in 1893 when he addressed the meeting of the American Historical Association at Chicago. It was the year of the Columbian Exhibition, the World's Fair honoring (a year late) the four hundredth anniversary of Columbus's discovery of the New World. It was also just 3 years after the 1890 census had declared that there was no longer a definable frontier of settlement in the West.

Turner theorized that the most important factor in the growth of distinctively American institutions and culture was the influence of the frontier, an area of unexplored free land where every man could carve himself a new life and a new home. Since 1893, Turner's thesis has been debated, rejected, redefined, supported, fussed over, and fought over by legions of American historians. It is to this day the most important single contribution of any individual to the study and interpretation of American history.

194.8 **WISCONSIN DELLS** *221.9.* Here the Wisconsin River has cut its way through high rock walls, forming a natural scenic spot of impressive beauty. A major resort complex has grown up around the Dells that is far and away Wisconsin's top tourist attraction. Amtrak passengers catch a quick glimpse of the river as the train crosses a high bridge just after leaving the station. The best view is to the north (right side, going west).

The Dells aren't the only attraction in this area, either. About 12 miles away is Baraboo, site of the unique Circus World Museum and former home of the Ringling Brothers Circus. The Circus World

Museum is more than a collection of antiquities—it also offers small-scale circus performances.

Also nearby is the International Crane Foundation, where research on these rare and beautiful birds is carried on. And a few miles west, at North Freedom, you can ride into the past behind a steam locomotive at the Midcontinent Railroad Museum. Indeed, there's something for everybody in the Dells area.

221.0 **New Lisbon** *195.7.* This is the junction with a freight-only line that runs up the Wisconsin River valley to the resort area of northern Wisconsin, where fishermen cast for muskie and bears come to dinner at the local garbage dumps.

239.8 **TOMAH** *176.9.* Tomah is the station for Fort McCoy Military Reservation and for the entire Kickapoo valley region of western Wisconsin. This is a beautiful, hilly area that was never ground into flat farmland by the glaciers, unlike much of Wisconsin.

243.2 **Tunnel City** *173.5.* The last thing the layman would expect to find in Wisconsin is a tunnel; but the western part of the state is far from flat, and a tunnel there is, right on the main line.

256.2 **Sparta** *160.5.* The town is named for the Greek city-state famous for its harsh living conditions and sturdy soldiers. A look at the rocky soil and the winter temperatures gives you the idea that modern Spartans must be just as tough as their ancestors.

280.8 **LA CROSSE, WIS.** *135.9.* Named by the French explorers as a symbol of their faith, La Crosse is a railroad division point and the most important station between Milwaukee and the Twin Cities. It is a crew-changing point on both the Milwaukee and Burlington Northern railroads, whose payrolls help to support the community.

La Crosse, on the Mississippi River, just below the mouth of the Black River, has a population of about 100,000. It has one nationally known industry—the G. Heilmann Brewing Company, which markets a number of popular beer brands including Old Style and Blatz.

After leaving the passenger station, Amtrak trains cross the Mississippi River, the border between Wisconsin and Minnesota.

282.8 **Bridge Switch, Minn.** *133.9.* At the west end of the Mississippi River bridge, Amtrak trains turn north toward the Twin Cities. Secondary freight lines continue from this point west to South Dakota and south to Iowa.

307.5 **WINONA** *109.2.* The town, pronounced *Wye-nona,* was named after a legendary Indian maiden who, it is said, threw herself into Lake Pepin over losing her lover. Winona is the site of St. Mary's College. The Amtrak station serves the Mayo clinics at Rochester, Minnesota, 50 miles west. These clinics, founded in 1889 to help tornado victims and staffed at the time by only a few doctors, now treat 175,000 patients every year.

340.5 **Wabasha** *76.2.* For the entire distance from La Crosse to Hastings, Minnesota, 110 miles, there are beautiful views of the Mississippi from the east side of the train (right side, going north). The finest scenery, however, is beyond Wabasha, where the river widens into Lake Pepin—not a true lake but a good deal bigger and more impressive than most. According to Indian legend, Winona jumped into the water from a high precipice on the Wisconsin side called Maiden Rock. Thus, the Indians called this wide place in the great river ''the lake of tears.'' Today, Lake Pepin is the scene of happier pastimes—fishing, boating, and water-skiing.

353.0 **Lake City** *63.7.* At this pretty town beside Lake Pepin, the railroad tracks unfortunately run inland, so passengers do not get a good view of the lakeshore.

369.9 **RED WING** *46.8.* From the Twin Cities south, the Army Corps of Engineers has built and maintains a series of dams on the Mississippi that have tamed the raging floods that used to develop on the river. Lock and Dam number 3 is here at Red Wing. The town is known for the Red Wing Shoes that are made here and sold widely throughout America. It's a picturesque place, with the Amtrak station located right along the riverfront.

390.3 **Hastings** *26.4.* North of the Hastings station, the railroad crosses back to the east bank of the Mississippi. The St. Croix River empties into the Mississippi at this point.

391.5 **St. Croix Tower** *25.2.* A short distance beyond the Mississippi River bridge, the Milwaukee Road and Burlington Northern lines meet. Once upon a time, each railroad had a single track from here to St. Paul. Many years ago, however, they entered into a joint-track agreement; so now the two single tracks are operated as one double-tracked railroad. To take advantage of easier grades, all traffic leaving St. Croix Tower normally operates on the left track, closest to the river—this is Burlington Northern property.

401.8 **Newport** *14.9.* At this tower the Burlington and the Milwaukee used to crisscross. Consequently, by staying on the left track, Amtrak trains return to the Milwaukee Road.

407.3 **St. Paul Yard** *9.4.* This is the Milwaukee's major freight terminal at St. Paul. Adjacent to it is the Burlington Northern's colorfully named Pig's Eye Yard—a reminder of the fact that St. Paul was once officially known as Pig's Eye, Minnesota! Indeed, nearby is Pig's Eye Lake. South St. Paul is across the river to the west. Holman Field, the city's downtown airport, is a little farther north.

409.9 **St. Paul** *6.8.* St. Paul's old Union Depot is no longer in use, but Amtrak trains pass through it heading for the new Midway Station. The state capitol and the other buildings of downtown St. Paul are just to the north and up the hill (right side of the train, going west); the Mississippi is on the south. The tracks run along the base of a bluff. At the crest of this hill is fashionable Summit Avenue, the street where James J. Hill and St. Paul's other turn-of-the-century nabobs had their houses. F. Scott Fitzgerald, the writer, grew up in St. Paul and was always frustrated because he could never quite keep up with the Summit Avenue social set.

414.9 **Snelling Avenue** *1.8.* Old Fort Snelling, on the Mississippi to the south, was built to protect the Falls of St. Anthony from attacks by Indians and British troops. Today it is a museum.

415.7 **Merriam Park** *1.0.* Here Amtrak trains turn onto the Minnesota Transfer Railroad, a mighty-mite switching line along whose tracks the new Twin Cities station is located. Just before reaching the station, trains cross University Avenue—the main street connecting St. Paul and Minneapolis—on an overhead bridge.

416.7 **MINNEAPOLIS-ST. PAUL (Midway Station)** *0.0.* Amtrak has concentrated its Twin Cities operations at the new Midway Station, right in the middle of the metropolitan area. For information on the cities, see section 2.27. For west-coast bound (Seattle or Portland) passengers, see section 3.45.

3.39   Minneapolis-St. Paul—Duluth

Amtrak service between the Twin Cities and the Twin Ports has had a precarious existence for some time. The *North Star* depends on a subsidy from the State of Minnesota. It survived a 1982 funding crisis by the narrowest of margins and was actually canceled a few months later, only to be revived again on a limited basis after 2 weeks.

At present, the service operates daily during the summer months and Fridays, Saturdays, and Sundays only for the rest of the year. Superliner coaches are used, and there is snack and beverage service but no checking of baggage. Connections are made at Minneapolis-St. Paul with the *Empire Builder* to and from points in the Pacific Northwest. The train has been attracting sizeable passenger loads, but without ensured funding its future is uncertain.

0.0 **MINNEAPOLIS-ST. PAUL (Midway Station)** *154.0.* For information on the Twin Cities, see section 2.27.

1.1 **St. Anthony** *152.9.* At St. Anthony tower, Amtrak trains leave the tracks of the Minnesota Transfer Railroad and turn westward onto the Burlington Northern.

The name of St. Anthony is closely associated with the history of

Minneapolis. In 1678 a French priest, Father Hennepin, explored the upper Mississippi until he reached a waterfall that barred navigation farther north. This fall he named for his patron saint—the Falls of St. Anthony. Later, flour mills were built at the falls, using the power of the dropping water to turn the grinding machinery. Around the mills a town grew up, called Minneapolis, Greek for "city of waters." The

MINNEAPOLIS-ST. PAUL—DULUTH

Northbound/miles   *miles/Southbound*

Northbound		Southbound
0.0	MINNEAPOLIS-ST. PAUL (Midway Station)	154.0
1.1	St. Anthony	152.9
2.4	Union	151.6
4.9	Hennepin Avenue	149.1
5.1	First Street North	148.9
5.7	Fourteenth Avenue North	148.3
6.9	Mulberry Junction	147.1
9.5	Northtown	144.5
11.3	Interstate	142.7
17.0	Coon Creek	137.0
22.9	Andover	131.1
34.8	Bethel	119.2
40.8	Isanti	113.2
46.5	CAMBRIDGE	107.5
51.4	Grandy	102.6
53.8	Stanchfield	100.2
57.3	Braham	96.7
62.5	Grasston	91.5
67.9	Henriette	86.1
73.7	Brook Park	80.3
82.0	Hinckley	72.0
90.7	SANDSTONE	63.3
96.6	Askov	57.4
105.0	Bruno	49.0
110.7	Kerrick	43.3
117.2	Nickerson, Minn.	36.8
129.2	Foxboro, Wis.	24.8
140.5	Boylston	13.5
143.5	Saunders	10.5
145.5	Central Avenue	8.5
149.7	SUPERIOR, WIS.	4.3
154.0	DULUTH, MINN.	0.0

name could not be more apt, for the city contains not only the Mississippi but also twenty-two lakes.

2.4 **Union** *151.6.* This tower marks the approximate boundary between St. Paul and Minneapolis. Grain elevators line the right-of-way to the south (left side of the train, going west).

The tracks pass beneath a series of streets in an opencut subway.

Above is the campus of the University of Minnesota, one of America's great state universities, with an enrollment of nearly 50,000. After passing the campus, the tracks cross the Mississippi just above the falls on a long, stone-arch bridge. This bridge, which has been carrying trains for a hundred years, is a monument to James J. Hill, the "empire builder," the man who promoted the Great Northern railroad in the nineteenth century. Though a Canadian by birth, Jim Hill became one of St. Paul's leading citizens. His mansion is now being restored and will be open to the public as a museum.

4.9 **Hennepin Avenue** *149.1.* This is the site of the old Great Northern passenger station, which was torn down a few years ago. Downtown Minneapolis is a few blocks away.

6.9 **Mulberry Junction** *147.1.* Just beyond this point the rails swing east across the Mississippi River. Here the Mississippi looks nothing like the impressive Father of Waters; it's just another average-size river.

9.5 **Northtown** *144.5.* Here is a junction with the freight-only line that comes directly from St. Paul, cutting off the slow run through Minneapolis. A major Burlington Northern (former Northern Pacific) freight yard is here.

11.3 **Interstate** *142.7.* This is the north end of the freight yard and beginning of the main line. At last, the train picks up speed.

17.0 **Coon Creek** *137.0.* This is the junction where the Duluth line branches off from the main line westward to Seatle, used by Amtrak's *Empire Builder.*

22.9 **Andover** *131.1.* There is a strong New England flavor to many place names along this line. Andover, Minnesota, is named after Andover, Massachusetts. Other New England names to be found along this line include Bethel, Cambridge, Holyoke, Foxboro, and Boylston.

46.5 **CAMBRIDGE** *107.5.* Seat of Isanti County and with a population of around 3,000, Cambridge is the biggest town between Coon Creek and Superior.

82.0 **Hinckley** *72.0.* Hinckley is of special note because it was the site of one of the worst forest fires, and most heroic rescues, in American history. A state monument now marks the site.

90.7 **SANDSTONE, MINN.** *63.3.* Amtrak's station for all of east-central Minnesota. Thirty miles away are Father Hennepin State Park and Mille Lacs, with an Indian reservation and a wildlife area.

149.7 **SUPERIOR, WIS.** *4.3.* Superior, of course, is named for Lake Superior, on which it lies. The lake well deserves its name. Some 350 miles long and 160 miles wide, it is the largest freshwater lake in the world. Lake Superior covers more than 30,000 square miles, is fed by 200 rivers, and reaches a depth of more than 1,300 feet. It is connected to Lake Huron at the Soo Locks, at its extreme eastern end. The busiest locks in the world, they handle an estimated 100 million tons of shipping each year, much of it ore and grain loaded at Duluth and Superior, the so-called Twin Ports.

Superior is the southernmost of the two ports, and it has the more important docking facilities. The big commodity is iron ore, which comes down from the mines in railroad cars; here it is loaded onto lake ships for the voyage down the Great Lakes to the steel mills at Chicago, Gary, and Pittsburgh. To make steel in the nineteenth century, several tons of coal were needed for each ton of iron ore. It was therefore more cost efficient to move the ore a long distance than to move the coal, and so the steel mills were built near the coal fields. Although the technology has changed since then, the geographical pattern remains.

154.0 **DULUTH, MINN.** *0.0.* Minnesota's third-largest city, Duluth has a population of 100,000 and is among the world's most important inland ports. The city was named for Daniel Greysolon, Sieur Duluth, a French explorer who visited the site in 1679 and claimed it in the name of Louis XIV. The present settlement dates from 1817, when John Jacob Astor established a trading station of his American Fur Company here. The city's real growth, however, began with the start of ore mining at the Mesabi Range in the mid-nineteenth century.

The iron range, 60 miles northwest of Duluth, extends for more than a hundred miles. What made it so important was, first, that the ore was close to the surface and could be easily dug, and second, that the range was such a short distance from cheap water transportation to the mills. Thus it was mainly Minnesota ore that made America the world's industrial giant.

Other sources of iron ore are now more important; but the range still ships pellets of it to the mills every year, rushing the ore down through the Twin Ports during the warm months before the lakes are blocked by ice.

3.40   The Great Cruise Trains of the West

The West is a land of great distances, spectacular scenery, and relatively sparse population. Four Amtrak routes cross the Great Plains and rugged mountains: The *Sunset Limited* connects New Orleans with Los Angeles, by way of Houston and San Antonio; the *Eagle* runs from Chicago and St. Louis through Arkansas to Dallas and San Antonio, where through cars join the *Sunset Limited* for California. The *Southwest Limited* angles from Chicago and Kansas City through

Colorado and New Mexico, following the historic Santa Fe Trail on its way to Los Angeles. The *California Zephyr* runs from Chicago and Denver through the heart of the Colorado Rockies, then across the Utah salt flats and the Nevada desert and over the Sierras to San Francisco Bay. The *Desert Wind* and the *Pioneer* branch off from the *California Zephyr* to serve Los Angeles and the Pacific Northwest, respectively; and the *Empire Builder* connects Chicago, Porland, and Seattle by way of the northern-tier states. Finally, the *Coast Starlight* follows the Pacific rim all the way from Los Angeles to Seattle.

All these trains travel great distances and take 40 hours or more en route. Therefore they must offer more elegant accommodations than are necessary on short runs. Amtrak meets this demand with its fleet of 284 Superliner cars—the biggest, heaviest, costliest passenger equipment in the world. Assigned exclusively to runs west of Chicago, they are about as close as a train can come to offering the amenities of a cruise ship. Unfortunately, current economies in the dining-car department have reduced the level of meal service to something more reminiscent of an airplane than a ship.

On the long-distance Western streamliners, you'll find something of the atmosphere of a cruise liner, too. People who are in a hurry don't ride these trains: they fly. But people who want to enjoy the magnificient scenery, people who like to meet other people in a congenial atmosphere, and people who just want to get away from it all will find the Amtrak cruise trains a wonderful way to cross the continent. In fact, if you've never seen the American West, you'll find that there's no better way to appreciate the size, scope, and natural beauty of this enormous area than by rail.

3.41   *Chicago—Los Angeles via Albuquerque*

Of all the railroads operating passenger service in the last years before Amtrak, one—the Santa Fe—stood out. The Santa Fe cared about its patrons, and it kept up the highest standards of service on its *Super Chief* until the very end.

Today the train that used to be the *Super Chief* is called the *Southwest Limited,* and it still runs via the Santa Fe all the way from Chicago to Los Angeles by way of Kansas City and Albuquerque, New Mexico. It's not as fast or as elegant as it used to be, but the *Southwest* is still a fine train and a pleasant way to see the Old West en route from Chicago to the Pacific Coast.

Like all the cruise trains, the *Southwest Limited* now has bilevel and Superliner cars. Reservations are required for all space, both coach and sleeping car, and the train has a tendency to sell out in the heavy travel periods; so make your travel plans well in advance.

From the windows of the *Southwest Limited* passengers see an unmatched panorama of plains, mountains, and desert scenery. At Albuquerque, Indian women still sell handmade jewelry to passengers during the stop. And on the second morning out of Chicago, there is southern California—an endless sea of stucco houses, swimming pools, and fast-food restaurants.

0.0 **CHICAGO** *2239.2*. Until the advent of Amtrak in 1971, passenger trains on the Santa Fe line used the cramped old Dearborn Station. Today the *Southwest Limited* runs from Union Station, and Dearborn's site is a housing development.

1.6 **21st Street** *2237.6*. At this junction the *Southwest* crosses the South Branch of the Chicago River on a lift bridge, then curves sharply to the right and threads its way through a warehouse district. Beyond Halsted Street the right of way begins to parallel the Drainage Canal. (See section 3.35, above.) At Corwith, about 6 miles out of Union Station, the Santa Fe has its main Chicago freight yards. A short distance beyond, the tracks swing to the right, cross the Drainage Canal and the paralleling Des Plaines River, and run along the north bank

CHICAGO—LOS ANGELES VIA ALBUQUERQUE

Westbound/miles		miles/Eastbound
0.0	CHICAGO (Union Sta.)	2239.2
1.6	21st St.	2237.6
12.7	McCook	2226.5
17.4	Willow Springs	2221.8
25.1	Lemont	2214.1
29.3	Romeo	2209.9
32.7	Lockport	2206.5
37.5	JOLIET	2201.7
46.1	Millsdale	2193.1
48.2	Drummond	2191.0
52.8	Lorenzo	2186.4
58.2	Coal City	2181.0
61.9	Gorman	2177.3
66.1	Mazon	2173.1
70.8	Verona	2168.4
74.8	Kinsman	2164.4
79.7	Ransom	2159.5
84.8	Kernan	2154.4
89.6	STREATOR	2149.6
93.9	Moon	2145.3

374.3	Bosworth	1864.9
382.1	Standish	1857.1
386.4	Carrollton	1852.8
396.6	Norborne	1842.6
405.4	Hardin	1833.8
411.3	Henrietta	1827.9
416.9	Camden	1822.3
421.7	Floyd	1817.5
426.7	Sibley	1812.5
434.0	Atherton	1805.2
439.4	Courtney	1799.8
442.6	Sugar Creek	1796.6
446.3	Sheffield	1792.9
451.1	KANSAS CITY, MO.	1788.1

451.1	KANSAS CITY, MO.	1788.1
455.3	Argentine (Kansas City, Kans.)	1783.9
461.0	Morris	1778.2
464.2	Holliday	1775.0
475.4	DeSoto	1763.8
483.4	Eudora	1755.8
490.8	LAWRENCE	1748.4
501.7	Lecompton	1731.5
512.6	Tecumseh	1726.6
516.9	TOPEKA	1722.3
523.4	Pauline	1715.8
533.9	Carbondale	1705.3
537.6	Scranton	1701.6
542.9	Burlingame	1696.3
551.1	Osage City	1688.1
562.7	Reading	1676.5
578.2	EMPORIA	1661.0
589.5	Saffordville	1649.7
597.8	Strong City	1641.4
604.4	Elmdale	1634.8
611.7	Clements	1627.5
616.8	Cedar Point	1622.4
623.0	Florence	1616.2
634.4	Peabody	1604.8
644.4	Walton	1594.8
651.2	NEWTON	1588.0

651.2	NEWTON	1588.0
660.7	Halsted	1578.5
670.2	Burrton	1569.0
684.1	HUTCHINSON	1555.1
695.1	Partridge	1544.1
701.2	Abbeyville	1538.0
706.8	Plevna	1532.4
712.5	Sylvia	1526.7
717.2	Zenith	1522.0
723.1	Stafford	1516.1
732.1	St. John	1507.1

743.7	Macksville	1495.5
751.0	Belpre	1488.2
768.5	Kinsley	1470.7
776.5	Offerle	1462.7
782.1	Bellefont	1457.1
787.9	Spearville	1451.3
796.5	Wright	1442.7
804.3	DODGE CITY	1434.9

804.3	DODGE CITY	1434.9
809.4	Sears	1429.8
813.2	Howell	1426.0
823.0	Cimarron	1416.2
829.1	Ingalls	1410.1
835.8	Charleston	1403.4
841.9	Pierceville	1397.3
854.2	GARDEN CITY	1385.0
860.8	Holcomb	1378.4
868.8	Deerfield	1370.4
876.1	Lakin	1363.1
883.4	Hartland	1355.8
894.0	Kendall	1345.2
905.7	Syracuse	1333.5
920.6	Coolidge, Kans.	1318.6
926.7	Holly, Colo.	1312.5
933.3	Barton	1305.9
937.1	Granada	1302.1
943.2	Grote	1296.0
948.7	Clucas	1290.5
954.1	LAMAR	1285.1
962.2	Prowers	1277.0
973.0	Caddoa	1266.2
978.6	Hilton	1260.6
987.8	Las Animas	1251.4
992.9	Riverdale	1246.3
1006.7	LA JUNTA	1232.5

1006.7	LA JUNTA	1232.5
1024.2	Timpas	1215.0
1043.4	Delhi	1195.8
1051.7	Thatcher	1187.5
1060.8	Tyrone	1178.4
1070.0	Earl	1169.2
1077.7	Hoehne	1161.5
1083.8	El Moro	1155.4
1088.1	TRINIDAD	1151.1
1090.0	Jansen	1149.2
1093.4	Starkville	1145.8
1099.6	Morley	1139.6
1103.2	Wootten, Colo.	1136.0
1104.2	Lynn, N.Mex.	1135.0
1110.9	RATON	1128.3
1122.4	Hebron	1116.8

for the next 13 miles. The original Chicago Portage, used by the French explorers as early as 1673, is just west of Harlem Avenue in the forest preserve north of the railroad.

12.7 **McCook** *2226.5.* Here the train crosses the tracks of the Indiana Harbor Belt and the Baltimore and Ohio Chicago Terminal railroads, two of the several freight lines that connect the many railroads entering Chicago and expedite the movement of cars through the city. At McCook a huge stone quarry is visible to the north of the tracks (right side, leaving Chicago).

17.4 **Willow Springs** *2221.8.* Hidden behind the trees to the north of the right-of-way (right side, going west) is the Argonne National Laboratory, where for many years scientists have done important research in nuclear physics. Just before reaching Lemont, the tracks swing south and recross the Des Plaines River and the Drainage Canal. They also cross the old Illinois and Michigan Canal, built in the 1830s as the first effort to connect the Great Lakes with the Mississippi River system.

29.3 **Romeo** *2209.9.* Add this one to your list of Shakespearean town-names in America.

32.7 **Lockport** *2206.5.* Founded by the builders of the Illinois and Michigan Canal, this town is today the site of the main locks that control the Drainage Canal, which reversed the flow of the Chicago River.

37.5 **JOLIET** *2201.7.* Legend has it that the original name of this industrial city was Juliet, making it a twin to nearby Romeo, but it was really named for the French explorer Louis Joliet.

Leaving Joliet, the train also leaves the Des Plaines valley and takes off through the U.S. Army's Elwood Arsenal. About 14 miles from Joliet the Kankakee River is crossed. This joins with the Des Plaines to form the Illinois, a major tributary of the Mississippi.

58.2 **Coal City** *2181.0.* No need to ask how this town came into being—the name says it all. Coal was to the nineteenth century what oil is to the twentieth, the lifeblood of industrial society. Wherever deposits were found, mines were opened to exploit them.

89.6 **STREATOR** *2149.6.* A center of glass manufacturing, Streator is also another of those important but little-known railroad junctions. Eastbound cars can be sent around Chicago from this point over the Kankakee Belt Line, avoiding the city altogether. At Streator, trains cross the Vermilion River. A few miles north, where this river flows into the Illinois, a tall bluff called Starved Rock overlooks the big river. According to tradition, a party of Illinois Indians besieged here by a hostile tribe chose starvation rather than accept the humiliation of surrender. The site is now a state park.

130.1 **CHILLICOTHE** *2109.1.* Just before reaching this station the rails cross the Illinois River on a long steel bridge and a high fill.

About 20 miles downriver (south) is the city of Peoria. The station here is patronized mostly by people from that area, for Chillicothe itself is a town of only 5,000 inhabitants. It was named for Chillicothe, Ohio, the hometown of its early settlers.

163.3 **Dahlinda** *2075.9.* It's hardly more than a creek, but at Dahlinda the train crosses the Spoon River, immortalized by Edgar Lee Masters in the title of his book of free-verse poetry, *Spoon River Anthology,* in which the people of a typical Midwestern small town speak from their graves.

177.5 **GALESBURG** *2061.7.* For notes on this town, see section 3.36.

Amtrak has two stations in Galesburg: The *Southwest Limited* uses the former Santa Fe facility on North Broad Street, while the *California Zephyr* and *Illinois Zephyr* stop at the Burlington Station a mile or so away on Seminary Street.

183.3 **Surrey** *2055.9.* The 2.7 miles between Surrey and Cameron recall one of the most famous "speed runs" in all railroad history—the 1905 run of Death Valley Scotty's *Coyote Special.*

At that time the best schedule from Chicago to California was 57 hours, but that wasn't fast enough for Death Valley Scotty. He walked into the office of John J. Byrne, general passenger agent of the Santa Fe in Los Angeles. "Mr. Byrne," he said, "I want to go to Chicago in 46 hours. Kin you do it?"

Byrne took $5,000 of Scotty's money and made the deal, and the *Coyote Special* was off. As a matter of fact, the Santa Fe beat Scotty's schedule: The *Coyote* made the Los Angeles to Chicago run in 44 hours and 54 minutes. The fastest part of that record run was right here between Cameron and Surrey. Scotty's special covered that 2.7 miles in 95 seconds, an average speed of 106 miles per hour. For 1905 that was truly remarkable running.

Today's *Southwest Limited* won't reach that speed anywhere en route, yet its schedule for the 2,239 miles between Chicago and Los Angeles beats Scotty's record by more than 3 hours—stops included. Sustained speed over long distances, rather than short bursts at record speed, are the reason.

218.9 **Lomax** *2020.3.* Still another of those important junctions nobody but freight-traffic managers and railroaders has ever heard of. At Lomax the Santa Fe connects with the Toledo, Peoria and Western, which takes freight traffic to and from the East, avoiding Chicago and its congested yards.

231.0 **East Fort Madison, Ill.** *2008.2.* Between this point and Fort Madison the Santa Fe crosses the Mississippi River on a double-decker steel bridge. Trains are on the lower level, while autos cross on the upper level. The bridge is three fifths of a mile long, although in my opinion this crossing of the Mississippi is less impressive than the one at Burlington used by the *California Zephyr.*

Nine miles south, on the Illinois shore, is one of the most interesting and little-known historic spots in America—Nauvoo, where the Mormons established themselves about 1840.

The Church of Jesus Christ of Latter-Day Saints was founded by Joseph Smith in his native western New York, but the community soon moved to Ohio, and then Missouri, before settling at Nauvoo. Here the Mormons prospered, and here they built a temple similar to the one now standing at Salt Lake City. Nauvoo was for a time the biggest city in Illinois, but the jealousy of the neighbors and their fear of the Mormon institution of polygamy made the Latter-Day Saints people unpopular. Thus when Joseph Smith moved to silence a Mormon editor who had criticized his leadership, he was arrested, together with his brother Hyrum, and lodged in a cell at Carthage, Illinois. Here they were lynched and shot by a mob on June 27, 1844. After the death of Joseph Smith, the Mormon Church split, the larger part of the community following Brigham Young to Utah.

234.6 **FORT MADISON, IOWA** *2004.6.* Trains pass through, but no longer serve, the old station on the waterfront in the Fort Madison business district. Instead, they stop at what used to be called Shopton, site of the Santa Fe yards and shops 2 miles farther west along the river.

The original Fort Madison was built in 1808 and named for the new president. Its purpose was to offer protection from Indian raids and to assert American control of the Mississippi. It was burned in 1813 (during the War of 1812) when the Indians, with British support and encouragement, took the offensive against American settlers in the trans-Allegheny region. The current town dates from 1833, the heyday of Mississippi River steamboating.

263.1 **Medill, Mo.** *1976.1.* The town is named for the founder and editor of the *Chicago Tribune,* Joseph Medill. The builders of the Santa Fe often honored important journalists by naming new towns for them, as a way of assuring favorable publicity.

312.7 **LA PLATA** *1926.5.* Although La Plata itself has barely a thousand residents, it serves as the station for nearby Kirksville, home of Northeast Missouri State University. College students make up a sizable part of Amtrak's passenger load, because they travel often and frequently don't have cars.

347.3 **MARCELINE** *1892.9.* A village of fewer than 3,000 inhabitants, Marceline is still of some importance because it was the boyhood home of Walt Disney. Walt was born in Chicago, but when he was two, his father decided to get the children away from the big city. Walt's uncle was already living in Marceline, running a locomotive from here to Fort Madison on the Santa Fe, and it was to this little town that the family moved, in 1903. Walt Disney remained a railroad enthusiast throughout his life—a visit to Disneyland is ample proof of that.

354.6 **Boothville** *1884.6.* Fifteen miles northwest is the boyhood home of General John "Black Jack" Pershing, commander of the American Expeditionary Force in Europe during World War I. The home is now a state historic site.

411.3 **Henrietta** *1827.9.* About 30 miles northwest of here, at the little town of Kearney, Missouri, Jesse James was born. Jesse has become famous as a sort of nineteenth-century Robin Hood, though it's hard to tell now where the facts leave off and the legend begins. It is certain that Jesse was a Confederate irregular during the Civil War, that he robbed banks and trains after the war, and that he was shot by Robert Ford in 1882. It's probably also fair to say that Robin Hood or no, his minister father would have disapproved of Jesse's career.

421.7 **Floyd, Iowa** *1817.5.* The only member of the Lewis and Clark expedition who did not return safely was Sergeant Charles Floyd, who developed appendicitis on the westward trip and died near the present site of Sioux City, Iowa.

Between Floyd and Sibley, the rails cross the Missouri River, which Lewis and Clark explored in 1803.

451.1 **KANSAS CITY, MO.** *1788.1.* With a population of more than half a million, Kansas City is the largest community en route between Chicago and California. For information on the city, see section 2.21.

455.3 **Argentine (Kansas City, Kans.)** *1783.9.* Argentine is the name of the huge Santa Fe freight yard in Kansas City, Kansas, which marshals cars from all over the west and southwest and classifies them for shipment to Chicago and the East.

464.2 **Holliday** *1775.0.* The town was named for Cyrus K. Holliday, banker and builder of the Santa Fe system. Holliday is a junction: from here, one line (used by Amtrak trains) continues west through Lawrence and Topeka, while a second—called the Ottawa Cutoff—goes southwest. The two lines rejoin at Emporia.

490.8 **LAWRENCE** *1748.4.* Home of the University of Kansas, Lawrence was founded by New Englanders who came to Kansas determined to keep the area from becoming a slave state. The town was named for Lawrence, Massachusetts, which in turn was named for textile magnate Amos Lawrence, a notable antislavery man. In 1856 a posse of proslavery Missourians sacked the town, burning, looting, and killing. In revenge, John Brown—later notorious for his raid on Harpers Ferry, West Virginia—murdered five proslavery settlers at Osawatomie. The trouble came to be called "Bleeding Kansas," and it was a preview of the Civil War.

501.7 **Lecompton** *1731.5.* This is another town in the valley of the Kaw River that has a notable place in history. Proslavery Kansans met here in 1857 to draft a proposed state constitution that permitted slavery, but when the Lecompton constitution was submitted to the voters of the territory, it lost—three times—by big margins. Clearly a majority of Kansans did not want slavery in their state. Despite the maneuvers of President Buchanan, Kansas entered the Union as a free state in January 1861, after some Southern congressmen had already left Washington.

516.9 **TOPEKA** *1722.3.* Topeka is the capital of Kansas and the state's third largest city. It was founded in 1854 by antislavery Kansans and became capital in 1861. It is also the site of huge railroad shops; the home of the Menninger Clinic, specializing in treatment of mental illness; and a major farm marketing and distribution center.

533.9 **Carbondale** *1705.3.* Together with its neighboring town, Scranton, Carbondale's name recalls the Pennsylvania anthracite coal region.

578.2 **EMPORIA** *1661.0.* "Emporia" means "stores," and the town is in fact a trading center for the surrounding farmlands. It is the junction where the Topeka line and the Ottawa Cutoff rejoin.

Emporia is best known as the home of the award-winning journalist William Allen White, editor of the *Emporia Gazette* and the prototype of the independent, honest, forthright small-town newspaperman. White was known for his editorials, especially "What's the Matter with Kansas?" I like him best for his reluctant salute to Franklin Delano Roosevelt: "We who hate your gaudy guts—salute you!"

597.8 **Strong City** *164.4.* Named for William Barstow Strong, one-time president of the Santa Fe Railroad, Strong City never grew much. But Barstow, California, named for the same executive, has prospered so well that his middle name, at least, will never be forgotten.

651.2 **NEWTON** *1588.0.* Settled by Russian Mennonite immigrants in 1872, Newton was for a time the end of the Chisholm Trail, over which the cowboys drove the longhorn herds from Texas to the railroad. The Russian farmers who settled here brought with them Turkey Red wheat. This important contribution to American agriculture has flourished in Kansas.

Today Newton is a railroad town, with engine facilities, freight yards, and shops. It is also the junction between the original Santa Fe main line through Colorado and the low-grade line through the Texas panhandle used by most freight trains from California so as to bypass the Rockies. Newton is the closest Amtrak station to Wichita, the largest city in Kansas, 16 miles south.

660.7 **Halsted** *1578.5.* This is another town whose name honors a journalist: this time Murat Halsted, a nineteenth-century writer.

684.1 **HUTCHINSON** *1555.1.* Seat of Reno County, the largest wheat-producing county in the wheat-producing state of Kansas, Hutchinson is on the Arkansas River, sometimes pronounced *Ar-kan'-sas* instead of the conventional *Ar'-kan-saw*. Hutchinson is sometimes called "Salt City," because it lies in the midst of one of the world's most important salt-producing areas. The town also has oil and gas wells nearby.

804.3 **DODGE CITY** *1434.9.* Talk about the Wild West—this was it. The first settlement on the site was a trading post; during the Civil War, this was supplemented by a fort. In 1872 the railroad arrived, and by 1875 the Texas longhorn herds were being driven to Dodge City. Those were the days when anything went in Dodge City. Bat Masterson and Wyatt Earp served as sheriffs here, and Boot Hill got its reputation as a cemetery. A cowboy statue stands there today, and the town's Front Street has been rebuilt to look as it did during the cattle-drive days. Outside of tourism, Dodge City's business is wheat. The town likes to call itself "the buckle on the Kansas wheat belt."

854.2 **GARDEN CITY** *1385.0.* Garden City is another wheat town in the Arkansas River valley. It claims to have the world's largest grain elevator and the world's largest known field of natural gas.

Incidentally, if you think the train seems to be running exceptionally fast along here, you're right. The whole stretch between Dodge City and La Junta is high speed track: 90 miles per hour is the norm.

860.8 **Holcomb** *1378.4.* It looks like every other little Kansas farm town—a few stores clustered around the railroad depot, houses on the outskirts, a water tank, and then the wheat fields again. But Holcomb is different, for this was the scene of the Clutter murders described by Truman Capote in his best-selling book *In Cold Blood*.

From Dodge City all the way into Colorado, the rails follow the Arkansas River. And while you can't tell it from the terrain, the train is climbing steadily. The elevation at Dodge City is 2,400 feet; at La Junta, it's over 4,000.

920.6 **Coolidge, Kans.** *1318.6.* The town was named for a banker and railroad man named Thomas Jefferson Coolidge, and though he shared his name with two presidents, the only thing he ever presided over was the Santa Fe Railroad.

954.1 **LAMAR, COLO.** *1285.1.* The town was named for Lucius Quintus Cincinnatus Lamar, secretary of the interior under Grover Cleveland and the possessor of the most elegant name in the history of American politics. A native of Mississippi, he drafted that state's secession ordinance in 1861, but after the Civil War, Lamar was noted for his efforts to reconcile the North and South.

The town of Lamar is near the site of Bent's Second Fort, once an Indian trading post. Forty miles north is another Indian site, but

314

this is one few people remember. Here, along Sand Creek, a large number of Indians were massacred by overzealous militia under the command of a colonel named Chivington.

992.9 **Riverdale** *1246.3.* West of here are the ruins of Bent's Old Fort, Mr. Bent's first local venture in the trading-post business. Kit Carson, the scout, once worked here.

1006.7 **LA JUNTA** *1232.5.* La Junta (pronounced, as in Spanish, "La Hunta") is a railroad town that grew up with the Santa Fe and still makes its living by it today. The name is Spanish for "the junction," and in fact the Santa Fe splits here into two prongs: The northern fork goes west to Pueblo, then north to Denver, while the other line (used by Amtrak) goes south to New Mexico. La Junta is home to the Koshare Kiva, an organization of Pueblo Indians who perform their ritual dances for visiting tourists.

On clear days you can see Pike's Peak, 100 miles to the northwest. It's not the tallest mountain in the United States—in fact, it's not even the highest in Colorado—but Pike's Peak is almost surely the best-known mountain in America. It is named for Captain Zebulon Pike, who saw it from a distance while exploring the headwaters of the Arkansas River in 1805. Today you can drive a car to the top or go up by cog railroad, if you prefer.

Originally, the promoters of the Santa Fe had planned to build right up the Arkansas into the heart of the Rockies, pointing for the gold and silver mining town of Leadville. West of Pueblo, however, the Arkansas flows through a canyon so deep and narrow that there was hardly room for one railroad. The Denver and Rio Grande, originally planned as a link to Mexico, had reached Pueblo and its owners were also thinking about heading for Leadville. There was a race for the Royal Gorge, with surveyors from both sides shooting at each other while trying to get there first. The Rio Grande won possession of the gorge, thus turning west, and the Santa Fe, shut out of the Arkansas River gorge, was deflected south toward New Mexico. The one practical pass was Raton (in Spanish, "the rat"), and the Rio Grande had eyes on that too. But this time, with the aid of locating engineers Ray Morley and Lewis Kingman, and a rough-and-tough mountain man known as "Uncle Dick" Wootton, whose ranch was at the crest of the pass, the Santa Fe was first to grade through Raton—beating the Rio Grande, it is said, by 20 minutes.

1088.1 **TRINIDAD** *1151.1.* The name is Spanish for "trinity." Spanish place names are common in this region. Although Trinidad was a stop on the old Santa Fe Trail, its real growth dates from the discovery of coal fields at nearby El Moro about 1870. The entire surrounding area is rich with coal. Only a few miles north of Trinidad, at Ludlow, the bitterest labor violence in American history occurred during a 1914 miners' strike resulting in 10 days of fighting between strikers and troops.

From Trinidad to the summit of Raton Pass, the rails climb 1,600 feet in just 16 miles; the grade is 3.5 percent, one of the steepest on a main line in the United States. No wonder most freight trains go by way of Texas.

1099.6 **Morley** *1139.6*. The site was named for Ray Morley, one of the locating engineers who pushed the Santa Fe tracks over Raton Pass in 1878. As the rails climb up the pass, they hug the western side; therefore, the best views are from the left-side windows, going west.

1103.2 **Wootten, Colo.** *1136.0*. "Uncle Dick" Wootten's ranch was near the summit of Raton Pass. The tracks describe a big half-circle curve here, and a sign erected by the Santa Fe Railroad marks the location.

1104.2 **Lynn, N.Mex.** *1135.0*. At the top of Raton Pass, which is also the Colorado–New Mexico state line, twin tunnels half a mile long take the train from the watershed of the Purgatoire River on the north to that of the Canadian River on the south. The summit of the pass is 7,834 feet above sea level, the highest point on the Santa Fe line from Chicago to California.

1110.9 **RATON** *1128.3*. Raton is the jumping-off place for Taos, with its Indian pueblos and ski slopes. The aspect of the country changes here. For the next 110 miles to Las Vegas the tracks cross a high plain bordered by distant mountain peaks.

1193.6 **Shoemaker** *1045.6*. Keep an eye out for traces of the old Santa Fe Trail, which appear occasionally along the railroad right-of-way—a weedy roadway, or the ruins of a stage station.

1220.7 **LAS VEGAS** *1018.5*. Don't confuse this little town with the Nevada gambling capital; they have little in common besides the name, which is Spanish for "the meadows." Beyond Las Vegas, which is a crew-changing point, the tracks begin to climb again—this time, up Glorieta Pass, whose summit is only 400 feet lower than that of Raton. The 64 miles between Las Vegas and Lamy are probably the scenic highlight of the entire trip.

1239.2 **Chapelle** *1000.0*. About 7 miles west of this point, the rails form a giant S curve as they fight for altitude on the climb up Glorieta. The best views are from the left side, going west.

1266.0 **Rowe** *973.2*. Most of the way up the east side of the pass, Glorieta presents a deceivingly benign aspect. The terrain resembles a mountain plateau, flanked by tree-lined hills. Actually, the rails are climbing on a continuous stiff grade up toward the summit.

About 4 miles west of Rowe, watch for the Pecos Mission, founded in 1617, to the north side of the tracks (right side, going west). A sign erected by the Santa Fe Railroad marks the spot.

...[one] of America's fast growing southwestern cities, Albuquerque, New Mexico. The downtown is a few short miles from the mountains. First settled in 1706, the city has an Indian, Spanish, and pioneer American heritage combined with "high-technologies" stemming from its closeness to White Sands proving grounds. (See section 3.41.)

El Morro National Monument in Ramah, New Mexico.

1275.2 **Glorieta** *964.0.* The summit here is 7,400 feet above sea level—1,000 feet up from Las Vegas to the east, and 1,000 feet down to Lamy, 10 miles west.

The steep descent on the west side of Glorieta Pass, through twisting, shallow, narrow Apache Canyon, encompasses the most rugged terrain encountered on the entire trip. At some points Apache Canyon is so narrow that the train seems to squeeze between the rock walls like toothpaste coming out of a tube.

1284.9 **LAMY** *954.3.* Pronounced *Lay'me,* and named after the one-time archbishop of the local diocese. (He is the central figure in Willa Cather's novel *Death Comes for the Archbishop.)*

There's not much to see of Lamy—a few houses, a church, an old adobe, and the Legal Tender Saloon—but the town is more important than it appears. It is the railroad station for romantic Santa Fe, the capital of New Mexico and the oldest city in the Southwest.

Santa Fe, high up in the mountains 18 miles north of Lamy, was founded by Spanish explorers lured from Mexico by Indian tales of the "Seven Cities of Gold," said to lie somewhere in the north. It was nearly 2 centuries old when the United States won her independence, and did not become an American city until after the Mexican War. The climate is magnificent, the location picturesque, and the local ambience surprisingly cosmopolitan.

1315.3 **Domingo** *923.9.* The Santo Domingo Indian pueblo here is one of many in the area. The location is marked by a sign to the west of the tracks (right side, going west). New Mexico's Spanish and Indian heritage is so dominant that the state became the first in the Union to elect a Hispanic-American governor.

1352.1 **ALBUQUERQUE** *887.1.* For information on the city, see section 2.1. Trains stop here for 20 minutes while they change crews, inspect the equipment, and wash the windows. So if you want to stretch your legs, buy a late newspaper, make a phone call, or check out the Indian jewelry sold on the platform, this is the place.

1364.7 **Isleta** *874.5.* Just north of this Albuquerque suburb, the tracks cross the Rio Grande—yes, the same river that flows down through Texas and forms part of the international boundary between the United States and Mexico. It actually rises in the Colorado Rockies and flows mostly due south until it empties into the Gulf of Mexico near Brownsville, Texas.

1378.7 **Dalies** *860.5.* This is the junction at which the low-grade freight line through Texas rejoins the original Santa Fe main line that has come over Raton Pass. From here to Barstow, California, all traffic is funneled over a very busy stretch of double-tracked, heavy-duty railroad.

1480.4 **Thoreau** *758.8.* Four miles west of this hamlet is Campbell Pass, 7,247 feet above sea level and the Santa Fe's crossing of the Continental Divide, the spine of the continent. If Glorieta is deceiving, Campbell is completely mystifying, because you'd never know from looking at the scenery that you were crossing the roof of North America. There are no canyons or towering spires, the grade is gentle, and the speed is high.

1512.4 **GALLUP, N.MEX.** *726.8.* The name is good for all kinds of jokes, but actually it has nothing at all to do with the gait of a horse. Gallup is named for an official of the Atlantic and Pacific Railroad, the company that built this stretch west of Albuquerque back in the 1880s and that has since been absorbed by the Santa Fe. From the train you see an endless parade of garish neon signs strung out along the main street of the town. Gallup's population is largely Indian, with Navajo and Hopi the largest tribes. The only remaining pueblo of Zuni is 30 miles away.

Gallup is the closest Amtrak stop to the beautiful but desolate Four Corners region of New Mexico; to southern Colorado, with its stunning mountain scenery and amazing Mesa Verde National Park; and to the Petrified Forest and the Painted Desert, which lie to the west across the Arizona state line. It makes a convenient headquarters city for exploring the entire area.

1607.3 **Holbrook, Ariz.** *631.9.* To the north, the Navajo and Hopi reservations spread over some of the loneliest, most desolate territory in the entire United States. To the south are the Apaches. At Holbrook, the 72-mile Apache Railway connects the Santa Fe main line to the reservation at McNary.

1616.4 **Joseph City** *622.8.* The huge electric-power station here is brilliantly lit at night and can be seen for miles.

1639.6 **WINSLOW** *599.6.* Winslow sits at the base of the long descent from the Continental Divide to the east. It is also at the base of the shorter but steeper grade leading up to Bellemont, the mountain summit west of Flagstaff. It is therefore a railroad town—a division point where crews change, with freight yards, shops, and engine-servicing facilities.

1665.9 **Canyon Diablo** *573.3.* At this point the train crosses the canyon on a 544-foot steel bridge without even slowing down.

A few miles south is the site of Meteor Crater. In prehistoric times a large meteorite fell to earth, and its impact created a huge and beautiful crater.

West of Canyon Diablo the country changes. Instead of the sagebrush and chaparral through which the train has passed all the way from Albuquerque, you now see tree-covered mountain slopes.

1698.1 **FLAGSTAFF** *541.1.* Almost 7,000 feet above sea level, Flagstaff is the metropolis of northern Arizona. Just north of the town the San Francisco Peaks rise to heights of better than 12,000 feet; beyond them, 120 miles from Flagstaff, is the Grand Canyon National Park, probably the number-one natural scenic attraction in the United States. To the south is Oak Creek Canyon and the old silver-mining town of Jerome, where the buildings cling to ledges cut into the edge of a steep hill. Artists have found this a congenial place, and a number of them live and work here.

A mile out of Flagstaff is the Lowell Observatory, named for its founder, Percival Lowell. He was convinced that a ninth planet must lie outside the orbit of Neptune, and he built this private astronomical observatory especially to search for it. Lowell died without finding the planet he was sure existed, but in 1930 an assistant at the observatory named Clyde W. Tombaugh justified Lowell's conviction by discovering Pluto. The astronomical symbol for that planet is PL; the letters not only represent the Greek god of the underworld but are also the initials of Percival Lowell, the man who devoted his life to its discovery.

1710.2 **Bellemont** *529.0.* ''Bellemont'' is French for ''beautiful mountain,'' and at 7,300 feet above sea level this point is actually higher in elevation than the crossing of the Continental Divide at Campbell Pass. From here to Needles, in the valley of the Colorado River, it's downgrade all the way for westbound trains. Eastbound, it's a steady 220-mile climb of more than 6,000 feet in altitude from Needles to Bellemont.

1782.1 **SELIGMAN** *457.1.* Another railroad town, Seligman is named for the construction engineer who built the original railroad through here in 1881. The town is a division point and crew-change station; the railroad virtually supports the 900 inhabitants single-handedly.

1869.7 **KINGMAN** *369.5.* This town is named for Lewis Kingman, the engineer who, along with Ray Morley, was responsible for pushing the Santa Fe over Raton Pass. Kingman is convenient to two major Colorado River dams: Hoover (also called Boulder), 80 miles northwest; and Davis, 26 miles straight west. Both huge structures have created artificial lakes (Mead and Mojave, respectively) offering excellent outdoor recreation facilities including fishing and houseboating.

1918.4 **Topock, Ariz.** *320.8.* At Topock the railroad crosses the Colorado River and enters California at last. Twenty miles downriver is the resort community of Lake Havasu City, made notable by its purchase of London Bridge.

1930.8 **NEEDLES, CALIF.** *308.4.* The town is named for a rock formation on the Arizona side of the river. Needles is hotter than Hades in the summer, and just about as godforsaken. It sits on the edge of the Mojave Desert, and only water from the Colorado River gives life to the trees that make the place barely livable. Needles is a railroad division point: Crews change here, and some trains refuel at this station.

Between Needles and Barstow the Santa Fe railroad crosses the heart of the Mojave, 160 miles of rocks, sand, and snakes that has to be some of the cruelest country on earth. A person in this desert without food or water wouldn't last two days. The best way to cross the Mojave is at night, as Amtrak passenger trains do in both directions.

2089.6 **Daggett** *149.6.* At this important railroad junction the Union Pacific's line from Salt Lake City and Las Vegas, used by Amtrak's *Desert Wind,* joins the Santa Fe main line. The two railroads share track from here to San Bernardino.

Daggett is the site of an experimental solar power station as well as a conventional power plant and some military facilities. A few miles away is the ghost town of Calico—once a mining center and now restored as a tourist attraction.

2098.4 **BARSTOW** *140.8.* They named Strong City, Kansas, and Barstow, California, for the same man—William Barstow Strong, once president of the Santa Fe. Barstow is another railroad town, the point where the Santa Fe main line splits: One fork goes on over Tehachapi Pass to San Francisco; the other (used by Amtrak) turns south by way of Cajon Pass to the Los Angeles basin. The freight yards here are so big that in 1920 the railroad bought up the whole Barstow business district and moved it up onto the hills to make more room for tracks. Note the old hotel next to the station—while it's now in derelict condition, it was once one of the chain of Harvey Houses that used to spring up wherever the Santa Fe went. Fred Harvey believed in high standards of hotel and restaurant service; his Harvey Houses brought a touch of class to the Old West. And his pretty waitresses became such a legend that MGM made a Judy Garland musical about them—*The Harvey Girls.*

2135.1 **Victorville** *104.1.* Although you can't tell it by looking out the window—this high desert country looks monotonously the same—there is a steady upgrade from Barstow to Cajon Pass summit. The tracks here follow the bed of the Mojave River, usually dry.

2154.3 **Summit** *84.9.* The top of Cajon (pronounced *Cuh-hone',* don't say *Kay-john*) Pass, 3,822 feet above sea level, this is one of only two gateways through the San Gabriel Mountains into the Los Angeles basin. The east side of Cajon is nothing much to look at—but oh, the west side! Here the rails wind and twist, and at times it looks as if the Cajon walls are so fully terraced that there's no room for the rocks. The descent from Cajon is very steep—some 6 miles of 3 percent grade and 16 miles of 2.2 percent. From Summit to San Bernardino, the tracks drop 2,800 feet in 25 miles. Passenger trains share

The San Francisco peaks are the highest in Arizona, rising to over 12,000 feet above sea level. (See section 3.41.)

The Grand Canyon, near Flagstaff, Arizona. (See section 3.41 and Part 4, for traveling instructions.)

the pass with Route I-15 and a Southern Pacific freight line from Palmdale.

While descending the pass, you may actually see the brown southern-California smog closing in on you. The mountains tend to hold the polluted air, and at the far eastern end of the Los Angeles basin the smog collects in thick, eye-stinging, throat-itching clouds. It's particularly bad in August and September, when wind currents tend to blow off the desert and when high temperatures and frequent brush fires add to the smog.

2179.7 **SAN BERNARDINO** *59.5.* At San Bernardino, often called "San Berdoo" for short, Amtrak trains swing sharply to the west, pointing for Los Angeles.

San Bernardino was named by a group of missionaries who first visited the site in 1810 on May 20, the feast day of San Bernardino of Siena. Mormon interests established a community here in 1851, and construction of the line over Cajon Pass gave the town much of its present character as a railroad center. Today military facilities help support San Bernardino: Norton and March Air Force Bases are nearby.

2187.2 **Fontana** *52.0.* About the last thing you'd expect to find in southern California is a fully integrated steel mill—but that's exactly what you'll see to the south side of the tracks (left side, going west). This mill is owned by Kaiser steel.

2196.1 **Cucamonga** *43.1.* Remember the old Jack Benny gag about "Anaheim, Azusa, and Cucamonga?" Well, this is Cucamonga, and Azusa is 20 miles or so farther west. Anaheim is in Orange County, southeast of Los Angeles.

Until relatively recent times, the area between San Bernardino and Pasadena was a land of fruit trees, farms, and wineries called "the Orange Empire." Today it's mostly tract houses and shopping centers, though California's oldest winery is still in the vicinity.

2203.2 **Claremont** *36.0.* Claremont is a college town, the home of the six associated Claremont colleges (Pomona, Scripps, Pitzer, Harvey Mudd, Claremont, and Claremont Graduate).

2205.1 **POMONA** *34.1.* Formerly a citrus center, Pomona was named for the Roman goddess of fruit. Today it's best known as the site of the annual Los Angeles County Fair, which draws more than a million visitors each September. The station here serves all of the San Gabriel Valley and is convenient for people whose homes are east and south of Los Angeles. Freeways give Pomona easy access to many towns in Los Angeles and Orange counties.

2215.3 **Azusa** *23.9.* Somebody is sure to tell you that Azusa stands for "A to Z in the U.S.A." It makes a good story, but don't believe it. West of the station the rails cross the San Gabriel River (usually just a dry wash), which gives its name to this whole area east of Los Angeles proper.

2224.2 **Santa Anita** *15.0.* This land was once owned by "Lucky" Baldwin, who made his money in Comstock mining, then bought a ranch here and began to race horses on it. Today Santa Anita is one of the nation's top racetracks, with a winter meeting traditionally beginning the day after Christmas. The track is to the south of the railroad (left side, arriving in Los Angeles), but the most you'll see of it is a distant glimpse. Incidentally, there is no town of Santa Anita—the racetrack is in the city of Arcadia.

Between Santa Anita and Pasadena the tracks occupy the median strip of the Colorado Freeway. Amtrak passengers can enjoy the novel experience of pacing speeding autos from a Pullman room.

2230.1 **PASADENA** *9.1.* Leaving the freeway median strip, the tracks curve sharply to the left, tunnel under the eastbound lanes, and thread their way down an alley between shops and office buildings to reach the passenger station. In the past, when Hollywood stars rode the trains, they would often use the Pasadena station to avoid the crowds at Los Angeles's Union Terminal. And while the stars don't shine here much anymore, Pasadena remains a convenient place to catch the train. Here's a tip: If you're afraid you're going to miss your departure from L.A. Union, you may still catch your train by driving lickety-split up the freeway to Pasadena.

Pasadena sounds like another Spanish place name, but it's actually a Chippewa Indian word meaning "crown of the valley." It was settled originally by Easterners with money as a sort of winter retreat. To encourage new real-estate investment, Pasadena began the Tournament of Roses back in the 1890s. For a few years chariot races were the featured attraction, but they were soon replaced by an annual New Year's Day football game, the Rose Bowl.

Pasadena has always had a refined cultural atmosphere. The magnificent Huntington Library, art gallery, and gardens—one of the premier attractions in all of southern California—are in adjacent San Marino. The Norton Simon art gallery displays an outstanding collection of paintings, drawings, and sculpture in a stunning building within walking distance of the Amtrak station, and Pasadena also has its own symphony orchestra. Cal Tech, world famous for mathematics and physics research, where much work on rocketry has been done, is within walking distance of the Amtrak station. In the vast concrete ocean of southern California, Pasadena retains a special character all its own.

2232.1 **South Pasadena** *7.1.* After crossing the Pasadena Freeway on an overhead bridge, the tracks run practically through the backyards of some fine homes. Beyond this residential area is a high bridge across the Arroyo Seco, the ravine that divides South Pasadena from the city of Los Angeles.

2234.3 **Highland Park** *4.9.* Trains wind along a curving right of way through this area of Los Angeles. Rock-throwing kids occasionally are a problem along here. The tracks cross the Los Angeles River on a trestle bridge; the river is concreted and channeled as a flood-control measure. Trains then follow the river's west bank for a short distance to Mission Tower, curve sharply to the right past the Los Angeles County Jail (left side, entering Los Angeles), and enter the Union Passenger Terminal.

2239.2 **LOS ANGELES (Union Passenger Terminal)** *0.0.* Built in 1939, Union Passenger Terminal is a masterpiece of harmony between the Spanish and Art Deco styles. Fortunately, it's due for purchase by the state and a thorough rehabilitation. It needs it—the building hasn't been painted since it was built. It already serves Trailways bus passengers as well as Amtrak patrons, and will someday be a transportation center for all forms of travel.

For information on the city, see section 2.23.

3.42 New Orleans—Los Angeles

This is the route of the *Sunset Limited;* with a stayover in New Orleans, and by using the *Crescent* to New York, you have a nice alternative to going through Chicago.

The *Sunset Limited* has been running under the same name since 1894, and passengers on the westbound trip often see two spectacular sunsets en route—over the Louisiana bayous and in the New Mexico mountains. And there is no better way to appreciate the immense size of Texas than to cross it in this train. From Orange in the east to El Paso in the west is a distance of 922 miles, farther than from New York to Chicago—and all in Texas.

This train currently operates only three days a week in each direction, leaving New Orleans each Monday, Wednesday, and Saturday and departing Los Angeles each Sunday, Wednesday, and Friday.

The *Sunset Limited* is equipped with Superliner cars, and all space must be reserved in advance. Through coaches and sleeping cars also operate from Chicago and St. Louis to Los Angeles. These cars are switched from the *Eagle* to the *Sunset Limited* at San Antonio.

0.0 **New Orleans** *2031.5.* For information on the city, see section 2.28.

5.8 **East Bridge Junction** *2025.7.* This junction controls the approaches to the Huey Long Bridge, the mammoth structure that spans the Mississippi River to connect New Orleans with the West. Until this bridge was built, ferryboats had to be used to get passengers and freight across the broad, treacherous river; but today Amtrak riders enjoy a majestic view from the towering bridge. Downriver (left side of the train, leaving New Orleans) the great river loops to the south, beginning the curve that has given New Orleans its nickname, the "Crescent City." The bridge is named for the flamboyant senator and governor Huey P. Long, who ruled Louisiana from 1928 to 1935.

Incidentally, at the site of the bridge the Mississippi actually flows northeast, which means that the sun rises over the *west* bank.

11.1 **West Bridge Junction** *2020.4*. Here westbound trains curve to the right and set out across the Louisiana bayou country. There are many French names here, a reminder of the people who first settled this area in 1718. To this day Louisiana civil law is based on the French Code Napoleon, rather than on the English Common Law.

32.2 **Des Allemands** *1999.3*. The name is French for "from the Germans." Just to the south is Lake Salvador and the town of Lafitte—this area was the headquarters of the legendary pirate (or privateer, as you prefer) Jean Lafitte, who flourished in Louisiana around the turn of the nineteenth century. Lafitte dealt in smuggled goods, slaves, rum, and guns. He freely acknowledged that he attacked ships of "a

NEW ORLEANS—LOS ANGELES

Westbound/miles		miles/Eastbound
0.0	NEW ORLEANS	2031.5
2.4	Carrollton Ave.	2029.1
5.8	East Bridge Jct.	2025.7
11.1	West Bridge Jct.	2020.4
24.8	Boutte	2006.7
32.2	Des Allemands	1999.3
40.8	Raceland Jct.	1990.7
55.6	SCHRIEVER	1975.9
80.7	Morgan City	1950.8
82.4	Berwick	1949.1
96.2	Bayou Sale	1935.3
101.6	Franklin	1929.9
105.7	Baldwin	1925.8
113.1	Jeanerette	1918.4
126.2	NEW IBERIA	1905.3
132.7	Cade	1898.8
139.0	Broussard	1892.5
145.1	LAFAYETTE	1886.4
145.1	LAFAYETTE	1886.4
150.3	Scott	1881.2
160.6	Rayne	1870.9

167.1	Crowley	1864.4
175.4	Midland	1856.1
180.7	Mermentau	1850.8
185.8	Jennings	1845.7
192.0	Roanoke	1839.5
195.9	Welsh	1835.6
207.8	Iowa	1823.7
219.9	LAKE CHARLES	1811.6
237.6	Edgerly	1793.9
242.8	Vinton, La.	1788.7
252.5	Echo, Tex.	1779.0
257.7	Orange	1773.8
281.4	BEAUMONT	1750.1
281.4	BEAUMONT	1750.1
294.2	China	1737.3
299.1	Nome	1732.4
309.5	Devers	1722.0
314.6	Raywood	1716.9
322.0	Liberty	1709.5
328.0	Dayton	1703.5
341.9	Crosby	1689.6
346.6	Sheldon	1684.9
363.6	HOUSTON	1667.9
363.6	HOUSTON	1667.9
365.2	Chaney Junction	1666.3
368.1	Eureka	1663.4
372.3	Bellaire Jct.	1659.2
377.4	West Jct.	1654.1
383.2	Missouri City	1648.3
389.5	Sugar Land	1642.0
394.2	Harlem	1637.3
400.7	Rosenberg	1630.8
416.6	East Bernard	1614.9
426.9	Lissie	1604.6
433.3	Eagle Lake	1598.2
438.8	Ramsey	1592.7
446.0	Alleyton	1585.5
449.4	Columbus	1582.1
451.9	Glidden	1579.6
463.7	Weimar	1567.8
471.9	Schulenberg	1559.6
484.8	Flatonia	1546.7
495.5	Waelder	1536.0
504.2	Sandy Fork	1527.3
508.6	Harwood	1522.9
518.1	Luling	1513.4
528.9	Kingsbury	1502.6
538.8	Seguin	1492.7
541.3	Nolte	1490.2
552.9	Cibolo	1478.6
559.9	Randolph Field	1471.6
567.0	Kirby	1464.5

572.2	East Yard	1459.3
574.1	SAN ANTONIO	1457.4
574.1	SAN ANTONIO	1457.4
583.6	Withers	1447.9
589.3	Macdona	1442.2
599.8	LaCoste	1431.7
613.1	Dunley	1418.4
623.3	Hondo	1408.2
635.5	Seco	1396.0
643.4	Sabinal	1388.1
654.4	Knippa	1377.1
665.9	Uvalde	1365.6
679.9	Obi	1351.6
689.5	Odlaw	1342.0
698.4	Anacacho	1333.1
706.5	Spofford	1325.0
719.4	Pinto	1312.1
727.6	Amanda	1303.9
734.9	Johnstone	1296.6
743.3	DEL RIO	1288.2
743.3	DEL RIO	1288.2
756.2	Amistad	1275.3
766.9	Feely	1264.6
775.7	Comstock	1255.8
785.5	Lull	1246.0
793.7	Shumla	1237.8
804.9	Langtry	1226.6
818.7	Pumpville	1212.8
827.8	Malvado	1203.7
839.1	Shaw	1192.4
845.1	Dryden	1186.4
854.1	Mofeta	1177.4
862.3	Fedora	1169.2
869.2	SANDERSON	1162.3
869.2	SANDERSON	1162.3
878.2	Emerson	1153.3
886.3	Longfellow	1145.2
893.7	Rosenfeld	1137.8
899.3	Maxon	1132.2
905.7	Tesnus	1125.8
913.2	Haymond	1118.3
920.7	Warwick	1110.8
929.2	Marathon	1102.3
937.4	Lenox	1094.1
945.0	Altuda	1086.5
953.8	Strobel	1077.7
960.4	ALPINE	1071.1
973.3	Paisano	1058.2
986.0	Marfa	1045.5
996.1	Aragon	1035.4
1004.8	Ryan	1026.7

1013.2	Quebec	1018.3
1021.0	Valentine	1010.5
1033.1	Wendell	998.4
1044.3	Lobo	987.2
1056.9	Collado	974.6
1067.8	Hot Wells	963.7
1079.3	Mallie	952.2
1090.1	Sierra Blanca	941.4
1099.3	Lasca	932.2
1104.5	Small	927.0
1110.2	Finlay	921.3
1119.4	McNary	912.1
1132.9	Iser	898.6
1143.3	Tornillo	888.2
1149.5	Fabens	882.0
1157.3	Clint	874.2
1164.5	Belen	867.0
1172.1	Alfalfa	859.4
1177.0	Cotton Avenue (CT)	854.5
1178.6	EL PASO, TEX. (MT)	852.9

1178.6	EL PASO, TEX. (MT)	852.9
1185.9	Anapra, N.Mex.	845.6
1190.3	Lizard	841.2
1196.8	Strauss	834.7
1216.8	Afton	814.7
1227.8	Aden	803.7
1237.8	Dona	793.7
1246.8	Akela	784.7
1256.3	Carne	775.2
1267.8	DEMING	763.7
1277.8	Tunis	753.7
1287.8	Gage	743.7
1298.8	Wilna	732.7
1308.8	Separ	722.7
1316.8	Lisbon	714.7
1322.8	Ulmoris	708.7
1327.5	LORDSBURG	704.0
1335.0	Gary	696.5
1342.1	Mondel	689.4
1346.9	Steins, N.Mex.	684.6
1353.8	Vanar, Ariz.	677.7
1361.4	San Simon	670.1
1369.0	Olga	662.5
1377.2	Bowie	654.3
1384.6	Luzena	646.9
1393.0	Raso	638.5
1400.9	Willcox	630.6
1411.7	Cochise	619.8
1421.7	Dragoon	609.8
1428.4	Tully	603.1
1434.1	Sibyl	597.4
1438.9	Fenner	592.6

1441.7	BENSON	589.8
1446.0	Chamiso	585.5
1450.6	Mescal	580.9
1478.0	Wilmot	553.5
1488.9	TUCSON	542.6

1488.9	TUCSON	542.6
1493.5	Stockham	538.0
1498.1	Kino	533.4
1505.9	Rillito	525.6
1514.4	Naviska	517.1
1521.4	Red Rock	510.1
1528.6	Wymola	502.9
1536.1	Picacho	495.4
1553.8	Coolidge	477.7
1565.6	Magma	465.9
1577.3	Germann	454.2
1587.5	Gilbert	444.0
1590.9	McQueen	440.6
1592.7	Mesa	438.8
1600.1	Tempe	431.4
1603.4	Kendall	428.1
1608.5	PHOENIX	423.0

1608.5	PHOENIX	423.0
1610.5	23rd Avenue	421.0
1616.4	Fowler	415.1
1618.8	Tolleson	412.7
1621.5	Cashion	410.0
1624.8	Litchfield	406.7
1638.8	Buckeye	392.7
1648.8	Dixie	382.7
1653.2	Arlington	378.3
1663.5	Gillespie	368.0
1673.4	Saddle	358.1
1692.2	Hyder	339.3
1712.0	Kofa	319.5
1733.6	Roll	297.9
1744.5	Wellton	287.0
1761.0	Dome	270.5
1763.8	Kinter	267.7
1770.7	Fortuna	260.8
1781.6	YUMA, ARIZ. (MT)	249.9

1781.6	YUMA, ARIZ. (MT)	249.9
1782.4	Colorado, Calif. (PT)	249.1
1787.3	Araz	244.2
1793.6	Dunes	237.9
1802.0	Cactus	229.5
1808.5	Clyde	223.0
1816.2	Glamis	215.3
1824.2	Acolita	207.3
1832.3	Regina	199.2
1839.9	Iris	191.6

1846.8	Niland	184.7
1854.2	Wister	177.3
1858.7	Frink	172.8
1867.5	Bertram	164.0
1874.7	Ferrum	156.8
1881.0	Mortmar	150.5
1889.1	Mecca	142.4
1894.8	Thermal	136.7
1899.9	Coachella	131.6
1903.4	INDIO	128.1
1907.8	Myoma	123.7
1915.3	Thousand Palms	116.2
1919.2	Rimlon	112.3
1922.7	Salvia	108.8
1926.2	Garmet	105.3
1931.7	West Palm Springs	99.8
1935.7	Fingal	95.8
1938.1	Mons	93.4
1940.2	Cabazon	91.3
1946.1	Banning	85.4
1948.8	Pershing	82.7
1952.3	Beaumont	79.2
1971.7	Loma Linda	59.8
1975.3	Colton	56.2
1978.6	West Colton	52.9
1984.6	South Fontana	46.9
1990.5	Guasti	41.0
1994.1	Ontario	37.4
1996.5	Montclair	35.0
2000.0	POMONA	31.5
2007.5	Walnut	24.0
2010.8	Marne	20.7
2013.6	City of Industry	17.9
2017.0	Bassett	14.5
2019.7	El Monte	11.8
2022.6	San Gabriel	8.9
2026.6	Alhambra	4.9
2030.6	East Bank Jct.	0.9
2030.9	Mission Tower	0.6
2031.5	LOS ANGELES	0.0

European power'' (England), but always denied that he engaged in common piracy. Lafitte supplied many of the weapons used by Andrew Jackson's army at the battle of New Orleans, the smashing victory that ended the War of 1812 and secured American control of the Mississippi. Ironically, pressure from the U.S. Government eventually forced Lafitte to leave Louisiana. He re-established his ''business'' at Galveston, Texas, for a few years, then disappeared forever.

55.6 **SCHRIEVER** *1975.9.* This is the station for Thibodaux, site of Nicholls State University, which is 4 miles north.

80.7 **Morgan City** *1950.8.* At this point the rails bridge the Atchafalaya River connecting Grand Lake with the sea. This stretch of track used to be called Morgan's Louisiana and Texas Railroad—the Morgan, of course, was J. P. Morgan, the most important financier in U.S. railroad history.

126.2 **NEW IBERIA** *1905.3.* Spain (old Iberia) once owned Louisiana. Nearby, at Avery Island, the McIlhaney Company produces its ubiquitous Tabasco Sauce, whose principal ingredient is hot peppers. Not far north is the Longfellow-Evangeline State Park, recalling the narrative poem about the Acadians, French-speaking natives of Nova Scotia who were forcibly expelled from Canada by the British around 1760. Some of them came to Louisiana, where "Acadian" was corrupted to "Cajun."

145.1 **LAFAYETTE** *1886.4.* The first division point west of New Orleans, Lafayette is named for the Marquis de Lafayette, the young French nobleman who came to the United States to aid in the struggle for independence.

Lafayette, which contains the nearest Amtrak station to the state capital, Baton Rouge, 50 miles east on Route I-10, is the site of the University of Southwestern Louisiana.

West of Lafayette the country changes: The bayous are behind, and so is the French heritage, which diminishes between here and Jennings and disappears altogether after you leave Acadia Parish.

219.9 **LAKE CHARLES, LA.** *1811.6.* Sulfur is the big industry in this town, which is also the site of McNeese State University.

252.5 **Echo, Tex.** *1779.0.* The Sabine River forms the Louisiana-Texas boundary. Farther south it flows through Sabine Pass into the Gulf of Mexico.

257.7 **Orange** *1773.8.* Twenty miles southwest is Port Arthur—located not on the Gulf itself but on Sabine Lake—birthplace of the late rock singer Janis Joplin.

From Orange to El Paso is 922 miles, farther than from New York to Chicago—and all in Texas. Just gives you an idea how enormous the Lone Star State really is.

281.4 **BEAUMONT** *1750.1.* The name means "beautiful mountain" in French, but don't bother looking for the mountain—the elevation here is 24 feet above sea level.

The modern history of Texas began near Beaumont in 1901, when the Spindletop Oil Field began producing. The multibillion-dollar petroleum industry has dominated the state's economy ever since. Today the Spindletop Museum at Beaumont houses artifacts and photographs about the original Texas oil discovery.

341.9 **Crosby** *1689.6.* A few miles south is the San Jacinto Battleground Historic Park, marking the site of Sam Houston's decisive victory over the Mexicans under Santa Ana on April 21, 1836, which secured the independence of Texas from Mexico. Texas remained an independent republic for 10 years, until it joined the United States in 1846. The state park features a 570-foot tower and the permanent mooring place of the battleship U.S.S. *Texas*.

363.6 **HOUSTON** *1667.9*. For information on the city, see section 2.18.

389.5 **Sugar Land** *1642.0*. Here the train crosses the Brazos River. As the name implies, this is sugarcane country. The Brazos marks roughly the dividing line between East Texas, which is more Southern than Western in attitude, and the Great Plains.

574.1 **SAN ANTONIO** *1457.4*. For information on the city, see section 2.43.

665.9 **Uvalde** *1365.6*. One doesn't think of Texas as a mountainous area, but West Texas has some hills as high as 8,000 feet. From Uvalde west, the railroad begins to climb over the Anacacho Mountains. Cline Mountain rises 1,250 feet overhead.

743.3 **DEL RIO** *1288.2*. Del Rio is on the Rio Grande, which for more than 1,200 miles forms the border between the United States and Mexico. Across the river from Del Rio is Ciudad Acuna in the Mexican state of Coahuila.

Just west of Del Rio is the Amistad Dam; behind it, the Rio Grande was backed up to form the Amistad Reservoir, more than 50 miles long and, at one point, 20 miles wide.

775.7 **Comstock** *1255.8*. A few miles west the railroad crosses the legendary Pecos River just before it empties into the Rio Grande. The Pecos high bridge marks what were once the limits of civilization in Texas.

804.9 **Langtry** *1226.6*. Remember the movie *The Life and Times of Judge Roy Bean?* Well, this was where he established his saloon and law office, the place where he declared himself to be "Law west of the Pecos." He named the place after Lillie Langtry, the actress he declared to be the lady of his dreams; unfortunately she preferred the Prince of Wales. Judge Roy's saloon and museum are now the chief attractions of Langtry.

West of Langtry the Rio Grande loops far to the south, while the railroad heads straight west.

869.2 **SANDERSON** *1162.3*. This is a railroad division point where train crews change. Talk about being in the middle of nowhere— Sanderson is 300 miles from San Antonio and 300 miles from El Paso.

878.2 **Emerson** *1153.3*. Somebody high in Southern Pacific management evidently had a fondness for New England writers. This station is called Emerson, and the next one is Longfellow.

905.7 **Tesnus** *1125.8*. When you run out of names, try spelling backward. "Tesnus," of course, spells "Sunset" when you turn it around.

929.2 **Marathon** *1102.3.* The historic Marathon was the plain in Greece where the Athenians defeated a Persian army in 490 B.C. Marathon, Texas, is a little town at the base of the climb over the Glass and Del Norte mountains, whose peaks reach nearly 7,000 feet above sea level. For the next 31 miles the tracks follow a pass between Cathedral Mountain to the north and Mount Ord to the southwest.

960.4 **ALPINE** *1071.1.* You can tell from the name alone that this is a mountain town. Sul Ross State University, named after an old-time Indian fighter, is here.

973.3 **Paisano** *1058.2.* At an elevation of 5,074 feet above sea level this is the summit of the pass through the Del Nortes and is the highest point en route between New Orleans and Los Angeles. From here, westbound trains descend toward El Paso.

1021.0 **Valentine** *1010.5.* To the east, Mount Livermore rises 8,300 feet.

1090.1 **Sierra Blanca** *941.4.* Here the Southern Pacific line from San Antonio, used by Amtrak, joins the Texas and Pacific, which comes straight across West Texas from Fort Worth. The two railroads share the tracks for the next 88 miles to El Paso, and behind this arrangement is a story.

Unlike most other transcontinental lines, the Southern Pacific was built from California toward the east. It was pushed by Collis P. Huntington, who was intent on dominating Texas the way his line already ruled California. In his way, however, stood Tom Scott, president of the Texas Pacific. (It became Texas *and* Pacific later.) Scott, who was also boss of the Pennsylvania Railroad, was pushing the Texas Pacific westward, trying to cut Huntington off at El Paso. This joint line was a compromise.

Sierra Blanca Peak, 6,970 feet high, lies north of the town.

1119.4 **McNary** *912.1.* Here at last the rails leave the mountains behind and reach the Rio Grande valley again, though the river is out of sight to the west much of the way into El Paso.

1178.6 **EL PASO, TEX.** *852.9.* El Paso is a railroad division point, and Amtrak trains stop here for 20 minutes—long enough to stretch your legs and bask in the sun, which shines in El Paso nearly every day.

For information on the city, see section 2.17.

After leaving El Paso, Amtrak trains now follow a route through Deming and Lordsburg, but years ago the *Sunset Limited* used to go by way of the former El Paso and Southwestern line through Columbus, New Mexico, just above the international border. This old line followed the original survey for a "southern Pacific railroad" that had been prepared at the order of Congress back in 1850. It was then

History come to life at the Alamo in San Antonio. (See section 3.42.)

Old engine #200 at the Texas State Railroad Historical Park in Rusk, Texas.

believed that only one railroad to the West Coast would ever be built. Consequently, the Northern and Southern states debated furiously about its terminal and its route.

One of the strongest Northern arguments against the proposed southern line was that its survey passed through Mexican territory for many miles west of El Paso. To remove this objection, the secretary of war, Jefferson Davis—later to be president of the Confederacy and always a strong advocate of Southern interests—arranged for the purchase of the strip of land south of the Gila River through which the proposed railway would run. Davis's envoy, James Gadsden, was able to make the deal for $10 million. The territory thus acquired in 1853 is known as the Gadsden Purchase. It comprises the southern parts of New Mexico and Arizona, and it was the scene in 1916 of Pancho Villa's raid on Columbus, New Mexico, which cost nineteen American lives. It was purchased just so the railroad could be built through it; ironically, that line has been abandoned now for more than two decades.

1267.8 **DEMING, N.Mex.** *763.7.* The town is at the crest of the Florida and Cooke's ranges, the highest mountains in southern New Mexico. This is the lowest crossing of the Continental Divide between Mexico and Canada.

New Mexico is the fifth-largest state in land area but only thirty-seventh in population. It's the most heavily Spanish state in the Union; more than a quarter of the population is Spanish-speaking, and New Mexico was the first state to elect a Hispanic governor and a Hispanic senator. The Spanish influence can be seen everywhere in architecture and language.

1327.5 **LORDSBURG, N.MEX.** *704.0.* Lordsburg is the last station in New Mexico, and here a question of time arises. Arizona has steadfastly refused to adopt Daylight Savings Time, though New Mexico does. This means that from October to April, the clocks in New Mexico and Arizona say the same thing. From April to October, however, Arizona is an hour behind New Mexico and on the same time as California.

1377.2 **Bowie, Ariz.** *654.3.* This town was named for Fort Bowie, a military outpost a few miles south, which was built to guard the approaches of Apache Pass. Its site is now a national historic landmark.

The fort was named for the frontiersman Jim Bowie, who was active in the Texas independence movement and died at the Alamo in 1836. Bowie (whose name is pronounced *Boo-ey*) is also credited with having designed the hunting knife that bears his name.

1411.7 **Cochise** *619.8.* This hamlet is named for the Apache chief who led the Chiricahua band of his tribe in a bitter 10-year war against the whites. He had plenty of provocation. First, the U.S. Army hanged a number of defenseless Indian prisoners in 1861, and then a cavalry officer tried to capture Cochise while under a flag of truce. From 1861 to 1871 Cochise made war on the white settlers of Arizona. A treaty arranged in 1871 was supposed to provide a reservation for the Apaches; but when Cochise learned that the army intended to uproot his tribe and move it to New Mexico, he took up arms again. The next year the Apaches were finally given lands in Arizona, where today one-seventh of all American Indians live. In fact, there are so many members of Cochise's tribe here that Arizona is sometimes still called the "Apache state."

1421.7 **Dragoon** *609.8.* Just 6 or 7 miles southeast of this town, deep in the Dragoon Mountains, Cochise had his stronghold. The spot is now a state historic site, but it's nearly inaccessible for casual visitors.

Incidentally, even after Cochise gave up the struggle, other Apaches, led by Geronimo, continued to fight the U.S. Army as late as 1886. The Indian warfare in Arizona was both savage and long-lived, and it presented real problems for the whites despite their tremendous advantages in numbers and technology.

1441.7 **BENSON** *589.8.* Copper is mined about 35 miles from here, at Bisbee. Also close to Benson is Tombstone, the old silver-mining town that was the site of the "Gunfight at the O.K. Corral." Tombstone got its name because the town's founder, a prospector called Ed Schieffelin, had been told that he'd find nothing at the site except his tombstone. Instead he found silver ore, and the place became a lawless boomtown. The leading desperados in the vicinity were the Clanton Gang, who did a thriving business in cattle rustling with a little robbery on the side. The Clantons met their end, though, in a shoot-out with the Earp brothers and Doc Holliday. The date was October 26, 1881.

1478.0 **Wilmot** *553.5.* In 1846, while the Mexican War was still going on, David Wilmot, a Democratic congressman from Pennsylvania, proposed an amendment outlawing slavery in any territory acquired from Mexico. This so-called Wilmot Proviso was passed in the House but repeatedly defeated in the Senate. It raised the most explosive of all issues in American political history: the question of what to do about slavery in the newly acquired territories. Antislavery Northerners supported the Wilmot Proviso; proslavery Southerners denied that Congress had any power to interfere with slavery. On this point there could be no agreement and no compromise. It was decided at last by the Civil War.

1488.9 **TUCSON** *542.6.* For information on the city, see section 2.48.

1498.1 **Kino** *533.4.* The town was named for Padre Eusebio Kino, a Jesuit missionary who established twenty-four missions, including San Xavier del Bac, a few miles south of this point.

334

1505.9 **Rillito** *525.6.* West of here is the Saguaro National Monument, including the Arizona–Sonora Desert Museum. The saguaro is a giant cactus that can grow as high as 40 feet; it sends out an extensive root system that stores water by expansion. This cactus provides food and homes for all manner of desert creatures and is the basis of the ecological system in this harsh environment.

1521.4 **Red Rock** *510.1.* West of here are the Picacho Mountains; the railroad breasts them at Picacho Pass, 1,800 feet high. Picacho Peak rises more than 3,300 feet above sea level to the south.

1536.1 **Picacho** *495.4.* This is a junction point on the railroad. Here the direct line continues northwest to Casa Grande, then turns due west toward Yuma. Amtrak passenger trains, however, turn north here, running by way of Coolidge to reach the Phoenix metropolitan area.

1553.8 **Coolidge** *477.7.* Just north of the city and to the west of the railroad (left side, going west) is the Casa Grande Ruins National Monument. *Casa Grande* is Spanish for "big house," and here are found the remains of a four-story Indian apartment building, together with the traces of an extensive canal system used for irrigation. The ruins are in an excellent state of preservation. The big question is why the Indians who built them suddenly abandoned them and never returned.

1590.9 **McQueen** *440.6.* To the northeast (right side of the train, westbound) Queen Creek comes down from the Superstition Mountains. Somewhere deep in these hills, legend says, is the Lost Dutchman Mine. A mysterious German prospector named Jacob Waltz worked this fabulous silver vein; he left some clues to its location, and on his death a legion of fortune hunters began to search for his mine. None of them ever found it—or, if they did, never lived to tell about it.

1592.7 **Mesa** *438.8.* Here the rails swing westward into the valley of the Salt River. Some miles east, back in the mountains, is the Theodore Roosevelt Dam, an early federal reclamation project that irrigates the area.

1600.1 **Tempe** *431.4.* Midway between Mesa and Phoenix, Tempe is best known as the site of Arizona State University. The campus is north of the railroad (right side of the train, going west). At Tempe trains make a sharp curve to the right, then cross the Salt River, which is usually dry—except when it's in flood. Then there's another curve to the left, and the train passes the Sky Harbor International Airport (left side, going west) to enter Phoenix proper.

1608.5 **PHOENIX** *423.0.* For information on the city, see section 2.32.

1621.5 **Cashion** *410.0.* A little way south, the Salt River flows into the Gila, which in turn flows west across the rest of Arizona to meet the Colorado near Yuma. The Gila marks the northern edge of the Gadsden Purchase, the 1853 real-estate deal that transferred what is now southern Arizona from Mexico to the United States.

1733.6 **Roll** *297.9.* To the north is the Yuma Proving Ground, where the U.S. Army tests weapons none of us know much about. Just west of Roll the rails cross the Gila River. From here to Yuma the route runs through what was, until the Gadsden Purchase, Mexican territory.

1744.5 **Wellton** *287.0.* Here the passenger route from Phoenix rejoins the freight line that comes directly from Picacho, saving 43 miles by avoiding Phoenix altogether.

1781.6 **YUMA, ARIZ.** *249.9.* There may be hotter, drearier places than Yuma, but you'd have to look pretty hard to find one. The town lies at the train crossing of the Colorado River, 25 miles north of the Mexican border and 200 miles from anything else. It's a railroad division point and crew-changing station and is the place where, from October to April, you reset your watch.

The next 65 miles to Niland, through the Sand Hill and Chocolate mountains, is one of the most desolate stretches in North America: There is literally nothing here except rocks and heat. Fortunately, Amtrak trains go through at night in both directions.

1846.8 **Niland, Calif.** *184.7.* Niland is the gateway to the Imperial Valley, which lies to the south. This was once also barren desert, but around the turn of the century the construction of the All American Canal brought Colorado River water to the valley. Now in its blazing heat grow huge crops of lettuce and other fruits and vegetables.

West of Niland the line passes along the east shore of the Salton Sea, 235 feet below sea level. This huge lake, covering almost 400 square miles, is what remains of a great flood early in the twentieth century, when the Colorado threatened to inundate the whole Imperial Valley. Heroic efforts over a period of years forced the river back into its channel, leaving the Salton Sea to cover some of the lowest-lying land.

1899.9 **Coachella** *131.6.* North of the Salton Sea, the railroad runs through another fertile, irrigated area: the Coachella Valley, where grapefruits and dates are grown.

1903.4 **INDIO** *128.1.* This is the station for the Palm Springs–Rancho Mirage–Palm Desert recreation area, as well as for the Coachella Valley. The Little San Bernardino Mountains rise to the east; the Santa Rosa Mountains are in the distance to the west.

1931.7 **West Palm Springs** *99.8.* Palm Springs, which might best be described as Beverly Hills in the desert, is a triumph of promotion over environment. This ultrachic resort has no natural advantages except its sunny desert climate and its clean air. Cleveland Amory once said that it resembled "an abandoned Cecil B. De Mille movie set."

Palm Springs actually dates back to the nineteenth century, but it became a glamour resort only after the movie colony discovered it around 1920. Rudolph Valentino and Charlie Chaplin were two of the first big-name stars to come to Palm Springs. After them came almost everybody else. These days the place is not only a winter resort but is bursting with new condominiums and permanent year-round residents.

Beyond West Palm Springs, Mount San Jacinto rises 10,000 feet to the south, while San Gorgonio Mountain towers 11,000 feet to the north. Between the peaks the railroad runs through San Gorgonio Pass and the towns of Cabazon and Banning toward the summit at Beaumont.

1952.3 **Beaumont** *79.2*. This is the summit of the pass; from here on it's downgrade all the way to Los Angeles. West of Beaumont the railroad curves into San Timoteo Canyon, through which the rails descend into the Los Angeles basin.

1971.7 **Loma Linda** *59.8*. Here you may see some of the orange groves that once were everywhere in southern California. Today many of them have been replaced by tract homes, but at the extreme end of the basin a number of groves remain.

1975.3 **Colton** *56.2*. Colton lies between San Bernardino to the north and Riverside to the south. This is actually the beginning of the sprawling Los Angeles metropolitan area. The Southern Pacific's huge freight yards extend east from Colton for 4 miles.

2000.0 **POMONA** *31.5*. The town is named for the Roman goddess of fruit. Amtrak has two stations in Pomona. The Sante Fe station on North Garey Avenue is used by trains running through San Bernardino, while trains going by way of Colton use the Southern Pacific station on Commercial Street. For more notes on Pomona, see section 3.41.

2013.6 **City of Industry** *17.9*. A short distance to the southwest is Whittier, which was named for the poet and is the birthplace of former President Richard Nixon.

2019.7 **El Monte** *11.8*. The name means "the mountain" in Spanish, and Mount Wilson towers to 5,700 feet, due north of the town.

Between El Monte and Los Angeles there are two routes. One goes through San Gabriel, past the old mission founded there by Fra Junipero Serra. The other, which is usually used by Amtrak trains, goes straight down the middle of the San Bernardino Freeway. Don't be surprised to see a truck rolling along beside your window.

2030.6 **East Bank Junction** *0.9*. The two lines from El Monte come together here, then cross the concrete-channeled Los Angeles River, pass Mission Tower, and curve to the left past the county jail and into Los Angeles's Union Passenger Terminal.

For information on Los Angeles, see section 2.23.

3.43   Los Angeles—Oakland—Sacramento —Portland—Seattle

When the original Amtrak system was planned back in 1970, the long Pacific Coast route from Los Angeles to Seattle was omitted. As a result of some intensive lobbying, however, it was later designated a part of the basic Amtrak System, and it has proved the most successful of all the NRPC's long-distance routes.

Before Amtrak, you had to change trains twice to make the Los Angeles—Seattle run, and one of the changes required a transbay bus ride at San Francisco. Today the Superliner *Coast Starlight* goes all the way through, treating its passengers to some magnificent scenery en route—113 miles of the Pacific Coast shoreline, plus the spectacular Cascade Mountains. In addition, it now serves the state capital, Sacramento, and makes convenient connections at Los Angeles for San Diego.

For information on Los Angeles, see section 2.23.

0.0 **LOS ANGELES** *466.6.* In 1769, 12 years before Los Angeles was founded, a Franciscan priest called Fra Junipero Serra set out to establish a chain of missions extending up the California coast. Each mission was to be a day's journey by horseback from the last; the road connecting them came to be called El Camino Real, "the Royal Road." Los Angeles was established where the Camino Real crossed the Los Angeles River, midway between Mission San Gabriel Arcángel and Mission San Fernando Rey de España, both of which are still standing. The present-day railroad route up the coast closely follows the Camino Real. In fact, the Los Angeles railroad station sits right in the middle of the original route.

0.9 **East Bank Junction** *465.7.* Just after leaving the station, the train crosses the Los Angeles River, usually just a dry concrete channel except during the flood season. Trains run along the river's east bank, past the Southern Pacific's freight facility, Taylor Yard.

5.7 **GLENDALE** *460.9.* This suburban station is convenient for residents of Pasadena, Burbank, and other communities north of Los Angeles proper. The station building is almost unchanged from its appearance when constructed back in the early part of the twentieth century. Note the unusual heavy doors.

11.2 **Burbank Junction** *455.4.* At this point the Coast Line leaves

Northbound/miles   *miles/Southbound*

Northbound		Southbound
0.0	LOS ANGELES	466.6
0.9	East Bank Jct.	465.7
2.1	Dayton Ave. Tower	464.5
5.7	GLENDALE	460.9
11.2	Burbank Jct.	455.4
15.5	Hewitt	451.1
18.4	Gemco	448.2
24.0	Northridge	442.6
28.4	Chatsworth	438.2
36.4	Santa Susana	430.2
46.8	Moorpark	419.8
57.3	Camarillo	409.3
66.1	OXNARD	400.5
70.7	Montalvo	395.9
75.7	Ventura	390.9
85.3	Seacliff	381.3
92.7	Carpenteria	373.9
96.6	Ortega	370.0
103.2	SANTA BARBARA	363.4
111.1	Goleta	355.5
115.0	Ellwood	351.6
118.9	Naples	347.7
124.0	Capitan	342.6
134.5	Gaviota	332.1
139.1	Sacate	327.5
142.9	San Augustine	323.7
148.6	Conception	318.0
156.6	Sudden	310.0
164.7	South Vandenburg	301.9
166.0	Honda	300.6
171.2	Surf	295.4
176.7	Tangair	289.9
180.7	Narlon	285.9
186.4	Casmalia	280.2
187.4	Devon	279.2
193.2	Waldorf	273.4
197.4	Guadalupe	269.2
201.5	Bromela	265.1
204.0	Callender	262.6
208.0	Oceano	258.6
209.7	Grover	256.9
211.1	Pismo	255.5
219.1	East San Luis Obispo	247.5
221.8	SAN LUIS OBISPO	244.8
221.8	SAN LUIS OBISPO	244.8
223.3	Hathaway	243.3
225.9	Goldtree	240.7
227.6	Chorro	239.0
230.5	Serrano	236.1

235.0	Cuesta	231.6
238.4	Santa Margarita	228.2
245.9	Henry	220.7
252.1	Templeton	214.5
257.6	Paso Robles	209.0
263.0	Wellsona	203.6
266.9	San Miguel	199.7
270.1	McKay	196.5
278.0	Bradley	188.6
284.2	Wunpost	182.4
291.0	San Ardo	175.6
301.5	San Lucas	165.1
310.2	King City	156.4
325.6	Harlem	141.0
330.3	Soledad	136.3
338.8	Gonzales	127.8
344.8	Chualar	121.8
353.6	Spreckels Jct.	113.0
355.7	SALINAS	110.9
363.5	Castroville	103.1
373.5	Watsonville Jct.	93.1
380.7	Logan	85.9
387.5	Corporal	79.1
390.7	Carnadero	75.9
393.2	Gilroy	73.4
396.9	Rucker	69.7
407.6	Perry	59.0
410.8	Coyote	55.8
418.6	Lick	48.0
423.6	SAN JOSE	43.0
424.3	College Park	42.3
425.7	Santa Clara	40.9
428.8	Agnew	37.8
431.4	Alviso	35.2
436.4	Albrae	30.2
439.9	Newark	26.7
445.2	Alvarado	21.4
450.3	Russell	16.3
455.0	Mulford	11.6
457.1	Elmhurst	9.5
460.8	Fruitvale	5.8
464.6	Magnolia Tower	2.0
465.6	West Oakland	1.0
466.6	OAKLAND (Connecting bus to San Francisco)	0.0

the San Joaquin Valley route. Both eventually wind up in the same place, but the two routes run parallel to each other some 60 miles apart, with the Coast Range in between. They eventually reunite at Oakland.

18.4 **Gemco** *448.2.* Not the name of a discount department store, "Gemco" is a contraction of "General Motors Co.," which has an auto-assembly plant here.

24.0 **Northridge** *442.6.* This is the heart of the San Fernando Valley, politically a part of Los Angeles but actually a world of its own, with more than a million residents, its own daily newspaper, its own radio stations, and its own distinct world view. The valley is separated from Hollywood and Beverly Hills by a low range of mountains and is drained by the Los Angeles River. The railroad enters it from the east, along the watercourse.

28.4 **Chatsworth** *438.2.* Although the scenery is quite rural—it looks like the old *Cisco Kid* TV series—this is still part of the city of Los Angeles, which sprawls without apparent reason from the ocean at San Pedro all the way to the dry ranch country around Chatsworth. It is possible to drive 50 miles without ever leaving the corporate limits of Los Angeles.

At Chatsworth there is a sweeping curve to the left. Just beyond, the rails begin to climb Santa Susanna Pass, the exit from the San Fernando Valley. A tunnel (1½ miles long) makes this mountain crossing an easy one.

66.1 **OXNARD** *400.5.* Here is the station for Ventura, on the coast nearby, as well as for Malibu, 30 miles south along the ocean. Oxnard is in a rich agricultural area. Although people from the Midwest may find it hard to believe, California is far and away the leading producer of foodstuffs among all the American states. Indeed, agriculture is California's biggest industry, and the value of its farm products dwarfs that of the gold that brought settlers here in the first place.

Between Oxnard and Ventura the tracks cross the Santa Clara River. Usually this is just a dry bed—except in spring, when torrents of water come down from the mountains.

75.7 **Ventura** *390.9.* The town takes its name from Mission San Buenaventura, the last mission founded by Fra Junipero Serra in person. It is still standing and may be visited today.

Just beyond Ventura the rails reach the Pacific Ocean, and they hug the shoreline for the next 113 miles. The ocean is in sight nearly all the way to San Luis Obispo—as spectacular a ride as you'll find anywhere. Take a left-side window, going north.

85.3 **Seacliff** *381.3.* The odd-looking contraptions out in the water are not boats. They are oil rigs, and this is one of the oldest offshore oil fields in America. A couple of piers extend out into the shoals, and you may see the walking beams at work pumping oil from beneath the Pacific as the train glides by.

Look far out to sea, and you'll probably make out the hazy forms of the Channel Islands, 30 miles offshore across the Santa Barbara Channel. These unspoiled islands became America's newest national park in 1980.

103.2 **SANTA BARBARA** *363.4.* This lovely city on the Pacific grew up around Mission Santa Barbara, founded in 1786 and widely regarded as the most beautiful of the California missions along the Camino Real. It is often called the "queen of the missions." Santa Barbara still celebrates its Spanish heritage with an annual festival, though it actually has a much smaller percentage of Spanish-speaking population than does Los Angeles.

Just north of the station building, on the east side of the tracks (right side, going north) stands one of the most magnificent trees I have ever seen. It's an Australian Moreton Bay fig tree, planted in 1877, and today its branches spread out 180 feet, making it the largest specimen of this species in the United States.

134.5 **Gaviota** *332.1.* At this point Route 101, the main coast road from Los Angeles to San Francisco, turns inland. Only by train can you continue to follow the coastline with its beautiful views of the Pacific.

148.6 **Conception** *318.0.* At Point Conception the coastline, which has been running in an east-west direction, now turns north. This, then, is the farthest "corner" of the United States.

171.2 **Surf** *295.4.* About 10 miles south of this little town is Point Arguello, where the United States has a satellite-tracking station. Just north of town the train crosses the Santa Ynez River.

187.4 **Devon** *279.2.* Near here the 113-mile run along the Pacific finally ends, as the rails turn inland. There will still be occasional glimpses of the ocean, but north of here the rails do not follow the shoreline as they do from Devon to Ventura.

221.8 **SAN LUIS OBISPO** *244.8.* This city was built around Mission San Luis Obispo de Tolosa, on the Camino Real, 8 miles from the Pacific. San Luis Obispo is a railroad division point, sitting as it does at the base of Santa Margarita Pass, over which the rails must climb to reach the interior of California.

This station is Amtrak's jumping-off place for the Hearst Castle at San Simeon, 40 miles up the coast. William Randolph Hearst, probably America's best-known press lord, wasn't very serious about his Harvard studies and got himself thrown out of school for his pranks. He went to New York and studied the success of Joseph Pulitzer's *New York World*; then he approached his father, George Hearst, and got permission to take over the family's sagging San Francisco newspaper. Using the sex-and-scandal approach he had learned in New York, Willie Hearst turned the moribund publication into a profitable paper. George Hearst, a farsighted man, had originally purchased the vast tract of land along the ocean where San Simeon now stands, and on it his son set out to build what is surely the most fantastic home in the United States. Millions of dollars were spent to bring art treasures to the Hearst Castle. This was Hearst's home and palace, where he

The Old Mission Santa Barbara—frequently called "Queen of the Missions"—is one of the more impressive of the mission chain, combining Greco-Roman, Spanish, Moorish, Mexican, and Native American influences. A tour of the mission includes a history of the mission site from the first explorations in 1542 to the founding of the Presidio in 1782 and of the mission four years later. (See section 3.43.)

The Santa Barbara County Court House was built in the 1920's as a showcase of Spanish-Moorish architectural styles.

entertained lavishly with the movie commedienne Marion Davies as his hostess. Today San Simeon is a state historic monument, open to the public. There are conducted tours, or you can see it by yourself (reservations are advised, especially in summer).

Immediately after leaving the station at San Louis Obispo, the diesel engines begin to roar and the train begins the slow, steep climb over Santa Margarita Pass. For the next 16 miles the track twists and winds up the mountainsides toward the summit. There are five tunnels in this stretch, as well as a horseshoe curve every bit as spectacular as the one in Pennsylvania, if less well known.

235.0 **Cuesta** *231.6.* *Cuesta* is Spanish for "hill," and this station is near the top of the climb from San Luis Obispo. The summit is in the middle of Tunnel Six, nearby. Cuesta is also near the halfway point in the trip from Los Angeles to Oakland.

301.5 **San Lucas** *165.1.* Nearby in miles, but on the other side of a mountain, is Mission San Antonio de Padua. The missions along the Camino Real were located, wherever possible, on the sites of Indian settlements to facilitate the conversion of the native population. Historians have been quite critical of the treatment of the mission Indians. Conversion to Christianity and close contact with white men brought slavery and virulent disease, and the Indian population declined rapidly after the padres came.

355.7 **SALINAS** *110.9.* This is the center of a large agricultural area, where lettuce is a key crop. Salinas (pronounced *Sa-le´-nas*) contains the Amtrak station for the Monterey Peninsula, where Carmel and Monterey are famous seaside communities. Big Sur is a little farther down the coast along the spectacular Route 1, the highway that winds along the cliffs hundreds of feet above the Pacific.

Salinas was the home of Nobel Prize–winning novelist John Steinbeck. Several of his books are set in the area, including part of *The Grapes of Wrath,* probably his best-known work.

363.5 **Castroville** *103.1.* Welcome to the self-styled artichoke capital of the world. From Castroville a branch line leads down to Monterey.

373.5 **Watsonville Junction** *93.1.* The junction is with a branch to Santa Cruz. Nearby is Mission San Juan Bautista, another stop on the Camino Real.

423.6 **SAN JOSE** *43.0.* Here is the station for the Santa Clara Valley. At this point passengers may change to commuter trains for points on the San Francisco peninsula, including Palo Alto, San Mateo, and San Francisco itself.

San Jose was founded in 1777 and was the first capital of California after the state was admitted to the Union in 1849. It was known for its fruit-processing plants, although the additional industry that has moved into the area since World War II has doubled the size of the city. San Jose is now about as big as Cincinnati.

425.7 **Santa Clara** *40.9.* This is the site of Mission Santa Clara and Santa Clara University. At this point the railroad divides: One branch goes on up the peninsula to San Francisco; the other (used by Amtrak trains) follows the eastern shore of San Francisco Bay to Oakland.

439.9 **Newark** *26.7.* Fremont is just to the east; San Francisco Bay is out of sight to the west. Near here is the San Mateo Bridge, which carries auto traffic across the Bay.

457.1 **Elmhurst** *9.5.* The Metro Oakland Airport is nearby. Paralleling the railroad tracks are the Nimitz Freeway, named for the World War II admiral, and the Bay Area Rapid Transit line. Look for the Oakland–Alameda County Coliseum complex, west of the track (left side of train, heading north).

466.6 **OAKLAND (16th Street)** *0.0.* For notes on Oakland and the East Bay area, see section 3.44. For information on San Francisco, see section 2.45. For connecting service to Salt Lake City, Denver, or Chicago, see section 3.44.

0.0 **OAKLAND (16th Street)** *737.1.*

For notes on the route from Oakland to Roseville, see section 3.44 from mile 675.6 to 779.8.

104.2 **Roseville** *632.9.* At Roseville the line to Portland branches off from the main line to the east and turns up the Sacramento valley heading north.

138.4 **MARYSVILLE** *598.7.* This is the station for nearby Yuba City and for Oroville, 30 miles north. Near Oroville is the Oroville Dam on the Feather River, one of the main components of California's controversial multimillion-dollar state water project designed to move fresh water from the north, where the rivers are, to the south, where the people are.

181.8 **CHICO** *555.3.* The name is Spanish for "little boy." Chico State University is here, and the station also serves the rest of the upper Sacramento valley. The Coast Range is to the west, and the high Sierras are to the east.

209.3 **Tehama** *527.8.* This is just a railroad junction where the East Valley line (used by Amtrak) meets the West Valley line, which runs due south to Davis, avoiding Sacramento. The *Coast Starlight* used this track until 1981, when it was rerouted to serve the more important population centers along the East Valley line.

221.0 **Red Bluff** *516.1.* The elevation here is 309 feet above sea level, but so steeply do the Sierras rise from the valley floor that not 50 miles away are summits over 10,000 feet.

The Golden Gate bridge, gateway to San Francisco harbor.

The C.P. Huntington reached California on a sailing vessel that came around Cape Horn. It was put into operation in 1863 by Danforth, Cook, and P.T. Hudson and is one piece of rolling stock on display at the restored Central Pacific Railroad Station in old Sacramento. (See section 3.43.)

OAKLAND—PORTLAND VIA ROSEVILLE

Northbound/miles   *miles/Southbound*

0.0	OAKLAND	737.1
1.1	Emoryville	736.0
1.5	Shellmound	735.6
3.7	Berkeley	733.4
7.6	Stege	729.5
9.5	RICHMOND	727.6
11.1	San Pablo	726.0
13.4	Giant	723.7
17.5	Pinole	719.6
18.3	Hercules	718.8
20.0	Rodeo	717.1
20.8	Oleum	716.3
21.6	Tormey	715.5
22.0	Selby	715.1
23.4	Crockett	713.7
26.8	Benica	710.3
27.5	Ozol	709.6
29.1	MARTINEZ	708.0
35.5	Bahia	701.6
46.4	Suisun-Fairfield	690.7
49.4	Tolenas	687.7
52.9	Cannon	684.2
56.9	Elmira	680.2
65.0	Dixon	672.1
67.1	Sucro	670.0
69.3	Tremont	667.8
73.1	DAVIS	664.0
76.6	Swingle	660.5
77.9	Webster	659.2
83.8	Mikon	653.3
85.6	West Sacramento	651.5
86.5	SACRAMENTO	650.6
87.6	15th St.	649.5
89.4	Elvas	647.7
92.5	Benali	644.6
97.0	Walerga	640.1
100.4	Antelope	636.7
104.2	Roseville	632.9

104.2	Roseville	632.9
110.4	Sunset-Whitney	626.7
114.6	Lincoln	622.5
116.0	Clayton	621.1
118.6	Ewing	618.5
119.7	Brock	617.4
128.8	Earle	608.3
131.8	Ostrom	605.3
136.5	Rupert	600.6
137.4	Dantoni Junction	599.7
138.4	MARYSVILLE	598.7

346

418.3	KLAMATH FALLS	318.8
422.9	Wocus	314.2
427.7	Algoma	309.4
436.0	Modoc Point	301.1
445.5	Chiloquin	291.6
459.1	Kirk	278.0
463.3	Fuego	273.8
472.2	Lenz	264.9
481.4	Yamsay	255.7
486.8	Diamond Lake	250.3
492.1	CHEMULT	245.0
503.6	Mowich	233.5
512.8	Umli	224.3
517.4	Crescent Lake	219.7
525.5	Cascade Summit	211.6
529.6	Abernathy	207.5
534.8	Cruzatte	202.3
540.1	Frazier	197.0
543.6	Fields	193.5
549.2	Wicopee	187.9
533.0	Heather	184.1
558.1	McCredie Springs	179.0
564.1	Pryor	173.0
569.3	Oakridge	167.8
574.4	Lookout	162.7
579.7	Hampton	157.4
584.2	Crale	152.9
589.4	Minnow	147.7
593.1	Dexter	144.0
598.7	Dougren	138.4
600.8	Fall Creek Junction	136.3
603.9	Natron	133.2
607.8	Mohawk Junction	129.3
609.2	Springfield	127.9
610.4	Springfield Jct.	126.7
611.2	Judkins	125.9
613.4	EUGENE	123.7
613.4	EUGENE	123.7
619.1	Irving	118.0
626.0	Swain	111.1
626.7	Junction City	110.4
633.1	Alford	104.0
639.9	Halsey	97.2
645.1	Shedd	92.0
654.1	Hallawell	83.0
656.0	Page	81.1
657.0	ALBANY	80.1
661.5	Millersburg	75.6
670.3	Marion	66.8
680.8	Renard	56.3
684.3	SALEM	52.8
688.3	Labish	48.8

698.2	Gervais	38.9
701.3	Woodburn	35.8
707.7	Hito	29.4
712.9	Canby	24.2
716.9	Coalca	20.2
726.1	Clackamus	11.0
730.2	East Milwaukie	6.9
731.3	Willsburg Junction	5.8
733.0	Brooklyn	4.1
734.0	Haig	3.1
736.4	East Portland	0.7
737.1	PORTLAND	0.0

255.8 **REDDING** *481.3.* This is the crossroads of north-central California, and the north end of the Sacramento River valley. From here on, the railroad must climb over the Cascade Range to reach Oregon.

Redding is the station for Mount Lassen National Park and ski area, 50 miles east by car. Until Mount St. Helens erupted in 1980, Mount Lassen was considered the only active volcano in the continental United States; it last erupted in 1921.

Just north of Redding is Shasta Dam, a huge hydroelectric and flood-control project that holds back the Sacramento, McCloud, Squaw, and Pit rivers. Behind the dam is Lake Shasta, 30 miles long.

275.2 **O'Brien** *461.9.* Here the railroad crosses the Pit River (at this point, actually an arm of Lake Shasta) on the highest double-decked bridge in the world. It's 500 feet tall from the base of its piers to its deck, but you'd never know it: Nearly the whole bridge is submerged under water.

This bridge marks the southern end of the Sacramento River Canyon, a narrow defile where the rails cross the river 18 times in 32 miles. At the northern end of the canyon is the Cantara Loop, a hairpin turn where the engineer can look across the curve and wave to the rear brakeman.

312.8 **DUNSMUIR** *424.3.* Dunsmuir may be just a little village, but it's an important division point on the Southern Pacific. All trains stop here to change crews. Ahead lies the toughest portion of the Oakland–Portland run: 195 mountain miles over the Cascade Range to Eugene, Oregon.

In addition to its operating significance, Dunsmuir serves as Amtrak's station for the Mount Shasta ski area and the Whiskeytown-Shasta-Trinity National Recreation Area.

327.4 **Mount Shasta** *409.7.* Glistening Mount Shasta, 14,160 feet high, is the queen peak of the Cascade Range. Like Mount Lassen, it is another in the chain of volcanos extending down the Pacific Coast into California. It is considered extinct today—but then, they thought

Mount St. Helens was extinct, too, a few years ago. You can see glaciers and the scars of lava flows on its slopes.

335.4 **Black Butte** *401.7*. In the shadow of a 6,343-foot peak of volcanic rock is Black Butte station, a railroad junction where the Southern Pacific splits. One fork goes on to Eugene by way of Ashland and Grants Pass, Oregon. This is called the Siskiyou Line. The other fork turns east and goes to Eugene by way of Klamath Falls. Amtrak passenger trains and most heavy freights use this route, the so-called Cascade Line.

The Siskiyou route was built first. When it was finished, in 1887, it gave Portland and the Northwest their first rail link with Oakland. But in 1927, barely half a century ago, the Southern Pacific completed the new Cascade route, which has easier grades than the original route. Happily for Amtrak passengers, the Cascade Line also has the more spectacular scenery.

358.7 **Grass Lake, Calif.** *378.4*. Grass Lake is at the top of the long grade up from Dunsmuir. At 5,063 feet above sea level, it is the highest point en route from Oakland to Portland. From here to Crescent Lake the railroad crosses a high, barren, windswept mountain plain.

418.3 **KLAMATH FALLS, OREG.** *318.8*. At this stop, crews change, locomotives are refueled if necessary, and the car inspectors go down the train with their hammers, tapping the wheels, looking for cracks or evidence of metal fatigue. The station at Klamath Falls serves all of southern Oregon, including the nearby town of Altamont.

445.5 **Chiloquin** *291.6*. Here the train crosses the Sprague River. To the northwest is Crater Lake, where an ancient volcano has filled with water to make an unusual and strikingly beautiful scenic attraction. Crater Lake National Park is about a 30-mile drive from Chiloquin.

492.1 **CHEMULT** *245.0*. This is the station for Bend, Oregon, and its surrounding natural recreation areas, including Bachelor Butte Ski Area. Connecting bus service is available.

517.4 **Crescent Lake** *219.7*. This is a pretty mountain lake near the summit of the Cascade Range.

525.5 **Cascade Summit** *211.6*. Here the elevation is 4,885 feet above sea level, at the crest of Willamette Pass and summit of the Cascade Range. Unlike the level mountain plain on the south side of the pass, the north side drops 3,600 feet in the next 44 miles to Oakridge. Southbound freight trains must climb this hill on grades as stiff as 1.7 percent, through 19 tunnels totaling almost 4 miles in length. In winter snowslides are a problem. They have been known to reach a depth of 25 feet. Slide detectors, which look like fences, have been installed along the tracks at likely slide locations. If one of these is knocked down, it sends a warning signal and the plows and snow shovelers come out to clear the tracks. The area is also subject to violent windstorms and howling blizzards—not the most pleasant corner of the world in winter.

But is it beautiful! Near the summit you get a stunning view of the Cascade Range and Salt Creek Canyon, down which the railroad winds and loops as it seeks a lower elevation. Northbound, this entire section is covered in daylight, and once you see it you'll not soon forget it.

569.3 **Oakridge** *167.8.* This town is at the bottom of the big hill from Cascade Summit. From this point to Eugene, the rails follow the Willamette River (pronounced *Will-lam'-ette,* with the accent on the second syllable).

589.4 **Minnow** *147.7.* To the north of the train (right side, going north) is Lookout Point Lake, backed up behind Meridian Dam. This huge flood-control project, built in 1953, caused the relocation of 22 miles of track; the original right-of-way is now underwater.

613.4 **EUGENE** *123.7.* This is the second largest city in Oregon and home of the University of Oregon. Most of the state's population lives in the corridor that extends from Eugene north to Portland, along the valley of the Willamette River. The Coast Range separates this valley from the Pacific shore, which lacks the natural harbors that have made San Francisco and Seattle port cities. By contrast, Oregon is sparsely settled along the coast, and its leading port, Portland, is accessible only by the Columbia River.

657.0 **ALBANY** *80.1.* This town was named after Albany, New York. Most of the pioneers in Oregon were fervent antislavery people from the New England states or New York, and they naturally gave many of their new communities the names of the towns from which they had come. Albany contains the station for adjacent Corvallis, home of Oregon State University.

684.3 **SALEM** *52.8.* Salem is the capital of Oregon, lying as it does midway between Portland and Eugene, the state's two largest cities. The town was founded in 1840 by Methodist missionaries in what was then the Oregon Territory. Willamette University, founded in 1842, has the honor of being the oldest college in the Pacific Northwest. Salem was territorial capital of Oregon during the 1850s, and when Oregon entered the Union as the thirty-third state in 1859, it assumed the role of state capital easily enough. The current population is around 100,000.

730.2 **East Milwaukie** *6.9.* It may be "Milwaukee" in Wisconsin; but it's "Milwaukie," with an *i,* in Oregon. And by the way, don't say, *Ora-gon.* The natives pronounce the name *Ora-gun.*

736.4 **East Portland** *0.7.* This is the junction with the Union Pacific's Columbia River line, used by Amtrak's Salt Lake City—Portland *Pioneer.*

Beyond the junction, passenger trains cross the Willamette River on a double-decked steel bridge. Autos use the top level of this structure; trains use the lower deck. Coming off the bridge, there is a sharp right curve leading directly into Portland's Union Station.

737.1 **PORTLAND.** *0.0.* For information on the city, see section 2.34.

0.0 **PORTLAND** *186.4.*

4.3 **Willbridge** *182.1.* The name is a contraction of "Willamette Bridge." Here trains cross the river to the east bank and pass through the northwest corner of Portland. Near Willbridge is the port area of Portland, reached from the Pacific by the Columbia River.

7.0 **East St. John's, Oreg.** *179.4.* North of here the tracks pass Delta Park (left side of the train, going north) and the Multnomah County Expo Center, then cross the Columbia and enter the state of Washington.

10.0 **VANCOUVER, WASH.** *176.4.* A British seaman, Captain George Vancouver, surveyed Puget Sound in 1792; and a fort named after him was established on the north bank of the Columbia. Around

PORTLAND—SEATTLE

Northbound/miles		miles/Southbound
0.0	PORTLAND	186.4
2.0	Lake Yard	184.4
4.3	Willbridge	182.1
7.0	East St. John's	179.4
8.1	North Portland, Oreg.	178.3
10.0	VANCOUVER, WASH.	176.4
13.1	Vancouver Jct.	173.3
24.3	Ridgefield	162.1
29.7	Woodland	156.7
38.8	Kalama	147.6
45.2	Longview Jct.	141.2
49.0	KELSO-LONGVIEW	137.4
50.5	Rocky Point	135.9
52.8	Ostrander	133.6
59.0	Castle Rock	127.4
69.3	Vader	117.1
75.0	Winlock	111.4
81.3	Napavine	105.1
88.6	Chehalis	97.8
92.3	CENTRALIA	94.1
96.8	Wabash	89.6
99.6	Bucoda	86.8
102.8	Tenino Jct.	83.6
111.4	EAST OLYMPIA	75.0

116.5	Kyro	69.9
118.1	St. Clair	68.3
121.9	Nisqually	64.5
128.6	Ketron	57.8
130.7	Steilacoom	55.7
136.3	Titlow	50.1
143.6	McCarver Street	42.8
146.0	U.P. Jct.	40.4
146.3	TACOMA	40.1
148.2	Reservation	38.2
154.5	Puyallup	31.9
155.9	Meeker	30.5
157.4	Sumner	29.0
164.9	Auburn	21.5
170.1	Kent	16.3
174.2	Orillia	12.2
176.9	Black River	9.5
178.5	South Seattle	7.9
183.1	Argo	3.3
186.4	SEATTLE (King Street Sta.)	0.0

Bus Connection to Vancouver, B.C.

the fort a town grew up; and while Vancouver, Washington, has never rivaled its namesake city in Canada, it is nevertheless a thriving place. The Fort Vancouver National Historic site is just east of the town.

From Vancouver to Kelso-Longview the route parallels the Columbia River, which at this point flows northward, although the river is seldom in sight of the rails.

49.0 **KELSO-LONGVIEW** *137.4.* The station here serves both adjoining towns. Here the Columbia swings west toward Astoria and the Pacific Ocean, while the railroad continues northward to Seattle.

To the east (right side, going north) 30 miles away is Mount St. Helens. Nearly 10,000 feet high, this volcano was considered extinct until 1980, when it staged several spectacular eruptions. It continues to be active. It was named for Alleyne Fitzhugh, first Baron St. Helens, once British ambassador to Madrid. He negotiated the treaty by which England acquired Spanish claims to the Pacific Northwest.

92.3 **CENTRALIA** *94.1.* A look at the mileage table tells you how Centralia got its name. It's midway between Portland and Seattle. Off in the distance to the east (right side of the train, northbound) towers the majestic snow-covered bulk of Mount Rainier. Just its height—14,410 feet above sea level—would make Mount Rainier impressive. But what makes this extinct volcano truly spectacular is the way it seems to float in air. The mountain is white because it's covered with glaciers—26 of them, blanketing 40 square miles of slopes.

111.4 **EAST OLYMPIA** *75.0.* Ask the next hundred Americans you meet to name the capital of Washington, and if they aren't from

352

The majestic beauty of the Olympic peninsula in Washington state.

Lake Chelan, in the Lake Chelan National Recreation Area, is the gateway to the North Cascade mountains.

the Northwest, they'll probably say Seattle or Tacoma. Actually, the capital is Olympia, just west of this station.

From here to Seattle the rails skirt the shore of Puget Sound, one of the world's great natural harbors. The sound is separated from the Pacific by the Olympic Peninsula and connected with it by the broad Strait of Juan de Fuca.

130.7 **Steilacoom** *55.7.* Lumbering still is the big industry in this part of Washington. The state's forests provide lumber for construction as well as pulpwood for papermaking. You may see lines of freight cars loaded with raw logs or finished boards, ready for shipment east or for export from the ports of Seattle and Tacoma.

146.3 **TACOMA** *40.1.* Tacoma is the third-largest city in Washington, with a population of more than 150,000. It is a major Puget Sound port and also an industrial center. It owes its growth to the arrival of the Northern Pacific Railroad, opened for transcontinental traffic in 1883.

164.9 **Auburn** *21.5.* This is the junction with the line from Spokane via Stampede Pass, formerly the main line of the Northern Pacific. This route used to be served by Amtrak's *Empire Builder* before it was shifted to the Cascade Tunnel line late in 1981. Stampede Pass sees relatively light traffic now; most of the through freight trains also go by way of the Cascade Tunnel and Wenatchee. At Auburn is an old roundhouse where locomotives and snow-fighting equipment are kept, ready for use in Stampede Pass.

170.1 **Kent** *16.3.* Kent is a tidy town in a pretty dairy-farming area. Mount Rainier is still visible, south and east of the train (look back from the right-side windows, going toward Seattle).

183.1 **Argo** *3.3.* Mention Seattle and someone is bound to bring up the Boeing Company, the aerospace firm that has its headquarters and factories there. Entering Seattle, Amtrak trains pass some of the Boeing facilities (left side of the train, going north). Not far from here is Sea-Tac Airport, which serves both Tacoma and Seattle and accounts for low-flying air traffic overhead.

186.4 **SEATTLE** *0.0.* As the train enters the city, the large cranes that unload ships in the harbor can be seen towering overhead to the west side of the train (left side, going north). The Kingdome, Seattle's indoor baseball, football, and basketball stadium, sits on a parcel of land adjacent to the King Street Station, Amtrak's Seattle facility.

For information on the city, see section 2.47.

3.44   Chicago—Denver—Salt Lake City— Oakland

This is the route of the *California Zephyr,* which runs daily between Chicago and San Francisco Bay through some of the most spectacular scenery in the United States. The *Zephyr* uses the Burlington Northern's tracks from Chicago to Denver, then goes through the heart of the Colorado Rockies and across the Utah deserts via the tracks of the Denver and Rio Grande Western Railway to Salt Lake City. The train skirts Great Salt Lake, races across the Nevada sagebrush during the dark hours, and pauses at Reno. Then it climbs over the Sierras using tracks of the Southern Pacific Railroad—part of the original transcontinental railroad of 1869. Through coaches and sleeping cars for Los Angeles and the Pacific Northwest operate on the *Zephyr* east of Salt Lake, giving passengers for those points a chance to enjoy the majestic Rocky Mountains en route. You cannot say that you have seen the United States until you have taken this trip. It's the experience of a lifetime.

For notes on the route from Chicago to Galesburg, see section 3.36.

162.4 **GALESBURG** *871.4*.   The *California Zephyr* uses the former Burlington Route passenger station on Seminary Street. After leaving the station, look to the right side of the train (going west) for a quick glimpse of the Knox College campus.

179.1 **Monmouth** *854.7*.   Monmouth is a quiet little town, home of a small college, and a trading center for the surrounding farms. But it did attract some national attention in 1961, when during one hot summer week the town experienced a series of spectacular fires. Arson was the obvious cause, and for four consecutive blazing nights the Monmouth Firebug was at work. The town was like an armed camp, alive with police, state patrolmen, and civilian volunteers conducting a round-the-clock vigil to protect the town. They never found the arsonist, but he has never struck again.

Monmouth also has one other claim to fame: Wyatt Earp, one of the most famous heros of the Old West, was born here in 1848.

190.6 **Biggsville** *843.2*.   Here the rails enter the valley of Cedar Creek, following it on an easy downgrade to the Mississippi.

202.5 **Connet, Ill.** *831.3*.   The last miles before the Mississippi River bridge are built through marshy bottom lands. Depending on the season, much of this ground can be underwater.

This is perhaps Amtrak's most picturesque crossing of the great Mississippi, the Father of Waters. The river is broad here, giving a feeling of serenity as well as of majestic power as it flows relentlessly beneath the great steel bridge. It's easy to imagine a white steamboat coughing its way upriver.

205.4 **BURLINGTON, IOWA** *828.4. Iowa* is an Indian word meaning "the land beyond"—beyond the Mississippi, that is. Burlington's roots go all the way back to Indian times, when the site was a fur-trading post. Later, as steamboating developed on the Missis-

CHICAGO—DENVER

Westbound/miles		miles/Eastbound
0.0	CHICAGO (Union Sta.)	1033.8
1.7	Halsted St.	1032.1
3.7	Western Ave.	1030.1
6.9	Cicero	1026.9
8.5	Clyde	1025.3
9.0	LaVergne	1024.8
9.6	Berwyn	1024.2
10.0	Harlem Avenue	1023.8
11.0	Riverside	1022.8
11.7	Hollywood	1022.1
12.2	Brookfield	1021.6
13.0	Congress Park	1020.8
13.8	La Grange Rd.	1020.0
14.1	Stone Avenue	1019.7
15.4	Western Springs	1018.4
16.3	Highlands	1017.5
16.8	Hinsdale	1017.0
17.8	West Hinsdale	1016.0
18.2	Clarendon Hills	1015.6
19.4	Westmont	1014.4
20.3	Fairview Avenue	1013.5
21.1	Downers Grove	1012.7
22.6	Belmont	1011.2
24.4	Lisle	1009.4
28.4	Naperville	1005.4
33.4	Eola	1000.4
37.8	AURORA	996.0
40.0	Montgomery	993.8
45.5	Bristol	988.3
51.5	Plano	982.3
55.9	Sandwich	977.9
59.2	Somonauk	974.6
65.3	Leland	968.5
72.1	Earlville	961.7
78.1	Meriden	955.7

82.7	Mendota	951.1
91.4	Arlington	942.4
95.3	Zearing	938.5
98.4	Malden	935.4
104.2	Princeton	929.6
110.7	Wyanet	923.1
116.6	Buda	917.2
123.0	Neponset	910.8
131.0	Kewaunee	902.8
139.3	Galva	894.5
146.7	Oneida	887.1
155.1	Wataga	878.7
157.7	Bishop	876.1
162.4	GALESBURG	871.4

162.4	GALESBURG	871.4
168.3	Graham	865.5
171.4	Cameron	862.4
179.1	Monmouth	854.7
184.0	Kirkwood	849.8
190.6	Biggsville	843.2
196.1	Gladstone	837.7
202.5	Connett, Ill.	831.3
204.2	Illinois Jct., Iowa	829.6
205.4	BURLINGTON	828.4
212.5	Dayman	821.3
218.3	Danville	815.5
224.6	New London	809.2
233.2	MOUNT PLEASANT	800.6
243.7	Lockridge	790.1
250.2	Beckwith	783.6
255.2	Fairfield	778.6
266.1	Batavia	767.7
273.4	Agency City	760.4
279.6	OTTUMWA	754.2
290.8	Dudley	743.0
301.9	Maxon	731.9
303.7	Albia	730.1
307.5	Halpin	726.3
318.6	Melrose	715.2
326.9	Russell	706.9
334.3	Chariton	699.5
341.7	Shannon	692.1
359.7	OSCEOLA	674.1
370.4	Murray	663.4
375.9	Thayer	657.9
379.8	Talmadge Jct.	654.0
383.6	Afton	650.2
392.9	CRESTON	640.9

392.9	CRESTON	640.9
398.6	Cromwell	635.2
406.7	Prescott	627.1
413.7	Corning	620.1

422.7	Nodaway	611.1
427.4	Villisca	606.4
435.2	Stanton	598.6
442.4	Red Oak	591.4
448.1	McPherson	585.7
451.7	Emerson	582.1
456.9	Hastings	576.9
461.7	Malvern	572.1
467.9	Balfour	565.9
471.4	Glenwood	562.4
475.0	Pacific Jct.	558.8
480.7	Folsom	553.1
486.0	Island Park	547.8
492.1	CB Yard	541.7
493.2	BN Jct. Iowa	540.6
496.1	OMAHA, NEBR.	537.7
499.6	South Omaha	534.2
503.7	Ralston	530.1
510.6	Chalco	523.2
516.9	Gretna	516.9
520.5	Melia	513.3
526.4	Ashland	507.4
533.2	Greenwood	500.6
538.6	Waverly	495.2
543.2	Baird	490.6
545.8	Havelock	488.0
550.9	LINCOLN	482.9

550.9	LINCOLN	482.9
551.4	Hall	482.4
552.7	Hobson	481.1
554.7	Cushman	479.1
558.7	Cobb	475.1
561.2	Denton	472.6
568.0	Berks	465.8
571.5	Crete	462.3
579.8	Dorchester	454.0
588.9	Friend	444.9
597.5	Exeter	436.3
604.7	Fairmont	429.1
611.5	Grafton	422.3
619.6	Sutton	414.2
623.9	Saronville	409.9
632.3	Harvard	401.5
639.1	Inland	394.7
643.6	Halloran	390.2
646.5	Brick Yard	387.3
647.8	HASTINGS	386.0
649.6	Gaines	384.2
654.2	Juniata	379.6
662.5	Kenesaw	371.3
670.2	Heartwell	363.6
679.8	Minden	354.0
689.4	Axtell	344.4

357

695.9	Funk	337.9
702.5	HOLDREGE	331.3
709.9	Atlanta	323.9
718.4	Mascot	315.4
725.5	Oxford	308.3
733.3	Edison	300.5
740.0	Arapahoe	293.8
745.9	Holbrook	287.9
754.3	Cambridge	279.5
762.1	Bartley	271.7
768.0	Indianola	265.8
779.6	McCOOK (CT)	254.2

779.6	McCOOK (MT)	254.2
784.2	Perry	249.6
790.8	Culbertson	243.0
801.0	Trenton	232.8
812.8	Stratton	221.0
822.4	Max	211.4
830.8	Benkelman	203.0
841.3	Parks	192.5
852.8	Haigler, Nebr.	181.0
869.2	Wray, Colo.	164.6
876.6	Robb	157.2
883.8	Eckley	150.0
896.4	Yuma	137.4
906.0	Calhoun	127.8
907.5	Otis	126.3
914.7	Platner	119.1
922.5	AKRON	111.3

922.5	AKRON	111.3
929.3	Xenia	104.5
935.6	Pinneo	98.2
946.5	Brush	87.3
950.1	Lodi	83.7
956.0	FORT MORGAN	77.8
960.4	Bijou	73.4
970.6	Wiggins	63.2
980.7	Crest	53.1
987.0	Roggen	46.8
992.4	Tampa	41.4
996.9	Keensburg	36.9
1004.5	Hudson	29.3
1016.0	Barr	17.8
1023.4	Irondale	10.4
1026.9	Commerce City	6.9
1028.3	Sand Creek	5.5
1032.6	31st Street	1.2
1033.8	DENVER	0.0

sippi, Burlington became a river port, and the geography of the old town still reflects its former orientation toward river trade. The Amtrak station is on the riverbank just south of the central business district.

After leaving the station, trains curve to the left, cross several streets, and begin to assault the stiff grade up from the river valley, which is known as West Burlington Hill. This is a historic spot; in tests conducted on this grade, George Westinghouse demonstrated the effectiveness of his air brake—probably the greatest single safety improvement developed in the railroad business since wheels first turned on rails. At the top of the hill are the buildings of the West Burlington shops, built by the predecessor Chicago, Burlington and Quincy railroad.

233.2 **MOUNT PLEASANT** *800.6.* This little town, site of Iowa Wesleyan College, is best known for its Old Settlers and Threshers Heritage Museum, whose collection of antique steam-driven farm machinery is sure to delight you. Each September Mount Pleasant plays host to the Old Settlers' Reunion, which attracts thousands of visitors.

Iowa is an appropriate spot for a farming museum, for this state produces 10 percent of all the foodstuffs raised in the United States. The biggest crop, of course, is corn, much of which is fed to cattle and hogs.

Mount Pleasant contains the closest Amtrak station to Iowa City, site of the University of Iowa, which lies 50 miles north.

273.4 **Agency City** *760.4.* The name derives from an Indian agency, or trading post, having been located here. Agency City is the burial place of Chief Wapello, an important Indian leader.

279.6 **OTTUMWA** *754.2.* Ottumwa rises on terraces above the Des Moines River, a tributary of the Mississippi, which bisects the town. Its name is said to derive from Indian speech as mispronounced by the early French explorers. At Ottumwa the rails cross the Des Moines, then turn up the river and run parallel to it for 8 miles to Chillicothe before turning west again.

303.7 **Albia** *730.1.* Because "Iowa" and "farming" are so nearly synonymous in the public mind, most folks don't realize that the state is far from flat. Rather, it's full of small hills and coursed by rivers and streams—and in some of those hills is coal. The area south of Albia once was a flourishing coal field, though it is less important today. Sixty miles north of Albia is Grinnell, a college town named for Josiah B. Grinnell, the young man to whom Horace Greely is supposed to have said, "Go West, young man." Of course, Greely never actually said it—but Grinnell went west anyhow and founded this town. Grinnell College enjoys an outstanding reputation among small liberal-arts institutions.

359.7 **OSCEOLA** *674.1.* Osceola was a famous Seminole war chief. The town contains Amtrak's station for Des Moines, Iowa's capital and largest city, which is 50 miles north.

392.9 **CRESTON** *640.9.* Creston's name is self-explanatory: At 1,300 feet above sea level, it is the highest point on the Burlington Northern line east of the Missouri River, and is built on the summit of a ridge between the Des Moines and Missouri River valleys—a perfect place for a railroad town. That's exactly what Creston is—a division point and, in steam days, an engine-changing point. Today's diesels roll right through, but crews still change here.

From Creston to Pacific Junction, in the Missouri valley, it's a steady downgrade all the way. There are many curves, especially farther west, as the track snakes around the hills to achieve a gentler pitch.

475.0 **Pacific Junction, Iowa** *558.8.* Three Burlington Northern routes converge here. One goes south to Kansas City; a second goes north to Council Bluffs; and the third (presently used by Amtrak) goes straight west to cross the Missouri River. "P Junction," as the railroaders call it, also has freight yards and other railroad facilities.

West of the junction is the Missouri River bridge leading to Plattsmouth, Nebraska. Here Amtrak trains turn north parallel to the river for the run up to Omaha, using tracks owned by the Missouri Pacific.

496.1 **OMAHA, NEBR.** *537.7.* For information on the city, see section 2.30. Leaving Omaha, the rails climb up out of the Missouri valley by winding along the side of a bluff.

526.4 **Ashland** *507.4.* This is the junction with a freight-only cutoff that comes straight west from Plattsmouth, bypassing Omaha altogether.

545.8 **Havelock** *488.0.* The railroad shops here build and repair equipment for the entire Burlington Northern system.

550.9 **LINCOLN** *482.9.* Capital of Nebraska, Lincoln is the state's second-largest city and the home of the University of Nebraska (whose football stadium can be seen to the south). The city was originally called Lancaster but was renamed in honor of Abraham Lincoln in 1867, when Nebraska was admitted to the Union and the state capital was established here. (The territorial capital had been at Omaha.)

The capitol building is unique. Instead of the usual Greek- or Romanesque-style building, it is a tower 400 feet high, capped with a dome. It houses an unusual form of government as well, for Nebraska has a unicameral legislature—only one house.

From the railroading point of view, Lincoln is the hub of Burlington Northern lines west of the Missouri, with tracks spreading out in six directions. It is a crew-change and servicing stop for Amtrak trains.

568.0 **Berks** *465.8.* Take a careful look at the list of stations between this point and Minden (111 miles). The railroad's management named town sites in alphabetical order, with some exceptions, as it built across the unsettled prairie.

From about this point all the way to Denver the land gradually slopes up toward the Rockies. The rise is imperceptible, but between the Missouri and the Rockies the gain in elevation is nearly a mile. The land looks different, too—no longer the green, fertile farmland of Illinois and Iowa. When the first white settlers came, Nebraska was a nearly treeless plain. The Rockies tend to hold the rain clouds, so the Great Plains east of the mountains get very little natural moisture; wheat farming is carried on today by means of irrigation and dry-farming methods. Still, those great empty stretches are awesome—and lonesome—even now.

647.8 **HASTINGS** *386.0.* This is a railroad division point 20 miles south of Grand Island. Forty miles south, Red Cloud, the home of author Willa Cather, is preserved as a memorial to the pioneers who settled on this hostile prairie.

679.8 **Minden** *354.0.* The Pioneer Village, a historical re-creation that displays more than 30,000 items relating to early life on the prairies, is here. The valley of the Platte, the great natural pathway to the West, along which the old Oregon Trail ran, is 10 miles north. From this point on, however, Burlington Northern rails run southwest and leave the Platte Valley behind.

725.5 **Oxford** *308.3.* At this little town the tracks enter the valley of the Republican River, which they will follow all the way into Colorado. The river was named for the political party that led the Union war effort and passed the Homestead Act, the Transcontinental Railroad Bill, the Land Grant College Act, and the ordinance that admitted Nebraska to the Union.

779.6 **McCOOK** *254.2.* This is a railroad division point and home of the former Nebraska senator George Norris. Senator Norris was the father of the Federal Reserve Banking system and was a leader in the Progressive movement's attempts to reform American politics. He was also the author of the Twentieth Amendment to the U.S. Constitution, which eliminated the so-called lame duck session of Congress.

McCook is the dividing line between the Central and Mountain time zones. Set your watch accordingly.

852.8 **Haigler, Nebr.** *181.0.* Not only is this the westernmost town in southern Nebraska, but it's also within a mile of the Kansas state line to the south.

869.2 **Wray, Colo.** *164.6.* It's easy to think of Colorado in terms of the spectacular high peaks of the Rockies, but a third of the state is arid and relatively flat, given over to cattle grazing and wheat farming. Wray is a small trading town for the surrounding ranches and farms. At this point, after following the Republican River and the North Fork for 143 miles, the railroad finally leaves the river to strike westward across country.

922.5 **AKRON** *111.3.* *Akron* is a Greek word meaning "high"—though this part of Colorado is not nearly as elevated as the Rocky Mountain area west of Denver. If the weather is clear, you may get your first glimpse of the high mountains somewhere along here. They look deceptively tiny from a distance, but don't be fooled—Colorado contains more than a thousand peaks above the 10,000-foot level.

Akron is a railroad crew-changing point, which accounts for the stop here at a town whose total population is less than 2,000. In addition to the railroad payroll, the town is supported by agriculture, mainly cattle grazing and sugar-beet farming.

956.0 **FORT MORGAN** *77.8.* Fort Morgan, on the south bank of the South Platte River, likes to call itself the bean capital of America. Jack's Bean Company stands right beside the tracks (north side).

1026.9 **Commerce City** *6.9.* On the way into Denver, look for the big stockyards of the nation's largest sheep market. There are also grain elevators, oil depots, and other industrial facilities along here.

1033.8 **DENVER** *0.0.* Amtrak trains enter Denver from the northeast and stop at the Union Station at the foot of 17th Street, within walking distance of the central business district and convenient to all parts of the metropolitan area. The *California Zephyr* makes a half-hour stop here, allowing passengers time to stretch their legs.

For information on the city, see section 2.15.

0.0 **DENVER** *570.0.* When the first transcontinental railroad was surveyed, Denver, having been founded before the Civil War, fully expected to be an important station on that line. However, Grenville M. Dodge, boss of the Union Pacific, found the mountains directly west of the city to be too rugged for a railroad. He decided to route the Union Pacific 100 miles north of Denver, leaving the Colorado capital stranded away from any main-line railroad to the west.

For more than 30 years angry Denverites fumed, but scheme after scheme failed to get Denver on a main route to the West. One of those angry Denverites was David Moffat, who had arrived from New York in 1860 when he was twenty-one and Denver was two. He had already made and lost a fortune in banking and real estate back home, and he was soon in business in his new city—first running a store, then as a leading banker. There was hardly a major civic project in which he did not have a hand over a 40-year period. In all this time, however, he was never able to accomplish his ultimate dream: to rectify General Dodge's decision and put Denver on a main line to the west.

In February 1902 Moffat—then sixty-three years old and in semiretirement—made a momentous decision: He would build a new main line to Utah which would compete with the Union Pacific, and in the process he would challenge the main range directly west of Denver.

The rails climb the sheer face of the Rockies, enter South Boulder Canyon high on its southern wall, and wind among crags and crevices and through twenty-nine tunnels before reaching the Moffat Tunnel under the Continental Divide. Then the tracks follow the Fraser River to Granby, and follow the Colorado westward from there through Byers and Gore canyons to Bond Station. Today this railroad line is David Moffat's enduring monument. He called his new line the Denver, Northwestern and Pacific, and now it forms the spectacular first 129 miles of Amtrak's direct route west from Denver.

3.3 **Utah Junction** *566.7.* Nothing came easily for Moffat, including his entrance into Denver. The Union Pacific used all its con-

DENVER—SALT LAKE CITY

Westbound/miles		*miles/Eastbound*
0.0	DENVER	570.0
3.3	Utah Jct.	566.7
6.8	Ralston	563.2
12.9	Leyden Jct.	557.1
17.8	Arena	552.2
24.3	Plainview	545.7
27.1	Scenic	542.9
31.5	Crescent	538.5
33.5	Miramonte	536.5
36.9	Pine Cliff	533.1
41.7	Rollinsville	528.3
46.9	Telland	523.1
50.0	East Portal	520.0
	Moffat Tunnel (6.2 mi.)	
56.9	Winter Park	513.1
57.9	Vasquez	512.1
62.1	Fraser	507.9
65.9	Tabernash	504.1
75.5	GRANBY	494.5
86.1	Hot Sulphur Springs	483.9
91.0	Parshall	479.0
98.0	Troublesome	472.0
103.2	Kremmling	466.8
105.8	Gore	464.2
116.1	Radium	453.9
126.1	State Bridge	443.9
129.3	BOND (Orestod)	440.7
129.3	Bond	440.7
134.9	Glen	435.1
144.6	Burns	425.4
148.8	Sylvan	421.2
157.7	Sweetwater	412.3
166.8	Dotsero	403.2
175.4	Shoshone	394.6

siderable influence to try to keep Moffat out of the city, and they did keep his new line out of the Union Station for many years. Utah Junction was the site of the old Moffat line's shops, which were torn down after Moffat's line became part of the Rio Grande.

At this point the rails swing to the west (left) on a broad curve and begin to climb the long 2 percent (106 feet up for every mile forward) grade that extends all the way to the Moffat Tunnel, 47 miles away. In this stretch the rails must gain 4,000 feet of altitude—one of the toughest sustained climbs in America.

6.8 **Ralston** *562.9.* The railroad climbs through suburban Denver parallel to Ralston Creek, going upgrade along a natural escarpment known as the Leyden Ramp. Use of this natural incline up toward the base of the mountains was a master stroke by H. A. Sumner, the brilliant locating engineer employed by David Moffat to find a route for his new railroad. It meant that the tracks achieved a maximum altitude possible before reaching the face of the Rockies—and anything gained here is a tremendous help farther on.

12.9 **Leyden Junction** *557.1.* To the south (left side, going west) are traces of the Leyden coal mines and the Denver Tramways electric line that served them until 1950. This was once another of David Moffat's many properties. He was forced to sell his stock in it to help pay for his railroad line.

17.8 **Arena** *552.2.* This is the top of the natural Leyden Ramp. Ahead lie the almost sheer Rockies. One would have thought that Sumner would immediately turn his survey northward along the face of the Front Range. Instead he achieved another master stroke at this point: a sweeping horseshoe-and-a-half curve that winds around to the south before turning back north. This curve, with a radius of 10 degrees, enables the railroad to gain a precious 200 feet in altitude before beginning its climb along the mountain walls. Because of its radius, this is called the ''Big Ten'' curve.

The south side of the Big Ten is high on an embankment, and high winds have been a problem here; gusts have occasionally blown trains right off the track. Consequently, the Denver & Rio Grande railroad has parked a long string of hopper cars filled with rock on a spur track beside the main line, where they serve as an impromptu wind screen.

Not far beyond the Big Ten is the mouth of Coal Creek Canyon, too wide and deep to be bridged. Here Sumner employed a favorite trick of railroad builders in the mountains: He turned his line up the canyon for a mile or so, crossed it on a high bridge, then worked his way back along the opposite side until the tracks reached the face of the Front Range again—but this time, many feet higher than on the other side of the canyon.

In turning out of Coal Creek Canyon, Sumner drilled the first of some twenty-nine tunnels that had to be built in the next 13 miles to Pine Cliff. Although some of these have since been bypassed or dynamited, the *California Zephyr* still does a lot of popping into and out of tunnels ranging from 60 feet to a third of a mile in length.

24.3 **Plainview** *545.7.* No need to ask how this place got its name—the rails are now high enough on the Front Range to provide spectacular views of the east (right side of the train, leaving Denver). It is said that on a clear day one can see a hundred miles or more across the plains. Coming into Denver at night, the sight of the city lights is equally arresting.

About 3 miles beyond Plainview the tracks curve through Tunnel Eight and enter South Boulder Canyon. At this point the stream bed is 500 feet below the railroad grade, which hangs along the south rim of the canyon like a steel thread, still climbing at the same steady rate of 106 feet per mile. The canyon floor rises much more steeply, however, so the defile appears to get shallower as you go westward.

31.5 **Crescent** *538.5.* The site is named for Crescent Mountain, over 8,000 feet high, which rises to the south. At this point there is a series of curves, and the main range of the Rockies suddenly comes into view directly ahead. Below in the canyon, a dam has created a big reservoir, part of Denver's water-supply system. Between Crescent and Pine Cliff a succession of tunnels carry the rails through the huge granite spurs that make up the canyon wall.

36.9 **Pine Cliff** *533.1.* At this point the stream and the railroad are at last side by side, still on a grade of 2 percent. From Pine Cliff to Rollinsville, the road runs through a shallow gorge.

41.7 **Rollinsville** *528.3.* The town is named for its founder, a pioneer by the name of J. G. Rollins who built a wagon road from here over what was then called Boulder Pass, a staggering 11,680 feet above sea level. Later the pass was renamed in his honor, and it is called Rollins Pass today.

From this point west for the next 6 miles, the tracks run along South Boulder Creek through an open, flat valley—but the pitch is still the same, 106 feet up for every mile, leading up the main range of the Rockies that now looms straight ahead.

Alongside the tracks runs a dirt road. This is the Rollins Pass Highway, maintained by the U.S. Forest Service. It crosses Rollins Pass on the grade originally built by the Denver, Northwestern and Pacific as an interim measure until a tunnel could be constructed. But Moffat ran out of money, the tunnel project was abandoned for 20 years, and trains fought their way over Rollins Pass on the highest standard-gauge railroad ever built in North America. Today you can drive over this route.

46.9 **Tolland** *523.1.* Here the valley of the South Boulder opens into a mountain meadow, or "park." At this point the Moffat line once had an engine house and other facilities for servicing the locomotives used to help trains over Rollins Pass. There was also an eating house, a dance hall, and a hotel run by a Mrs. Toll, who gave her name to the community.

Ahead and to the right (going west) you will see a forested mountain. Across it are three distinct lines, the three levels of the "Giants' Ladder," the series of loops by which Moffat and Sumner began the staggering climb over Rollins Pass. You will notice that the top level is angled more steeply than the lower two; this is because the lower rungs were intended to lead to a tunnel under the summit, and are thus on a 2 percent grade. The top rung, however, was meant to be temporary; thus it was built on a grade of 4 percent, or 211 feet to a mile—the steepest grade considered operable with standard-gauge equipment. This "temporary" track remained in service for 24 years, carrying trains across the roof of the continent.

Beyond Tolland the railroad continues west along the South Boulder Creek for another 3 miles, right to the base of the main range.

50.0 **East Portal** *520.0.* Here the canyon closes in. The old Rollins Pass line curves sharply away to the north (right side, going west) and begins to climb the Giants' Ladder, while dead ahead is the concrete portal of the Moffat Tunnel.

David Moffat died in 1910, his dream railroad across the Rockies still unfinished. But in 1923 Denver's growing demand for water led to construction of two tunnels under James Peak at an altitude of 9,000 feet. One was for water, the other for the railroad.

Construction took five years, while the Moffat Road's trains continued to fight their way through snowdrifts 30 feet high on Rollins Pass. But at last, in February 1928, the first train ran through the Moffat Tunnel—the third longest bore in the Western Hemisphere.

The tunnel, 6.2 miles long, slopes gradually upward from both ends toward the apex, where it is 9,239 feet above sea level. It is 16 feet wide, 24 feet high, and totally dark inside. The trip through the Moffat takes about ten minutes. By way of comparison, freight trains used to take five or six hours to get over Rollins Pass. Incidentally, the temperature inside the tunnel remains constant all year at about 50 degrees.

56.9 **Winter Park** *513.1.* The western end of the Moffat Tunnel is at Winter Park, one of Colorado's most popular ski areas. U.S. 40 passes directly over the tunnel portal on its way over the 11,000-foot-high Berthoud Pass.

Just beyond the exit from the tunnel there is a sweeping curve to the north, which takes the railroad into the valley of the Fraser River, a tributary of the Colorado.

57.9 **Vasquez** *512.1.* This site is named for Vasquez Creek, which empties into the Fraser here. On the east side of the train (right side, going west) can be seen the remains of the old roadbed as it curves sharply away to begin the long, steep climb over Rollins Pass. The present Rollins Pass auto road ends here at its junction with U.S. 40.

62.1 **Fraser** *507.9.* A broad, flat plain opens up here. With perverse pride, Fraser calls itself "the Icebox of America." Frigid winds sweeping down along the Fraser, coupled with the absence of trees and other windbreaks, can bring the winter temperatures down to –50° F.

65.9 **Tabernash** *504.1.* Tabernash was the name of a local Indian chief. Before the Moffat Tunnel opened in 1928, this was a major operating point where helper engines were stationed to aid trains crossing Rollins Pass. Remains of the old enginehouse stood until recent years. Beyond Tabernash the grade eases to 1 percent as the tracks follow the Fraser River through shallow Fraser Canyon and on to the Colorado at Granby.

Tabernash is just as cold as Fraser—temperatures of -60° F. have been recorded, and standing trains have been known to freeze to the rails.

75.5 **GRANBY** *494.5.* Granby is at the confluence of the Fraser and the Colorado. From this point the railroad follows the Colorado River for 238 miles, all the way into Utah.

Granby is a station stop for the Rocky Mountain National Park, 15 miles north. Visitors to Colorado might do well to take the scenic train ride from Denver to Granby, then arrange to rent a car here and drive up through the park, returning to Boulder and Denver by Route 36. There are a number of dude ranches in the Granby vicinity that offer a different sort of vacation experience.

86.1 **Hot Sulphur Springs** *483.9.* This was a resort town even before the railroad was built. At Hot Sulphur the tracks cross from the south side of the Colorado to the north bank.

Between Hot Sulphur Springs and Parshall lies Byers Canyon—narrow, dark, and winding. The roadbed had to be blasted out of the canyon wall at more than one spot in this short defile.

91.0 **Parshall** *479.0.* This is at the west exit of Byers Canyon. The track continues to descend westbound at grades of 1 percent or less.

103.2 **Kremmling** *466.8.* At Kremmling the highways to the west—U.S. 40 and Route 84—turn north toward their crossings of the Park Range at Gore and Muddy passes. The railroad, however, following the Colorado, pushes straight ahead toward the forbidding entrance of Gore Canyon.

Gore is an amazing place. The sheer rock walls rise a thousand feet above the narrow defile through which the rails and the river run. Electric fences warn of rockslides, which are a not infrequent occurrence. The sun barely strikes the canyon floor, and then only for a short time around noon. There is no more spectacular spot in North America than this fearsome gorge, and it's only natural to feel relieved when the train bursts out of the canyon and back into the sunshine.

126.1 **State Bridge** *443.9.* This bridge carries Route 131 over the Colorado River. Route 131 comes up from Wolcott 15 miles south in Eagle River Canyon, where it connects with U.S. 6 and U.S. 24.

129.3 **Bond (Orestod)** *440.7.* There is no town here, just a railroad junction and division point where engine crews change.

Technically there are two stations here: Bond, on the main line, and Orestod, a few feet away and up the hill (right side of the train, going west). Orestod serves the branch line that begins climbing here to cross from the Colorado River valley to the Yampa. This was once the Moffat line's main line, which went as far as Craig, in northwestern Colorado, but never reached Utah. After 1928, however, it had two tremendous assets: its beautifully engineered line from Denver to the Moffat Tunnel and from Winter Park to Orestod, and the Moffat Tunnel itself. Moreover, at Dotsero, just 38 miles down the Colorado River, ran the main line of the Denver and Rio Grande Western, which detoured from Denver all the way south to Pueblo before turning west. By connecting Orestod and Dotsero, the east end of the Moffat Road and the west end of the Rio Grande could be brought together to create David Moffat's dream railroad—a main line directly west from Denver to Utah and the Pacific Coast. The cutoff was constructed in 1934, and in 1947 the Rio Grande absorbed the Moffat line altogether.

A word about names: "Orestod," you will note, is "Dotsero" (see next entry) spelled backward. And "Dotsero" derives from a survey of the Colorado River that began at its confluence with the Eagle. That point appeared on the surveyor's report as mile .0—and "dot zero" soon became "Dotsero."

166.8 **Dotsero** *403.2.* This is the west end of the Dotsero Cutoff, where it joins the Rio Grande's old main line from Pueblo. Here too the Eagle River flows into the Colorado. Just before the junction, trains from the cutoff cross the Eagle upstream from its mouth.

Between Dotsero and Glenwood Springs the train passes through the fourth major canyon since Denver, Glenwood Canyon. Glenwood is neither so deep nor so forbidding as Gore Canyon, but it's perhaps more colorful and beautiful. There used to be an unusual monument beside the tracks here: While riding through Glenwood Canyon in the cab of a diesel locomotive, a General Motors executive realized that passengers would enjoy the same view he was getting, and thus was born the Vista Dome car. Amtrak runs a number of them on various routes, but not currently on this one.

185.0 **GLENWOOD SPRINGS** *385.0.* Glenwood lies at the point where the Roaring Fork River empties into the Colorado. For generations before the white men came, the Indians brought their sick to the hot springs at this site.

The modern town was founded in 1883 and was named for Glenwood, Iowa, birthplace of one of the founders. A few years later the elegant Hotel Colorado, with its big outdoor swimming pool, was built just across the Colorado River from the railroad station. It can be seen from the north side of the train as it stops in Glenwood (right side, going west). The hotel's pool is a delight.

Glenwood Springs is also the railroad station for Aspen, the old silver-mining town that has been reborn as a ski center in winter and a cultural festival site in summer.

For several miles west of Glenwood Springs, the rails are on the south bank of the Colorado as a result of a line relocation made necessary by the construction of Route I-70. This stretch is built on the abandoned grade of the old Colorado Midland, once the arch-competitor of the Rio Grande, which went out of business in 1918.

197.6 **New Castle** *372.4.* Most people aren't likely to think of Colorado as a coal-mining state, but in fact bituminous coal has long been a major product of its mines. This town is named after the English coal-mining city of Newcastle. As the train rounds the curves east of New Castle, some black dumps may be seen on the mountains south of the river (left side of the train, going west). These dumps mark the site of the Vulcan Mine, a fine producer but a dangerous shaft. In 1896 a terrific explosion in the Vulcan killed fifty-four miners. So powerful was the blast that heavy mine timbers were thrown as much as 400 feet into the river. The mine was reopened and expanded, but in 1913 a second explosion killed every man in the works. This time the toll was thirty-seven miners. Again, the Vulcan was reopened, but after World War I the demand for Western Slope coal declined and the mine was closed for good. Only the sinister signs of the dumps remain.

211.5 **Rifle** *358.5.* This ranching town, long a cattle-shipping point, has now become a center of uranium mining and shale-oil production as well.

228.9 **Grand Valley (Parachute)** *341.1.* Originally called Parachute, this town was known for many years as Grand Valley. Until 1921 the Colorado River was called the Grand, for which the town was named. But in 1980 the name was changed back to Parachute after nearby Parachute Mountain.

Parachute experienced a remarkable boom in the early 1980s, when a couple of major oil companies established shale-oil–extraction facilities here. The population jumped from 300 to 3,000 nearly overnight, and it was thought that the site might someday support as many as 25,000 residents. But the stabilization in oil prices has reduced the expected demand for shale oil, and the boom is off—at least for now.

241.5 **De Beque** *328.5.* North of the railroad the Book Cliffs extend for many miles, all the way into Utah. These hills are not the granite and basalt rocks that form the ramparts farther east; they are limestone and shale, and they bear strata marks that give clear evidence that this land was once underwater. Indeed, the whole of western Colorado and eastern Utah was once a shallow sea, with heavy tropical vegetation. This was the home of the dinosaurs, and the area has produced more dinosaur fossils than any other part of the United States.

The Book Cliffs also contain enormous deposits of shale oil. Experiments in extracting the oil from the rock began as early as 1917.

About 10 miles west of De Beque is Beaver Tail Tunnel, drilled through a shale cliff to avoid the sharp curves and the rockslides that used to occur here. Beyond the tunnel, look for the Cameo Mine to the north side of the tracks (right side, going west). This coal mine has been worked continuously since the turn of the century, and since 1957 its output has gone to fuel a large electric-power plant built right at the mine site. This is the ultimate in efficiency: Instead of carrying the coal to the user, the power plant has come to the coal mine.

261.9 **Palisade** *308.1.* The area between here and Grand Junction is known for its wonderful fruit. Nothing tastes better than a big, fresh Grand Valley peach, and this is where they grow.

To the south looms the bulk of Grand Mesa with its table-flat top, extending 40 miles eastward.

274.5 **GRAND JUNCTION** *295.5.* Grand Junction was founded in 1881 and takes its name from its site at the junction of the Grand (now Colorado) and Gunnison rivers. It was originally a cattle town, but irrigation of the Grand Valley has turned Grand Junction into a center of agriculture.

The remarkable Colorado National Monument is just outside the town, with as amazing a lesson in the story of the earth as you'll find anywhere. Dinosaur bones have been discovered here as well as at the Dinosaur National Monument 100 miles farther north.

Grand Junction is also the station for the Gunnison River valley. Sixty miles south is the city of Montrose, and near it the Black Canyon National Monument—another scenic wonder that in some ways equals the Grand Canyon itself. Farther south are Ouray and the spectacular vistas of Red Mountain Pass; and beyond it are Silverton and Durango and the Mesa Verde National Park.

Grand Junction is also the most important freight-classification facility between Denver and Salt Lake City. A huge, modern switchyard is just east of the town; this is the hub of operations on the Denver and Rio Gande Western.

285.4 **Fruita** *284.6.* The town is named for the Grand Valley's leading crop, fruit. Across the river is the western entrance to the Colorado National Monument.

293.8 **Mack, Colo.** *276.2.* In years gone by, this was the junction with the narrow-gauge Uintah Railway, which climbed rugged Baxter Pass to the north on an astounding 7 percent grade. This line was abandoned and torn up many years ago. Between Mack and Westwater the rails run through Ruby Canyon, so named because of the red color of its rocks. The Colorado-Utah state line is marked by a large sign painted on the canyon wall to the north of the track (right side, westbound).

313.3 **Westwater, Utah** *256.7.* The Rio Grande tracks leave the Colorado River here after following it for 238 miles from Granby. From Westwater to Green River the railroad crosses the most desolate stretch of land this side of the moon.

353.0 **THOMPSON** *217.0.* This is absolutely the middle of nowhere—yet Thompson is the station for Moab, the Arches National Park, and its neighbor, Canyonlands National Park.

380.1 **Green River** *189.9.* Coming down from Wyoming to join the Colorado, the Green River offers a welcome oasis from the harsh desert to the east. Here the railroad turns north to begin the long climb up to the crest of the Wasatch Range at Soldier Summit. Green River is, in fact, the lowest point en route between Denver and Salt Lake City.

406.3 **Woodside** *163.7.* Here the rails begin to follow the Price River, a tributary of the Green, whose headwaters rise at Soldier Summit 70 miles northwest and 3,000 feet higher.

444.0 **Price** *126.0.* This is the largest town in the Price River valley and the biggest community since Grand Junction. There is no stop here, however. Passengers for Price use the station at Helper, 7 miles farther up the river.

451.4 **HELPER** *118.6.* This is one of those towns that owe their existence to the railroad. Helper is pure D & RGW. It is not only a division point where engine crews change, but it also serves as the base for the pusher engines that help heavy freight trains up the hill to Soldier Summit.

453.7 **Utah Railway Junction** *116.3.* The Utah Railway is a little-known line that shares the track over Soldier Summit to Provo. Its primary function—almost its only function—is to carry mountains of coal from the rich mines around Hiawatha, southwest of Helper, to the steel mills near Provo.

455.2 **Castle Gate** *114.8.* A rock formation resembling a medieval castle seems to guard the "gate" that opens into the mountains at this point. The rails continue to follow the Price River as the climb to Soldier Summit begins in earnest.

469.4 **Colton** *100.6.* Here the Price is left behind. Indian Head Peak, 9,800 feet high, rises to the east. Between Colton and Soldier Summit the tracks cross a high, wind-swept plateau.

476.3 **Soldier Summit** *93.7.* This is the crest of the Wasatch Range. There's nothing pretty about Soldier Summit, but just getting heavy trains across it is an engineering work of art.

So steep is this pass that the original narrow-gauge crossing, built about 1882, had to employ 4 percent grades and a series of switchbacks to get over the top. These expedients would not do for a heavy-duty main line, however, so the entire pass had to be re-engineered and rebuilt to meet twentieth-century standards. Even today there are stretches where the grade reaches 2.4 percent, and that means 140 feet of vertical rise for every mile forward. On the west side of the pass, the rails describe a huge S as they descend the mountain.

505.8 **Thistle** *64.2.* Thistle, which was a tiny village at the upper end of Spanish Fork Canyon, no longer exists. In April 1983 a massive landslide dammed up the creek, causing Thistle to disappear under the waters of a big new lake. The Rio Grande Railway's main line was blocked for three months until a 6-mile-long bypass could be built. This involved construction of a 3,400-foot tunnel through Billy's Mountain, east of the site of Thistle. Slightly shorter than the old route, the new line rejoins the former alignment several miles below the town site in Spanish Fork Canyon. The new tunnel is single-tracked, which makes it a bottleneck. But a planned second bore will eliminate the problem.

About 7 miles west of Thistle the canyon ends abruptly, and the rails debouch onto the floor of the Salt Lake valley.

526.1 **PROVO** *43.9.* Utah's third-largest city, Provo stands at the base of Y Mountain—that's really its name—and is best known as the home of Brigham Young University, the Mormon Harvard. The city is also important as an industrial center, most notably for nearby Geneva Steel.

Provo is the southern anchor of the 100-mile-long corridor, extending north to Brigham City, that contains most of Utah's population and nearly all of its commerce. Settlement began in 1847 at Salt Lake, when Brigham Young declared to his followers, "This is the place!" From Provo north, the railroad runs through a string of small towns that, in effect, make up one continuous semiurban area.

532.1 **Geneva** *37.9.* Here the Geneva Steel plant lies west of the railroad (left side, going north). The town of Orem is to the east.

538.6 **American Fork** *31.4.* The American Fork River comes down from the Wasatch Mountains to empty into Utah Lake, smaller and less well known than its neighbor, Great Salt Lake, which lies farther north.

554.1 **Riverton** *15.9.* Hidden behind the mountains directly to the west are the huge copper mines of Bingham Canyon, one of which is said to be the largest open-pit mine in the world.

The Salt Lake valley, or the Jordan valley—the Jordan River runs through it—is a prosperous agricultural area and has one of the prettiest natural settings in North America. There are mountains to the east and west, some of them snowcapped, and the whole valley gives you a sense of serenity and security. This is the best natural location for a settlement between the Rockies and California, so it seems that Brigham Young really had divine guidance when he planted the Mormons here.

567.4 **Roper** *3.6.* The D & RGW's main Salt Lake area freight yards are here. Connections are made at Salt Lake with the Union Pacific and Western Pacific railroads for points on the Pacific Coast.

570.0 **SALT LAKE CITY** *0.0.* For information on Salt Lake City and Great Salt Lake see sections 2.42 and 3.49. Passengers continuing on to Portland should refer to section 3.50; for Seattle, see 3.50 and the last part of section 3.43. For Los Angeles–bound travelers, see section 3.49.

0.0 **SALT LAKE CITY** *814.8.* For information on the city, see section 2.42.

15.3 **Garfield** *799.5.* Here the railroad approaches the southern shore of Great Salt Lake. The Bingham Canyon copper mines are a short distance south.

20.2 **Lago** *794.6.* *Lago* means "Lake" in Italian. Great Salt Lake is left behind after this point.

113.2 **Salduro** *701.6.* Salduro lies right in the middle of the Great Salt Desert, which is 60 miles long, 8 miles wide and from 1 to 13 feet thick. This huge salt deposit is 98 percent pure sodium chloride (salt). The Bonneville Speedway is on the salt flats just north of this station.

122.2 **Wendover, Utah** *692.6.* Wendover is a railroad division point, and although not an Amtrak passenger station, the California *Zephyr* pauses here for a few minutes to change crews. The town lies at the western end of the salt flats, just east of the Nevada state line; beyond, the rails begin the climb over the Toana and Pequop ranges.

156.4 **Silver Zone, Nev.** *658.4.* Silver Zone Pass is the highest point on the pass through the Toana Mountains, at an elevation of 5,819 feet above sea level. From this point the rails drop 300 feet in the next 6 miles to Shafter, then climb again over the Pequop Range.

162.2 **Shafter** *652.6.* Shafter is a junction, where the Union Pacific (formerly the Western Pacific) line used by Amtrak crosses the Nevada Northern Railway. The Nevada Northern was for many years a major copper hauler, but since the mines near Ruth (south of Shafter) were closed, it has been almost dormant. Coal, however, has been discovered in the area, and the Nevada Northern may soon be back in business. West of Shafter,

SALT LAKE CITY—OAKLAND

Westbound/miles		miles/Eastbound
0.0	SALT LAKE CITY	814.8
15.3	Garfield	799.5
20.2	Lago	794.6
31.3	Burmerster	783.5
35.2	Ellerbeck	779.6
42.0	Timpie	772.8

375

569.0	Vista	245.8
571.9	SPARKS	242.9
571.9	SPARKS	242.9
575.2	RENO	239.6
586.4	Verdi, Nev.	228.4
595.6	Floriston, Calif.	219.2
609.9	TRUCKEE	204.9
625.8	Norden	189.0
632.3	Troy	182.5
637.6	Cisco	177.2
646.5	Emigrant Cap	168.3
651.2	Blue Canyon	163.6
656.1	Midas	158.7
664.6	Gold Run	150.2
670.8	Cape Horn	144.0
675.1	COLFAX	139.7
688.8	Bowman	126.0
692.7	Auburn	122.1
697.6	Newcastle	117.2
700.6	Penryn	114.2
703.3	Loomis	111.5
706.6	Rocklin	108.2
710.6	Roseville	104.2
714.4	Antelope	100.4
717.8	Walerga	97.0
722.3	Benali	92.5
725.4	Elvas	89.4
727.2	15th St.	87.6
728.3	SACRAMENTO	86.5
728.3	SACRAMENTO	86.5
729.2	West Sacramento	85.6
731.0	Mikon	83.8
736.9	Webster	77.9
738.2	Swingle	76.6
741.7	DAVIS	73.1
745.5	Tremont	69.3
747.7	Sucro	67.1
749.8	Dixon	65.0
757.9	Elmira	56.9
761.9	Cannon	52.9
765.4	Tolenas	49.4
768.4	SUISUN-FAIRFIELD	46.4
779.3	Bahia	35.5
785.7	MARTINEZ	29.1
787.3	Ozol	27.5
788.0	Benica	26.8
791.4	Crockett	23.4
792.8	Selby	22.0
793.2	Tormey	21.6
794.0	Oleum	20.8
794.8	Rodeo	20.0

796.5	Hercules	18.3
797.3	Pinole	17.5
801.4	Giant	13.4
803.7	San Pablo	11.1
805.3	RICHMOND	9.5
807.2	Stege	7.6
811.1	Berkeley	3.7
813.3	Shellmound	1.5
813.7	Emoryville	1.1
814.8	OAKLAND	0.0

Bus connection to San Francisco via Bay Bridge

the rails climb more than 300 feet to their highest point in the Pequop Mountains, at the tunnel near Jasper, about 10 miles further on.

210.6 **Wells** *604.2.* The nearby Humboldt Wells are natural springs that are one source of the Humboldt River. Wells lost much of its former importance as a railroad town with the coming of diesel locomotives and new technology, but one relic of boom times remains—Donna's brothel, right beside the tracks. Prostitution is legal in Nevada, except in Reno and Las Vegas.

214.5 **Alazon** *600.3.* For the next 183 miles to Weso, the Union Pacific and Southern Pacific railroads share their tracks. As a rule, westbound trains use the former while eastbound trains are on the latter.

228.5 **Deeth** *586.3.* From just east of Deeth all the way to Lovelock, 245 miles, the right-of-way parallels the Humboldt River—one of the most unusual in America because it literally flows from nowhere to nowhere. The Humboldt rises in the desolate mountains of northeastern Nevada and ends in the dread Humboldt Sink in the western part of the state. It never empties into another river, and its waters never reach the sea. This peculiar stream was discovered in 1828 and is named for Baron Alexander von Humboldt, a brilliant German naturalist, explorer, and diplomat who lived from 1769 to 1859.

241.4 **Halleck** *573.4.* The site was named for Henry Wager Halleck, Union general and chief of staff during the Lincoln administration, who spent part of his long and active life in the West prospecting for gold and silver. He is best remembered for his Civil War military role, but that was only a small part of his unusually varied career.

261.9 **ELKO** *552.9.* *Elko* is an Indian word meaning "white woman." Until recently, the town was bisected by railroad tracks, but a federally financed line relocation has now moved rail traffic out of the center of town, eliminating seventeen grade crossings. This project included construction of a new Amtrak station, replacing two former buildings.

Between Elko and Carlin, trains pass through rugged Carlin Canyon. Extensive gold-mining was once carried on here, but nearly all traces of it have long since disappeared.

283.6 **Carlin** *531.2.* Carlin is another town named for a Union officer—W. P. Carlin, a general in the Army of the Potomac.

309.9 **Beowawe** *504.9.* The name is pronounced *Bay-o-wow-ee*. Three miles east of the town, on the south side of the tracks (left side, going west) is a large weathered white cross. This is the so-called "Maiden's Grave," which marks the final resting place of eighteen-year-old Lucinda Duncan, who died at this spot while making the westward trek about 1851. Her grave was marked only by a rude wooden board until the Central Pacific grade was built about 1868. At that time the railroaders put up a stone and a large cross, and the site has been cared for ever since. Today it is part of the local graveyard.

342.3 **Battle Mountain** *472.5.* Battle Mountain takes its name from a fight between pioneers and Indians that took place nearby in 1857. There are copper mines in the vicinity.

390.0 **Golconda** *424.8.* Though named for the legendary Hindu city known for its great wealth, Golconda, Nevada, hasn't produced much wealth for anybody. The name, bestowed during prospecting days, turned out to be more optimism than description.

397.2 **Weso** *417.6.* This is the western end of the joint track agreed on between the Western Pacific and Southern Pacific that extends 183 miles from Alazon. The name is a contraction of the two railroad names. The Western Pacific in now part of the Union Pacific.

400.8 **WINNEMUCCA** *414.0.* Winnemucca, chief of the Piute Tribe, believed that red men and white could live in peace. He was respected by both races, so much so that the whites called him the "Napoleon of the Piutes" and proudly named this town after him. Butch Cassidy and his gang robbed the local bank in 1900.

440.9 **Humboldt** *373.9.* Nearby is the Rye Patch reservoir, which collects the water of the Humboldt River and distributes it for irrigation before it disappears into the Humboldt Sink—a sandy stretch where pioneer wagons sank to their hubcaps.

452.1 **Rye Patch** *362.6.* Rye Patch Dam (right side of the train, going west) creates a reservoir and recreation area in the midst of the bleak sagebrush desert.

473.8 **Lovelock** *341.0.* Just southwest is the Humboldt Sink, where the Humboldt River ends. Nearby is the larger Carson Sink, which absorbs the Carson River. Pony Express riders used to consider this stretch the worst part of the entire trail from Missouri to California.

542.0 **Fernley** *272.8.* Here the rails reach the Truckee River, whose course they follow up the eastern side of the Sierras. About 20 miles south is the Fort Churchill historical site, marking the military post that guarded the Comstock Lode from Indian raids. Fort Churchill was also the eastern end of the telegraph line to San Francisco during the autumn of 1860, and it was here that the Pony Express delivered the news of Lincoln's election for transmission to the Pacific Coast.

571.9 **SPARKS** *242.9.* Actually a suburb of Reno, Sparks is named for John Sparks, once governor of Nevada; since 1905 it has been synonymous with Southern Pacific. This station marks the end of the long run across the desert from Salt Lake City and the beginning of the stiff climb over the Sierras at Donner Pass. Helper engines and snow plows used on the mountain are stationed here, and crews change on Amtrak passenger trains. If you're looking for a place to stretch your legs, you might want to take advantage of the 20-minute stop here.

In addition to its railroading significance, Sparks has one additional claim to fame—it's the site of Harrah's Automobile Collection, the biggest and most complete museum of autos in the country. The collection was put together by the same man who ran Harrah's Casino in nearby Reno, and it includes more than a thousand vehicles. A free bus comes out from Reno, if your're planning to stay in the area.

575.2 **RENO, NEV.** *239.6.* For information on the city, see section 2.37.

In 1857 the Comstock Lode, a fabulous mountain of gold and silver, was discovered 20 miles south of Reno. It took its name from an early prospector, Henry Comstock; and the leading town of the area was christened "Virginia" by a tipsy miner who hailed from the Old Dominion. Within three years of its first discovery the Comstock was turning out ore assayed, in 1860 dollars, at $5,000 a ton. In all, the mines in and around Virginia City produced at least $600 million in gold and another half billion in silver; it was the richest mining property ever discovered in the United States. Comstock ore built the mansions of San Francisco, made the merchants of Reno prosper, and was so important to financing the Union war effort that Nevada was admitted to the United States even though it had nowhere near the required number of residents. It is still the most thinly populated of the forty-eight continental states.

West of Reno the rails ascend the Sierra Nevada range following the Truckee River. These mountains are aptly named: *Sierra* means "jagged" or "rugged" in Spanish, while *Nevada* translates as "snow-covered." These peaks are both. From Reno to the summit at Donner Pass the rise in elevation is 2,500 feet in just 50 miles.

609.9 **TRUCKEE, CALIF.** *204.9* The headwaters of the Truckee River are nearby, giving the town its name. Truckee is Amtrak's station for the resorts on the California side of Lake Tahoe, 20 miles south.

Between Truckee and Norden the rails circle Donner Lake. The Donner party was stranded here by snow in the winter of 1846–47.

Of the eighty-two pioneers in the group, forty-seven survived—by eating the flesh of their dead companions.

625.8 **Norden** *189.0*   This is at 7,000 feet, near the crest of the Sierras. The facilities here are covered by a huge snow shed, which helps keep operations going during the winter.

The 85 miles from Norden to Roseville is probably the most famous section of mountain railroad in America; trainmen call it simply the "Hill." It was built mostly by hand labor, and it took three excruciating years of work to construct. Not enough local help was available, so Chinese labor was employed, reluctantly at first. Soon, however, construction boss Charles Crocker realized the value of the Chinese trackmen: They were small but tough and seemingly tireless. They ate little and drank less, were happy with wages of a dollar a day, and—best of all—endured the brutal labor day after day and kept coming back for more. Soon Crocker was sending agents to Canton to recruit more of these hardy workmen. Some thirteen thousand Chinese were brought to America to work on the Central Pacific. Many of their descendants now live in San Francisco's Chinatown.

Some of the most spectacular mountain scenery in the United States is found in the 50 miles between Norden and Colfax. The rails wind along the mountainsides, high above the American River, whose canyon they follow down to Sacramento.

670.8 **Cape Horn** *114.0.*   Here the roadbed rounds a curve high on the side of a mountain, using a shelf blasted out of the rock by Chinese workmen suspended from the top of the cliff in bosun's chairs.

675.1 **COLFAX** *139.7.*   This town was named for Schuyler Colfax, a powerful Republican politician who was speaker of the House of Representatives and later vice-president in the scandal-ridden Grant Administration. Colfax was up to his ears in railroad politics. He accepted stock from the Crédit Mobilier, the crooked construction company that bilked the taxpayers out of millions of dollars in Union Pacific money. No wonder the builders of the Central Pacific honored him by naming a town after him—he was just too powerful to ignore.

From Colfax to Sacramento the worst of the mountain grades are behind. It speaks for the persuasive powers—or the political connections—of the Big Four (Mark Hopkins, Charles Crocker, Leland Stanford, and Collis P. Huntington, builders of the original Central Pacific) that they were able to get all this track accepted as mountain mileage, thus increasing the federal subsidy from $16,000 to $48,000 per mile.

692.7 **Auburn** *122.1.*   While many of the old gold-rush towns did not survive the mining mania, Auburn is one that did. Appropriately, it's only 25 miles from Sutter's Mill, where James Marshall made the original California gold strike in 1848.

710.6 **Roseville** *104.2.* Sitting at the base of the Hill, Roseville has always been a railroad town. It is also the junction with the Sacramento Valley line to Oregon, used by Amtrak's *Coast Starlight.*

728.3 **SACRAMENTO** *86.5.* From the train you can see the new California State Railroad Museum, just west of the station (left side, going west). This museum commemorates the developers of the Central Pacific Railroad, who lived in Sacramento, the railroad's original terminus. For information on the city, see section 2.39.

741.7 **DAVIS** *73.1.* Davis is the home of one of the eight campuses of the University of California. This branch, with a good liberal-arts college, specializes in agriculture and veterinary medicine.

768.4 **SUISUN-FAIRFIELD** *46.4.* This station serves not only the two towns in its name but also other nearby communities including Napa, Vacaville, and Vallejo. Travis Air Force Base is nearby.

779.3 **Bahia** *35.5.* The water to the east side of the train (left side, going west) is Suisun Bay, an inlet of San Francisco Bay. Here can be seen row after row of mothballed U.S. Navy vessels.

At the mouth of Suisun Bay the tracks cross the Carquinez Strait on the Martinez–Benicia Bridge, more than a mile long. Not finished until 1930, this structure replaced a ferry service that used to carry whole trains across the straits.

785.7 **MARTINEZ** *29.1.* Pronounced the Spanish way, *Mar-teen-es,* this station is convenient to Walnut Creek, Concord, and the other suburban communities east of the Berkeley Hills. At Martinez the *San Joaquins* from Bakersfield and Fresno join the main line for the rest of the way to Oakland.

Martinez was the home of the naturalist and conservationist John Muir (1838–1914), who came to Wisconsin from Scotland in 1849 and spent the later years of his life here. His home is now a state historic site.

West of Martinez the railroad follows the shoreline of San Pablo and San Francisco bays most of the way to Oakland.

805.3 **RICHMOND** *9.5.* Richmond is a particularly convenient station because it is the transfer point between Amtrak trains and the Bay Area Rapid Transit (BART) system. Richmond is also handy for Marin County communities, which are easily reached by car via the Richmond–San Rafael bridge. The big industry in Richmond is refining; Standard Oil has a major facility here.

811.1 **Berkeley** *3.7.* This is the site of the main campus of the University of Calfornia. Berkeley currently enrolls 20,000 students in more than 100 different departments; its library contains 5 million books. The first of the big student demonstrations of the 1960s took place here.

Just beyond Berkeley, look for the Golden Gate Fields racetrack by the shore of the bay (right side of the train, approaching Oakland).

814.8 **OAKLAND** *0.0.* Gertrude Stein probably summed up Oakland's dilemma best when she said, "There's no THERE there." Even though it is a major commercial and industrial city and one of America's leading ports, Oakland tends to be obscured by its glamorous neighbor, San Francisco, across the bay.

A cautionary note: Amtrak's 16th Street station is in one of the worst areas of town, some distance from the central business district. Do not go wandering around here, especially after dark.

Trains terminate here, and buses take passengers from trackside on to San Francisco across the Bay Bridge.

For information on San Francisco, see section 2.45. For passengers continuing on to Los Angeles or San Diego, see the first part of section 3.43 and section 3.51. For passengers going north to Portland or Seattle, see the latter part of section 3.43.

3.45 (Chicago—Milwaukee)— Minneapolis-St. Paul—Seattle—Portland

From Chicago and Milwaukee across fertile Wisconsin and up the Mississippi Valley to the Twin Cities, then across the endless plains of North Dakota and Montana, over the Rockies and the Cascades, and down to the Pacific—this is the route of Amtrak's *Empire Builder.*

The train is named after James J. Hill, builder of the Great Northern Railroad, who was called the "empire builder" because he did so much to develop the resources of the far Northwest. It runs daily through some of the most spectacular scenery in North America, including Glacier National Park and the Cascade Mountains. And, since late 1981, a Portland section has operated from Spokane along the Columbia River valley to the Oregon city, giving direct service to the East. In addition, connections can be made to Vancouver, British Columbia, via bus from Seattle.

The *Empire Builder* has Superliner sleeping cars, coaches, a dining car, and a glass-roofed lounge. Reservations are required for all space. Make your plans early if you're going to travel in the summer, because the train usually runs full.

If this isn't Amtrak's best long-distance run, it certainly rates up there with any other. A trip on the *Empire Builder* is an experience to remember.

For the route segments from Chicago, see the sections for

Chicago—Milwaukee (3.37) and Milwaukee—Minneapolis-St. Paul (3.38).

For the section of the route from Minneapolis-St. Paul to Coon Creek, Minnesota, see section 3.39.

17.0 **Coon Creek** *1777.5.* This is the junction between the Burlington Northern main line used by Amtrak (the former Northern Pacific) and the branch line to Duluth-Superior.

The Northern Pacific was finished in 1881 with the aid of federal land grants. It was merged, along with its competitor, the Great Northern, and two other lines, into the Burlington Northern system, and the resulting combine is America's longest railroad. By virtue of its large landholdings and mineral rights, it is also probably the richest.

22.7 **Anoka** *1771.8.* Here the tracks cross the Mississippi River for the third time since Minneapolis. The railroad plays tag with the river all the way from the Twin Cities to Little Falls; in all, it crosses the Mississippi seven times in this 102-mile stretch.

69.9 **ST. CLOUD** *1724.6.* Thirty miles west is Sauk Centre, once the home of Nobel Prize–winning author Sinclair Lewis. His best-known work, *Main Street,* depicts life in small towns such as this one half a century ago.

101.6 **Little Falls** *1692.9.* This is the boyhood home of aviator Charles A. Lindbergh. Lindy was actually born in Detroit, but that was only because his mother, a Michigan native, did not trust the birthing facilities in her husband's town. Lindbergh developed an interest

MINNEAPOLIS-ST. PAUL—SPOKANE

Westbound/miles		*miles/Eastbound*
0.0	MINNEAPOLIS-ST. PAUL	1794.5
1.1	St. Anthony	1793.4
2.4	Union	1792.1
4.9	Hennepin Ave.	1789.6
5.1	First St. North	1789.4
5.7	14th Ave. North	1788.8
6.9	Mulberry Jct.	1787.6
9.5	Northtown	1785.0
11.3	Interstate	1783.2
17.0	Coon Creek	1777.5
22.7	Anoka	1771.8
29.8	Dayton	1764.7
34.6	Elk River	1759.9
43.7	Big Lake	1750.8
51.5	Becker	1743.0
58.6	Clear Lake	1735.9
67.3	Reformatory	1727.2
69.9	ST. CLOUD	1724.6

413.9	DEVILS LAKE	1380.6
421.0	Grand Harbor	1373.5
426.9	Penn	1367.6
432.9	Church's Ferry	1361.6
444.3	Leeds	1350.2
450.6	York	1343.9
456.6	Knox	1337.9
462.1	Pleasant Lake	1332.4
471.1	RUGBY	1323.4
476.4	Tunbridge	1318.1
482.7	Berwick	1311.8
490.1	Towner	1304.4
498.9	Danbigh	1295.6
511.0	Granville	1283.5
517.9	Norwich	1276.6
525.1	Surrey	1269.4
532.3	MINOT	1262.2

532.3	MINOT	1262.2
545.8	Des Lacs	1248.7
554.6	Berthold	1239.9
571.1	Blaisdell	1223.4
578.0	Palermo	1216.5
585.8	STANLEY	1208.7
593.1	Ross	1201.4
605.1	White Earth	1189.4
613.0	Tioga	1181.5
618.5	Temple	1176.0
624.8	Ray	1169.7
630.1	Wheelock	1164.4
635.1	Epping	1159.4
646.6	Avoca	1147.9
652.2	WILLISTON (CT)	1142.3

652.2	WILLISTON (CT)	1142.3
664.1	Trenton, N.D. (MT)	1130.4
678.1	Snowden, Mont.	1116.4
690.1	Bainville	1104.4
704.4	Culbertson	1090.1
709.9	Blair	1084.6
723.6	Brockton	1070.9
737.6	Poplar	1056.9
753.0	Macon	1041.5
758.8	WOLF POINT	1035.7
770.1	Oswego	1024.4
777.4	Frazer	1017.1
782.5	Kintyre	1012.0
793.9	Nashua	1000.6
808.4	GLASGOW	986.1

808.4	GLASGOW	986.1
820.2	Tampico	974.3
834.3	Hinsdale	960.2
847.0	Saco	947.5

860.7	Bowdoin	933.8
874.0	MALTA	920.5
883.6	Wagner	910.9
891.5	Dodson	903.0
906.8	Savoy	887.7
918.6	Harlem	875.9
930.4	Zurich	864.1
939.7	Chinook	854.8
947.8	Lohman	846.7
961.4	HAVRE	833.1

961.4	HAVRE	833.1
965.4	Pacific Jct.	829.1
971.1	Burnham	823.4
980.7	Kremlin	813.8
990.8	Gildford	803.7
996.7	Hingham	797.8
1002.7	Rudyard	791.8
1008.9	Inverness	785.6
1012.7	Joplin	781.8
1015.7	Buelow	778.8
1022.8	Chester	771.7
1035.9	Lothair	758.6
1041.9	Galata	752.6
1047.9	Devon	746.6
1056.5	Dunkirk	738.0
1066.0	SHELBY	728.5
1068.2	Teton	735.8
1079.0	Ethridge	715.5
1090.2	CUT BANK	704.3
1116.4	Blackfoot	678.1
1123.7	BROWNING	670.8
1132.7	Spotted Robe	661.8
1137.1	GLACIER PARK	657.4
1142.2	Bison	652.3
1148.7	Summit	645.8
1150.7	Marias	643.8
1155.7	Blacktail	638.8
1163.0	Java	631.5
1166.9	Essex	627.6
1171.0	Pinnacle	623.5
1175.3	Paola	619.2
1182.8	Red Eagle	611.7
1185.7	Nyack	608.8
1193.4	BELTON (West Glacier)	601.1
1201.3	Coram	593.2
1205.7	Conkelly	588.8
1208.6	Columbia Falls	585.9
1216.2	WHITEFISH	578.3

1216.2	WHITEFISH	578.3
1221.6	Vista	572.9
1228.0	Lupfer	566.5
1239.2	Radnor	555.3

1246.3	Stryker	548.2
1249.7	Brimstone	544.8
1260.4	Twin Meadows	534.1
1270.0	Rock Creek	524.5
1279.0	Wolf Prairie	515.5
1286.9	Tamarack	507.6
1294.8	Fisher River	499.7
1303.7	Riverview	490.8
1310.7	Ripley	483.8
1317.9	LIBBY	476.6
1328.9	Kootenai Falls	465.6
1336.1	Troy	458.4
1342.8	Yakt, Mont.	451.7
1349.6	Leonia, Idaho	444.9
1363.1	Crossport	431.4
1367.4	Bonners Ferry	427.1
1378.8	Naples	415.7
1386.2	Elmira	408.3
1400.1	Boyer	394.4
1402.1	Sandpoint Jct.	392.4
1402.2	SANDPOINT	392.3
1409.4	Algoma	385.1
1416.1	Cocolalla	378.4
1428.7	Athol	365.8
1436.0	Ramsey	358.5
1441.7	Rathdrum	352.8
1443.1	Hauser	351.4
1448.7	Hauser Jct., Idaho	345.8
1454.5	Otis Orchards, Wash.	340.0
1460.4	Irvin	334.1
1464.0	Parkwater	330.5
1465.2	Yardley	329.3
1468.7	SPOKANE	325.8

in aviation while still very young, and dropped out of college to become a pilot. In time, he got a job flying the U.S. mail between Chicago and St. Louis. Then Lindbergh heard of a $25,000 prize offered to the first pilot to fly across the Atlantic from New York to Paris. While other fliers were failing, he arranged with the Ryan aircraft plant in San Diego to fly a little monoplane with additional fuel tanks. He called it "The Spirit of St. Louis." Lindbergh took off from Roosevelt Field on Long Island on May 20, 1927, and landed in Paris the following night. The French received him with a glorious celebration, but it was nothing to the welcome the young flier got when he returned—by ship—to the United States. Lindbergh never lived in Minnesota again, but the state has not forgotten him.

135.3 **STAPLES** *1659.2.* Staples is the little town that survives as the first crew-changing point after the Twin Cities; a lot of people here work for the railroad.

197.3 **DETROIT LAKES** *1597.2.* "Detroit" is French for "strait." An early fort, Fort Detroit, was built on this site, and the town grew up around it. The area is dotted with many of Minnesota's ten thousand lakes, left over from glacial times.

245.9 **Moorhead, Minn.** *1548.6.* Between Moorhead and Fargo the train crosses the Red River of the North, which forms the boundary between Minnesota and North Dakota. The Red is unusual because it flows north, emptying into Lake Winnipeg in Canada.

247.0 **FARGO, N.D.** *1547.5.* Named for William G. Fargo, best known as the second half of the Wells Fargo express company. Fargo is primarily a railroad town—a junction city, with the usual yards and engine servicing facilities. Crews change at this division point. Fargo is also a livestock trading center and distribution point for the surrounding area.

Between the Twin Cities and Fargo, the *Empire Builder* uses the former Northern Pacific. West of Fargo, it runs over the old Great Northern for 1,150 miles. This was the railroad built by James J. Hill, the "empire builder" himself. He intended his line to tap the trade of the Orient, and he pushed it to completion without a cent of federal aid or an acre of land-grant support.

Leaving Fargo, the *Empire Builder* runs straight north for 78 miles to Grand Forks before turning west again.

322.6 **WEST GRAND FORKS** *1471.9.* Grand Forks is Amtrak's station for northwestern Minnesota, as well as for Winnipeg, Canada, which is two hours farther north by car. The new station here, on the western outskirts of town near the campus of the University of North Dakota, eliminated a backup move into town and saved 30 minutes in the *Builder's* schedule.

413.9 **DEVILS LAKE** *1380.6.* You wouldn't expect to find a resort area in the middle of the Dakota wheat fields—but here it is.

444.3 **Leeds** *1350.2.* Like many other western railroads, the Great Northern was built largely through unsettled land. Thus it fell to the railroad builders to name the towns as they went. It's easy to see where the Great Northern men looked for inspiration. From Leeds to Minot almost every town is named after a place in Great Britain.

471.1 **RUGBY** *1323.4.* Although it's just like hundreds of other little farm towns in every other way, Rugby has one unique distinction: It stands at the exact geographical center of the North American continent. This makes you realize how much land there is in Canada.

532.3 **MINOT** *1262.2.* This railroad division point, where crews change, must be one of the coldest places in America in winter. It lies on a wide, open plain, 50 miles below the Canadian border, where the chilling winds sweep in from the north six months a year. If you're thin-blooded, don't get off the train to stretch your legs in Minot between November and May.

.   *585.8* **STANLEY** *1208.7.* Stanley marks the eastern end of the rich Williston Basin, which produces millions of barrels of oil every year and contains immense fields of lignite coal as well. It's an energy treasure trove, just now being exploited for the first time.

613.0 **Tioga** *1181.5.* This is where the oil boom began when the first successful well began producing in 1951. Today there are over a thousand wells pumping in the Williston Basin, and some geologists think that most of the fields there have yet to be opened up.

652.2 **WILLISTON** *1142.3.* On the north bank of the Missouri River at its junction with the Little Muddy, Williston is the center of the North Dakota oil fields, a wheat-marketing center, and a railroad division point. It marks the border between the Central and Mountain time zones. Reset your watch here.

664.1 **Trenton, N.D.** *1130.4.* Nearby is the site of Fort Buford, where Sitting Bull, the Sioux chief, finally surrendered to the U.S. Army. Fort Buford and its companion, Fort Union, were established to guard the junction of the Yellowstone and Missouri rivers, a strategic spot, especially before the railroad was built.

758.8 **WOLF POINT, MONT.** *1035.7.* The Wolf River empties into the Missouri at this point. This is Indian country. The Fort Peck reservation stretches for miles around the town.

808.4 **GLASGOW** *986.1.* Named after the Scottish metropolis, Glasgow is on the Milk River a few miles above its junction with the Missouri. The Milk owes its name to Lewis and Clark, who thought its cloudy waters resembled a nice, cold glass of milk.

From Glasgow to Malta the rails follow the course of the river. An irrigation project has reclaimed more than 150,000 dry acres for farming.

847.0 **Saco** *947.5.* Saco (and neighboring Bowdoin) are named after towns in Maine. Just west of town is a memorial to the cowboy artist Charles M. Russell, who lived and worked in this area around the turn of the century.

874.0 **MALTA** *920.5.* Fifty miles south, in a large wilderness area, is the Charles M. Russell National Wildlife Range. It extends along both sides of the Missouri River for many miles.

961.4 **HAVRE** *833.1.* The name means "harbor" or "haven" in French. Near here the Indian leader Chief Joseph and his Nez Percé followers were forced to surrender to the U.S. Army. Havre is a division point where trains are inspected and refueled and where crews change. There is always an extended stop here, long enough to stretch your legs or go into the station for a newspaper and a cup of coffee. The Bear Paw Mountains dominate the horizon to the south.

990.8 **Gildford** *803.7.* This is another town name to make a

Britisher feel right at home. Within the next 60 miles are five more: Hingham, Inverness, Lothair, Devon, and Dunkirk.

1066.0 **SHELBY** *728.5.* This is the station for Great Falls, Helena, and Butte, all to the south. In the other direction, it's just 35 miles to the Canadian border and a 3-hour drive from there to Calgary, Banff, Lake Louise, and the Yoho National Park, all in Canada.

Shelby isn't much to look at, even today—so you can imagine what it must have been like back in 1923. At that time, the census credited the place with 537 inhabitants (it has 3,000 today). But some of them happened to be wealthy oil men, cattlemen, and bankers intent on putting Shelby on the map, and they decided that the way to do it was to stage a World's Heavyweight Championship fight in the town. They approached Doc Kearns, manager of Jack Dempsey, who agreed to have the champ fight Tommy Gibbons in Shelby—for a guarantee of $300,000. The fight was held on July 4, 1923. Dempsey won by a decision and kept his title, but the promotion was a disastrous failure. Only ten thousand spectators showed up, and many of them crashed the gate. Kearns slipped out of town under cover of darkness, carrying the $300,000 in cash in a couple of shopping carts. As a result four Montana banks failed.

1090.2 **CUT BANK** *704.3.* The town takes its name from the Cut Bank River, one of three that join to form the Marias, itself a tributary of the Missouri.

We have Meriwether Lewis to thank for the name Marias. He named this river after a young lady whose name was Maria Wood, but the apostrophe from "Maria's River" was somehow lost. There is a monument to Lewis west of Cut Bank; look to the south side of the train (left side, going west).

1123.7 **BROWNING** *670.8.* The Museum of the Plains Indians, commemorating a vanished culture and life-style, is here.

A few miles west of Browning, look for Triple Divide Peak to the north (right side, going west). This mountain, 8,000 feet high, takes its name from the fact that its runoff eventually reaches three oceans—Atlantic, Pacific, and Arctic.

1137.1 **GLACIER PARK (East Glacier)** *657.4.* This station stands at the east entrance to the park; the Glacier Park Lodge is nearby. The mountains seem almost ordinary from this vantage point—but don't despair, the really magnificent views lie ahead.

1148.7 **Summit** *645.8.* The Continental Divide is crossed here, at the top of Marias Pass; the elevation at the crest is 5,236 feet above sea level, the lowest pass between New Mexico and Canada. Marias Pass Summit is lower than Denver, which is at the *base* of the Colorado Rockies!

1150.7 **Marias** *643.8.* The Indians told stories of a broad, flat pass across the Divide; but at the time Jim Hill was building his Great Northern Railroad toward the Pacific, no white man had yet seen it. To find out if such a pass really existed, Jim Hill sent an engineer named John Paul Stevens to Montana. Alone, and in –40° weather, Stevens found that legendary pass. Today a statue at the summit honors him (right side of the tracks, going west).

The rails descend the west side of Marias Pass on a stiff 1.8 percent grade, winding around the mountain spurs and twisting and looping under concrete snowsheds and between electric slide-fences for 12 tortuous miles.

1163.0 **Java** *631.5.* Here the tracks reach the Middle Fork of the Flathead River, which they follow down from the pass. Mount St. Nicholas, 9,300 feet above sea level, towers overhead.

1166.9 **Essex** *627.6.* This is a helper station on the west side of the pass, where freight trains used to get additional engines to boost them over the Divide.

1193.4 **BELTON (West Glacier)** *601.1.* This is the end of the beautiful ride through Glacier Park. The Lake McDonald and other Glacier hotels are accessible from this station.

1208.6 **Columbia Falls** *585.9.* A huge sawmill is here; you'll see raw tree trunks going in at one end and finished lumber emerging at the other.

1216.2 **WHITEFISH** *578.3.* This is a division point; crews change here, and there's time to get out and stretch. Breathe the pure, invigorating air! And note the unusual Whitefish station—it's styled like a Swiss chalet.

Near Whitefish are Whitefish and Flathead lakes and the Big Mountain ski area with its 6,800-foot chair lift.

1246.3 **Stryker** *548.2.* West of here the original grade followed the valley of the Kootenai River. This has been inundated by water backed up behind the Libby Dam, and 65 miles of track have been relocated. The scenery along this stretch is extremely beautiful.

1317.9 **LIBBY** *476.6.* Blue Mountain, 6,000 feet high, towers over the town. In fact, Libby is surrounded by mountains. The Purcells are to the north; the Cabinets, to the south. The Kootenai River flows through the town, and the railroad follows it westward into Idaho.

1336.1 **Troy, Mont.** *458.4.* Extensive lumbering is carried on here; one industry is raising Christmas trees. At Troy you cross from the Mountain to the Pacific Time Zone; reset your watch accordingly.

1367.4 **Bonners Ferry, Idaho** *427.1.* At Bonners Ferry the Canadian border is only 20 miles away—this is the most northerly point en route. Here the tracks leave the Kootenai Valley and turn south.

1402.2 **SANDPOINT** *392.3.* Sandpoint lies on the north shore of Lake Pend Oreille, the largest lake in Idaho. It's in the narrowest portion of the Idaho panhandle, which projects up between Montana on the east and Washington on the west. From Sandpoint to Spokane, the *Empire Builder* uses the former Northern Pacific line. After the Burlington Northern merger, a number of operating changes and consolidations were made to increase efficiency, and this was one.

1441.7 **Rathdrum, Idaho** *352.8.* Ten miles south is Coeur d'Alene, now an attractive resort area but once the site of Idaho's silver boom.

Silver was discovered at Coeur d'Alene in 1884, and the strike was so successful that large-scale mining soon began. The Western Federation of Miners, a radical labor union associated with the IWW—the "Wobblies"—attempted to organize the miners, and in 1892 violence broke out. Order was restored when troops were called in. Seven years later there was another outbreak of shooting. Governor Frank Steunenberg declared martial law and called federal soldiers into the region. Then, in 1905, Steunenberg, no longer governor, was murdered by a bomb planted at his front gate, and a man named Harry Orchard, already suspected of bombings in other states, was arrested. His confession implicated several officials of the Western Federation of Miners, and the State of Idaho brought the union leaders to trial. Attorney Clarence Darrow saw the case as a trial of the whole labor movement. He came to Coeur d'Alene to conduct the defense and won acquittal for his clients. One of America's historic trials, it was one of Darrow's greatest victories.

1468.7 **SPOKANE, WASH.** *325.8.* With more than 200,000 people, Spokane is the biggest city between Minneapolis and the Pacific Coast. It is often called the "capital of the Inland Empire," the stretch of rich farmland and timberland walled in by the Rockies on one side and the Cascades on the other. The city takes its name from an Indian word meaning "children of the sun." It is bisected by the Spokane River. A park along the banks was the site of the Spokane World's Fair in 1974.

One hundred miles away is the Grand Coulee Dam, the largest manmade structure in the Western Hemisphere. This giant Columbia River dam provides electricity for Spokane and its industries, particularly two large aluminum plants.

SPOKANE—SEATTLE

0.0 **SPOKANE, WASH.** *325.8.* At Spokane the *Empire Builder* splits into two sections. One goes to Portland by way of Pasco and the Columbia River valley; the other continues westward to Seattle by way of Stevens Pass and the Cascade Tunnel.

1.1 **Sunset Junction** *324.7.* Here the eastbound Portland section of the *Empire Builder*, coming from Pasco, joins the main line.

SPOKANE—SEATTLE VIA WENATCHEE

Westbound/miles   *miles/Eastbound*

0.0	SPOKANE	325.8
1.1	Sunset Jct.	324.7
1.9	Latah Jct.	323.9
9.7	Lyons	316.1
15.1	Fairchild	310.7
19.2	Espanola	306.6
31.4	Edwall	294.4
40.5	Bluestem	285.3
48.0	Harrington	277.8
63.1	Lamona	262.7
73.3	Odessa	252.5
85.8	Gibson	240.0
96.3	Wilson Creek	229.5
109.4	Adrian	216.4
119.4	EPHRATA	206.4
124.5	Naylor	201.3
135.7	Quincy	190.1
146.4	Trinidad	179.4
155.7	Columbia River	170.1
161.4	Rock Island	164.4
164.7	Malaga	161.1
171.6	WENATCHEE	154.2

171.6	WENATCHEE	154.2
182.6	Cashmere	143.2
190.4	Pehastin	135.4
193.6	Leavenworth	132.2
207.1	Winton	118.7
213.7	Merritt	112.1
220.7	Berne (Cascade Tunnel)	105.1
229.7	Scenic	96.1
242.5	Skykomish	83.3
246.3	Grotto	79.5
250.1	Baring	75.7
264.6	Gold Bar	61.2
277.3	Monroe	48.5
285.2	Snohomish Jct.	40.6
290.1	Lowell Jct.	35.7
291.6	PA Jct.	34.2

291.6	PA Jct.	34.2
293.0	EVERETT	32.8
293.8	Everett Jct.	32.0
297.6	Mukilteo	28.2
308.4	EDMONDS	17.4
318.6	Ballard	7.2
321.2	Interbay	4.6
324.7	North Portal	1.1
325.6	South Portal	0.2
325.8	SEATTLE (King Street Sta.)	0.0

Bus connection to Vancouver, B.C.

1.9 **Latah Junction** *323.9.* The westbound Portland section of the *Empire Builder* turns off here, bound for Pasco over track that used to belong to the Spokane, Portland and Seattle railway. This is in keeping with current operating practice, which sends all westbound trains betwen Spokane and Pasco over that route and all eastbound trains over the former Northern Pacific.

31.4 **Edwall** *294.4.* All the way from Spokane to Wenatchee, the rails cross the so-called Columbia Plateau, a semiarid, treeless plain created by lava flows and cut with deep trenches called coulees. This unhospitable country is crossed by night in both directions.

96.3 **Wilson Creek** *229.5.* The Grand Coulee Dam is about 30 miles north of here, on the Columbia River. Washington leads the nation in the production of hydroelectric power, though only half of its potential has yet been exploited.

119.4 **EPHRATA** *206.4.* Ephrata is a farming community. Agriculture is Washington's second-largest industry, wheat being the leading crop. Irrigation has reclaimed a million acres of dry land for farming in the area around Ephrata.

155.7 **Columbia River** *170.1.* The tracks run beside the Columbia for the next 30 miles. The Columbia is the great river of the Pacific Northwest, rising in British Columbia and flowing through Washington to the Pacific.

171.6 **WENATCHEE** *154.2.* This region is among the leading apple-growing areas in the world, and Washington leads all states in apple production. Wenatchee is also a railroad division point (crews change here) and is the beginning of the long climb over the Cascade Mountains. The next 22 miles of track follow the Wenatchee River to Leavenworth, at the base of Stevens Pass.

193.6 **Leavenworth** *132.2.* The really tough climb begins here—27 miles of grades as steep as 2.2 percent as the train works its way up Tumwater Canyon to the Cascade Tunnel. There is a rise of more than 100 feet for each mile of forward progress—a stiff challenge for railroad engines.

220.7 **Berne (Cascade Tunnel)** *105.1.* When the original Great Northern line was built, the plans called for a tunnel under Stevens Pass, the road's crossing of the Cascades. But construction of a tunnel would take years, and Jim Hill didn't want to wait. So John Paul Stevens—the same engineer who found Marias Pass—laid out a temporary track over the top of the pass. It was a precarious route that required six switchbacks and grades of 4 percent, up which a steam engine could stagger with five or six cars. In 1900 the long-planned tunnel was finally opened. It was 2½ miles long and eliminated the switchbacks and some of the worst grades, but there was still plenty of steep 2.2 percent grade. Accumulations of 30 feet of snow were common, and slides were an ever present danger. But John Paul Stevens had the answer to these problems: the new Cascade Tunnel, the longest bore in the Western Hemisphere. He was chief engineer on the project, and he lived to see it opened for traffic in 1929.

The new Cascade Tunnel is 7.79 miles long. It eliminated 500 feet of altitude, shortened the Great Northern's main line by 9 miles, eliminated the fear of avalanches, did away with 40,000 feet of expensive snowsheds, and best of all, bypassed much 2.2 percent grade on the mountainside. The tunnel is concrete-lined throughout and is equipped with a complicated ventilating system that allows diesel engines to operate through it.

229.7 **Scenic** *96.1.* This is the west portal of the Cascade Tunnel. From here to Skykomish lie 13 miles of 2.2 percent grade. The rails drop from 2,883 feet above sea level at the tunnel to 39 feet at Everett, on Puget Sound, in just 65 miles; that's how steeply the Cascade Range rises above tidewater.

242.5 **Skykomish** *83.3.* In the days before modern diesel locomotives, Skykomish was a busy railroad town. Here powerful electric locomotives were coupled onto trains going up to Scenic and through the Cascade Tunnel, where steam locomotives were a hazard because of smoke and gas fumes. The electrified section extended all the way to Wenatchee, a distance of 71 miles. It was removed in 1956, when diesels made electrical operation unnecessary.

The rails follow the Skykomish River down an easy grade west from Skykomish to Monroe, passing through some of Washington's famous forests. Indeed, because of its great stands of pine and fir trees, Washington is sometimes called the "Evergreen State."

291.6 **PA Junction** *34.2.* Here the Cascade Mountain line joins the Burlington Northern (former Great Northern) track that comes down from Vancouver, Canada, along the shore of Puget Sound.

293.0 **EVERETT** *32.8.* This is a picturesque port town, known for its fishing fleet. Lumbering and papermaking are important local industries. From Everett south to Seattle, the tracks skirt the shore of Puget Sound (right side of the train, coming into Seattle).

308.4 **EDMONDS** *17.4.* This station serves the northern suburbs of Seattle and is also the transfer point for ferryboats to the Olympic Peninsula, the wild area across Puget Sound.

321.2 **Interbay** *4.6.* This is the site of Balmer Yard, Burlington Northern's main Seattle freight facility. Seattle is a major ocean port, being the closest mainland harbor to both Alaska and the Orient.

324.7 **North Portal** *1.1.* A mile-long tunnel under Seattle's hilly downtown area brings trains from the north into the King Street passenger station.

325.8 **SEATTLE** *0.0.* For information on the city, see section 2.47.

SPOKANE—PORTLAND

0.0 **SPOKANE** *377.7.* Between Spokane and Pasco, all westbound trains use the former Spokane, Portland and Seattle tracks, through Kahlotus, while all eastbound traffic goes over the former Northern Pacific line through Ritzville. The eastbound line is about a mile shorter.

1.1 **Sunset Junction** *376.7.* Eastbound trains from Pasco join the main line here.

Latah Junction *375.9 (eastbound).* Westbound trains turn off here, headed for Pasco.

16.3 **Cheney** *(eastbound).*

South Cheney *360.8 (westbound).* Eastern Washington University is at Cheney. Beyond this point the eastbound and westbound lines diverge. They remain about 15 to 20 miles apart until they come together.

Kahlotus *277.7 (westbound).* Just west of here, some heavy construction was necessary to bring the rails into the valley of the Snake River, which they follow to Pasco. A tunnel takes trains from the plains near Kahlotus into Devil's Canyon; and a 5-mile descent leads to a second tunnel, half a mile long, which opens into the Snake River valley at its far end.

SPOKANE—PASCO

Westbound/miles		Eastbound/miles	
0.0	SPOKANE	231.3	PASCO
1.0	Sunset Junction	238.9	Glade
1.8	Latah Junction	243.6	Sagemoor
5.6	Overlook	248.6	Eltopia
9.8	Scribner	261.5	Cactus
11.9	Fish Lake	266.8	Connell
16.9	South Cheney	279.1	Cunningham
22.1	Mock	284.0	Beatrice
33.3	Rodna	287.1	Providence
41.9	Lamont	295.0	Lind
53.8	Macall	302.7	Pasha
65.9	Benge	312.1	Ritzville
77.5	Hooper	320.4	Tokio
85.9	Washtucna	325.9	Keystone
100.0	Kahlotus	335.7	Sprague
108.1	Farrington	346.0	Fishtrap
114.4	Burr	355.5	Babb
120.5	Snake River	360.4	Cheney
123.4	Votaw	367.7	Marshall
132.4	Levey	374.1	Empire
139.0	Martindale	375.6	Sunset Junction
143.6	Ainsworth	376.7	SPOKANE
145.4	PASCO		

145.4 **PASCO** *231.3*. Pasco stands in the fork between the Columbia River and its most important tributary, the Snake, which empties into it here. The town's name is said to be an abbreviated version of "*Pa*cific *S*teamship *Co*mpany." It is the farthest point up the Columbia that can be reached by seagoing ships.

The Amtrak station at Pasco also serves Walla Walla, Washington. The U.S. atomic energy facility at Hanford is just a few miles upstream.

PASCO—PORTLAND

Westbound/miles		miles/Eastbound
145.4	PASCO	231.3
147.5	Kennewick	229.2
152.6	Finley	224.1
156.8	Hover	219.9
163.3	Yellepit	213.4
178.5	Berrian	198.2
181.4	North McNary	195.3
183.8	Plymouth	192.9
187.8	King	188.9
196.2	Paterson	180.5
206.0	Whitcomb	170.7
214.4	Alderdale	162.3
218.8	McCredie	157.9
230.0	Roosevelt	146.7
235.9	Sundale	140.8
246.1	Goodnoe	130.6
257.8	Cliffs	118.9
262.4	Maryhill	114.3
270.6	WISHRAM	106.1
273.9	Avery	102.8
282.7	Northdalles	94.0
291.4	Lyle	85.3
301.1	BINGEN-WHITE SALMON	75.6
304.0	Underwood	72.7
310.9	Cooks	65.8
319.0	Carson	57.7
322.9	Stevenson	53.8
327.9	North Bonneville	48.8
333.9	Skamania	42.8
338.9	Prindle	37.8
344.5	Mount Pleasant	32.2
349.1	Washougal	27.6
352.3	Camas	24.4
357.4	Fisher	19.3
366.7	VANCOUVER, WASH.	10.0
368.1	North Portland, Oreg.	8.6
369.7	East St. John's	7.0
372.4	Willbridge	4.3
374.7	Lake Yard	2.0
376.7	PORTLAND	0.0

It is said that the Columbia River water used for cooling the nuclear reactor here comes out a couple of degrees warmer than it goes in, so intense is the heat generated.

At Pasco westbound trains must back into the passenger station. Eastbound trains just pull in from the west and continue on their way. West of the station the railroad crosses the Columbia River on a long bridge.

147.5 **Kennewick** *229.2.* Here the Portland line turns southeast, following the north bank of the Columbia all the rest of the way to Portland. Another line goes west from this point, through Yakima and over Stampede Pass to Seattle. This, the former Northern Pacific main line, was the route of the Seattle section of the *Empire Builder* until October 1981, when it was switched to the Cascade Tunnel route via Wenatchee, which is some 70 miles shorter.

163.3 **Yellepit** *213.4.* In October 1805 Lewis and Clark met a local Indian chief named Yellepit (accent the second syllable) and exchanged tokens of friendship. The station name commemorates the chief. Near here, John Jacob Astor's fur-trading expedition finally reached the Columbia River in 1812, after nearly perishing from fatigue and starvation on the way across the mountains.

181.4 **North McNary** *195.3.* This is the site of McNary Dam, one of the many power and flood control structures on the Columbia. This one is named for Charles L. McNary, U.S. senator from Oregon for more than 25 years. The dam is visible from the south side of the train (left side, going west). In fact, this side has the best views all the way to Portland as the railroad follows the north bank of the Columbia for nearly 200 miles.

183.8 **Plymouth** *192.9.* Across the Columbia is the town of Umatilla, Oregon, where the Umatilla River empties into the Columbia. This was the point where the old Oregon Trail finanally reached the big river after crossing the Blue Mountains. Over this route the first pioneers came to Oregon in the 1840s.

206.0 **Whitcomb** *170.7.* The town of Boardman, Oregon, is on the south side of the river. The Union Pacific's line from Portland to Salt Lake City, used by Amtrak's *Pioneer,* follows the south bank from here on to the outskirts of Portland.

262.4 **Maryhill** *114.3.* At Maryhill you'll find the Sam Hill peace museum, called Maryhill Castle. It contains relics from the courts of Europe. And just up the hill from the railroad tracks is a most unusual monument to the dead of World War I—a replica of Stonehenge, the mysterious circle of stones on Salisbury Plain, England. This, too, was created by Sam Hill.

270.6 **WISHRAM** *106.1.* Wishram takes its name from an Indian village once on this site; it's currently a crew-changing point. The Dalles,

Oregon, is 14 miles west across the river; and while it has its own station (served by Amtrak's *Pioneer*), the Wishram station gives residents of The Dalles an additional train each way daily.

The Dalles of the Columbia River, just west of Wishram, are a series of deep, narrow channels so dangerous that Lewis and Clark portaged around this stretch rather than risk running the river.

282.7 **Northdalles** *94.0.* The Dalles, Oregon, is on the south bank; a bridge crosses the Columbia to reach the city.

Between Northdalles and Lyle the train passes through four tunnels.

301.1 **BINGEN-WHITE SALMON** *75.6.* These two adjacent towns are opposite Hood River, Oregon, across the river. Mount Hood, the highest point in Oregon, with an elevation of 11,235 feet, can be seen to the south (left side of the train, going to Portland).

327.9 **North Bonneville** *48.8.* Built between 1937 and 1943, the giant Bonneville Dam is more than half a mile from end to end and cost more than $80 million before inflation. It generates a tremendous amount of electricity; note the power lines leading away from the dam.

One problem engineers encountered when building Bonneville was the salmon who come up the Columbia from the ocean to spawn. In order to give these fish access to their breeding grounds, fish ladders were provided; and these can be seen just below the tracks. If you're lucky, you may catch a glimpse of determined salmon working their way up these ladders to reach the upper Columbia—the only place in the world where they will lay their eggs.

The scenery in the Columbia River valley is particularly beautiful in these last 100 miles east of Portland, and it gets progressively more impressive as you get closer to the sea.

333.9 **Skamania** *42.8.* Pacific Ocean tides reach up the Columbia to a point just east of here. Beacon Rock, an 800-foot basalt formation named by Lewis and Clark, towers overhead, while St. Peter's Dome, 2,000 feet high, stands across the river.

338.9 **Prindle** *37.8.* Three miles west of Prindle is Cape Horn, the westernmost rampart of the Cascade Range. The railroad passes through it by means of a 2,400-foot-long tunnel.

349.1 **Washougal** *27.6.* The name means "running water" in Indian language.

352.3 **Camas** *24.4.* The camas plant, a blue flower with a sweet-tasting bulb, was a favorite food of the local Indians. At Camas is a big paper and pulp mill.

366.7 **VANCOUVER, WASH.** *10.0.* Look to the north (right side, going west), and you'll see Mount St. Helens in the distance. To the river side (left side, going west) are the Kaiser shipyards, birthplace of many World War II vessels.

The town grew up around Fort Vancouver, the Hudson's Bay Company fur-trading post that was established here in 1825. This fort, in turn, was named for George Vancouver, the British sea captain who surveyed the site and claimed the area for England in 1792.

At Vancouver the line from Spokane joins the Burlington Northern's Seattle–Portland route, used by several Amtrak trains including the *Coast Starlight*. For notes on the 10 miles between Vancouver and Portland, see section 3.43.

3.46   *The Rest in the West*

In addition to the classic trains described in the last chapter, Amtrak also operates a number of other lines west of the Mississippi. Some are long, some are short; some have Superliner-equipped trains with through cars from Chicago, some are virtually commuter runs operated with Amfleet cars. These various runs are arbitrarily grouped together on the basis of geography alone, for what they all have in common is their unmistakably Western character.

3.47   *St. Louis—Kansas City*

Twice each way daily, Amtrak trains flash along the Missouri River between St. Louis and Kansas City, connecting the two largest cities in the state. En route, this line serves Jefferson City, the capital of Missouri, and a number of smaller communities as well.

Service is reasonably fast (under 6 hours for the 280-mile trip), and the Amfleet cars assigned are appropriate for the run. The trip along the Missouri is quite scenic. Amcafe cars provide snack and beverage service, but on this line there is no checking of baggage; anything you want to take along, you must carry on board. Seats on the St. Louis—Kansas City trains are unreserved, so get to the station early if you're traveling during a peak period.

0.0 **ST. LOUIS**   *279.2*   For information on St. Louis, see section 2.40.

Leaving the new Amtrak station, trains run due west through the heart of the city. Unfortunately most of the major landmarks, like the Anheuser-Busch Brewery and Forest Park, are not visible from the train.

2.9 **Tower Grove** *276.3.* No longer a passenger stop, this point marks the junction between the lines west to Kansas City and south to Arkansas and Texas.

6.6 **Maplewood** *272.6.* Just outside the St. Louis city limits, the suburb of Maplewood is also an important railroad junction where the Missouri Pacific's main line to the west crosses the Terminal Railroad Association of St. Louis's belt line around the city. Freight cars use the belt line to avoid congestion.

9.5 **Webster Groves** *269.7.* Several years ago the CBS television network chose this suburb for its study of typical American teen-agers.

12.9 **KIRKWOOD** *266.3.* This is a convenient suburban station serving the western and southern regions around St. Louis. West of the Kirkwood station the route passes the site of the National Museum of Transport, which contains one of the finest collections of historic railroad equipment in the United States.

27.3 **Eureka** *251.9.* In ancient Greek the work *eureka* means "I have found it!" Archimedes is said to have exclaimed "Eureka" upon discovering the principle of displacement of water while reclining in his bathtub. The highway paralleling the rails is I-44.

29.5 **Allenton** *249.7.* To the north (right side of the train, going west) is the Six Flags theme park.

39.3 **Gray Summit** *239.9.* This is the crest of the grade up from St. Louis. Beyond, the tracks descend again to the Missouri River near

ST. LOUIS—KANSAS CITY

Westbound/miles		miles/Eastbound
0.0	ST. LOUIS	279.2
2.9	Tower Grove	276.3
6.6	Maplewood	272.6
9.5	Webster Groves	269.7
12.9	KIRKWOOD	266.3
15.9	Barretts	263.3
18.3	Valley Park	260.9
23.3	Jedburg	255.9
27.3	Eureka	251.9
29.5	Allenton	249.7
34.2	Pacific	245.0
39.3	Gray Summit	239.9
51.0	Washington	228.2
54.9	Dewey	224.3
63.5	New Haven	215.7
71.4	Berger	207.8
77.3	Hermann	201.9
84.8	Gasconade	194.4

Washington. The builders of the Missouri Pacific chose to surmount this hill rather than follow the looping Missouri all the way from St. Louis.

51.0 **Washington** *228.2* A few miles east of Washington, the tracks come alongside the Missouri River and follow its south bank for 70 scenic miles. The river is on the north side of the train (right side, going west).

North of the river and not far east is the site of Daniel Boone's last home. He always did get to feeling hemmed in when the nearest neighbor settled less than 10 miles away, and eventually Kentucky got too crowded for him. So Dan'l moved on across the Mississippi and died near here in 1820 at age eighty-six.

77.3 **Hermann** *201.9.* Hermann, a tribal chieftain who fought the Romans in the first century A.D., was the first national hero of Germany.

96.5 **Chamois** *182.7.* A few miles northwest of Chamois, across

402

the river, is the tiny town of Fulton, site of Westminster College. Here, in 1946, Winston Churchill declared in a commencement address that "from Stettin on the Baltic, to Trieste on the Adriatic, an Iron Curtain has descended over Eastern Europe." In all his great speeches, Churchill never coined a more graphic or more memorable term.

113.5 **Osage** *165.7.* The Osage River rises in the Lake of the Ozarks resort area to the southwest and winds through the central part of Missouri to flow into the Missouri River here.

121.5 **JEFFERSON CITY** *157.7.* By virtue of its location at the dead center of the state, Jefferson City is the capital of Missouri. It's a pretty town, built on the bluffs rising high above the south bank of the river. The Amtrak station is right beside the river, below the center of town.

Jefferson City contains the closest Amtrak station to Columbia, home of the University of Missouri and Stephens College, about 30 miles north.

West of this point the rails leave the banks of the winding Missouri River and strike directly across the state toward Kansas City.

204.3 **Knob Noster** *74.9.* This is only one of a number of oddly named towns in Missouri; others include Tightwad, Fairdealing, Pure Air, and Walnut Shade.

214.6 **WARRENSBURG** *64.6.* Central Missouri State University, with an enrollment of 10,000, is here.

245.5 **Pleasant Hill** *33.7.* Approaching Kansas City from the southeast, the rail line makes an abrupt turn and actually runs around the east side of the metropolitan area before turning west again to enter the city.

256.1 **LEE'S SUMMIT** *23.1.* This is a newly established Amtrak stop, serving eastern and southern suburbs of Kansas City including Raytown and Grandview.

269.5 **INDEPENDENCE** *9.7.* Independence contains the home of Harry S. Truman, president of the United States from 1945 to 1953. Truman was a native of Lamar, Missouri, but spent most of his adult life in and around Independence. He was the last president to come up the hard way—he never went to college—and his blunt, down-to-earth style endeared him to "the little man." While his last years in office were marred by scandals, historians today rate him high among American presidents. The Truman Library at Independence houses his correspondence and state papers.

Entering Kansas City, the rails run through a depressed, concrete-lined trough, which makes it impossible to see much of the city.

279.2 **KANSAS CITY (Union Station)** *0.0.* Amtrak trains use Kansas City's Union Station, a nice old terminal that, oddly, faces away from the city. For information on Kansas City, see section 2.21.

3.48 (Chicago)—St. Louis—Little Rock— Dallas-Fort Worth—San Antonio— (Los Angeles)

The *Eagle* connects the Midwest with Texas and California. Operated with Superliner equipment, it runs daily between Chicago and St. Louis and three days a week between St. Louis and San Antonio, where it connects with the *Sunset Limited* for Phoenix and Los Angeles. Through sleeping-car and coach service is offered between Chicago and southern California, although the trip is considerably longer than on the *Southwest Limited, California Zephyr* or *Desert Wind*.

Departures from St. Louis are on Sundays, Tuesdays, and Thursdays; those from San Antonio, on Sundays, Tuesdays, and Fridays. Make travel plans accordingly.

For notes on the route from Chicago to St. Louis, see section 3.35.

0.0 **ST. LOUIS** *493.4*. For information on the city see section 2.40.

2.9 **Tower Grove** *490.5*. This used to be a stop for through passenger trains, but it was closed when Amtrak took over in 1971. Just beyond the station the Texas line branches away from the Missouri Pacific's Kansas City route, also served by Amtrak. The station takes its name from nearby Tower Grove Park.

Close at hand are the Missouri Botanical Gardens, also called the Shaw Gardens. Henry Shaw, a St. Louis businessman struck by the beauty of London's Kew Gardens while visiting Britain in 1855, determined that his native city should have a similar touch of class and donated the property for that purpose. The gardens contain rare orchids and tropical lily plants as well as many other plant species.

Beyond Tower Grove, trains circle through South St. Louis, where the letter *o* is pronounced as an *a*—you eat with a "fark" in South St. Louis. This is the site of the Anheuser-Busch Brewery, the biggest in the United States, where the Budweiser flows day and night.

9.6 **Broadway** *483.8*. One of the longest streets in St. Louis, Broadway parallels the riverfront all the way from the northern city limits to the southern suburbs. Four blocks east the train curves to the right and crosses the River Des Peres Drainage Works Canal just before it empties into the Mississippi.

Four miles due west of this point is Grant's Farm, the homestead

Southbound/miles   *miles/Northbound*

Southbound		Northbound
0.0	ST. LOUIS	493.4
2.9	Tower Grove	490.5
9.6	Broadway	483.8
12.8	Jefferson Barracks	480.6
24.0	Kimmswick	469.4
26.1	Sulphur Springs	467.3
29.7	Riverside	463.7
35.1	Silica	458.3
38.8	Hematite	454.6
45.4	De Soto	448.0
54.3	Blackwell	439.1
64.1	Mineral Point	429.3
72.8	Irondale	420.6
78.6	Bismarck	414.8
84.0	Iron Mountain	409.4
86.4	Middlebrook	407.0
91.9	Ironton-Arcadia	401.5
99.6	Hogan	393.8
111.1	Annapolis	382.3
115.5	North Des Arc	377.9
129.9	Piedmont	363.5
136.4	Leeper	357.0
148.7	Williamsville	344.7
155.8	Hendrickson	337.6
168.8	POPLAR BLUFF	324.6
168.8	POPLAR BLUFF	324.6
176.4	Harviell	317.0
183.8	Neelyville, Mo.	309.6
195.2	Corning, Ark.	298.2
201.7	Knobel	291.7
217.6	O'Kean	275.8
228.1	WALNUT RIDGE	265.3
229.5	Hoxie	263.9
242.1	Alicia	251.3
255.1	Tuckerman	238.3
262.6	Diaz	230.8
264.9	NEWPORT	228.5
281.3	Bradford	212.1
291.4	Bald Knob	202.0
295.8	Judsonia	197.6
299.6	Kensett	193.8
302.9	Higginson	190.5
311.4	McCrae	182.0
315.9	Beebe	177.5
323.6	Austin	169.8
326.2	Cabot	167.2
335.2	Jacksonville	158.2
347.4	North Little Rock	146.0

348.9	LITTLE ROCK	144.5

348.9	LITTLE ROCK	144.5
361.9	Alexander	131.5
371.9	Benton	121.5
380.5	Traskwood	112.9
391.9	MALVERN	101.5
402.8	Donaldson	90.6
413.3	Daleville	80.1
414.2	Arkadelphia	79.2
427.5	Smithson	65.9
429.5	Gurdon	63.9
445.6	Prescott	47.8
461.0	Hope	32.4
474.5	Fulton, Arkansas	18.9
493.4	TEXARKANA, ARK.-TEX.	0.0

where U. S. Grant worked the land before he became famous during the Civil War.

12.8 **Jefferson Barracks** *480.6.* An important military post dating back to the early nineteenth century, Jefferson Barracks was once the prison of Blackhawk, the Sac chief who was defeated in 1832. Today the site includes a historical park with two museums concerning the military and the opening of the west, a veterans' hospital, and a national cemetery. South of the barracks the rails run for 17 miles along the Mississippi to Riverside.

45.4 **De Soto** *448.0.* Named for Hernando De Soto, the Spanish explorer who, in May 1541, was the first European to see the Mississippi.

64.1 **Mineral Point** *429.3* The names of the towns through the next 30 miles (Irondale, Iron Mountain, Hematite, etc.) tell you plainly that this was a mining region. Indeed, it still claims to be the world's largest lead-mining district, although in earlier days the principal ore dug here was iron. As a matter of fact, the railroad over which Amtrak operates was originally called the St. Louis and Iron Mountain, before it was absorbed into the Missouri Pacific system many years ago.

Missouri is also far more rugged than is generally realized. It may not have peaks like Colorado's, but offshoots of the Ozarks are present. Because of the rough terrain, freight trains are sent from St. Louis by way of the Illinois shore of the Mississippi—a longer route, but one that avoids the grades and curves of the former Iron Mountain line.

91.9 **Ironton-Arcadia** *401.5.* Taum Sauk Mountain, at 1,772 feet the highest point in Missouri, is about 3 miles west of these twin towns. From here south it is downgrade all the way to Poplar Bluff.

136.4 **Leeper** *357.0.* Here the rails reach the valley of the Black River, which they follow the rest of the way to Poplar Bluff, 22 miles. Much of the trip is made through the middle of the Mark Twain National Forest.

168.8 **POPLAR BLUFF, MO.** *324.6.* This is a railroad division point and junction with the freight line from St. Louis that runs around the hills of Iron County.

195.2 **Corning, Ark.** *298.2.* Arkansas is a beautiful state with a colorful history, but it needs a good press agent—it's one of the least-known states in the Union. The state is named after the Arkansas Indians, whose name meant "downstream people"; French influence is clear in the spelling and pronunciation. Arkansas has long been a leading cotton state but is presently enjoying an industrial boom that has reversed a long-term population decline. It has the Ozark Mountains, offering pretty recreation areas. In fact, about the best way to describe Arkansas is to say that it has a little of everything.

228.1 **WALNUT RIDGE** *265.3.* This station serves adjacent Hoxie.

264.9 **NEWPORT** *228.5.* Memphis, Tennessee, is 60 miles east. This is the most convenient Amtrak station for passengers heading from Memphis to Texas and California.

347.4 **North Little Rock** *146.0.* The town is separated from Little Rock by the Arkansas River, one of the important tributaries of the Mississippi. The Arkansas rises in the Colorado Rockies near Leadville and flows 1,500 miles through Colorado, Kansas, Oklahoma, and Arkansas before reaching the Mississippi.

348.9 **LITTLE ROCK** *144.5.* Arkansas' capital and largest city, Little Rock grew from a trading post established on this site in 1722 by a French explorer, Bernard de la Harpe. He named the spot for a small outcropping of rock overlooking the Arkansas River, and it's been Little Rock, in French or English, ever since.

Probably the most national publicity the city ever got was when Governor Orval Faubus attempted to prevent desegregation of Central High School in 1957. Fortunately, Arkansas has changed since those days.

Little Rock is today not only the market for the state's principal crops—cotton and rice—but also a manufacturing and distributing city with a diversified economy.

The passenger station is a masterpiece of urban restoration. When the Amtrak system began in 1971, the Texas service ran by way of Oklahoma City, and Little Rock was left without passenger trains. The elegant old station building seemed headed for the wreckers' ball. But a farsighted local group managed to save it and restore it to first-class condition, and it went back into service when Amtrak rerouted its Texas trains through Arkansas.

371.9 **Benton** *121.5.* Directly west of Benton is Hot Springs National Park, one of the first sites in the nation to be set aside for conservation. In 1832 Congress passed a law ensuring that Hot Springs would remain public land, and it became a national park in 1921. The springs themselves bubble at a constant 143 degrees, making a natural hot tub that attracts visitors the year round. Lakes Hamilton and Catherine and the nearby Ouachita National Forest are additional attractions.

391.9 **MALVERN** *101.5.* This is the closest Amtrak stop to Hot Springs, 23 miles away. Malvern also serves as a station for Pine Bluff, 50 miles east.

414.2 **Arkadelphia** *79.2.* Henderson State and Ouachita Baptist universities are here. Passengers for Arkadelphia use the station at Malvern.

Note that from North Little Rock to Texarkana, the railroad is built across the natural drainage pattern. Four major rivers are crossed in this 143-mile stretch (the Arkansas, Ouachita, Little Missouri, and Red). The railroad is always either climbing out of one valley or dropping into the next.

493.4 **TEXARKANA, ARK.-TEX.** *0.0.* As its name suggests, Texarkana straddles the state line. Half of it is in Arkansas, the rest in Texas. West of Texarkana the track is owned by the Texas and Pacific Railroad, affiliated with the Missouri Pacific but legally a separate company.

No state has a more interesting history than Texas, which has waved six flags since the first white settlers arrived in the sixteenth century. It has been Spanish, French, Mexican, Confederate, and independent, in addition to flying the U.S. banner twice. It is one of three states recognized as having been independent republics (Hawaii and Vermont are the others—California declared its independence but was not recognized) before becoming part of the United States. Until the admission of Alaska, Texas was the biggest state in the Union; in the minds of Texans it still is.

0.0 **TEXARKANA, ARK.-TEX.** *249.0.* Leaving Texarkana the line curves southward, around the east edge of Lake Texarkana. You don't think of Texas as lake country, and of course most of it isn't. But here, in the extreme northeast corner of the state, there are a number of lakes and some of them are pretty good-sized bodies of water.

66.8 **MARSHALL, TEX.** *182.2.* This is the station for Shreveport, Louisiana, about 35 miles east on I-20. A line from New Orleans, now freight only, joins here.

90.5 **LONGVIEW** *158.5.* Longview is a real railroad town and one of the most important junctions in all of Texas. From Longview, Missouri Pacific and Texas and Pacific rails run west to Dallas, Fort Worth, and beyond; southwest to Austin, San Antonio, and Mexico; south to Houston and Galveston; east to New Orleans; and north to St. Louis. No wonder Longview is the hub of the system. It is also

Westbound/miles   *miles/Eastbound*

0.0	TEXARKANA, ARK.-TEX.	249.0
8.1	Sulphur, Tex.	240.9
21.2	Queen City	227.8
23.9	Atlanta	225.1
30.8	Bivins	218.2
37.1	Kildare	211.9
42.1	Lodi	206.9
51.2	Jefferson	197.8
66.8	MARSHALL	182.2
80.6	Hallsville	168.4
90.5	LONGVIEW	158.5
90.5	LONGVIEW	158.5
103.0	Gladewater	146.0
113.1	Big Sandy	135.9
118.8	Hawkins	130.2
136.4	Mineola	112.6
149.5	Grand Saline	99.5
159.9	Edgewood	89.1
167.2	Wills Point	81.8
176.3	Elmo	72.7
182.7	Terrell	66.3
186.8	Lawrence	62.2
194.2	Forney	54.8
202.5	Mesquite	46.5
207.1	Orphans Home	41.9
217.4	DALLAS	31.6
217.4	DALLAS	31.6
223.3	Eagle Ford	25.7
229.6	Grand Prairie	19.4
235.9	Arlington	13.1
242.5	Handley	6.5
249.0	FORT WORTH	0.0

the Amtrak station for Tyler, 26 miles west, and Kilgore, 12 miles south. Kilgore is best known for its Rangerettes ensemble, which has been performing at half-time shows of major football games for many years.

West of Longview the railroad follows the Sabine River for 50 miles through more unexpected lake country. The stations at Gladewater and Hawkins are both named after nearby lakes. This whole area was once inhabited by the Caddo Indians, whose name is reflected in several other East Texas towns, such as Lake Caddo and Caddo Mills.

202.5 **Mesquite** *46.5.* This is pronounced *Mes-keet,* and if you say *Mes-kwite,* you'll mark yourself as a tenderfoot. Once a separate town, Mesquite is now a suburb of Dallas, which has grown out to meet it.

409

Look for the Texas State Fairgrounds, site of the Cotton Bowl stadium, on the way into Dallas proper.

217.4 **DALLAS** *31.6.* For information on the city, see section 2.14.

229.6 **Grand Prairie** *19.4.* This is the site of the Fireman's Hall of Fame and the Six Flags Over Texas theme park. Irving, home of the Dallas Cowboys' Texas Stadium, is just to the north.

235.9 **Arlington** *13.1.* The town is the home of the University of Texas-Arlington and of the Texas Rangers' baseball team, whose stadium is also here.

249.0 **FORT WORTH** *0.0.* Thirty-one miles from Dallas, but light years away in atmosphere, Fort Worth stands on the West Fork of the Trinity River. It was founded in 1849 as an outpost against Indian attacks, and as Dallas grew up with cotton, Fort Worth was a cattle town where Texas longhorns were driven to the stockyards and rail yards. Indeed, the largest meat-processing facilities in the Southwest are in Fort Worth.

Like Dallas, however, Fort Worth has become an oil capital and an important industrial center. Aircraft, boats, electronic equipment, and mobile homes are manufactured here. Dallas may have more glamour, but Fort Worthers prefer the more down-home character of their own smaller city.

0.0 **FORT WORTH** *128.2.*

28.7 **CLEBURNE** *99.5.* Although most people think of Texas as a Western, rather than a Southern, state, it did secede and join the Confederacy in the Civil War. It's not surprising, then, to find a Texas town named after a general—Pat Cleburne—who was one of the best and most popular officers in the Confederate army.

Cleburne is a railroad town. The Santa Fe has a diesel shop here.

102.9 **McGREGOR** *25.3.* This station serves Waco, home of Baylor University, 20 miles northeast on the Brazos River.

128.2 **TEMPLE** *0.0.* At this railroad junction, Amtrak trains leave the Santa Fe rails and head south via the Missouri-Kansas-Texas line,

FORT WORTH—TEMPLE—TAYLOR—SAN ANTONIO

Southbound/miles		miles/Northbound
0.0	FORT WORTH	128.2
12.5	Crowley	115.7
20.9	Joshua	107.3
28.7	CLEBURNE	99.5
36.7	Rio Vista	91.5
43.1	Blum	85.1
51.2	Kopperl	77.0
58.4	Morgan	69.8
65.8	Meridian	62.4

76.1	Clifton	52.1
87.2	Valley Mills	41.0
96.2	Crawford	32.0
102.9	McGREGOR	25.3
112.9	Moody	15.3
120.9	Pendleton	7.3
128.2	TEMPLE	0.0
0.0	TEMPLE	39.0
7.6	Little River	31.4
12.0	Sparks	27.0
16.8	Holland	22.2
22.8	Bartlett	16.2
28.1	Granger	10.9
39.0	TAYLOR	0.0
0.0	TAYLOR	115.3
8.6	Hutto	106.7
16.8	Round Rock	98.5
21.2	McNeil	94.1
31.2	Camp Mabry	84.1
35.4	AUSTIN	79.9
46.4	Manchaca	68.9
50.6	Buda	64.7
57.4	Kyle	57.9
66.0	SAN MARCOS	49.3
73.3	Hunter	42.0
79.4	Goodwin	35.9
83.7	New Braunfels	31.6
89.2	Dittlinger	26.1
91.4	Corbyn	23.9
97.4	Bracken	17.9
104.4	Wetmore	10.9
115.3	SAN ANTONIO	0.0

often call "the Katy" for short. The MKT is actually a St. Louis to Texas railroad, but much of its track is not suitable for high-speed passenger operations. Amtrak uses just 39 miles of the Katy as a bridge between the Santa Fe at Temple and the Missouri Pacific at Taylor.

0.0 **TEMPLE** *39.0.* Between Temple and Taylor the train crosses two small rivers that like most in East Texas, flow southeast toward the Gulf. The northernmost is the Little River; the other is the San Gabriel.

28.1 **Granger** *10.9.* The MKT divides here. The west fork goes to San Antonio, but Amtrak uses the east fork, which goes to Taylor and eventually beyond to Houston and Galveston.

39.0 **TAYLOR** *0.0.* Taylor deserves a footnote in the encyclopedia; for it was the birthplace (in 1903) of Bill Pickett, the black cowboy who invented bulldogging. That's the rodeo event where the man wrestles the calf *mano a mano*, so to speak. Pickett was an active cowpoke and also acted in the Tom Mix Westerns until his untimely death in 1932 at age twenty-nine.

At Taylor the *Eagle* makes a sharp turn onto the Missouri Pacific and runs due west to Round Rock, 17 miles; there it turns south to Austin.

0.0 **TAYLOR** *115.3.*

35.4 **AUSTIN** *79.9.* Capital of Texas and home of the University of Texas, Austin owes its importance to its location near the center of the big triangle formed by Dallas-Fort Worth at the northern tip, Houston at the southeast, and San Antonio at the southwest. The city was founded in 1838 and named Waterloo, but when it became the capital of the new Republic of Texas the following year, it was renamed in honor of Stephen F. Austin.

Following a plan first proposed by his father, Moses, Stephen Austin obtained a land grant from the Mexican authorities and settled three hundred American families in Texas in 1822. The Mexicans seem to have thought that inviting American settlement would help increase their tax revenues from Texas. In fact, the flood of Americans resulted in demands for an independent Texas, which Austin first presented in 1833. Three years later, Texas won its independence on the battlefield of San Jacinto, and Austin was made secretary of state of the new republic. He died shortly afterward.

Austin was the childhood home of William Sidney Porter, the short story writer better known by his pen name, O. Henry. The house in which he lived has been preserved as a museum.

Fifty miles west, along the Perdenales River, lies the LBJ ranch at Johnson City—the home of Lyndon B. Johnson, President of the United States from 1963 to 1968 and one of the most important political leaders of the twentieth century. Johnson's Great Society may have ended in the Vietnam War, but some of the accomplishments of his administration—notably the Civil Rights and Voting Rights acts—were landmarks in the struggle to give all Americans an equal chance for a better life.

66.0 **SAN MARCOS** *49.3.* The town takes its name from the San Marcos River, which is bridged here.

115.3 **SAN ANTONIO** *0.0.* For information on the city, see section 2.43. For passengers continuing on to Los Angeles (westbound) or New Orleans (eastbound), see section 3.42.

412

3.49 (Chicago—Denver)—Salt Lake City—
Las Vegas—Los Angeles

Amtrak calls its daily train on this run the *Desert Wind,* and it certainly does cover enough desert en route. Practically the whole line from Salt Lake City to San Bernardino, more than 700 miles, goes through desolate areas. The only important intermediate city is Las Vegas, where you might just have time to visit the casino at the Union Plaza Hotel during the stop.

The *Desert Wind* is a Superliner-equipped train, offering through coach and sleeping-car service from Chicago to Los Angeles in conjunction with the *California Zephyr.* Only the absence of a glass-roofed lounge car keeps the *Wind* from being a fair approximation of the old *City of Los Angeles,* which served this route until the advent of Amtrak in 1971.

The *California Zephyr* or *Desert Wind* offers a good alternative to the busy *Southwest Limited* between Chicago and Los Angeles. It takes about seven hours longer, but it offers marvelous Colorado scenery. You can go one way and return the other.

For information on the route from Chicago to Salt Lake City, see section 3.44.

01.0 **SALT LAKE CITY** *775.2.* For information on the city, see section 2.42.

15.3 **Garfield** *759.3.* Garfield is on the shore of Great Salt Lake, 15 miles west of Salt Lake City. The lake is fed by three streams but loses water only by evaporation. Its salt content is so high that it is

SALT LAKE CITY—LAS VEGAS—LOS ANGELES

Westbound/miles		miles/Eastbound
0.0	SALT LAKE CITY	775.2
5.6	Buena Vista	769.6
15.3	Garfield	759.3
17.7	Smelter	757.5
19.6	Lake Point	755.6
27.9	Erda	747.3
31.9	Shields	743.3
36.4	Warner	738.8
39.1	Bauer	736.1

41.0	Stockton	734.2
47.9	St. John	727.3
51.3	Clover	723.9
61.3	Faust	713.9
67.0	Pehrson	708.2
73.5	Lofgren	701.7
79.6	Boulter	695.6
86.1	Tintic	689.1
92.2	McIntyre	682.0
98.7	Jericho	676.5
108.6	Champlin	666.6
118.5	Lynndyl	656.7
122.9	Cline	652.3
125.8	Strong	649.4
134.1	DELTA	641.1
144.3	Van	630.9
152.9	Clear Lake	622.3
166.8	Bloom	608.4
174.3	Cruz	600.9
184.6	Black Rock	590.6
194.2	Read	581.0
199.4	Murdock	575.8
207.3	MILFORD	567.9
207.3	MILFORD	567.9
212.7	Upton	562.5
222.6	Thermo	552.6
233.4	Latimer	541.8
242.3	Lund	532.9
252.4	Zane	522.8
257.9	Beryl	517.3
267.9	Heist	507.3
273.9	Modena	501.3
283.0	Uvada, Utah	492.2
290.3	Crestline, Nev.	484.9
294.5	Brown	480.7
299.9	Acoma	475.3
308.5	Islen	466.7
312.1	Little Springs	463.1
319.6	Eccles	455.6
324.2	CALIENTE	451.0
329.3	Etna	445.9
334.2	Stine	441.0
338.9	Boyd	436.3
345.7	Elgin	429.5
349.6	Leith	425.6
365.4	Carp	409.8
370.7	Vigo	404.5
381.3	Hoya	393.9
386.0	Rox	389.2
391.1	Farrier	384.1
401.1	Moapa	374.2
410.0	Ute	364.9

715.7	SAN BERNARDINO	59.5

715.7	SAN BERNARDINO	59.5
719.3	Rialto	55.9
726.2	Kaiser	49.0
728.1	Etiwanda	47.1
732.1	Cucamonga	43.1
735.3	Upland (Ontario)	39.9
739.2	Claremont	36.0
741.1	POMONA	34.1
744.6	San Dimas	30.6
748.8	Glendora	26.4
751.3	Azusa	23.9
756.8	Monrovia	18.4
758.6	Arcadia	16.6
761.7	Chapman	13.5
766.1	PASADENA	9.1
768.1	South Pasadena	7.1
770.3	Highland Park	4.9
773.8	Broadway	1.4
775.2	LOS ANGELES	0.0

about four times as briny as the ocean, and no fish can live in it. Along the shores of the lake a number of giant extraction plants take 100,000 tons of salt a year from the water.

17.7 **Smelter** *757.5.* What gets smelted here is copper—and copper is largely responsible for the existence of the Salt Lake to Los Angeles railroad in the first place.

Just a little south of Great Salt Lake is Bingham Canyon, site of the world's largest open-pit copper mine. Its developers, seeking a Pacific Coast outlet, built the San Pedro, Los Angeles and Salt Lake Railroad from the new port of San Pedro, just south of Los Angeles, to Utah. This line is the present-day Union Pacific route now used by Amtrak.

19.6 **Lake Point** *755.6.* Here the rails turn inland, leaving Great Salt Lake behind and pointing south along the edge of the Salt Lake desert. From this point to Las Vegas there is not a single town of more than 1,000 population—more than 400 miles of nearly uninhabited land!

131.1 **DELTA** *641.1.* So steep are the mountains and so harsh the desert west of the Salt Lake valley that there is not even a highway between Salt Lake and Delta. Here the railroad crosses U.S. 6 and 50, the first east-west highway since Salt Lake City. The *Desert Wind* now stops at Delta.

207.3 **MILFORD** *567.9.* This is a railroad division point, and if it weren't for the Union Pacific, the town probably wouldn't exist.

Directly west is the site of Frisco, an old mining town at the base of 9,000-foot-high Frisco Mountain. South and east is Cedar City, jumping-off point for Zion and Bryce Canyon national parks. Although

Milford is the closest Amtrak station to the parks, they are a tough 2 to 3 hours away by car and are more easily reached from Las Vegas on I-15.

283.0 **Uvada, Utah** *492.2.* This site is just east of the Utah-Nevada state line, amid the barren mountains that make up so much of the topography of this part of the country. To the north is Mount Ellenore; to the south, Mount Hawkins, both over 7,500 feet high.

290.3 **Crestline, Nev.** *484.9.* As its name indicates, Crestline marks the summit of the pass through Needle Range. The grade up to Crestline from Milford is gentle enough; but coming eastward, up from Caliente, it is a taxing climb. Thirty miles to the northwest is Pioche, one of Nevada's mining towns. Silver, lead, and zinc have been mined here.

299.9 **Acoma** *475.3.* Here the rails enter the valley of the Claver Wash, which they follow down to Caliente.

324.2 **CALIENTE** *451.0.* No need to bother with the weather forecast here: *Caliente* is Spanish for "hot." From here the rails pass through Rainbow Canyon, formed by Meadow Wash, for 62 miles. Unfortunately, Amtrak trains usually make this run in darkness.

386.0 **Rox** *389.3.* This is at the end of the canyon. From here the rails strike across country to Las Vegas, still on a descending grade. The mountains to the east are the Mormon Range. On the Utah side of these peaks Brigham Young once had a winter home.

441.5 **Valley** *333.7.* A spur line runs from here to Nellis Air Force Base, a major facility to the east.

449.8 **LAS VEGAS** *325.4.* Amtrak passengers get a quick introduction to Vegas—the passenger station is inside the Union Plaza Hotel, a few steps from a casino. The hotel occupies the site of the former depot at the foot of glittering Fremont Street.

For information on Las Vegas, see section 2.22.

Today, most of the biggest hotels are south of town along Las Vegas Boulevard—the famous "Strip." You can see them from the east side of the train (left side, going toward Los Angeles). The lights at night are a unique sight.

456.7 **Boulder Junction** *318.5.* From here a 22-mile branch extends to Hoover Dam and Boulder City, which lie to the east of the main line. Hoover Dam, on the Colorado River, is the highest in the country; it holds back Lake Mead, which irrigates more than a million acres of farmland.

482.8 **Jean, Nev.** *292.4.* There is no town here, but a building that is the quintessence of Nevada—a combination roadhouse, gas station, and casino!

526.2 **Cima, Calif.** *245.1.* This is the summit of the Providence Mountains. Eastbound trains must fight up a 2.2 percent grade from Kelso to reach this point.

548.7 **Kelso** *226.5.* Helper engines used to be stationed here to push heavy freights up to Cima. West of here the railroad crosses a harsh stretch of rocky desert aptly called the Devil's Playground.

621.0 **Yermo** *154.2.* There are freight yards here. The old mining town of Calico, now restored as a tourist attraction, is nearby.

625.6 **Daggett** *146.6.* At Daggett is the junction with the Santa Fe main line from the east.

For notes on the route from Daggett to Los Angeles, see section 3.41.

3.50   (Chicago—Denver)—Salt Lake City —Portland—Seattle

Amtrak's *Pioneer* serves parts of Utah, Idaho, and Oregon, and in conjunction with the *California Zephyr* it provides an alternative route between Chicago and the Pacific Northwest. Superliner coaches and sleeping cars operate all the way through from Chicago to Seattle, and the *Pioneer* now offers complete dining-car service. Baggage may be checked to some, but not all, stations en route.

The train is scheduled to pass through the most scenic parts of the route in daylight. Highlights are the crossing of the Blue Mountains between Pendleton and La Grande, and the 165-mile run down the south bank of the Columbia River from Boardman to Portland. For a scenic circle trip second to none, take the *California Zephyr* and *Pioneer* from Chicago to Seattle and return via the *Empire Builder*. You'll see the Colorado Rockies, the Columbia River valley, the Cascades, Glacier National Park and the Mississippi Valley, all during one vacation.

For information on the route from Chicago to Salt Lake City, see section 3.44.

0.0 **SALT LAKE CITY** *896.2.* For information on the city, see section 2.42.

36.0 **OGDEN** *860.2.* Named after trader and fur trapper Peter Skene Ogden, this is the second-largest city in Utah. It has always been a railroad center, where the lines from the east meet the Southern Pacific line to California. But there is more to Ogden than trains. Though less well known than its larger neighbor to the south, Ogden is as much a Mormon city as Salt Lake City. Ogden's street plan resembles Salt Lake City's, with an unadorned grid pattern centering on Tabernacle Square. Weber State University, one of Utah's four major institutions

418

Westbound/miles		miles/Eastbound
0.0	SALT LAKE CITY	896.2
3.3	Becks	892.9
4.7	North Salt Lake	891.5
6.4	Pioneer	889.8
8.2	Woods Cross	888.0
10.4	Centerville	885.8
14.5	Farmington	881.7
20.4	Kaysville	875.8
21.4	Layton	874.8
25.9	Clearfield	870.3
30.1	Roy	866.1
36.0	OGDEN	860.2
40.7	Harrisville	855.5
41.8	Wip	854.4
42.3	Randall	853.9
45.0	Hot Springs	851.2
50.6	Willard	845.6
53.3	Perry	842.9
57.1	Brigham City	839.1
66.4	Honeyville	829.8
71.7	Dewey	824.5
76.3	Collinston	819.9
80.0	Wheelon	816.2
84.6	CACHE JUNCTION	811.6
91.8	Cottle	804.4
92.6	Trenton	803.6
96.6	Cornish, Utah	799.6
99.8	Anderson, Idaho	796.4
101.4	Weston	794.8
107.4	Dayton	788.8
111.2	Clifton	785.0
114.8	Coulam	781.4
120.4	Swan Lake	775.8
131.0	Downey	765.2
136.4	Virginia	759.8
140.8	Arimo	755.4
147.2	McCammon	749.0
157.6	Inkom	738.6
170.1	POCATELLO	726.1

170.1	POCATELLO	726.1
175.9	Don	720.3
182.4	Schiller	713.8
186.0	Bannock	710.2
194.6	American Falls	701.6
198.2	Borah	698.0
205.9	Quigley	690.3
211.9	Wapi	684.3
216.2	Dewoff	680.0

419

792.0	Biggs	104.2
795.4	Miller	100.8
803.9	Dune	92.3
808.6	Seufert	87.6
810.9	THE DALLES	85.3

810.9	THE DALLES	85.3

814.1	Crates	82.1
819.2	Rowena	77.0
826.7	Mosier	69.5
832.7	HOOD RIVER	63.5
837.4	Meno	58.8
846.0	Wyeth	50.2
852.8	CASCADE LOCKS	43.4
857.8	Bonneville	38.4
862.5	Dodson	33.7
869.5	Bridal Veil	26.7
879.2	Sandy	17.0
880.6	Troutdale	15.6
883.3	Fairview	12.9
884.4	Rockwood	11.8
888.4	Clarnie	7.8
891.8	Graham	4.4
895.6	East Portland	0.6
896.2	PORTLAND	0.0

of higher education, is here. Incidentally, ''Weber'' is pronounced ''Weeber,'' not ''Webber.'' This is because the name is a corruption of ''Weaver''—James G. Weaver, a nineteenth-century populist who was an unsuccessful candidate for the presidency. Somehow his name was misspelled on the maps.

By the way, neither Ogden nor Salt Lake City is on the shore of Great Salt Lake. Both are several miles east of the lake.

57.1 **Brigham City** *839.1.* This town is named for Brigham Young, the man who led the Mormon trek across the continent and established the Latter-Day Saints in Utah, having taken over from founder Joseph Smith after Smith's death in 1844. As president of the Church of Jesus Christ of Latter-Day Saints, Young directed the development of industry and agriculture, in addition to performing his religious duties. He was territorial governor of Utah for 7 years, and somehow found time to entertain twenty-seven wives. He died in 1877.

84.6 **CACHE JUNCTION, UTAH** *811.6.* The station here serves Logan, 18 miles to the east via Route 30, which is the home of Utah State University, one of the four major universities in the state.

147.2 **McCammon, Idaho** *749.0.* This is an important railroad junction where the line from Salt Lake, used by Amtrak, meets the cutoff from Granger, Wyoming, which is used by freight trains en route to and from Omaha and Chicago. The Skyline ski area is nearby, and

422

a few miles northeast is the Blackfoot Indian Reservation. The Blackfeet were the most powerful and warlike tribe of the Northwest. Skillful horsemen and crack riflemen, they dominated an area extending from southern Idaho all through Montana and up into Canada. The decline of the buffalo herds, a smallpox epidemic, and military pressure from the U.S. Army weakened the tribe and forced its remaining people onto the reservation by 1890.

170.1 **POCATELLO** *726.1.* At an altitude of 4,464 feet above sea level, Pocatello is the largest city in southeastern Idaho (and second largest in the state). The town is named for Chief Pocatello, an Indian leader who helped the railroad builders obtain a right-of-way through his lands. A large phosphate industry, producing fertilizers for farm use, is centered in this area. Pocatello is also the home of Idaho State University and site of a major railroad freight yard and terminal. From Pocatello to Huntington, Oregon, the railroad follows the Snake River.

194.6 **American Falls** *701.6.* The American Falls dam on the Snake River has created a reservoir that serves both hydroelectric and irrigation demands.

198.2 **Borah** *698.0.* The town is named for William E. Borah, Republican politician and U.S. senator from Idaho for thirty-three years. Though a progressive on domestic matters, Borah is best known for this stance against the League of Nations and as a spokesman for isolationism during Franklin Roosevelt's administration. He died in 1940 at age seventy-five.

223.3 **Hawley** *672.9.* This place is named for James Hawley, who served with Senator Borah on the prosecution staff in the famous 1906 trial of Big Bill Haywood. Haywood, the outspoken and controversial president of the Western Federation of Miners, was accused of conspiracy in the bomb murder of Idaho's former governor, Frank Steunenberg. Together with two other WFM officials, he was represented by Clarence Darrow and eventually acquitted.

277.7 **SHOSHONE** *618.5.* Here is the station for the Sun Valley ski area around Ketchum, 30 miles north. Sun Valley was developed as a winter resort by the Union Pacific Railroad, which did an excellent job of promoting the area. Ernest Hemingway lived at Ketchum, the nearest town, and it was here that he shot himself in 1961, ending a literary career that culminated with both the Nobel and Pulitzer prizes.

The Shoshones, or Shoshoni, were not a tribe but a group of Indian peoples that included such disparate branches as the Diggers, who had no horses and ate nuts, and the Comanches. At their height the Shoshones ranged from California to Wyoming, but today there are fewer than ten thousand living on reservations.

293.6 **Gooding** *602.6.* The town is named for the governor of

Idaho at the time of the Haywood trial. Like Borah and Hawley, he was rewarded by the railroad company with a whistle-stop in his name.

305.9 **Bliss** *590.3.* The Bliss Dam on the Snake River aids in flood control and irrigation.

338.6 **Hammett** *557.6.* Hammett sits at the base of Medbury Hill, 10½ miles of tough upgrade that takes the rails out of the Snake Valley and up toward Boise. This grade demanded pusher engines back in the steam days.

349.2 **Reverse** *547.0.* Reverse is at the summit of Medbury Hill. The place may have gotten its name because pusher engines were cut off here and sent back down the hill.

357.7 **Mountain Home** *538.5.* Mountain Home Air Force Base is just outside the town.

379.5 **Orchard** *516.7.* At this junction between the main line and the Boise Cutoff, through freight trains save 11 miles and avoid some steep grades by going directly on to Nampa via Kuna, but Amtrak passenger trains run up to Boise.

404.6 **BOISE** *491.6.* For information on the city, see section 2.5.

423.8 **NAMPA** *472.4.* This is the junction point where the Boise Cutoff rejoins the main freight line from Orchard. Nampa is a shipping point for sugar beets, dairy products, and fruit, as well as for Idaho's familiar potatoes.

432.7 **Caldwell** *463.5.* This was the site of the Steunenberg murder, on December 30, 1905, which ultimately led to the Haywood trial.

453.1 **Apple Valley, Idaho** *443.1.* Beyond here the railroad crosses to the Oregon side of the Snake River.

465.9 **ONTARIO, OREG.** *430.3.* This is the station for all of eastern Oregon and the fruit belt of western Idaho. Beyond Ontario the railroad recrosses the Snake River back to Idaho and follows the east bank for 35 miles.

469.7 **Payette, Idaho** *426.5.* Payette is the birthplace of baseball slugger Harmon Killebrew.

499.8 **Rock Island, Idaho** *396.4.* For the last time the railroad crosses the Snake River, returning to Oregon. Farther north the river plunges through Hells Canyon, the deepest gorge in North America. With sheer walls, 8,000 feet high, it is half again as deep as the Grand Canyon.

505.8 **Huntington, Oreg.** *390.4.* Though not a passenger stop, Huntington is a crew-changing point. Set your watch—this is the dividing line between the Mountain and Pacific time zones.

526.9 **Durkee** *369.3.* Durkee sits at the bottom of a 13-mile grade leading up to Encina, lower of the two summits of the Blue Mountains that the railroad crosses between Huntington and Pendleton. This grade, which averages 2.2 percent, or 115 feet up for every mile forward, is stiff enough to demand the use of helper engines on heavy freight trains even today. Out of Durkee there is a horseshoe curve that allows the passengers on the left side of the train (going west) to get a look at the engines up ahead.

540.4 **Pleasant Valley** *355.8.* The steep climb from Durkee levels out somewhat here, though it's still upgrade for another 3 miles to Encina.

543.7 **Encina** *352.5.* This is the top of the grade. Helper engines cut out here and return to Durkee for a new assignment. Passenger trains, however, usually do not need a helper. From Encina, 3,968 feet above sea level, the rails drop down on a 1.3 percent pitch to Baker.

553.8 **BAKER** *342.4.* Baker, in the Powder River valley between the twin summits of the Blue Mountains, is the gateway to the Hells Canyon national recreation area. Although lumbering and agriculture are the principal industries today, Baker began as a gold-mining camp. It was named for Colonel Edward Baker, a leading Republican politician and close friend of Lincoln's who was a U.S. senator from Oregon until he resigned to accept a Union Army commission. He should have stayed safely in the Senate: He was killed at Ball's Bluff, Virginia, early in the Civil War, while trying to attack a superior Confederate force.

573.4 **North Powder** *322.8.* Beyond here the rails climb out of the Powder River valley and up a 1 percent grade to Telocaset; they then descend along Catherine Creek into the Grande Ronde valley. Partway down the hill you pass Wind Hollow, where the wind has been known to blow freight cars right off the track.

605.4 **LA GRANDE** *290.7.* At an elevation of 2,766 feet above sea level, La Grande is the low point between the two summits of the Blue Mountains—Encina to the east, Kamela to the west. It is a railroad division point, with the usual freight yards, engine terminal, and shop facilities. In addition, La Grande is the home of Eastern Oregon State College and the major shipping point for the products of the Grande Ronde valley. Immediately west of town the rails resume the long climb to the summit of the Blue Mountains.

613.6 **Hilgard** *282.6.* Here the pusher engines are cut into freight trains, and the 2.2 percent grade, which extends for 11 miles up the mountain, begins. This is the toughest climb on the entire route from Salt Lake City to Portland: Freight trains may take as much as 2 hours to struggle up that tortuous 11 miles when snow and ice are on the track.

624.8 **Kamela** *271.4.* At 4,205 feet above sea level, Kamela is the highest point of the pass through the Blue Mountains; this marks the divide between the Snake River and Columbia River watersheds. Helper engines on heavy freight trains are cut off here to return to Hilgard. From Kamela down to Pendleton, passengers can enjoy some fine scenery with stands of pine and rushing mountain streams close by the tracks.

630.3 **Meacham** *265.9.* As picturesque a scene as you'd care to find. Just west of here, an old tunnel has been bypassed by a new right of way.

637.8 **Huron** *258.4.* This is at the bottom of the steep grade that leads to Kamela. The Umatilla Indian Reservation occupies many acres west of the railroad (left side, going west).

658.9 **Gibbon** *237.3.* Here the rails gain the valley of the Umatilla River, which they follow until they reach the Columbia and then the coast. Gibbon is another of the many towns named for Civil War officers—this time, General John Gibbon, commander of the Iron Brigade in the Union Army of the Potomac.

680.1 **PENDLETON** *216.1.* This is a quiet, pretty town on the Umatilla River. Fifty miles north is Walla Walla, Washington; the Blue Mountains can be seen in the distance to the east and south. An annual roundup is held at Pendleton each fall. The rich agricultural area around the town produces wheat and green peas.

710.5 **HINKLE** *185.7.* You won't find Hinkle on a highway map—as a town, it doesn't exist. Hinkle is a railroad junction 3 miles west of Stanfield and just south of Hemiston from which a long and important branch line runs north to Spokane and on to Canada. This junction is the site of one of the biggest and newest freight yards on the Union Pacific system, and everything about Hinkle looks raw and unfinished. Crews change here, which accounts for the stop.

716.9 **Ordnance** *179.3.* To the north of the tracks (right side, going west) is the Umatilla Army Depot.

748.9 **Heppner Junction** *147.3.* A branch line leads south to Heppner, Oregon. From this point, the tracks follow the south bank of the Columbia River all the way into Portland. The best scenery is on the north side of the train (right side, going west).

783.2 **Goff** *113.0.* Nearby is John Day Dam, one of many dams on the Columbia that provide flood control, irrigation, and hydroelectric power to the Northwest region.

795.4 **Miller** *100.8.* For a few miles west of this point, the railroad tracks are laid on a causeway between the westbound and eastbound lanes of I-80N, an unusual arrangement.

808.6 **Seufert** *87.6.* This is the site of The Dalles Dam, another major Columbia River project administered by the U.S. Army Corps of Engineers.

810.9 **THE DALLES** *85.3.* The town clings to both sides of the Columbia River. Lumbering is an important industry here. On clear days, travelers may be able to see Mount Hood, 11,235 feet high, to the southwest.

814.1 **Crates** *82.1.* One look at the gigantic sawmills here—Martin-Marietta Corporation has a major plant—and you'll know how this siding was named.

826.7 **Mosier** *69.5.* After rounding the sharp curve here, watch for the interesting rock strata that show up on the mountainsides north of the Columbia. A short tunnel leads into the environs of Hood River.

832.7 **HOOD RIVER** *63.5.* Mount Hood, the highest point in Oregon, is directly south. Between Hood River and Portland is the most scenic part of the trip along the Columbia River, with the Gifford Pinchot National Forest on the Washington side and the Multnomah National Forest to the south. The rock ramparts of the river get steeper and more spectacular, and the ride is a truly beautiful one.

846.0 **Wyeth** *50.2.* Look for booms of logs in the river along here. They are floated down to the sawmills for processing.

852.8 **CASCADE LOCKS** *43.4.* Cascade Falls was a major barrier to navigation on the Columbia, but locks now get river traffic around the falls. The old locks can be seen on the river to the north side of the railroad (right side going west).

857.8 **Bonneville** *38.4.* This is the site of the Bonneville Dam, biggest of all the Columbia River dams (right side of the train, going to Portland), and its interesting fish ladder (see section 3.45).

869.5 **Bridal Veil** *26.7.* Another Columbia River waterfall is here. The mountains come down right to the water's edge—a pretty location.

880.6 **Troutdale** *15.6.* Here the passenger route into Portland leaves the Columbia River and turns inland. A freight-only line continues along the shore.

884.4 **Rockwood** *11.8.* A freeway parallels the tracks through the suburbs of Portland.

895.6 **East Portland** *0.6.* This is the junction with Amtrak's Oakland–Portland line, used by the *Coast Starlight*. For notes on East Portland, see section 3.43.

For information on Portland, see section 2.34. For notes on the route from Portland to Seattle, see section 3.43.

3.51   Los Angeles—San Diego

This route is Amtrak's biggest success story. In 1970 it saw three poorly patronized daily trains, made up of hand-me-down cars from elsewhere on the Santa Fe system. Today, with the aid of a subsidy from the State of California, there are seven daily trains each way, using Amfleet equipment and loading more passengers than this line carried in the peak years of World War II.

The *San Diegoan*s are all unreserved, so get to the gate early. Snack and beverage service, adequate for a run of less than 3 hours, is available on all trains, and baggage may be checked on certain runs (consult agent).

0.0 **LOS ANGELES** *128.0.* Los Angeles's Union Station is a stub-end terminal with the tracks entering from the north; so trains must back up to reach Mission Tower, on the banks of the Los Angeles River, where the terminal tracks join the main line to the south. The Los Angeles County Jail is to the east (left side of the train, leaving Los

LOS ANGLES—SAN DIEGO

Southbound/miles   *miles/Northbound*

0.0	LOS ANGELES	128.0
1.9	First St.	126.1
4.0	Redondo Jct.	124.0
6.3	Hobart	121.7
10.6	Bandini	117.4
12.0	Pico Rivera	116.0
13.9	Los Nietos	114.1
15.2	Santa Fe Springs	112.8
19.5	La Mirada	108.5
25.8	FULLERTON	102.2
29.5	ANAHEIM (Anaheim Stadium)	98.5
33.4	Orange	94.6
36.3	SANTA ANA	91.7
39.2	Irvine	88.8
43.6	Valencia	84.4
48.8	El Toro	79.2
53.3	Galivan	74.7
57.9	SAN JUAN CAPISTRANO	70.1
60.5	Serra	67.5
65.5	SAN CLEMENTE	62.5
69.9	San Onofre	58.1
84.8	Fallbrook Jct.	43.2
86.9	OCEANSIDE	41.1
87.9	Escondido Jct.	40.1
94.4	Ponto	33.6
98.6	Encinitas	29.4
104.6	DEL MAR	23.4
109.6	Sorrento	18.4
113.5	Miramar	14.5
118.4	Elvira	9.6
124.7	Old Town	3.3
128.0	SAN DIEGO	0.0

Angeles), between the station and Mission Tower.

1.9 **First Street** *126.1.* As the rails follow the west bank of the concreted Los Angeles River, they pass Amtrak's Los Angeles coach yard at First Street (right side of the train, leaving Los Angeles). You will probably see some Superliner cars on the yard tracks.

4.0 **Redondo Junction** *124.0.* At this point the Santa Fe main line meets the Los Angeles harbor branch. San Diego–bound trains swing to the east and cross the Los Angeles River.

The harbor line, which comes in from the south at Redondo Junction, has quite a history. It was built by the Santa Fe Railroad to connect its line with the newly dredged harbor at San Pedro. The route winds circuitously through south Los Angeles because, before the San Pedro site was chosen, there was talk of putting the harbor at Santa Monica. The railroad decided to play it safe and build to a point halfway between the proposed sites. Today, therefore, the Santa Fe's freight trains wander all over southern Los Angeles to reach the harbor; for, when the branch was begun, its builders literally did not know where it was going.

6.3 **Hobart** *121.7.* This is the site of the Santa Fe's main Los Angeles freight yard. From here trains are dispatched eastward in a never-ending stream, headed for Texas, Kansas City, and Chicago. Between Hobart and Fullerton passengers get a look at the side of Los Angeles few tourists are even aware of—for not only is Los Angeles the glamour capital of America, it is also the nation's third-largest industrial center.

25.8 **FULLERTON** *102.2.* Just across the Orange County line, Fullerton is the junction where the San Diego branch, often called the Surf Line because so much of it follows the Pacific Ocean beaches, diverges from the main freight line to the east. The Fullerton station also serves other suburban communities, such as La Mirada and La Habra, and is only a short drive from points in the San Gabriel valley.

29.5 **ANAHEIM (Anaheim Stadium)** *98.5.* Amtrak's new Anaheim station is adjacent to Anaheim Stadium, home of the California Angels and Los Angeles Rams. A few blocks west along Katella Avenue is Disneyland, the theme park created by Walt Disney back in 1955 when this area was just a big barley field. In those days nobody was building new amusement parks: Disney's Folly was looked on as a multimillion-dollar mistake. From its opening day, however, Disneyland—carefully planned, smoothly run, and brilliantly promoted—caught the nation's fancy and became one of the top tourist attractions in America. And as it grew it transformed Anaheim from a sleepy farming village to the commercial capital of booming Orange County.

36.3 **SANTA ANA** *91.7.* Convenient to Huntington Beach,

Newport Beach, and other Orange County residential areas, Santa Ana station sees heavy commuter traffic into Los Angeles. Long Beach, where the *Queen Mary* rests at her dock and where the U.S. Navy has extensive facilities, is half an hour by freeway to the west.

39.2 **Irvine** *88.8*. The huge Irvine ranch has only recently been developed for residential and commercial use. The Irvine branch of the University of California is here.

48.8 **El Toro** *79.2*. "El Toro" means "the bull" in Spanish, but in southern California it means the United States Marine Corps, which has one of its most important bases here.

57.9 **SAN JUAN CAPISTRANO** *70.1*. Of the chain of missions along El Camino Real, San Juan Capistrano is undoubtedly the most famous because of the swallows who return here from South America to make their summer home each March. I was always bothered by the question of how the swallows managed to arrive in Capistrano exactly on Saint Joseph's Day, March 19. I now know the answer, but I'm sorry to say it's a bit disappointing. The birds do always come back around the third week in March—but those who arrive before March 19 are officially designated as "scouts," while those who show up later are, of course, "stragglers." In other words, even if the trees at the old mission are groaning with swallows on March 18, they don't count. You can see the mission, to the left side of the train, going south.

60.5 **Serra** *67.5*. Three miles down the valley from Capistrano the rails reach the Pacific Ocean at last. They curve to the left, cross the San Juan River, and come out right on the beach.

Serra, which lies a couple of miles south of the river mouth, is named after Fra Junipero Serra, the Father of the California Missions. Fra Serra set out from Mexico with a dual purpose: to convert the Indians to Christianity, and to strengthen Spain's tenuous hold on California by building a chain of missions all the way up the coast. He started with Mission San Diego de Alcala in 1769, and gradually worked his way north. Although he died before it was completed, Fra Serra's chain of missions eventually extended all the way to San Francisco, 600 miles from Mexico. For good or ill, his work had a tremendous impact on the history of California.

65.5 **SAN CLEMENTE** *62.5*. Until Richard Nixon entered the White House, few Americans outside southern California had heard of San Clemente. Then Nixon made this picturesque seaside town his vacation retreat, and all of a sudden the town became world famous. The Nixons are gone now; and their old property, Casa Pacifica, has been subdivided for homes. But San Clemente is as lovely as ever: Amtrak passengers get a glimpse of the town up on the hills as the train stops at the seaside station.

69.9 **San Onofre** *58.1*. Rising up from the sandy beach, right beside the tracks (to the right, going south) is the big, controversial San Onofre nuclear power plant. All nuclear plants are objects of debate these days, but San Onofre is paticularly controversial because of the question of what would happen to it if it were struck by a massive earthquake. Proponents of nuclear power say the reactor is perfectly secure; opponents raise a number of nightmarish possibilities. Meanwhile, the plant has never gone into full operation, although testing continues.

86.9 **OCEANSIDE** *41.1.* This is the station for Camp Pendleton. Because of this Marine base, the stretch between San Clemente and Oceanside has been kept closed to residential development. From Oceanside to San Diego, however, is a 40-mile-long string of seaside towns. Also because of the proximity of the Marine base, Oceanside was recently named one of the ten toughest towns in America by a national magazine.

98.6 **Encinitas** *29.4.* This is one of those beautiful seaside residential villages where the rails hug the shoreline. The body of water is technically the Gulf of Santa Catalina, a bay of the Pacific. This is probably the nation's ideal residential area, with a perfect climate 365 days a year and without the fires, floods, smog, and crime that plague Los Angeles.

104.6 **DEL MAR** *23.4.* All out for the races! The Del Mar track (left side of the train, going south) offers Thoroughbred racing during the summer in an ideal seaside setting.

Beyond Del Mar station the railroad leaves the beaches and swings into the mountains to the east, winding through the canyons to descend the 200-foot drop to San Diego. This slow detour may someday be replaced by a tunnel, if plans for the high speed Los Angeles—San Diego trains now on the drawing board are carried out.

124.7 **Old Town** *3.3.* This is the original San Diego settlement, now restored. Between Old Town and the central business district is Lindbergh Field, the local airport (right side, going south).

128.0 **SAN DIEGO** *0.0.* For information on the city, see section 2.44.

3.52   (Los Angeles)—Bakersfield—Oakland

This combined bus-rail line offers an alternative Los Angeles—Oakland route by way of California's San Joaquin valley. The rail portion, from Bakersfield north to Oakland, sees twice-daily service in each direction, scheduled for the convenience of travelers going to the Bay Area.

As a result, one of the Los Angeles bus connections leaves and arrives in the wee hours of the morning, but one schedule in each direction does operate at a convenient time for through travelers. A separate bus ticket is not necessary, and the connecting coaches arrive and leave from the railroad stations in both Los Angeles and Bakersfield. Other bus connections serve Sacramento and San Francisco.

The *San Joaquin*s are Amfleet trains. Coach seats are unreserved, there is snack and beverage service but no full dining car, and there is no checking of baggage. While the San Joaquin valley scenery doesn't match that on the coast line, this bus-rail-bus route is actually *faster* from Los Angeles to Oakland than the all-rail *Coast Starlight*.

The *San Joaquin*s serve Yosemite, Sequoia, and Kings Canyon national parks.

Los Angeles—Bakersfield, via motor coach.

0.0 **BAKERSFIELD** *311.6*. It's hard to believe that hot, dry Bakersfield is only 100 miles from glittering Los Angeles. Oil is an important industry here, and so is ranching. Bakersfield is also, incongruously, the gateway to Sequoia National Forest, with its ski areas and mountain climate. The National Forest is also accessible from Fresno (below). See Part 4 for information.

25.3 **WASCO** *286.3*. This is a ranching and farming town near the southern end of the San Joaquin valley, one of the richest agricultural areas on earth.

80.2 **HANFORD** *231.4*. Hanford is the station for Visalia and Tulare, each about 15 miles away. This is the southern gateway to the

(LOS ANGELES)—BAKERSFIELD—OAKLAND

Northbound/miles		miles/Southbound
0.0	LOS ANGELES	111.0
	via motor coach	
111.0	BAKERSFIELD	0.0
0.0	BAKERSFIELD	311.6
17.8	Shafter	293.8
25.3	WASCO	286.3
44.3	Allensworth	267.3
54.4	Angiola	257.2
63.2	Corcoran	248.4
80.2	HANFORD	231.4
88.3	Laton	223.3
107.5	Calwa	204.1
110.4	FRESNO	201.2
110.4	FRESNO	201.2
118.0	Figarden	193.6
131.9	MADERA	179.7

142.6	Sharon	169.0
153.8	Le Grand	157.8
159.6	Planada	152.0
168.4	MERCED (Yosemite)	143.2
184.0	Ballico	127.6
191.9	Denair	119.7
198.1	Hughson	113.5
201.5	Empire	110.1
208.6	RIVERBANK (Modesto)	103.0
213.9	Escalon	97.7
224.8	Burnham	86.8
233.7	STOCKTON	77.9

233.7	STOCKTON	77.9
241.6	Holt	70.0
247.1	Middle River	64.5
249.1	Orwood	62.5
255.3	Knightsen	56.3
258.4	Oakley	53.2
264.4	Antioch	47.2
268.1	Pittsburg	43.5
275.9	Port Chicago	35.7

275.9	Port Chicago	35.7
279.1	Avon	32.5
281.2	Mococo	30.4
282.5	MARTINEZ	29.1
284.1	Ozol	27.5
284.8	Benicia	26.8
288.2	Crockett	23.4
289.6	Selby	22.0
290.0	Tormey	21.6
290.8	Oleum	20.8
291.6	Rodeo	20.0
293.3	Hercules	18.3
294.1	Pinole	17.5
298.2	Giant	13.4
299.5	San Pablo	11.1
302.1	RICHMOND	9.5
304.0	Stege	7.6
307.9	Berkeley	3.7
310.1	Shellmound	1.5
310.5	Emoryville	1.1
311.6	OAKLAND	0.0

Bus connection to San Francisco via Bay Bridge

Sequoia National Park and Kings Canyon National Park (also accessible from Fresno).

The sequoias, found only in California and Oregon, are the biggest living things in the world and probably the oldest as well. There are two kinds of sequoia trees: the redwoods, concentrated in north-

433

ern California, and the giant sequoias. Some of them may be as much as 3,500 years old.

The sequoias are named for one of the most remarkable men in American history—the Cherokee Indian chief Sequoya, who invented a written language for his people. In 1821, after 12 years of work, he reduced the Cherokee speech to eighty-five sounds, then developed a system of notation to express them. After the tribe had been removed to Oklahoma by the U.S. government, he published a newspaper in his own Cherokee written language. He was a giant—it is fitting that the giant trees be named for him.

110.4 **FRESNO** *201.2*. With a metropolitan-area population of half a million people, Fresno is the great inland city of California and the capital of the San Joaquin valley agricultural complex. The valley produces grapes, figs, grain, fruit, and everything else that grows, and Fresno's main business is the packing and processing of these products. Wine is produced here from the grape crop, and the world's largest raisin plant is here.

168.4 **MERCED** *143.2*. Merced is the station for Yosemite National Park, one of the wonder spots of the world. Nowhere is there a more beautiful place than the Yosemite Valley, with its peaks and waterfalls. The park draws so many visitors that its facilities are strained during the high seasons. But don't let that stop you from coming— Yosemite is a must for visitors to California.

208.6 **RIVERBANK** *103.0*. Don't look for much of a town here— there isn't any. Riverbank, however, is the station for Modesto, 7 miles west, and for Oakdale and the gold-rush country to the east.

233.7 **STOCKTON** *77.9*. Named for Captain Robert Stockton of the U.S. Navy, an early bearer of the American flag in California, Stockton was founded during the gold-rush days. It is the seat of San Joaquin County, home of the University of the Pacific, and accessible to ocean vessels coming up from San Francisco Bay, making it a shipping center for San Joaquin valley agricultural products.

Leaving Stockton, the railroad turns west, threading its way between the hills and crossing a number of streams that flow down to San Francisco Bay.

275.9 **Port Chicago** *35.7*. At this little town the train leaves the Santa Fe to operate over the Southern Pacific from Port Chicago to Oakland. The right-of-way follows the shore of the bay most of the way.

281.2 **Mococo** *30.4*. On the right side (going toward Oakland) passengers can see the Martinez-Benicia Bridge, which carries rail traffic (including Amtrak trains) across San Francisco Bay. At Mococo the line from the San Joaquin valley joins the bridge tracks, which come from Sacramento. The two lines share the right of way to Oakland.

For notes on the route from Martinez to Oakland, see section 3.44.

3.53 Independent Rail Lines

Alaska

Alaska's rail service is outside the Amtrak network. The principal line is that of the Alaska Railroad (ARR), between Anchorage and Fairbanks. It is owned by the U.S. Government, but Congress has authorized its purchase by the state if a price can be agreed on. The streamliner *Au-Ro-Ra* (named after both the aurora borealis and the ARR) runs daily in summer and twice a week in winter, serving Mount McKinley National Park en route.

The only other passenger service in the state is on the White Pass and Yukon Railway, a scenic little narrow-gauge line connecting the port of Skagway with Whitehorse in the Yukon Territory of Canada. It follows the Sourdough Trail, the route of the miners to the Yukon goldfields during the bonanza of 1898; and until 1983 it ran passenger trains in the summer months only. The slump in copper prices that year, however, led to closure of the mines on which the company depends for freight traffic, and without the ore traffic it did not pay to operate the railroad at all. Consequently, no passenger trains ran on the line in 1983, and the service may not be resumed in the summer of 1984 if the mines remain closed. Check the situation before making plans to travel on this line.

Neither of the Alaskan lines has any physical connection with the rest of the North American railroad network, and both are impossibly out of the way for most travelers. I have not, therefore, gone in detail about them.

South Shore Line

One other American passenger carrier doesn't fit neatly into any category. This is the South Shore electric line, America's last interurban.

In the first decade of the twentieth century, thousands of miles of intercity electric railways were built in the United States. They were an outgrowth of the city streetcar systems, and they were designed primarily to offer cheap, frequent, short-distance passenger service to people in rural communities and small towns. Most of these lines were sketchily built, and the development of the automobile and the spread of paved roads doomed many of them as early as the 1920s. The Depression killed off most of the remaining companies, and although some systems were kept running by wartime restrictions on auto travel, by the mid-1960s the South Shore Line was the only interurban line left.

It survived because of its strategic location in the heavy-industry district at the southern end of Lake Michigan and because its farsighted management realized early in the game that there was no future in the local passenger business and concentrated on building up the company's freight operations. Today the South Shore is owned by the Chessie system, which runs its profitable freight trains while electric passenger trains continue in cooperation with the Northern Indiana Commuter Transportation District. A fleet of brand-new cars was delivered in 1983, permitting retirement of the old equipment, which was built as far back as 1926.

The South Shore Line is a study in contrasts. Physically it is not one railroad but three—all in fewer than 90 miles fom one end to the other. Between Chicago and Gary, Indiana, the South Shore is a modern, heavy-duty freight line with frequent commuter passenger business. In this first 30 miles the current operation betrays its interurban past only in a series of incredibly sharp curves at Hammond, Indiana. At East Chicago, where the main line once ran down the center of the city's main street, the South Shore now enjoys a new right-of-way constructed in 1956.

East of Gary the South Shore assumes a second character. Here it is a single-track rural railroad through the beautiful, ever shifting sand dunes. At Tremont the railroad serves the Indiana Dunes state park.

Through Michigan City one gets a feeling of the 1940s, for here the South Shore still does run down the city streets. Trains fight for space with parked cars and pause dutifully for traffic lights. The line's shops and operating headquarters are on the east edge of the city.

Finally, between Michigan City and South Bend the C S S & S B really resembles the old-time interurban lines as its lightly traveled tracks meander along lake shores to New Carlisle, then parallel the Conrail right-of-way to South Bend. There used to be another mile or so of street running there, but this has been eliminated by terminating all trains at Bendix Drive on the western edge of the city, where the South Shore shares its station facility with Amtrak.

436

PART 4

Major Attractions:
How to Get There by Train

Rainbow Bridge rises to a height of 309 feet and is the world's largest known natural bridge. It is located near Lake Powell at the northern end of the Grand Canyon. Flagstaff, Arizona, is the nearest station.

Major Attractions:
How to Get There by Train

The following has been compiled to aid travelers in finding the easiest method of getting to many of America's major attractions by train. Where there is no station in the immediate vicinity, the trip will generally be by train and interconnecting bus. In some cases, however, attractions can only be reached by car, because they are not serviced by public transportation. In others (e.g., Acadia National Park, Zion National Park, etc.), travelers would be well advised to consider using air transportation because of the attraction's remoteness from railroad lines. Readers should note that the stations listed are not necessarily the closest; rather, they have been chosen for their access to interconnecting buses or convenient taxi or car-rental facilities.

Abraham Lincoln Home. Station: Springfield, Ill. Abraham Lincoln Home National Historic Site, 426 S. 7th St., Springfield, IL 62701. 217-789-2357. The visitors' center is about 10 blocks from the station.

Acadia National Park. Station: Boston, Mass. (275 miles). Superintendent, Acadia National Park, RFD 1, Box 1, Bar Harbor, ME 04609. 207-288-3338. Greyhound buses run twice a day from Boston to Ellsworth, Maine, about 20 miles from the park. Take a taxi from Ellsworth to the park, or rent a car at the Avis counter at the Bar Harbor Airport, in Trenton, about 8 miles from the bus station (Avis: 207-667-5421). Also, Bar Harbor Airlines offers flights from Logan Airport, Boston, to Bar Harbor, Maine, which is near the park.

Alamo. Station: San Antonio, Tex. See under San Antonio, section 2.43.

Alcatraz Island. Station: San Francisco, Calif. See under San Francisco, section 2.45.

Arches National Park. Stations: Grand Junction. Colo. (90 miles), or Green River, Utah (65 miles). Rent a car from Avis (303-244-9170) or Hertz (303-243-0747) in Grand Junction. From Green River, you can raft to the park along the Green River (call Alice Schabb River Trips, 801-564-3369, or Moki-Mac, 801-564-3361). If you don't want to float the river, you can still arrange to have one of the rafting companies shuttle you to the park in a van.

Arizona-Sonora Desert Museum. Station: Tucson, Ariz. See under Tuscon, section 2.48.

Astrodome. See Houston Astrodome, below.

Atlantic City. Station: Philadelphia, Pa. (60 miles). Atlantic City Convention and Visitors' Bureau, 16 Central Pier, Atlantic City, NJ 08404. 609-345-3305. Transport of New Jersey (215-569-3100) runs frequent bus service to Atlantic City and Cape May from its Philadelphia terminal.

Baseball Hall of Fame. Station: Utica, N.Y. (45 miles). Main St., Cooperstown, NY 13326. 607-547-9988. Greyhound (315-735-4471) and Trailways (315-797-2550) run two buses each to Cooperstown daily. The Trailways buses leave from the Utica railroad station. The museum is 2 blocks from the bus stop.

Berkeley Plantation. Station: Richmond, Va. See under Richmond, section 2.38.

Big Sur. Stations: Salinas (45 miles) or San Luis Obispo, Calif. (100 miles). Coastlines Bus Tours (408-649-4700) runs twice-a-day service along the coast highway. Buses leave from the Greyhound stations in Monterey and San Luis Obispo and make several stops along the way. If you leave the train at Salinas, take Monterey-Salinas Transit (408-899-2555) to Monterey. (The Coast Highway is closed indefinitely because of mud slides. The town of Big Sur is accessible only from the north, but there is no bus service.)

Biltmore Estate (Vanderbilt Home). Station: Spartanburg, S.C. (60 miles). Asheville, NC 28813. 704-274-1776. Trains arrive late at night in Spartanburg; so visitors will probably want to spend the night there and take a bus to Asheville in the morning. Greyhound (803-583-1471) and Trailways (803-583-3669) both offer service to Asheville; public transportation is available from the bus station to the estate.

Bronx Zoo. Station: New York, N.Y. See under New York, section 2.29.

Busch Gardens, the Dark Continent. Station: Tampa, Fla. (10 miles). Busch Blvd. and 40th St., Tampa, FL 33612. 813-971-8282. Take a taxi from the station, about 25 minutes' drive away.

California Wine Country. Station: San Francisco, Calif. There are more than 100 vineyards in Napa and Sonoma counties, north of San Francisco, many open to the public. Rent a car to tour the wineries, and be sure to buy a guide that describes the vineyards and how to find them.

Capitol. Station: Washington, D.C. See under Washington, section 2.49.

Carlsbad Caverns. Station: El Paso, Tex. (200 miles). Headquarters, Carlsbad Caverns National Park, 3225 National Parks Highway, Carlsbad, NM 88220. 505-885-8884. Rent a car in El Paso; no other transportation available.

Crater Lake National Park. Station: Klamath Falls (60 miles). P.O. Box 7, Crater Lake, OR 97604. 503-594-2211. Avis car rental is available in Klamath Falls (503-882-7232).

Cypress Gardens. Station: Winter Haven, Fla. (5 miles). 813-324-2111. Take a taxi from the station.

Disney World. See Walt Disney World, below.

Disneyland. Stations: Anaheim (Anaheim Stadium) (2 miles), Fullerton (5 miles), or Los Angeles, Calif. (30 miles). 1313 Harbor Blvd., Anaheim, CA 92802. 714-999-4565. Public transportation is available from all three stations. For bus routes and schedules, call RTD (213-626-4455) in Los Angeles or OCTD (714-636-7433) in Fullerton or Anaheim.

Dodge City (Boot Hill). Station: Dodge City, Kans. Dodge City Convention and Visitors' Bureau, 4th and Spruce Sts. (P.O. Box 1474), Dodge City, KS 67801. 316-227-2176. Within walking distance of the station.

Empire State Building. Station: New York, N.Y. See under New York, section 2.29.

Fisherman's Wharf. Station: San Francisco, Calif. See under San Francisco, section 2.45.

Fort McHenry. Station: Baltimore, Md. See under Baltimore, section 2.3.

Fort Sumter. Station: Charleston, S.C. See under Charleston, section 2.8.

Fort Ticonderoga. Station: Fort Ticonderoga, N.Y. Ticonderoga, NY 12883. 518-585-2821. Within walking distance of the station.

Gateway Arch. Station: St. Louis, Mo. See under St. Louis, section 2.40.

Gettysburg National Military Park. Stations: Harrisburg, Pa. (30 miles), or Baltimore, Md. (45 miles). Gettysburg National Military Park Visitors' Center, Route 134, Gettysburg, PA 17325. 717-334-1124. Trailways runs one bus each day from Harrisburg; Greyhound runs one each day from Baltimore. The park is within walking distance of the Gettysburg tour center (717-334-6296), where buses arrive. To see the extensive battleground, however, take one of the bus tours offered by the tour center.

Glacier National Park. Stations: Glacier Park Station (East Glacier) or Belton (West Glacier), Mont. Superintendent, Glacier National Park, West Glacier, MT 59936. 406-888-5441. Stations are on the borders of the park. Shuttle buses run between the stations, the lodges, and other points in the park.

Gold Rush Towns (Nevada City, Calif. and Virginia City, Nev.). Stations: Sacramento, Calif. (55 miles from Nevada City), and Reno, Nev. (20 miles from Virgina City). To visit Nevada City, rent a car in Sacramento; for Virginia City, see under Reno, section 2.37.

Graceland Manor (Elvis Presley Home). Station: Memphis, Tenn. See under Memphis, section 2.24.

Grand Canyon National Park. Stations: Flagstaff (80 miles) or Phoenix, Ariz. (220 miles). Superintendent, Grand Canyon National Park, Grand Canyon, AZ 86023. 602-638-2310. Greyhound and Trailways run buses from Phoenix to Flagstaff. Bus service is available from Flagstaff to the Grand Canyon from Nava-Hopi Tours (602-774-5003).

Grand Teton National Park. Stations: Pocatello, Idaho (185 miles). Superintendent, Grand Teton National Park, Drawer 170, Moose, WY 83012. 307-733-2880. Cars can be rented in Pocatello: Avis (208-232-3244), Hertz (208-233-2970).

Great Smokey Mountains National Park. Station: Greenville, S.C. (120 miles). Superintendent, Great Smokey Mountains National Park, Gatlinburg, TN 37738. 615-436-5615. Car rental is available in Greenville from Hertz (803-877-4261) or Avis (803-877-6456).

Greenfield Village and Henry Ford Museum. Station: Dearborn, Mich. See under Detroit, section 2.16.

Harpers Ferry National Historical Park. Station: Harpers Ferry, W.Va. Superintendent, Harpers Ferry National Historical Park, P.O. Box 65, Harpers Ferry, WV 25425. 304-535-6371. Within walking distance of the station.

Hearst Castle. Stations: San Luis Obispo (40 miles) or Salinas, Calif. (110 miles). Hearst-San Simeon State Historic Monument, Route 1, San Simeon, CA 93452. Coastlines Bus Tours (408-649-4700) runs two buses each day in each direction between the Greyhound stations in Monterey and San Luis Obispo. If coming from Salinas, take Monterey-Salinas Transit (408-899-2555) to Monterey; frequent service is available. Tickets to the house are available through Ticketron or the Coastlines bus driver or at the gate. (Tours are often sold out during busy seasons.) (Until further notice, the Coast Highway will be closed from the south. Coastlines Bus Tours will not operate until the highway reopens.)

Hershey. Station: Harrisburg, Pa. (15 miles). Hershey Information Center, Hershey, PA 17033. 717-534-3005. Several buses go to Hershey each day from the Trailways bus station in Harrisburg (717-232-4251), located in the railway station. The bus brings passengers to within a few blocks of Hershey Park and other attractions.

Hollywood. Station: Los Angeles, Calif. 213-876-8742. Public transportation available from the Los Angeles station.

Hoover Dam. Station: Las Vegas, Nev. See under Las Vegas, section 2.22.

Hot Springs National Park. Station: Little Rock, Ark. (70 miles). Superintendent, Hot Springs National Park, P.O. Box 1960, Hot Springs, AR 71901. 501-624-3383. Frequent Trailways bus service is available from Little Rock (501-372-1861). Take a taxi from the bus station to the park.

Houston Astrodome. Station: Houston, Tex. See under Houston, section 2.18.

Independence Hall. Station: Philadelphia, Pa. See under Philadelphia, section 2.31.

Indianapolis 500 Motor Speedway. Indianapolis, Ind. See under Indianapolis, section 2.19.

Johnson Space Center. See Lyndon B. Johnson Space Center, below.

Kennedy Space Center and Cape Canaveral. Station: Sanford, Fla. (50 miles). Kennedy Space Center Tours, Visitors' Center, Kennedy Space Center, FL 32899. 305-452-2121. Greyhound buses (305-322-1421) run from Sanford to Titusville, and taxis are available to bring visitors from there to the space center.

Kentucky Derby. Station: Cincinnati, Ohio (100 miles). Churchill Downs, 700 Central Ave., Louisville, KY 40208. 502-636-3541. Greyhound runs buses between Cincinnati and Louisville (513-352-6000).

Kitty Hawk. Station: Newport News, Va. (100 miles). Wright Brothers National Memorial, P.O. Box 427, Kill Devil Hills, NC 27948. 919-441-7430. Greyhound offers bus service between Newport News and Norfolk (804-599-3900). Trailways (804-622-7181) runs three buses a day from Norfolk to Roanoke Island; these buses will stop at the national memorial.

Knotts Berry Farm. Station: Los Angeles (20 miles) or Fullerton (5 miles), Calif. Knotts Berry Farm, 8039 Beach Blvd., Buena Park, CA 90620. 714-952-9400. For public transportation from Los Angeles, call RTD (213-626-4455); for public transportation from Fullerton, call OCTD (714-636-7433).

Lake Placid Olympic Arena. Station: Westport, N.Y. (45 miles). Lake Placid Chamber of Commerce, Lake Placid, NY 12946. 518-523-2445. Lake Placid Sightseeing (518-523-4431) will meet passengers at the railway station if they have advance reservations.

Lexington and Concord Battlefields. Station: Boston, Mass. See under Boston, section 2.6.

Liberty Bell. Station: Philadelphia, Pa. See under Philadelphia, section 2.31.

Lincoln Home. See Abraham Lincoln Home, above.

Lincoln Memorial. Station: Washington, D.C. See under Washington, section 2.49.

Lost Sea. Station: Atlanta, Ga. (150 miles). Sweetwater, TN 37874. 615-337-6616. See car rentals under Atlanta (section 2.2); no other transportation available.

Lyndon B. Johnson Space Center. Station: Houston, Tex. See under Houston, section 2.18.

Mardi Gras. Station: New Orleans, La. See under New Orleans, section 2.28.

Marineland. Stations: Deland (45 miles) or Jacksonville (45 miles), Fla. Route 1, Box 122, St. Augustine, FL 32084. 904-471-1111. Rent a car in Jacksonville (see under Jacksonville, section 2.20) or in Deland (Hertz: 904-736-8091; pick-up service). No other transportation available.

Mariners' Museum. Station: Newport News, Va. Museum Dr., Newport News, VA 23606. 804-595-0368. Call 804-723-3344 for information on public transportation in the city.

Mark Twain's Boyhood Home. Stations: West Quincy (30 miles) or St. Louis (120 miles), Mo. 208 Hill St., Hannibal, MO 63401. 314-221-9010. Trains arrive in West Quincy late in the evening; so visitors may wish to spend the night there. Trailways buses run once during daylight hours in each direction between nearby Quincy and St. Louis, stopping at Hannibal en route. In West Quincy, call Trailways at 217-223-1010; in St. Louis, call 314-231-7181.

Mesa Verde National Park. Station: Gallup, N. Mex. (150 miles). Superintendent, Mesa Verde National Park, CO 81330. 303-529-4461. Avis has a car-rental agency in Gallup (505-863-9309); no other transportation available.

Middleton Place. Station: Charleston, S.C. See under Charleston, section 2.8.

Mississippi River Boats. Station: St. Louis, Mo., or New Orleans, La. See under St. Louis (section 2.40) and New Orleans (section 2.28).

Monticello (Jefferson home). Station: Charlottesville, Va. See under Charlottesville, section 2.9.

Mormon Tabernacle. Station: Salt Lake City, Utah. See under Salt Lake City, section 2.42.

Mount Hood. Station: Portland, Ore. (60 miles). Timberline Lodge, Timberline Lodge, OR 97028. 503-272-3311. From May through October, Gray Line buses run on a day trip from Portland (503-226-6755). Hood River, a closer station, offers no transportation or car rentals.

Mount Rainier. Station: Tacoma, Wash. (90 miles). Superintendent, Mount Rainier National Park, Tahoma Woods – Star Route, Ashford, WA 98304. 206-569-2291. From Tacoma, rent a car (Hertz: 206-627-2426); see also under Seattle, section 2.47.

Mount Rushmore. No convenient access by train.

Mount Saint Helens. Station: Portland, Ore. (65 miles). See under Portland, section 2.34.

Mount Vernon (George Washington home). Stations: Washington, D.C. (15 miles), or Alexandria, Va. (8 miles). Mount Vernon Estate, Mount Vernon, VA 22121. 703-780-2000. Bus 11A runs to the estate from Washington, D.C. Call 202-637-2437 for route and schedule information.

Mystic Seaport. Station: Mystic, Conn. Greenmanville Ave., Mystic, CT 06355. 203-572-0711. Within walking distance of the station.

Natural Bridge. Station: Lynchburg, Va. (45 miles). US Route 11, Natural Bridge, VA 24578. 703-291-2272. Rent a car in Lynchburg (Avis: 804-237-5959); no other transportation available.

Newport. Station: Providence, R.I. (35 miles). See under Providence, section 2.35.

Niagara Falls. Station: Niagara Falls, N.Y. Niagara Falls Convention and Visitors' Bureau, 300 4th St., Niagara Falls, NY 14302. 716-278-8010. Take a taxi from the station.

Norfolk Submarine Base. Station: Newport News, Va. (25 miles). Norfolk Naval Station, 9809 Hampton Blvd., Norfolk, VA 23511. 804-444-4071. Call 804-723-3344 for information on city buses.

Old Sturbridge Village. Station: Springfield, Mass. (30 miles). Visitors' Information, Old Sturbridge Village, Route 20, Sturbridge, MA 01566. 617-347-3362. Peter Pan Bus lines runs three buses each day between Springfield and Sturbridge (413-781-3320).

Opryland, USA, and Grand Old Opry. Station: Memphis, Tenn. (210 miles). Opryland Information Center, 2802 Opryland Dr., Nashville, TN 37214. 615-889-6611. Trailways (901-523-0200) and Greyhound (901-523-7676) both offer frequent bus service to Nashville (see under Memphis, section 2.24). For information on public transportation in Nashville, call 615-242-4433.

Ozark Folk Center. Station: Little Rock, Ark. (85 miles). Route 382, Box 500, Mountain View, AR 72560. 501-269-3851. Rent a car in Little Rock (Hertz, 501-378-0777; Avis, 501-375-1102).

Pennsylvania Dutch Country. Station: Lancaster, Pa. Lancaster Chamber of Commerce, 30 W. Orange St., Lancaster, PA 17601. 717-397-3531. Rent a car to tour the countryside.

Petrified Forest National Park and Painted Desert. Stations: Winslow, Ariz. (60 miles), or Gallup, N. Mex. (70 miles). Superintendent, Petrified Forest National Park, AZ 86028. 602-524-6228. From Winslow, arrange a taxi tour with the Greyhound office (602-289-2171) or take a Trailways bus to the park entrance (602-289-2936). From Gallup, rent a car (Avis: 505-863-9309).

Pike's Peak (highway and cog train). Station: Denver, Colo. See under Denver, section 2.15.

Presley Home. See Graceland Manor, above.

San Diego Zoo. Station: San Diego, Calif. See under San Diego, section 2.44.

San Juan Capistrano Mission. Station: San Juan Capistrano, Calif. See under Los Angeles, section 2.23.

Sea World. Station: San Diego, Calif. See under San Diego, section 2.44.

Sequoia National Park and King's Canyon National Park. Station: Fresno, Calif. (80 miles). Superintendent, Sequoia National Park, Giant Forest, CA 93262. 209-565-3456. Rent a car in Fresno (Avis, 209-251-5001; Hertz, 209-251-5055).

Shenandoah National Park. Station: Charlottesville, Va. (30 miles). See under Charlottesville, section 2.9.

Six Flags over Georgia. Station: Atlanta, Ga. See under Atlanta, section 2.2.

Six Flags over Texas. Stations: Dallas or Fort Worth, Tex. See under Dallas, section 2.14.

Smithsonian Institution. Station: Washington, D.C. See under Washington, section 2.49.

Statue of Liberty. Station: New York, N.Y. See under New York, section 2.29.

Stone Mountain. Station: Atlanta, Ga. See under Atlanta, section 2.2.

United Nations. Station: New York, N.Y. See under New York, section 2.29.

Universal Studios. Station: Los Angeles, Calif. See under Los Angeles, section 2.23.

Valley Forge. Station: Philadelphia, Pa. (25 miles). Valley Forge National Historical Park, Valley Forge, PA 19481. 215-783-7700. A bus tours the park in spring and summer, but there is no public transportation to the park. See car rentals under Philadelphia, section 2.31.

Vanderbilt Home. See Biltmore Estate, above.

Vieux Carré (French Quarter). Station: New Orleans, La. See under New Orleans, section 2.28.

Walt Disney World. Stations: Orlando (10 miles) or Kissimmee (15 miles), Fla. P.O. Box 40, Lake Buena Vista, FL 32830. 305-824-4321. Take a taxi from either station.

Washington Monument. Station: Washington, D.C. See under Washington, section 2.49.

White House. Station: Washington, D.C. See under Washington, section 2.49.

Williamsburg. Station: Williamsburg, Va. Tourist Information, Box C, Colonial Williamsburg Foundation, Williamsburg, VA 23187. 804-229-1000, ext. 2751. Within walking distance of the station.

Wisconsin Dells. Station: Wisconsin Dells, Wis. Olson Boat Co., 815 River Rd., Wisconsin Dells, WI 53965. 608-254-8500. Take a taxi from the

446

station. Boats run mid-April through mid-October.

Yellowstone National Park. Station: Pocatello, Idaho (180 miles). Yellowstone National Park, WY 82190. 307-344-7381. Greyhound runs several buses a week from Pocatello to West Yellowstone (208-232-5365), and you can rent a car in Pocatello (Avis, 208-232-3244; Hertz, 208-233-2970).

Yosemite National Park. Station: Merced, Calif. (60 miles). Superintendent, P.O. Box 577, Yosemite National Park, CA 95389. 209-372-4461. California-Yosemite Tours runs a daily bus between the park and the Amtrak station in Merced; call 209-383-1563; reservations required.

Zion National Park. Station: Las Vegas, Nev. (160 miles). Rent a car in Las Vegas (see car rentals under Las Vegas, section 2.22), or take a short flight from Las Vegas to Cedar City (Sky West: 702-736-7376), from which Color Country Tours (801-586-9916) will transport you to the park. That firm offers tours of Zion and other southwestern parks.

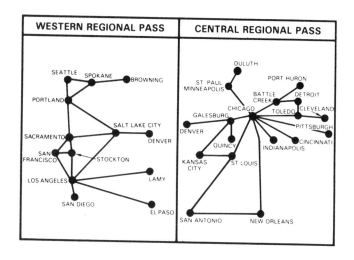

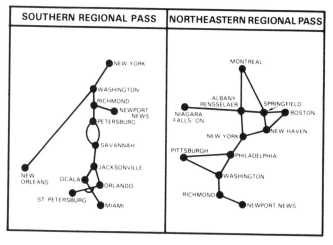

The maps indicate authorized routes for travel on each of the
Regional U.S.A. RAIL PASSES

APPENDIX I: U.S.A. RAIL PASSES

This pass is issued by Amtrak-authorized agencies only to permanent residents of countries outside North America that are not U.S. possessions. The pass may be used only by the person whose name is on it. The traveler must begin to use his pass within 90 days after the date of issue. To get a pass, purchasers must have a valid passport with a nonimmigrant visa. If you can't find an Amtrak-authorized agency, write to Amtrak International Sales, 400 North Capitol Street, NW, Washington, DC, U.S.A.

USA RAIL PASS TARIFFS

U.S.A. RAIL PASS	ADULT FARE (12 years old or over)	CHILD 2-11
7-days (Nationwide)	$265.00	$133.00
14-days (Nationwide)	$400.00	$200.00
21-days (Nationwide)	$535.00	$268.00
30-days (Nationwide)	$665.00	$333.00
14-days (Northeastern Regional)	$125.00	$ 63.00
14-days (Southern Regional)	$215.00	$108.00
14-days (Central Regional)	$215.00	$108.00
14-days (Western Regional)	$215.00	$108.00

APPENDIX II: BRITISH & AMERICAN RAILROAD TERMS

British and many European travelers familiar with British terminology should find the following helpful in communicating with American station and train personnel. Be sure to use the American term or you will not be understood.

British term	Equivalent American term
Booking hall	Ticket office
Single ticket	One-way ticket
Return-trip ticket	Round-trip ticket
Carriage	Coach
Pullman car	Parlor (or club) car
Sleeping car	Pullman car (or sleeping car, or sleeper)
Sleepers	Cross ties
Luggage van	Baggage car
Guard	Conductor or trainman
Engine driver	Engineer
Permanent way	Right of way, roadbed, or track
Level crossing	Grade crossing
Goods train	Freight train

24-HOUR TIME CONVERTER

Courtesy of Thomas Cook Ltd.
Thomas Cook International Timetable
Peterborough, England

APPENDIX III: AMTRAK FOREIGN AGENCIES

Readers outside the United States can obtain information, timetables, U.S.A. Rail Passes, tour brochures, and tickets from the various agents listed below.

ARGENTINA
Organfur, S.A., Cangallo 725, 10° Piso, 1038 Buenos Aires

AUSTRALIA
Allied Travel Services, Woden Plaza, Ground Floor, Phillip, Canberra
Business Holiday Travel Pty Ltd., 636 St. Kilda Road, Melbourne, Victoria 3004
Coulter Tours, 17 Albert Street, 1st Floor, Sydney, N.S.W. 2096
Destination Holidays, 34 Main Street, Croydon, Victoria 3136
Travelwise Travel Agency, Wynyard House, 4th Floor, 291 George Street, Sydney, N.S.W. 2000
World Travel Headquarters Pty, Kindersley House, 22 Bligh Street, Sydney, N.S.W. 2000

AUSTRIA
Austria Reiseservice, Wien 1, Himmelpfortgasse #3, Vienna

BELGIUM
Wirtz Travel Agency, 44 De Keyserlei, B 2000 Antwerp

BRAZIL
Deluxe Destinations, Av. N.S. Copacabana, 500-GR601, Rio de Janeiro CEP 22.020

CANADA
Any VIA *station*; for information call 1-800-665-8630 (from Canada only). U.S.A. Rail Passes not issued.

CHILE
Viajes Ecuador, Huerfanos, 1160-Oficina 405, Santiago 1

CHINA
Travel Advisers Ltd., 1105 Swire House, 11 Charter Road (G.P.O. Box 8136), Hong Kong

DENMARK
DSB Rejsebureau, Nytorv 11 DK 1450, Copenhagen
Dane Tours, Bredgrade 27, 1260 Copenhagen K

ENGLAND
Albany Travel, 190 Deansgate, Manchester M3 3WD
Thomas Cook, Ltd., P.O. Box 36, Thorpe Wood, Peterborough, PE3 6SB
TWA City Ticket Office, 200 Piccadilly, London

FINLAND
Area Travel Agency, Pohjoisesplanadi 2 (P.O. Box 227), 00131 Helsinki
United Travel Ltd., Eerindato 7A, 00100 Helsinki 10

FRANCE
Wingate Travel, 19 Bix Rue Du Mont Thabor, 75001 Paris

GERMANY (WEST)
A.B.R. (Amtliches Bayerisches Reiseburo), 8 Munchen 2, Postfach 200-125, Im Hauptbahnhof
D.E.R. (Deutsches Reiseburo), 6 Frankfurt am Main, Eschersheimer, Landstrasse 25-27
N.U.R. Touristic GMBH, Hochhaus am Baseler Platz, Postfach 11 13 43, 6000 Frankfurt 11
Vobis Reisen, Landsberger Strasse 478, D-8000 Munchen 60

GUAM
Marianas Travel Agency, Ground Floor, GITC Building, Tamuning 96911

HONG KONG (see **CHINA**)

INDIA
Sita World Travel, F-12 Connaught Place, New Delhi 110 001

ISRAEL
Uni 2000 Ltd., 90A Hayarkon Street, Tel Aviv 63903

ITALY
American Express Company, Societa Per Azioni Italiana, Piazza Di Spagna, No. 38, Rome
Caleidoscopio SRL, 15 Via Fatebene, Fratelli, Milan 20121

451

Gastaldi Tours, 1, Via Cairoli, P.O. Box 1855, 16124 Genova

Travel United S.R.L., Viale Montenero, 6, 20135 Milano

JAPAN

Executive Travel, Diani Eiwa Building 5F, 2-26 Dojima 2 Chome, Kita-Du, Osaka 530

Japan Travel Bureau, 1-6-4 Marunouchi, Chiyoda-ku, Tokyo, 100

Kintetsu International, 19-2 Matsunga-Cho, Kanda Chiyoda-ku, Tokyo, 101

Travel Plaza International, No. 8 Tokyo Kaiji Building 1-5-13, Nishi-Shimbashi, Minatu-Ku, Tokyo, 105

NETHERLANDS

De Zuid-Europa Stichting, Van Baerlestraat 76, 1071 BB Amsterdam

Incento B.V., Stationsplein 1 (P.O. Box 457), 1400, A1 Bussum

NBBS Jongeren & Studentenreizen, Rapenburg 8 2311 EV, Leiden

NEW ZEALAND

Atlantic and Pacific Travel, Parnell Place, 164 Parnell Road, Auckland 1

Hunts Carefree Holidays, Ltd., 83 Kitchener Road, Milford, P.O. Box 31250, Auckland 9

NORWAY

Norwegian State Railways (Norges Statsbaver), P.O. Box 9115 Vaterland, Oslo 1

PAKISTAN

American Express International Banking Corp., Standard Insurance House, 1.1 Chundrigar Road (P.O. Box 4847), Karachi No. 2

PANAMA

Gordon Dalton Travel, Box 8691, Panama 5

PERU

Trips International, Nicolas de Pierola 677 OF. 603, Lima

PHILIPPINES

Expertravel and Tours, Inc.1971-1973A Mabini Street, Malate, Metro Manila

PUERTO RICO

Agencias Solder, P.O. Box 13321, San Juan 00908

Viajes Caribe, Canals, Roosevelt, San Juan 00918

SCOTLAND

Thistle Air, 22 Bank Street, Kilmarnock, Ayrshire

SINGAPORE

Diners World Travel, 7500 E Beach Road, 02-201 Merlin Plaza 0719

Siakson Coach Tours, 26028 Prinser Street, 7

SOUTH AFRICA

Holiday Tours (Pty) Ltd., 112 President Street (P.O. Box 8576), Johannesburg, 2000

World Travel Agency Pty Ltd., Commissioner Street (P.O. Box 4568), Johannesburg, 2001

SPAIN

Giras S.A., Gran Via 88, Grupo 3-3-8, Madrid 13

Viajes Ecuador, Gran Via 81-2, Bilboa 11

SWEDEN

Reso Travel Agency, Vastmannagatan 2, S-101-21 Stockholm

SFS Resor Agency, P.O. Box 45072, 104 30 Stockholm

SWITZERLAND

Kuoni Travel Ltd., Neue Hard, Neugasse 231, Zurich

SSR-Reisen, Backerstrasse 40/52, P.O. Box CH-8026, Zurich

TAIWAN

Taiwan Orchid Express Ltd., 35 Chung Hsiao E. Road, Sec. 1 Taipei 100

THAILAND

S.M.I. Travel Company, Ltd., 404 Phyathai Road, Patumwan Bangkok

URUGUAY

Turisport, Mercedes 942 (P.O. Box 6447), Montevideo

VENEZUELA

Turven, S.A., Sabana Grande, Edificio Union, Caracas

APPENDIX IV: STUDENT & YOUTH INFORMATION

Students and other young travelers may find the following organizations useful when seeking inexpensive accommodations, etc. The *American Youth Hostels Councils,* like their counterparts in Europe and elsewhere, have many hostels and other facilities all over the country, including national and state parks. Foreigners should note, however, that distances between hostels may be much greater than in Europe and that bicycling or hiking from one hostel to another may not always be practical. The AYH is a membership organization. For further information, write to AYH National Administrative Offices, 1332 I Street, N.W., Suite 800, Washington, DC 20005, or the principal local councils below:

WESTERN STATES

Arizona AYH Council, 14049 N. 38th Place, Phoenix, AZ 85032

Golden Gate AYH Council, Bldg. 240, Ft. Mason, San Francisco, CA 94123

Los Angeles AYH Council, 1502 Palos Verdes Dr., N., Harbor City, CA 90710

San Diego AYH Council, 1031 India St., San Diego, CA 92101

Rocky Mt. AYH Council (Colorado & New Mexico), 1107 12th St., P.O. Box 2370, Boulder, CO 80306

Oregon State AYH Council, 4212 S.W. Primrose St., Portland, OR 97219

Washington State AYH Council, 4730 ½ University Way N.E., Suite A, Seattle, WA 98105

MIDWESTERN STATES

Metro Chicago AYH Council, 3712 N. Clark St., Chicago, IL 60613

Ozark Area AYH Council (Kansas, Southern Illinois, Missouri), 1908 S. 12th St., St. Louis, MO 63104

Metro Detroit AYH Council, 3024 Coolidge, Berkley, MI 48072

Minnesota AYH Council, 475 Cedar St., St. Paul, MN 55101

Columbus AYH Council, 103 West Park St., Apt. B, Westerville, OH 43081

Tri-State AYH Council (Kentucky, Southern Ohio, Southeastern Indiana), 5400 Lanius Lane, Cincinnati, OH 45224

MID-ATLANTIC STATES

Delaware Valley AYH Council (Pennsylvania and New Jersey), 35 South 3rd St., Philadelphia, PA 19106

Potomac Area AYH Council (Washington, Virginia, Maryland), 1332 I Street, N.W., Suite 451, Washington, DC 20005

Metropolitan New York AYH Council, 132 Spring Street, New York, NY 10012

NEW ENGLAND

Greater AYH Boston Council (Massachusetts, New Hampshire, Rhode Island), 1020 Commonwealth Ave., Boston, MA 02215

The *Council on International Educational Exchange,* while mostly equipped to help American students traveling abroad, is able in some ways to assist foreign students visiting the United States. The Council issues International Student I.D. Cards. For information, contact:

NEW YORK

(Mail and telephone only:) CIEE, 205 East 42nd St., New York, NY 10017; 212-661-1450

(In-person inquiries only:) New York Student Center, 356 West 34th St., New York, NY

BOSTON

CIEE, 1278 Massachusetts Ave. (#21) Harvard Square, Cambridge, MA 02138; 617-497-1497

MIAMI

CIEE, 3401 Main Highway, Miami, FL 33133; 305-444-8829

LOS ANGELES

CIEE, 1093 Broxton Ave., Los Angeles, CA 90024; 213-208-3551

SAN FRANCISCO

CIEE, 312 Sutter St., San Francisco, CA 94108; 415-421-3473

SAN DIEGO

CIEE, UCSD Student Center B-023, La Jolla, CA 92093; 619-452-0630

SEATTLE

CIEE, 1314 Northeast 43rd St., Seattle, WA 98105; 206-632-2448

APPENDIX V: NAMED TRAINS AND THEIR ROUTES

NAME OF TRAIN	ROUTE & SECTIONS
Adirondack	New York—Albany—Montreal, 3.4, 3.5
Ann Rutledge	Chicago—St. Louis—Kansas City, 3,35, 3.47
Bankers	Springfield, Mass.—New Haven—New York—Washington, 3.3, 3.6, 3.8
Bay State	Boston—New York—Philadelphia, 3.3, 3.8
Bear Mountain	New York—Albany, 3.4
Benjamin Franklin	Boston—New York—Philadelphia, 3.3, 3.8
Big Apple	Harrisburg—Philadelphia—New York, 3.8, 3.15
Blue Ridge	Washington—Martinsburg, W.Va., 3.16
Broadway Limited	New York—Philadelphia—Pittsburgh—Chicago, 3.8, 3.15, 3.17
California Zephyr	Chicago—Galesburg, Ill.—Oakland, 3.36, 3.44
Calumet	Chicago—Valparaiso, Ind., 3.17
Capitol	New York—Washington, 3.8
Capitol Limited	Washington—Pittsburgh—Chicago, 3.16, 3.17
Cardinal	New York—Washington—Cincinnati—Chicago, 3.8, 3.18, 3.19
Chesapeake	Philadelphia—Washington, 3.8
City of New Orleans	Chicago—New Orleans, 3.33
Clocker Service	New York—Philadelphia, 3.8
Coast Starlight	Los Angeles—Oakland—Sacramento—Seattle, 3.43, 3.44
Colonial	Boston—New York—Washington—Richmond—Newport News, 3.3, 3.8, 3.9, 3.10
Congressional	Washington—New York, 3.8
Connecticut Valley Service	Springfield, Mass.—New Haven, 3.6
Connecticut Yankee	Springfield, Mass.—New Haven—New York—Washington, 3.3, 3.6, 3.8
Crescent	New York—Washington—New Orleans, 3.8, 3.28
Desert Wind	Salt Lake City—Los Angeles, 3.41, 3.49
Eagle	Chicago—St. Louis—San Antonio, 3.35, 3.48
Electric City Express	New York—Albany—Schenectady, 3.4, 3.12
Empire Builder	Chicago—Milwaukee—Minneapolis-St. Paul—Pacific Northwest, 3.37, 3.38, 3.45
Empire State Express	New York—Albany—Buffalo—Niagara Falls, 3.4, 3.12, 3.13
Garden State Special	New York—Washington, 3.8
Herald Square	Washington—New York, 3.8
Hoosier State	Chicago—Indianapolis, 3.32
Hudson Highlander	New York—Albany, 3.4
Illini	Chicago—Champaign, Ill., 3.33
Illinois Zephyr	Chicago—Galesburg, Ill.—West Quincy, Mo., 3.36
Independence	New York—Washington, 3.8
Indiana Connection	Chicago—Valparaiso, Ind., 3.17
International Limited	Chicago—Toronto, 3.13, 3.31
Jeffersonian	New York—Washington, 3.8
Kansas City Mule	St. Louis—Kansas City, Mo., 3.47
Keystone Service	Philadelphia—Harrisburg, Pa., 3.15
Keystone Executive	Philadelphia—Harrisburg, Pa., 3.15
Lake Cities	Chicago—Detroit—Toledo, 3.30
Lakeshore Limited	Boston—Albany; New York—Albany—Buffalo—Chicago, 3.2, 3.4, 3.12, 3.14
LaSalle	Chicago—Milwaukee, 3.37
Manhattan Limited	Washington—New York, 3.8
Maple Leaf	New York—Albany—Buffalo—Toronto, 3.4, 3.12, 3.13
Marquette	Chicago—Milwaukee, 3.37

454

Merchants Limited	Boston—New York—Washington, 3.3, 3.8
Metroliners	New York—Washington, 3.8
Michigan Executive	Ann Arbor—Detroit, 3.30
Minute Man	Boston—New York—Washington, 3.3, 3.8
Mohawk	New York—Albany—Buffalo—Niagara Falls, 3.4, 3.12, 3.13
Montrealer	Montreal—New Haven, Conn.—New York—Washington, 3.3, 3.6, 3.8
Mount Rainier	Portland, Oreg.—Seattle, 3.43
Mount Vernon	New York—Washington, 3.8
New England Metroliners	New York—Boston, 3.3
New England Zip	Washington—New York—Boston, 3.3, 3.8
Niagara Rainbow	Niagara Falls—Buffalo—Albany—New York, 3.4, 3.12, 3.13
Nicollet	Chicago—Milwaukee, 3.37
Night Owl	Boston—New York—Washington, 3.3, 3.8
North Star	Minneapolis-St. Paul—Duluth, Minn., 3.39
Palmetto	New York—Washington—Richmond—Savannah, 3.8, 3.9, 3.21, 3.23
Patriot	Boston—New York—Washington, 3.3, 3.8
Pennsylvanian	New York—Philadelphia—Pittsburgh, 3.8, 3.15
Pioneer	Salt Lake City—Portland, Oreg.—Seattle, 3.43, 3.50
Potomac	New York—Washington, 3.8
Radisson	Milwaukee—Chicago, 3.37
Rip Van Winkle	New York—Albany, 3.4
St. Louis Mule	Kansas City, Mo.—St. Louis, 3.47
San Diegoans	Los Angeles—San Diego, 3.51
San Joaquins	Los Angeles—Chicago—Oakland, 3.44, 3.52
Shawnee	Chicago—Carbondale, Ill., 3.33
Silver Meteor	New York—Washington—Richmond—Savannah—Jacksonville—Miami—St. Petersburg, 3.8, 3.9, 3.21, 3.23, 3.24, 3.25, 3.26
Silver Palm	Miami—Tampa, 3.27
Silver Star	New York—Washington—Richmond—Savannah—Jacksonville—Miami—St. Petersburg, 3.8, 3.9, 3.22, 3.23, 3.24, 3.26
Southwest Limited	Chicago—Los Angeles, 3.41
Spirit of California	Los Angeles—Oakland—Sacramento, 3.43, 3.44
Statehouse	Chicago—St. Louis, 3.35
Storm King	New York—Albany—Schenectady, N.Y., 3.4, 3.12
Sunset Limited	New Orleans—Los Angeles, 3.42
Susquehanna	New York—Philadelphia—Harrisburg, Pa., 3.8, 3.15
Tidewater	Newport News, Va.—Richmond—Washington—New York, 3.8, 3.9, 3.10
Twilight Limited	Chicago—Detroit, 3.30
Valley Forge	New York—Philadelphia—Harrisburg, Pa., 3.8, 3.15
Verrazano	Washington—New York, 3.8
Wolverine	Chicago—Detroit, 3.30
Yankee Clipper	Boston—New York—Washington, 3.3, 3.8

Index of Amtrak Stations

Index of Amtrak Stations

Cities in italics are discussed in detail in Part 2, where they appear in alphabetical order. The numbers below indicate where stations are mentioned in Part 3 only.

BED & BREAKFAST
1982/83
The Great American Guest House Book

JOHN THAXTON

If your local bookseller, gift shop, or country inn does not stock a particular title, ask them to order directly from Burt Franklin & Co., Inc., 235 East 44th Street, New York, New York 10017, U.S.A. Telephone orders are accepted from recognized retailers and credit card holders. In the United States, call, toll free, 1-800-223-0766 during regular business hours. (In New York State, call 212-687-5250.)

THE COMPLEAT TRAVELER'S READER REPORT

To: *The Compleat Traveler*
  c/o Burt Franklin & Company, Inc.
  235 East 44th Street
  New York, New York 10017 U.S.A.

Dear Compleat Traveler:

I have used your publication *America by Train,* and I would like to make the following ☐ recommendation, ☐ comment, ☐ suggestion, or ☐ criticism:

Date of rail trip: _____

Route and train: _____

From (name): _____

Address: _____

_____ Telephone: _____